Mortgage-Backed Securities

Products, Analysis, Trading

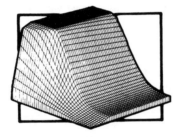

William W. Bartlett
Vice President, Product Management
Shearson Lehman Hutton

Françoise Dearden
Developmental Editor

New York Institute of Finance

Library of Congress Cataloging-in-Publication Data

Bartlett, William W.
    Mortgage-backed securities : products, analysis, trading / William
W. Bartlett.
        p.   cm.
    Includes index.
    ISBN 0-13-725516-0 : $39.50
    1. Mortgage-backed securities--United States.   I. Title.
HG5095.B35 1988
332.63'244--dc19

                                                            88-28866
                                                                CIP

The views expressed in this book are the author's own and do not necessarily reflect the views of Shearson Lehman Hutton Inc. or its clients.

This publication is designed to provide accurate and authoritative information in regard to the subject matter covered. It is sold with the understanding that the publisher is not engaged in rendering legal, accounting, or other professional service. If legal advice or other expert assistance is required, the services of a competent professional person should be sought.

From a Declaration of Principles Jointly Adopted by
a Committee of the American Bar Association and a
Committee of Publishers and Associations

© 1989 by NYIF Corp.
A Division of Simon & Schuster, Inc.
70 Pine Street, New York, NY 10270-0003

Printed in the United States of America

10   9   8   7   6   5   4

New York Institute of Finance
(NYIF Corp.)
70 Pine Street
New York, New York 10270-0003

In Memory of My Father
Hall Bartlett

For whom words, and writing, were the essence of life.

Contents

PREFACE xix

ACKNOWLEDGMENTS xxiii

I

THE MORTGAGE WORLD

1

Historical Highlights of the Secondary Mortgage Market

THE ANCIENT HISTORY OF MORTGAGES 3

A BRIEF HISTORY OF MORTGAGE BANKING............................... 4
    The Depression Era 5
    The Post-World War II Era... 7
    Birth of a Secondary Market 8
    The Evolution of Conduits.. 9

EVOLUTION OF FEDERAL AGENCY MBSs PROGRAMS 11
    Benefits of Federal Agency Sponsorship of MBSs Programs 12
    Introduction of Freddie Mac Participation Certificates (PCs) 13
    1981—A Year of Innovation 14
    1983—CMO and ARM Initiatives................................ 14
    1984—Federal Agency Programs Foster Standardization of the
    Secondary Market 15
    Federal Agency Programs Under Siege........................... 17
    1986—Resurgence of Federal Agency Initiatives 17

THE TAX REFORM ACT OF 1986................................. 18
    REMIC: In Brief... 20

SAVINGS INSTITUTIONS 23
    Savings Deregulation 24
    The Impact of RAP Accounting 25
    1987 Legislative and Regulatory Activity Expanded 35

OTHER INSTITUTIONAL INVESTORS.. 36
Mutual Funds 37

THE PRIMARY DEALER MARKET... 39
A Tandem Plan for Projects 41
Federal Agencies Join Forces with Wall Street................................. 41
Troubles of the Early 1970s 42
Derivative MBSs Products 44
Asset-Backed Securities 44

2

The Mortgage Market and Mortgage Banking: Mortgage-Backed Securities Trends to the Twenty-first Century

THE MBSs MARKET AND ITS DERIVATIVES 56
A Call to ARMs 58
Attractiveness of ARMs 59

THE HISTORICAL PERFORMANCE OF MBSs................................. 59
MBSs Sector Analysis 61
Mortgages Outperformed Treasuries and Corporates 61
Fixed-Rate Pass-Through Issuance Threatened by ARMs 62
Mortgage-to-Treasury Yield Spreads Stabilized 64
1988 MBSs to Treasury Spreads Narrow Further 65

THE PRIVATE PASS-THROUGH MARKET 66
Composition 68

THE WHOLE-LOAN MARKET 70
Alternative Mortgage Instruments (AMIs)...................................... 71
The Conventional Residential Loan Market..................................... 72
Project Loans.. 72

THE MORTGAGE BANKING BUSINESS 73
Servicing... 73
The Origination Process 74
Warehousing 77
Marketing.. 77
Servicing... 78
Managing the Mortgage Pipeline 79
Increased Leverage and Decreased Risk... 84

THE WHOLE-LOAN SECONDARY MARKET 90
The Whole-Loan Trading Mechanism 91

TRENDS TO THE TWENTY-FIRST CENTURY.................................... 91
Assessing Housing Demand and Financing Needs............................. 92
The Outlook for S&Ls.. 93
The Mortgage Banking Outlook 96
A New Breed of Investors 100
Future Sources of Mortgage Capital.. 101
The Mortgage Instruments of the Future 102
The Primary Dealer Market.. 103

II
DYNAMICS OF MORTGAGE POOL CASH FLOWS

3
Federal Agency Mortgage-Backed Securities Programs

MBSs POOL CHARACTERISTICS 108
Pass-Through Rate and Servicing Spread.. 108
Weighted Average Coupon (WAC) 108
Issue Date.. 109
Maturity Date 109
Weighted Average Maturity (WAM).. 110
Payment Delay.. 110
Pool Factor 112

FEDERAL AGENCY-SPONSORED PROGRAMS 112

GOVERNMENT NATIONAL MORTGAGE ASSOCIATION (GINNIE
MAE)... 115
GNMA-I 115
GNMA-II 118
Other Ginnie Mae-Sponsored Programs 120

FEDERAL HOME LOAN MORTGAGE CORPORATION (FREDDIE
MAC)... 123

FEDERAL NATIONAL MORTGAGE ASSOCIATION (FANNIE MAE)....... 131

4
Uniform Practices for Delivery and Settlement of Agency-Guaranteed Mortgage-Backed Securities

SETTLEMENT 137
   Dealer Settlement Procedures... 137
   Variance Rule 137
   Denominations 138
   Pieces.. 138
   Investor Considerations.. 138

TBA VERSUS SPECIFIED TRADES 139
   Specified TBA 139

RECEIVE AND DELIVER (R&D) 139

THE 48-HOUR RULE 140
   Due Bills... 141
   Reclamations 141

5
Calculating Principal and Interest: Measuring and Predicting Prepayments

FUNDAMENTALS OF POOL CASH FLOW 143
   Mortgage Cash-Flow Calculations 146
   Calculating the Remaining Principal Balance (RPB) 146
   Calculating Principal and Interest (P&I) Payments 147
   Adjustments to Cash Flows for Mortgage Securities 148
   Adjusting for Servicing Spread.. 150
   Adjusting for Prepayments... 150
   The Average-Life Concept 152

MEASURING PREPAYMENT SPEED 153
   FHA Experience 154
   Constant Prepayment Rate (CPR).. 155
   The PSA Standard... 155
   Interest-Rate Changes Influence Speed 156
   Impact of Age... 157
   Seasonal Impact on Speed 159
   Impact of WAM 162
   WAC Effect on Speed.. 164
   Impact of Housing Turnover Rate 165

CALCULATIONS OF PREPAYMENT SPEEDS 167
  Calculation of SMM 167
  Calculation of CPR... 168
  Converting between CPR and PSA..................................... 169
  Calculation of FHA Experience 172
  Delayed Issuance Pools.. 173

6
Determinants of Price and Yield

DETERMINANTS OF PRICE.. 176
  Price to 12-Year Prepaid Life 176
  Price to Cash-Flow Yield 176
  Derivation of Principal Amortization (AM) and Prepayments (PP) 178
  Derivation of Interest Portion (Int) 178
  Pricing Discount MBSs.. 179
  Pricing Par-Priced MBSs... 179
  Pricing Patterns of Premium-Priced MBSs 179

THE IMPLIED CALL OPTION OF THE MBS 181
  Valuing the Call Option... 181

TOTAL-RETURN ANALYSIS... 182
  Reinvestment Impact on Value... 182
  Impact of Volatility 184
  MBS versus Treasury Cash Flows... 185

HOLDING-PERIOD RETURN ANALYSIS.. 186
  Bull and Bear Market Impact on HPR................................. 187

BREAKEVEN PREPAYMENT RATE... 189

7
Duration, Convexity, and Volatility Properties
of Mortgage Securities

DURATION.. 193
  Duration Measures Time to Receipt of Value 195
  Using Duration to Measure Price 197
  Coupon Impact on Duration 198
  Modified Duration... 198

CONVEXITY 200
  Negative Convexity of MBSs 203

ALTERNATIVE DURATION MEASURES 204
   CPR-Adjusted CFY 205
   Volatility-Implied Duration 205
   The Implied-Volatility Framework 207
   Prepayment-Sensitive Model.. 208
   Option-Adjusted Spread 209
   OAS Analysis Applied to MBS Pricing 212
   Conclusion... 213

8
Measuring Value without the Black Box

A RISK-VALUATION FRAMEWORK.. 215
   Investing with a Market View.. 215

RIDING THE MORTGAGE YIELD CURVE 216
   Discussion of Figure 8.1 217
   Seeking and Holding Basis-Point Spread 218
   Bull Market Investing.. 219
   Bear Market Investing 222
   Sector Analysis 224
   Some Guidelines for Swaps... 226
   You May Be Able to Buy Cheap Bonds 228

III
SPECIAL MORTGAGE PROGRAMS

9
Fifteen-Year, Manufactured Housing, and
Graduated-Payment Mortgage Securities

CHARACTERISTICS OF 15-YEAR MORTGAGES 232
   Rising Popularity of 15-Year Mortgages 232
   Significantly Lower Default Rates.................................... 236
   Issuance and Outstanding Volume.................................... 238
   Aggressive Agency Participation...................................... 240
   Prepayment Rates... 241
   Cash Flows 242
   Relative Value Analysis 243
   Liquidity 246
   Derivative Mortgage Securities....................................... 247

TYPICAL INVESTORS 248
   Insurance Companies 248
   Savings Institutions... 249

GINNIE MAE MANUFACTURED HOUSING PASS-THROUGHS 249

CONVENTIONAL PASS-THROUGHS... 250
   Investment Characteristics of MH-Backed Pass-Throughs....................... 251
   Credit Considerations 252
   Credit-Rating Considerations 254
   Future Developments 255

GRADUATED-PAYMENT MORTGAGES 255
   GPM Plans 256
   The Ginnie Mae GPM Program... 259

10

Adjustable-Rate Mortgage Securities

ARM STRUCTURAL CHARACTERISTICS 262
   Initial Rate.. 262
   Indexes 262
   Margin.. 264
   ARM Caps.. 264

FEDERAL AGENCY-BACKED ARM SECURITIES 267
   The Ginnie Mae ARM Security.. 267
   Fannie Mae 268
   Freddie Mac 269

THE PRIVATE ARM MARKET... 270
   Whole Loans—100 Percent Participations.. 272
   Private Pass-Through ARM Securities 272

ARM VALUATION 274
   Factors Affecting ARM Security Valuation 274
   Net Effective Margin 275
   Effects of Mortgage Characteristics on ARM Security Prices................... 276
   Impact of Prepayments 277
   Sensitivity of Net Effective Margins and Prices to Changes in Interest
   Rates, Prepayments, and Index Volatility 277
   Interest Rates... 278
   Index Volatility 280

THE SLH ARM PRICING MODEL 281

ACCOUNTING CONSIDERATIONS—FASB 91 282
  Overview 282
  Accounting Provisions 282

APPENDIX: VOLATILITY 283

11
Multifamily and Project Loan Securities

MULTIFAMILY LENDING AND LOAN STRUCTURES 286

FEDERAL MORTGAGE PROGRAMS 287
  FHA Insurance and Co-Insurance Programs 287
  Put Option 290
  Section 8 Lower-Income Rental Assistance 290
  Interest-Rate Subsidy Programs 290
  Conventional Loans 291

MULTIFAMILY MORTGAGE-BACKED SECURITIES 291
  Ginnie Mae 291
  Freddie Mac and Fannie Mae Multifamily MBSs 292

THE FREDDIE MAC MULTIFAMILY PC PROGRAM 292
  The Plan-B Mortgages 292
  The Plan-B Loan Terms 293
  Call-Protection Feature 293
  The Multifamily PC 293

PRIVATELY ISSUED POOLS 294

INVESTMENT CONSIDERATIONS 294

THE PREPAYMENT HORIZON FOR MULTIFAMILY PROJECT
LOANS 295
  Methods for Valuing Multifamily Projects 296
  Determining the Likelihood of Prepayment 297

APPENDIX 300
  Section 207: Multifamily Rental Housing 300
  Section 213: Cooperative Housing 301
  Section 221(d)(3): Rental and Cooperative Housing for Low- to
  Moderate-Income Households 302
  Section 221(d)(4): Rental Housing for Low- to Moderate-Income
  Households 304

Section 223(f): Loans to Purchase or Refinance Existing Multifamily
Projects... 305
Section 231: Rental Housing for the Elderly or Handicapped.................. 306
Section 232: Nursing Home and Intermediate-Care Facilities.................. 307
Section 236: Interest-Rate Subsidy Plan for Low- to Moderate-Income
Households and Elderly Individuals 308
Section 242: Hospitals 309

IV
DERIVATIVE MORTGAGE-BACKED SECURITIES PRODUCTS: THEIR PROPERTIES AND USES

12
CMO Investing and Trading

UNDERSTANDING THE CMO 313
    Collateral Considerations.. 314
    Number and Size of Tranches... 315

CMO STRUCTURE 315
    The Pricing Process 317
    CMO Cash-Flow Structure... 317
    Z-Bond Class Structure.. 317
    The Stated Maturity 320
    The Reinvestment Assumption 320

CMO PRICING AND INVESTMENT 320
    Tracking Yield Spreads.. 321
    Collateral Type 321
    Price Considerations 322
    Prepayment-Speed Considerations 322
    Summary of Key Points.. 323
    Measuring Risk/Reward in CMO Investing 324
    Synthetic Discount CMOs... 325

SELECTING THE CMO INVESTMENT.. 326
    Techniques of Investing 326

FLOATING-RATE CMOs... 327
    The Variety of Floater Caps 327
    CMO Superfloaters: A New Hedging Vehicle..................................... 328
    Inverse Floaters 330
    Investment Strategies 331
    Considerations by Investor Class 331

PLANNED-AMORTIZATION CLASS (PAC) CMO TRANCHES 332
  Investor Considerations with PAC CMOs 333
  The First Class of a PAC CMO 334
  Third-Class CMOs (Intermediate-Term Average Lives) 336
  Fourth-Class Z-Bonds 337
  Pricing Considerations 339
  Targeted Amortization Class (TAC) Tranches 340
  Turbo POs: Derivative of Derivatives 340

13
IOs and POs: Stripped Mortgage-Backed Securities Cash Flows

RISK/REWARD IN STRIP INVESTING 344

UNDERSTANDING STRIP CASH FLOWS 345
  Principal-Only (PO) Cash Flow 345
  Hedging Prepayment Risk with POs 351
  Interest-Only (IO) Cash Flow 353
  Illustrating Strip Cash Flows 357
  IO Projected Price Performance 361
  PO Projected Price Performance 362

TOTAL RETURNS AND HOLDING-PERIOD RETURNS OF STRIPS 363
  Traditional Holding-Period Returns for Strips 364
  Dynamic Total-Return Analysis 366

MORTGAGE-DURATION CHARACTERISTICS OF STRIPS 368
  Mortgage Duration of PO Strips 369
  The Negative Duration of IOs 369
  Hedging with Strips 371

INVESTOR CONCERNS WITH SMBSs 373

SMBS PRICING METHODOLOGY 374

REGULATORY CONCERNS WITH SMBSs 374

APPENDIX A:
Guidelines for Selection of Securities Dealers and Unsuitable
Investment Practices 376

APPENDIX B:
Federal Income Tax Considerations 384

APPENDIX C:
  FNMA Synthetic-Coupon SMBSs 392

14
Residuals: The Ultimate Derivative

EVOLUTION OF THE RESIDUAL SECONDARY MARKET 396
  The Owner-Trust Vehicle 396
  The TIMs Initiative 397
  The REMIC Impact 397

SOURCES OF RESIDUAL CASH FLOWS.. 398
  Fixed-Rate CMO Residuals—Bear Market Bias 398
  Residual Income Sensitivity to Prepayment Spread............................. 399
  Other Sources of Residual Cash Flow 400

FIXED-FLOATER RESIDUALS—VOLATILITY ADVERSE................... 402
  Rating-Agency Considerations 403

RESIDUAL CASH-FLOW SENSITIVITY ANALYSIS............................ 404
  Residual Friendly-Floater Structures 406
  All-Floater Residuals—Bull Market Biased 406
  Techniques for Hedging Residuals 408
  Available Tools for Hedging Residuals... 408
  Other Types of Assets 410

15
Structured Arbitrage Strategies

OVERVIEW OF STRUCTURED ARBITRAGE STRATEGIES.................. 414

CONSIDERATIONS IN USING IOs 420
  Interpreting the SAT Evaluation Model... 421
  Yield-Basis Risk 424

SAT PERFORMANCE MEASURES 426
  Book-Based Measures 427
  Cash-Based Measures... 428
  Cash- versus Book-Based Measures... 430
  Rebalancing 431

RISK CONSIDERATIONS 432

16
Using Mortgage Collateral as a Source for Earning Power

USES OF MORTGAGE COLLATERAL 437
Sale of Assets 437
Financing Transactions 438
Bond and Stock Offerings 441

ARPS, MMPS, AND MMNs 443
ARPS 443
MMPS 446
MMNs 448

DOLLAR ROLLS: TRANSACTION DESCRIPTION 449
Economic Basis 450
Accounting Treatment 451
Profit Evaluation 451
Prepayment Risk 454
The Delivery Put Option 455

FEDERAL HOME LOAN BANK BOARD R MEMORANDUM:
OPINION AND CLARIFICATION 456

17
Accounting Issues

ACCOUNTING BY INVESTORS FOR INVESTMENTS IN IOs, POs,
AND RESIDUALS 459
Background—Different Accounting Methods 459
Accounting for Investments in IOs 462
Accounting for Investments in POs 462
Accounting for Investments in Residuals 462
Other Issues 463

THE EFFECTS OF A REMIC ELECTION ON THE ACCOUNTING
BY THE ISSUER OF MBSs 464

AN EVOLVING AREA 465
Example 1: Applying the Constant-Yield Method With and Without
Assumed Prepayments 466
Example 2: Investor's Accounting with Estimated Prepayments 467
Example 3: Investor's Accounting Based on Contractual Cash Flows 467

GLOSSARY.. 469

INDEX 479

Preface

Mortgage-Backed Securities: Products, Analysis, Trading is an overview of the structural characteristics and the cash-flow dynamics of mortgage-backed securities. The book has been written for practitioners at all levels of experience.

Practical applications are emphasized while key concepts relating to the prepayment phenomenon and option characteristics of mortgage securities are explored in depth, together with their related analytical techniques. The text is presented from the viewpoint of a practitioner who has had to put it together every day on the trading floor for almost 20 years.

Market participants with some mastery of the basics of mortgage cash flows can use the chapters in whatever order is appropriate. The book is organized to progress from the simple to the complex, from the verbal introduction of basic concepts through graphically illustrated explanations to mathematical definitions and applications of concepts. Although the text flows from an introductory level to more complex techniques of trading and portfolio valuation, each chapter stands on its own to cover a specific aspect of the MBS product.

The text is a readable guide to complex but essential concepts—such as the various forms of duration, negative convexity, the implied call option imbedded in the MBS, and the interest-rate–path dependency of prepayment patterns. Key valuation techniques such as option-value-adjusted spread, breakeven analysis, and the derivation of net effective margin are illustrated with graphics and easily followed examples of their application to investing and trading.

Other sections focus on actual transactions. Examples demonstrate specific trading techniques ranging from basic coupon swaps, dollar spread trades, and dollar rolls to the more rigorous techniques of risk-controlled arbitrage transactions.

Part I—"The Mortgage World"—consists of two chapters that highlight the historical evolution, composition, and performance of the secondary mortgage market.

Chapter 1 emphasizes the principal themes governing the interface between the private sector and federal agency participants in the development of the secondary market from the 1930s to the present. Critical legislative and regulatory events of the past decade are emphasized—those that have shaped the market as it stands today and into the 1990s.

Chapter 2 evaluates the performance of MBSs relative to the universe of fixed-income securities and the likely trends of mortgage finance into the twenty-first century.

Part II—"Dynamics of Mortgage Pool Cash Flows"—spans six chapters.

Chapter 3 outlines the specifics of the Ginnie Mae, Fannie Mae, and Freddie Mac MBSs programs.

Chapter 4 covers practical concerns relating to good delivery and settlement procedures, including, for example, how to comply with the 48-hour rule.

Chapter 5 is an extensive analysis of prepayments, the factors that induce prepayments, and the impact of prepayments on price and yield. Sophisticated aspects of prepayment analysis, such as the prepayment lag response, defining the threshold for refinancing, differentiating the prepayment sensitivity of new versus seasoned loans, and the impact of pool age on prepayment patterns are introduced here.

Chapters 6 and 7 explain pricing techniques, the implied call inherent in the MBS, and the option-valuation process. Total-return analysis and measuring risk/reward to a holding period are also reviewed. A special presentation on measuring the power of reinvestment income—unique in this text—is included in Chapter 6. Chapter 7 focuses on alternative definitions and applications of duration.

Part III—"Other MBS Products"—explains 15-year, adjustable-rate, and project loan MBS forms. Manufactured housing and graduated payment mortgages are also defined. Particular attention is given to the latest techniques for pricing adjustable-rate mortgage securities to a net effective margin.

Part IV—"Derivative MBSs, Structural Characteristics and Uses" —concludes the book with Chapters 12 through 17.

Chapters 12 through 14 describe CMOs, strips, and residuals. The focus is on the alternative structural forms of these securities, with a thorough analysis of their sensitivity to varying prepayment scenarios. The investment risk considerations of strips and residuals are fully explored as well as the application of these forms to a number of hedging techniques.

Chapter 15 examines the dynamics of structured arbitrage, with illustrations and examples demonstrating several ways to maximize earnings and the return on assets of financial institutions. Chapter 16 outlines ten ways to utilize mortgage securities collateral to maximize earnings, with particular focus given to dollar rolls. Finally, Chapter 17 discusses accounting applications relating to strips and residuals.

FEATURES

With the end-of-book glossary—and with glossary terms identified in the text in boldface type—*Mortgage-Backed Securities* is a ready reference tool.

A detailed Contents lists all major topic headings.

For the busy practitioner, a quick reference guide has been included following the index. Among these one can find a conversion table of monthly mortgage yields to CBE and a comparative summary of the principal terms relating to the three federal agency programs: Ginnie Mae, Fannie Mae, and Freddie Mac.

Acknowledgments

First, my thanks to Françoise Dearden, who as Developmental Editor was a full partner in this effort—reading every line of copy many times over and contributing especially to the organization and clarity of the text. In addition, many talented and knowledgeable people contributed to this book. I am grateful to the following:

My special appreciation is due the staff members of the federal agencies for their thorough editing of the sections relating to the Freddie Mac and Fannie Mae programs: especially at Freddie Mac, the analytic staff in the Corporate Communications Department; and at Fannie Mae, Frank Demarais, Director of MBS Product Acquisition, and Janice Mitchell, Senior MBS Representative. To Jim Marshall and Roger McMahon of James C. Marshall PC I owe thanks for providing assistance with the glossary.

I owe my gratitude to Cassie Dana, Bill Halapin, Ron Keusch, Kevin McDermott, Mary Parker, Mark Rudnitsky, Vincent Moore, and Harold Zeitlin of Shearson Lehman Hutton; in particular I wish to thank Mike Conway, Ron "Jesse" Juster, Steve Turner, Townsend Shean, and Paul Williams, for their help at the Shearson end; to Leon Baudouin of Goldman Sachs; to Robert McGovern of Thomson McKinnon Securities; to Bill Reagan of Stern Brothers; and to Rodger Shay of U.S. League Investment Services. All contributed to the book in various ways.

Very special thanks are due the publishing staff at the New York Institute of Finance. First, for initiating the project and lending the encouragement to proceed, I thank Mark Greenberg, who was at the time NYIF Vice President of Publishing and is now Executive Vice President of Marketing at Simon & Schuster Publishing and Information Services. Second, I am grateful to Fred Dahl, Managing Editor, who provided the encouragement to help me see the project to conclusion. Fred Eickelberg, Director of Marketing, and Dan Gonzalez who succeeded him, gave life to the marketing effort and inspired the design of the cover. And a special blessing for Jeanmarie Brusati, Production Editor, who was primarily responsible for the fine job of coordinating the many facets of the production process and keeping us on schedule.

Finally, a most important vote of thanks to the principal consultants who gave generously of their time in reading various parts of the manuscript and for their thoughtful comments.

Principal Consultants

Steven J. Carlson
Vice President and Director
Transaction Strategies Group
Shearson Lehman Hutton

Wesley R. Edens
Vice President, MBS Trading
Shearson Lehman Hutton

Eric Fix
Senior Associate
Transaction Strategies Group
Shearson Lehman Hutton

Thomas Fultz
Vice President
Transaction Strategies Group
Shearson Lehman Hutton

Joseph C. Hu
Executive Vice President
 and Director
Mortgage Securities Research
Shearson Lehman Hutton

Theodore P. Janulis
Vice President, MBS Trading
Shearson Lehman Hutton

Peter M. Kunigk
Corporate Bond Sales
Shearson Lehman Hutton

Nicole A. Lowen
Vice President
Mortgage Securities Research
Shearson Lehman Hutton

T. Barrett Moore
Senior Vice President
Product Management Group
Shearson Lehman Hutton

Benjamin S. Neuhausen
Partner
Arthur Andersen & Company
Chicago

David A. Olson
Vice President, Research
SMR Research Corporation
Budd Lake, NJ

Harry Panagos
Vice President
Government Securities Department
The First Boston Corporation

William D. Riley
Director/Operations
Government Securities Department
The First Boston Corporation

William A. Wildhack
President
William Wildhack & Associates
Washington, D.C.

Peter H. Wallace, CFA
Vice President, Mortgage Sales
Shearson Lehman Hutton

John M. Winters
Vice President, SLCPI
Shearson Lehman Hutton

I

THE MORTGAGE WORLD

1
Historical Highlights of the Secondary Mortgage Market

2
The Mortgage Market and Mortgage Banking: Mortgage-Backed
Securities Trends to the Twenty-first Century

1

Historical Highlights of the Secondary Mortgage Market

THE ANCIENT HISTORY OF MORTGAGES

Some secondary market participants view the first issuance of Ginnie Mae securities in February 1970 as the beginning of the secondary market as we know it today. Others might say that the Depression era of the 1930s with legislation establishing the federal housing-related agencies such as the Federal Housing Administration (FHA) in 1934 and Fannie Mae in 1938 marks the birth of modern-day mortgage finance.

But, in fact, about five thousand years ago, the Babylonians used the device of employing land as security to encourage the development of dikes and dams critical to agriculture on the Euphrates River plain. The ancient Egyptians used surveys to describe land plots of varying fertility ranked by successive levels of Nile River flooding. And the Romans introduced the *fiducia*, a document that was an actual conveyance of land and a transfer of title as described under Roman law. In the late Roman Empire, the *pignus* evolved as a concept in the exchange of property rights whereby in lieu of transfer of title the land was pawned. The Roman law definition of *hypotheca*—or "pledge"— was remarkably similar to the lien theory that exists in most American states today.

Following the decay of the Roman Empire, Germanic law developed the concept of using land as security for performance under borrowers' agreements. This idea of using land as a security deposit was called a *gage*.

In feudal times the king was the owner of all lands, and he granted his lords the right to use portions of his domain in return for their military fealty. In turn, these overlords granted use rights to lesser lords or allowed serfs to cultivate the land.

When William of Normandy introduced the Germanic *gage* system into early English law the French word *mort* ("dead" or "frozen") was combined with *gage* to signify a "locked pledge," or *mort-gage*, on property.

As Europeans came to America they brought with them these ancient legal practices that were to form the basis of U.S. mortgage law. These practices included the lien theory that title remains with the mortgagor, or borrower, while the mortgagee, or lender, holds a lien that can be enforced upon nonperformance by the borrower.[1]

A BRIEF HISTORY OF MORTGAGE BANKING

The roots of mortgage banking reach back to the settlement of the Midwest by farmers in the nineteenth century and the establishment of mortgage companies to finance land purchases. These early mortgage banks obtained lending capital by issuing debenture bonds that were bought by insurance companies. By the turn of the century there was about $4 billion of farm mortgages outstanding originated by some 200 mortgage companies. The loans had loan-to-value ratios of about 40 percent, were short term, paid interest semiannually, and involved a balloon payment, often as short as three or five years. In part it was the nonamortizing nature of these balloon mortgages that contributed to the high default rates of the Depression years.

The Farm Mortgage Bankers Association was formed in 1914 by these 200-odd mortgage companies. By the 1920s, the lending activities of these mortgage banks were increasingly extending into urban areas; in 1923, in recognition of a more urban lending market, the Association changed its name to the Mortgage Bankers Association.

The 1920s brought a real estate boom and high profits to both institutional and individual investors of mortgages. The evolution of this early secondary mortgage market of sorts spawned a new type of mortgage banking entity that guaranteed to these investors the payment of principal and interest on the mortgages sold to them. This business quickly evolved into a form of mortgage participation bonds sold to individuals in units of $500 or $1,000. A trustee held the physical mortgage and enforced foreclosure if necessary.

The guarantee by the mortgage companies was backed by the short-term, nonamortizing loans, of course, and in 1929 the real estate boom crashed with the stock market. Mortgage companies foreclosed on one property after anoth-

---

[1]See Marshall W. Dennis, "Evolution of an Industry" (Washington, D.C.: Mortgage Bankers Association of America, n.d.).

er, flooding the severely depressed real estate market with thousands of new properties for sale. Mortgage guarantee companies, now mostly operating out of New York State, were unable to pay on their mortgage bonds, and the loss to individual investors was crushing. A majority of the investors lost all their cash savings. It had not occurred to anyone to be concerned with the real economics of the mortgages backing the participation bonds. The universal assumption was that the real estate boom had an assured future and inflation would bail out the bad loans. In the early 1920s, real estate was appreciating annually a stunning 50 percent to—at times—75 percent.

Virtually all of all the mortgage guarantee companies went out of business, with only a few managing to survive. Some of the survivors are today's giants of the mortgage banking industry.

The Depression Era

Although the entire U.S. economy was in grave danger of collapse during the late 1920s and early thirties, and real estate values had plunged to half the levels of 1927–28, foreclosures on first mortgages were actually rare. The majority of all foreclosures during the 1930s was by second and third mortgagees, who needed to foreclose immediately upon defaulted property to protect what little security they may have had. The highest number of foreclosures occurred between 1931 and 1935, averaging 250,000 annually. With the increasing number of foreclosures, especially on family farms in the Midwest, came the beginning of compulsory moratoriums. In the Midwest, where economic deterioration was combined with the Dust Bowl storms, the cry for moratoriums reached the stage of near-rebellion, and violence resulted in some instances. In Iowa, one of the farm states most affected by the wave of foreclosures, civil courts were suspended and replaced by military justice. Reacting to the hysteria sweeping the Farm Belt as well as some cities, many mortgagees voluntarily instituted moratoriums, some for as long as two years. The first actual law requiring a mortgage moratorium became effective on February 8, 1933, in Iowa. Within 18 months, 27 states had enacted legislation suspending foreclosures. Most of the moratorium laws enacted during this period were to last for two years or less, although some were re-enacted and allowed to continue until the early 1940s.

In response to the plight of the homeowners of that era, in 1933 the federal government established the Home Owners' Loan Corporation (HOLC), which used the proceeds of government-guaranteed bond sales to refinance homeowners' indebtedness. HOLC acquired defaulted mortgages, reinstituted them, and put the loans on a monthly payment schedule. This action on the part of the government not only helped to restabilize the economy but in converting loans to an amortized basis prevented thousands of homes from falling into foreclosure. The first three years witnessed the refinancing of over one million homes.

In 1934 the government created the Federal Housing Administration (FHA) to insure long-term, fixed-rate loans to provide homeowners with viable financing. From its beginning the primary objectives of the FHA were (1) to encourage the improvement of the nation's housing standards and conditions; (2) to provide an adequate home financing system; and (3) to exert a stabilizing influence on mortgage and residential real estate markets. This program furthered the concept of amortizing loans and provided a system whereby funds could flow from capital-rich to capital-poor areas. The reason the FHA could be used in setting up this conduit system for funds was that it established certain minimum standards for both the house and the borrower.

The FHA was not popular with the financial communities when it first appeared. Many people feared the practice of government guaranteeing of mortgages because large numbers of people had been severely burned by the mortgage guarantee companies of the 1930s. Others believed that government intrusion into the housing market would, in the long run, be detrimental to private capitalism. In the vanguard of those who were critical and suspicious of the FHA were most of the managing officers of the nation's savings and loans (S&Ls) business. To this day S&Ls have little to do with the origination of FHA-insured mortgages.

The FHA-insured mortgage provided the elements of dependability, transferability, and minimal risk, which were vital to the development of a national mortgage market. The correspondence system between mortgage bankers and the insurance companies, in existence since the 1920s, helped pave the way by using FHA standards to move mortgage investment funds from prosperous localities to poor ones. Undoubtedly, the mortgage banking industry as it exists today owes its unparalleled growth to this basic decision by life insurance companies to engage in national lending, with the FHA providing the insurance. About 80 percent of today's independent mortgage banking companies were formed after the creation of the FHA—dramatically pointing out the FHA's impact on the mortgage banking industry. In 1938, the Federal National Mortgage Association (FNMA, or Fannie Mae) was formed by an act of Congress for the purpose of providing a secondary mortgage market for FHA-insured loans; 30 years later, Fannie Mae was reorganized as a private corporation; and today it is the largest holder of single-family mortgages.

In the 1930s, too, attention turned to the private sector, raising the question of how to address the collapse of the New York-based mortgage guaranty insurance industry. In 1934, an investigative committee focused on why the industry had failed. The study cited two related causes of the collapse: (1) 100 percent mortgage insurance coverage that proved impossible to honor and (2) the weak capital structure of the mortgage insurance companies. The committee's recommendations, together with the FHA's experience, were used decades later to write and construct legislation governing private mortgage guaranty insurance companies.

The Post-World War II Era

Between 1926 and 1946, with the Depression and World War II, single-family home construction was minimal. At the end of the war, five million men came marching home, creating a tremendous demand for housing. The government, as part of its responsibility to returning veterans, passed the Servicemen's Adjustment Act. One program under this act was the Veterans Administration (VA), which provided veterans with the means for financing homes. From the start, the most distinguishing feature of the VA program has been the lack of down-payment requirements. Rates have been pegged at or slightly below the FHA rate, with no mortgage insurance premiums to be collected from the participants. Unlike the FHA, the VA program was not meant to be self-supporting. The second large factor contributing to the rapid expansion of single-family dwellings following World War II was the highly liquid position of the financial institutions. In 1945, over half of financial institution assets were tied up in the riskless but low-yielding bonds they had been obligated to purchase during the war. At the end of the war, these bonds could be converted into higher returns in mortgage debt.

With the built-in demand for housing, and with the FHA and VA available as financing vehicles, the way was made ready for the greatest boom in housing construction in the history of this country. A new form of housing construction took the form of developments such as Levittown, New York. These huge developments of homogeneous homes offered great economies of scale and thereby low-cost but sound housing. Starting with this post-war boom and continuing today, the mortgage market has been the largest user of long-term credit. The mortgage banker was the logical person to develop funds for this boom and to handle the servicing. From 1946 until the 1960s, mortgage banking companies grew from small, family-owned companies to multibillion dollar corporations.

The face of the real estate market changed in the 1960s, with the credit crunch and a shift in the investment philosophy of institutional investors from residential housing production to income-property production. Many institutional investors, especially life insurance companies, lost interest in single-family lending when they were able to realize larger yields in commercial properties. In 1955, three out of every four dollars invested by life insurance companies in long-term mortgages were in single-family. By 1960, the ratio had changed to two out of four new dollars invested in single-family. During the first half of the 1970s, almost all new dollars invested by insurance companies were in commercial mortgages. During this transition period for life insurance companies, thrift institutions increasingly assumed the major responsibility for financing the single-family mortgage, with the help of the new, dynamic mortgage banking industry.

Birth of a Secondary Market

At the outset, the most common investors available to mortgage bankers were life insurance companies. In the post-World War II era, mutual savings banks were the most active purchasers of loans. Fannie Mae's first purchases of VA mortgages in 1948 may mark the beginning of the secondary market. Insurance companies soon retreated from single-family mortgage lending, shifting their attention to large-income property loans, with mutual savings banks following suit about 10 years later. By the late 1950s, S&Ls had become the primary investors in single-family residential mortgages.

The mortgage insurance industry was reborn with the founding of Mortgage Guaranty Insurance Corporation (MGIC) in 1957. The re-emergence of private mortgage insurance laid the foundation necessary for growth of the institutional secondary mortgage market. Without mortgage insurance many mortgages would not have been marketable.

The FHA then approached its loan correspondents—which by now were taking on mortgage banking functions—opening the door for other non-supervised lenders to become FHA-approved mortgagees. This development, together with the presence of a secondary mortgage market created by the federal government through the housing-related federal agencies, gave the mortgage bankers their start in exploiting the opportunity presented by government support of the mortgage market, a business that was turned down by both the commercial banks and S&Ls.

The Federal Home Loan Bank Board (FHLBB) assured continued growth of institutional sales when, in 1957, it issued regulations permitting institutions insured by the Federal Savings and Loan Insurance Corporation (FSLIC) to make or purchase conventional loans on the security of properties located beyond their regular area (usually defined as out of state). Until this ruling such institutions needed special approval to buy conventional loans.

In 1968, congressional legislation spun off Fannie Mae as a government-chartered private corporation. The Government National Mortgage Association (GNMA, or Ginnie Mae) was also created to assume Fannie Mae's special-assistance functions of overseeing loan subsidies and below-market purchase programs. Ginnie Mae was also given the guaranty authority that resulted in the introduction of the Ginnie Mae guaranteed mortgage-backed securities (MBSs) program. The Federal Home Loan Mortgage Corporation (FHLMC, or Freddie Mac) followed shortly with its PC program in 1971.

Fannie Mae continued with its market-rate mortgage purchase programs, evolving into the major private secondary market support factor that it is today. A few years later, in 1981, Fannie Mae introduced its own MBSs program.

With the introduction of the Ginnie Mae security in 1970, the residential mortgage market was opened to a broad range of investors, enabling the secondary mortgage market to blossom into a multibillion dollar industry. The still-fledgling mortgage banking industry together with the housing-related agencies were the cornerstones of what would soon become the most spectacular phenomenon in the history of fixed-income securities.

Today, the mortgage banking community includes—in addition to the many still-independent mortgage bankers—savings institutions, commercial banks, and other lenders; even some insurance companies are engaged in originating and servicing home mortgages.

A major evolution of the mortgage banking business has been the development of mortgage conduits. A **conduit**, simply defined, is an organization that buys mortgages from correspondents, packages the loans into collateral pools held by a trustee, and sells mortgage securities through the capital markets.

The Evolution of Conduits

The first conduits were public bodies usually structured as state housing finance agencies that sold tax-exempt "housing bonds" and made the proceeds available to mortgage originators. These state-sponsored agencies passed on the benefit of raising low-cost funds through the tax-exempt market to middle-income home buyers through banks and savings institutions. In 1979, Congress severely limited the issuance of tax-exempt housing bonds, so that these agencies are no longer a dominant factor in residential housing finance. In a real sense Freddie Mac was the first conduit in that the agency purchases mortgages from thousands of mortgage originators across the country and forms giant loan pools against which it issues its Cash program PCs.

Bank of America, building on Ginnie Mae's success, issued the first privately issued pass-through MBS in 1977. The Crocker National Bank of San Francisco and the First Federal Savings and Loan Association of Chicago soon followed. Other private-sector conduits of the early 1980s included Maggie Mae, created by Mortgage Guaranty Insurance Corp. (MGIC), the giant private mortgage insurer of the time and still a leader in that business today. Maggie Mae was innovative because it was set up as a turnkey for mortgage originators, complete with documentation and the requisite loan-by-loan private mortgage insurance as well as the blanket-pool policy required by the rating agencies. The National Home Builders created a conduit called HOMAC (Home Mortgage Access Corp.), which provided mortgage financing obtained from Fannie Mae to homebuilders.

The First Modern Conduits

The first conduit to access directly the Wall Street capital markets was Residential Funding Corporation (RFC), formed in 1982. RFC specialized in "jumbo" mortgages—those that exceed the statutory limit for loan size eligible for purchase by Fannie Mae or Freddie Mac. MGIC underwrote and insured the individual loans and provided the pool policy, and Salomon Brothers issued mortgage securities backed by the pooled loans. Still very active today, RFC is one of the largest as well as the oldest operating conduit, purchasing loans from some 400 correspondents nationwide. RFC issued real estate mortgage investment conduit (REMIC) mortgage securities at a rate of approximately $100 million a month during 1987.

In 1983, Sears Mortgage Securities Corporation attempted to make secondary market history with a $500 million offering of collateralized mortgage obligations (CMOs) that were structured as pass-throughs. Such a structure had long been sought by the conduits in order to achieve sale-of-asset status rather than adding an ever-growing mountain of debt, as was required under the CMO builder-bond structure.

Pre-REMIC Multiclass MBSs Efforts

The Sears structure, in the eyes of the Treasury Department, represented a multiclass pass-through, which was not allowed under the tax law of the time. The existing legislation stipulated that a grantor trust would be exempt from taxation at the mortgage pool level only if there were only one class of securities issued against the trust. The dispute lent stimulus to a series of legislative initiatives, including the TIMS (Trusts for Investment in Mortgages) proposal. TIMS would have amended the tax law and the Securities and Exchange Acts of 1933 and 1934 specifically to permit the issuance of multiclass pass-throughs. TIMS failed to come to fruition, primarily because it prohibited the housing-related federal agencies to share in the exemption. The need for such an instrument became increasingly compelling, however, and ultimately led to inclusion of the REMIC legislation in the 1986 Tax Reform Act.

Evolution of Builder Bonds

The builder-based conduits grew rapidly with the evolution of the CMO as a financing mechanism. The key to the appeal of the CMO was that it enabled the builder to sell mortgages at a low financing cost because of the CMO's sequential bond-class structure. The first few bond classes typically carried shorter average lives—two, three, or five years—which sold at a yield spread off the Treasury yield curve. In other words, the builder created an arbitrage in effect by originating, or buying, mortgages at a yield off the long-maturing end of the yield curve, while much of the financing was obtained at rates pegged off the short (two to seven years) spectrum of the yield curve. This arbitrage would soon be recognized as a commodity of value and traded by Wall Street dealers under the label *residual*.

An added incentive was the builder's ability to elect installment-sale treatment for tax purposes if the mortgages he originated were financed and not sold. By using the mortgages as the proceeds from the sale of the homes he built, the builder could amortize the profit on the sale of a house over the life of the mortgage—in essence recognizing the sale proceeds in installments represented by the mortgage payments. The trick was, by using the mortgages as collateral for the CMO they were deemed to have been financed and not sold, thereby entitling the builder to the installment-sale, or tax deferral-of-income, treatment. The Tax Reform Act of 1986 drastically reduced the ability of the builder to take this attractive tax credit, and by mid-year 1987 builder-bond CMOs began to taper off.

Introduction of REMIC

The REMIC provision of the Tax Act was a boon for some conduit builder-bond issuers—notably Ryland Mortgage Securities Corporation, the financing subsidiary of the Ryland Group, one of the biggest of the builders. Ryland found it could pass on to smaller S&Ls the advantageous REMIC election of taking sale treatment for tax-loss purposes while retaining financing treatment for generally accepted accounting procedures (GAAP). Under this election, S&Ls with underwater loans in portfolio may create a REMIC subsidiary to which the loans are transferred with tax-loss-on-sale treatment. However, the loans are then used as collateral for funding securities, which could either be issued to a Fannie Mae REMIC or a Ryland REMIC to become part of a larger CMO-type REMIC financing. The program became so popular that only 5 percent of the collateral backing Ryland's REMIC bond issues in late 1987 and 1988 was from Ryland's own builder activities. In addition to RFC and Sears, other major conduit operations include Gemico (a General Electric Mortgage Capital subsidiary), GMAC Mortgage Corp, Citibank, Shearson Lehman Mortgage Corp, Travelers, and Prudential.

EVOLUTION OF FEDERAL AGENCY MBSs PROGRAMS

Many investors buy MBSs who would not consider owning whole mortgage loans or who are restricted by statute from such ownership. Initially the largest buyers of these securities were also the largest holders of mortgages. Traditionally, mortgages have been held by investors with long-term liabilities and by financial institutions that intermediate between short-term liabilities and long-term assets. In 1950, for example, long-term investors held about 40 percent of outstanding residential mortgage debt, and depository institutions held 60 percent. But long-term investors stopped accumulating mortgages because of higher returns and lower transaction costs on corporate and government bonds. By 1970, depository institutions' share of mortgage debt amounted to 75 percent of total residential loans originated.

Benefits of Federal Agency Sponsorship of MBSs Programs

The development of MBSs by Ginnie Mae, Freddie Mac, and Fannie Mae has served three functions for the housing-finance system. First, ownership of mortgages can become readily transferable once the mortgages are packaged into instruments with characteristics comparable to other fixed-income securities regularly traded in the financial markets. Thus, while an individual mortgage is of uncertain maturity and risk, the federal agency guaranty converts the mortgage pool into a mortgage pass-through security (MPTS) that may be compared to government bonds of similar maturity. Too, the secondary mortgage market for MBSs is able to assume many of the characteristics of other securities that include the more familiar spectrum of all the other fixed-income securities on the market.

Second, the Ginnie Mae experiment demonstrated that elimination of credit concerns through the federal agency guaranty and broadening of market acceptance via standardized product type would bring such liquidity to the mortgage market that the cost of mortgage financing to the homeowner would be visibly reduced. Not only is the interest required on the mortgage itself less. Transaction costs to originate the loan have also been greatly reduced as the financial intermediaries that originate mortgages have gained access to the Wall Street-sponsored capital markets with their ability to market mortgages in bulk—literally by millions of dollars in minutes. The evolution of federal agency-guaranteed mortgage securities has therefore dramatically enhanced home affordability.

Third, the federal agencies contributed in a singular fashion to the innovation of new mortgage forms, further opening options to both home buyers and institutional investors of mortgage product. Not only was Ginnie Mae the first of the housing-related federal agencies to issue MBSs, it was also early in bringing innovations to the MBSs market. By the early 1970s, Ginnie Mae had already introduced a broad range of MBSs programs that expanded beyond the familiar single-family MBS. These innovations were led by a series of "Tandem plans" wherein Ginnie Mae purchased below-market-rate loans on homes and apartment buildings to assure affordable housing for low- to moderate-income families. Fannie Mae oversaw the origination of the loans through its field offices, and so Ginnie Mae and Fannie Mae were said to be working in tandem to support the program. The Tandem program led to the issuance of project loan securities that financed the construction of hospitals, nursing homes, and a host of multifamily apartment programs. Also early to appear on the Ginnie Mae MBSs menu were securities backed by manufactured housing loans—also referred to as mobile home securities. These programs are all actively used today. Other experiments by Ginnie Mae did not survive, such as its early attempt to create a serial note Ginnie Mae. But the dream of having a MBS with a range of maturities within a single-pool issuance never died. It was given a real life by Freddie Mac in 1983 with its first CMO issuance.

Introduction of Freddie Mac Participation Certificates (PCs)

Freddie Mac joined the MBSs' parade in 1971 with its participation certificate (PC) program, opening the federally guaranteed MBSs market to conventional mortgages (loans not insured by FHA or guaranteed by VA). Freddie Mac furthered the innovation effort in 1975 with the creation of a mortgage security designed to look like a corporate bond. The guaranteed mortgage security (GMC)—"motorcycle" as it was nicknamed by the Wall Street traders, always quick with catchy plays on acronyms—reduced the risk of prepayment volatility by guaranteeing a minimum average life. In addition, the GMC was structured with semiannual payments of principal and interest (P&I) in an effort to make the mortgage security more attractive to nontraditional investors who objected to the monthly remittance of P&I that is characteristic of the pass-through.

Throughout the 1970s Fannie Mae and Freddie Mac further supported the secondary mortgage market by acting as aggressive purchasers of loans originated by approved mortgage bankers and S&Ls. By 1973, Fannie Mae had inaugurated a bi-weekly standby auction program, which offered significant relief from market risk to the mortgage bankers. Under this program, Fannie Mae every two weeks invited mortgage bankers to bid for the right to sell FHA/VA mortgages to the agency over a subsequent four-month period. The mortgage bankers paid a fee to have the right to sell (or "put") the mortgages to Fannie Mae, but the right to sell was optional for the mortgage bankers. Mortgage bankers who held the puts—called standbys, at the time—were able to withstand periods of volatility in mortgage rates. Fannie Mae thereby contributed enormously to the stability of the mortgage market in periods of high interest rates. In 1983, Fannie Mae suspended the four-month commitment auction program as part of its undertaking to restructure and reduce its own exposure to interest-rate risk.

In 1975, the Chicago Board of Trade announced the opening of a futures market in Ginnie Mae securities, adding a further avenue for the hedging of market risk by mortgage originators and investors. Following soon after was the listing of options on Ginnie Mae futures. Fannie Mae and Freddie Mac in 1981 introduced their swap programs, whereby approved financial institutions could package loans held in portfolio and, following submission of the appropriate documentation, receive back on "swap" mortgage securities issued by these agencies. The securities are backed by the loans held in portfolio by the private institution that initiated the swap. Initially the swap program was used primarily by S&Ls, which held seasoned loans in portfolio and took advantage of the program to add liquidity to their mortgage portfolios. The S&Ls were stimulated to do so under 1981 FHLBB regulations allowing S&Ls (under special regulatory accounting procedures called RAP) to dispose of fixed-rate, long-term assets as part of a regulatory mandated effort to restructure the S&L industry. Under the stimulus of these swap programs billions of dollars of MBSs backed by seasoned loans were introduced to the marketplace, thereby creating the two-tiered market for seasoned versus new production loans that exists today.

1981—A Year of Innovation

The year 1981 was pivotal for the now-surging secondary market for mortgages and mortgage securities. Foremost was Fannie Mae's introduction of its adjustable-rate mortgage (ARM) purchase program. Under the program, Fannie Mae announced eight experimental ARM purchase programs representing a number of indexes and a variety of program characteristics. Two plans are indexed to the six-month Treasury bills; four are indexed to Treasury securities with rate-adjustment intervals of 1, 3, and 5 years; and two are indexed to the FHLBB series for closed-loan contracts. At about the same time, the FHLBB and the controller of the currency issued regulations permitting regulated financial institutions to originate ARMs. At first Freddie Mac limited its ARM purchases to loans indexed to the FHLBB mortgage contract rate.

Finally, 1981 launched the age of the conduit when RFC began operation in the private secondary market with a program to purchase mortgage loans exceeding the statutory loan limits on the maximum loan size eligible for purchase by Fannie Mae and Freddie Mac. Under the program, RFC originated the loans, MGIC insured them, and Salomon Brothers issued securities backed by the mortgages.

And in 1981 the lowest mortgage rate in Freddie Mac's primary mortgage market survey was 15 percent, with the highest rate 18.63 percent. Certainly 1981 was a year of both crisis and innovation in the mortgage market.

1983—CMO and ARM Initiatives

After 17 months of recession and one of the longest and most severe housing slumps of the post-World War II years, 1983 ushered in a new round of innovation by the housing-related agencies. A key was the previously mentioned issuance of the first CMO by Freddie Mac: a $1 billion issue, the largest single issue of a mortgage-related security in the U.S. market up to that time. The burgeoning ARM market also underwent refinement as Fannie Mae cut its eight programs to three, all indexed to the market yields of U.S. Treasury securities. Freddie Mac in 1983 also initiated purchases of ARMs indexed to Treasury securities. The ARM market—born of a need to offer affordable mortgage financing to homeowners and at the same time an interest-rate-responsive mortgage instrument to S&Ls top-heavy with fixed-rate as-sets—now became highly standardized. After a period of almost runaway innovation in ARM mortgage structures—one count at Fannie Mae showed 120 different types in the mortgage market—the need to refine the instrument to the strictures of the secondary market took control.

Ginnie Mae in 1983 modified its standard MBSs program with the introduction of GNMA-II, which provided for payments to investors through a central paying agent. Another objective of the GNMA-II program was to encourage the creation of jumbo pools to offer greater diversification of pool demographics and make it possible for large institutional Ginnie Mae investors to receive one check for multimillion dollar holdings of the security. The targets were pension accounts and bond funds, but the program did not become as popular as was hoped because of the additional interest-free time delay that is integral to the GNMA-II security.

An early step toward the CMO-type structure was the issuance in 1983 of sequence bonds by Lehman Brothers Kuhn Loeb (predecessor firm of Shearson Lehman Hutton). The offering was made in the form of serial bonds issued under a real estate investment trust called Investors Ginnie Mae Mort-gage-Backed Securities Trust (Investors GNMA Trust) using pools of Ginnie Mae MBSs as the collateral. There were a total of 10 different projected maturities ranging from 1.9 to 30 years. The projected maturities, as they were referred to in the prospectus, equaled what we would call today the average life of a tranche in the CMO.

1984—Federal Agency Programs Foster Standardization of the Secondary Market

The thrust to standardization of the mortgage market was furthered by Freddie Mac in 1984 when it introduced tape-to-tape transfer of mortgages in a transac-tion of 6,600 loans from the Howard Savings Bank of Livingston, New Jersey. Shortly thereafter Freddie Mac transacted the first dial-up transfer when 1,079 loans were delivered in 12 minutes with an average processing time of 5 seconds per loan. Both Fannie Mae and Freddie Mac now routinely conduct tape-to-tape electronic transfers of large mortgage portfolios.

In 1984, too, American Southwest Financial Corporation, a conduit for homebuilders, sold the first CMO backed by agency-guaranteed securities as well as nonsecuritized conventional mortgages. Thus began a new era in home-builder financing.

Other agency innovations that year were the introduction of the Ginnie Mae ARM security, the beginning of the conversion of Freddie Mac PCs to book-entry transfer, and the birth of the 15-year MBS with issuance of Freddie Mac PCs called Gnomes.

The Secondary Market Enhancement Act (SMEA)

In October 1984, Congress passed the Secondary Market Enhancement Act (SMEA), which vastly broadened Fannie Mae and Freddie Mac programs. The legislation also resolved the controversy surrounding due-on-sale, making the clause a federal jurisdiction. Prior to the SMEA, the ability of financial institutions to enforce the due-on-sale clause was subject to the individual state legislatures.

The SMEA defined a mortgage-related security as one that is:

- Collateralized by first mortgages on residential property (single- or multiple-family, including manufactured home paper).
- Rated in either of the top two categories by a nationally recognized bond-rating service.
- Sold under a registration statement filed with the SEC.

Mortgage securities that so qualify are:

- Legal investment for depository institutions.
- Exempt from any state Blue Sky Law restriction.
- Free from any state law restrictions on investment by insurance companies, private pension funds, and "plan asset" funds.

SMEA Definition of Mortgage-Related Security

The SMEA legislation defined a mortgage-related security as one that is rated in one of the two highest categories by at least one nationally recognized credit-rating agency. In addition, the security either (1) represents ownership of one or more promissory notes or other instruments that are secured by a first lien on property on which is located a residential or mixed residential and commercial structure, or on a residential manufactured home, that were originated by an institution supervised and examined by federal or state authority or by a mortgage lender approved by the secretary of HUD; or (2) is secured by one or more instruments meeting the requirements set forth above that by its terms provides for payments of principal in relation to payments or reasonable projections of payments. The definition further requires that the securities be sold under a registration statement filed with the SEC.

After the mid-1980s innovativeness in mortgage securities shifted to the primary Wall Street dealers, who used the CMO MBS structure to bring about dramatic changes in mortgage finance for massive builder-bond underwritings and to serve as a vehicle for continuing the restructuring of S&L balance sheets.

Federal Agency Programs under Siege

The federal agencies, in the meantime, came under attack by the Reagan Administration. Toward the end of 1985 and into 1986, a number of privatization efforts were made to reduce the involvement of the federal government and its agencies in the housing market. The push for privatization was based in large part on efforts to reduce the mounting federal deficit by slashing housing-subsidy programs. Some people also urged that user fees be imposed on the housing-related agencies in order to generate revenue to the Treasury based on the guaranty authority of the agencies.

Among the proposals was the sale of the FHA to private ownership (which proved to be impractical) and the dismantling of Fannie Mae into several totally private entities. Congress did pass legislation imposing taxation on Freddie Mac beginning in January 1985.

The user-free proposal included a schedule of fees to be charged the agencies based on the volume of mortgage securities they issued. Additionally, the Office of Management and Budget (OMB) proposed a fee on the amount of debt borrowed by Fannie Mae and Freddie Mac to finance purchases of mortgages.

None of the substance of the proposals came to pass, but the distraction within the agencies of responding to the proposals and preparing reports for White House and legislative staff hearings and inquiries caused the innovation process to slacken during 1985 and into 1986.

1986—Resurgence of Federal Agency Initiatives

The agencies did not languish long, however. In July 1986, Fannie Mae issued its first synthetic MBS. The collateral for the pool carried a gross weighted average coupon (WAC) of 11.50 percent with a unique two-class structure dividing the pool P&I cash flow unevenly. In this division 99 percent of the principal and 45 percent of the interest payments were allocated to the A-1 class bonds and 1 percent of the principal and 55 percent of the interest to the A-2 class. The A-1 class bonds carried a discount coupon of 5 percent and the A-2 class a super-premium coupon of 605 percent. This synthetic discount/premium structure evolved into Fannie Mae's issuance in February 1987 of its Trust 1 stripped MBS, which for the first time consisted of 100 percent principal-only and interest-only classes. Goldman Sachs & Company was the underwriter for both the July 1986 and February 1987 Fannie Mae issues.

Freddie Mac meanwhile expanded its project loan program, beginning with the purchase of loans on multifamily rental apartment projects in August 1985. In September 1986, Freddie Mac issued PCs backed by the project loans. The issues were well received by institutional investors as a result of Freddie Mac's innovative structure, which included 5 years of total call protection and balloon maturities of 10 years and 15 years.

Also in March 1986, Freddie Mac inaugurated a PC program for ARMs. The PC ARMs, auctioned weekly, have come to be the most broadly traded of the securitized ARM products.

Figure 1.1 and Table 1.1 present the total MBSs issuance by the three federal agencies from 1970 to 1987.

THE TAX REFORM ACT OF 1986

The Tax Reform Act of 1986 (the Act), enacted early in 1987, affected the secondary mortgage market and its participants in a number of ways. It provided a new vehicle, a real estate mortgage investment conduit (REMIC),

FIGURE 1.1
Annual Issuance of GNMAs, FHLMC PCs, and FNMAs, 1970–87*

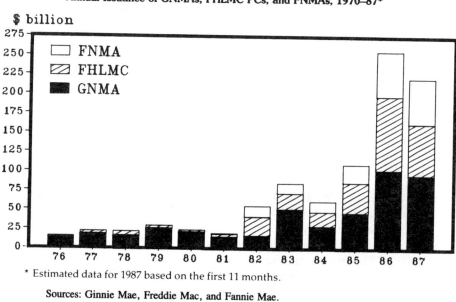

\$ billion

* Estimated data for 1987 based on the first 11 months.

Sources: Ginnie Mae, Freddie Mac, and Fannie Mae.

TABLE 1.1
Summary of Federal Agency Issuance, 1970–87
($ billion)

	1970	1971	1972	1973	1974	1975	1976	1977	1978
Ginnie Maes	0.5	2.7	2.6	2.9	4.6	7.5	13.8	17.4	15.4
30-year single-family	0.5	2.7	2.4	2.6	4.3	7.3	13.1	16.7	14.6
Level-payment	0.5	2.7	2.4	2.6	4.3	7.2	13.1	16.7	14.6
Other[a]	—	—	0.2	0.3	0.3	0.2	0.7	0.7	0.8
FHLMC PCs	—	0.1	0.5	0.3	*	0.5	1.0	4.1	5.7
FNMAs	—	—	—	—	—	—	—	—	—
Grand total[b]	0.5	2.8	3.1	3.2	4.6	8.0	14.8	21.5	21.1

	1979	1980	1981	1982	1983	1984	1985	1986	1987[c]
Ginnie Maes	24.9	20.6	14.3	15.5	50.5	28.2	46.2	101.7	95.2
30-year single-family	24.0	19.7	13.3	14.3	45.1	25.0	40.9	89.5	84.0
Level-payment	22.1	17.4	11.4	12.2	40.3	22.1	38.7	88.3	83.1
Graduated-payment	1.9	2.3	1.9	2.1	4.8	2.9	2.2	1.2	0.9
15-year	—	—	—	*	2.6	1.2	2.9	7.6	5.5
Adjustable-rate	—	—	—	—	—	*	0.1	1.0	1.9
Other[a]	0.9	0.9	0.9	1.2	2.9	2.0	2.2	3.6	3.7
Freddie Mac PCs	3.8	2.5	3.5	24.2	20.0	18.9	38.9	95.6	68.8
30-year	3.8	2.5	3.5	24.2	20.0	17.3	31.3	73.7	55.9
15-year	—	—	—	—	*	1.2	6.9	21.9	12.9
Adjustable-rate	—	—	—	—	—	—	0.2	*	*
Other[a]	—	—	—	—	—	0.4	0.4	*	*
Fannie Maes[a]	—	—	0.7	14.0	13.3	13.6	23.1	58.1	61.0
30-year	—	—	0.7	14.0	13.2	10.2	15.9	43.6	43.7
15-year	—	—	—	—	0.1	0.2	3.0	8.8	8.6
Adjustable-rate	—	—	—	—	*	2.8	4.0	5.3	8.3
Other[a]	—	—	—	—	*	0.4	0.3	0.4	0.4
Grand total[b]	28.7	23.1	18.5	53.7	83.8	60.7	108.2	255.4	225.0

*Less than $50 million.

[a]Includes mobile homes, project and construction loans for Ginnie Maes, and multifamily loans for Freddie Mac PCs and Fannie Maes.

[b]Components may not add to total due to rounding.

[c]Data for 1987 are estimated based on actual data through November.

Note: Issuance of graduated-payment Ginnie Maes, 15-year pass-throughs, and adjustable-rate pass-throughs began in 1979, 1982, and 1984, respectively.

Sources: Ginnie Mae, Freddie Mac, and Fannie Mae.

for the issuance of multiple-class pass-through MBSs. REMICs provide easier access to capital markets because they are simpler and more efficient issuing vehicles than previously existing structures for issuing CMOs. Put simply, the Act minimizes tax considerations when issuing multiple-class MBSs through REMICs. The tax consequences are the same regardless of how the REMIC is structured. As a result, issuers were quick to adopt the REMIC structure and began to issue multiple-class pass-throughs. The Act allows both Fannie Mae and Freddie Mac to issue multiple-class securities through REMICs, and both agencies—as well as Ginnie Mae—now guarantee these securities. Nevertheless, the Act allows a five-year transition period during which time multiple-class pass-through MBSs may be issued through other structures under prior regulations. Beyond that period REMICs will become the exclusive means of issuing multiple-class MBSs without the imposition of two levels of taxation.

REMIC securities appeal to a broader group of investors than existing CMOs, however. The Act removes impediments that may have prevented certain investors—particularly savings institutions and foreigners—from purchasing CMOs or residual interests in CMOs sold through structures such as owner trusts. In addition, multiple-class pass-throughs are generally more desirable investments than single-class pass-throughs because they allow better management of the prepayment risk in the underlying pool of mortgages.

REMIC: In Brief[2]

- REMIC creates a new pass-through tax entity that can hold mortgages secured by any type of real property and issue multiple classes of ownership interests to investors in the form of pass-through certificates, bonds, or other legal forms.

- REMIC allows multiple-class (fast-pay/slow-pay) mortgage pass-throughs, similar to the Sears–Dean Witter structure that was outlawed by IRS regulations in 1984.

- REMIC allows senior/subordinated mortgage pools for all real estate mortgages, with no restrictions on trading the subordinated piece.

- REMIC allows CMOs to be structured with "zero" equity and immediate pay through of monthly bond payments, to eliminate all reinvestment risk.

- REMIC allows mortgage pass-throughs to establish reserve funds for added credit enhancement.

- REMIC allows thrift institutions and others with underwater mortgages to sell mortgages while treating the sale as a *financing* for accounting purposes, avoiding unwanted accounting losses.

- REMIC allows mortgage-backed cash-flow bonds structured like CMOs to qualify as real estate investments for thrifts and REITs.

[2]This analysis of the REMIC legislation was prepared by Donald Susswein, tax-law partner in the Washington office of Thacher Proffitt & Wood. Thacher Proffitt & Wood was the leading law firm in developing and shepherding the REMIC provisions through the congressional tax legislative process.

- REMIC applies to all real estate mortgages and to public as well as private offerings.
- REMIC reduces "phantom income" on discount CMOs by clarifying how the OID rules apply to debt with uncertain maturities.
- REMIC also creates new information-reporting requirements for CMOs and similar debt obligations, even when they are sold to corporations.

REMIC Building Blocks

The building blocks of REMIC transactions come in two basic categories: the underlying mortgage collateral that goes into the REMIC entity and the investment certificates the REMIC issues to investors.

REMIC Collateral

The basic and predominant type of collateral is an extremely broad category called a Qualified Mortgage. It encompasses whole loans; 100 percent participation certificates and pass-throughs; partial participations and interests in pass-throughs; stripped coupons such as a stream of interest only on a mortgage, mortgage participation, or pass-through; stripped mortgages such as the principal and part of the interest that remains after stripping off a stripped coupon; and senior and subordinated participations in mortgage pools. It also includes certain interests in other REMIC pools.

Qualified Mortgages (whichever of the above-mentioned forms are selected) must be secured by an interest in real property. Thus both commercial and residential mortgage loans qualify, but not automobile loans or installment receivables.

The second type of collateral is called a Cash-Flow Investment. In essence, it is a short-term investment in a passive, interest-bearing asset made solely for the purpose of reinvesting cash flows received from Qualified Mortgages between regular scheduled payments to investors. Cash-Flow Investments need not be mortgage related in any way. They may be actual short-term securities or third-party investment arrangements such as guaranteed-investment contracts.

The third type of collateral is called a Qualified Reserve Fund. It includes longer-term investments that may be set aside if a reserve fund is required solely to fund the expenses (if any) of running the REMIC pool or to insure investors against the risk of default on Qualified Mortgages. These investments may include mortgage securities or nonmortgage securities and may also include third-party contractual guarantees to fund expenses or insure against default, such as letters of credit or pool insurance.

In addition, in the event of default on Qualified Mortgages, real property acquired in connection with foreclosure can be held for up to one year.

REMIC Interests Sold to Investors

Once the REMIC collateral is selected, interests in the pool can be created for investors. As with other aspects of REMICs, the hallmark of the law is substance, not form. Permissible REMIC interests can be called bonds, participations, pass-through certificates, or even corporate stock or partnership interests. The important rules relate to the economic differences among different types of REMIC interests that can be sold to investors or retained by issuers.

Regular Interests The predominant form of investor participation in a REMIC is called a Regular Interest. Regular Interests can best be thought of as the economic equivalent of bonds, although they may be issued in the form of pass-throughs as well as debt obligations. In essence, a Regular Interest must represent an amount corresponding to the principal of a debt obligation. It may also—but need not—provide for coupon interest on the outstanding principal amount.

Regular Interests may be issued in multiple classes. Thus, in a mortgage pool subject to prepayment, the earliest mortgages to prepay can be assigned to the fast-pay Regular Interests while the last mortgages to pay off can be assigned to the slow-pay Regular Interests, just as with a CMO. Regular Interests may also be issued with differing priorities in the event of defaults on Qualified Mortgages. Thus, senior and junior participations in mortgage pools can be created and issued as multiple classes of Regular Interests. The advantage of a REMIC senior/junior arrangement (as compared with similar arrangements under the grantor trust rules) is that Congress has explicitly clarified that both the senior and the junior classes may be freely traded. Prior to REMIC there had been some uncertainty whether junior interests in a traditional grantor trust participation or pass-through could be traded without losing pass-through treatment.

Residual Interests The second type of investment in a REMIC pool is called a Residual Interest. Residual Interests are statutorily defined—somewhat cryptically—as investments that are designated as Residual Interests and that are not Regular Interests. Although some points remain to be clarified in Treasury regulations, Residual Interests are generally intended to encompass rights to payments that are contingent on a certain speed of prepayments (for example, excess servicing that will be extinguished if prepayments accelerate or "excess" mortgage principal in an overcollateralized structure that will be used up to make interest payments to Regular Interest holders if prepayments are slower than anticipated).

In addition, Residual Interests may include the right to earnings on Qualified Reserve Funds or Cash-Flow Investments that are not needed to pay the amounts guaranteed to holders of Regular Interests. In general, no restrictions apply with regard to the size of Residual Interests because the purpose of the law is to permit the elimination of "equity" from CMO-like transactions. There must, however, always be one—and only one—class of Residual Interests. Thus, any payments that are contingent in amount on the income earned on Cash-Flow Investments, or the risk that Qualified Reserve Funds will be called upon to pay unexpected expenses, must all be allocated to the single class of investors who own the Residual Interests. Although different investors may own different portions of the Residual Interest, all of their interests must be undivided, pro-rata interests.

The REMIC legislation has had a singular impact on the private pass-through market by permitting greater flexibility in the use of the senior/subordinated structure for enhancing the credit considerations related to privately issued pass-throughs. When issued as a REMIC, the subordinated class may be issued as a marketable bond class structured as a pass-through security. Before REMIC, creation of a subordinated participation on a pass-through security would have violated the tax-law prohibition on multiple-class pass-throughs.

The senior/subordinated structure has become popular with issuers of private pass-throughs because it avoids the expense of the pool insurance and bank letter of credit enhancements that were common to the privately issued MBSs of the past decade. Many investors prefer the senior/subordinated structure because the credit enhancement relies on the subordination of a participation in the underlying collateral pool. The weakening of the private mortgage insurance industry in the mid-1980s (highlighted by the Epic Mortgage Company default) and the recent downgrading of many commercial bank credit ratings have subjected deals with third-party credit enhancement to "event" risk.

The major breakthrough for the structure came in a $127 million senior/subordinated 1987 REMIC issue by RFC, underwritten by Salomon Brothers. RFC sold both the senior and subordinated classes in the same transaction, which was rated AA by both Standard & Poor's and Moody's without the requirement of mortgage-pool or special-hazard insurance or a bank letter of credit.

SAVINGS INSTITUTIONS

S&Ls, savings banks, and credit unions perform a vital function in the U.S. economy, linking consumers who have funds to save or invest with those who want to borrow. They accept savings deposits from the public and then use the funds to make various types of investments.

Savings institutions are specialized but extremely important members of a class of institutions known as financial intermediaries. This broad classification includes such diverse organizations as commercial banks, insurance companies, credit unions, and finance and investment companies. As a group, these institutions offer investors and savers a wide variety of financial options and make funds available to borrowers for many purposes.

At one time, savings associations and savings banks were distinct types of institutions with unique purposes and forms of operation. With the FHLB restructuring initiatives of the early 1980s, however, these distinctions have largely disappeared. A convergent trend first appeared a number of years ago, and with the enactment of the Garn-St Germain Depository Institutions Act in October 1982, most of the remaining gaps were closed. Among many other distinction-blurring provisions, the Garn-St Germain Act authorized savings associations to convert easily to savings bank form, and vice versa.

Savings Deregulation[3]

The single most important factor that has changed the structure of the savings industry in recent years has been deregulation. In the 1960s, savings institutions and commercial banks were totally regulated as to the kinds of deposit plans and terms they could offer. In essence, this body of regulations gave every institution the same product line, except that savings institutions could pay 1/4 of 1 percent more than could commercial banks on most account classes. This differential in favor of thrift institutions was intended to help the thrifts attract funds for housing, since they could not offer the full range of consumer financial services that commercial banks could.

These savings account regulations both simplified savings choices for consumers by limiting options and prevented rate wars among depositories. During the 1970s, however, consumers increasingly reacted to limited choices and controlled-rate ceilings by moving their funds out of depository institutions and into alternative, unregulated intermediaries and direct market investments.

The regulators dealt with these problems by authorizing a greater variety of accounts, raising ceilings on some accounts and tying the ceilings on others to market indicators such as Treasury obligations. Consumers responded by moving an unprecedented amount of money at an unprecedented rate into some of the new types of accounts.

In 1980, the power to set interest-rate ceilings and authorize new types of accounts was shifted from the individual federal banking and thrift regulatory agencies to the Depository Institutions Deregulation Committee (DIDC). The overall mission of this body was to phase out interest-rate ceilings and most other regulations applying to savings accounts.

On October 1, 1983, the DIDC removed rate ceilings and minimum

---

[3]This discussion is reprinted from the U.S. League of Savings Institutions, *Savings Information Sourcebook* (Chicago: 1987).

balance requirements on all new accounts with maturities longer than one month. At the same time, it reduced early-withdrawal penalties.

On January 1, 1984, the 1/4 of 1 percent thrift institution differential was ended. This equalization of rates was mandated by the Garn-St Germain Act of 1982, which also granted broad new powers to savings institutions.

On January 1, 1985, the remaining minimum balance requirement on savings accounts was lowered to $1,000 and a year later was phased out altogether. Three months later, on March 31, 1986, the last interest-rate ceilings (on passbook accounts) were eliminated—and the DIDC went out of existence.

The Impact of RAP Accounting

A landmark ruling by the FHLBB in October 1981 introduced regulatory accounting procedures (RAP), a ruling that triggered a massive restructuring of S&L balance sheets, forever altering the face of the S&L industry. Under RAP, S&Ls could dispose of long-term, fixed-rate assets and amortize the loss over the remaining life of the assets sold. And RAP permitted the S&Ls to sell underwater loans without taking immediate recognition of the loss.

Until the RAP ruling, S&Ls had been unwilling to sell loans held in portfolio at a loss because the consequent write-down to net worth would have been devastating—in fact, many S&Ls would have slipped below the minimum net worth required to maintain eligibility for FSLIC insurance. Following RAP, S&Ls disposed of fixed-rate loan portfolios by the hundreds of millions of dollars per institution, with some selling over 50 percent of their fixed-rate loans held in portfolio. The process was accelerated by the loan swap program introduced in 1981 by Fannie Mae and Freddie Mac. Under these swap programs, S&Ls could exchange their mortgages for securities issued by one of the federal agencies. These securities could then be sold into the now highly liquid MBSs secondary market or used as collateral for short-term borrowing under a repurchase agreement or even to issue a mortgage-backed bond or CMO.

The proceeds from these asset sales were reinvested for the most part in assets that would give the S&Ls a better asset-to-liability match than had their fixed-rate loans. The S&L crisis was precipitated in the first place by decades of long-term lending of fixed-rate mortgages that were carried against short-term, variable-rate liabilities, primarily CDs. The S&Ls now sought assets that would be variable rate, or shorter term if fixed rate.

This major redirection in S&L investing and lending patterns took two major thrusts. One was to shift S&L portfolio lending practices to ARMs. Fixed-rate mortgages were increasingly originated for immediate resale into the secondary market. Most S&Ls simply sold the loans to the Freddie Mac Cash auction window. Some, however, evolved into mortgage banking entities, becoming major competitors of the independent mortgage bankers. The S&L had an advantage in that it could still perform as a portfolio lender when it was competitively advantageous to do so. It also enjoyed a lower cost of loan warehousing (the trade term for the interim financing of mortgages prior to sale to the secondary market).

The second thrust was a headlong charge by some S&Ls to income-property lending for condominiums, shopping centers, hotels, and a host of commercial projects. The allure of income-property lending was short-term loans at high returns. Most of these loans were for construction, or for ''miniperms''—postconstruction loans for two to three years designed to carry the project from completion of construction through lease-up until, as a proved economic entity, a permanent loan could be secured from an insurance company or similar lending source. The income-property loans made by the S&Ls were for the most part balloon loans, many made at low interest rates in return for a percentage of the capital gain anticipated on resale of the property.

And so a new crisis for the S&L industry was bred by the acquisition of billions of dollars of commercial loans, large numbers of which ultimately proved to be bad assets. Many S&Ls found they had simply substituted credit risk for the market risk of the old fixed-rate residential loans. The onset of inflation in the 1970s and early eighties brought about the initial destruction of S&L net worth by discounting the market value of the long-term, fixed-rate residential loans. Ironically, it was the absence of inflation in the mid-1980s that brought to an end the real estate boom—a surge that was built on expectations that ever-rising real estate prices would bail out projects of questionable economic viability. Perhaps the death blow was the Tax Reform Act of 1986, which pulled the rug out from under the tax shelter-oriented syndicators who had found it easy to raise equity-based money to start projects for which there was no real demand. Many S&Ls that did not have income-property underwriting expertise were caught off guard.

Table 1.2 summarizes S&L secondary market activity from 1980 through 1987. The table reflects the sudden jump in sales of residential loans starting in 1982 at $51.5 billion. Much of the activity through 1984 represented disposition of underwater loans, largely through the Freddie Mac Guarantor swap program, although some was also done through Fannie Mae. By 1985, the sale of seasoned loans subsided as the restructuring process ran its course. Since 1985, most S&L loan sales have represented mortgage banking style sale of new production loans not originated for holding in portfolio.

The growth in loans purchased for portfolio since 1983 has increasingly consisted of ARMs. According to U.S. League of Savings Institutions data, from 1983 to mid-1987, S&L portfolio holdings of ARM loans increased by 18

TABLE 1.2
How Savings Institutions Have Performed in the Secondary Market[a]

	1980	1981	1982	1983	1984	1985	1986	1987
Sales of residential loans	$15.6	$12.3	$51.5	$52.8	$56.4	$91.3	$165.4	$124.2
Sales of other mortgages	0.3	0.3	1.9	2.6	7.4	6.3	4.4	3.8
Total sales	$15.9	$12.6	$53.4	$55.4	$63.8	$97.6	$169.8	$128.0
Purchases of residential loans	$12.5	$10.0	$20.4	$37.4	$48.6	$49.7	$ 62.5	$ 59.4
Purchases of other mortgages	0.5	0.5	2.9	8.4	15.6	12.5	6.6	5.3
Total purchases	$13.0	$10.5	$23.3	$45.8	$64.2	$62.2	$ 69.1	$ 64.7
Net loan sales	$ 2.9	$ 2.1	$30.1	$ 9.6	($ 0.4)	$35.4	$100.7	$ 63.3
As a percentage of assets	0.5%	0.3%	4.4%	1.2%	−0.0%	3.3%	8.6%	5.0%

[a]FSLIC-insured institutions only; dollars in billions.

Source: U.S. League of Savings Institutions.

percent, from $201 billion to $237.5 billion. More than 80 percent of this increase was after the interest-rate spike in the spring of 1986—an indication of how sensitive S&Ls have become to interest-rate risk exposure.

The listing of major legislative highlights includes the key legislative and regulatory events that shaped the S&L industry from the 1960s through the mid-1980s.

Major Legislative Events Affecting Savings Institutions

1932	Federal Home Loan Bank Act	Established the Federal Home Loan Banks (FHLB) under the supervision of the Federal Home Loan Bank Board (FHLBB) to provide a central credit facility for home financing institutions.
1933	Banking Act	Created the Federal Deposit Insurance Corporation (FDIC) to insure demand and time deposits at commercial banks and savings banks.
1933	Home Owners' Loan Act	Authorized the creation under the FHLBB of a system of federally chartered and supervised savings and loan associations.

1934	National Housing Act	Established the Federal Savings and Loan Insurance Corporation (FSLIC) to insure savings accounts at member associations; created the Federal Housing Administration (FHA) to insure mortgages and other loans made by private lenders.
1944	Servicemen's Readjustment Act (The G.I. Bill of Rights)	Established a program of loan guarantees under Veterans Administration (VA) auspices to encourage private lending on generous terms to veterans of the armed forces.
1949	Housing Act	Established national housing goals of "a decent home and suitable living environment for every American family"; provided grants to municipalities for public housing and slum clearance; set up a program of financial assistance for rural areas under the Farmers Home Administration.
1961	Housing Act	Authorized new programs for federal involvement in housing, including subsidized rental housing for low- and moderate-income families; expanded funding for Fannie Mae special-assistance functions.
1968	Housing and Urban Development Act	Gave federal associations the authority to invest in mobile home and home-equipment loans; expanded their authority to issue a wide variety of savings plans, notes, bonds, and debentures.
1970	Emergency Home Finance Act	Created the Federal Home Loan Mortgage Corporation (Freddie Mac), under the FHLBB, to provide a secondary market for conventional, FHA, and VA mortgages.
1974	Housing and Community Development Act	Liberalized the types and amounts of loans a federal association may make.

1974	Real Estate Settlement Procedures Act	Provided comprehensive guidelines for loan closing costs and settlement practices.
1975	Home Mortgage Disclosure Act	Required most financial institutions to disclose the numbers and dollar amounts of mortgage loans made, by geographical area.
1976	Tax Reform Act	Reduced certain allowable federal income tax deductions for savings institutions and increased the minimum tax rate; liberalized IRA and Keogh account provisions.
1977	Housing and Community Development Act	Liberalized association lending limits; required financial institution regulatory agencies to take into account an institution's record of serving the credit needs of its community when evaluating applicants for new facilities, mergers, and other matters.
1978	Financial Institutions Regulatory and Interest Rate Control Act	Increased FDIC and FSLIC insurance limits for IRA and Keogh accounts from $40,000 to $100,000; provided for FHLBB chartering of federal savings banks; amended Consumer Credit Protection Act establishing rights and responsibilities for electronic fund transfers.
1980	Depository Institutions Deregulation and Monetary Control Act	Shifted deposit account authority from individual depository institution regulators to a Deregulation Committee; increased FSLIC and FDIC insurance for all accounts from $40,000 to $100,000; gave the Federal Reserve authority to set reserve requirements on short-term accounts at all depository institutions; extended the federal override of state usury ceilings on various loans; authorized NOW accounts nationwide.

1982	Garn-St Germain Depository Institutions Act	For all depository institutions, preempted or severely limited state due-on-sale clause and alternative mortgage loan restrictions; granted broader powers to the Federal Deposit Insurance Corporation; mandated the phaseout of the savings interest-rate differential by 1/1/84. For insured institutions with deficient net worth, provided for FSLIC and FDIC assistance to bring net worth to required levels, in the form of insurance corporation notes exchanged for net worth certificates issued by the institution. For savings institutions, eased charter and conversion limits. For federal associations, created or expanded lending and investment authority; authorized the acceptance of demand deposits from business and agricultural loan customers; removed mortgage loan-to-value ratio limits.
1984	Deficit Reduction Act	Reduced the tax benefits from certain corporate tax-preference items; simplified tax credit rules; extended the tax exemption for qualified mortgage subsidy bonds; phased out graduated tax rates for large corporations; created new reporting procedures for mortgage interest, property foreclosure, or abandonment, and IRAs.
1986	Tax Reform Act	Reduced top corporate tax rate from 46 percent to 34 percent and also reduced the percentage of taxable-income bad-debt deduction from 40 percent to 8 percent; provided for 3-year carrybacks and 15-year carryforwards for savings institution net operating losses; extended to 8

years the carryover period for net
operating losses incurred in taxable
years beginning after December 31,
1981, and before January 1, 1986.

1986 Tax Reform Impact on Savings Institutions[4]

Savings institutions are among the businesses heavily affected by the Tax
Reform Act of 1986. The law created substantial tax-planning challenges and
opportunities for savings institutions as a result of key changes involving
corporate tax rates, bad-debt calculations, and the treatment of net operating
losses.

One change reduced the top tax rate from 46 to 34 percent for all
corporations, including savings institutions. The law established an effective
date of July 1, 1987, for rate reductions, producing maximum blended rates of
about 40 percent for calendar year 1987.

The main feature of the Internal Revenue Code for savings institutions is
the availability of a special tax deduction for additions to reserves for bad debts.
The new law substantially changed the size and applicability of this deduction.
Under the previous law, an institution generally qualified as a savings and loan
association for tax purposes as long as it held at least 60 percent of its assets in
cash, U.S. government or agency securities, and housing-related investments
such as loans secured by real estate. A maximum 40 percent of taxable-income
bad-debt deduction applied but was subject to a pro-rata reduction to the extent
qualifying assets comprised less than 82 percent of total assets.

The 1986 tax law reduced the percentage of taxable-income bad-debt
deduction from 40 to 8 percent for tax years beginning after December 31,
1986. In addition, it eliminated the 82 percent qualification for the maximum
deduction. Instead, a standard 60 percent threshold was established in order to
qualify as a savings association.

Under another provision of the 1986 tax law, savings institutions' net
operating loss carrybacks and carryforwards will be covered by the same rules
that generally apply to other corporations. Formerly, institution net operating
losses could be carried back 10 years and carried forward 5 years. The new tax
law provides for 3-year carrybacks and 15-year carryforwards.

The 1986 tax law also provides for the creation of a new mortgage-backed securities pooling mechanism conduit, or REMIC. A REMIC
security is similar to a CMO but qualifies for more favorable tax and accounting
treatment. Issuers may opt for either debt financing or sale-of-assets treatment

---

[4]This discussion of tax act impact is from U.S. League of Savings Institutions, *The Savings
Institution Sourcebook* (Chicago: 1987).

in structuring a REMIC issue. The REMIC statute has enabled savings institutions to become bigger participants in the multiclass mortgage securities market because REMIC securities qualify for purposes of the asset-composition test.

New Net Worth Requirements of S&Ls

In August 1986, the FHLBB issued extensive amendments to its net worth regulation for FSLIC-insured institutions. The new regulation, which became effective January 1, 1987, imposed significantly tighter capital account discipline on the savings institution business. Over time, the regulation will require savings institutions to build their capital ratios from 3 to 6 percent of liabilities. When the 6 percent level will be reached is to be determined by two main conditions: each institution's level capital as of December 31, 1986, and the overall profitability of the business. Officially, the new regulation replaced the term "net worth" with "regulatory capital." In practice, however, "net worth" will likely remain in use.

The new capital rules will have the least impact on savings institutions with strong net worth ratios. Some institutions will have to adjust their capital ratios more quickly than others.

Savings institutions today have evolved into full-service financial institutions. Most S&Ls and savings banks now approach fixed-rate mortgage lending from a mortgage banker's perspective. The majority of S&Ls sell their conforming-size fixed-rate loans to both Freddie Mac and Fannie Mae. Increasingly, however, these institutions avail themselves of the federal agency programs to swap loans for MBSs to achieve the flexibility and generally better pricing available by selling the fixed-rate loans as agency-guaranteed mortgage securities to the Wall Street-sponsored MBSs dealer market. ARM production is, however, largely retained for portfolio because of the excellent asset-to-liability match it represents.

Some institutions have transformed their balance sheets into largely fully hedged combinations of assets and liabilities. Assets owned are financed in any way that is most advantageous, from reverse repurchase agreements to various types of structured financings, with the mortgage assets serving as collateral. Often the assets include derivative mortgage products such as CMO residuals, CMO floaters, or stripped MBSs that shorten the duration of the assets. Similarly, the liabilities may include interest-rate swaps that extend the duration of the liabilities or other forms of financing through subordinated capital notes, adjustable-rate preferred stock, or term CDs. The S&L ideal has become to achieve the optimum asset-to-liability match.

FASB 91 Statement Impacts Financial Institutions

In December 1986 the Financial Accounting Standards Board (FASB) climaxed an extensive examination of the accounting for loan-origination fees and costs with the issuance of Statement of Financial Accounting Standards Number 91 (SFAS 91). The SFAS statement, titled *Accounting for Nonrefundable Fees and Costs Associated with Originating or Acquiring Loans,* had a major impact on S&L income accounting.

SFAS 91 in Summary[5] SFAS 91 affects all lending and leasing transactions entered into, and commitments granted, in fiscal years beginning after December 15, 1987.

It applies to accounting and reporting for nonrefundable fees and costs associated with various lending activities, such as:

- Points
- Application fees
- Management fees
- Restructuring fees
- Origination fees
- Commitment fees
- Syndication fees.

SFAS 91 also applies to all types of loans and lenders—including banks, thrift institutions, mortgage bankers, insurance companies, and other financial and nonfinancial institutions.

Whatever their designations, all fees associated with lending activities are now classified in one of the three following categories:

1. Loan-origination fees
2. Commitment fees
3. Syndication fees.

Loan-Origination Fees Under SFAS 91 origination fees are to be deferred and recognized over the life of the loan as an adjustment of yield (interest income) using the interest method.

The incremental direct cost of loan acquisition or origination is treated as a reduction in the yield of the respective loan using the interest method of amortization.

The current practice of recognizing that part of fee income equal to original cost is not permitted.

---

[5]This analysis of SFAS 91 by Richard A. Sprayregen, partner in the Los Angeles office of Kenneth Leventhal & Company, was published in *Secondary Marketing Executive* (L.D.J. Corporation, Waterbury, CT) in February 1988.

There are three problems associated with accounting for such fees in that manner.

1. The statement presumes that each loan will be accounted for separately. Aggregated treatment is allowed only if the resulting amortization is not materially different from the amount determined on a loan-by-loan basis.

2. The life of the loan is presumed to be the contract term. In the event of premature payoff, any unamortized fee is recorded in the period of early payoff.

3. Application of the interest method will consider only periodic payments required by the contract. Prepayments of principal are not to be anticipated. Prepayment penalties, negative amortization of the loan, and variable-rate mortgages only complicate calculations.

Commitment Fees Under SFAS 91 commitment fees are to be deferred, and if the commitment is exercised, the fee is recognized by the interest method over the life of the new loan.

If the commitment expires unexercised, the fee is recognized as income upon expiration of the commitment. There are exceptions, however:

- If the lender's experience indicates a remote likelihood of the loan commitment being exercised, the fee may be recognized as income over the commitment period on a straight-line basis. If the commitment is exercised, the unamortized fee is recognized using the interest method over the life of the loan.

- If the commitment fee is determined retrospectively as a percentage of a previously unused line of credit that was (a) below market when paid and (b) at market rates when the loan was made, the commitment fee is recognized as service-fee income as of the determination date.

Syndication Fees Syndication fees are now to be recognized when the syndication is complete unless the syndication retains a portion of the syndication loan.

If the yield on the retained portion, after taking into account fees passed through by the syndication, is less than the average yield to the participants, the syndicator must defer a portion of the fee.

Special treatment is also accorded fees and costs in refinancings or restructuring loans if the terms are at least as favorable to the lender as are comparable loans other than refinancings. The fee is then accounted for as with a new loan.

The effective yield of the new loan must be the current market yield when compared to other new, nonrestructured loans. Any unamortized net fees or costs—including prepayment penalties—from the original loan must be recognized in interest income when the new loan is granted. New fees are deferred according to guidelines for all new loans.

Fees received in connection with a modification of terms of a troubled debt restructuring under FASB 15 are now treated as a reduction of the recorded investment in the loan. All related costs, including direct loan cost, are charged to expense as incurred. Deferred net fees or costs cannot be amortized during periods in which interest income is not being recognized.

Impact of SFAS 91 on S&Ls The new requirements for prepayment and cost accounting may encourage some lenders to sell loans. When a loan is sold, the excess of origination fees over costs may be recognized immediately. In addition, if MBSs are purchased, accounting for prepayments may be simplified because prepayments for MBSs are easier to track than are those for a large number of separate whole loans.

The new standards for cost accounting could result in deferral of up to 50 basis points of origination income for loans that are not sold. In 1988, FSLIC-insured thrifts are expected to originate about $150 billion in mortgage loans. If loan sales continue at the 1987 pace, FASB 91 could result in a deferral of $250 million in income that would have been reported in 1988 under the previously accepted accounting standards. In the third quarter of 1987, the latest for which data are available, solvent thrifts earned a total of $713 million, while all FSLIC-insured thrifts lost $1.6 billion.

1987 Legislative and Regulatory Activity Expanded

In addition to being a year of economic transition, 1987 was an active period for housing- and mortgage-related legislation and regulation. After several months of negotiations, Congress passed and the President signed a housing appropriations bill in December. The bill authorized $30 billion in spending over the next two years on a variety of housing-development programs. Included in the bill were a number of provisions relating to the secondary mortgage market:

1. Maximum limits on FHA-insured loans were raised in high-cost areas from $90,000 to $101,250.
2. The insurance premium on FHA loans was frozen at 3.8 percent of the mortgage balance.
3. User fees were prohibited on federally sponsored credit agencies.
4. The limit on FHA-insured loans that may carry adjustable mortgage rates was raised from 10 percent to 30 percent.

The other major piece of legislation affecting the mortgage markets was the enactment in August of the Competitive Equality Banking Act (CEBA) of 1987. The act authorized the FSLIC to raise up to $10.8 billion in capital through a newly chartered financing corporation. In addition, a one-year moratorium was placed on exits from FSLIC, and regulatory relief was granted to some thrifts unable to meet current capital requirements. In December, the FHLBB issued final regulations to implement provisions of the CEBA pertaining to thrifts. The regulations covered uniform accounting standards, classification of assets, qualified thrift lender tests, troubled debt restructuring, capital forbearance, and regulatory capital requirements.

Two regulatory and accounting proposals relating to the risk associated with mortgage securities were made in 1987. The Federal Reserve Board issued a proposed regulation requiring that a risk-based capital measure be used in conjunction with changes in the definition of primary capital. The regulation groups bank assets into categories and assigns "risk weights" according to credit liquidity and interest-rate risks. Ginnie Maes have a 25 percent weight, compared to 50 percent for Fannie Mae MBSs and Freddie Mac PCs. The weights range from zero percent for cash to 100 percent for claims on private entities.

A separate proposal by the Financial Accounting Standards Board (FASB) would require that companies using generally accepted accounting principles disclose the risks associated with their holdings of financial instruments. Disclosure encompasses four areas of possible risk: credit, cash flow, interest rate, and market value. Holdings of mortgage securities are covered by the proposal.

Both the Federal Reserve regulation and the FASB proposal, if adopted, could lead to a reassessment of the relative values of mortgage securities and possible shifts of portfolio holdings. In the case of the FASB proposal, these shifts are likely to take place before the end of accounting periods. The lower capital requirements for MBSs are not expected to have a sizable impact on the portfolio management of large commercial banks because mortgage securities generally constitute only a small portion of their assets. Among smaller banks, however, the impact may be greater because mortgage securities are often a significant portion of total assets. The new regulation may induce capital-deficient banks to swap out of Freddie Macs and Fannie Maes into Ginnie Maes.

OTHER INSTITUTIONAL INVESTORS

Pension funds were initially reluctant to invest heavily in mortgage securities, but beginning in the 1980s their investment posture changed significantly. Through the 1970s, pension funds (public and private) held from 5 to 11 percent of outstanding Ginnie Mae MBSs. By 1986, the percentage had increased to perhaps 35–40 percent, representing a substantial increase in pension fund participation in Ginnie Maes.[6]

The public pension funds have for some time, as a social benefit, invested portions of their funds in home mortgages. Private pension funds, however, are less fixed-income–oriented than are their public counterparts and are less prone to support public causes.

Pension funds most recently have participated in three principal segments of the MBSs market: pool-specific discount-coupon MBSs collateralized by seasoned loans; the broadly traded generic current-coupon sector; and the longer-maturing classes of the CMOs, in particular the Z-bond class.

The seasoned discount sector offers the pension funds a steady cash flow assured by the seasoning of the underlying loans. The discounts also offer considerable call protection because of the relatively lower mortgage coupon rates inherent in the discounts collateral. Most pension funds interested in seasoned discount-coupon MBSs invest on a pool-specific basis because they prefer to analyze the historical profile of an actual pool with respect to its demographic and prepayment-speed characteristics.

Most pension funds that buy MBSs for the yield spread they offer to comparable-maturing Treasury and agency securities invest primarily in the current-coupon sector of the MBSs market. The current-coupon MBS represents current new production mortgage securities produced by the primary obligation market. It is readily available to investors in large pools and represents a higher liquid market.

The Z-bond class of the CMO represents the ultimate in call protection because prepayments from the collateral pool underlying the CMO are passed through first to the holders of the earlier CMO classes. In addition, many pension funds face a heavy cash-flow stream to be invested and prefer the Z-bond, which makes no principal or interest payments for several years. Pension fund assets are expected to quadruple during this decade, rising from their $600 billion 1980 level to an anticipated $2.25 trillion by 1990.

Mutual Funds

In the early 1980s the mutual and bond funds added Ginnie Mae funds to their stable of products. Ginnie Mae mutual funds have lent additional liquidity to the MBSs market as major institutional buyers of the mortgage security product but also from time to time have introduced high volatility when they have engaged in mass selling.

The difficulty stems from the sensitivity of these mutual funds to the

---

[6]Ginnie Mae holdings specifically identified as pension funds were reported as 6.9 percent, but it is believed the 36.6 percent held in the "nominees" category is largely represented by pension fund investments.

reactions of their individual investors to sudden changes in investor sentiment. When interest rates are seen to be rising, mutual fund investors tend to redeem their shares in a mass exodus of sorts, forcing the funds to liquidate some of their holdings to meet the redemptions. All institutional investors trade their portfolios in keeping with their market outlook; but the Ginnie Mae funds cause more volatility in the market than others because heavy redemptions force them to sell securities for reasons unrelated to pure portfolio strategy.

The Investment Company Institute estimates that government bond and Ginnie Mae funds grew in asset size from about $58 billion in 1980 to almost $450 billion by the end of 1987.

SEC Advertising Ruling Affects Ginnie Mae Funds[7]

The ability to report a high-yield performance is critical to mutual funds in their effort to maintain competitive standing with fixed-income investors. For these funds, of course, advertising is the prime marketing tool, with emphasis placed on their ability to claim a yield return superior to other funds over as long a time as possible. As a consequence, Ginnie Mae funds in particular have favored investing in high-coupon MBSs where, based on a current-yield calculation, these premium-priced MBSs would demonstrate the highest yield performance. The difficulty is that if prepayments accelerate, the yield realized on premium-priced MBSs can be substantially below the calculated current yield.

In response to this practice, the SEC in March 1988 issued new regulations governing the manner in which yields and performance claims are represented in mutual fund advertising. The rule requires that the calculated yield must be based on the actual income received over the most recent 30-day period. The calculation must reflect amortization of discount and premium, using a market value, not cost basis. The consequence, of course, would be a reduction in the reportable net income of premium-priced MBSs held in the mutual fund portfolio if an acceleration of prepayment speed caused the loss of unamortized premium. An acceleration in prepayment speed of a discount-coupon MBS, with the early return of principal at par, obviously enhances the realized yield and would benefit the mutual funds.

The consequence of the ruling—effective May 1, 1988—has resulted in a shift in the investment orientation of the Ginnie Mae funds from one of current yield to total return. (For a discussion of the techniques for calculating the yield and total return of an MBS, see Chapter 6.)

A summary of holders of Ginnie Mae MBSs through 1986 is given in Table 1.3.

[7]This discussion of mutual fund advertising is based on information contained in Drexel Burnham Lambert, *The New SBC Mutual Fund Advertising Rules*, March 1988.

TABLE 1.3
Type of Ginnie Mae Holder to Total in Percentage, 1986
($ billions)

	Jan.	Feb.	Mar.	Apr.	May	June	July	Aug.	Sept.	Oct.	Nov.	Dec.
Mutual savings banks	4.2	4.2	4.1	4.1	3.9	3.8	3.9	3.7	3.6	3.4		
Commercial banks	3.6	3.5	3.4	3.3	3.3	2.8	2.8	2.9	2.9	2.8		
Savings & loans	9.5	9.1	9.5	9.6	9.1	9.6	9.3	8.9	8.4	8.0		
Public pension funds	6.7	6.6	6.4	6.2	5.9	5.7	5.5	5.4	5.2	5.1		
Private pension funds	0.5	0.5	0.5	0.6	0.5	0.5	0.5	0.5	0.5	0.5		
Mortgage bankers	0.7	0.7	0.7	0.7	0.7	0.7	0.7	0.8	0.7	0.7		
Broker/dealers	9.5	9.6	8.7	8.0	8.9	8.4	7.6	7.8	7.9	8.1		
Nominees	47.1	47.5	47.8	49.1	49.1	50.3	50.0	50.7	51.7	52.3		
Corps./ partnerships	3.8	3.9	3.6	3.4	3.5	3.3	3.2	3.2	3.2	3.3		
Individuals	2.7	2.6	3.1	2.9	2.8	2.8	4.6	4.5	4.3	4.6		
Credit unions	0.9	0.8	0.8	0.7	0.7	0.7	0.7	0.6	0.6	0.6		
Life insurance cos.	3.0	3.2	3.3	3.2	3.3	3.3	3.2	3.1	3.0	2.9		
Other insurance cos.	0.5	0.5	0.5	0.5	0.5	0.5	0.5	0.5	0.5	0.5		
State/local govts.	0.7	0.7	0.6	0.6	0.6	0.6	0.6	0.5	0.5	0.5		
Fiduciary individual	0.4	0.4	0.4	0.4	0.4	0.4	0.4	0.4	0.4	0.4		
Fiduciary institutional	3.8	3.8	4.1	4.1	4.1	4.0	3.9	3.9	3.8	3.7		
Others	1.5	1.5	1.5	1.5	1.5	1.6	1.6	1.6	1.6	1.6		
Terminated issues	1.0	1.0	1.0	1.0	1.1	1.1	1.1	1.1	1.0	1.1		
Total issues in billions of dollars	272.2	277.7	282.8	289.7	295.5	303.7	313.9	320.8	333.6	343.8		

Source: Mortgage Commentary Publications.

THE PRIMARY DEALER MARKET

Wall Street dealers were quick to pick up on an idea where the government would guarantee the credit of the mortgage market. Some of the first Ginnie Mae dealer market makers were actually mortgage brokers by origin—Huntoon Paige and Company and G. Adrian Thompson, among the notables. F. S. Smithers, Merrill Lynch, Salomon Brothers, and First Boston were among the early Wall Street securities firms to join the Ginnie Mae dealer ranks.

A number of issues had to be resolved to form an organized secondary trading market. Among the first—and thorniest—was how to reach a common maturity assumption for pricing purposes. Common ground was found in the FHA studies of mortgage mortality experience with FHA Section 203 single-family mortgages, which were found to have an average survivorship of 12 years. Thus was born the 12-year average-life assumption, which became the pricing convention through most of the first decade of Ginnie Mae trading. Another issue was how to book a trade for a security that could not be deferred precisely until some time after the ticket was written. The difficulty arose because mortgage bankers were anxious to sell the Ginnie Mae pool as soon as they knew they had the mortgages in hand to fill it. But the exact settlement dollars could not be determined until Ginnie Mae actually issued the pool and any loan fallout or paydowns had been accounted for. The exact settlement date could not be specified either—it depended on when the actual certificate could be issued by Ginnie Mae and delivered to the originating mortgage banker. Trades were simply booked for a specified month for delivery, and settlement day was whenever the certificate was physically presented to the dealer.

To resolve these issues the pioneering Ginnie Mae dealers in 1972 formed the GNMA Mortgage-Backed Security Dealers Association, chaired by Rodger Shay, then head of the Government Securities Department at Merrill Lynch. William D. Riley, who was then and still is First Boston's Government Securities Operations head, invented the TBA (to be announced) form of ticket to avoid the need to cancel and correct the original terms of the trade upon determining the final details of the pool, sometimes not known until actual delivery.

Other pioneers of that era were W. Stevens Sheppard of F. S. Smithers (later merged with Paine Webber), who was among the first to analyze each new Ginnie Mae program as it was announced; and Robert Schiffer of Huntoon Paige, who of the group best understood the dynamics of the mortgage aspects of the business. The other founding members were Paul Leonard and Robert Dall, Salomon Brothers; Kurt Kettenman, Citibank; Edward Hess, Bache & Company; Steve Hegemann, Blyth Eastman Dillon; and William Bartlett, The First Boston Corporation.

In 1974 Ginnie Mae initiated a series of auctions to sell the FHA 203 and 235 loans it had accumulated in portfolio. About once a month the agency made available lists of the loans that would be offered at sale. All of the loans were eligible to be pooled as Ginnie Mae securities. For this reason the loans were particularly attractive to mortgage bankers, who bid aggressively for such loans as a fast way to build their Ginnie Mae servicing portfolios. Thus for the first time there was an auction market of sorts for mortgage servicing. At the very least, it was these Tandem auctions of the 1970s that caused the mortgage banking industry to evaluate servicing as a marketable commodity. By the 1980s, the outright purchase and sale of large servicing portfolios amounting to hundreds of millions of dollars had become commonplace.

The auctions also had a salutary impact on the volume of secondary trading in Ginnie Mae securities within the primary dealer market. Wall Street dealers formed syndicates to bid the mortgage bankers for the Ginnie Mae securities they would issue from the pools of mortgages purchased in the Tandem auctions (the dealers could not bid for the loans directly—only HUD-approved mortgagees could do so). The result was to focus the dealers more precisely on competitive pricing and mass marketing efforts. At the same time, the availability of large blocks of Ginnie Mae securities issued from a common large pool attracted the attention of big institutional investors such as large thrifts and pension funds. The high water mark for the Tandem auctions was the sale of $304,996,790 Ginnie Mae MBSs in January 1975, the largest single offering in Ginnie Mae up to that time. First Boston was the lead manager for the winning syndicate. It can be said that it was the Tandem auctions that brought the MBSs secondary market to an age of maturity.

A Tandem Plan for Projects

Under an extension of the Tandem plans in 1975, the federal government added its subsidies to the low- and middle-income rental housing market by directing Ginnie Mae to purchase at par FHA-insured loans on multifamily projects. Ginnie Mae purchased $14.5 billion in the HUD-insured project loans with rates as low as 3 percent. The predominant program, however, involved loans with a 7.5 percent mortgage rate. Beginning in 1978, Ginnie Mae initiated a program whereby these Tandem project loans were sold at auction to the secondary market at a substantial discount. Between 1978 and the end of 1985, the majority of these project loans were sold.

Federal Agencies Join Forces with Wall Street

A milestone of the 1970s was the selection by Freddie Mac of a primary dealer marketing group in 1977 to sell its PCs. The joining of forces between the federal agencies and the dealer community was forged by this action and blossomed in the 1980s, especially with the several Fannie Mae issues underwritten by Wall Street firms in the mid-1980s. The new era in derivative products was initiated by the series of Fannie Mae synthetic-coupon issues that began in July 1986 and that by 1987 had evolved into the Fannie Mae stripped MBS program.

Troubles of the Early 1970s

Early in the 1970s the dealers initiated a forward-delivery market so mortgage bankers could reduce their market risk by selling a month's mortgage loans for delivery two or three months later. The forward-sale time rapidly extended to six months or even more as the mortgage bankers used the forward-sale option to issue financing commitments to builders. And before very long, some speculators took advantage of the dealer-sponsored forward-delivery privilege to play the market.

The early 1970s saw a number of frauds perpetrated by private speculators and schemers who found various ways to trade the dealer-sponsored forward-delivery market—and in some cases actually intercept the remittance of P&I from servicer to investor, as was the case in the infamous University of Houston scandal.

The bulk of the frauds perpetrated in the mid-1970s were not as colorful as those related above. Most were the result of outright speculation. The fall of Heritage Mortgage Corporation of Beverly Hills, California, a relatively small mortgage banker, in the early 1970s was among the first to involve a number of dealers; the firm failed simply from overextending. When the Reliance Mortgage Company of Denver went down in the mid-1970s, the failure was a major one that affected virtually the entire MBSs dealer community. A direct result was the formation of credit departments within the dealer firms to evaluate each account, with trading limits established before business could be conducted beyond an initial trade. Winters & Company, a regional dealer operating in southern Florida, was perhaps the first dealer to fail in the early 1970s, followed later by ESM of Fort Lauderdale.

The "standby" option that the dealers borrowed from the traditional mortgage market caused a number of thrift failures in the early and mid-1970s—notably Westside Federal Savings & Loan of Lima, Ohio. The standby was born of the mortgage market of the 1960s and was in effect a put option. Mortgage originators would pay a fee to the thrift institution to have the right—but not the obligation—to deliver loans at a future date at the price agreed to at the time the fee was paid. The fee taker, or thrift in this instance, was said to "stand by" awaiting notification of delivery. In the low-volatility markets of those days prices and yields of bond and mortgage investments changed little over long periods of time, and the fee income was attractive to the thrift. Most mortgage market standbys were actually delivered, but as market volatility escalated in the later 1970s, standbys became hedging and trading devices for the dealers. The latter used standbys to carry what would be otherwise speculative positions and "put" the Ginnie Mae securities to the thrift at a later date—usually six months to a year and at prices that in some cases were 10 points or more above the market. The practice became so ruinous to the S&Ls that in the late 1970s the FHLBB prohibited its member thrifts from writing puts that caused the S&L to be at risk by being forced to buy mortgages or MBSs that could be priced below market value at the time of delivery.

The standby, nevertheless, was the precursor of the now dealer-sponsored and widely traded over-the-counter (OTC) options market. Robert McGovern, head of Thomson McKinnon Securities GNMA department, was the first trader to make a two-way market in Ginnie Mae puts and calls while he was trading for Kuhn, Loeb & Company in 1975. Today single trades in OTC options for Ginnie Mae, Freddie Mac, and Fannie Mae securities of $50 million and more are not uncommon, and there are even options on options (called the split-fee options). Options on Ginnie Mae futures contracts are now listed and traded on the Chicago Board of Trade (CBT). In fact, it was the existence of the Wall Street-sponsored OTC options business that inspired Dr. Richard Sandor, when he was a professor of finance at the University of California at Berkeley, to contemplate a commodities-based market for Ginnie Mae futures contracts. Dr. Sandor pursued his idea, joined the Chicago Board of Trade as its economist, and in 1975 was responsible for initiating the trading of Ginnie Mae futures contracts on the CBT.

By the end of the 1970s, Wall Street firms that had committed significant resources to the computerized analysis of mortgage prepayments had accumulated sufficient data to track the prepayment patterns of mortgages through several interest-rate cycles. The now-arcane 12-year prepaid-life assumption was displaced with a new concept, that of a cash-flow yield based on a specific speed assumption. First Boston coined it the "Honest to God Yield" in 1978. After the turn of the decade and into the early 1980s, interest focused increasingly on the homeowner's held option to refinance or to prepay the mortgage at any time. Wall Street research turned to the analysis of prepayments and the derivation of methods for calculating and predicting prepayment rates, also known as speed. Terms such as "constant prepayment rate" (CPR) and "single monthly mortality" (SMM) became commonplace in secondary market terminology, culminating with the introduction of the PSA speed model in July 1985. (For a full discussion of the methods for measuring prepayment speed, see Chapter 5.)

Since the mid-1980s increasing attention has been placed on the valuation of the implicit call in the MBS, which derives from the homeowner's right to prepay the mortgage at his option. Much of the research effort focused on ways to derive a duration calculation that takes into account the prepayment characteristics of mortgage pools. More recently, attention has been directed to evaluation of the implied call option itself, resulting in the evolution of models that endeavor to assign a specific value to the option itself, either in terms of an actual dollar price or expressed as an option value-adjusted basis spread to that of the price/yield curve of Treasury securities. (For an analysis of duration and valuation of the prepayment-related call option, see Chapter 7.)

Derivative MBSs Products

The introduction of derivative MBSs in the mid-1980s has dramatically changed the face of the MBSs market. Derivative MBSs products initially appeared in the form of the now familiar CMO. Modifications of the CMO structure classed as derivatives include the planned amortization (PAC) bond class of the CMO and CMO floaters. The PAC bond drastically reduces the prepayment risk to the investor of the PAC through a sinking fund structure that stabilizes the average life of the PAC within a wide range of prepayment speeds. The floater form of CMO class has been further refined with inverse floaters and superfloaters. Another refinement of the CMO was the creation of deep-discount-coupon bonds of CMOs collateralized by current-market-rate MBSs, or even premium-priced MBSs. Finally, the residual of the CMO has become perhaps the ultimate derivative MBSs product of the 1980s.

The introduction of stripped mortgage securities in July 1986 opened up whole new possibilities for investors. With the interest-only (IO) and principal-only (PO) components of the stripped MBS, investors have new instruments for hedging and leverage opportunities to exploit anticipated changes in interest rates.

Chapters 13 through 16 of this book describe and analyze the growing family of derivative MBSs products.

Asset-Backed Securities

In May 1985, the process of aggregating loans as a pool to collateralize securities was extended to the nonmortgage arena with the issuance of CARS by Marine Midland Bank. The CARS issue was a $60.2 million asset-backed security, with the asset consisting of automobile receivables. General Motors Acceptance Corporation followed with its own $524.7 million offering of an automobile receivables asset-backed offering.

In January 1987, the Republic Bank of Delaware issued a variation of the asset-backed security with credit-card receivables as the collateral. The total of asset-backed deals of all types reached $29.4 billion by mid-1988. Of the total, auto and truck receivables amounted to $19.5 billion, and credit-card receivables were $4.9 billion. The balance represented commercial loans, lease contracts, and unsecured consumer loans.

With few exceptions the asset-backed deals have been rated AAA by Standard & Poor's and are usually issued with short maturities and an average life of between one and four years. The prepayment experience of the automobile and credit-card receivables-backed deals has proved to be less volatile than that with mortgages. For the most part, asset-backed collateral consists of consumer installment loan receivables, which typically are not sensitive to interest-rate changes. The consumer does not have the clear option to refinance a car loan that he has with a home mortgage.

Historical Landmarks
of the Secondary Mortgage Market[8]

1914   Farm Mortgage Bankers Association formed in Ohio by 200 mortgage banks to provide mortgage financing for farmers.

1916   Federal Land Bank established to provide farm credit.

1920s   Evolution of mortgage banks in Ohio to finance farm loans.

1923   Farm Mortgage Bankers Association renamed The Mortgage Bankers Association in recognition of extension of its business to urban markets.

1933   Home Owners' Loan Corporation (HOLC) established as a federal agency to refinance the short-term balloon loans common to the era and which suffered high default rates on the heels of the Depression.

1934   Federal Housing Administration (FHA) formed to provide federal backing for home mortgage loans.

1938   Federal National Mortgage Association (Fannie Mae) chartered as a subsidiary of the Reconstruction Finance Corporation (RFC).

1944   Veterans Administration (VA) chartered to provide mortgage loan guarantees.

1948   Fannie Mae completes first secondary market transaction with purchase of VA loans.

1949   Prudential Federal, Salt Lake City, consummates first private secondary market transaction with sale of $1.5 million FHA/VA loans to First Federal, New York, at a yield of 3.56 percent.

1954   Fannie Mae rechartered as a part privately held corporation, part federal.

1956   U.S. League of Savings Institutions holds organizational meeting to address secondary marketing concerns of S&Ls.

1957   Federal Home Loan Bank Board (FHLBB) issues regulations for FSLIC-insured institutions to purchase 50 percent participations on residential mortgages (up to 20 percent of assets).

1963   FHLBB and FSLIC issue nationwide lending regulations permitting S&Ls to purchase conventional residential loans (up to 5 percent of assets).

Tax law amended to remove restrictions confining S&Ls to making loans only to association members.

1968   Fannie Mae restructured as a privately held corporation and mandated to purchase market-rate mortgage loans.

Ginnie Mae chartered to oversee special-assistance and mortgage-subsidy programs.

Ginnie Mae granted authority to guarantee timely payment of P&I on securities issued by lenders of FHA-insured and/or VA-guaranteed loans. Ginnie Mae guarantee to be backed by the full faith and credit of the U.S. Treasury.

1970   Ginnie Mae in February guarantees first issue of its pass-through backed by FHA-insured and VA-guaranteed mortgages. IDS mortgage was the servicer and the State of New Jersey Pension Fund the buyer.

Ginnie Mae launches its series of Tandem plans to purchase mortgages at below-market rates to provide affordable housing. The first plans were for FHA 235 single-family residential mortgages and FHA 236 subsidy loans for rental apartments. The 235 loans were later the source of multimillion dollar auctions under which the loans could be packaged as Ginnie Mae MBSs.

Federal Home Loan Mortgage Corporation (Freddie Mac) chartered as the secondary marketing arm of the 12-bank FHLB system.

Fannie Mae granted authority to purchase conventional mortgages.

Secondary mortgage activity totals $16 billion—$6 billion of which is attributed to Ginnie Mae, Fannie Mae, and Freddie Mac.

1971   Freddie Mac issues first guaranteed mortgage participation certificate, or PC, backed by conventional mortgages. Sales of $67 million the first year.

Freddie Mac issues criteria to qualify private mortgage insurers. Action prompted private-lender acceptance of private mortgage insurance as credit enhancement for secondary market transactions, including conventional mortgages. Start of the era of the high-balance 95 percent LTV (loan-to-value) mortgage loan.

Freddie Mac and Fannie Mae introduce uniform loan documents—a landmark step leading to standardization of secondary market transaction activity.

1972   Freddie Mac commences purchase of conventional single-family and multifamily mortgages.

Fannie Mae commences purchase of single-family conventional loans.

1974   Emergency Home Purchase Act (Brooks–Cranston) establishes Tandem plan for conventional mortgages.

1975   Freddie Mac sells $500 million of guaranteed mortgage certificates (GMCs). The GMC was structured to attract traditional bond buyers to the mortgage securities market.

Chicago Board of Trade opens futures trading in Ginnie Mae MBSs to broaden builders and mortgage bankers in hedging activities.

Ginnie Mae MBSs hit $20.8 million total outstanding.

1976   Fannie Mae purchases of conventional mortgages ($2.5 billion) for the first time exceed FHA/VA purchases ($820 million).

Total secondary market activity exceeds $43 billion for the year. Ginnie Mae guarantees $14 billion MBSs; sales by private mortgage insurance (PMI) companies reported at $2.9 billion.

1977   Freddie Mac forms Wall Street dealer group to market its PCs; previously, PC sales were handled by Freddie Mac sales representatives.

Bank of America, San Francisco, and First Federal of Chicago issue the first private pass-throughs. Total sales of private pass-throughs total $728 million.

Conduit issuers first appeared on the heels of the success of the private pass-through initiative of 1976. Conduits marketed MBSs backed by conventional mortgages assembled by many primary originators with PMI on the individual loans and a pool policy as credit enhancement to cover losses on foreclosure in excess of the base loan-by-loan PMI.

1978   Eligibility to sell loans to Freddie Mac expanded from federally insured thrifts to include FHA-approved mortgage bankers.

1979   Interest rates spike to dramatically reduce home affordability. Mortgage bankers, traditionally oriented to FHA/VA lending, shift for the first time with focus on conventional mortgage lending.

Median home sale price, stimulated by the worst inflation seen in the post-World War II era, significantly exceeds the median household income—further worsening the affordability gap.

1980   Ginnie Mae issuance tops the $100 billion mark at mid-year. Freddie Mac issuance hits $21.2 billion at year-end.

Housing starts decline to a low water mark of 1.3 million, confirming the longest housing slump of the decade. Bank prime rate hits 20 percent, the CPI 13.5 percent.

1981   Fannie Mae introduces its guaranteed MBSs program for conventional mortgages.

FHLBB and FSLIC issue new net worth accounting regulations to encourage S&Ls to restructure by disposing of fixed-rate mortgage assets to reinvest in ARMs and shorter-term assets. Regulatory accounting procedures, RAP, as it was called, permitted S&Ls to amortize the loss on sale of long-term, fixed-rate assets over the economic remaining life of the asset. S&Ls thus embarked on a restructuring effort to match the duration of assets to liabilities—dramatically altering the nature of the thrift business.

Disposition of multimillion dollar seasoned loan portfolios by S&Ls stimulates interest in the value of short weighted average maturity (WAM) seasoned loan products.

Freddie Mac and Fannie Mae initiate loan swap programs whereby S&Ls may exchange loans held in portfolio for MBSs issued by the participating agency, giving birth to the Freddie Mac Guarantor as a separate MBSs program. $5.5 billion of loans were swapped for Guarantor PCs, a second-tier market among the Wall Street dealers for seasoned, short WAM MBSs.

Fannie Mae announces eight ARMs it will buy.

FHLBB issues regulations for ARM loans that may be originated and sold by S&Ls.

A multiple of ARM loan types swamps the market—providing both home affordability and confusion within the secondary market. Lack of product standardization and credit concerns with issues such as negative amortization raise doubts for the future of ARM lending.

Statutory loan-size limit amended to permit annual adjustment based on a formula tied to the Freddie Mac national lender survey at the median loan contract size.

Housing starts dip to a 15-year low to 854,000. Lowest average mortgage contract rate in the Freddie Mac index was 15 percent; the highest, 18.63 percent. Stimulus for interest-rate spike was exceeding the "one" trillion federal deficit benchmark.

1982   Freddie Mac Guarantor activity soars to $25 billion in conventional mortgages swapped for PCs.

Residential Funding Corporation (RFC) enters the market as the first capital markets-oriented conduit. Its purchase activity centers on *jumbo* loans—loans that exceed the statutory loan size permitted for purchase or inclusion in agency-guaranteed MBSs programs. MGIC performs the underwriting in the field as well as the PMI and pool policy. Salomon Brothers, operating under a broad-based shelf registration with the SEC, underwrites privately issued MBSs.

Bond market yields decline; national average mortgage contract rate declines to 13.57 percent. Housing starts soar to a new high of 1.4 million.

1983   Ginnie Mae introduces the GNMA-II program to attract pension fund money with the availability of large, homogeneous pools and designation of Chemical Bank of New York as central transfer and paying agent for the GNMA-II securities.

FSLIC eliminates restrictions on S&L investing in loans outside its normal lending area.

Freddie Mac issues first collateralized mortgage obligation (CMO). This landmark offering transforms the builder-bond market and accelerates the growth of conduit-based mortgage financing.

Fannie Mae discontinues its weekly auction of forward optional commitments, or "standbys"—as mortgage bankers called it.

Housing starts climb to a 1.7 million annual level, extending the recovery in the housing market.

Freddie Mac initiates an ARM purchase program for mortgages indexed to the 1-, 3-, and 5-year constant maturity Treasury (CMT) index.

Fannie Mae reduces its eight ARM plans to three, all CMT-based and with caps on the annual rate adjustment. Combined actions of Freddie Mac and Fannie Mae set the pattern for standardization of ARM loans, lending stimulus to the secondary market for ARM loans.

Fannie Mae and Freddie Mac commence universal enforcement of the due-on-sale provision in their mortgage documents. Congress passes legislation exempting Fannie Mae, Freddie Mac, and federally chartered financial institutions from state law restrictions on enforceability of due-on-sale. These actions stimulate a two-tier market based on differing prepayment-speed expectations for the conventional loan-backed securities issued by the two agencies that enforce due-on-sale versus the Ginnie Mae mortgage security backed by FHA/VA loans that permit loan assumptions.

National average mortgage rate declines to 12.55 percent, the lowest since August 1980.

$85 billion of mortgage pass-throughs are issued for the year, an increase of $31 billion over the 1982 level.

1984   ARM mortgages represent nearly half of all residential home loans closed, according to the Freddie Mac national survey for 1984. Three years earlier the ARM had barely been heard of.

Sears Mortgage Securities Corporation opens its mortgage conduit in January 1984, the first to include 15-year mortgages as well as 30-year—primarily jumbos up to $500,000 in loan size.

Freddie Mac Cash purchase window adds 10-day commitment period in addition to its 30-, 60-, 90-, and 120-day mandatory delivery periods. The $100,000 minimum loan package requirement is eliminated, allowing loan-by-loan sale to the Cash window.

Ginnie Mae MBSs issuance reaches the $200 billion mark.

Chicago Board of Trade initiates GNMA-II futures contracts with the fifth heaviest opening day of the commodity new entry.

Freddie Mac completes the first tape-to-tape transfer of mortgages in a 6,600-loan transaction from Howard Savings Bank, Livingston, New Jersey. In a subsequent electronic transfer, 1,079 loans were delivered in 12 minutes from the UMIC service bureau.

American Southwest Financial Corporation, a consortium of homebuilders, issues the first CMO backed by collateral that included whole loans as well as agency-guaranteed MBSs.

Coast Savings and Loan, Las Vegas, issues first adjustable preferred stock through Shearson American Express (now Shearson Lehman Hutton) as the underwriter.

Norwest Corporation sells mortgage securities backed by manufactured housing loans in a private-placement transaction arranged by Shearson Lehman Brothers (Shearson Lehman Hutton).

Ginnie Mae issues its first ARM MBS backed by FHA-insured ARM loans.

Passage of the Secondary Market Enhancement Act (SMEA), which broadened the eligibility of mortgages for purchase as investments for institutional investors.

Congress passes legislation to tax Freddie Mac.

Deficit Reduction Act of 1984 repeals the 30 percent withholding tax on interest paid to foreign investors of U.S.

Freddie Mac initiates the process of shifting to book-entry clearance and transfer of its PCs through the Federal Reserve Bank of New York.

Freddie Mac introduces its 15-year PC, called Gnomes.

1985   Freddie Mac shifts to a book-entry system for selling PCs and CMOs, thus eliminating definitive securities.

Freddie Mac's Accelerated Remittance Cycle (ARC) is introduced to provide lenders with increased flexibility in handling the temporary investment of principal and interest payments.

The first security backed exclusively by multifamily mortgages is introduced by Freddie Mac.

Fannie Mae announces its new Buy/Sell program under which it buys 15-year mortgages exclusively for resale as MBSs.

Freddie Mac enters the foreign investor market with the sale of both PCs and CMOs to the European and Japanese markets.

HUD reported that in 1985 secondary market trading hit the second highest level for any year, with a total of 52 percent of originations sold into the secondary market.

1986   Fannie Mae introduces Par Plus, a new mortgage purchase program that allows lenders to sell premium loans at prices above face value.

FSLIC establishes the Federal Asset Disposition Association to help liquidate assets the FSLIC has acquired from failed thrift institutions.

Freddie Mac issues its first CMO backed by 15-year mortgages.

Bear Stearns and Company starts a new mortgage conduit, Bear Stearns Mortgage Capital Corporation, to securitize jumbo loans.

Freddie Mac introduces the first PC backed by ARMs.

The role of Freddie Mac and Fannie Mae in the secondary market, including privatization and a loan-limits freeze, becomes the subject of industry scrutiny.

Fannie Mae introduces a three-year rate-capped ARM program with 2 percent per adjustment-rate caps and 6 percent life-of-loan caps.

Salomon Brothers is the top mortgage-backed securities underwriter for the first three quarters of 1986.

A record of $48 billion of CMOs are offered by 50 different CMO issuers in 1986.

Fannie Mae issues the first stripped securities, giving investors additional ways to purchase combinations of mortgage cash flows which meet their investment needs.

Centex Collateralized Mortgage Corporation, Dallas, issues the first CMO floating class in September. The floater was given the trademark *firsts* by Shearson Lehman Hutton who designed and underwrote the issue.

MDC Mortgage Funding Corporation, Denver, Colorado, issues in August the first CMO with a PAC (Planned Amortization Class). The PAC provides the investor in that class with protection to a wide range of prepayment speeds. Underwritten by Morgan Stanley.

1987   Fannie Mae introduces multiple-lender pools to participants in their MBSs program whereby participants can submit pool packages of at least $250,000 and receive securities backed by larger multiple-lender pools.

Freddie Mac introduced its first stripped PC through a swap transaction with the California-based American Savings and Loan Association.

Freddie Mac in July launches an ARM Guarantor program whereby lenders sell their ARMs to Freddie Mac in exchange for a like amount of ARM PCs representing interests in ARM mortgages.

Fannie Mae receives HUD authority to issue REMICs (Real Estate Mortgage Investment Conduits).

Interest rates fall on 30-year conventional, fixed-rate mortgages to 9.08 percent, the lowest point since January 1978.

Fannie Mae begins purchasing 10- and 20-year residential mortgages on a regular basis.

Convertible ARMs make a comeback in the marketplace. Fannie Mae begins purchasing them on a regular basis.

[8]Based on information provided by Federal Home Loan Mortgage Corporation.

2

The Mortgage Market and Mortgage Banking: Mortgage-Backed Securities Trends to the Twenty-first Century

INTRODUCTION

The residential mortgage market, totaling about $2 trillion in outstandings as of mid-year 1988, is synonymous in most people's minds with the common residential home mortgage. The mortgage market has become the mother of a rapidly evolving universe of mortgage securities products that now constitute the largest and most complex aspect of the fixed-income securities market—exceeded in size only slightly by the total of the equity market (see Figures 2.1 and 2.2).

Twenty years ago the mortgage securities market had not even been created, and until about five years ago the only form of MBS traded was that made up of pools of 30-year, fixed-rate mortgages (with the exception of a relatively small collection of mobile home and project loan securities). Even 10 years ago, 1978 issuance of Ginnie Mae, Fannie Mae, and Freddie Mac MBSs came to only $22.5 billion. By 1983, the total federal agency issuance level was $84.5 billion and included a few CMOs. In just the few years that followed, the MBSs family expanded to include adjustable-rate mortgages (ARMs) and 15-year and stripped MBSs with annual issuance volumes of $255 billion in

FIGURE 2.1
Size of the Capital Markets
(as of December 1987)

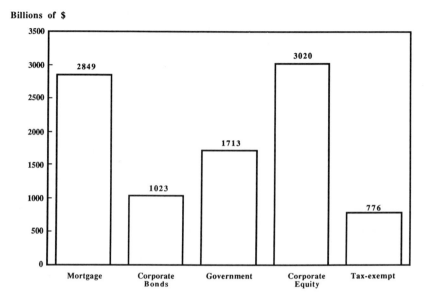

FIGURE 2.2
Composition of the Mortgage Market
(as of December 1987)

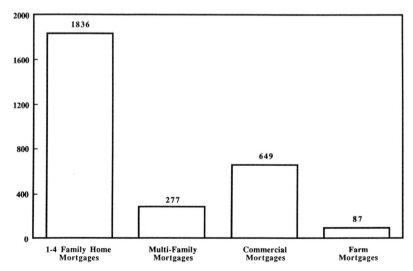

1986 and $225 billion in 1987. Concomitant with that growth was the introduction of complexity. Yet, behind all the apparent complexity the familiar single-family home mortgage remains as the central source of mortgage pool cash flows. Even with the initially bewildering terminology—negative convexity, volatility-implied duration, option value-adjusted spread—the common denominator is the single-family homeowner and his mortgage. So in spite of the evident complexity, a new initiate to today's analytical tools can go a long way toward understanding mortgage cash flows by simply asking what action he would take as a homeowner in a given economic and interest-rate environment.

THE MBSs MARKET AND ITS DERIVATIVES

Of the more than $2 trillion of one- to four-family home mortgages outstanding at mid-year 1988, almost half, or $708 billion, has been securitized. Almost half of the total securitized market consists of Ginnie Mae MBSs ($320 billion), which are all backed by government-insured mortgages; about $370 billion are accounted for by Fannie Mae and Freddie Mac MBSs and PCs, which are for the most part backed by conventional mortgages. The remaining $19 billion is made up of privately issued MBSs (see Figures 2.3 through 2.5 for 1987 year-end totals).

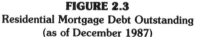

FIGURE 2.3
Residential Mortgage Debt Outstanding
(as of December 1987)

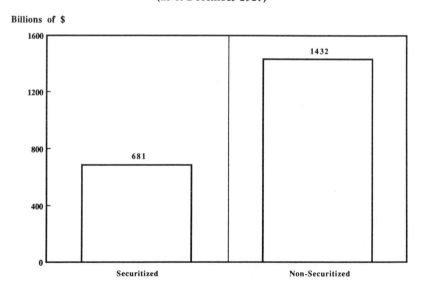

FIGURE 2.4
Profile of Securitized Mortgage Market
(as of December 1987)

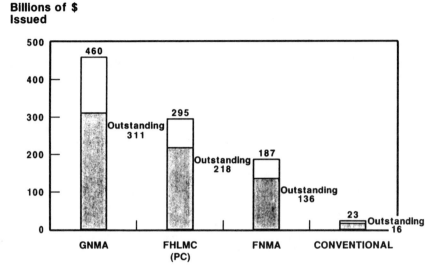

FIGURE 2.5
Securitization and Origination of One- to Four-Family Mortgages

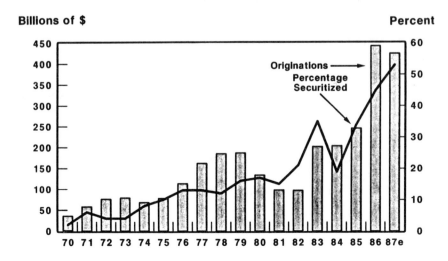

The phenomenon of just the past few years has been the introduction of derivative mortgage products. According to a report on the mortgage market,[1] issuance of derivative mortgage securities using mortgage pass-throughs and whole loans as collateral further proliferated in 1987 and 1988. Total issuance of derivative securities jumped 50 percent from $53 billion in 1986 to $78 billion in 1987 and exceeded $100 billion by mid-year 1988. Derivatives constituted 35 percent of total pass-through issuance in 1987—an increase of 15 percentage points over 1986. In March 1988 the issuance level of derivative MBSs for the first time actually exceeded the issuance level of standard MBSs and constituted 80 percent of total MBS issuance volume by mid-1988.

Derivative MBSs took many new forms, principally as CMOs, which have evolved into innovative structures such as floating-rate classes and deep-discount and principal-only bonds. The issuance of CMOs grew from less than $6 billion in 1984 to about $60 billion in 1987. In 1988 the CMO issuance level was about $38 billion for the first half, doubling the 1987 pace of issuance for standard pass-throughs.

Residuals, formerly considered by-products of CMOs, have attracted increasing interest as stand-alone investments. Other derivative securities that have gained wide investor acceptance are stripped mortgage securities (about $12 billion new issuance in 1987). The issuance level of stripped MBSs slowed somewhat in the winter and spring of 1988 as the office of the comptroller of the currency (OCC) and select district banks of the FHLB system issued restrictive guidelines for investment in derivative MBSs products by regulated financial institutions (see Chapter 14). Following implementation of the REMIC legislation in 1987, about 30 percent of derivative securities were issued with the REMIC election, according to Shearson's report. Figure 2.5 compares total residential loans to the portion securitized from 1970 through 1987.

A Call to ARMs

Another variation in the secondary market was the issuance of MBSs backed by ARMs. The ARM was introduced early in the 1980s as a culmination in the search for a mortgage affordable to the homeowner that would at the same time represent an attractive investment for institutional investors. Of the approximately $425 billion total residential loan originations in 1987, an estimated $130 billion—almost 40 percent—were accounted for by ARMs. Through the first half of 1988, ARMs accounted for about 60 percent of total residential loan originations. From being virtually unheard of in 1981, the ARM soared in popularity in its first years in the mortgage market. In the high-interest-rate

---

[1]Shearson Lehman Hutton, *The 1988 Outlook for the Housing and Mortgage Markets*, January 1988.

environment of 1984, ARMs represented over 60 percent of total single-family conventional loan originations.

The securitization of the ARM has not kept pace with the market share that ARMs represent in the primary originations market. This is so in large part because thrift institutions represent the bulk of ARM originations, and S&Ls generally would rather hold ARMs in portfolio as a good match against their variable-rate liabilities than securitize them for sale into the secondary market. However, in the two years 1986 and 1987, $20 billion of ARMs had been securitized as federal agency-guaranteed MBSs. In the first half of 1988, issuance of ARM securities increased more than 40 percent from the 1987 level to $10 billion, or 18 percent of total MBSs issued through the second quarter. As the ARM achieves greater acceptance in the MBSs secondary market, the volume of ARM securities is expected to increase significantly.

Attractiveness of ARMs

Three aspects of the ARM make it appealing to both the home buyer and the investor. First, the initial rate on the ARM is generally from 2 to 3 percentage points below that of 30-year, fixed-rate mortgages. Since the home buyer qualifies for the mortgage at the initial loan rate, the ARM permits a greater number of potential home buyers to qualify for a mortgage loan. At the same time, the home buyer can qualify for a much larger house if the financing is with the ARM. The investor often does not mind that the ARM rate is lower because the loan rate can adjust higher with interest-rate volatility. The adjustment interval is usually monthly or annually, but may be for any period agreed on by the borrower and lender.

Second, the index plus margin used to adjust the rate is usually tied to a widely recognized and published index—for example, the constant maturity Treasury (CMT) index, which is published weekly by the Federal Reserve Bank, or a cost of funds index published by the FHLBB. These measures make it easy for secondary market investors to price and hedge the ARM.

Third, the interest-rate adjustments permitted by the ARM are capped, thereby protecting the consumer from loan payment shock during prolonged periods of rising interest rates. Figure 2.6 illustrates the average spread between fixed and adjustable mortgage rates from 1984 through the first half of 1988.

THE HISTORICAL PERFORMANCE OF MBSs

MBSs outperformed 10-year Treasury bonds by 304 basis points in yield each year during the six-year period 1982–1987, and by about 150 basis points in the first half of 1988, according to the Shearson Lehman Mortgage-Backed Securi-

FIGURE 2.6
Average Spread Between Fixed and Adjustable Mortgage Rates,
1984 through June 1988

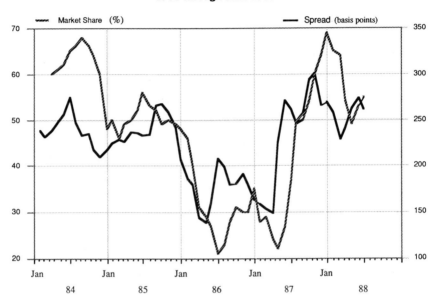

Source: Shearson Lehman Hutton Mortgage Research.

ties Index (SL Index). They also outperformed the Shearson Lehman Government/Corporate Index by 287 basis points a year over the same six-year period. In fact, MBSs did better than the S&P 500 by 80 basis points during the greatest equities bull market in the past 50 years (1982–87).

Table 2.1 gives the annualized returns of MBSs for the five years from 1982 through 1986 and the six years from 1982 through 1987. The table shows MBSs were surpassed during both periods only by the junk bond index, which did so by only 115 basis points a year over the six-year period 1982–87. The

TABLE 2.1
Annualized Returns (in percents)

	(5-Years) 1982–86	(6-Years) 1982–87
• SL MBSs index	20.96	18.01
• 10-Year Treasury	18.99	14.97
• Junk bond index	22.22	19.16
• SP 500	19.80	17.21
• SL Govt/Corp	17.89	15.14

Source: Shearson Lehman Hutton Mortgage Research.

only major exception to the record of consistent superior performance by the MBS sector was in the spring of 1986, when more than 50 percent of all MBSs were premium-priced coupons, and market yields fell by some 400 basis points. The resulting sudden explosion in prepayment rates caused a devaluation of the premium-priced MBS sector during that period.

MBSs Sector Analysis

Figure 2.7 illustrates the performance of various sectors of the MBSs market for 1987. The base return rate for the figure is the SL Index. In the figure, MBSs with returns higher than the SL Index are charted to the right of the SL Index and those that underperformed the SL Index to the left.

Mortgages Outperformed Treasuries and Corporates[2]

For 1987, the cumulative total rate of return for mortgage pass-throughs, as measured by the SL Index, exceeded returns on the government and corporate indexes (see Figure 2.7). Mortgage securities generally outperform comparable-maturity fixed-income securities in periods of rising interest rates, as occurred in 1987. During the first four months, rates of return on all three fixed-income securities were fairly close. Then, for the next five months, mortgages substantially outperformed the other two types of securities. The cumulative return for the entire year on the mortgage-backed index was 4.28 percent, compared with cumulative returns of 2.20 and 2.56 percent for the government and corporate indexes, respectively.

For the first six months of 1988 the SL Index showed a total return of 6 percent, 1.5 percent better than the SL Government/Corporate Index. Returns on both the mortgage and government/corporate indexes were higher for January and February than for March and April, with mortgage products outperforming corporates and governments early in the year and somewhat underperforming in March and April. By July, mortgages outperformed governments by a considerable margin, as demonstrated by the narrowest yield spread between the current-coupon Ginnie Mae and the 10-year Treasury (110 basis points) seen in several years.

Among mortgage securities, there was a wide dispersion of total rates of return in 1987. However, mortgage securities outperformed comparable-maturity Treasuries by wide margins. Premium-coupon securities performed best in the rising interest-rate environment that characterized most of the year. For example, total returns in 1987 for GNMA 13s, 12s, and 11s were 8.3, 7.5, and

[2]This discussion was taken in part from Shearson Lehman Hutton, *The 1988 Outlook for the Housing and Mortgage Markets,* January 1988.

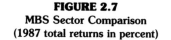

FIGURE 2.7
MBS Sector Comparison
(1987 total returns in percent)

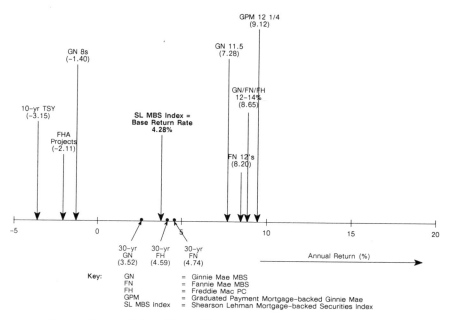

Source: Shearson Lehman Hutton Mortgage Research.

5.7 percent, respectively. The comparable 2-, 3-, and 5-year Treasuries, on the other hand, returned only 2.0, 0.9, and − 1.8 percent, respectively. Coupons with longer-weighted average lives did not perform as well. GNMA 8s had total returns in 1987 of − 2.0 percent, while GNMA 10s returned 3.1 percent. The comparable 10-year Treasury returned a total return of − 7.1 percent for the year.

Table 2.2 illustrates the quarterly actual returns of MBSs for 1987, and Table 2.3 presents the quarterly data from 1982 through 1986. Figure 2.8 illustrates the total returns of MBSs versus Treasuries for the first six months of 1988.

Fixed-Rate Pass-Through Issuance Threatened by ARMs[3]

Total issuance of fixed-rate mortgage pass-throughs (Ginnie Maes, Freddie Macs, and Fannie Maes) totaled $225 billion for 1987. The breakdown was: $98.3 billion, Ginnie Mae; $75.0 billion, Freddie Mac; and $63.2 billion, Fannie Mae. The 1988 first half issuance level of agency-guaranteed MBSs

---

[3]This discussion was taken from Shearson Lehman Hutton, *The 1988 Outlook for the Housing and Mortgage Markets,* January 1988.

FIGURE 2.8
MBS Total Returns versus Treasuries, January–June 1988

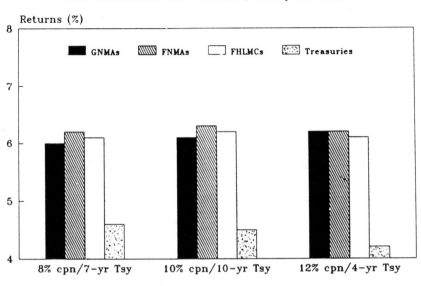

Source: Shearson Lehman Hutton Mortgage Research.

was only $68 billion, down dramatically from about $140 billion for the first half of 1987, with the 1988 monthly issuance level averaging only $10 billion versus the 1987 $20 billion a month pace. In 1986, total MBSs monthly issuance volumes of $30 billion were not uncommon.

The drop in the 1987 and 1988 MBSs issuance levels is attributed in large part to the increasing share of adjustable-rate mortgages as a percent of total residential loan originations. From a low origination share of 10 percent in early 1987, adjustables increased their share to 60 percent of the total by summer of 1987. In the spring of 1988 the adjustable share was commanding about 60 percent of total residential loan originations.

Monthly issuance of Ginnie Maes generally constituted between 40 and

TABLE 2.2
Actual Returns, 1987

	SL Index	10-Yr. Tsy.	SP 500	SL Junk Bond Index (Comp.)	SL Govt./Corp
● Q1	2.21%	−0.01%	21.32%	7.08%	1.47%
● Q2	−1.38	−3.80	4.94	−1.54	−1.89
● Q3	−2.08	−5.95	6.58	−2.29	−2.92
● Q4	5.65	7.06	−22.54	1.90	5.84
1987	4.28%	−3.15	5.10	4.98	2.29

Source: Shearson Lehman Hutton Mortgage Research.

TABLE 2.3
Actual Returns, 1982–86

		MBS Index	10-Yr. Tsy.	SP 500	SL Junk Bond Index	SL Govt./Corp
1982	1	5.12	4.49	−7.4	0.25	3.25
	2	3.56	1.77	10.6	5.05	2.76
	3	19.33	16.84	11.6	16.52	13.76
	4	8.81	11.28	18.3	10.64	8.29
1983	1	4.49	0.56	10.0	10.72	3.15
	2	1.10	0.58	11.1	3.53	1.62
	3	2.09	−0.11	−0.1	1.41	1.54
	4	2.76	0.89	0.4	2.99	1.47
1984	1	0.38	−0.76	−2.4	−1.74	0.51
	2	−3.95	−3.86	−2.7	−4.43	−1.70
	3	10.68	11.15	9.7	8.57	8.35
	4	8.50	8.95	1.8	3.59	7.45
1985	1	2.63	2.65	9.20	5.16	2.14
	2	10.18	10.78	7.30	5.74	8.24
	3	2.63	2.15	−4.10	8.06	2.00
	4	8.33	9.98	17.10	6.75	7.57
1986	1	4.67	12.21	14.09	8.18	8.53
	2	.31	1.35	5.88	5.67	1.32
	3	4.13	1.86	−6.98	2.06	2.02
	4	3.76	3.67	5.59	2.52	3.07

Source: Shearson Lehman Hutton Mortgage Research.

50 percent of the total in 1987. At the beginning of the year, issuance of Freddie Macs exceeded Fannie Maes. Later in the year, this pattern was reversed, with Fannie Maes composing nearly one-third of the total.

In early December, both Fannie Mae and Freddie Mac announced that effective January 1, 1988, the maximum loan amounts on conventional mortgages eligible for their mortgage programs would be raised to $168,700 from the 1987 limit of $153,100. This increase of 10.2 percent is lower than the 1987 increase of 14.9 percent. For both years, however, the increases exceeded the percentage price appreciation of new and existing homes. The significant rise in loan purchase limits will slightly reduce the secondary market share of nonconforming or jumbo loans.

Mortgage-to-Treasury Yield Spreads Stabilized[4]

The yield spread between current-coupon Ginnie Maes and the 10-year Treasury was fairly stable for the first half of 1988 as well as for most of 1987,

[4]This section was taken in part from Shearson Lehman Hutton, *The 1988 Outlook for the Housing and Mortgage Markets,* January 1988.

ranging between 110 and 135 basis points the first half of 1988, compared to a range of 130 and 150 basis points for all of 1987. These spreads contrast with those of 1986, when the spread rose from 100 basis points at the beginning of the year to nearly 250 basis points in mid-year and dropped to 100 basis points in the final quarter. The spread narrowed to less than 90 basis points in January 1987—the tightest spread of the year. At that time, the yield volatility of the 10-year Treasury was in a downward movement which had started in September 1986. After widening to 160 basis points in May, the yield spread remained in a range of 130–150 basis points for the rest of the year, despite fluctuations in Treasury yield volatility.

In the week following the October 1987 stock market crash, the spread widened to as much as 161 basis points. At the same time, the 10-year Treasury yield averaged 9.4 percent, with volatility reaching its yearly peak at nearly 35 percent. (Volatility may be interpreted as a measure of yield fluctuations. For example, an expected 35 percent volatility over the next year means that there is approximately a two-thirds chance that at any time during the period the 10-year Treasury yield will be within 35 percent of 9.4 percent.) Within a month after the sell-off, however, volatility fell to less than 15 percent, and the yield spread returned to its pre-October level.

In 1988, the current-coupon Ginnie Mae MBSs yield spread to the 10-year Treasury ranged from a high of 135 basis points early in the year to a narrow of 110 basis points by June.

The principal factors causing the tightening of spreads were the growing stake of ARMs as a percentage of total residential mortgage originations, the absorption of much of the MBSs production as collateral for CMOs, and a decline in market volatility, which dropped to 6.5 percent by the second quarter of 1988.

The spread-tightening phenomenon was exemplified in April when more than half of that month's total issuance of Ginnie Maes was claimed as collateral for structured financings, mostly CMOs. The explosive growth in demand for MBSs as collateral for structured financings was reported in a study by Drexel Burnham Lambert in May 1988. The study indicated that through the first four months of 1988, $9.87 billion of Ginnie Maes, $6.45 billion of Freddie Macs, and $5.62 billion of Fannie Maes had been absorbed as collateral for financings. A Kidder Peabody study on MBSs to Treasury spreads observed that the tighter yield spreads may also be attributed to market anticipation of less volatility in prepayment speeds for the period ahead than has been the case in the high-volatility markets of the past several years.

1988 MBSs to Treasury Spreads Narrow Further

Perhaps the most remarkable phenomenon of 1988 was the narrowing of the spread between primary mortgage market rates and comparable-maturity

Treasuries. By May 1988, with primary mortgage rates averaging 10.3 percent and the Treasury long bond yielding 9.15 percent, the spread had narrowed to 115 basis points. Of particular note, the first year, or initial, rate on ARM loans averaged 7.6 percent in May, compared to the one-year Treasury yield of 7.3 percent, a spread of a mere 30 basis points. With ARMs representing about 60 percent of total primary residential originations by the spring of 1988, and with CMO issuance for the first time exceeding that of standard MBSs, the stage appeared set for major changes in the traditional patterns of the primary and secondary mortgage markets.

In recent years the Ginnie Mae basis-point spread to the 10-year Treasury yield has typically widened in times of uncertainty as to the future direction of prepayment rates. For example, in the spring and early summer of 1986, the spread widened to over 240 basis points while the yield of the 10-year Treasury fell 400 basis points. When Treasury yields are stable or increasing moderately, the Ginnie Mae to 10-year Treasury spread tends to narrow to 100 basis points or less.

This pattern of widening and narrowing of the basis-point yield spread between Ginnie Maes—and for that matter all MBSs—and the Treasury yield relates directly to the secondary market's assessment of the probability of the loss in yield suffered by MBSs when these securities trade to premium prices at the same time that prepayments accelerate. (This phenomenon and the valuation of the option to prepay the mortgage held by the homeowner are the focus of Section II of this book.)

THE PRIVATE PASS-THROUGH MARKET[5]

The private MBSs market in 1987 and 1988 experienced the largest increase in activity of any segment of the mortgage-related securities market. Private MBSs public offerings totaled more than $11 billion in 1987, a 60 percent increase over the 1986 issuance level, and in the first half of 1988, $7 billion were offered. In 1987, some 21 issuers came to market with private MBSs offerings compared with 9 issuers in 1986 (see Table 2.4 and Figure 2.9).

Almost half of the private MBSs issues in 1987 utilized the senior/subordinated and/or stripped-coupon MBSs structures, and most were expected to do so in 1988. In 1986, 90 percent of the private MBSs that year were structured as single-class offerings.

Although Citicorp was the largest issuer of private MBSs in 1987 with $3

---

[5]This section is based on a study of the private MBSs market published in Financial World Publications, *Inside Mortgage Capital Markets,* Washington, D.C., January 22, 1988.

TABLE 2.4
Ranking of Publicly Offered Privately Issued MBSs in 1987
($ in millions)

Rank	Issuer	Amount	Number of Issues	1st Qtr. Volume	2nd Qtr. Volume	3rd Qtr. Volume	4th Qtr. Volume	1986 Volume
1	Citicorp & affiliates	$ 1,677.98	17	$1,332.50	$ 345.48	—	—	$3,140.50
2	Salomon Bros. Mortgage Securities	$ 1,395.44	11	$ 958.87	—	$ 100.00	$ 336.57	$1,922.74
3	Citicorp Mortgage Securities Inc.	$ 1,281.00	17	—	$ 932.00	$ 309.00	$ 40.00	—
4	Residential Funding Corporation	$ 1,229.43	15	$ 84.70	$ 502.36	$ 546.24	$ 96.70	—
5	First Boston Corporation	$ 1,029.50	5	$ 846.90	$ 110.00	$ 72.60	—	—
6	Imperial Savings Associations	$ 778.64	4	$ 443.45	$ 147.00	$ 188.19	—	—
7	Travelers Mortgage Services	$ 701.51	8	$ 458.75	$ 104.76	—	$ 57.00	$ 642.75
8	Security Pacific National Bank	$ 652.40	5	$ 615.00	—	$ 81.00	$ 37.40	—
9	Kidder Peabody Acceptance Corp.	$ 590.00	4	$ 300.00	—	$ 290.00	—	—
10	Merrill Lynch Mortgage Investors	$ 272.65	3	—	—	$ 160.35	$ 112.30	—
11	Sears Mortgage Securities Corp.	$ 219.26	3	$ 77.70	$ 92.00	$ 49.56	—	$ 633.86
12	Great Western Savings	$ 204.00	1	—	—	$ 204.00	—	—
13	Home Owners Federal S&L (LA)	$ 200.00	2	—	—	—	$ 200.00	—
14	Columbia Savings & Loan Association	$ 194.49	1	—	—	—	$ 194.49	—
15	Republic Federal S&L (LA)	$ 145.73	3	$ 53.00	—	—	$ 92.83	—
16	ComFed Savings Bank (Lowell, Mass.)	$ 135.00	2	—	—	—	$ 135.00	—
17	California Federal S&L	$ 113.00	1	—	—	—	$ 113.00	$ 89.44
18	Dean Witter Mortgage Capital Corp.	$ 102.00	1	$ 102.00	—	—	—	—
19	Countrywide Funding Corporation	$ 102.00	2	—	—	—	$ 102.00	—
20	Mechanics and Farmers Savings Bank	$ 76.00	1	$ 76.00	—	—	—	$ 160.00
21	Home Savings of America	$ 0.00	0	—	—	—	—	$ 403.37
	TOTALS IN 1987:	$11,100.03	106	$5,348.87	$2,233.60	$2,000.94	$1,517.29	$6,992.66

Source: Financial World Publications, *Inside Mortgage Capital Markets*, January 22, 1988.

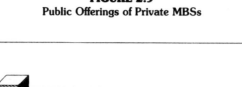

FIGURE 2.9
Public Offerings of Private MBSs

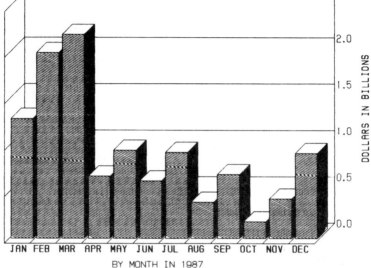

BY MONTH IN 1987

Source: Financial World Publications, *Inside Mortgage Capital Markets,* January 22, 1988.

billion in offerings, the investment banking category suggested a new trend may be taking form as the securities dealers accounted for $3.4 billion—or almost one-third of the 1987 total private MBSs offerings. Of the issues by securities dealers, 60 percent were structured as stripped MBSs using federal agency-guaranteed MBSs as the collateral. Also, the securities dealers as a category accounted for the majority of the stripped MBSs that were privately issued (see Figures 2.10 and 2.11).

Composition

The majority of the 1987-issued private MBSs were pass-throughs, although several small offerings by S&Ls were structured as CMOs. For the most part, the CMOs represented disposition of seasoned loans by S&Ls as part of their asset-liability restructuring efforts. There is a growing trend to ARM-backed offerings in the private pass-through market.

The major structural trend in the private MBSs market appears to be to the senior/subordinated form of credit enhancement. The impetus for the trend stems from the REMIC legislation that was passed as part of the 1986 Tax

FIGURE 2.10
Private MBSs Market by Issuer
(1987)

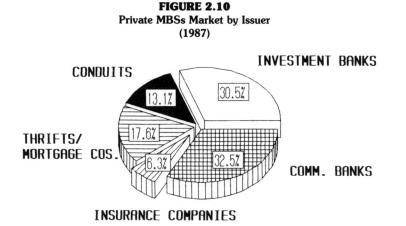

Source: Financial World Publications, *Inside Mortgage Capital Markets*, January 22, 1988.

Reform Act. Under a REMIC election the debt financing may include a second-class bond as a subordinated class and still have the pass-through structure to the offering. The senior/subordinated structure has become increasingly popular, not only for its simplicity. It is much less expensive than the traditional forms of deal credit enhancement, which included high levels of overcollateralization and/or special-hazard insurance, a pool policy, and possi-

FIGURE 2.11
Private MBSs Market by Structure
(1987)

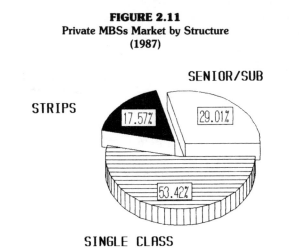

Source: Financial World Publications, *Inside Mortgage Capital Markets*, January 22, 1988.

bly a commercial bank-issued letter of credit. In addition to the greater expense associated with the latter credit enhancements, both the ills plaguing the private mortgage insurance industry and the downgrading of commercial bank credit ratings have raised concerns on the part of rating agencies and institutional investors, who purchase the bulk of private MBSs offerings.

The senior/subordinated trend first became apparent in the fourth quarter of 1987 when of the 19 private pass-throughs offered during the period, 15—more than 75 percent—used the senior/subordinated structure. S&Ls, which accounted for almost half of the issues utilizing the senior/subordinated form, were represented primarily by Imperial Savings of San Diego, which issued four offerings totaling $778.6 billion.

Another form of credit enhancement used with private MBSs is self-guarantees by some strong issuers in lieu of either the pool policy or senior/subordinated credit enhancements. About 40 percent of 1987 private MBSs involved self-guarantees by the issuer. Citicorp, the largest issuer of private MBSs in 1987, was also the largest user of the self-guaranteed credit enhancement. Others were issued by Travelers Insurance and Security Pacific.

THE WHOLE-LOAN MARKET

The residential mortgage is a multitiered universe made up of government-insured loans and conventional loans. And, in turn, the conventional loan market is divided between **conforming loans** and **jumbo loans**. (The term "conforming" refers to loans that are within the statutory size limit eligible for purchase or securitization by the federal agencies: the statutory limit in 1988 was $168,700.)

The government-insured market includes FHA-insured or VA-guaranteed loans. Virtually all government-insured mortgages are sold to the secondary market under one of the federal agency-guaranteed MBSs programs, with the vast majority securitized as Ginnie Mae pass-throughs. In 1987, FHA/VA loans represented about 20 percent of total residential loan originations, about the same percentage as in 1985 and 1986, according to HUD data. Because the FHA/VA market is highly sensitive to the relative threshold of affordability, the ARM as a mortgage form will take a significant share of the middle-income housing market, which is largely the domain of government-insured loans. For example, in 1984 FHA/VA mortgages captured only 14 percent of total originations when 61 percent of all conventional loans were fixed rate, according to Shearson Lehman Hutton Mortgage Research Department information.

The residential mortgage market is further defined into fixed-rate mortgages for 30-year, 15-year, and bi-weekly terms.

Alternative Mortgage Instruments (AMIs)

There is also a growing population of **alternative mortgage instruments (AMIs)**. The AMI constituency includes adjustable-rate and variable-rate mortgages (ARMs and VRMs), graduated payment mortgages (GPMs), reverse-annuity mortgages (RAMs), and several seldom-used variations such as growing-equity and shared-appreciation mortgages (GEMs and SAMs). These newer mortgage plans offer consumers a range of options. **Graduated-payment mortgages (GPMs)** have monthly payments that increase periodically at a predetermined rate during the early years of the loan—a help to young home buyers who anticipate that their incomes will rise. With **growing-equity mortgages (GEMs)** the increased payments are applied to the principal, thus building the borrower's equity in the home and paying off the loan more quickly than a traditional mortgage. The SAM provides mortgage financing through a combination of a fixed-rate payment, which would be at a below-market rate with the lender participating in a share of any appreciation in value realized on sale of the house.

There are also **buydowns**, which provide for an escrow account that may be held by a regulated depository institution. Funds are deposited to the escrow account by a third party, which may be the seller, a builder, a relative, or a friend of the buyer. Monthly predetermined amounts are withdrawn from the escrow account to subsidize the P&I payments the borrower makes, thereby in effect reducing the cost of the mortgage. The escrow may cover a portion of the loan payments for a specified term—such as two, three, or five years—or may be deposited in an amount sufficient to subsidize the loan for its full contractual life. **Balloon loans** are usually written for terms of three or five years. Their contracts call for regular monthly payments based on a 30- or 15-year amortization but stipulate one large (balloon) payment at the maturity date for the full remaining unpaid principal balance of the loan.

According to a U.S. League of Savings Institutions estimate, there are up to 100 distinct types of loans in existence today. Most of the AMIs were designed during periods of high interest rates to address an affordability crisis in times of stress in the housing market. As a consequence, they are seldom used in times of stable and affordable interest rates. A notable exception, of course, is the ARM—certainly an invention of the affordability crisis of the 1981–83 period. But the ARM remains attractive because of the substantial rate advantage it has over the fixed-rate mortgage. And payment shock is largely avoided because of the interest-rate or payment-rate caps structured into most ARM loans. **Reverse-annuity mortgages (RAMs)** are filling a special need for elderly and retired homeowners on limited incomes who want to draw on the builtup equity in their homes. With the RAM, the bank makes a loan for an amount equal to a percentage of the appraised value of the home. The loan is then paid to the homeowner in the form of an annuity. The annuity is usually funded by the lender with an insurance company who pays the annuity directly to the homeowner. If the homeowner outlives the loan, and its annuity, a new RAM can be created if the property has enjoyed further appreciation.

The AMI forms that have become broadly securitized and actively traded in the secondary market are discussed in Chapters 9–11. The 15-year mortgage has been securitized under all three federal agency MBSs programs and is described in Chapter 9. GPMs are analyzed in Chapter 10 and ARMs in Chapter 11.

Under a federal agency guarantee, only conventional loans that are conforming in size and underwritten to Fannie Mae/Freddie Mac standards may be federal agency-securitized.

The Conventional Residential Loan Market

One- to four-family residential mortgage originations totaled $449 billion in 1987. This volume approached the 1986 record level of $454 billion. However, the composition of originations in 1987 differed substantially from that of 1986 when fixed-rate mortgages accounted for 69 percent of all conventional loan originations. ARM originations reached an estimated $130 billion in 1987, almost 40 percent of all conventional loans closed.

Origination activity slowed late in 1987 and into 1988, with fixed-rate mortgages declining sharply. As the spread between fixed and adjustable rates widened from below 200 basis points in March 1987 to over 300 basis points in the first half of 1988, the market share of ARMs expanded from about 20 percent to over 60 percent, a trend that persisted into the second half of 1988.

About 10 percent of total residential loans do not conform to federal agency loan-size restrictions. Technically, any loan above the agency statutory size limit is a jumbo loan. The secondary market for jumbos is totally private for obvious reasons. Much of the private market for conventional loans excludes jumbo loans in excess of $500,000—particularly in privately issued MBSs which are to be rated. In addition, the rating agencies generally require that the loans used as collateral for rated offerings have loan-to-value (LTV) ratios of 80 percent or lower. However, there is a whole-loan secondary market for large jumbo loans, as well as for loans with LTVs in excess of 80 percent up to 95 percent (referred to as high-ratio loans).

Project Loans

Multifamily projects are primarily rental apartments constructed for families of low to moderate incomes, and multifamily mortgage loans are considered part of the residential market. FHA has a long-standing program for insuring multifamily projects, and FHA-insured projects have been securitized under the Ginnie Mae MBSs program since the early 1970s. Freddie Mac instituted a purchase program for conventional multifamily projects in 1972 and initiated its securitized multifamily PC program in 1985. Project loans and project loan securities carry unique structural average-life characteristics, which are described in detail in Chapter 11.

THE MORTGAGE BANKING BUSINESS

Mortgage bankers are financial intermediaries in the **origination** and closing of mortgage loans. Their role includes making a credit review of the prospective borrower and appraising the property before the loan closing. Most mortgage originators employ an approved outside appraiser to evaluate the property proposed as the security for the mortgage. The mortgage banking process also encompasses warehousing the loans. **Warehousing** refers to the interim holding period from the time of the closing of the loan to its subsequent marketing to secondary market investors. The period from the taking of applications from prospective mortgage borrowers to the point of marketing the loans is collectively referred to as the **mortgage pipeline**. Finally, the mortgage banking business is the ongoing management or **servicing** of loans through the loan's repayment term. Mortgage bankers generate revenue in each of the four stages of the mortgage banking process: origination, warehousing, marketing, and servicing.

Servicing

Servicing involves collecting principal, interest, and escrow funds for taxes and insurance on the mortgaged property from the borrowers and paying these taxes and premiums; paying P&I to the investors of the loans; and in many if not most cases advancing uncollected P&I payments to the mortgage loan investors. Finally, servicing also includes supervising foreclosures in the event of remedied defaults and performing all related accounting and reporting activities.

Servicing generates cash income in the form of fees, which represent a percentage of the declining principal amount of the loans serviced plus any late charges. Servicing income is reduced by the normal amortization of the servicing spread as the loans pay down over time. Retention or purchase of servicing rights creates a cash-flow stream of servicing spread which lasts throughout the life of the mortgage loan.

Mortgage bankers also generate income through the sale of servicing rights, for which there is an active secondary market. Servicing value is usually determined by estimating the expected present value of the income stream associated with the servicing of a given loan. Factors that may affect this value include the amount of the servicing spread, the relative size of the loan balances, loan types, and of paramount consideration, the estimated average life of the loans. Other factors that affect the value of servicing include escrow balances, delinquency and foreclosure history, projected servicing costs, and existing or expected liabilities related to borrower delinquencies.

The Origination Process

Mortgage bankers may originate mortgages by processing applications taken directly from prospective borrowers (called **spot lending**) or by purchasing loans originated by others, with the servicing rights released to the buyer (called **wholesale mortgage banking**).

Spot Originations

Spot lenders typically originate mortgage loans through referrals from real estate brokers, builders, developers, customers, and other sources, as well as through media advertising. A number of referral agencies and electronic referral systems provide a centralized source of detailed information regarding mortgage commitment programs available from mortgage lenders and investors, as well as listings of potential borrowers and lenders. Referrals through real estate brokers represent the largest source of the mortgage bankers' loan originations. Extensive advertising in the local markets where the mortgage banker's offices are located is also a source of originations. Most mortgage banking firms have a number of branch offices distributed throughout a regional, and in many cases a national, lending market.

Each branch is responsible for processing loan applications, preparing loan documentation, and determining that loans comply with the firm's underwriting requirements. After approval of a loan application, the firm issues the buyer a commitment specifying the amount of the loan, the prevailing interest rate on that date, the fees to be paid the firm, and the expiration date of the commitment. The actual interest rate of the loan is usually established about three days prior to loan closing based upon the then-prevailing interest rate unless the borrower has purchased a rate lock. A **rate lock** is an agreement between the mortgage banker and the loan applicant guaranteeing a specified interest rate for a designated period, generally about 60 days. Commitment terms usually change with market conditions.

Each branch office typically has a sales manager, whose compensation is based in large part on the principal amount of loans originated at the branch. The branch is staffed with mortgage loan originators, whose remuneration is usually based on commissions paid as a percentage of the principal amount of loans they originate.

Underwriting personnel in each branch office approve mortgage loans according to the requirements for sale of the loans into the secondary market as securitized pools of MBSs or to private investors as whole loans or participations. Some mortgage bankers believe they can more sensitively respond to their customers if the underwriting function is performed at the branch level, subject to review by the firm's head office. Others require all loan applications to be referred to a regional underwriting department or to the head office itself. Underwriting personnel are usually compensated by salary plus incentive bonus compensation but with the incentives based on the firm's profitability, not on loan-by-loan origination volume per se.

Branches also employ salaried clerical personnel to process loan applications. The firm's origination, underwriting, processing, and servicing functions ideally are accomplished through a comprehensive data and communications network linking the branches to the firm's head office.

The branch is managed by a branch manager with overall responsibility for administering the office and directing the underwriting function. Branch managers are usually compensated without incentives based on volume.

Advertising and Promotion The firm is likely to emphasize aggressive media advertising throughout its market area. It usually runs at least one weekly newspaper advertisement in each locality where it maintains an office. Periodically it distributes information concerning its current mortgage rates and its financing arrangements to real estate brokers in its lending territory.

Correspondent Lending Most mortgage firms have established a correspondent program throughout their lending areas with small mortgage firms, thrift institutions, and commercial banks. Under a correspondent program, the firm may either make mortgage loans originated by the correspondents directly to borrowers or purchase mortgage loans from the correspondents. Purchased loans are accepted subject to satisfying the underwriting criteria applied to loans originated by the firm directly.

Types of Loans Loans originated by mortgage bankers include conventional mortgage loans (not guaranteed or insured by FHA or VA), which are secured by one- to four-family residential properties (including townhouses and condominiums) and generally comply with the requirements for sale or conversion to MBSs issued by Fannie Mae and Freddie Mac. Such loans are referred to as being in compliance with Fannie Mae documentation—and conformance is critical for the loans to be acceptable for secondary marketing. Conformance to Fannie Mae and Freddie Mac documentation is mandatory if the loans are to be included as collateral for a structured financing such as a REMIC, CMO, or privately issued pass-through.

Mortgage bankers also originate FHA-insured and VA-guaranteed mortgage loans for sale in the form of Ginnie Mae pass-throughs. In addition, firms usually originate conventional loans exceeding the maximum amounts qualifying for sale to Fannie Mae (jumbo loans) but otherwise complying with Fannie Mae requirements, as well as a limited number of loans for multifamily units.

The typical mortgage banking firm is an approved FHA nonsupervised mortgagee and an approved seller–servicer with the VA, Ginnie Mae, Fannie Mae, and Freddie Mac.

Wholesale Mortgage Banking

Wholesale mortgage bankers purchase some or all of their loans from other originators. Loans are usually purchased from correspondent sources that have been preapproved by the mortgage banker or conduit who is the wholesale buyer. Purchase commitments are generally given by the buyer to the seller based on telephone or verbal confirmation that all of the loans conform to a specification memorandum provided by the buyer. The memorandum specifies the loan type (fixed-rate or adjustable, 30- or 15-year, conventional or government-insured), maximum loan size, and perhaps a range of loan sizes—with the maximum percentage each loan-size category may represent of the total loan package.

The maximum permissible LTV ratio for each loan size is specified, as well as preferred locations, including especially locations that may not be permitted. Detailed underwriting criteria are provided with respect to various loan-to-income tests to be met and methods for conducting employee verification and credit checks. The buyer may use the services of a private mortgage insurance company or even a title company to screen the loans to be purchased, although the latter practice is more typical of a full-blown conduit purchaser. All loans are purchased subject to final review of the loan documentation by the buyer's loan underwriting staff.

Purchase commitments may be available in a number of ways. Sometimes the purchasing mortgage company or conduit agrees to a single purchase amount—such as $50 million—and when it buys that amount the purchase program is suspended until the buyer wishes to purchase another block of mortgages. At the opposite extreme, some mortgage purchasers, particularly conduits, operate an open-ended purchase program for their established correspondents. Generally, for each correspondent a monthly purchase amount is agreed on, with a delivery schedule that is usually mandatory. Some loan purchasers offer a **production-flow commitment** permitting the monthly loan quota to be delivered in batches, or even loan by loan. Sometimes the purchase commitment yield is held firm for a specified period of time, such as a week or a month. Longer flow commitments may be given with the purchase yield tied to an index such as the Fannie Mae contract purchase yield as of a certain date or the Fannie Mae purchase yield plus a margin. Arrangements like these are sometimes referred to as an indexed-flow purchase commitment.

Warehousing

Pending sale and delivery to the secondary market, the firm's mortgage loans are usually funded by borrowing from banks under warehousing lines of credit. The mortgage firm typically holds mortgage loans for a period of 30 to 60 days after closing in order to prepare the loans for sale to the secondary market. The borrowed funds are repaid when the firm receives payment from the sale of the loans. Accordingly, the mortgage banker is dependent on loan sales to free warehousing credit lines so that new loans can be closed without exceeding available credit limits.

The firm usually pays interest on funds advanced under the lines of credit at the prime rate prevailing at the lending bank or more often at a margin above the prime rate. Under the terms of the warehousing lines of credit, the firm is almost always required to maintain at the warehousing bank compensating balances that can usually be satisfied in whole or in part with escrowed funds held in custodial accounts for taxes and insurance due on the loans serviced. By maintaining balances in excess of the minimum requirements, mortgage bankers can—and frequently do—borrow funds under the warehousing lines at reduced interest rates. This method of reducing costs of borrowing may significantly improve the profitability of warehousing mortgage loans.

Some mortgage firms also obtain short-term financing through a type of reverse repurchase agreement called a **gestation repo** arranged with financial institutions and securities dealers. Under these agreements, the firm sells federal agency-guaranteed MBSs and simultaneously agrees to repurchase them at a future date at a fixed price. Mortgage bankers then use the proceeds of the repos to repay borrowings under their bank lines of credit. The effective cost of funds under repurchase agreements is typically lower than for borrowings under the warehousing lines of credit, although at times it has been higher.

Marketing

Marketing, the offering, the sale, and the packaging and delivery of closed mortgage loans to investors are the activities that distinguish mortgage bankers as financial intermediaries from portfolio lenders or permanent investors. Marketing mortgage loans is the most complex aspect—both financially and operationally—of the mortgage banking business. It requires matching the needs of the retail origination market (home buyers and homeowners seeking new mortgages) with those of the secondary market for mortgage loans (securities dealers, thrifts, insurance companies, pension funds, and other institutional investors).

Conventional mortgage loans are packaged for direct sale to private investors or to Fannie Mae or Freddie Mac. Loans that conform in size to the statutory limit of the agencies ($168,700 in 1988) are frequently submitted for conversion to a MBS issued by Fannie Mae or Freddie Mac through their respective loan swap-for-securities programs in pools of $1 million or more. MBSs issued by Fannie Mae or Freddie Mac are primarily sold by mortgage banking firms directly to securities dealers.

FHA-insured and VA-guaranteed mortgage loans are packaged for sale as pass-through MBSs guaranteed by Ginnie Mae and sold also primarily to securities dealers. In addition, there is an active private market for mortgage loans that have not been pooled or securitized, including especially jumbo loans.

Factors that may influence the market value of packaged loans include the general level of interest rates, the type of loan (for example, conventional mortgage loans or jumbo loans), interest payment and principal amortization schedules (self-amortizing or balloon, fixed- or adjustable-rate), and type of mortgaged property (one- to four-family detached, row or townhouse, condominium or planned unit development). Other considerations include the ratio of loan proceeds to appraised property value (LTV), property location, borrower credit profile, and whether the loans are packaged in pools to be securitized or sold separately on a whole-loan basis.

The sale of mortgage loans produces a net gain or loss equal to the sum of (1) the difference between the principal amount of the loans and the net price at which the loans are sold (the cash gain or loss on sale) and (2) the present value of the difference (the "premium on sale of mortgage loans") between the gross mortgage interest rate collected by the mortgage banker from the borrowers and the pass-through interest rate remitted by the mortgage banker to the purchasers of the loans, net of a normal servicing spread.

Servicing

Retention of Servicing

When the firm sells the mortgage loans it has originated, it generally retains the rights to service those loans and receive the related fees. Servicing agreements relating to the MBSs programs of Fannie Mae, Freddie Mac, and Ginnie Mae require the firm to advance funds to make scheduled payments of principal, interest, taxes, and insurance—whether or not these payments have been received from borrowers.

Many whole-loan sales now also require that the mortgage banker maintain the payment of all P&I due, whether it is collected or not. This practice is almost always mandatory if the loans are to be used as collateral for a structured financing—particularly if there are bonds issued in connection with the financing that are to be rated. The requirement that the mortgage servicer maintain payment of the full amount of contractually due P&I payments is often referred to as **MBS servicing** because the practice is required by Fannie Mae for seller–servicers who swap their loans with Fannie Mae for MBSs.

Managing the Mortgage Pipeline[6]

It is crucial for the pipeline manager to have accurate reporting of the status of the pipeline and how it is likely to perform in varying interest-rate environments. Pipeline management requires the manager to make a series of choices, such as how much risk to take in view of the outlook for interest rates and how much to pay to hedge against interest-rate risk. Hedging requires familiarity with several hedging strategies, many of which introduce risks of their own.

The challenge of pipeline management is twofold: knowing how to hedge and making the decision of when to hedge. The pipeline manager must also address the question of how changing the make-up of the pipeline can affect his net exposure to interest-rate volatility. The pipeline manager must decide how to balance the risks, rewards, and costs of different pipeline-management strategies.

Sources of Interest-Rate Risk

There are three principal sources of pipeline risk:

- Many risks result from timing delays between the setting of loan terms for borrowers and the setting of terms for sale to the secondary market.
- Another source of risk is the inconsistency that often occurs between origination and sale commitments. Closing and delivery of loans can be either mandatory or optional, depending on terms agreed upon with borrowers and investors.
- Finally, it is never certain how the market will value specific loans in a lender's pipeline if rates have moved substantially in one direction or another. This uncertainty can result from changing prepayment expectations on fixed-rate loans or the impact of interest-rate adjustment caps, which characterize many new adjustable-rate loans.

It is important to distinguish between the loan production and inventory periods, because a lender's risks on a loan already closed and warehoused are different from those associated with a loan that has not closed and might never close.

Loan Terms Affecting Price

To determine the precise nature of interest-rate risk in the pipeline, we need to know at what point in the process the lender commits to terms that affect loan prices. These terms are:

[6]The following discussion of managing the mortgage pipeline is taken in part from Federal National Mortgage Association, *Managing Your Pipeline* (Washington, D.C.: 1985).

- Nature of the loan (fixed- or floating-rate, conventional or government).
- Maturity of the loan (or time to first repricing).
- Note rate.
- Closing and delivery dates.

We also need to know whether closing/delivery of the commitment is required or optional.

In some markets, lenders are forced by competitive pressures to commit themselves to specific loan terms when they advertise or take applications from borrowers. These lenders have different risks than those who do not fix terms, especially note rates, until closing.

Differences also occur in the marketing of loans to investors. The lender can commit to sell loans under particular terms before, after, or simultaneously with the setting of terms for the borrower. It is important to remember that the lender commits to loan terms twice: once to the borrower and once again to the secondary market.

Table 2.5 provides a matrix of pipeline-risk exposure.

Types of Pipeline Risk

Fallout risk is generally created when the terms of the loan to be originated are set at the same time as the sale terms are set. Although the timing of commitment is the same, the risk is that either of the two parties (borrower or investor) fails to close and the loan "falls out" of the pipeline. This can occur either because the commitment does not require closing/delivery or because one contracting party does not live up to a firm commitment.

TABLE 2.5
Summary of Pipeline Risks

If terms to the borrower are set at time of:	And terms of sale to the investor are set at time of:	Then pipeline risk can be defined as:
Application	Application	Borrower and/or investor fallout
Application	Closing or sale	Price/product risk or investor fallout
Closing	Closing	Investor fallout
Closing	Sale	Price/product risk or investor fallout
Closing	Application	Borrower fallout and/or reverse price risk

The catalyst for pipeline fallout is generally related to changes in interest rates. The amount and type of fallout a pipeline manager experiences depend on the direction of interest rates and on which party fails to close. The result, however, is always the same: the lender must sell loans at an unexpected discount and record a marketing loss.

- When rates fall, the applicant might not close. The lender with a mandatory delivery commitment at a higher rate must then purchase a market-rate loan and deliver it to the investor at a discount to provide the required yield.
- When rates rise, the investor may fall out. The lender must then find a new investor for the closed loan, which is now at a below-market yield. A new investor will expect to purchase the loan at a discount.

Price risk is the more familiar type of pipeline risk because it reflects exposure only to rising rates. Such risk is created in the production segment when loan terms are set for the borrower in advance of terms being set for secondary market sale. If the general level of rates rises during the production cycle, the lender probably will have to sell his originated loans at a discount.

Price risk occurs during the inventory period for loans previously originated but not yet sold. This situation affects any loan that could be sold at some future date.

Reverse price risk also results from mismatched commitment timing, but exposes a lender to the risk of falling rates. It occurs when a lender commits to sell loans to an investor at rates prevailing at application but sets the note rates when the borrowers close. When rates fall, the lender must deliver loans at a discount to provide the investor with the required yield previously established.

Product risk is a corollary of price risk. It occurs when a lender has an unusual loan in production or in inventory but does not have a sale commitment at a prearranged price.

- The value of a specific loan depends on general market rates and on the market's assessment of the financial characteristics of the loan.
- It is possible, therefore, that the value of a loan can change even when market rates remain constant.

Product risk can be considered a special form of price risk, assuming a lender can always find an investor for a ''nonstandard'' loan—at a price.

The process of managing the pipeline begins by identifying the risks associated with both the production and inventory segments. Once these risks have been identified, one can select the most appropriate tools for eliminating these risks.

Methods of Hedging Price and Product Risk

There are two methods for efficiently hedging price risk: forward sales and substitute sales. These are accomplished by advancing the setting of loan sale terms to the time final terms are set for the borrower.

A **forward sale** is an agreement between a lender and an investor to sell particular kinds of loans at a specified price and future time. The most common type of forward sale is a mandatory delivery commitment or a similar contract with an investor or dealer.

Advantages of Forward Sales Forward sales of production permit lenders to eliminate both price and product risk by establishing simultaneously the terms of origination and sale. Forward sales of inventory provide similar protection from the time the sales decision is made.

Forward sales insulate lenders from movements in market rates and in the relationship between rates in general and the market price for the loans in question. Furthermore, the costs of hedging are known with certainty at the time of sale.

Disadvantages of Forward Sales In situations where both closing and delivery are certain, forward sales represent a "perfect hedge"—one that provides complete, reliable protection and introduces no additional risks. There is always the possibility of borrower fallout during the production cycle, however, in which case the lender can be penalized for failing to deliver.

Likewise, the potential for investor fallout if rates rise could render a forward sale ineffective as a hedge. Thus, it is important for a lender to be confident of the investor's willingness and ability to live up to his part of the agreement.

A **substitute sale**, or what is more commonly considered a hedge, is an alternative to the forward sale that effectively creates a similar pipeline. Substitute sales are accomplished with debt-market instruments such as futures, which are traded on regulated exchanges, or by selling borrowed securities through dealers.

Advantages of Substitute Sales Substitute sales can be a valuable alternative to forward sales.

- Futures and related hedges are very liquid instruments because of their standardized terms and the ease of offsetting hedge contracts in lieu of making delivery. This liquidity enables lenders to respond to changing product preferences of borrowers and investors.
- The expected costs of substitute sales sometimes can be judged to be less than forward commitment fees and yield premiums.

Disadvantages of Substitute Sales As with forward sales, the use of futures hedges addresses price risk but introduces fallout risk in the production pipeline. Hedging with futures or similar instruments, however, does not protect against product risk and entails its own costs and risks.

- Futures exchanges and some cash dealers require that margins be posted and maintained, which can lead to sudden cash needs for lenders.
- Hedging requires an investment in fixed resources to manage the operation.
- Substitute sales and related hedges introduce basis risk, a critical factor.

Basis Risk While hedging with substitute sales helps reduce exposure to market-rate movements the strategy can introduce a risk of its own—**basis risk**. The "basis" is the relationship between the price of the item being hedged (like a mortgage pipeline) and that of the hedge tool (for example, Treasury bond futures). The risk is that the price of the hedge tool does not move as expected relative to the increase or decrease in the market price of the hedged loan.

The principal basis risk associated with using Treasury bond futures is that the mortgages being hedged might react to changes in interest rates with a very different price response than would Treasury bonds. Chapters 6 and 7 explore these differences in detail, and the pipeline hedger should clearly understand them before attempting to put on a hedge utilizing bond futures contracts.

Hedge tools such as futures contracts are based on securities such as Treasury bills, notes, and bonds or Ginnie Mae futures contracts. Market forces cause the yields and prices of specific mortgages to move differently from those of such securities for a number of reasons. Among them are changing expectations of mortgage prepayments, which vary with loan coupon and market conditions. (See Chapter 5 for a discussion of the causes and impact of prepayments.)

- **Yield Curve Shape:** Another source of basis risk is the shape of the yield curve. Lenders may hedge 30-year mortgages with 30-year Treasuries. However, if we assume a 12-year mortgage prepayment, the yield/price of the mortgage will perform closer to that of a Treasury instrument with a comparable-maturity duration.

  A 1-basis-point change in yield causes a significantly greater change in price on a 30-year instrument than on a shorter instrument. This inequality must be taken into account when constructing hedges. Additionally, because yield curve changes cause the rates on securities with differing maturities to move out of step with each other, there is a risk that even a properly constructed hedge will be inefficient.

- **Cash-to-Futures Basis:** This basis reflects price changes in Ginnie Mae or Treasury futures contracts relative to the change in price of the underlying market for these cash securities. As with other basis factors, some changes can be anticipated. The risk is that this component moves contrary to expectations.

- **Hedging with OTC Options:** Some lenders have avoided yield curve and cash-to-futures basis risk by hedging with substitute forward sales of securities that are of similar maturity to loans in the pipeline, but are of different duration (see Chapter 7). These are over-the-counter (OTC or nonexchange traded) positions. Examples are Ginnie Mae forwards used to hedge conventional fixed-rate loan production or constant maturity Treasury index contracts used as ARM hedges. This technique eliminates cash-to-futures basis risk and minimizes yield curve and sector risk. However, the lender continues to experience product risk between his specific loans and the security used in constructing the hedge. Such OTC positions are also less liquid than futures and can entail credit risk.

Increased Leverage and Decreased Risk[7]

A **split-fee option** is an option on an option. Two types are now available: a call on a call option and a call on a put option. In other words, the buyer of the split-fee option will be buying a "window on the market"—an opportunity to look at the market for a specified period of time for a smaller premium than would be paid for a standard put. For builders, mortgage bankers, and other market participants this is an attractive vehicle that enhances the leverage of conventional options.

The Language

- **Front fee**—the fee initially paid by the buyer upon entering the split-fee option contract.
- **Extension date**—the day on which the first option either expires or is extended.
- **Back fee**—the fee paid on the extension date if the buyer wishes to continue the option.
- **Strike price**—the price at which the mortgages will be sold if the option is exercised.
- **Notification date**—the day the second option is either exercised or expires.

[7]Shearson Lehman Hutton, *Increased Leverage and Decreased Risk: The Split Fee Option,* March 1986, prepared by Richard Kaplan.

How Split-Fee Options Work

An investor buying a split-fee option determines how much he wishes to pay initially (the front fee), the strike price, the length of the "window," and the final notification date of the option. On the basis of these factors, the option seller calculates the cost of the second fee. When the extension date arrives (the window on the market is about to close), the investor can either pay the additional premium (the back fee) to continue the option until the notification date or let the option expire worthless (hence the term "split fee").

This type of option offers tremendous leverage to both hedgers and other market participants because of the smaller premium risk. For a better understanding of these advantages, compare a conventional option and a split-fee option with similar maturity dates and strike prices.

Example A builder wishes to purchase four-month protection on a future closing using put options on current-coupon Ginnie Maes.

Assume

- It is currently August.
- December GNMA 9s are trading at 100.00.
- A conventional December put option on a GNMA 9 (100.00 strike price) costs 1⅝ points.
- A split-fee put option on GNMA 9s (100.00 strike price) with an extension date in October and a notification date in December has a front fee of ⅞ point and a back fee of 1 point.

	Conventional Put Option	Compound Put Option
Initial premium/front fee	1⅜	⅞
Strike price	100.00	100.00
Extension date	N/A	October
Notification date	December	December
Total cost (Rates fall/prices rise)	1⅝	⅞
Total cost (Rates rise/prices fall)	1⅝	1⅞

Scenario I: Interest Rates Fall (Prices Rise)

- The conventional option expires worthless in December for a loss of 1⅝ points.
- The split-fee option expires worthless in October for a loss of ⅞ point (a savings of ¾ point over the conventional option). At this point, the option buyer can purchase an additional put option for the remaining two months of market exposure at a better strike price.

Scenario II: Interest Rates Rise (Prices Fall)

- The conventional option is exercised in December, allowing the put-option buyer to sell GNMA 9s for an effective price of $100 - 1\frac{5}{8}$ (premium) = $98\frac{3}{8}$.

- The split-fee option was extended in October for a back fee of 1 point. In December, the option is exercised, allowing the put-option buyer to sell GNMA 9s for an effective price of $100 - 1\frac{7}{8} = 98\frac{1}{8}$.

    The builder in this example—by entering into a split-fee put-option contract rather than a conventional put-option contract—has given himself the chance to save $\frac{3}{4}$ of a point for identical protection versus the possibility of paying $\frac{1}{4}$ point more, a potential savings of 300 percent. The builder has effectively controlled the same amount of bonds with considerably less premium at risk for the first two months (the window on the market). The buyer can determine his own boundaries with respect to the extension and notification dates.

    This analysis can provide the advantages of the split-fee option over the conventional option, namely, leverage benefits and additional flexibility. More important, however, is the opportunity the investor has to save money in an unfriendly market. This instrument is popular with pipeline hedgers and other market participants.

Choosing Between Forward and Substitute Sales[8]

When should an originator use a substitute sale in place of a forward sale? The decision should be made by comparing the expected basis risk or maximum sustainable net loss on a substitute sale to the known cost of a forward sale, which is essentially free of basis risk. The decision as to which hedge tool is better depends on the lender's confidence in managing hedges and the value placed on certainty.

    In some circumstances, an originator has access only to substitute sales, a situation that often occurs with new mortgage products. In such cases, the golden rules of hedging apply:

- Hedge only when you believe the general market risk from which you want protection is greater than the expected basis risk to which your hedge exposes you.

- Not hedging is as important a choice as hedging. The decision of whether or not to hedge is unavoidable and should not be made by default.

---

[8]This section contains material taken from Federal National Mortgage Association, *Managing Your Pipeline* (Washington, D.C.: 1985).

Hedging Fallout Risk

As described earlier in this chapter, two types of fallout introduce risk into the mortgage pipeline. One is **investor fallout** and the other is **borrower fallout**. These risks occur in pipelines with simultaneous commitments to borrowers and investors, which are often created as a result of having constructed hedges against price risk.

- **Investor Fallout:** Originators can experience investor fallout risk during the pipeline period, when the originator commits loan terms to the borrowers and gets commitments from investors at the time of application. Also, investor fallout risk occurs when both sets of terms are made at closing. If interest rates rise subsequently, investors may renege on their promises to buy lower-yielding mortgages at par. Originators, therefore, should be certain of the investors' ability and willingness to live up to their commitments.
- **Borrower Fallout:** The problem of borrower fallout risk is likely to occur if a pipeline is hedged against price risk during the production cycle. This risk occurs in pipelines in which the terms of loan sale to the secondary market are established before the loan is closed. Furthermore, the originator's forward sale or other hedge requires that a loan be delivered, while his origination commitment is generally not binding on the borrower.

Borrowers may fail to close for a number of reasons. It is most common for them to do so when rates fall and opportunities arise for more advantageous forms of financing. Thus, when originators hedge against price risk to protect against rising rates, they set themselves up for possible losses if rates fall. (Of course, originators will not have fallout risk if they have decided to remain at risk on price.)

Protecting against borrower fallout risk is a matter of creating an **additional hedge** to be placed in tandem with the forward or substitute sale. This is an **option not to deliver** under the terms of the original sale or hedge.

Types of Hedges against Borrower Fallout An originator can obtain an option not to deliver in two ways:

- By paying a fee determined at the time the option for nondelivery is exercised.
- By paying an agreed-upon up-front fee for the option not to deliver.

As with choices involving any insurance policy, the originator's decision should be based on a desire to avoid risk and from his view on which fee is likely to be the less costly—the contingent or the known.

The **"Contingent-Cost" Nondelivery Hedge** There are two ways to establish an option not to deliver hedged loans at a cost contingent on market conditions.

- A substitute sale, such as a futures hedge, that can be liquidated at any time.
- A forward-sale contract that allows for a buy-back or **pairoff** to liquidate the sale. Under this contract, the originator "pairs off" his previous sale commitment with a purchase at current market yields that liquidates the contract. When rates fall (prices rise) the originator suffers a net loss.

In either case, the cost of exercising the right not to deliver is determined by the extent the market moves from the time the sale price is first established to the time the sale or hedge is terminated.

The Fixed Up-Front Fee (Put) Option

Buying an option along with a price-risk hedge (forward sale) allows the originator to establish two hedges from the outset.

- A specific sale price, to protect against upward rate movements.
- The right not to deliver, which protects against downward rate movements.

Mechanically, these two hedges are combined to create the put option. A **put option** gives the originator the right, but not the obligation, to deliver a loan or security at a prearranged price within an agreed-upon period.

The originator pays a "premium" or fee for a put option; this is the maximum cost for such a hedge. It offers protection to originators from rate swings that have the potential to make alternative hedges unexpectedly costly.

It is important to realize that the seller, or writer of the option, assumes that the buyer, or holder of the option, will use it to his best advantage. Thus, when market rates rise above the contract (or strike) rate, the investor expects that the lender will deliver. If rates fall, the investor will expect the lender to exercise his option not to deliver and to take advantage of better prices elsewhere for any loans that will still close.

The up-front fee (put) option has several advantages over the contingent-fee alternative. First, the maximum possible cost of the put option is known, although some people might gamble that the contingent-cost option will result in less expense. Second, originators using put options are able to take advantage of profit opportunities when loans unexpectedly close after rates fall, or when loans fall out after rates rise. When market rates fall, loans can be delivered profitably at new market yields without additional cost for not delivering into the original commitment. When rates rise, loans that fail to close can be replaced by higher-yielding loans for delivery into the commitment.

Creating Subpipelines

In order to minimize pipeline risk, the originator needs to hedge loans that will close and to be able to forego delivery of hedged loans that will not close. He must also contain his hedging costs, to remain both competitive and profitable. This is accomplished by knowing through experience what portion of the production pipeline is (1) likely to close, (2) not likely to close, and (3) truly unpredictable as to closing. This knowledge is translated into hedging strategies, as shown in Table 2.6.

As shown in the table, the originator divides his production segment pipeline into three subpipelines, each of which is hedged in the most cost-efficient manner. Loans that are certain to close can be sold forward at a yield that is set when the commitment is issued. Loans that never close because of credit, personal, or situational problems do not represent an interest-rate risk and, therefore, should not be hedged.

The critical category is the portion of loans in the pipeline for which closing is uncertain. This group represents:

- Borrowers who are rate-sensitive (those who might decide not to close in order to take advantage of lower rates).
- A random element of loans that do not close or close late due to unforeseen circumstances.

Hedging Inventory Risk Inventory risk is limited to price or product risk and is not subject to borrower fallout, assuming loans stay current while warehoused. The choice among available hedge vehicles—forward sales, substitute sales, or options—depends both on the lender's level of risk aversion and on his view of market rates. A cost differential between these alternatives also affects his choice of the optimal strategy for hedging inventory-period risk.

Using an Optional Hedge If the originator wishes to protect his inventory against rate increases (price decreases) but wishes to benefit from the rising

TABLE 2.6
Hedging Strategies

Portion of Pipeline	Hedge Method
Always closes	Forward sale or substitute sale
Never closes	Do not hedge
Uncertain as to closing	Forward sale or substitute sale with option not to deliver

value of that inventory should rates fall, an optional hedge will give him an appropriate position. Using optional hedges against inventory is a choice based on the originator's interest-rate outlook.

If rates rise, however, or do not fall enough to allow the originator to recoup the marginal cost of the option, the lender would be better off to hedge with a forward sale and avoid the options premium.

A final alternative is for the originator to sell options (calls) against his pipeline. Although some originators believe this is a hedge, it is not. Selling options merely increases the effective yield earned by the amount of the premium collected. If rates rise substantially, the inventory will still lose considerable value. If rates fall, his inventory will not benefit fully because the option holder will exercise his option to purchase the loans at the contract price.

THE WHOLE-LOAN SECONDARY MARKET

Long before the 1970s, when the federal agency securitization programs merged the secondary mortgage market with the Wall Street-sponsored capital markets, mortgage loans were bought and sold among financial intermediaries such as S&Ls, savings banks, and insurance companies. Following the initiative to securitization, the focus of the secondary market shifted to the trading of MBSs. Nonetheless, buyers and sellers of nonsecuritized whole loans remain a powerful force in today's secondary market. According to data provided by *Secondary Mortgage Markets,*[9] whole loans purchased by thrifts, mortgage bankers, commercial banks, pension funds, and life insurance companies totaled $57.6 billion in 1983, $81.9 billion in 1985, $138.7 billion in 1986, and $134.4 billion in 1987. These amounts compare surprisingly well with MBS issuance volumes of $83.8 billion in 1983, $60.7 billion in 1985, $255.4 billion in 1986, and $225 billion in 1987.

Thrift institutions accounted for $59.8 billion in loan purchases in 1986, representing less than half of all whole-loan purchases, down from 67 percent in 1985 when thrift whole-loan purchase volume was $55.1 billion. This figure may be an indication that thrifts have shifted their investment parameters to less emphasis on portfolio lending and purchases of whole loans. Thrift statistics may be too conservative, however, because purchases of whole loans by mortgage bankers increased from $21 billion in 1985 to $49 billion in 1987. And much of that amount was likely to be remarketed in the form of private-issue MBSs. It should be also noted an increasing share of whole-loan purchases by thrifts would have been purchases of ARMs by the S&Ls.

[9]Federal Home Loan Mortgage Corporation, *Secondary Mortgage Markets* (Washington, D.C.: Winter 1988).

The Whole-Loan Trading Mechanism

Whole-loan trades often start with a friendly call between long-time business associates. Institutions that have been in the whole-loan market for some time typically have established correspondent relationships with firms that have a proven record of reliability in underwriting and product delivery. Recently the conduits, with their access to the capital markets, have become a major factor as net purchasers of whole loans, which they then market in securitized form, usually in large public offerings of MBSs.

Other intermediaries include mortgage brokers and private mortgage insurers. Until the late 1970s, mortgage brokers were the principal intermediaries for the whole-loan secondary market. However, shortly after the Ginnie Mae program was initiated virtually all government-insured loans were marketed directly to securities dealers packaged as Ginnie Mae pass-throughs. By 1980, most conforming conventional loans were sold to or securitized through Fannie Mae or Freddie Mac. The securitized conventionals were in turn sold directly to securities dealers. And so the mortgage brokers were deprived of their bread and butter volume business. Unable to compete with the capital-intensive securities dealers for the MBSs business, the brokers turned to the placement of construction and permanent loans on commercial properties. The primary market for these commercial loan placements was the S&Ls, which by the mid-1980s had soured on the business as a result of having acquired too many bad assets.

Early in the 1980s, Wall Street securities dealers themselves increasingly moved into the whole-loan brokerage business. By the mid-eighties many securities dealers were purchasing whole loans as principal for their own trading positions. And so today the process has to a large degree come full cycle. Between the primary securities dealers and the proliferating conduits the secondary whole-loan market has become closely tied to the same capital markets that drive the securitized secondary market. The by-product of this market link is the increasing standardization of all mortgage products, with far greater emphasis placed on sound underwriting practices and reliable appraisals. And finally, with the greater access to the efficiency and liquidity of the capital markets, competition among mortgage originators has become intense. Greater emphasis is now placed on wholesale mortgage banking, with the competitive advantage lying with the large, highly computerized originators who operate in national and international markets.

TRENDS TO THE TWENTY-FIRST CENTURY

The trends that will shape the secondary mortgage market for the next decade and into the twenty-first century are rooted in several major events of the past two to three years that have changed the face of the U.S. economy and its financial institutions. The dampening of the pace of inflation in the mid-1980s has changed the market's perception of the ability of inflation to make bad loans and bad real estate investments turn good.

Major events transforming the financial community include the globalization of the securities markets; the conversion of old kinds of debt into new kinds of securities, exemplified by the emerging predominance of ARMs, CMOs, and floating-rate CMOs; and the erosion of clear distinctions among securities dealers, banks, and thrift institutions. Also, demographic patterns in the United States are changing dramatically. The baby boom and the baby boomer's baby boom are passing behind us. The aging of the population will dictate the emergence of a new profile in housing construction. And a shift to new types of financial instruments that will more quickly build—and utilize—home equity is likely to displace some traditional forms of home financing.

Assessing Housing Demand and Financing Needs

Existing home sales in 1985 totaled 3.49 million units, with new home sales of 1.75 million. The National Association of Realtors (NAR), using the 1985 data as the base year, projected residential home demand for the balance of this century as follows[10]:

- Total existing home demand is projected to range from 3.9 to 4.6 million units between 1990 and 2000.
- Total new home demand is projected to range from 1.9 to 2.2 million units between 1990 and 2000.

In assessing the demand for mortgage financing, NAR applied home price projections to the estimated housing consumption demands, making allowances for down payments and an 80 percent average LTV ratio. NAR further adjusted its projections to take into account the fact that new home purchases normally involve the sale of a previous home. It therefore derived a net demand figure reflecting estimates for new financing less the retirement of existing debt. The net demand for financing is estimated to increase by more than 50 percent over the five years from the 1985 base year to 1990. Total net demand for the full five years is estimated at $409 billion. By the year 2000, it is projected to double to almost $900 billion, according to the NAR study.

The NAR demographic projections indicate that the largest growth in net mortgage finance demand will be in metropolitan areas. Regionally, the South

[10]National Association of Realtors, *The Demand for Housing and Home Financing* (Washington, D.C.: September 1987).

is projected to show the greatest growth, increasing in its share of net demand to almost 37 percent by the year 2000. The West is projected for modest growth. The Northeast and Midwest are predicted to decline somewhat. The NAR projections are given in Table 2.7.

The Outlook for S&Ls

NAR foresees a continuation of the shakeout of the S&L industry stemming from a probable merging of the FDIC and the FSLIC. The result of such a union is likely to be an eventual phaseout of distinctions between thrift and commercial banking institutions. Continued rapid evolution of electronic banking and the mixing of savings, checking account, and consumer investments of all kinds into a universal, full-service account held by diverse financial institutions could accelerate the process.

The Impending Thrift Crisis

The combination of deregulation, propensity by many S&L managers for high-risk lending, and what many observers feel has been inadequate supervision has led to a probable major restructuring of the S&L industry and mechanisms for reducing deposit insurance. Estimates of the FSLIC loss required to bail out the now-ailing thrift industry range from the $40 billion acknowledged by M. Danny Wall, Chairman of the FHLBB, to $100 billion by some private analysts, with the taxpayers likely to foot most of the bill. Increasingly, banking and legislative leaders envision the creation of new classes of thrifts and possibly reregulation of deposit-based lending institutions. One cornerstone of the proposed restructuring would transform the S&Ls into conduits that would concentrate on the origination of consumer finance loans which would be packaged and sold into the growing secondary market for asset-

TABLE 2.7
Projected Net Finance Demand: 1985–2000
Metropolitan and Nonmetropolitan Areas, U.S. Census Regions
($ billions)

| Year | Metro Areas | Nonmetro Areas | Census Regions | | | | Net Finance Demand |
			Northeast	Midwest	South	West	
1985[a]	$201.0	$ 64.8	$ 55.3	$ 66.7	$ 90.1	$ 53.7	$265.8
1990	310.7	98.6	81.0	98.7	142.8	86.8	409.3
1995	466.7	145.0	116.2	141.6	219.4	134.5	611.7
2000	686.4	210.8	161.5	198.2	331.1	206.4	897.2

[a]Baseline.

Source: Estimates by Forecasting and Policy Analysis Division, National Association of Realtors.

backed securities. There is also growing pressure to reduce the scope of federal deposit insurance below the present $100,000-per-account level, with proponents arguing that few thrift depositors need the present high level of insurance protection. According to FHLBB data, the typical S&L depositor maintains an average savings balance of $7,300. It is suggested that private investment plans seeking large-balance deposits should be expected to make credit judgments regarding their choice of depository, and that such free-market scrutiny would ensure better discipline on the part of thrift managers.

Other restructuring proposals call for the banking regulators to close troubled banks and thrifts before they become insolvent and another claim on the already strained insurance fund. Proponents suggest closure when the institution's net worth plus subordinated debt falls below 2 percent of assets. Concurrent with this proposed foreclosure guideline would be an increase in capital standards to 8 or 10 percent of assets for all banks and thrifts (currently 6 percent for banks and 3 percent for thrifts).

The proposals for better examination and supervision call for monthly reporting by banks, especially thrifts, to regulators and a legislatively imposed requirement that *all* assets of banks as well as of thrifts be marked for market quarterly. Some leaders of the S&L business are calling for more liquid and frequent examination and supervision of thrifts in addition to the higher proposed capital requirements. Critics of the existing FHLBB monitoring process call it too bureaucratic and slow to respond to the fast-paced and highly competitive capital markets structure that has engulfed the financial institutions in the past few years. Critics, including the U.S. Savings League, say it is unrealistic to expect a regulatory body to accept responsibility to assess S&L industry transaction risks accurately, at least on the monthly review cycle some have proposed.

Proposed Mark-to-Market Regulations In June 1988, the FHLBB issued proposed regulations requiring federal S&Ls to differentiate securities held in portfolio between those designated for investment and those held for trading or intended for eventual sale.

The regulations are intended to encourage S&Ls to develop market-sensitive strategies appropriate to the intent of their investments. Under the new regulations, securities clearly held as long-term portfolio investments may be carried at amortized cost. Securities that may be identified with trading activity, however, will have to be marked to market, requiring the institution to recognize profits or losses whether or not securities are actually sold.

The loophole used to be that an S&L could buy securities and if able to trade them for a profit to book the earnings while at the same time bury trading losses by declaring underwater securities to be a "portfolio holding" that, under existing regulations, could be carried to maturity at original cost regardless of deterioration in market value. The FHLBB has indicated that any frequency of trading activity in a given category of investments will cause these securities to be classified as a trading account. In other words, the S&L will find it harder to be a trader in this month's bull market and become a long-term investor the next month.

Securities held for sale will be carried at the lower of cost or market. An example would be mortgages originated within a mortgage banking entity of the S&L. A typical pattern with many S&Ls engaged in mortgage banking has been to sell their fixed-rate mortgages if they could do so at breakeven or at a profit, but if prices fell to put the mortgages in the portfolio.

The impact of the regulations, if adopted as proposed, would likely be to reduce trading activity and/or encourage more active hedging of securities held for trading or sale. Securities that are effectively hedged will not incur an impact on the balance sheet because profits and losses in a hedged position may be netted one against the other.

The FHLBB has indicated that the regulations may become effective early in 1989 in substantially the form proposed, and that securities held prior to the effective date would be exempt from the mark-to-market requirement unless they are actively traded. However, the proposed regulations are highly controversial because they ask accountants and regulators to determine the intent of S&L management in investing practices.

S&Ls Vie for Origination Volume

On the brighter side, some S&Ls are competing effectively with mortgage bankers in the business of building servicing income in lieu of the traditional dependency on attempting to maximize income through fees and maintenance of a positive spread between yield on assets and costs of funds. As recently as March 1987, savings institutions claimed 41.2 percent of all U.S. residential mortgage originations versus 32.6 percent for mortgage banking firms. Presumably the majority of the S&L originations were either ARMs, which are a good asset match against their liabilities, or if fixed-rate, mostly sold into the secondary market. One particularly encouraging note is that Freddie Mac reported a 30 percent increase in auction sales of fixed-rate mortgages to their auction window; more S&Ls are becoming comfortable in using the Freddie Mac Guarantor swap program to access Wall Street as a source of mortgage financing.

Another factor that will put competitive pressures on all financial institutions, particularly S&Ls, is the FASB 91 ruling on accounting for loan-origination-fee income. For years S&Ls have focused on the generation of fee income as an immediate contribution to earnings. The ruling provides for a 1988–89 phase-in period to comply with the FASB requirement to amortize fee income over the life of the asset, unless the asset is sold. The FASB ruling is likely to put further pressure on thrift earnings, forcing S&Ls to sell as much of their originated assets as possible to recapture earnings. The move could thrust the S&L industry headlong into the mortgage banking arena where competition is already intense. Some remarkable events of 1987 and 1988, such as the asset liquidation of the once-giant FCA empire, the merge of Transohio with Amerifirst SB of Florida, and the consolidation by Citicorp of a number of thrifts into its St. Louis-based Citicorp Homeowners Inc. mortgage banking facility are illustrative of the consolidation of the thrift industry. On a brighter note, there appears to be a gradual shift to a higher savings rate stimulated by a growing conservatism among consumer financial management following the October 1987 stock market selloff. A gradual evaporation of inflation fears would also be a plus for the depository-based savings institutions. And the fact that Freddie Mac reported in 1987 a 30 percent increase in new thrift sellers of loans to its window is a positive trend.

The Mortgage Banking Outlook

SMR Research Corporation, a private research firm specializing in analysis of the financial services markets, defined some major trends of the mortgage origination business.[11]

The SMR study identified the record mortgage origination volume of 1986 as a high water mark for the mortgage banking business which is not likely to be duplicated for many years. According to the report, a unique set of economic circumstances led to the 1986 surge in mortgage originations:

1. Interest rates dropped so far and so fast in 1986 that six full years of loan originations (1980 through 1985) were susceptible to refinancing.

2. Affordable mortgage rates and a strong economy made home purchases particularly attractive.

3. The 1986 Tax Reform Act gave mortgage debt special tax-deductible status.

4. Intense competition within the mortgage banking industry combined with the threat of loss of servicing from refinancings led originators to take the initiative to offer refinancing through aggressive marketing programs.

5. The secondary market matured in size and liquidity, and with the innovation of a variety of mortgage-financing instruments there was assured an ample supply of funds to finance a high level of mortgage demand.

SMR estimates that of the $442 billion of total 1986 mortgage origina-tions, 40 percent consisted of refinancings. According to data provided by Joseph Hu, refinancings accounted for $120 billion of total 1986 originations

[11]SMR Research Corporation, *Giants of the Mortgage Industry* (Budd Lake, N.J.: 1987).

and $60 billion of the 1987 total. Dr. Hu estimates refinancings will account for less than $30 billion of 1988 originations. This refinancing boom led to an expansion of the mortgage banking firms in addition to origination and servicing staffs. It also resulted in a significant enlargement of the electronic data-processing capabilities of the large firms. As origination volume trailed off in 1987 and even more in 1988, the industry found itself with excess capacity, a development that squeezed the profit margins of the origination business and favored the large, efficient operators.

David Olson, Vice President, Research, SMR, with research following up the 1986 study, contributed the following discussion specifically for this chapter:

> The mortgage banking industry is highly cyclical, responding to macroeconomic cycles as well as shifting patterns within the financial intermediaries. During the recessionary years of 1981 and 1982, residential mortgage originations totaled about $98 billion each year, half the level of the previous peak year of 1979 when originations were $187 billion. By 1985 mortgage originations rebounded to $243 billion, then a record, which was surpassed by the 1986 high-water mark of $454 billion. Although 1987 total residential origination volume was close to the 1986 level, the increasing share of originations taken by ARMs, which are mostly held in portfolio by S&Ls, coupled with a decline in refinancings, dramatically reduced the level of mortgage originations available to the mortgage bankers.
>
> As origination volume changes over the cycles, so does the profitability of the mortgage bankers. According to the data provided by the Mortgage Bankers Association (MBA), return on equity (ROE) for all mortgage originators was 13.9 percent in 1986. It had been 11.4 percent in 1985, 14.2 percent in 1984, 22.5 percent in 1983, 19.1 percent in 1982, and only 10.6 percent in the 1981 recession year. SMR believes that ROE will be minimal in 1987, but the official figures published by the MBA (reflecting all types of mortgage banks) will not be available until September 1988.
>
> There appear to be three reasons for the decline in profitability. First, FASB 91 became effective in 1987. This ruling requires all lenders to amortize all front-end fees over the life of the loan. Second, the average servicing fee on a first mortgage fell from ⅜ percent in 1986 to ¼ percent in 1987 as a result of competitive pressures. Third, the volatility in interest rates led to hedging losses, especially in the second quarter of 1987.
>
> Origination volume is expected to be down in 1988 due to rising interest rates, and very little refinancing is expected during the year. The

MBA projects originations of $325 billion for all of 1988, compared to $449 billion in 1987. The combination of a decline in volume plus lower margins on that volume imply lower total profit during the year. It is true, however, that many mortgage banks in early 1988 cut overhead and greatly reduced their staff levels.

Another pressure affecting the mortgage banking industry is the strong competition from thrifts who are originating ARMs for portfolio. Thrifts are so determined to eliminate interest-rate risk from their portfolios that they are willing to originate ARMs at unprofitable yields in order to book them. The thrift industry ROE in 1987 was a negative 20 percent. It is clearly difficult for a mortgage bank to compete with that type of performance.

The securities market for ARMs is just beginning and is not nearly as efficient as the market for fixed-rate securities. This accounts in large part for the sharp decline in MBSs volume in 1987 and 1988. In 1986 there were some months when origination volume exceeded $30 billion. In 1987 volume averaged about $20 billion a month. By early 1988 monthly volume was down to $7.5 billion. In 1988, 60 percent of first mortgage originations have been ARMs, most of which are staying in thrift portfolios.

SMR does not see this trend continuing. "We don't think the thrift industry is viable for many more years. The strongest firms are changing their name to bank and seeking to convert to FDIC insurance. Many have diversified and now have almost identical powers as commercial banks. The large number of runs of depositors at thrifts indicates that depositors are losing confidence in FSLIC insurance, forcing thrifts to pay higher rates for their funds (especially CDs). This cost-of-funds differential and the higher cost of FSLIC insurance lead us to assume that the two funds will likely be merged in the future. The outlook for funding mortgages in thrift portfolios is not strong. We think that the pressures on the thrift industry will be to convert to a FDIC bank charter or become a mortgage bank. Thus it is likely that in late 1989 or 1990, there will be a resurgence in the mortgage banking and MBSs market."

Consolidation Trends of the 1980s

SMR reported that just the 10 largest mortgage originators in 1986 accounted for almost 15 percent of that year's total mortgage originations from all sources, which includes 19,000 origination firms. The 25 largest originators took 25 percent of the total U.S. mortgage volume in 1986. Citicorp, with its Citicorp Homeowners Inc. mortgage banking and Citi Mae conduit subsidiaries, topped the list with a 1986 origination volume of $13.4 billion and a market share of 3 percent of all U.S. originations. Some thrift institutions also headed the list, with HF Amanson, Great Western Financial, City Federal, Homeowners Federal, and Calfed Mortgage Company among the top 10. Citicorp remained as top originator in 1987, with $13.1 billion generated in residential loans, followed by Home Savings of America (Los Angeles), with $11.6 billion, and Western Bank FSB (Beverly Hills), with $9.5 billion.

SMR also identified a growing trend to wholesale banking, which is illustrated in Table 2.8.

Economics of Size

The SMR study found that a number of advantages fall to the larger originators; key among them is the ability to achieve a lower cost of funds for loan warehousing. Most of the largest originators are part of well-capitalized financial institutions whose backing gives the mortgage banking subsidiaries access to the commercial paper market. The ability to access the capital markets through the capacity to securitize large volumes of loans quickly and relatively inexpensively also gives these firms a marketing advantage. The marketing aspect of the business is possibly the most critical factor. With more than half of all conventional mortgages now marketed in securitized form, the mortgage market has become highly sensitive to the volatility of the bond markets. As a consequence, mortgage rates have become more volatile, with rates changing as much as 100 basis points in a week. Managing this trend to higher and more regular rate volatility requires a sophisticated secondary marketing department with a sound knowledge of hedging techniques.

Other considerations identified by SMR as favoring the largest operators

TABLE 2.8

Wholesale and Correspondent Purchased Loans as Components of Originations
($ billions)

Company	Total Originations	Purchased Loan Portion	Purchased Loans as % of Total
Citicorp	13.4	3.5[a]	26.1%
GMAC	7.3	4.2	57.5%
City Federal	6.07	3.44	37.2%
Fleet	5.1	3.4	66.7%
Sears	4.496	0.8	17.8%
Goldome	4.0	2.2	55.0%
First Union	3.241	0.156	4.8%
Fireman's Fund	3.0	1.8	60.0%
Countrywide Funding	2.814	0.970	34.5%
Commonwealth	2.8	0.305	10.9%
Imperial Savings	2.7	0.2	7.4%
Transohio	2.683	0.418	15.6%

[a]SMR estimate.

Source: SMR Research Corporation.

include servicing economies of scale, where the threshold for profitability may now exceed the $1 billion level in loans serviced; cross-selling opportunities; mass marketing techniques, including national advertising; and geographic diversification, which reduces the originator's exposure to the vagaries of regional economic cycles.

The Realty Ownership Connection

Finally, SMR regarded the ownership connection between mortgage originators and realty brokers as the single most important trend today in marketing mortgage origination services to the consumer. Since the realty broker represents the largest source of origination referrals to the mortgage originators, the opportunity to cross-sell between a large realty brokerage franchise and an affiliated mortgage banking firm is seen as the biggest opportunity enjoyed by the large originators today. Sears, with its ownership of Coldwell Banker, and Metropolitan Life, which owns Century 21, are illustrative of such combinations. Other examples include Empire of America, which owns Relocation Realty Service Corp.; Twin City Federal, which bought a major Realty World franchise; and Travelers Mortgage, with Equitable Relocation.

Thus the major trends of the S&L and mortgage banking industries suggest that consolidation, possession of capital, quick access to the capital markets, and cross-selling appear to point the way of the future.

A New Breed of Investors

Joseph Hu, Executive Vice President and Director of Mortgage Research at Shearson Lehman Hutton, in a presentation in Boston in July 1988 identified a new and growing breed of MBSs investors.

According to Dr. Hu, in recent years, increased sophistication in mortgage instruments, especially CMOs, has attracted nontraditional investors with liabilities of significantly shorter maturities. These investors include mutual funds; professional money managers for private savings, trusts, or pension funds; and foreign banks.

Over the past few years, the profile of secondary market investors has changed dramatically. The involvement of thrifts has declined steadily, from a little under 50 percent in 1978 to only 12 percent in 1982. Severe hemorrhaging of deposit flows during the 1981–82 period forced thrifts to withdraw from the mortgage market. During this period, commercial banks also lightened their investment in mortgages; however, they reversed this trend in 1986 and 1987, enlarging their market share to more than 25 percent. Life insurance companies have also stepped up mortgage activity to become more significant market participants, accounting for about 10 percent of total mortgage investment. Private and public pension funds have steadily added mortgages to their investment portfolios in recent years. Mutual funds became heavily involved in mortgages through purchasing Ginnie Maes starting in early 1985. In the rally market of 1986, they accounted for more than 10 percent of total net mortgage investments. When the rally ran out of steam after mid-1987, mutual funds' share plummeted by about 50 percent, thereby showing these funds to be a volatile, although important, new source of mortgage capital.

More important to the development of a wider investor base was the participation of money managers and foreign banks and insurance companies. Their investment activity is reported in the Federal Reserve's flow of funds under the broad category of CMO trust. No other details are available on buyers of CMOs; however, anecdotal evidence indicates that nontraditional investors purchased large amounts of CMOs. Usually they purchase floating-rate or short-tranche CMOs, but occasionally they are interested in CMOs with longer maturities. Their maturity preferences vary according to the relative market values of fixed-income securities. Over the past two years as the CMO market has become more sophisticated, these investors' involvement with residential mortgages has increased markedly.

Future Sources of Mortgage Capital

Against this historical background, several conclusions may be reached about the future of the residential mortgage market. First, the market has been remarkably capable of raising needed capital in the past 18 years to finance housing demand, and should continue to do so in the future. It is also likely to maintain its historical share of 20 to 30 percent of total funds raised by nonfinancial sectors. Recent demographic projections point to a steadily declining housing demand for the coming decade. With reduced demand, the mortgage market is more likely to raise the needed capital.

Second, thrift institutions will continue to be important mortgage investors, although their dominance will decline steadily. Commercial banks will be the leading challenger to thrifts. A recent international agreement on risk-adjusted capital requirements for banks appears to favor mortgages. These requirements are likely to encourage banks to expand their investment in mortgages.

Third, creative mortgage securities with multiclass maturity structures will become the major means of attracting mortgage capital. While the underlying mortgages will continue to have a fixed, 30-year maturity, the underlying cash flow will increasingly be recast to attract investors.

Finally, as the popularity of multiclass securities increases, the investor base will expand to include more nontraditional investors. Mutual funds, money managers, and foreign investors will become increasingly important sources of mortgage capital.

The Mortgage Instruments of the Future

The traditional 30-year, fixed-rate mortgage will continue as the financing instrument of choice for a large portion of home buyers. Its survival in the secondary market is increasingly dependent on the ability of the capital markets to transform the 30-year mortgage into other forms, however. The CMO was the first truly successful effort to alter mortgage cash flows in a security form that can appeal to a broad universe of investors. One trend is clear—the availability of mortgage forms in the primary mortgage market has become increasingly dependent on what can be sold into the secondary market. The 30-year, fixed-rate mortgage derived its support from the thousands of S&Ls that were encouraged by public policy of the fifties, sixties, and seventies to portfolio the fixed-rate mortgage but can no longer afford to do so. Therefore, the success of MBSs derivative products to repackage this traditional loan form into altered states will dictate its availability to homeowners of the future.[12]

ARMs

No longer a brand new instrument, the ARM is nevertheless in its adolescence, having been part of the secondary market for only five years. The points in favor of the ARM for both borrower and lender/investor were covered earlier in this chapter. Many people view the ARM postured much as the Ginnie Mae was in the early 1970s, predicting we will see an evolution of new forms that are difficult to contemplate today. One variation, which appeared in the spring of 1988, was the creation of an ARM indexed to the **London Interbank Offered Rate (LIBOR)**. The LIBOR ARM was first offered by WESAV Mortgage Corporation, the mortgage banking subsidiary of Western Savings and Loan in Phoenix, Arizona. In the spring of 1988, Shearson Lehman Mortgage Corporation added the LIBOR-based ARM to its package of purchase-eligible loans, and Shearson Lehman Hutton initiated purchase of LIBOR-based ARMs for its own position. Other mortgage banking and investment banking firms announced similar programs.

The WESAV ARM is to be securitized as a $150 million floating-rate CMO offering with three tranches of roughly equal amounts. It adjusts every six months to LIBOR plus a margin at 2.65 percent, with caps of 1 percent per six-month interval and a lifetime cap of 13.875 percent. The marriage of the ARM to the CMO was the result of the greater secondary market acceptance of the CMO floaters compared to the ARM securities. To date, some $30 billion of CMO floaters have been marketed over a period of less than a year and a half compared to $20 billion of securitized ARMs in over two years.

The LIBOR-based index is particularly popular with foreign investors,

---

[12]National Association of Realtors, *The Demand for Housing and Home Financing* (Washington, D.C.: September 1987).

who have bought a large share of the CMO floaters—so far, all LIBOR-based. Furthermore, the LIBOR plus margin rate to the borrower is typically lower than that of either the 1-year CMO or 11th District Cost of Funds ARM. Whatever acceptance this version of the ARM will gain in the marketplace, the ARM loan and evolving securitized versions of it appear assured in the market of the future.

RAMs

The RAM has been an instrument of limited availability to date, but demographic trends for the balance of this century suggest it is an instrument with a future. According to the Joint Center for Housing Studies of M.I.T. and Harvard, the number of heads of households aged 65 years and over will increase by 4.4 million between 1985 and 2000. Adding the 1.5 million projected increase in households aged 55 to 64, we find that the market of mature adults becomes 6 million. Many of these households will live on limited incomes, and a RAM will satisfy their need to convert home equity to cash. The apparent need for the RAM is clear; whether it will find acceptance in the secondary market—or at least attract a sufficient number of primary mortgage lenders—remains to be seen.

Bi-Weekly Mortgages

The bi-weekly mortgage is another instrument with high expectations among originators but which so far has gained little acceptance, except with a select group of lenders in New England and northeastern Canada. The bi-weekly is structured with a 30-year monthly amortization schedule, with the payments split into two payments every 14 days. The result, of course, is an acceleration in the paydown of the loan, shortening its term to 18 or 19 years.

The benefit to the borrower is twofold. A considerable interest savings is realized, and equity buildup in the home is accelerated. However, servicing has been a major problem so far, and there has been no secondary market activity to date.

15-Year Mortgages

The 15-year mortgage offers benefits to the homeowner similar to the bi-weekly in interest savings and equity buildup. The important difference is the 15-year mortgage has developed an active secondary market (see Chapter 9).

The Primary Dealer Market

Nowhere has consolidation been more apparent over the past few years than in the Wall Street dealer community. In 1987, there were devastating marketing losses among several primary dealers. Some notable losses occurred in stripped MBSs and in a form of CMO floater, collectively costing one firm close to $500 million. At another firm a mix-up between seasoned and new production loans resulted in losses reportedly in excess of $40 million. A controversy over the proper pricing of stripped MBSs persists, as does an ongoing debate among dealers regarding prepayment-speed projections. At the same time, it is the primary dealers who have led the way in MBSs product innovations, analytical tools, and MBSs portfolio-valuation techniques. There is no doubt but that the future of the MBSs secondary market rests first and foremost with the primary MBSs dealers. And the future of the dealers depends on access to vast capital resources, the availability of market and analytical information in seconds, in-depth and unbiased research, disciplined trading practices, and sound marketing. More so than with any other segment of the secondary market, the trends of the future are all with the biggest and best-managed of the dealer community.

Finally, innovation will continue to be a predominant trend among the dealers. However, the emphasis is likely to shift from MBSs product innovation to MBSs product utilization in the form of better ways to manage and hedge portfolios. Also, we will likely see a continuing flow in innovative forms of financing. The senior/subordinated structure under REMIC is likely to play a major role in evolving financing techniques and may add a spark of life to the private-issue MBSs sector, which in 1988 for the first time showed signs of gaining a meaningful share of the mortgage securitization business.

II

DYNAMICS OF MORTGAGE POOL CASH FLOWS

3
Federal Agency Mortgage-Backed Securities Programs

4
Uniform Practices for Delivery and Settlement
of Agency-Guaranteed Mortgage-Backed Securities

5
Calculating Principal and Interest:
Measuring and Predicting Prepayments

6
Determinants of Price and Yield

7
Duration, Convexity, and Volatility Properties
of Mortgage Securities

8
Measuring Value without the Black Box

3

Federal Agency Mortgage-Backed Securities Programs

INTRODUCTION

Mortgage pass-through securities (MPTSs) were the first form of pooled mortgage-collateralized securities to be issued and are the predominant form of mortgage-backed security (MBS) actively traded in the secondary market today. With a pass-through security, investors own an undivided interest in the pool of mortgages that collateralizes the MPTS. The pass-through is so called because principal and interest (P&I) is passed through to the investor as it is generated by the mortgages underlying the pool. Each pool has a coupon, or pass-through rate; an issue date; a final, or stated, maturity date; an average life; and a payment delay.

The first MPTS was issued in 1970 under the guaranty of the Government National Mortgage Association (Ginnie Mae). Since that historic event, several varieties of pass-through securities have evolved. The predominant form of MPTS has been that guaranteed and issued by the housing-related federal agencies. Following the Ginnie Mae initiative, the Federal Home Loan Mortgage Corporation (Freddie Mac) introduced its participation certificate (PC) program in 1971, and in 1981 the Federal National Mortgage Association (Fannie Mae) followed with its MBSs program.

The average life—the weighted average time to the receipt of the principal repayment—is often used by investors as a proxy for the effective maturity of the MPTS. The payment delay represents the period between the time the P&I is made on the mortgages and when it is passed through to the MPTS investor.

This chapter reviews the characteristics of pass-throughs and summarizes the specific pass-through securities programs of each federal agency.

MBSs POOL CHARACTERISTICS

Pass-Through Rate and Servicing Spread

The **pass-through rate** is the net interest rate passed through to investors after deducting servicing, management, and guarantee fees from the gross mortgage coupon. The pass-through rate, a single-coupon rate that is used in describing the mortgage-backed pass-through certificate, is always lower than the gross weighted average coupon (WAC) on the mortgages underlying the pool.[1] The difference between the net pass-through rate paid to investors and the mortgage rate paid by the homeowners is the servicing spread paid to the mortgage servicer and a management and guarantee fee remitted to the guaranteeing agency. The servicing fee represents the servicing institution's compensation for "servicing" the loans by collecting payments from homeowners and remitting the amounts due to investors, including advancing late payments. For example, in a GNMA-I pool with an 8.50 percent pass-through rate, the underlying mortgages carry a 9 percent gross mortgage interest rate. From the total servicing spread of 50 basis points annually (.50 percent), Ginnie Mae receives .06 percent for its guaranty, and the mortgage servicer retains .44 percent for servicing. *In this text the term "servicing spread" refers to the total basis-point spread between the security coupon and the gross mortgage rate. The term "servicing fee" refers only to that portion of the spread retained by the servicer.* MBSs practitioners are cautioned to be precise in use and interpretation of these terms; many market participants casually use the term "servicing fee" incorrectly to refer to the total servicing spread. Freddie Mac and Fannie Mae servicing spreads differ by program type, as described in the sections that follow.

Weighted Average Coupon (WAC)

The weighted average coupon (WAC) is calculated as a weighted average of the gross interest rates of the mortgages underlying the pool as of the pool issue date, with the balance of each mortgage used as the weighting factor. A WAC is needed only when the underlying mortgages have varying interest rates. Since GNMA-I pools (except AR, MH, and PL pools) consist of mortgages that all

---

[1]In very old Freddie Mac pools there may be some mortgages with rates below the coupon.

have the same interest rate, a calculation of WAC is not necessary. However, since Freddie Mac and Fannie Mae allow varying mortgage rates to be included within a single pool for fixed-rate mortgage securities, a WAC is necessary to evaluate Fannie Mae and Freddie Mac pools more accurately. Fannie Mae releases the original WAC as of the issuance date of the security for all its pools, and Freddie Mac releases it for pools issued after June 1983 in its Guarantor program.

Effective November 1, 1987, Freddie Mac began disclosure of updated WACs on most of its 15- and 30-year PCs issued under both its Cash and Guarantor programs, along with the **quartile** distribution of mortgage coupons in the pool. (Quartile identifies the lowest and highest mortgage coupons in each 25th percentile of the unpaid balance of the pools.) In most cases, the servicing spread can be approximated as the difference between the WAC and the pass-through rate. This information is useful in predicting future cash flows; however, since an updated WAC is not available for all pools, a 75 basis-point assumption for the servicing spread is often used for Freddie Mac- and Fannie Mae-issued securities. Over time, as principal is repaid at different rates on the underlying mortgages, the WAC may change.

Issue Date

The **pool issue date** is the date of issuance of the pass-through security, not the date of origination of the underlying mortgages. Ginnie Mae pools consist of mortgages issued within two years prior to the pool issue date. Fannie Mae and Freddie Mac pools may contain ''seasoned'' mortgages. Seasoned mortgages are generally regarded as those that for 30-year original term have been outstanding for five years or more and for 15-year original term are at least two years old. There is no industry-directed rule on the definition of seasoned loans, however, and investors are cautioned to clarify how the term is to be defined when trades involving seasoned loans are to be conducted among different dealers.

Maturity Date

The **pool maturity date** is the maturity date of the latest-maturing mortgage in the pool. In Ginnie Mae pools, most of the underlying mortgages carry maturity dates within a relatively narrow range. Because Fannie Mae and Freddie Mac pools can contain loans with various degrees of seasoning, and since these agencies do not impose any limits on the dispersion of the underlying mortgage maturity dates, the pool maturity date may be misleading. Pools backed by new production loans will generally have a fairly tight WAM range, but seasoned loan pools could have loans that differ in maturity by several years.

Weighted Average Maturity (WAM)

If an investor uses the maturity date of a Fannie Mae or Freddie Mac pool to compute cash flows and yields, the results may be erroneous. In the extreme case just described, such a security priced at a discount would be undervalued and priced at a premium would be overvalued. Fannie Mae and Freddie Mac provide additional information on the maturities of their pools by releasing a **weighted average maturity (WAM)**. As with WACs, Fannie Mae releases the original WAM on all pools, and Freddie Mac releases the original WAM on newly issued Cash and Guarantor pools. It also releases updated WARMs for all existing pools for which information is available and expects to update them annually. The WAM is calculated as a weighted average of the remaining term of the underlying mortgages as of the issue date and the WARM as of a subsequent date of recalculation, using the balance of each mortgage as the weighting factor.

Payment Delay

The **payment delay** refers to the time lag representing the number of days between the first day of the month following the month of issuance and the date the servicer actually remits the P&I to the investor. The payment delay differs for each pass-through type (see Figure 3.1). Since interest is calculated monthly, the payment delays result in interest-free delay periods of 14, 19, 24, and 44 days for GNMA-I, GNMA-II, Fannie Mae, and Freddie Mac, respectively, reflecting the actual number of days elapsed. For example, with a Ginnie Mae issued on June 1, the payment is delayed from June 30 to July 15, or 15 days. Since the payment would be expected to be made on July 1, the actual interest-free delay for a Ginnie Mae is 14 days. The interest so paid will have been accrued for the 30 days from June 1.

Payment delays are often stated in a misleading fashion. The stated delay is commonly specified as 45 days for GNMA-I, 50 days for GNMA-II, 55 days for Fannie Mae, and 75 days for Freddie Mac pools. Described in this way, the stated delay is the time lag from the issue date of the pass-through to the date of the first payment from the servicer to the investor. The number of days stated includes both the issue date and the first payment date. Subsequent P&I payments are passed through to the investor monthly on the same day of the month. To follow the example given above, with a GNMA-I issued on June 1, the stated delay is 45 days from June 1 to July 15.

Payment delays reduce the yield to the investor. The longer the delay, the greater the yield reduction on mortgage pools with otherwise identical characteristics. Unlike a current-coupon corporate bond, the yield at issue on a 9 percent pass-through-rate GNMA-I priced at par will not be 9 percent. For

FIGURE 3.1
How Payment Delays Work
(primary market)

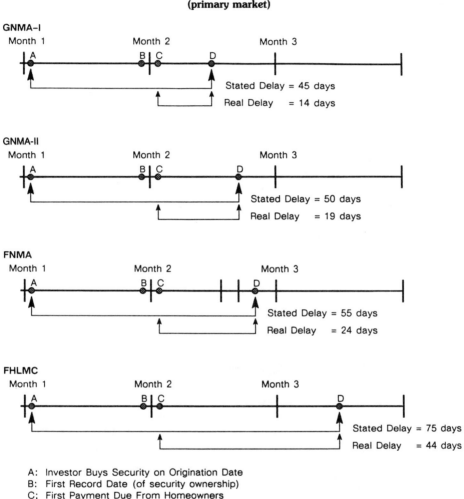

A: Investor Buys Security on Origination Date
B: First Record Date (of security ownership)
C; First Payment Due From Homeowners
D: First Payment Actually Made to Pass–Through Investor

Source: First Boston Corporation Fixed Income Research.

example, the cash-flow yield (CFY) of a 9 percent GNMA priced at par, using a **zero prepayment assumption** (assuming the scheduled P&I with no prepayments), will be 8.96 percent because of the payment lag. (The CFY represents the internal rate of return on the projected cash flow of the MBS using a prepayment assumption.) Because of this reduction in yield caused by the payment delay, **parity**, or the price that yields 9 percent for a 9 percent GNMA, is not 100—it is 99 21/32. In addition, the impact of payment delay is more pronounced in shorter-duration securities. Therefore, given two securities with the same yield, the security with the lower coupon, shorter maturity, or higher prepayment rate will produce a greater yield reduction for a given payment delay.

Pool Factor

The **pool factor** is the outstanding principal balance divided by the original principal balance. In a pass-through security the outstanding principal balance changes monthly, and usually it declines as the mortgages amortize. In pools that allow negative amortization on the underlying mortgages, the outstanding balance may increase. Thus, while the pool factor always starts at 1 (on the issue date) and finishes at 0 (at maturity), it may temporarily rise above 1 for pools that include negative amortization. When a pass-through investor owns only a portion of a pool, the pool factor is necessary to determine the current balance of the piece owned. For example, an investor may own a $100,000 original face value certificate in a pool that has an original principal balance of $1 million.[2] If the pool pays down to an outstanding principal balance of $951,839.01, the pool factor will be .95183901, and the investor's certificate will represent a current principal balance of $95,183.90.

FEDERAL AGENCY-SPONSORED PROGRAMS

The three housing-related federal agencies are the Government National Mortgage Association (GNMA or "Ginnie Mae"); the Federal Home Loan Mortgage Corporation (FHLMC or "Freddie Mac"); and the Federal National Mortgage Association (FNMA or "Fannie Mae"). Ginnie Mae is distinguished in two key respects: first, it is an instrumentality of the federal government, and its guaranty is that of the full faith and credit of the U.S. Treasury; second, Ginnie Mae uses only government-insured or guaranteed loans in its programs. Freddie Mac and Fannie Mae, by contrast, have quasi-federal agency status and use primarily conventional (nongovernment-insured) mortgages in their programs, although both issue some MPTSs backed by FHA/VA mortgages. Table 3.1 summarizes the characteristics of the primary MPTSs programs of the three agencies.

[2]MBS pools rarely come in even $1 million amounts because of loan principal paydowns in the pool collateral prior to the issuance of the certificate. The odd amount in the pool is referred to as the **tail**.

TABLE 3.1
Comparison of Primary GNMA, FNMA, and FHLMC Pass-Through Programs[a]

Feature	GNMA-I	GNMA-II	FHLMC PC	FNMA MBS
Collateral	Primarily single-family residential mortgages. Mortgages have FHA, VA, or FmHA default guarantees. Newly issued mortgages (less than two years old)	Same as GNMA-I	Mostly conventional loans (single-family fixed-rate mortgages without government guarantees). New or seasoned mortgages. Some seasoned FHA/VA pools	Similar to FHLMC
Maximum mortgage amount	$153,200	$153,200[b]	$168,700 (50%[b] more for Alaska, Hawaii, and Guam)	$168,700 (50%[b] more for Alaska, Hawaii, and Guam)
Original term	15–30 years	15–30 years	10–30 years (wide range of underlying maturities)	10–30 years (wide range of underlying maturities)
Guarantee	Full faith and credit of U.S. government for timely payment of P&I guaranteed by GNMA	Same as GNMA-I	Timely payment of interest and eventual repayment of principal guaranteed by FHLMC	Timely payment of interest and principal guaranteed by FNMA
Minimum pool size	$1 million ($500,000 for manufactured housing)	$250,000 multiple-issuer pools $1 million level custom pools $350,000 manufactured housing custom pools	$1 million for Guarantor $50 million for Cash, $500,000 for ARMs, $250,000 for Baby pools	$1 million ($250,000 for FNMA Majors)
Originator	Mortgage bankers, savings and loan associations, savings banks, commercial banks	Same as GNMA-I (multiple-issuer pools available)	Same as GNMA-I (single-issuer or FHLMC portfolio)	Same as GNMA-I (single- or multiple-issuer Majors or FNMA portfolio)
Usual servicing spread (basis points)	50 bp (except manufactured housing and project pools)	50–150 bp	37.5–250 bp[c]	50–250 bp
Payment frequency	Monthly	Monthly	Monthly	Monthly

TABLE 3.1 (cont.)

Comparison of Primary GNMA, FNMA, and FHLMC Pass-Through Programs[a]

Feature	GNMA-I	GNMA-II	FHLMC PC	FNMA MBS
Payment delay:				
actual	14 days	19 days	44 days	24 days
stated	45	50	75	55
Minimum certificate	$25,000	$25,000	$25,000	$25,000
Number of checks	One check for per month for each pool owned	One check per month for all pools	One check per month for all pools	One check per month for all pools

[a] This table refers only to single-family MBSs programs. ARM and project loan securities are covered separately in Chapters 10 and 11.

[b] The maximum loan amount for GNMA pools is the maximum VA loan, which maximum is adjusted administratively. The maximum loan eligible for FHLMC and FNMA pools is adjusted according to a formula tied to the Freddie Mac closed-loan contract index.

[c] The maximum allowable servicing spread differs between the Cash and Guarantor programs. As of May 2, 1988, the maximum spread is 200 basis points for the Cash program and 250 basis points for the Guarantor program.

Source: Ginnie Mae, Freddie Mac, Fannie Mae.

GOVERNMENT NATIONAL MORTGAGE ASSOCIATION (GINNIE MAE)

The **Government National Mortgage Association (Ginnie Mae)** is a wholly owned U.S. government corporation within the Department of Housing and Urban Development (HUD). By act of Congress Ginnie Mae is authorized to guarantee the timely payment of P&I on securities issued by approved servicers and that are collateralized by FHA-insured, VA-guaranteed, or Farmers Home Administration (FmHA)-guaranteed mortgages.

The Ginnie Mae pass-through security is called a fully modified pass-through security because the investor will be paid interest plus scheduled principal even if the borrowers of the underlying mortgages have not made their payments. Pass-through issuers are responsible for advancing funds for scheduled payments in arrears and for passing through early repayments of principal that have been received from the mortgage borrowers. All of these payments are guaranteed by Ginnie Mae; the Ginnie Mae guaranty is in turn backed by the full faith and credit of the U.S. government.

GNMA-I

Ginnie Mae began issuing pass-through securities in February 1970. Since then, the original **GNMA-I program** has developed into several programs, each of which securitizes different types of mortgages. All Ginnie Mae pools share certain characteristics. Most carry a 50 basis-point servicing spread and a 45-day stated delay. The original, basic Ginnie Mae MPTSs program is referred to here as GNMA-I to distinguish it from later modifications. The GNMA-I program packages current mortgages, which means mortgages are pooled within two years of issuance and are gathered into pools with matching coupons and maturities. As a result, new issuances of Ginnie Mae pools tend to track current market mortgage rates. For example, soon after homeowners borrow at 10.5 percent, Ginnie Mae pools with a 10 percent pass-through rate will become available to investors. GNMA-I pools are issued and serviced by mortgage bankers, S&Ls, savings banks, and to a lesser degree by commercial banks. Investors in GNMA-I pools receive a separate check each month for every certificate they own. Figure 3.2 illustrates the payment delay, prepayment period, and record and P&I distribution dates for GNMA-I securities. The payment-flow data for GNMA-II securities are identical, except that the P&I distribution date is the 20th of the month and the GNMA-II pool-factor data are typically available on the 6th business day of the month (A tape) and on the 8th business day (B tape). (See p. 112 for explanation of pool-factor data.)

Single-family (SF) pools, which comprise the largest number of pools and the largest outstanding balances, contain long-term, fixed-rate mortgages on residential properties. These securities are extremely liquid because of the

FIGURE 3.2
GNMA-I Schedule of Payment Flows—14-Day Delay

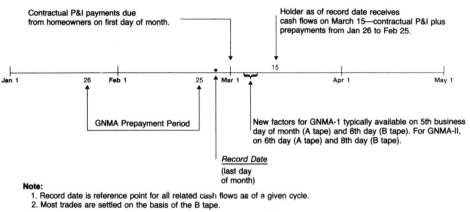

Note:
1. Record date is reference point for all related cash flows as of a given cycle.
2. Most trades are settled on the basis of the B tape.

Source: Shearson Lehman Hutton Mortgage Securities.

large number of issuances and the fungibility (that is, the interchangeability of like securities) of the pools. In trading, the participants may indicate a specific pool or a generic (**to be announced**, or **TBA**) pool. In a TBA trade, the seller may deliver any conforming pools within industry guidelines. Table 3.2 summarizes the Ginnie Mae security types by program.

GNMA-I MPTSs Product Summary

Guarantee Timely payment of P&I is guaranteed by Ginnie Mae under Section 306(g) of Title III of the National Housing Act. The section provides that "the full faith and credit of the United States is pledged to the payment of all principal and interest payments." An opinion of a U.S. Assistant Attorney General, dated December 9, 1959, states that such guarantees "constitute general obligations of the U.S. Government."

Pool Composition All mortgages in Ginnie Mae pools must be FHA-insured or FmHa- or VA-guaranteed. Mortgages must not be more than two years old from date of origination (except in the event the mortgages are owned by agencies of the federal government).

Payments GNMA-I payments are made on the 15th day of each succeeding month by the issuer directly to the MBS holder of record as of the last day of the month. One check is sent to each investor for his share of the P&I. The cutoff date for prepayments to be included is the 25th day of the month prior to remittance.

TABLE 3.2
Ginnie Mae Program Terms

Program	Stated Payment Delay (days)	Original Term (years)	Servicing Spread (basis points)	Coupon Range
GNMA-I[a]				
Single-family (SF)	45	30	50	Coupons equal
Graduated-payment (GP)	45	30	50	Coupons equal: GPM plans may be mixed.
15-year (Midget) (SF)	45	15	50	Coupons equal
Manufactured housing (MH)	45	12, 15, 18, 20	225–350	Vary
Buydown (BD)	45	30	50	Coupons equal
Project loan (PL)	45	40	25	Coupons equal
Construction loan (CL)	45	Varies[b]	25	Coupons equal
GNMA-II				
Single-family (SF)[c]	50	30	50–150	Within 1%
Graduated-payment (GP)	50	30	50–150	Within 1%
15-year (Midget) (SF)	50	15	50–150	Within 1%
Mobile home (MH)	50	12, 15, 18, 20	225–350	Vary
Adjustable-rate (AR)	50		50–150	Within 1%

[a] The two-character letter abbreviation in parentheses following the program identification is the suffix assigned to pool numbers issued under the program.

[b] Term not defined in years by statute; it is stated as to be not less than 150% of the estimated construction period.

[c] GNMA-II SF pools may and frequently do include buydown mortgages.

Source: Ginnie Mae.

Form of Settlement and Remittance As of this writing, some Ginnie Mae MBSs are settled by physical delivery of a certificate registered in the name of the security holder. Ginnie Mae is in the process of converting to a book-entry system, however, with full conversion expected to be completed during 1988.

Under book entry, monthly remittance of P&I for GNMA-I securities is made by the issuer–servicer to the Mortgage-Backed Securities Clearing Corporation (MBSSCC) on the 15th of the month. Checks are in turn mailed on the 15th by the clearing corporation to the security holder registered as of the record date, which is the last business day of the month. With GNMA-I securities under physical delivery, payments of P&I are remitted on the 15th of each month by the issuer–servicer directly to the security holder of record.

GNMA-II payments are made on the 20th day of each month by the central transfer and paying agent to the MBS holder of record as of the last business day of the month. One check is sent to each investor regardless of the number of pools held. The registered owner on the last day of each month (the record date) is entitled to that month's P&I.

   Settlement **Standard settlement** for the current-coupon Ginnie Mae is established under a uniform code of practices of the **Public Securities Association (PSA)**, the trade association for primary dealers in U.S. government securities, which includes MBSs dealers. Trades may be negotiated to settle on any day. Ginnie Maes, however, rarely settle between the 1st and 10th days of the month because Ginnie Mae issues a series of computer tapes that provide pool-factor data. The A tape is typically available on the 5th business day of the month for GNMA-I pools and on the 6th business day for GNMA-II, but the data are based on a limited universe of pools. The B tape, usually available on the 8th business day of the month for both GNMA-I and GNMA-II, lists pool factors on all outstanding Ginnie Mae pools and is the source usually used for settling trades. Settlement prior to publication of the factor report is made using factors from the previous month and is subsequently adjusted. Settlement for other coupons is made according to a schedule predetermined by the PSA.

GNMA-II

In July 1983, Ginnie Mae initiated a second pass-through program referred to as **GNMA-II**. The program includes single-family, graduated-payment, manufactured housing, and adjustable-rate pools. GNMA-II pools have a stated payment delay of 50 days, which offers increased float income to the servicers of the pool. The GNMA-II program was designed to address investor concerns relating to diversity and the cumbersome bookkeeping required from receipt of multiple-payment checks to holders of several small pools. The principal feature of the GNMA-II program is the availability of large, homogeneous multiple-issuer pools. These pools are usually larger and more geographically diverse than single-issuer pools. Also, the central transfer paying agent mechanism eliminates the need for multiple checks. GNMA-II investors receive a single check each month encompassing payments on all their GNMA-II investments.

   Table 3.3 presents in summary form a comparison of the GNMA-I and GNMA-II programs.

Pool Types

The GNMA-II program offers two approaches under which issuers may pool loans and issue securities.

   Multiple-issuer pools (also called Jumbo pools) are formed through the aggregation of individual issuers' loan packages. Under this option, packages

TABLE 3.3
Comparison of Ginnie Mae MBSs

	GNMA-I	GNMA-II
Issuer	GNMA-approved mortgage lender (single issuer)	GNMA-approved mortgage lender(s) (single and multiple issuers)
Underlying mortgages	Government-insured or guaranteed loans (FHA, VA, and FmHA)	Government-insured or guaranteed loans (FHA, VA, and FmHA)
Pool types	SF, GPM, GEM, MH, CL, PL, and BD	SF, GPM, GEM, and MH
Interest rate on underlying mortgages	All mortgages in a pool have the same interest rate (except manufactured home pools).	Mortgages in a pool may have interest rates that vary within a 1 percent range.
Guaranty	Full and timely payment of P&I, plus prepayments	Full and timely payment of P&I, plus prepayments
Guarantor	GNMA (full faith and credit of U.S. government)	GNMA (full faith and credit of U.S. government)
Principal and interest	Paid monthly to holders	Paid monthly to holders
Payment date	15th	20th
Maturity	Maximum 30 years, project loans to 40 years	Maximum 30 years
Minimum certificate size	$25,000	$25,000
Transfer agent	Chemical Bank	Chemical Bank
Paying agent	Individual issuers send checks to investors	Central paying/transfer agent sends check to investors

Source: Reprinted from a Ginnie Mae mortgage-backed securities pamphlet prepared by the Government National Mortgage Association.

submitted by various issuers for a particular issue date and interest rate are aggregated into a single pool which backs a single issue of securities.

The individual issuing firms are responsible for marketing securities in amounts equal to their own loan packages. Each security issued under a multiple-issuer pool is backed by a proportionate interest in the entire pool, rather than solely by the loan package contributed by any single issuer.

The purpose of the multiple-issuer pools under the GNMA-II program is to enable the creation of large pools that may have greater consistency in prepayments than custom pools. Also, multiple-issuer pools permit participation in the GNMA-II program by firms that may be unable to pool enough loans to establish a custom pool.

Under the single-issuer, or **custom pool**, approach, an individual issuer assembles a pool of mortgages against which he issues and markets securities, as in the GNMA-I program.

GNMA-II Programs

GNMA-II includes five separate programs characterized by the types of mortgages eligible for pooling. These programs, the minimum custom pool or loan package (for a multiple-issue pool) amounts, and the two-character prefix preceding the pool number for each are as follows:

1. Single-family, level-payment mortgages—SF (FHA, VA, or FmHA):
   - Custom pools: $1 million (may be $500,000 if used in connection with builder-bond financing)
   - Loan packages: $250,000
2. Graduated-payment mortgages—GP (5-year plan), GT (10-year plan) (FHA or VA):
   - Custom pools: $500,000
   - Loan packages: $250,000
3. Growing-equity mortgages—GA (4 percent annual increases), GD (any rate of annual increases) (FHA or VA):
   - Custom pools: $500,000
   - Loan packages: $250,000
4. Manufactured home loans—MH (FHA or VA):
   - Custom pools: $350,000
   - Loan packages: $250,000
5. Adjustable-payment mortgages—AR (FHA):
   - Loan packages: $250,000 (custom pools are not allowed under the AR program)

Generally, the same types of mortgages are eligible for the GNMA-II programs as for the comparable GNMA-I programs. All FHA-insured and VA-guaranteed home mortgages (except builder-operative loans) may be financed through one of the five GNMA-II programs. Buydown mortgages may be included in GNMA-II pools and loan packages without restriction. Fifteen-year mortgages are eligible under GNMA-II provided certain disclosures are made in the marketing of the securities. Multifamily mortgages are not eligible under GNMA-II.

Other Ginnie Mae-Sponsored Programs

In addition to the familiar single-family programs, Ginnie Mae also guarantees securities issued against a variety of types of mortgages—in fact, virtually any type of mortgage insured by FHA. The 15-year single-family securities are called **Midgets**. (For further information on the pool cash-flow characteristics of Midgets, see Chapter 9.)

Graduated-Payment Mortgages (GPMs)

Graduated-payment mortgages (GPMs) were initiated in the 1970s to provide an affordable mortgage in times of high interest rates and/or to accommodate middle-income home buyers who normally would not qualify for a standard, level-pay mortgage. The idea is that the GPM provides a significantly lower loan payment rate than fully amortizing level-pay mortgages because a portion of the interest payment is deferred for a period of time, usually five years. The deferred interest payment is added back to the balance due on the mortgage, resulting in negative amortization. In other words, the mortgage balance actually becomes larger during part of the period that some interest payments are deferred. At the end of the deferral period, the GPM becomes fully amortizing, although at a new, higher payment rate than would have been the case had the loan been level pay at the start. The rate is higher, of course, because of the need to pay off the negative amortization that has been added to the original mortgage loan amount. (GPMs and their cash-flow characteristics are discussed further in Chapter 9.)

Manufactured Housing Securities (MHs)

Manufactured housing securities (MHs), which include loans on manufactured homes, are frequently referred to as mobile home securities even though HUD draws a clear distinction in its regulations between mobile homes and manufactured housing, frequently referred to in the trade as mobile homes. By contrast, manufactured homes are prefabricated homes built to HUD specifications. Typically, they are transported to the site on a flat-bed truck and secured to a slab or other foundation; in fact, manufactured homes are not very mobile at all.

MH securities are frequently used as a proxy for 15-year securities and are issued with final maturities of from 12 to 20 years, with most MH securities having a stated maturity of 15 years. (MHs cash-flow characteristics are discussed further in Chapter 9.)

Ginnie Mae Project Loans

Ginnie Mae project loan securities are those backed by a variety of FHA-insured project loan types, notably multifamily apartment buildings, hospitals, and nursing homes. The flagship apartment project loan programs are those insured under Section 221 d-4 of the Housing Act. These projects for middle-income families contain a number of amenities, including security systems, elevators, and sometimes even swimming pools. Section 236-insured apartments are projects assisted with interest-rate subsidies for low-income families. The 236 program has been discontinued.

Rental apartment project loans have stated maturities of 40 years. Section 223f, now used largely for rehabilitation projects, was initiated to make financing available for conventionally financed apartment projects that had lost their original financing because of insolvency of the lender. 223f loans have 35-year maturities. Hospitals are insured under Section 242, with 40-year maturities, and nursing homes under Section 232, with 20- or 40-year maturities. FHA also provides for insured construction loan advances, sometimes securitized under the Ginnie Mae program as **construction loan certificates (CLCs)**, which are issued monthly during the construction phase. (These certificates are issued with the suffix "CL" following the pool number.) Upon completion of the project and final endorsement of the permanent loan by FHA, the CLCs may be exchanged for a **permanent loan certificate (PLC**, issued with a suffix "PL"). CLCs are not commonly issued today because of the uncertainty of the timing and amounts for which they may be issued, but a sizable amount of PLCs is outstanding for all the project types described above. (For information on Ginnie Mae project loan securities, see Chapter 11.)

Adjustable-Rate Mortgages (ARMs)

Adjustable-rate mortgages (ARMs) insured under FHA were first securitized under the GNMA-II program in 1984. The ARM security is indexed to adjust annually to the 1-year constant maturity Treasury (CMT) index. Ginnie Mae sets the security or pass-through margin to the index quarterly at 100 or 150 basis points over the index. The CMT is calculated weekly by the Federal Reserve Bank as the yield of all U.S. Treasury securities with a remaining maturity of 1 year or less. The ARM security has annual interest-rate caps of 1 percent and a lifetime cap set generally 5 points above the initial, or first-year, rate of the ARM. The first-year rate is set by the mortgage originator at the time of the closing of the loan and is not directly related to the index plus margin value that will govern the rate of the loan, and of the ARM security, from its first anniversary date to its maturity. However, at each adjustment the mortgage margin must be at least 50 basis points higher than the security margin but not more than 150 basis points higher. (Ginnie Mae ARM securities are designated by the prefix "AR.") (For greater detail on ARMs, see Chapter 10.)

Dormant Programs

The growing-equity mortgage (GEM) and serial note (SN) programs were Ginnie Mae initiatives that resulted in only $237 million GEMs and $639 million SN being issued under the programs (as of April 1, 1988) and remain dormant. Therefore, they are not discussed in this text.

Buydowns (BDs) represent loans which a third party (usually the builder or a relative) has deposited in escrow to cover part or all of the monthly P&I payments.

Ginnie Mae Mortgage Purchase (Tandem) Programs

Historical Background Ginnie Mae mortgage purchase programs, which entail secondary mortgage market operations, were authorized in 1954 as part of government special-assistance functions. The programs were carried out by Fannie Mae until 1968, when their direction was transferred to Ginnie Mae. The **Tandem** programs were so named because under them mortgage funds were provided at below-market rates to residential mortgage buyers with FHA Section 203 and 235 loans and to developers of multifamily projects with Section 236 loans initially and later with Section 221 d-4 loans as well. Ginnie Mae provided interest-rate subsidy by purchasing the low-rate mortgages at par, while Fannie Mae did the fieldwork: underwriting the loans and issuing commitments to qualified builders. Thus Ginnie Mae and Fannie Mae were working "in tandem" to assist the housing market. Tandem commitments ceased in 1983. Most of the mortgages purchased under the program have been sold out of the Ginnie Mae portfolio into the secondary market. However, there is a substantial floating supply of project loan securities collateralized by Tandem loans. Many Tandem plan-subsidized projects also received Section 8 assistance in the form of a Housing Assistance Payments (HAP) contract. The HAP contract was written directly between HUD and the developer and made up the difference between what the tenant could afford to pay and the then-market-rate rentals. The Section 8 program has also been discontinued.

FEDERAL HOME LOAN MORTGAGE CORPORATION (FREDDIE MAC)

The Federal Home Loan Mortgage Corporation (Freddie Mac) is a corporate instrumentality of the U.S. government, with its common stock owned by the 12 Federal Home Loan Banks that make up the Federal Home Loan Bank system. Its participating preferred stock is now owned by thrift institutions, but regulation has been introduced that would allow the preferred stock to be publicly traded in 1989. The Emergency Home Finance Act of 1970, which created Freddie Mac, mandated the agency to increase liquidity and available credit for the conventional mortgage market by establishing and maintaining a secondary market for conventional mortgages. To satisfy this mandate, Freddie Mac purchases mortgages, manages several pass-through programs, and issues debt, including collateralized mortgage obligations (CMOs). (CMOs are discussed in detail in Chapter 12.)

Freddie Mac began issuing pass-through securities in 1971, although new issues in large quantities were not available until 1976. It has designated its

MPTSs as **participation certificates**, and therefore its pass-throughs are universally referred to as **PCs**. The underlying mortgages in the PCs carry fixed or adjustable coupon rates and original maturities of between 10 and 30 years. As a practical matter, however, most maturities are 15 or 30 years for new originations.

The Freddie Mac pass-throughs differ from Ginnie Mae pass-throughs in several ways (see Table 3.1). First, Freddie Mac guarantees timely payment of interest and eventual repayment of principal[3] on its obligations, thus giving its securities "U.S. Agency" status, meaning the credit markets consider the credit of Freddie Mac to be equivalent to that of securities issued by agencies of the U.S. government. Freddie Mac securities, however, are not backed by the full faith and credit of the U.S. government. Second, Freddie Mac pools have a 44-day actual and 75-day stated interest-free delay. Third, many Freddie Mac pools use seasoned mortgages primarily under its Guarantor program, so that the underlying mortgage maturities may vary from pool to pool over a wide range. Usually they are close within a pool, although they do not have to be. Finally, the rates on the mortgages in a pool may vary up to 100 basis points from the highest to lowest note rate, with a maximum spread between the pass-through rate and the highest note rate of 250 basis points. Freddie Mac operates two pass-through programs: the Cash program and the Guarantor program. Figure 3.3 illustrates the Freddie Mac Guarantor PC payment flows.

Cash Program PCs

Under the **Cash program**, Freddie Mac purchases from savings and loan associations (S&Ls), mortgage bankers, and other originators' mortgages that meet Freddie Mac's quality, size (maximum single-family loan size in 1988 was $168,700), mortgage-type, and property-type requirements. Freddie Mac then packages these loans into PCs issued under **jumbo pools**, in which the mortgage rates may be above or below the pass-through rate. The agency auctions its Cash program PCs directly to the primary dealers who make up the dealer group for Freddie Mac.

WAC Range For Cash program PCs the maximum servicing spread is 2 percent, and the maximum range between mortgage coupon rates is 1 percent. For example, if the PC security rate is 9 percent, the maximum allowable mortgage rate eligible to be included in the pool is 11 percent. In that case, the minimum mortgage rate that could be included would be 10 percent. If the highest mortgage rate were 10½ percent, then the minimum would be 9½

---

[3]An exception to the guaranty is a special series of PCs designated with the prefixes "26" and "32" through "34" under which timely payment of principal is guaranteed. This special series was inaugurated in 1986 to enhance the use of PCs as collateral for CMO issues that require timely payment guarantees of both P&I to secure AAA rating on the CMO.

FIGURE 3.3
FHLMC Guarantor PCs Schedule of Payment Flows—44-Day Delay

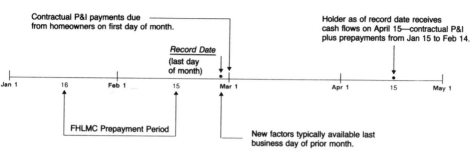

Note:
1. Record date is reference point for all related cash flows as of a given cycle.

Source: Shearson Lehman Hutton Mortgage Securities.

percent, and so on. Finally, the minimum mortgage rate must allow for the Freddie Mac guaranty fee to be included within the servicing spread. The guaranty fee may be negotiated to some degree but is a minimum of 1/8th percent.

Guarantor Program PCs

In the **Guarantor program**, a single issuer (usually an S&L) aggregates collateral to form a qualifying pool, and Freddie Mac exchanges a PC for the mortgages. Cash PCs tend to be larger and more diverse geographically than Guarantor PCs because the mortgages come from Freddie Mac's national portfolio and are aggregated into jumbo pools before being auctioned to primary dealers. The Guarantor PCs by contrast represent PC pools aggregated by a single issuer consisting either of seasoned loans that have been carried in the portfolio of an S&L or of new production loans originated by an S&L, mortgage banker, or bank that are converted to PCs by the issuer and marketed directly in much the same fashion as Ginnie Maes. Because of the way they are originated, these PCs are often referred to as Guarantor swap PCs, meaning that the issuer has "swapped" mortgages for PCs, in contrast to the Cash program, in which the mortgages are sold outright to Freddie Mac by the originator.

Because Freddie Mac has an active Guarantor swap program for seasoned loans, many PC securities have WAMs that are significantly shorter than the stated 15- or 30-year original maturity. The collateral may consist of whole loans or participations in whole loans (partial interest in the mortgages), and payments received by Freddie Mac are passed through to the investor. The Freddie Mac PC was the first MBSs program to securitize conventional mortgages under a federal agency guarantee. Freddie Mac also issues a limited number of PCs backed by FHA-insured mortgages. In 1988 Freddie Mac added ARM and multifamily loans to its Guarantor swap program.

WAC Range With Guarantor program PCs the maximum servicing spread is 2.5 percent, and there is no restriction on the range of mortgage coupons that may be included in the pool as long as the Freddie Mac guaranty fee is allowed for.

Investors and traders should be aware that before June 1, 1987, there was no limit on the Cash program servicing spread, and the Guarantor program servicing spread was capped at 2 percent. Between June 1, 1987 and May 2, 1988, the maximum servicing spread for both Cash and Guarantor programs was 2 percent, and the maximum spread between mortgage rates was 1 percent for both.

Freddie Mac Product Types

In 1984, in response to the increased popularity of 15-year fixed-rate mortgages, Freddie Mac added a 15-year pass-through to its product line. Freddie Mac **Gnomes**, as they have been nicknamed, are issued under the Cash program.

Freddie Mac in October 1983 expanded its multifamily loan purchase program. In August 1985 it launched a multifamily-backed PC auction program, which was suspended in October 1987. The multifamily PCs are issued as 30-year amortizing securities with balloon maturities in 10 or 15 years. They generally also carry five years of call protection. (For more detail on multifamily PCs, see Chapter 11.)

In March 1986 Freddie Mac inaugurated its PC ARMs programs and now holds twice-monthly auctions of these securities on a 30-day forward-delivery basis. The PC ARMs are indexed to the 1-year constant maturity Treasury index with a 150 or 175 basis-point spread over the index. They typically carry caps of 2 percent per interval with a lifetime cap of about 5 percent over the initial coupon rate for the first year of issuance. (Securitized ARMs are covered in greater detail in Chapter 10.)

In addition to PCs, Freddie Mac issues collateralized mortgage obligations. **Collateralized mortgage obligations (CMOs)** are debt issues with multiple classes, called **tranches**, of bonds. Each tranche may have a different coupon rate, final maturity date, and average life. All Freddie Mac CMOs have had semiannual bond payments. Also, they have all used 100 percent fixed-rate mortgages as collateral and a guaranteed sinking fund to establish minimum principal prepayments. (Chapter 12 covers CMOs in greater detail.)

Freddie Mac Program Terms[4]

Each Cash program PC represents an undivided interest in mortgages that Freddie Mac purchased from a number of sellers and formed into a PC pool.

---

[4]This section and the following section on Strip PCs are based on information provided by Federal Home Loan Mortgage Corporation.

Pool prefixes "36" and "38" reflect new restrictions on the mortgages backing the related Cash PC pools as follows: the minimum interest rate on any mortgage is to be equal to or greater than the related PC coupon, and the maximum interest rate on any mortgage is to be no greater than the related PC coupon plus 200 basis points. In addition, the range of the interest rates on the mortgages within any particular PC pool with a "36" or "38" prefix is to be no more than 100 basis points.

Each Guarantor program PC represents an undivided interest in mortgages that Freddie Mac purchased from a single seller in exchange or on swap for PCs representing undivided interests in the same mortgages.

Each different type of Freddie Mac PC is assigned a distinct two-digit prefix to identify the types and original terms of the mortgages underlying the PCs and/or the program under which the mortgages were purchased, as summarized in Table 3.4.

Freddie Mac Strip PCs

Each **strip mortgage participation certificate (Strip PC)** represents ownership interests in specified mortgages that Freddie Mac purchased from a single seller in exchange for Strip PCs representing interests in the same mortgages. The mortgages are fixed-rate, first lien, conventional residential mortgages secured by one- to four-family dwellings with original terms of maturity of 15 years or less or from more than 15 years to 30 years.

Each Strip PC represents an undivided interest in all of the principal received on the related mortgages (principal only, or PO Strip PCs) or an undivided interest in interest received on the mortgages, to the extent of the applicable Strip PC coupon (interest only, or IO Strip PCs). IO Strip PCs are sold in a notional amount, that is, the amount upon which interest is calculated at the applicable Strip PC coupon. Although an IO Strip PC holder owns none of the principal of the related mortgages, the notional amount of an IO Strip PC is equal in amount to an identical pro-rata share of the aggregate unpaid principal balance of the related mortgages, the principal of which is owned by holders of the related PO Strip PCs. Freddie Mac assigns two-digit numbers to each Strip PC pool, which identify the type of interest owned (PO or IO), the original terms of the mortgages underlying the Strip PCs, and the program under which the mortgages were purchased. The prefixes are summarized in Table 3.5.

Freddie Mac Giant Program to Consolidate Pools

The Freddie Mac Giant PC exchange program was introduced in the spring of 1988 to form large Guarantor PCs from smaller pools now outstanding. Freddie Mac expects that the program, aimed at illiquid Baby pools (original balance of $250,000 or less) and small pieces of significantly paid-down pools, will lower

TABLE 3.4
Freddie Mac Group Number Prefixes and Program Terms[a]

Pool Prefix	Program	Maximum Mortgage Term (years)	Mortgage Type	Minimum Original Pool Balance	Scheduled Principal Guarantee
14	Guarantor	30	FHA/VA	$ 1,000,000	No
15	Cash	30	FHA/VA	10,000,000	No
16	Cash	30	Conventional	10,000,000	No
17	Cash	30	Conventional	50,000,000	No
18, 25, 27–29	Guarantor	30	Conventional	1,000,000	No
20	Cash	15	Conventional	50,000,000	No
21	Guarantor	15	Conventional	1,000,000	No
22	Cash	10–15	Multifamily	1,000,000	No
23	Guarantor	10–30	Multifamily	1,000,000	No
26	Guarantor	30	Conventional	1,000,000	Yes
31	Guarantor	30	Multifamily (variable interest rate)	1,000,000	No
32	Guarantor	15	Conventional	1,000,000	Yes
33	Guarantor	30	FHA/VA	1,000,000	Yes
34	Guarantor	40	Conventional (variable interest rate)	1,000,000	Yes
35	Cash	30	Conventional (2% annual capped ARM)	1,000,000	No
36	Cash	30	Conventional	50,000,000	No
38	Cash	15	Conventional	50,000,000	No
42	Guarantor	40	Conventional (11th District Cost-of-Funds)	1,000,000	No
43	Guarantor	30	Conventional	250,000	No
44	Guarantor	15	Conventional	250,000	No
45	Guarantor	30	FHA/VA	250,000	No
46	Guarantor	30	Conventional	250,000	Yes
47	Guarantor	15	Conventional	250,000	Yes
48	Guarantor	30	FHA/VA	250,000	Yes
49	Cash	10	Multifamily	1,000,000	No
80	Guarantor	30	Principal only	10,000,000	No
82	Guarantor	15	Principal only	10,000,000	No
90	Guarantor	30	Interest only	10,000,000	No
92	Guarantor	15	Interest only	10,000,000	No

[a] Program information provided by Federal Home Loan Mortgage Corporation.

repo and administrative costs for investors. The first Giant offering was a large multiple-servicer, 9.5 percent fixed-rate pool made up from the whole and partial pools submitted during the eligibility period (May 18–19). The terms of the exchange program are:

TABLE 3.5
Freddie Mac Strip PC Program Terms[a]

Pool Prefix	Program	Maximum Mortgage Term (years)	Mortgage Type	Minimum Original Pool Balance	Scheduled Principal Guarantee
80	Guarantor	30	Conventional	$10,000,000	No
82	Guarantor	15	Conventional	10,000,000	No
90	Guarantor	30	Conventional	10,000,000	No
92	Guarantor	15	Conventional	10,000,000	No

[a] From program information provided by Federal Home Loan Mortgage Corporation.

- Only wireable pools backed by fixed-rate, one- to four-family, conventional loans (including timely pay pools) are eligible.
- Only the Freddie Mac dealer group may submit pools, and if less than $1 million is submitted, no exchange will take place.

While the Freddie Mac Giant program appears to be a response to the Fannie Mae Majors program, it is directed at a different segment of the MBSs market. The Majors program allows issuers to participate directly in creating large pools, while the Giant exchange involves only previously created securities. Under Fannie Mae's Majors program, issuers submit loan packages as small as $250,000. Participants receive certificates for a pro-rata share of a large, liquid Majors pool, thereby avoiding the creation of Baby pools. The average Majors pool size is $80 million. The program has been very popular; since inception in January 1987, $6.2 billion of Majors pools have been issued, $2.5 billion of them in 1988.

Freddie Mac also intends to start a negotiated exchange program that would swap one investor's Guarantor PCs of various coupons (quarter and odd coupons included) for a whole Giant pool with a full or half coupon and an IO strip.

Original WARM and WAC

The **WARM,** or **weighted average remaining maturity,** is used by Freddie Mac and Fannie Mae in lieu of WAM. The WARM of the mortgages in a PC pool or Strip PC pool formed under the Guarantor program is stated as of the formation of the pool. The WARM is expressed in months and calculated based on sellers' reports of the final scheduled monthly payment due on the mortgages. The original WARM of the mortgages in a PC pool formed under the Cash program is stated as of the formation of the PC pool expressed in months and calculated based on the note dates of the mortgages.

The WAC of a PC pool is expressed as a percentage carried to three decimal places. The original WAC reported for any PC pool is computed as of the date of the PC pool formation. Accordingly, the original WACs do not reflect principal payment activity on the mortgages after the "as-of" date.

On October 1, 1986, Freddie Mac began providing WACs for PC pools comprised of single-family, fixed-rate mortgages formed under the Cash program. The interest rates on the mortgages used to compute the WACs reflect those on the mortgages purchased by Freddie Mac based on information obtained from the seller upon the delivery of the mortgages. Under the Cash program mortgages are delivered to Freddie Mac in groups. A weighted average interest rate for each mortgage group is calculated using the mortgage coupons and unpaid principal balances of each mortgage in the group as of the date of delivery of the mortgages for purchase. Each of these weighted average interest rates for each mortgage group included in a PC pool is then weighted, using the unpaid principal balance of each respective mortgage group as of the date of PC pool formation to produce the associated WAC for the entire PC pool.

For Cash PC pools, WACs are provided for those formed on or after June 1, 1987, for those with a "20" prefix, and for those with the prefix "17" beginning with PC pool number 17-0082. WACs are *not* provided for Cash PC pools 17-0083, 17-0084, 17-0093, and 17-0094 and may not be provided for Guarantor PC pools formed before July 1983.

PC Product Summary

Since PCs formed from Freddie Mac's mortgage portfolio (Cash program) and those originated under the Guarantor swap program differ in certain respects, they are differentiated in secondary market trading. Cash program PCs are generally referred to as *Cash program PCs* and Guarantor PCs as *Guarantors*.

Guarantee Freddie Mac unconditionally guarantees the timely payment of interest at the PC pass-through rate on the unpaid principal amount and the eventual payment of all principal. Servicers are required to advance monthly interest payments to Freddie Mac whether or not they are received from the mortgagors until foreclosure is approved. Under the Freddie Mac statute, however, principal is required to be passed through only as collected.

PCs are not guaranteed by the United States or by any Federal Home Loan Bank and do not constitute a debt or obligation of the U.S. government or any FHLB.

Pool Composition PC pools, or groups, are composed of whole loans, or in some instances, 50–95 percent participations.

- *Cash program PCs* The minimum pool size is $50 million, and pools generally consist of from 500 to 1,500 mortgages. The geographic distribution of mortgages in a specific PC group depends on Freddie Mac's mortgage portfolio at any particular time.

- *Maximum Cash program servicing spread* The maximum servicing spread is 2 percent; the maximum range between mortgage coupons is 1 percent.

- *Guarantor swap program PCs* The aggregate unpaid principal balance and number of mortgages in Guarantor PC groups depend on the amount and number of loans put up for swap. Minimum pool size is $1 million, with the average size between $5 and $10 million except for ARM PCs with a $500,000 minimum pool size and Baby pools for which the minimum is $250,000. Since Guarantor PCs are typically composed of mortgages originated by one institution—usually an S&L—they tend to be geographically concentrated.

- *Maximum Guarantor servicing spread* The maximum servicing spread is 2.5 percent; there is no restriction on the maximum mortgage coupon range.

Maturity All PCs have a stated maturity equal to that of the longest mortgage in the underlying pool.

Payments A single check is sent to each certificate holder of record on the 15th of each month regardless of the number of pools held by the investor of record as of the last business day of the previous month. The cutoff date for prepayments to be included is the 20th day of the month prior to the remittance.

All Freddie Mac PCs are wireable securities and are now traded under book entry.

Freddie Mac Guaranteed Mortgage Certificates (GMCs)

Freddie Mac issued the first **guaranteed mortgage certificates (GMCs)** in 1975 in an attempt to capture a new segment of the investor market. Similar to PCs, GMCs represent undivided interest in specified conventional whole loans and participations previously purchased by Freddie Mac. Unlike PCs, however, the GMC is structured like a corporate bond, with cash flow made up of semiannual interest and principal payments. Freddie Mac guarantees the scheduled interest and minimum principal payments. If the loans in the underlying pool repay principal more rapidly than the guaranteed minimum, the investor receives the full principal repayment. If they prepay less rapidly, Freddie Mac makes up the difference. The security was designed to appeal to investors desiring the yield and relative safety of mortgage pass-throughs packaged in a traditional bond structure.

FEDERAL NATIONAL MORTGAGE ASSOCIATION (FANNIE MAE)

The **Federal National Mortgage Association (Fannie Mae)** is a federally chartered, privately owned corporation that was established in 1938 to expand the liquidity of the mortgage market. In 1968, under the Housing Act amendments that gave Ginnie Mae its guarantee authority, Fannie Mae was rechartered as a privately held corporation authorized to purchase and sell conventional, FHA-insured and VA-guaranteed loans. Fannie Mae introduced its guaranteed mortgage securities pass-through program in 1981. As with Freddie Mac, the majority of Fannie Mae MBSs are issued against pools of conventional mortgages, although Fannie Mae does issue some MBSs with FHA-insured or VA mortgages. Such pools are referred to as **GLs** (for government loans).

Fannie Mae guarantees the timely payment of both principal and interest on its MBSs whether or not the payments have been collected from the borrower. The guarantee encompasses principal payments resulting from foreclosure or prepayment. While Fannie Mae obligations are not backed by the full faith and credit of the U.S. government, they carry U.S. Agency status in the credit markets.

Pass-through securities may contain mortgages from Fannie Mae's own portfolio or those aggregated by a single issuer, which are then swapped for Fannie Mae MBSs. The pass-through rate is lower than the rates on the mortgages, with the underlying mortgages usually fixed-rate, conventional mortgages that have been outstanding for one or more years. The original maturities within a pool range from either 8 to 15 years or 20 to 30 years, although most are 15 or 30 years. Fannie Mae MBSs with underlying 15-year mortgages are referred to as **Dwarfs**. Like the Freddie Mac PCs, the mortgage coupons within a Fannie Mae MBSs pool may also vary widely. Fannie Mae pools have a 24-day actual and 55-day stated payment delay. Both Fannie Mae and Freddie Mac operate smaller pass-through programs for seasoned FHA/VA mortgages. (Figure 3.4 illustrates the Fannie Mae payment cash flows.)

Fannie Mae Majors Program

In January 1987, Fannie Mae introduced a multiple-issuer program to form large, diversified pools of mortgage collateral. The **Fannie Mae Majors** program is used in its lender swap network, which is more comparable to the

FIGURE 3.4
FNMA MBSs Schedule of Payment Flows—24-Day Delay

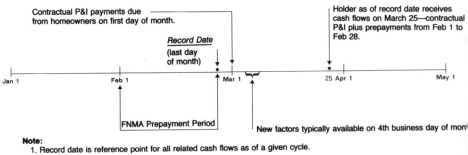

Note:
1. Record date is reference point for all related cash flows as of a given cycle.

Source: Shearson Lehman Hutton Mortgage Securities.

Freddie Mac Guarantor swap program. As a program feature, the WAC and WAM restrictions on Fannie Mae Majors pools are tight, with the WAC held within 1 percent and the WAM within a few months.

All loans submitted for swap into Fannie Mae Majors MBSs must have an original term of 25 to 30 years, resulting in a tight range of WAMs. Furthermore, the loans may be no older than 12 months. Since all the loans are required to have been originated within the 1-year time frame, it is expected the WAC range will generally also be fairly tight, unless mortgage rates were highly volatile during the period the swapped loans were originated. The minimum aggregate amount of loans that may be submitted for swap is $250,000. The payment delay is the same as that for all Fannie Mae MBSs. (See Table 3.1 for a summary of Fannie Mae MBSs characteristics.)

In July 1984, Fannie Mae issued its first securitized ARM. Fannie Mae holds a substantial portfolio of ARM loans, but most of the Fannie Mae ARM securities are issued against pools of ARM loans assembled by S&Ls and mortgage bankers who swap these pools for Fannie Mae MBSs. ARM swaps are issued against the 11th District Cost of Funds index, the 1-, 3-, and 5-year constant maturity Treasury index, and other indexes. (For further details on Fannie Mae ARM MBSs programs, see Chapter 10.) In 1986, Fannie Mae inaugurated a program of issuing stripped MBSs (see Chapter 13).

Megapools

In the spring of 1988 Fannie Mae revealed details for a Megapool program (which is different from the Majors program). Holders of at least $25 million in Fannie Mae pools of the same type and coupon can participate. Like Freddie Mac's Giant program, Megapools must be created in cooperation with a dealer. The other requirements are as follows:

- Pools included may not have WACs more than 150 basis points higher than the pass-through coupon.
- Pools included must have WAMs within a 24-month range from shortest to longest (adjusted for time outstanding).
- Minimum denomination for pool pieces is $1,000 original face.
- Fannie Mae will charge 1/8 of a point for the swap.

Both the Giant and Megapool programs allow holders of pools with small remaining balances to consolidate their holdings. The resulting large pools should command better execution in both the cash and repo markets.

Fannie Mae MBSs Product Summary

MBSs formed from mortgages in Fannie Mae's portfolio and from those swapped with originators are not normally distinguishable in the capital markets.

Guarantee Fannie Mae guarantees timely payment of all scheduled principal and interest due MBSs certificate holders, whether or not the payments have been collected from mortgagors. The MBSs guarantee is the obligation of Fannie Mae and not the U.S. government; nevertheless, the Secretary of the Treasury has discretionary authority to purchase up to $2.25 billion Fannie Mae securities at any time. Most Fannie Mae MBSs are backed by pools of one- to four-family conventional mortgages or FHA/VA loans as well as conventional ARMs. On a limited basis, Fannie Mae has originated pass-throughs backed by multifamily, adjustable-rate, and California variable-rate mortgages (precursors of ARMs).

Pool Composition Each pool contains only one type of loan. Minimum pool size is $1 million, with no maximum. All conventional loan MBSs issued before 1984 contain only single-family loans. Servicing spreads range by pool from .5 to 2.5 percent.

Pool Number Each individual issue of guaranteed MPTSs is assigned a separate number. The pool number contains a two-character prefix which identifies the types of loans and the original terms underlying the securities. Unless a special prospectus supplement has been issued on a given pool, the prefixes are defined as follows:

- AB—Alaska Housing conventional growing-equity mortgages (GEMs).
- AM—Conventional ARMs, multifamily.
- AS—Conventional ARMs, single-family.
- CA—Conventional long-term, level-payment mortgages—fully assumable, current production.
- CI—Conventional intermediate-term, level-payment mortgages—maturing or due in 15 years or less.
- CL—Conventional long-term, level-payment mortgages—maturing or due in 30 years or less.
- CS—Conventional short-term, level-payment mortgages—maturing or due in 7 years or less.
- C3, C4, or C5—Conventional GEMs, with 3, 4, or 5 percent annual increases to the P&I payment—fully amortizing—8 to 15 years.
- GC—Conventional GPMs, single-family.
- GG—Government GPMs, single-family.
- GL—Government (FHA/VA) long-term, level-payment mortgages—maturing or due in 30 years or less.
- MA—Government (FHA) long-term, level-payment project loans—fully amortizing within 40 years.

- ML—Conventional long-term, level-payment mortgage, multifamily.
- MX—Conventional balloon-payment mortgages, multifamily.
- RL—Conventional long-term, reverse buydown mortgages—fully amortizing within 30 years.
- VL—Conventional long-term, California variable-rate mortgages—fully amortizing within 40 years.

Maturity The stated maturity of all Fannie Mae MBSs is that of the longest-maturing mortgage in the underlying pool. All FHA/VA loans have been outstanding more than one year.

Payments Fannie Mae sends a single check on the 25th day of the month to each certificate holder of record regardless of the number of pools owned. The record date is the last day of each month, and the prepayment cutoff date is the 25th for lender swap and Majors MBSs and the last day of the second previous month for MBSs issued from Fannie Mae's portfolio of purchased loans. All Fannie Mae MBSs are wireable securities and are traded under book entry.

4

Uniform Practices for Delivery and Settlement of Agency-Guaranteed Mortgage-Backed Securities

INTRODUCTION

This chapter examines **good delivery and settlement procedures** for agency-guaranteed MBSs. An MBS may be traded for **immediate settlement** (within five business days of the trade date) or for **forward delivery**. Forward delivery is settlement beyond corporate settlement for the same month as that in which the trade has occurred, or for any future month mutually agreed to by buyer and seller. Immediate settlement is a form sometimes used for the sale and purchase of specific pools—that is, for outstanding MBSs with known pool numbers and pool factors and for which the original and current, or paid-down, face amounts may be determined.

Forward-delivery settlements are typically employed by mortgage originators with a known quantity of eligible mortgages that are yet to be pooled. The MBSs are sold into the forward-delivery market with pool information details to be provided on a **to-be-announced (TBA)** basis.

The uniform practices for good delivery and settlement have been set forth by the PSA.[1] Certain standard forms designed by HUD and the guaranteeing agency to expedite physical delivery of the MBS, and later the remittance of P&I by the servicer, are also described. This chapter reviews the definitions of settlement for the various classes of MBSs, the variance and

---

[1]Public Securities Association, "Uniform Practices for the Clearance and Settlement of Mortgage-Backed Securities," 1988.

136

48-hour rules, and other investor considerations relating to making good delivery.

SETTLEMENT

Settlement is an arrangement between firms and their customers for payment or receipt of cash or securities. It represents the consummation of a securities transaction on the delivery date. Settlement with Freddie Mac PCs and Fannie Mae MBSs is through electronic book entry. Some Ginnie Mae securities are settled through book entry while others are settled with physical delivery of the certificate.

Dealer Settlement Procedures

The primary dealers coordinate settlements through three administrative functions: (1) allocations, (2) receive and deliver (R&D), and (3) P&I. The allocations department of the dealer firm is responsible for apportioning MBSs received against scheduled deliveries to be made in accordance with uniform PSA procedures governing four key aspects of the transaction: (1) variance, (2) number of pieces, (3) pool information cutoff, and (4) denominations.

The receive and deliver department (R&D) is responsible for taking and delivering securities. R&D must prove the balance of settlement dollars against the securities that are received and/or delivered.

The principal and interest (P&I) department maintains the books for the firm's P&I payments for the MBSs held in inventory. It is also incumbent on P&I to verify that all P&I payments due the firm have been properly received. P&I checks that all positions are factored properly and processes all claims.

The discussion of uniform practices fairly represents practices as known as this writing, but these procedures are subject to change at any time.

Variance Rule

The first consideration for the allocations department is the **variance rule**. TBA trades are commonly executed in round dollar amounts—$1 million, $500,000, and so on—but mortgages are not originated in round amounts. Therefore, a so-called $1 million pool is not likely to be issued for exactly $1 million. The PSA has therefore defined the maximum allowable variance as 2.499999 percent of $1 million—in other words, not less than $975,000.01 nor more than $1,024,999.[2] Furthermore, no certificates may be delivered for more than $1 million (plus or minus the variance).

[2]Unless both parties to the transaction have agreed to different terms and conditions for settlement.

Denominations

The minimum denomination is $25,000 in increments of $5,000, with the exception of one allowed piece—designated the tail piece—that may be delivered intact, in one piece.

Pieces

A. There may be a maximum of three or four separate pieces, which may consist of different pools (unless otherwise specified), depending on coupons as follows:

   - 12 percent coupons and above—maximum four pools per $1 million.

   - 11.99 percent coupons and below—maximum three pools per $1 million.

B. *Deliveries for trades of less than $1 million* If the trade is for less than $500,000, one piece must be delivered to fill the trade. If the trade is for $500,000 or more but less than $1 million, not more than two pieces may be delivered, of which one piece must be for $500,000 or not less than $487,500.01 nor more than $512,499.99. The second piece must be for the amount that fills the trade.

C. *Deliveries for trades greater than $1 million* If the trade is for more than $1 million, as many pieces of $1 million or multiples thereof as are required to fill the trade must be delivered (each $1 million lot may not be for more than the maximum number of pieces allowed for a $1 million delivery, as described in paragraph A). If the trade is in excess of $1 million but includes a portion of the balance which is for less than $1 million, that portion must be filled in conformance with the rule applicable for trades of less than $1 million described in paragraph B.

Investor Considerations

The MBSs buyer must keep in mind several important considerations with respect to how the settlement may be treated by the dealer's allocations department.

A prime consideration is the variance rule. The dealer is likely to overallocate if market prices have fallen (to pass on as much market loss as possible to the buyer) or underallocate if prices have risen. The alert institutional seller should attempt to take the same advantage of the allocations rule when preparing his certificates for delivery. Another consideration is that failure to make good delivery on settlement date is expensive—interest runs from the original settlement date to the time of actual delivery (referred to as a "fail"— that is, failure to deliver on time). Investors must remember that all settlements are paid for by Fed Funds wired through the Federal Reserve system. Checks or clearinghouse funds are not acceptable.

In addition, the 48-hour rule (described below) can be costly if not adhered to. Attention to detail and preparation prior to delivery are perhaps the key concerns. Mistakes made in rendering pool information or wiring instructions can lead to a fail. Finally, checking all confirms on the date received is critical. An error not corrected for several days (or weeks) creates time-consuming—and expensive—research to correct after the fact.

TBA VERSUS SPECIFIED TRADES

The variance rule applies to TBA trades only. A trade done as a specified purchase or sale must be delivered and settled in the amount specified. For example, a trade for $675,000 must settle for that amount—there is no applicable variance.

Specified TBA

Some trades are done as TBA with certain aspects of the trade specified. This form is common when an account wishes to specify whether the pool is to be delivered as a seasoned or new production pool, but without specifying a pool number at the time of the trade. The specification is usually done by indicating either the year of stated maturity or the issue date of the pool, or preferably both. Stating maturing dates such as 2011 or earlier as seasoned versus 2012 or later as new, or specifying issue dates such as 1972 (seasoned) or 1986 (new production) is the usual way to specify a TBA. Sometimes the distinction is made in terms of an original WAM of 2010 or sooner to specify seasoned.

Another form of specified TBA might relate to the number of pieces or denomination amount—for example, no more than two pools or no piece for less than $100,000.

RECEIVE AND DELIVER (R&D)

A key to R&D procedures is awareness of the difference between the settlement date and the delivery date. The settlement date does not change—interest accrues from the originally specified settlement date no matter when delivery is ultimately made. The delivery date is the date of the actual availability of the MBS certificate—ideally, the settlement date.

Settlement dates for all MBSs are set from time to time by the PSA several months in advance, with all MBSs segregated into three classes. The classes define settlement of MBSs using the settlement date of current-coupon Ginnie Maes as the benchmark reference date, which is the Wednesday that falls between the 14th and 20th of each month.

The following, subject to change at any time, is the settlement schedule as it existed mid-year 1988:

- *Class A*   The Monday before the third Wednesday of each month:
  Freddie Mac securities below 10 percent with the exception of multifamily, ARMs, and VRMs.
  Fannie Mae securities below 10 percent with the exception of multifamily, ARMs, and VRMs.

- *Class B*   The Tuesday before the third Wednesday of each month:
  Ginnie Mae securities below 10 percent with the exception of multifamily, ARMs, and VRMs and those listed in Class D.

- *Class C*   The third Wednesday of the month:
  All Freddie Mac securities 10 percent and above with the exception of multifamily, ARMs, and VRMs.
  All Fannie Mae securities 10 percent and above with the exception of multifamily, ARMs, and VRMs.

- *Class D*   The Thursday following the third Wednesday:
  All Ginnie Mae GPMs.
  All Ginnie Mae mobile homes.
  All Ginnie Mae-IIs with the exception of ARMs and VRMs.
  All Ginnie Mae, Fannie Mae, and Freddie Mac 15-year securities.

- *Class E*   The Monday following the third Wednesday of each month:
  Ginnie Mae securities—all coupons 10 percent and above except Ginnie Mae securities noted in Class D.
  All Ginnie Mae, Fannie Mae, and Freddie Mac ARMs.
  All Ginnie Mae, Fannie Mae, and Freddie Mac VRMs.
  All multifamily Freddie Mac, Ginnie Mae, and Fannie Mae securities.

THE 48-HOUR RULE

The **48-hour rule** defines the cutoff time for providing pool information. Final pool details of any TBA trade must be provided by the seller no later than 3 P.M. of the second business day before the settlement date, sometimes referred to as **pool day**. Any changes to be made with respect to information provided earlier than two days before pool day must be provided by 12:15 P.M. on pool day. Failure to conform to the 48-hour rule will result in delivery not taking place earlier than two business days after the information has been transmitted, which will cause a fail and interest to accrue from the scheduled settlement to the actual delivery date.

Due Bills

A **due bill** is a nontransferable demand note to pay to the recipient the appropriate P&I due on a pool delivered as a "fail." When the pool is delivered after the record date (last day of the month) and prior to the payment date for the pool, a due bill for the month's P&I must accompany the delivery. If delivery is made after both the record and payment dates, the P&I payment is due to be paid to the buyer on delivery of the pool.

Reclamations

Reclamations refer to deliveries that are turned back either because the wrong security (or wrong amount of security) was delivered or because the receiving party failed to receive instructions regarding the delivery. Reclamations are generally referred to as a "DK," or a "don't know" trade.

5

Calculating Principal and Interest: Measuring and Predicting Prepayments

INTRODUCTION

MBSs, of which the predominant form is the mortgage pass-through security (MPTS), discussed in Chapter 3, differ from all other fixed-income securities in two key respects. First, the MBS is made up of a series of cash flows (which for the MPTS is monthly) consisting of a portion of both P&I. Unlike a typical corporate or government-type bond with interest usually paid as a semiannual coupon with principal paid on maturity, the MPTS pays both P&I monthly.

Second, the cash flows vary in amount each month because they are derived from the P&I cash flows generated by the mortgages underlying the MBS issued against the pool. In addition to the contractual payments required of each of the mortgage loans in the pool, from time to time mortgages in the pool will prepay, thereby causing the MBS to pay to an average life rather than to a single stated maturity.

Since the MPTS is a pass-through, whatever applies to the mortgages in the pool is mirrored directly through the pool to the investor of the MBS. The mortgage security therefore is a hybrid consisting in part of a standard coupon bond and in part an implied call option—that is, the right of the homeowner to call, or prepay, the mortgage at any time. This chapter explores the demographic and interest-rate factors that induce prepayments; the models used to measure prepayment speed; the basic mathematics of mortgage pool cash-flow calculations; and the derivation of average life and calculation of prepayments.

FUNDAMENTALS OF POOL CASH FLOW

Before beginning an examination of mortgage pool cash flows it is necessary to understand the profile of MBS pool P&I payments assuming no prepayments.

Figure 5.1 illustrates the **contractual,** or **scheduled cash flows,** of P&I for a pool of 30-year, 10 percent mortgages. The total payment of P&I is in the same aggregate amount each month—a characteristic often referred to as the **level pay** of the standard mortgage. In the early years the P&I is weighted largely with interest, becoming increasingly weighted to principal payments with the passage of time. The area below the solid line representing the principal cash flows, which roughly resembles the shape of a triangle, represents the total of principal payments made for the mortgage pool. The area beneath the dotted line, roughly resembling a wide slice of pie, represents the total of interest payments.

Contrast the P&I patterns illustrated in Figure 5.1 with those of Figure 5.2, which introduces prepayment speed measured in terms of constant prepayment rate (CPR). CPR, a measure of prepayment activity, is explained later in this chapter.

FIGURE 5.1
Scheduled Mortgage Cash Flow
($100 million face; 9% pass-through)

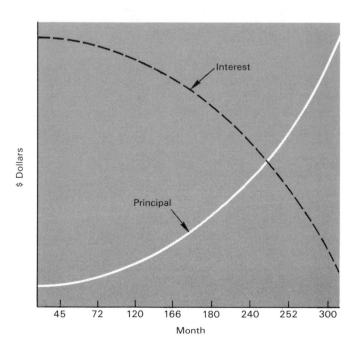

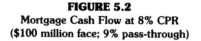

FIGURE 5.2
Mortgage Cash Flow at 8% CPR
($100 million face; 9% pass-through)

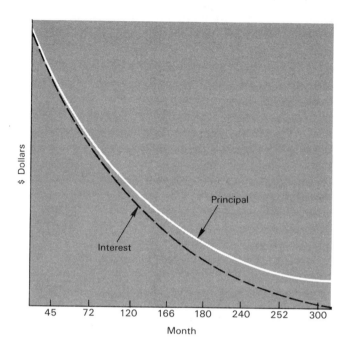

A key point to observe is that in Figure 5.2 the curve representing principal payments is a mirror image of the principal payments curve in Figure 5.1. The reason is that with an acceleration of prepayments, the principal cash flows are shifted forward. When a mortgage is prepaid early in its life, all the principal payments that would have been made over many months and years into the future are paid as a lump sum at the time of the prepayment.

There is another significant point to be observed from Figure 5.2. The triangle beneath the solid line denoting principal payments is the same size and represents the same amount as its corresponding triangle in Figure 5.1. That is, the total of principal payments is the same with or without prepayments, although with prepayments the principal is received much sooner. The pattern of cash flows is therefore altered, with the principal being received up front, as in Figure 5.2, rather than as a deferred annuity, as in Figure 5.1.

Now note the pattern of interest payments illustrated in Figures 5.1 and 5.2. The timing and total amount of interest in Figure 5.2 are quite different from those in Figure 5.1. That is, the total amount of interest received when prepayments are introduced (Figure 5.2) is less than in the base case of the scheduled cash flows illustrated in Figure 5.1. This pattern may be seen by noting that the space beneath the dotted line representing interest payments in Figure 5.2 is noticeably smaller than the comparable space in Figure 5.1. *A key tenet 'of MBSs cash-flow dynamics is that interest lives off principal, and without principal there is no interest.* Since prepayments accelerate the payment of principal, there is less and less principal remaining as time goes by from which interest may be generated.

Figures 5.3 and 5.4 illustrate the changing patterns of P&I as prepayments increase from zero prepayments (0 percent CPR) to a higher rate of prepayments.

Before further analyzing the impact of prepayments, we shall complete the examination of the cash-flow pattern of the mortgages underlying the pass-through MBS.

FIGURE 5.3
Principal Cash Flow at Various CPRs
($100 million face; 9% pass-through)

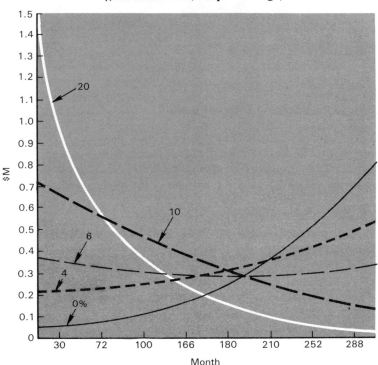

FIGURE 5.4
Interest Cash Flow at Various CPRs
($100 million face; 9% pass-through)

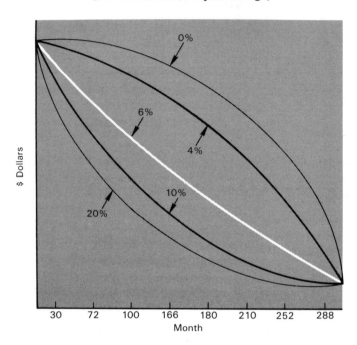

Mortgage Cash-Flow Calculations[1]

The key to understanding the pricing of mortgage securities is the process of discounting back to present value the future stream of cash flows representing the monthly P&I payments. The principal payments consist of both the scheduled amortization of the principal balance of the mortgage and repayments, which will be variable from month to month.

Calculating the Remaining Principal Balance (RPB)

The **remaining principal balance** (RPB) of the mortgage at any point during its term is calculated as in (1).

$$\text{BAL}_t = 1 - \frac{(1 + I)^t - 1}{(1 + I)^m - 1} \tag{1}$$

[1]This discussion of mortgage cash-flow calculations was contributed by H. Peter Wallace, Vice President, Shearson Lehman Hutton.

where BAL_t = the remaining balance of the loan at month t,

     t = time elapsed expressed in months,

     I = the periodic mortgage interest rate expressed as a decimal, and

     m = the number of months to original maturity.

Example Let us examine a standard 30-year original-maturity mortgage with a 10 percent mortgage rate. The balance remaining at the end of 90 months may be derived as follows:

$$I = 10/1200 = .008333.^2$$
$$m = 360$$
$$t = 90$$
$$BAL_t = 1 - \frac{(1.00833333)^{90} - 1}{(1.00833333)^{360} - 1} = 1 - \frac{1.110431067}{18.83739701}$$
$$BAL_{90} = .941051778$$

The .941051778 represents the principal balance expressed as a factor. For example, the actual dollar balance of the mortgage (or of the mortgage pool) may be determined by multiplying the original loan amount by the factor.

To illustrate, assume we had an original loan amount of $100,000. The remaining balance at 7.5 years (month 90) is $100,000 \times .941051778 =$ 941,051.78.

To calculate the **current loan balance** (current = month t, which is 90 months) we use equation (2).

In the equation, O will represent the original loan amount:

$$RB_t = O \cdot BAL_t \tag{2}$$

where RB_t = the remaining balance of the original loan amount at month t and

$$BAL_{90} = .941051778$$

Recall we assumed an original loan amount of $100,000:

$$RB_{90} = \$100,000 \times .941051778$$
$$RB_{90} = \$94,105.18$$

Calculating Principal and Interest (P&I) Payments

We have now derived the monthly pool factor (BAL_t), which is applied to the original loan amount to produce the current loan balance for any month during the term of the mortgage. We may then determine the P&I payments, which are a function of changes in the remaining principal balance.

It is important at this juncture to recall that mortgages *pay interest in arrears, and the interest amount that is paid is based on the remaining balance at the end of the month prior to the month in which the interest is paid.* In our example, then, the interest calculated on the remaining balance at month 90 is paid in month 91, as calculated in (3).

$$i_{t+1} = RB_t \times I \tag{3}$$
$$i_{91} = \$94,105.18 \times .00833333$$
$$i_{91} = \$784.21$$

where i_t = the interest payment at month t and

RB_t = the remaining principal balance at month t.

The principal payment that will be paid in month 91 is simply the difference between the remaining balance at month 90 (P_{90}) and that at month 91 (P_{90+1}).

$$P_{t+1} = RB_t - RB_{t+1} \tag{4}$$
$$P_{91} = \$94,105.18 - \$94,011.82$$
$$P_{91} = \$93.36$$

where P_t = principal payment at month t.

The total cash flow paid at month 91, C_{t+1}, is simply the sum of the P&I payments for that month:

$$C_{t+1} = i_{t+1} + P_{t+1}$$
$$C_{91} = \$784.21 + \$93.36$$
$$C_{91} = \$877.57$$

Adjustments to Cash Flows for Mortgage Securities

The calculations in equations (1) through (5) deal with determining the cash flows of individual mortgage loans, which are less complex than mortgage-backed pass-throughs. Pass-throughs are collective pools of individual loans. In evaluating the cash flows of the mortgage-backed pass-through, we must consider a number of differences between the MBS and the familiar corporate or Treasury bond. The key distinctions between the cash-flow characteristics of an MBS and those of a corporate or Treasury security are:

• Monthly receipt of P&I versus semiannual receipt of interest with principal paid on maturity.

- Servicing and guaranty fees deducted from the gross WAC of the aggregate mortgage P&I.
- Interest-free delays from the time of remittance of mortgage P&I to the pool and remittance of the pass-through P&I to the MBS investor.
- The phenomenon of prepayments, which alter the amount of monthly P&I cash flows.

Corporate bond equivalent (CBE) or **bond equivalent yield (BEY)** are notations used to indicate the fact that the MPTS P&I is received monthly, thereby enabling the more frequent reinvestment of cash flows. This more frequent reinvestment opportunity enables the MPTS investor to achieve a higher effective yield than would be realized with the semiannual- or annual-pay coupon normally received with a typical corporate or Treasury security.

The conversion of a monthly compounded yield to a CBE may be calculated as follows:

$$Y = \text{monthly compounded mortgage yield} \qquad (6)$$

$$Z = \text{CBE}$$

$$Y = 1200[(1 + Z/200)^{1/6} - 1]$$

$$Z = 200[(1 + Y/1200)^6 - 1]$$

Some illustrative CBE yields for comparable stated mortgage yields are given in Table 5.1.

TABLE 5.1
Conversion of Mortgage Yield
to Corporate Bond Equivalent (CBE)

Mortgage Yield (percent)	+	Increase in Yield (basis points)	=	CBE[a] (percent)
6.0		+ 8		6.08
8.0		+13		8.13
10.0		+21		10.21
12.0		+30		12.30
13.5		+39		13.89
14.0		+41		14.41
16.0		+54		16.54
18.0		+69		18.69

[a] The higher CBE reflects monthly compounding of the mortgage yield at the mortgage yield rate to an equivalent semiannual payment that includes reinvestment income.

Source: Shearson Lehman Hutton Mortgage Securities.

Adjusting for Servicing Spread

The servicing spread for an MBS actually represents both a guaranty fee paid to the agency (Ginnie Mae, Freddie Mac, or Fannie Mae) as well as the actual servicing fee itself. The fee is retained by the mortgage servicer as compensation for collecting the P&I due on the mortgage and remitting the appropriate pass-through equivalent P&I to the MBS investors. For example, a Ginnie Mae MBS with a 10.5 percent pass-through rate has total servicing of .50 percent (.44 percent retained by the servicer and .06 percent remitted to Ginnie Mae).

It is important to remember to use the correct interest rate when calculating MBS cash flows. The interest figure most visible to us is the pass-through rate, but of course the amortization of P&I is a function of the gross mortgage rate of the individual loans that make up the MBS pool. To correct for the presence of the servicing spread, we must redefine I in equation (1) as I_A:

$$I_A = I + s \tag{7}$$

where I = the monthly pass-through coupon rate (decimal) and
$\qquad s$ = the monthly servicing spread (decimal).

Example Assume a 10 percent pass-through coupon rate and a .5 percent annual servicing spread.

$$I_A = (10/1200) + (.5/1200)$$
$$I_A = .00833333 + .00041666$$
$$I_A = .008749990$$

For pools where a servicing spread is present, it is necessary to substitute I_A for I in equation (1).

Adjusting for Prepayments

Prepayments are the factor that introduces variability to the total P&I cash-flow stream of the MBS. Even though it is the phenomenon of prepayments that complicates the pricing and analysis of pass-throughs, in fact, only a minor adjustment is needed to the BAL_t calculation shown in (1).

In the discussion and examples that follow, prepayment speed is expressed as single monthly maturity (SMM). It is important to appreciate that the standard calculations of mortgage balances *assume that the SMM applied to the calculations has been the prepayment speed for each month since the issuance of the pool and will be assumed to continue for its remaining life.*

The remaining balance of a loan pool given a monthly prepayment rate, SMM, can be found by equation (8). Let A_t be the remaining balance at time t, adjusted for prepayments:

$$A_t = BAL_t F^t \tag{8}$$

where A_t = remaining balance at time t and
F = the function of prepayments.

$$F = 1 - (SMM/100)$$

Example Assume a 10 percent loan, 30-year term, aged 90 months, and .3 percent SMM.

$$F = 1 - (.3/100)$$
$$F = .997$$
$$A_{90} = .9410518 \times (.997)^{90}$$
$$A_{90} = .718088180$$

To properly apply (8), we must, from the current loan balance, derive the *original face value* of the loan. We need an original face value from which to derive the monthly cash flows. We shall let P_t represent the current principal balance of the loan at month t, and O shall represent the original face value.

$$O = P_t(BAL_t F^t)^{-1} \text{ or } O = P_t/A_t \tag{9}$$

Example Assume a $100,000 remaining balance.

$$O = P_t/A_t = 100,000/.718088180$$
$$O = \$139,258.66$$

The original balance as calculated in (9) is not, in fact, the actual original loan balance, but represents a derived original loan balance for a pool that has prepaid at a .3 percent SMM rate for each month from issuance of the pool to the month of calculation.

Using the derived original balance, we can then solve for the remaining balance, RB_t, by substituting the calculated original balance and the speed-adjusted remaining balance factor, A_t, in equation (2):

Example

$$RB_{90} = \$139,258.66 \times .718088180 = \$100,000.00$$

The Average-Life Concept

When considering the pricing methodology for a stream of mortgage pool cash flows we must look to some benchmark other than the stated maturity of the pool to weigh the value of the pool cash flows. The principal determinant of value with any investment relates to the concept of the present value of an annuity that will be received over time into the future. When considering the value of an investment in standard fixed-income securities, we simply weigh the value of the future dollars that will be received back on the maturity date of the bond. Since we will receive the principal payments on the MBS in the form of a variable-annuity cash flow, we need a mechanism for better estimating what alternate maturity benchmark to consider. Thus, the concept of **average life** was devised as a proxy for MBSs investors to use as a measure of time to the receipt of cash flows.

The average life of a MBS may be defined as the average number of years that each dollar of unpaid principal due on the mortgage remains outstanding. Average life is computed as the weighted average time to the receipt of all future principal payments due to be paid on the pool, using as weights the dollar amounts of the principal paydowns. The greater the amount of the anticipated principal payment, the heavier its weighted impact will be in the average-life calculation. Therefore, the greater the anticipated rate of prepayments, the higher the weights and the shorter the average life. The mathematical expression of weighted average life (WAL) is as follows:

$$
\text{WAL} = \frac{\sum_{i=1}^{m} P_i(i)}{12 \times \text{BAL}_t} \tag{10}
$$

where m = remaining term (months) to maturity (with seasoned loans the WAM may be used as m),

P_i = principal repayment in the ith month,

i = months 1, 2, ..., m ($i = 1$ to m),

BAL_t = principal balance outstanding at time t.

Equation (10) expresses our intuitive understanding of the WAL concept. The sigma (Σ) alerts us that we are adding a series of principal cash flows to the remaining maturity (or WAM) of the pool (m). The notation $i = 1$ simply reminds us that the series of principal cash flows is to be added until they equal the total, or 1 ($i = 1$).

We must take into account the factor of payment delay (14 or 45 days for Ginnie Maes, 24 or 55 for Fannie Mae MBSs, and 44 or 75 for Freddie Mac PCs. For a review of payment delays, see Figure 3.1 and the accompanying discussion in Chapter 3.)

MEASURING PREPAYMENT SPEED

The timing of principal repayment, or prepayment rate, in the Wall Street lexicon is **speed**. Certain universal considerations govern the rate of principal repayment. A significant factor affecting speed is the presence—or absence— of the due-on-sale[2] clause. FHA-insured and VA-guaranteed loans do not permit due-on-sale and are, therefore, fully assumable. Most conventional loans today, however, carry a provision for due-on-sale. The FHA/VA-backed Ginnie Mae securities, which do not have due-on-sale, prepay at a much slower rate than Fannie Mae and Freddie Mac securities backed by conventional loans. Table 5.2 gives a comparison of speeds for Ginnie Mae, Freddie Mac, and Fannie Mae securities. The principal methods of measuring speed (FHA, CPR, and PSA) are described on pages 154 and 155.

Note that Table 5.2 indicates the prepayment rate, or speed, in both PSA and CPR for 12 percent, 10 percent, and 8 percent coupons of various types of MBSs. We see that the Ginnie Maes prepay much more slowly for all coupons than the Fannie Mae and Freddie Mac securities with either the PSA or CPR as the speed standard. Ginnie Maes prepay more slowly for a number of reasons related to the fundamental differences between FHA/VA loans used as collateral for Ginnie Mae MBSs and nongovernment-insured conventional loans representing the collateral for most Freddie Mac- and Fannie Mae-issued MBSs.

In addition to the assumability issue just described, the FHA borrower tends to be a first-time home buyer; have a lower household income profile than the conventional borrower; be less demographically mobile—that is, less prone to move frequently; and be less aware of opportunities to refinance, trade up in house, and so on. In addition, FHA financing appears to be less available in the economically affluent and mobile communities such as the wealthy suburbs of money center cities and more available in rural and less wealthy communities in

TABLE 5.2
Speeds of Selected MBSs

		Ginnie Mae	Freddie Mac (Guarantor)	Fannie Mae
12%	PSA	268	238	280
	CPR	16.1	14.3	16.8
	PSA	116	133	134
10%	CPR	4.0	6.5	5.1
	PSA	68	92	92
8%	CPR	2.6	4.3	3.6

Source: Shearson Lehman Hutton Mortgage Securities.

[2]Due-on-sale refers to a requirement that the mortgage not be assumed by a new home buyer; that is, upon sale of the house the mortgage must be paid in full.

the Southeast and Midwest. The latter are also area types in which homeowners display a lower rate of housing turnover.

Prepayment speed, however, is consistently faster for higher coupons than for lower ones (for both FHA- and conventional-backed MBSs) as a function of the propensity of all homeowners to refinance, and therefore prepay, the mortgage when falling interest rates make it economically attractive to do so.

FHA Experience

The FHA-experience method of calculating prepayment speed is the familiar 12-year prepay benchmark developed years ago by FHA, based on the average FHA mortgage prepaying in about 12 years. The traditional FHA-experience method looks at prepayments relative to an index. The universal standard, in the case of MBSs, has been the prepayment experience of FHA-insured mortgage loans. HUD periodically issues new data on the termination experience of various insured mortgage programs. Investors usually look to the tables for 30-year, fixed-rate, fully amortizing mortgages. Unlike CPR, FHA experience looks at the actual prepayments (both voluntary and as a result of foreclosure) during each year a mortgage is outstanding. The FHA index for prepayment has a different value for each year since the date the mortgage pool was originated. Investors evaluate the performance of a particular pool relative to the FHA pattern. The evaluation is expressed as a percentage of the FHA index. One hundred percent FHA is the 12-year prepay assumption; 200 percent FHA means the pool is paying twice as fast, and so on.

The FHA 12-year Prepaid-Life Concept

The 12-year prepaid-life convention that was adapted by the investment industry when MBSs were introduced in the 1970s has some limitations in terms of its mathematical derivation. Under the 12-year prepaid concept, it is assumed that MBSs cash flows consist of the contractual P&I payments for the first 12 years of the life of the MBS pool. In the twelfth year the remaining principal balance is assumed to be prepaid in full. Stated another way, the mortgage yield calculations are predicated on the assumption of a single prepayment event, with the entire prepayment experience treated as a single maturity at the end of the twelfth year—as though the MBS were a corporate bond with monthly payments of P&I to a 12-year maturity. The cash flows up to the 12-year prepaid event are treated as a level-payment P&I schedule.

The obvious limitation of this approach is that with the volatile swings in interest rates of recent years, this assumed schedule of level cash flows does not conform to the schedule of cash flows now anticipated by the marketplace as changing patterns of interest rates cause frequent changes in prepayment expectations.

Constant Prepayment Rate (CPR)

Constant prepayment rate (CPR) was developed as an index that takes into account only principal repayments in excess of those contractually required. Therefore, many people view CPR as a more sensitive index of the rate of principal repayments. This index is particularly applicable when evaluating speed of the conventionally backed Fannie Mae and Freddie Mac pools. The CPR method expresses prepayments as a ratio to the prior month's outstanding principal balance. Typically, the result is stated as a percentage of the mortgage balance outstanding at the beginning of a period (for example, prior month or year) to a subsequent like period. This number is referred to as the CPR. The CPR includes only prepayments, not contractual amortization payments.

Measurements of prepayment rate may be expressed in terms of single monthly mortality (SMM), constant percent prepayment (CPP), or CPR. SMM reflects the percentage of outstanding principal balance prepaid each month; CPP expresses SMM on an annual basis; and CPR is simply SMM multiplied by 12. CPR reflects prepayment experience over a year, and the monthly rate may be calculated from the annual CPR rate. CPR thereby corrects for the compounding effect of SMM. When comparing rates of prepayments expressed as a percentage of FHA or as CPR, it is useful to bear in mind that for seasoned loans 6 percent CPR is roughly equivalent to 100 percent FHA. (For a more detailed discussion of the mathematical calculations illustrating the computation of FHA, CPR, and SMM, see "Calculations of Prepayment Speeds," p. 167.)

The PSA Standard

In July 1985, the PSA standardized all of the methods used to measure prepayment speed just described into a common standard for measuring prepayments, referred to as PSA. One hundred percent PSA is defined as follows: 0 percent CPR in month zero, increasing by .2 percent CPR monthly, rising to 6 percent CPR in month 30, and remaining at 6 percent CPR thereafter through maturity. Thus, 100 percent PSA is substantially equivalent to 100 percent FHA experience and to 6 percent CPR. Assuming a constant PSA or FHA percentage as a predictor implies that the prepayment rate (and the CPR) will change over time according to a predefined pattern.

The PSA method may be thought of either as an idealized FHA curve or as the CPR method adjusted for fewer prepayments in the early years. Prepayments are expressed as a percentage of the PSA standard: 50 percent PSA, 100 percent PSA, and so forth. Zero percent PSA is equivalent to 0 percent CPR or 0 percent FHA—that is, no prepayments. One hundred percent PSA or FHA means that the pool prepays at the same rate as the PSA or FHA standard.

The relationship between CPR and SMM may be given as:

$$CPR = 1 - (1 - SMM/100)^{12}$$

The PSA standard was developed to conform the very slow speed associated with newly produced loans to that of MBSs pools backed by loans that have been outstanding for two and a half years (30 months) or more.

Interest-Rate Changes Influence Speed

The general level of interest rates bears a strong influence on speed, in part because of refinancings. Mortgagors carrying a relatively high mortgage rate will refinance as rates decline. But refinancing is not the only reason that prepayments accelerate in a declining interest-rate environment. Lower interest rates stimulate home sales activity. At lower interest rates housing becomes more generally affordable and may trigger the trade-up to a bigger house. Also, lower interest rates stimulate general economic activity, thereby increasing disposable personal income and giving more people the wherewithal to go house hunting.

Varying Speed Paths

During its life a pool passes through varying paths of speed experience as interest rates rise and fall, inducing cycles of slowing speeds (as rates rise) and rising speeds (as rates fall).

Furthermore, as each subsequent cycle of falling rates stimulates a new round of refinancings, the impact of refinancings becomes less. Those mortgagors who were most sensitive to the refinancing opportunity will have done so in the first cycle of lower rates, so that in each subsequent cycle there are fewer and fewer people who prepay the mortgage strictly for an opportunity to refinance. Ultimately the pool is left with a certain number of mortgagors who do not refinance regardless of the opportunity to do so—perhaps because of contractual constraints relating to syndication of the properties, failure to realize sufficient equity in the home, or lack of available cash to execute a refinancing. Note that almost one-third of all GNMA 16 percent coupons are still outstanding in spite of ample opportunity to refinance over the last several years.

Threshold for Refinancing

The MBS is most subject to accelerating prepayment speed when the prevailing mortgage rate becomes 200 basis points below that of the mortgage rate on the loans underlying the pool. This event is referred to as the **threshold for**

refinancing. The speed of prepayments accelerates rapidly for four to six months and then tends to "burn out" as those most prone to prepay do so. An MBS that has been a premium-priced coupon for some time will stabilize at about 40 percent CPR after peaking at 60 percent CPR in the four to six months after becoming a premium.

Overshooting to Steady State

When mortgage rates fall 200 basis points or more, thereby pushing the WAC of an MBSs pool through the threshold for refinancing, prepayments increase dramatically (usually three months or so after the threshold has been reached). Past experience indicates that home borrowers most aware of the interest savings that can be realized with refinancing to lower rates will respond within 12 months, unless within that period mortgage rates once again rise to within 200 basis points of the WAC on the mortgages underlying the pool. This quick, initial response—referred to as **overshooting** of prepayments—lasts until about one-third of the pool has been paid down, a process that takes about a year.

Within that time most homeowners who are both inclined and able to refinance will have done so, and prepayment speeds then level off to a **steady state**. When rates again fall through the refinancing threshold, fewer homeowners remaining in the pool will be inclined to take advantage of the refinancing opportunity because most who are astute enough to recognize the value of refinancing did so in the first round. Of course, some homeowners who were not in a position to refinance in the first round will do so the second time. There will not, however, be enough to induce overshooting of prepayments to the extent experienced with a new pool the first time it falls through the refinancing threshold.

Impact of Age

The age of an MBSs pool has an impact on the prepayment experience of the pool, most markedly in the distinction between brand new and seasoned production loans. Prepayment studies indicate that interest-rate changes and other demographic considerations have little impact on prepayment speeds for the first two and a half years of the pool life. This observation is logical in that a homeowner who has just closed on a mortgage will be less willing and less financially able to undertake a refinancing shortly after having gone through the expense of a first closing. Furthermore, other demographic considerations that cause prepayments—job transfer, trading up, divorce, delinquency, and so on—are not likely to occur within a year or two of the home purchase. Stated another way, if a job transfer or divorce had been imminent, it is unlikely the family would have purchased the house. After three years or so the MBS pool begins to experience all the demographic factors that can lead to sale of the house—and the homeowner becomes increasingly prone to respond to refinancing opportunities.

Figure 5.5 graphically illustrates the combined impact of interest-rate changes and age. Interest-rate impact is shown on the left horizontal axis as the spread between current interest rates and pool WAC. The maximum spread is 8 points and declines to minus 2 points at the apex at the bottom of the figure. Age is shown at the right horizontal axis, ranging from 0 months at the bottom apex of the figure to 150 months at the right-hand end of the axis. Speed, measured in CPR, is the vertical axis and shows a range of from 0 to 10.00.

Overshooting is illustrated in Figure 5.5 by the rapid increase in CPR when the spread is at 8 points. Impact of age is illustrated by the fact that the SMM spread does not maximize unless the pool is at least 30 months old.

New Production versus Seasoned Pools

The implications of the impact of pure age (absent interest-rate changes to induce refinancing) are that new production loans will not exhibit normal

FIGURE 5.5
Prepayment Response to Age
and Interest-Rate Spread

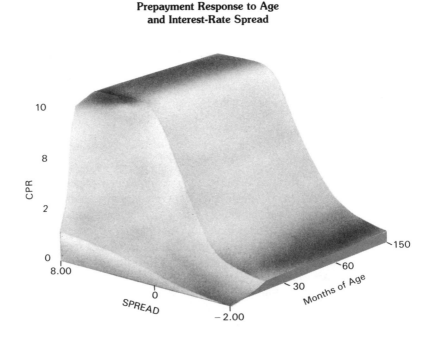

Source: Based on a model provided by Shearson Lehman Hutton Mortgage Research.

prepayment-speed patterns for two to three years. These loans will then experience an increase in prepayment speed, but will stabilize to a steady state over time. Discounts will experience an increase in speed from the fifth year or so and achieve a steady state after the eleventh year. Premiums will slow down after about 12 months to a steady state. The passage of the pool through successive cycles of falling interest rates will see prepayments accelerate to a peak CPR, which is lower for each prepayment cycle than that observed on the previous low-interest-rate path.

Lag Response of Prepayments

When evaluating the probable future direction of prepayment speeds it is important to note there is a lag of about three months from the time the threshold for refinancing is achieved to the time an increase in prepayment speed is actually observed (referred to as the **lag response of prepayments**). This lag is explained by the time required for the homeowner to respond to the opportunity to refinance, apply for a refinancing, and schedule a closing for the mortgage. The actual prepayment of a mortgage will then be reflected as a reduction in the balance of the pool at the end of the month in which the closing for a new loan took place.

Figure 5.6 illustrates the lag effect of prepayments in response to changes in interest rates. Note that when interest rates first fall, prepayments do not respond concurrently; they continue to accelerate for a time even after interest rates have again increased.

Seasonal Impact on Speed

Another major factor affects the speed of MBSs—the four seasons. The seasonal impact on speed is strong partially because of the impact it has on building activity. Many more homes are built in the summer than in the winter. Other major seasonal factors include family formation—more people get married in the spring and summer than in the winter—and the school cycle. Most families with school-age children prefer to move between the end of one school year and the start of another. And perhaps many people would rather buy a house and move in warm weather than when there is ice and snow to contend with.

The impact of the seasonal cycle on prepayments is a key consideration in deriving the trend of prepayments.[3]

The estimation of prepayments results based on the seasonally differentiated prepayment model indicates that strong seasonality is present in all four

[3]This discussion of a seasonal prepayment model has been abstracted from a Shearson Lehman Hutton research report issued in April 1986 (prepared by Andrew S. Carron). The purpose of the model was to isolate the impact of seasonal factors on a universe of MBSs. The model tested the seasonal impact on prepayment speeds on the MBSs sample from 1981 through 1985.

FIGURE 5.6
Prepayment Speeds Related to Interest-Rate Path

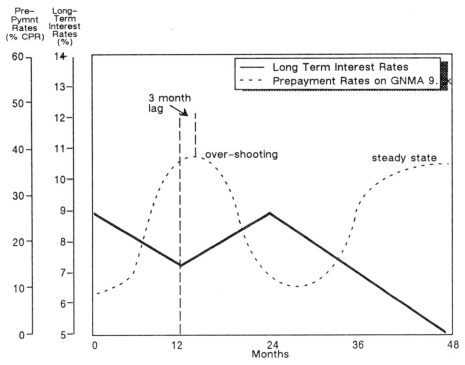

Source: Shearson Lehman Hutton Mortgage Securities.

security types—Ginnie Mae, Freddie Mac Cash and Guarantor, and Fannie Mae MBSs. Prepayments accelerate during April or May and remain high until August or September. Then they drop, reaching their lows between November and February. Figure 5.7 illustrates the seasonality of prepayment patterns.

The most interesting finding for each security type is that seasonality is not coupon-dependent. With the exception of super-premiums and a few deep discounts, seasonality is uniform across all coupons. The seasonality of the housing market is evident from housing starts, which typically reach their lows (not seasonally adjusted) between the late fall and the early spring. Another confirmation of the seasonal factor is that the rate of telephone installations in both homes and rentals is higher from June to October.

Super-premium pools (at the time of the study super-premiums were those with coupons above 13 percent) were present in the Ginnie Mae and Freddie Mac Cash samples that made up the universe of the study. Although their prepayment rates were higher during the spring/summer and lower during the

FIGURE 5.7
Seasonal Impact on Speed
(percent of average annual CPR)

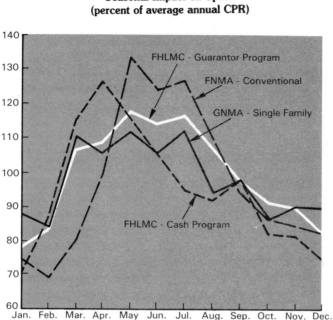

Source: Based on Shearson Lehman Hutton Mortgage Research.

fall/winter, the magnitude of underlying prepayment changes was much larger. Typically, there are "spikes," representing very high prepayment rates immediately after a decline in market interest rates, with prepayment rates above 45 percent CPR. Then they settle into a super-premium steady state around 30 percent CPR. The effect of overshooting in terms of the underlying trend is so powerful that it masks the true seasonal effect for these securities. Later, when the super-premium pools settle into a super-premium steady state, a constant seasonal pattern is likely to emerge.

The deep discounts, included in the Ginnie Mae and Freddie Mac Cash samples, tended to be more erratic in their seasonal behavior, probably because relatively few pools in a low-coupon range were included in the sample. The uniformity of prepayment rates across coupons indicates that households with higher mortgage rates are more likely to move. As interest rates drop, households with higher mortgage rates prepay with increasing probability. Typically, the average CPR speed ranges from below 6 percent for discounts to above 30 percent for super-premiums. A household will prepay if it expects to continue living in the house for more than a year or two, to recoup the costs of refinancing. On the other hand, if a household plans to move within this period, the prepayment will coincide with the sale of the house, and these sales are more likely to occur during the spring and summer. On this basis one would expect both an increase in prepayments and an increase in moves for households with higher original mortgage rates.

The well-defined acceleration of prepayments between the winter and spring is contrasted with the gradual decrease of prepayments in the fall. The difference can be attributed to weather conditions in the spring, implying that the housing market becomes more active as the weather improves. Conversely, the slowing of activity in the fall housing market may be linked to the beginning of the school year. In the fall the weather is not an important factor, and the deceleration in prepayments is more gradual and random.

Impact of WAM

As the pool ages, factors other than the relative level of interest rates become increasingly important. After five years or so, the house underlying the mortgage becomes a candidate for the resale market because of the propensity to trade the home after five to ten years. In addition, all the demographic factors that drive prepayments come into play. In general, the prepayment speed of the pool will stabilize to a steady state with age, thereby giving seasoned (short WAM) pools an attractive cash-flow pattern generated by a steady prepayment pattern.

Other WAM Considerations

All things being equal, some general rules apply to how the WAM changes over time:

1. Assuming no prepayments, the passage of time alone obviously reduces the WAM.
2. If a loan with an actual maturity longer than the calculated WAM of the pool prepays, the WAM will become shorter.
3. If a loan with a maturity shorter than the WAM prepays, the WAM will become longer.
4. Older mortgages amortize faster than new loans (the level amortization is mostly interest in the early years, with a shift to a greater percentage of principal in the later years). Therefore, the return of principal cash flows is heavier and (assuming the pool was purchased at a discount) more valuable with short WAMs.

There are, however, some difficulties associated with measuring pool value in terms of WAM. For one thing, the investor may not know from available information whether the loans that prepay have maturities that precede or follow the WAM date. Thus, estimating the WAM with the passage of time becomes increasingly difficult, except for those issues of Freddie Mac PCs for which updated WAC and WAM data are provided.

In general, the use of the WAM or the final stated maturity date of the pool as a proxy for the maturity of a single mortgage in the pool will result in an understatement of principal payments and an assumption of a higher remaining unpaid principal balance than is actually likely.

To illustrate, assume we had a single hypothetical pool consisting of two mortgages of like amount, and both 8 percent coupons. One has a remaining term of 15 years, the other a remaining term of 30 years. The final stated maturity of this pool would be 300 months. (As we have seen, the stated maturity of any pool is that of the longest-maturing loan in the pool.) The WAM at issuance would be 270 months—90 months less than the final maturity. Table 5.3 shows calculated pool balances for selected amortization periods using the WAM and final stated maturity of the pool as proxies for the maturity of an individual loan within the pool.

Table 5.3 reflects the dramatic differences between the remaining balances based upon reality and market expectations based upon considering the WAM or the final maturity of the pool as the ultimate maturity of a single mortgage loan. (For the sake of simplicity we have assumed only normal amortization of principal.)

TABLE 5.3
Principal Amortization Using WAM and Final Stated Maturity

$1,000,000 8.0% Pass-Through Pool
$500,000 8.0% 15-Year Loan
$500,000 8.0% 30-Year Loan

Remaining Balances at Year-End

Year	Actual	WAM	Final
1	$977,834	$983,445	$991,646
3	927,830	946,071	962,190
5	869,181	902,297	950,699
7	800,392	850,922	924,774
10	674,280	756,735	877,247
15	383,908	539,869	767,816
20	302,389	216,773	604,780
22	259,525	46,878	519,050
25	180,941	Matured	361,881
29	42,187	Matured	84,352

Source: Shearson Lehman Hutton Mortgage Securities.

Pricing Implications Mortgage loans, in their simplest form (assuming no delay or prepayments), are easy to price because the loan payments can be treated as a level-payment annuity. The payment of a level-payment annuity can be found by a simple formula, and subsequently the payments can be discounted to their present value. Using our previous example, we see that the three assumptions provide the monthly payments given in Table 5.4.

Depending on the investors' choice of either the WAM or final maturity of the pool as the maturity of a single mortgage loan, the investors' expectations are the equivalent of purchasing an annuity of $7,996.38 for 270 months or an annuity of $7,337.65 for 360 months, respectively. The actual pool provides payments of $8,447.08 a month for the first 180 months and payments of $3,668.82 a month for the next 180 months. Clearly, the cash flows from the actual pool differ rather dramatically from the investors' expectations. As a result, assuming the same yield, the present value of the expected cash flows will be different from the actual.

Table 5.5 gives the present value of the cash flows and the resulting bond price of the three alternatives.

In the example in Table 5.5, the WAM and final maturity produce a lower present value than the actual cash flows, indicating the investors have indeed profited from the market's incorrect expectations if they had purchased the pool based on its WAM or final maturity.

Prepayments on well-seasoned discounts such as 6½ coupons are affected by unique amortization patterns as well. Because the interest portion of the monthly payment is relatively small, the bulk of the payment is applied to amortizing the principal balance of the mortgage. Homeowners with seasoned discount mortgages are therefore less sensitive to interest-rate levels and more likely to prepay. Thus, these mortgages prepay at a faster rate than less seasoned and less deeply discounted loans.

WAC Effect on Speed

The pass-through rate observed on the MBS may be illusory. WAC is the governing factor. The investor in a GNMA 9 percent coupon can assume the underlying mortgage rate if the pool is all 9½ percent. However, for GNMA-II

TABLE 5.4
Assumed Monthly Payments

Months	Actual	WAM	Final
0–180	$8,447.08	$7,996.38	$7,337.65
181–270	$3,668.82	$7,996.38	$7,337.65
271–360	$3,668.82	Matured	$7,337.65

Source: Shearson Lehman Hutton Mortgage Securities.

TABLE 5.5
Present Value and Bond Price Assuming a 12 Percent Discount Rate

	Actual	*WAM*	*Final*
Present value	$754,809	$745,172	$713,354
Bond price	75.48	74.52	71.34

Source: Shearson Lehman Hutton Mortgage Securities.

and all Freddie Mac and Fannie Mae pools, the servicing spread between the net pass-through rate and the gross WAC may vary. (See Table 3.1 for a review of servicing spreads allowable for the principal types of MBSs.)

Note that a Freddie Mac MBS with a pass-through rate of 9 percent could be backed by mortgages as high as 11½ percent. The prepayment characteristics of a 9 percent MBS backed by loans as high as 11½ percent are very different from those of a 9 percent GNMA backed by all 9½ percent mortgages.

An additional consideration is that the WAC can change over time. As noted in the discussion of WAM, lower-coupon mortgages amortize faster than higher-coupon ones (absent prepayments). As they do so and pay out of the pool, the WAC tends to increase toward the rate of the remaining coupons. On the other hand, higher coupons prepay faster, and as they prepay the WAC tends to decline—a more likely case.

Impact of Housing Turnover Rate

Joseph Hu, Executive Vice President and Director of Mortgage Research, Shearson Lehman Hutton, has developed a method for predicting prepayment speeds utilizing the turnover rate of single-family housing stock.

A simple yet accurate method for projecting prepayment is to identify and forecast the sales turnover rate of the single-family housing stock.[4] Prepayments typically occur for two reasons: sales of the home or refinancing of the mortgage. For seasoned mortgage pass-throughs with coupon rates of 10 percent and below (low-coupon pass-throughs), housing activity almost dictates prepayments. There is a strong relationship between generic prepayments for low-coupon pass-throughs and the sales turnover rate of the single-family housing stock. Extrapolating from this relationship, we can project future prepayments based on a qualitative assessment of the outlook for housing sales activity.

The turnover rate for the single-family housing stock is defined as the ratio of sales of existing homes to the stock of single-family housing that is available for sales transactions (transaction housing stock). The specified housing stock should be adjusted downward by the number of houses sold in the

[4]This discussion is based on Joseph Hu, *Mortgage Banking*, October 1987.

past two years because houses that have recently sold are less likely to be for sale again within a certain period. Thus, the transaction stock is computed by assuming that homeowners will normally stay in a new residence for at least two years. Consequently, subtracting the sales of existing homes during both the current and the previous year from the specified housing stock gives an estimate for the transaction housing stock.

While mortgage prepayments are primarily caused by home sales, they can also result from defaults and disaster. If for any reason the mortgagor is unable to continue servicing the mortgage debt, the lender will eventually foreclose and sell the property, causing a prepayment. Statistics provided by the Federal Home Loan Bank Board indicate that annual default rates during the 1980s have increased steadily from .1 percent in 1980 to a current rate of about .8 percent. In addition, a small fraction of the housing stock is constantly being destroyed, by either natural disasters or human events, motivating further prepayments. The Annual Housing Survey reports that each year roughly .4 percent of the housing stock is permanently lost.

For seasoned, low-coupon pass-throughs, prepayment rates can be approximated by adding turnover, default, and disaster rates, which shall define the term "housing factors" as used here. The total of these rates can be summed to derive what Dr. Hu refers to as "the alternative prepayment projection." The alternative prepayment projection can be compared with prepayment rates of low-coupon Freddie Macs, Fannie Maes, and Ginnie Maes for the period 1977 to 1986. (Because both the Freddie Mac Guarantor and Fannie Mae MBSs programs were implemented in 1981, prepayments for Freddie Macs and Fannie Maes were not available until 1982.) In the strong housing market that prevailed between 1977 and 1979, the alternative projection modestly overestimated Ginnie Mae prepayment rates. This difference can be explained by the Ginnie Mae's underlying FHA/VA mortgages, which historically have financed only 20 percent of home purchases. Borrowers of FHA/VA loans, with significantly lower incomes in general, are less mobile than borrowers of conventional loans who have financed the other 80 percent of home purchases. The prepayment rates on Ginnie Maes, therefore, are lower than the housing turnover rate.

During the two years 1980 and 1983 the collective housing data overestimated prepayments by a wide margin. This large discrepancy was probably due to the assumption of existing mortgages by home buyers—a common practice in high-mortgage-rate periods. In the early 1980s, historically high mortgage rates substantially slowed housing activity and reduced prepayments. Moreover, in that environment there was strong incentive for sellers to provide financing to prospective buyers. A significant feature of this financing was the practice of sellers to allow buyers to assume existing home mortgages. Consequently, home sales were consummated without mortgage prepayments, further slowing prepayments. After 1984, as mortgage rates steadily dropped, the reduced incentive of seller financing together with more rigorous enforcement of due-on-sale enabled housing turnover rates again to closely approximate prepayments of seasoned low-rate mortgages.

CALCULATIONS OF PREPAYMENT SPEEDS

Prepayments represent principal payments made in addition to the P&I payments required under the scheduled amortization of the mortgage contract. In this section we shall examine the computation of prepayments first as SMM and then by relating the SMM calculation to annualized equivalents such as CPR.

Since prepayments are simply principal payments made in addition to the scheduled principal amortization, our starting point is the **amortization factor**, which was derived from equation (1) as BAL_t. Having determined the amortization factor for the pool, we need only compare the **reported factor** as of the end of a month to the contractual factor to determine if prepayments have occurred. The amount by which the reported factor exceeds the amortization factor is the prepayment amount. If the reported factor is the same as the amortization factor, there were no prepayments.

Calculation of SMM

SMM measures the monthly amount of principal payments for the pool between two periods. SMM measures the compound rate of reduction between the two periods and therefore tends to smooth the pattern of prepayments over the period measured. Thus, a single large prepayment in a single month is averaged out to an SMM percentage for the period, which theoretically could be distorted if one month experienced an abnormally large one-time prepayment. For that reason, some analysts prefer to examine the monthly reported factors to determine whether the monthly paydowns are steady or erratic before the calculated SMM for the period is accepted as a fair representation of the true prepayment pattern of the pool. SMM is calculated as in equation (11).

$$SMM_n = 100[1 - (SF_{t+n}/SF_t)^{1/n}] \qquad (11)$$

where n = the number of months between month t and month $t + n$.

To calculate SMM, we must compare the actual, or reported, factor to what the scheduled amortization would have been assuming no prepayments. If the reported factor is the same as the factor for the scheduled amortization, there were no prepayments; if the reported factor is less than the scheduled amortization factor (which, of course, is usually the case), there *were* prepayments.

We can determine the survival factor (SF) which is the percentage of loans that have survived (not prepaid) with calculation (12).

$$SF_t = F_t/BAL_t \qquad (12)$$

where F_t = the reported, or actual, pool factor at time t and
BAL_t = the amortization factor [from equation (1)].

Example Assume we wish to calculate the SMM rate of a 10 percent mortgage at the 24th month of its amortization schedule. Assume a beginning factor of 1.0000 and a reported factor of .9455 at the 24th month.

$$BAL_{24} = 1 - \frac{(1 + .0083333)^{24} - 1}{(1 + .0083333)^{360} - 1}$$

$$BAL_{24} = .9883$$

$$SF_0 = 1.000/1.000 = 1.0000$$

where SF_0 is at time zero, or the issue date of the pool.

$$SF_{24} = .9455/.9883 = .9567$$

where SF_t is at month 24.

Now having derived SF_0, which is 1 and SF_{24}, which is applied as SF_{t+n} in equation (11), we can calculate SMM as follows:

$$SMM_{24} = 100[1 - (.9567/1.0000)^{1/24}]$$

$$SMM_{24} = 100[1 - (.9567)^{.041666}]$$

$$SMM_{24} = .184$$

Calculation of CPR

Constant prepayment rates (CPR) are the annualized equivalent of SMM. CPR is calculated from SMM as follows:

$$CPR = 100\{1 - [1 - (SMM/100)]^{12}\} \qquad (13)$$

Following our earlier example, we see that

$$CPR = 100\{1 - [1 - (.1842963/100)]^{12}\}$$

$$CPR = 100\{1 - [.9981570]^{12}\}$$

$$CPR = 100\{1 - .9781068\}$$

$$CPR = 2.189319$$

Rounding to two decimals, CPR = 2.19. Conversely, SMM may be found, given CPR, by equation (14).

$$SMM = 100 \{1 - [1 - (CPR/100)]^{1/12}\} \tag{14}$$

Converting between CPR and PSA

It is often helpful to be able quickly to convert prepayment-speed data from CPR to PSA, or from PSA to CPR. When doing so, it is helpful to remember:

- 6 percent CPR = 100 percent PSA *but only with pools that are seasoned 30 months or more.*
- For loans that are of less than 30 months of age, the exact months of age must be known or assumed.
- At 100 PSA the model assumes speed increases .2 percent per month linearly, so be aware of the function of .2 percent related to months of age.
- Therefore, after 30 months, 100 percent PSA = 6 percent CPR.

Converting CPR and PSA of Seasoned Loans

To convert from PSA to CPR with loans seasoned 30 months or more we divide the PSA number by 100 to convert it to a decimal and multiply by 6 (100 percent PSA = 6 percent CPR).

$$\text{Pool age} > 30 \text{ months}$$

$$CPR = \frac{\text{Percent PSA}}{100} \times 6 \tag{15}$$

Example   Assume PSA = 150

$$CPR = \frac{150}{100} = 1.5 \times 6 = 9$$

$$CPR = 9$$

To convert CPR to PSA for pools seasoned 30 months or more, simply divide the CPR by 6 and multiply by 100.

$$\text{Pool age} > 30 \text{ months}$$

$$PSA = \frac{CPR}{6} \times 100 \tag{16}$$

Following our example, we see that

$$CPR = 9$$

$$PSA = \frac{9}{6} = 1.5 \times 100 = 150$$

$$PSA = 150$$

Converting CPR and PSA of New Production Loans

To convert CPR to PSA for pools aged less than 30 months, divide the CPR by the product of the age (m) times .2 percent (at 100 PSA the model increases the speed by .2 percent per month) and multiply by 100.

Pool age $<$ 30 months

$$PSA = \frac{CPR}{(.2) \times (m)} \times 100 \qquad (17)$$

From the example,

$$CPR = 2.4$$

$$m = 8$$

$$PSA = \frac{2.4}{.2 \times 8} = \frac{2.4}{1.6} = 1.5 \times 100 = 150$$

$$PSA = 150$$

The last example demonstrates the reason for the creation of the PSA model. Since pools of new production loans are not as sensitive to the demographics that influence seasoned pools, the application of the CPR method will result in a misleading speed assumption (in this case, a CPR of 2.4 percent, which is "slow" compared to the norm of 6 percent CPR). So, if the CPR method gives us a 2.4 percent CPR, when we convert to the PSA model we find that this pool is actually fast (150 PSA) relative to the PSA norm for a new production pool (100 PSA).

If the pool consists of new production loans, that is, with an age less than 30 months, we must take into account the number of months of age, since the PSA increases *.2 percent per month for each month up to (but not exceeding) 30 months*. Therefore:

Pool age < 30 months

$$CPR = (.2 \times m) \times \frac{PSA}{100} \qquad (18)$$

where m = months of age since issue.

Example Assume WAM = 352 months

$$m = (360 - 352) = 8$$

$$PSA = 150$$

Convert PSA to decimal:

$$\frac{150}{100} = 1.5$$

$$CPR = (.2 \times 8) \cdot (1.5) = 2.4$$

$$CPR = 2.4$$

Summary of calculations 15–18

If:

Pool age > 30 months

$$CPR = \frac{PSA}{100} \times 6 \qquad (15)$$

$$PSA = \frac{CPR}{6} \times 100 \qquad (16)$$

If:

Pool age < 30 months

$$PSA = \frac{CPR}{(.2\,m)} \times 100 \qquad (17)$$

$$CPR = (.2 \times m) \times \frac{PSA}{100} \qquad (18)$$

Calculation of FHA Experience

The calculation of FHA experience by hand is complex and tedious. The FHA-experience measure is derived from survivorship tables prepared by HUD. The tables are updated each year, thereby creating the complication of contending with a series of FHA prepayment-rate data. In other words, the historical pattern of prepayments will differ depending on whether one is using the 1970, 1971, or 1973 survivorship data. The tables are based on the survivorship data for FHA Section 203 loans and reflect the percentage of loans expected to survive at the end of each year. The benchmark table is that of 1970 loan originations, which is given in Table 5.6.

TABLE 5.6
HUD Survivorship Table

	End of Year		
1.	.979146	16.	.420510
2.	.922385	17.	.400371
3.	.864461	18.	.381225
4.	.814124	19.	.363140
5.	.765958	20.	.346147
6.	.717625	21.	.330249
7.	.629736	22.	.312694
8.	.629736	23.	.293805
9.	.588726	24.	.273931
10.	.558027	25.	.253429
11.	.532287	26.	.232429
12.	.508652	27.	.221931
13.	.485726	28.	.191573
14.	.463261	29.	.165401
15.	.441530	30.	.139902

The table as provided by HUD gives annualized data, thereby requiring interpolation to derive monthly values within a given year. The interpolation requires calculation of geometric decay rates. The process is illustrated in equation (19), with Q representing the annual figure from the table and j the interim month within year Q.

$$q_{T,j} = Q_T (Q_{T+1} Q_T^{-1}) J \qquad (19)$$

where $q_{T,j}$ = FHA survivorship for year T, month j.

$$J = j/12$$

Example Assume five years, six months of age.

a. Survivorship factor for year 5 = .765958 = Q_5
b. Survivorship factor for year 6 = .717625 = Q_6
c. $j = 6$

$$q_{5,6} = .765958 \left[(.717625/.765958)^{6/12} \right]$$

$$q_{5,6} = .741398$$

The practitioner is cautioned when using the FHA-experience method derived from the HUD survivorship tables on several counts. First, the data are not appropriately applicable to conventional loans, which are subject to demographic factors quite different from those that apply to FHA loans, as was pointed out earlier in this chapter. Second, in deriving the survivorship factors HUD did not concern itself with the influence of economic forces such as changing interest rates or the level of housing turnover—the two factors that most affect the speed of prepayments (aside from seasonal cycles). Third, the user of these data should be aware that the purpose of the survivorship tables from HUD's view was simply to assist FHA in calculating its actual insurance exposure.

Delayed Issuance Pools

Delayed issuance pools (DIPs) represent a special case in the MBSs pool population. **Delayed issuance pools** refer to MBSs that at the time of issuance are collateralized by seasoned loans originated well before the date of the pool. A good example of a DIP would be Freddie Mac Guarantor Program PCs issued against loans pooled by an S&L. The calculation of pool balances and current P&I are complicated by the fact that the loans would have experienced several periods of scheduled amortization prior to being pooled.

The calculations are vastly simplified if the exact date of origination of the loans is known, but this is usually not the case. Therefore, it is necessary to estimate the origination date by subtracting from the final maturity date of the pool the estimated original months of full term (presumably 30 years).

An added complication is that not all of the loans pooled into the MBS would necessarily have been originated in the same month. Therefore, a WAM will have to be substituted as the final maturity date.

Once an acceptable origination date has been selected, the assumed balance of the pool may be calculated by using the months elapsed since the assumed date of origination. The BAL_t factor derived from this process then is used to adjust the reported pool factors of the newly originated MBS pool.

The calculations of prepayment speeds can obviously be tedious and time consuming. Computers alleviate the need to perform these calculations by hand, allowing the computation to be done almost instantaneously—a critical factor that has enabled the MBSs secondary market to enjoy its present state of high liquidity.

6

Determinants of Price and Yield

INTRODUCTION

The price of any MBS is the present value of a future stream of cash flows generated by the security. Mortgages and MBSs are different from almost all other fixed-income securities, and to properly evaluate them the investor must change his point of view. Any attempt to approach MBSs pricing with a "coupon-bond mentality" will rapidly end in frustration.

The key to MBSs investing is an appreciation that the set of cash flows is a variable annuity whose variations are due to fluctuations in the rate of prepayments. And central to understanding the impact of prepayments on MBS pricing is to realize that there is an implied—or embedded—call option on the MBS.

Virtually all mortgage loans are structured so that the homeowner has the right to prepay the mortgage at any time. Hence, the homeowner, in effect, holds an option to call the mortgage. This right to prepay is referred to as the **implied call option of the MBS**. With a pass-through, whatever happens to the mortgages underlying the pool is reflected directly by the MBSs pool cash flows. Since the homeowner has the right to call the mortgage (and thereby call a pro-rata portion of the pool), the MBSs investor is in effect short the implied call. Furthermore, this implied call option is often referred to as an **irrational call** because not all homeowners exercise the call when it is **in the money** (when interest rates are at or below the threshold to refinance). In fact, approximately one-third of all MBSs that have been above the refinancing threshold for two or three years have not prepaid. Conversely, homeowners frequently exercise the call when it is **out of the money** because they elect to sell the home without considering refinancing implications.

This chapter reviews the determinants of price, including the 12-year prepay and cash-flow yield methods. Evaluation techniques such as total return, holding-period return, and breakeven CPR are explored. The impact of reinvestment income on total return is also emphasized.

DETERMINANTS OF PRICE

Price to 12-Year Prepaid Life

Pricing the MBS would be a simple matter were it not for the uncertainty of prepayments. (Prepayments are described in Chapter 5.) For the sake of simplicity, the first approach to the prepayment issue was to assume that the MBSs pool experienced no prepayments in the first 12 years of its life and then prepaid completely. This 12-year prepaid-life assumption was believed to be plausible because the original FHA survival tables, developed in the early 1970s, found that the average FHA mortgage prepaid in 12 years. Pricing to the 12-year prepay assumption sometimes provides an acceptable estimation of realized yield when the MBS is priced near par. The 12-year prepay assumption, however, tends to undervalue the early return of principal in discount MBSs. In reality, cash flows purchased at a discount which are later returned at par have a greater present value the sooner they are received. Conversely, if a premium price was paid for the cash-flow stream, the early return of the principal reduces the value of the cash flows because the investor gives back the premium (price paid over par) when the cash flows are returned at par sooner than had been expected. For example, if a premium-coupon MBS had been booked (at purchase) to a 12-year average life, then as the cash flows were returned at par sooner than had been expected, the investor would have had to take a book loss on the accelerated amortization of premium. The 12-year prepay assumption, therefore, overstates the value of premium-priced MBSs cash flows. The fact that the MBS has risen to a premium price tells us its coupon is above the present market discount rate. When the MBSs cash flows are returned sooner than anticipated, the opportunity to receive the higher coupon is diminished, and the cash flows returned must be reinvested at the lower rates then available in the market.

Price to Cash-Flow Yield

By the late 1970s, the marketplace understood the limitations of pricing to the 12-year prepay assumption. The more realistic technique of pricing to a constant prepayment-rate assumption was adopted by many market participants. (Prepayment-speed models are described in detail in Chapter 5.) This technique, which applies a speed estimation to the distribution of prepayments over time, assumes a cash-flow pattern based on period-by-period distributions and is referred to as **cash-flow yield (CFY)**. CFY, then, is the monthly **internal rate of return (IRR)** of the MBS priced to a projected stream of P&I cash flows as estimated by a speed model (FHA, CPR, or PSA).

The principal advantage of pricing to CFY is that the prepayment assumption can be varied to a level appropriate to the type of collateral (FHA versus conventional) and coupon sector (discount, par, or premium) under consideration. The cash flows are then discounted to their present values, using as the monthly distribution amount the schedule of P&I generated by the applicable speed model.

The computation of price, or **net present value (NPV)**, to cash-flow yield is done by summing the series of cash flows to their maturity, or in the case of a MBS backed by seasoned loans, to the weighted average maturity (WAM), as shown in (1).

$$\text{NPV} = \frac{CF_1}{(1 + r)^d} + \frac{CF_2}{(1 + r)^{d+1}} + \frac{CF_3}{(1 + r)^{d+2}} \cdots \frac{CF_m}{(1 + r)^{m+d-1}} \quad (1)$$

where CF = cash flows for periods 1, 2, and 3;
CF_m = cash flows at maturity, or WAM;
r = market discount rate; and
d = decimal fraction of month from settlement until first P&I payment is received.

The NPV as calculated in (1) discounts each monthly cash flow in the series by the market discount rate (r). As used here, r is the internal rate of return required by investors in the current market environment—for example, 10 percent. In practice, r is generally derived as the investor required basis-point-yield spread over that of the comparable-maturing Treasury security. The market discount rate is also weighted with more distant cash flows more heavily weighted $(1 + r$ is squared for CF_2, cubed for CF_3, and so on). Finally, the discount factor also takes into account the delay in days (d).

Equation (1) may be written in a slightly more condensed form using standard summation notation:

$$\text{NPV} = \sum_{t=1}^{m} \frac{CF_t}{\left(\dfrac{1 + y}{12}\right)^{t-1+d}} = (\text{Price} + \text{Accrued}) \quad (2)$$

where y = the annualized discount rate.

The components of CF are as follows.

CF_i = the components of cash flows, including scheduled principal, interest, and prepayments.

$CF_i = P_i + I_i + S_i$, where

P_i = scheduled principal payment in the ith month,

I_i = interest payment in the ith month, and

S_i = prepayments in the ith month expressed as SMM.

The components of CF are discussed below in greater detail.

Derivation of Principal Amortization (AM) and Prepayments (PP)

The principal amortization component consists of scheduled amortization (AM) and prepayments (PP):

$$AM_t = B_{t-1}(1 - R_t) \quad \text{and} \quad (3)$$

$$B_{t-1} = (A \cdot f_{t-1}) \quad (4)$$

where B_t = remaining principal balance of pool after t payments,

f_t = pool factor after t payments, and

A = original principal amount of pool.

Furthermore,

$$R_t = \frac{M_t}{M_{t-1}} \quad (5)$$

where

$$M_t = \frac{(1 + y/12)^N - (1 + y/12)^t}{(1 + y/12)^N - 1}$$

and N is original maturity (in months). M is simply an adjustment factor to correct prepayments for regular amortization.

Derivation of Prepayments

$$PP_t = B_{t-1} \cdot R_t \cdot S_{t-1 \cdot t} \quad (6)$$

$$S = SMM$$

Derivation of Interest Portion (Int)

The interest portion of CF, which consists of interest earned (Int) on the mortgage less servicing (SC), equals the pass-through coupon (C), as follows:

$$\text{Int}_t = B_{t-1} \cdot (r/12) \tag{7}$$

r = mortgage loan rate as a decimal.

$$\text{SC}_t = B_{t-1} \, (\alpha/12) \tag{8}$$

α = servicing spread in basis points.

$$C_t = B_{t-1} \left(\frac{r - \alpha}{12}\right) \tag{9}$$

Pricing Discount MBSs

CFY gives a good estimation of value for the discount MBSs sector because discounts are, for the most part, backed by seasoned mortgage loans which have achieved a steady state of prepayment speed. Under the CFY method, the prepayment speed is held constant to the WAM of the MBSs pool. (Note that in pricing with CFY, the remaining life, or WAM, is used together with a speed assumption that produces an appropriate average life, a method in marked contrast to the 12-year prepay approach, which always prices to the original maturity—usually 30 years—and to a 12-year average life.)

Pricing Par-Priced MBSs

The CFY method also gives a good value approximation for par-priced MBSs, with the exception of those backed by new production loans. Newly originated loans do not display typical prepayment patterns for the first two years or so of loan life. (See Chapter 5, particularly "The PSA Standard" and "Impact of Age.") However, if the PSA model is used, the approximation should be close enough. After all, variations in cash-flow speeds have little impact on the yield of a security purchased at par.

Pricing Patterns of Premium-Priced MBSs

Premium-priced MBSs display a price structure that defies the pattern of discount or par-priced MBSs—or, for that matter, of any other fixed-income security. In Figure 6.1 the price/yield curve of the 10-year Treasury is plotted against that of a 10 percent MBS.

Note from Figure 6.1 that as yields fall and the Treasury and MBS price curves move to a price between par (100) and 105, the MBS price curve diverges from that of the Treasury into first a flat and then a downward slope. The MBS curve here illustrates what is referred to as the **price compression of premiums**. Price compression occurs because as yields fall through the

FIGURE 6.1
Mortgage-Backed and Treasury Price/Yield Curve

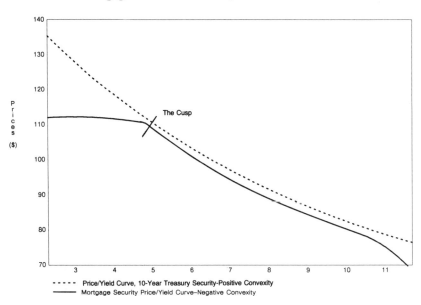

threshold to refinance, the MBS crosses the cusp on the price/yield curve. The **cusp**, shown in Figure 6.1, represents the point where the acceleration in prepayments causes the MBS investors to anticipate that the average life of the MBS will be shortened dramatically. At the same time there will be a loss of premium points as cash flows are returned at par more rapidly than had been expected. As investors anticipate an accelerating rate of prepayments, they command a higher stated yield in compensation for the risk of losing unamortized premium points as prepayment speeds increase. That is, investors discount the price of the MBS by the amount of potential yield loss at the worst-case prepayment-speed assumption. Stated another way, price compression occurs when and after the MBS trades up onto the cusp.

It is worth noting that the price deviation of premium MBSs works both ways—in bear markets prepayment speeds are expected to slow down; and as investors recognize the inherent value in the retention of the high coupon, the premium MBS will hold its price while other fixed-income securities drop. The premium MBS is therefore referred to as a **cushion bond**. The price patterns of the premium in a bear market are also illustrated in Figure 6.1, which if read from left to right shows the MBS price holding flat while that of the 7-year Treasury is descending.

THE IMPLIED CALL OPTION OF THE MBS

Understanding the implied call option is the key to understanding the price behavior of a premium-priced MBS. Since with a mortgage pass-through whatever occurs to the underlying mortgages is reflected directly in the MBS pool cash flows, it follows that if the homeowner holds the option, the MBS investor is short the option. In other words, we now see that the MBS is a hybrid investment in which a portfolio holding of an MBS consists of one part a standard-coupon bond and one part a short call option. It further follows that the composite value of the MBS will have to be the value of the sum of its parts. Therefore, the MBS composite value, or price, is as follows.

MBS Value = Noncallable Bond Value − Call Option Value

It further follows that since the value of the call option is a minus in deriving the composite price of the MBS, the increasing value of the call option will inhibit the ability of the composite value of the MBS price to increase. And the value of the call option obviously rises as prepayments increase.

Valuing the Call Option

Finding a way to value the implied call is central to deriving the fair market value of the premium-priced MBS. A number of approaches may be used to find the value of the implied call, most of them variants on the application of duration. (Chapter 7 explores the properties and applications of duration.) Table 6.1 gives prices of several MBS coupons ranging from discounts to premiums and demonstrates a simple way to appreciate the impact of the call option on the composite price of the MBS.

The composite price is the actual market price of several Ginnie Mae MBS coupons as of January 1988. The coupon-bond price is that of a compara-

TABLE 6.1
The MBS Option Component
Ginnie Mae Prices for Various Coupons
MBS Composite Value = Noncallable Bond Value − Call Option Value

Coupon	Price Composite	Call Option Value	Coupon Bond Value
16%	114.00	50.00	164.00
14%	108.25	39.40	147.65
12%	107.00	24.93	131.93
9%	99.56	8.70	108.26
8%	95.66	5.89	101.55

Source: Shearson Lehman Hutton Mortgage Securities.

ble Treasury security and reflects what the MBS price might be without the implied call. The implied value of the call option is the difference between the actual market price of the MBS and what the price should be without the call option. (A further discussion of the valuation of the implied call option within the application of duration is given in Chapter 7.)

TOTAL-RETURN ANALYSIS

The calculation of price based on total return involves calculating the net present value of the cash flows at an explicit reinvestment assumption. This approach differs from the CFY (or internal rate of return) method where the monthly P&I stream is implicitly reinvested at the cash-flow yield rate. Reinvestment proceeds can be a major component of the ultimate total performance of the investment, particularly in the case of mortgage securities, which return a large monthly cash flow available for reinvestment.

Reinvestment Impact on Value

The impact of reinvestment of the coupon return of a bond can be demonstrated in a simple way by comparing a 3-year return on investment for two bonds, each paying total interest of $1,200 in the three years, as shown in Figure 6.2. Bond A pays $600 in years 1 and 3. Bond B pays only the $1,200 in year 2. Since both bonds pay a total coupon of $1,200, how can we determine which is the better investment? As shown by the total-return calculations at the bottom of Figure 6.2, bond A gives us a return of 9.78 percent, 24 basis points better than bond B. The reason is simply that we had the $600 coupon from bond A to reinvest in the first and second periods. Because of the compounding of reinvesting interest earned on interest, the bond with the more frequent payment of the coupon is the better investment. The compounding effect is reflected in the $1 + r$ calculations, with $1 + r$ squared the first year and cubed the third year.

Note that in calculating total return,

$$NPV = Price + Accrued$$

The difficulty is that when we are evaluating reinvestment value, we do not know what the reinvestment rate will be. Table 6.2 illustrates the NPV at the three periods for the A and B bond investments with the compounding of interest on interest. Note that in the second period ($t = 2$) bond A earns a reinvestment rate on the $600 coupon paid at $t = 1$, and in $t = 3$ bond B earns

FIGURE 6.2
Comparison of 3-Year Investment

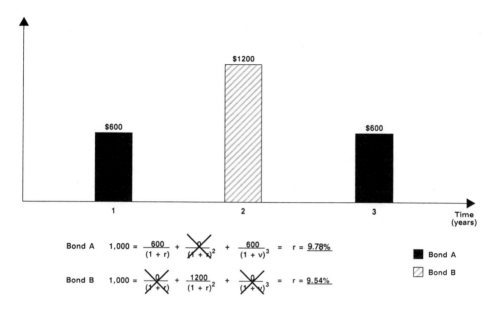

TABLE 6.2
Yield to Maturity
Sensitivity of Yield to Maturity to Reinvestment Rates

Initial Investment		Present Value at Different Times		
$t = 0$	$t = 1$	$t = 2$	$t = 3$	
A 1,000	600	$600(1 + r_1)$	$600(1 + r_1)(1 + r_2) + 600$	
		Reinv $= 600 \cdot r_1$	Reinv $= 600(r_1 + r_2 + r_1 \cdot r_2)$	
B 1,000	—	1200	$1200(1 + r_2)$	
		Reinv $= \phi$	Reinv $= 1200 \cdot r_2$	
A $1,000 = \dfrac{600(1 + r_1)(1 + r_2) + 600}{(1 + R)^3}$				
B $1,000 = \dfrac{1200(1 + r_2)}{(1 + R)^3}$			$NPV = \displaystyle\sum_{j=1}^{n} \dfrac{(CF_j + Reinv_j)}{(1 + R)^j}$	

another $600 coupon plus another reinvestment on the $t = 2$ reinvestment. Bond B does not get its first opportunity to reinvest its coupon until $t = 2$.

Table 6.3 shows the impact of realizing different reinvestment rates over the period of reinvestment. As the table indicates, if the reinvestment rate is 6.5 percent for both bonds for both reinvestment periods, bond A does better than B because A started reinvesting its coupon sooner.

Impact of Volatility

Note how volatility in reinvestment rates for r_1 and r_2 impacts total return, and how the impact is magnified for bonds A and B because A reinvests its coupon sooner than B. For example, if r_1 were 9 percent and r_2 6.5 percent, because A gets to reinvest r_1 and B does not, the returns in this scenario are 9.04 percent for bond A and 8.52 percent for bond B. The difference between a reinvestment rate of 6.5 percent for both periods and 9 percent for both gives A a 98 basis-point advantage in total return.

The implied forward reinvestment rates are, therefore, critical to the investment decision. The shape of the yield curve will also have a critical bearing on the investment. For example, it would be appropriate to assume that interest income would be reinvested in short-term securities pending accumulation of sufficient total cash flow to make a longer-term portfolio commitment. However, if the outlook is for a steep yield curve, that will have an influence on the reinvestment-rate assumption. Volatility will also influence the implied reinvestment rate. If volatility is expected to be high, then there will be more or less equal opportunity to reinvest at higher rates to offset the risk of a lower reinvestment rate. On the other hand, if volatility is low, then overall market direction will dictate the reinvestment rate. *The most compelling consideration regarding reinvestment income is that because of its compounding, the reinvestment income will make up at least 50 percent and up to 70 percent of the NPV of a long-term bond.*

TABLE 6.3
Total-Return Analysis, Bonds A and B

Reinvestment Scenarios		$R = IRR$ for Bonds A and B	
r_1	r_2	Bond A	Bond B
6.50	6.50	8.59	8.52 ←
6.50	9.00	9.04	9.36
9.00	6.50	9.04	8.52
9.00	9.00	9.50	9.36

↑ = 98 basis points

Source: Shearson Lehman Hutton Mortgage Securities.

MBS versus Treasury Cash Flows[1]

Because the MBS produces monthly cash flows, the opportunity (and risk) to reinvest is much higher with the MBS than with the Treasury. Table 6.4 compares total returns to cash-flow yields of a Ginnie Mae versus a Treasury bond. From Table 6.4 note the cash-flow yield of the Ginnie Mae is 9.17 percent versus 9 percent for the Treasury because its yield is expressed as bond equivalent yield (BEY), which recognizes the compounding of earnings on the monthly cash flows of the MBS. (Note that in CFY calculations it is assumed that the coupon interest received is reinvested at a rate which is the same as the pass-through rate of the MBS. This assumption, of course, is unrealistic but has been adopted for ease of calculation.)

TABLE 6.4
Comparative Analysis of Total Returns and Cash-Flow Yields:
Treasury Bond versus Ginnie Mae Security

	Treasury Bond	Ginnie Mae Security
Price	100–00	99–21 (parity)[a]
Coupon	9.0%	9.0%
Maturity	30 yrs.	30 yrs.

Security	Cash-Flow Yield	Total Rates of Return: Reinvestment-Rate Scenario			Total Return Minus Cash-Flow Yield		
		7.0%	9.0%	11.0%	7.00%	9.00%	11.00%
Treasury bond	9.00%	7.77%	9.0%	10.33%	−1.23%	.00%	1.33%
Ginnie Mae security							
0.0% CPR	9.17%	7.77%	9.17%	10.66%	−1.40%	.00%	1.49%
5.0% CPR	9.17	7.57	9.17	10.82	−1.60	.00	1.65
10.0% CPR	9.17	7.46	9.17	10.93	−1.71	.00	1.76
30.0% CPR	9.17	7.26	9.17	11.10	−1.91	.00	1.93

[a] The parity price of a pass-through security is the price at which the mortgage yield equals the coupon rate. Because of the impact of payment delay, the yield on a pass-through priced at par is less than the coupon rate, making it effectively a premium security. (For further information on payment delays, see Chapter 3.)

Note: All rates of return (cash-flow yields and total returns) are expressed as bond equivalent yields (BEY).

Source: Kidder Peabody & Company, 1986.

[1]This discussion of total-return analysis, holding-period return, and breakeven analysis is derived in part from Kidder Peabody & Company, *Total Return Analysis of Mortgage Securities*, October 1986, written by John F. Tierney, CFA and Vice President.

Now note the comparative returns under the different reinvestment scenarios illustrated in the table. First, in the 7 percent reinvestment scenario both the Ginnie Mae and the Treasury show a total return well below the CFY because the CFY assumes reinvesting at the underlying coupon rate. However, when the reinvestment opportunity rises to 11 percent, the Ginnie Mae outperforms the Treasury because of its more frequent reinvestment opportunity. And the Ginnie Mae earns the highest total return at the 30 percent CPR rate because the high speed assures the maximum cash flow to be reinvested.

The preceding observation should not be confused with the point made earlier in this chapter regarding yield loss on premium securities. Here we are simply showing a parity-priced Ginnie Mae at high speed for illustrative purposes—which, granted, may be an anomaly. In fact, an increase in speed would imply that rates are declining, suggesting that the total return would be closer to the 7.26 percent figure based on a 7 percent reinvestment rate at 30 percent CPR.

Table 6.5 clearly illustrates the impact of reinvestment on total return. Even at a 7 percent reinvestment assumption, reinvestment income makes up almost 70 percent of the total return of a Treasury security. The percentages are even more impressive for the Ginnie Mae. *Note that at an 11 percent reinvestment rate at 30 percent CPR, 99 percent of the return on the Ginnie Mae is from reinvestment income.*

HOLDING-PERIOD RETURN ANALYSIS

With the combination of price volatility and increasing pressure to maximize portfolio performance, many investors prefer to price to a holding period assuming the investment will be sold, for better or worse, at the end of the holding period.

TABLE 6.5
Coupon and Reinvestment Income Components of Total Return:
Treasury Bond versus Ginnie Mae Security

	Components of Total Return: Reinvestment-Rate Scenario					
	7.0%		9.0%		11.0%	
Security	Coupon	Reinvestment	Coupon	Reinvestment	Coupon	Reinvestment
Treasury bond	30.5%	69.5%	20.7%	79.3%	13.8%	86.2%
Ginnie Mae security						
0.0% CPR	21.7%	78.3%	14.0%	86.0%	8.9%	91.1%
5.0% CPR	13.5	86.5	8.2	91.8	5.0	95.0
10.0% CPR	9.1	90.9	5.3	94.7	3.1	96.9
30.0% CPR	3.3	96.7	1.8	98.2	1.0	99.0

Source: Kidder Peabody & Company, 1986.

The total return of the holding period will then include market gain or loss as well as reinvestment income and, of course, return of P&I. The holding-period analysis is generally restricted to a six-month or one-year horizon because projecting reinvestment rates and market prices beyond a year or so becomes increasingly uncertain (due to the growing variance in the stochastic interest-rate process).

The holding-period return calculation is based on a scenario-horizon analysis assuming flat, bull, and bear markets. The selection of appropriate changes in prepayment speed for the up- and down-market scenarios is, of course, key to a proper horizon analysis.

Table 6.6 illustrates a holding-period analysis for a one-year horizon assuming rates rise 100 basis points, remain unchanged, and fall 100 basis points. The up-100 and down-100 interest-rate assumptions in Table 6.6 assume parallel shifts in the yield curve, meaning the change in interest rate is instantaneous and is for the same basis-point change across all sectors of the yield curve. The curve points used as the benchmark for the various sectors of MBSs are adjusted to reflect changes in the average life of the MBS. Thus, if a GNMA new production 10 percent coupon at 158 percent PSA is benchmarked to the 10-year Treasury at its yield in the flat market, in the down-100 (bull market) scenario the CPR speed is accelerated to 298 percent PSA, shifting the GNMA 10 to the 6-year Treasury as its new benchmark for pricing. Changes in the shape of the yield curve (steepening or flattening) are not reflected, however.

Bull and Bear Market Impact on HPR

Table 6.6 shows that the best values in terms of current yields were the middle coupons—those from 9 percent up to 10.5 percent. It is also interesting to note that while these coupons perform relatively well in the bull market (rates fall 100 basis points), the best performers are the discounts. For example, the new production 8 percent coupon, returning 15.5 percent in the rates-down scenario, gives one of the best projected yields. The investor who is neutral to somewhat bullish can do well with the 9 percent new production loan pool, which offers a return of 9.7 percent, assuming interest rates remain unchanged, and a projected 14.7 percent return in the bull market. An outright bull investor would fare better with the 7 percent coupon with its projected 15.7 percent bull market return, but would earn a smaller current return of 9.3 percent. The higher return on the discount is realized, of course, because the PSA speed accelerates from 43 PSA for new production GNMA 7s to a projected 56 PSA.

Under the bear market scenario, neither the middle- nor discount-coupon investor does well. Table 6.6 shows that the return on 9 percent coupons falls to a projected 4 percent in the rates-rise 100 basis-point scenario—and the deeper discounts do even worse. A bear market investor would fare better with the premium coupons, such as 13 percent or higher, which show projected returns

TABLE 6.6

Holding-Period Return (HPR) to One-Year Horizon

What Are the One-Year Total Returns If Treasury/Mortgage Yields . . . ?

GNMA 30-yr.	Rise 100 Basis Points		Remain Unchanged		Fall 100 Basis Points	
	Projected PSA Rate	Projected HPR	Projected PSA Rate	Projected HPR	Projected PSA Rate	Projected HPR
15.00	478	7.3	644	7.1	723	6.9
14.00	478	7.3	644	7.4	723	7.3
13.50	420	7.2	596	7.5	727	7.1
13.00	361	7.1	533	8.0	699	7.5
12.50	295	6.9	454	8.3	635	8.0
12.00	237	6.4	379	8.7	564	8.7
11.50	192	6.0	304	9.1	471	9.8
11.00	144	5.5	229	9.4	368	10.9
10.50S	118	5.0	181	9.6	299	11.8
10.50N	122	4.9	210	9.6	380	11.8
10.00S	102	4.7	144	9.5	229	12.7
10.00N	94	4.5	158	9.8	298	13.0
9.50S	93	4.4	121	9.4	180	13.3
9.50N	65	4.1	110	9.8	224	14.0
9.00S	91	4.1	109	9.1	149	13.6
9.00N	71	4.0	93	9.7	153	14.7
8.50S	87	3.9	99	8.6	126	13.3
8.50N	47	3.6	61	9.6	101	15.3
8.00S	88	3.8	96	8.5	114	13.3
8.00N	43	3.6	57	9.5	80	15.5
7.50S	85	3.6	92	8.3	104	13.2
7.50N	37	3.4	52	9.4	67	15.5
7.00S	82	3.9	89	8.1	98	12.5
7.00N	26	2.8	43	9.3	56	15.7

N = new production loans.

S = seasoned loans.

Source: Shearson Lehman Hutton Mortgage Securities.

of 7 percent or higher when rates rise. The yield returns of premium coupons hold up well because in the bear market the PSA speed slows down from over 600 PSA for the premium sector to 400 or below. The current return for these higher coupons is only about 7 percent, however.

Table 6.6 illustrates that an important consideration when investing is to consider your point of view regarding the direction of interest rates and what impact rising or falling rates will have on your investment. Perhaps most important, the task clearly shows that MBSs investing is not a static endeavor.

The yield quoted to you based on the presently observed speed can be very misleading—*remember, the presently observed speed is history when you see it, but your money is invested for tomorrow and will earn a return based on tomorrow's PSA speed.*

The total return of a pass-through security over a given holding period is the sum of the following components:

1. Coupon interest return.
2. Principal return (scheduled amortization plus prepayments) to speeds adjusted for the appropriate interest-rate scenario.
3. Reinvestment return based on implicit reinvestment rates adjusted for up and down scenarios.
4. Price or market value return adjusted for gains and losses.

Each component of return will vary given the conditions of each scenario: prepayment rate, coupon, age of the pool, amount of servicing, length of the interest-free delay period, reinvestment assumptions, and, of course, the prices at the beginning and end of the holding period.

In order to perform the horizon analysis on a given pool and to study the various components of return, the following assumptions must be provided:

1. Remaining balance of the pool at the time of purchase.
2. Coupon rate, servicing, and delay factor in payments.
3. Assumed prepayment rate.
4. Assumed reinvestment rate to be applied to cash flows.
5. Terminal yield or price at the end of the holding period.
6. Length of the holding period.

BREAKEVEN PREPAYMENT RATE

Breakeven prepayment-rate (BEPR) analysis is in effect a way to measure the value of the call option of the MBS. With BEPR analysis, the value measure is made in terms of the relative prepayment rates of the MBS population of coupons.

The benchmark prepayment rate is that of the coupon trading closest to par, or the **current-coupon** security. (The current-coupon Ginnie Mae is defined as the pass-through rate applicable to the maximum allowable VA mortgage rate in effect at the time. For example, if the VA maximum mortgage rate is 9.50 percent, the current-coupon Ginnie Mae will be 9 percent. With

Freddie Mac, the current coupon is the pass-through rate Freddie Mac elects to auction in its regular Cash market PC dealer auctions.)

The purpose for using the current coupon as the benchmark is to have a broadly traded MBS where the implied call is inoperative and therefore of little value. Newly originated mortgages are not likely to refinance or be called because of sale of the home within two or even two and a half years of the closing (see Chapter 5, "Impact of Age"). Therefore, the current coupon is the benchmark against which we may measure premiums or discounts.

Table 6.7 illustrates BEPR values as of February 5, 1988. The current

TABLE 6.7
Breakeven Prepayment Rate (BEPR) Analysis[a]

Ginnie Mae	Prices 2/5/88	Prepayments Projected %PSA	COMP Yield	WAL WAL	TSY BEPR In %PSA	BEPR CBE % at Projected PSA	BEPR Minus Proj
15.00	114–24	672	7.16	2.4	500	6.46	− 171
14.00	113–16	672	7.25	2.8	451	6.20	− 221
13.50	112–24	610	7.29	3.0	428	6.81	− 182
13.00	111–18	533	7.28	3.0	424	7.64	− 109
12.50	110–20	452	7.32	3.2	402	8.24	− 50
12.00	109–19	377	7.46	3.8	366	8.70	− 11
11.50	108–06	300	7.56	4.5	343	9.13	43
11.00	107–00	235	7.66	5.2	302	9.30	67
10.50S	105–12	183	7.68	5.4	291	9.40	108
10.50N	105–12	186	7.66	5.2	321	9.44	135
10.00S	103–04	143	7.36	3.4	468	9.46	325
10.00N	103–00	145	7.33	3.2	572	9.54	427
9.50S	100–30	117	6.58	1.1	1247	9.43	1129
9.50N	100–14	116	6.79	1.5	2671	9.54	2555
9.00S	99–08	101	7.71	5.6	539	9.25	438
9.00N	97–28	98	—	—	—	9.48	—
8.50S	97–13	91	7.86	6.5	156	9.09	64
8.50N	95–09	86	8.16	10.2	130	9.37	44
8.00S	95–03	90	7.88	6.7	151	9.04	61
8.00N	92–19	86	8.16	10.0	132	9.29	46
7.50S	93–09	89	7.85	6.5	165	8.87	76
7.50N	90–01	85	8.14	9.8	135	9.18	50
7.00S	89–31	95	7.94	7.1	101	9.23	6
7.00N	86–23	74	8.16	10.6	116	9.15	42

[a] The projected PSA speeds are from the Shearson Lehman Hutton prepayment-speed model.

N = new production loans.
S = seasoned loans.
Source: Shearson Lehman Hutton Mortgage Securities.

coupon for Ginnie Maes at the time was 9 percent. Note the 9 percent coupon is assigned no relative values in the BEPR analysis because it is the current coupon.

The breakeven analysis computes the prepayment rate of each MBS coupon so that it will have the same cash-flow yield as that of the benchmark coupon. Stated another way, the breakeven speed for premiums shows *the highest CPR or PSA that will allow that coupon to still produce the same CFY as that of the benchmark coupon.* For discounts the breakeven speed is *the lowest CPR or PSA that will still produce the CFY of the benchmark coupon.*

For discounts, the BEPR indicates the minimum prepayment speed that will allow the same results to be realized.

Looking at the table, we see that GNMA 9.5 new production pools could suffer an increase in speed to 2671 percent PSA before their CFY drops below 9.54 percent.

This suggests the 9.5 coupons enjoy excellent value. In contrast, the premium-priced coupons of 12 percent and above show a minus when the BEPR speed is subtracted from the projected PSA. This means either the projected prepayment speed is too high (a possibility, of course) or the MBS is overpriced. In the discounts, the seasoned 7½s appear to offer the best value with a BEPR of 165, and when the projected PSA speed of 89 is subtracted from the BEPR speed of 165, the 7½s have the highest rating—76—of any of the discounts. It is interesting to recall the 7½s also came up as the most favorable bull market investment on a holding-period return analysis. Breakeven prepayment analysis is really a form of option value-adjusted price analysis (see Chapter 7).

7

Duration, Convexity, and Volatility Properties of Mortgage Securities

INTRODUCTION

Duration is a valuation measure which helps to place a given security within a risk/reward framework. The framework used here is the price/yield curve for U.S. Treasury securities.

Duration was first defined in 1938 by Frederick Macaulay, but for several decades was largely ignored. With the advent of price volatility as a major market force in the 1970s, duration became popular with fixed-income investors as a means of defining the relation between a change in price and a change in yield. Duration, in fact, is the derivative of the price/yield curve. It measures the sensitivity of price to interest-rate changes, and each duration calculation defines a tangent point of the price/yield curve. By plotting a series of tangent points, a linear tangent line may be derived as an approximation of the relationship between price and yield. The chapter also defines duration in terms of implied volatility. Convexity explains the deviation between the actual price curve and the price predicted by plotting the duration tangent points. The chapter concludes with an explanation of pricing the MBS to an option-adjusted spread.

This chapter defines duration and convexity and examines how these analytic tools relate to the valuation of mortgage securities. Definitions are stated first in descriptive and easily understood terms; second, with illustrations; and finally, in mathematical expression.

DURATION

Duration is the average time to the receipt of value of all the cash flows of a security weighted by the present value of each of the cash flows. The duration calculation for the MBS is somewhat similar to that for weighted average life (WAL). Duration, however, measures the time to the receipt of value, whereas the WAL calculation measures the time to the receipt of the average principal dollar. Duration, then, is a measure of value as it relates to price risk.

A key concept, illustrated in Figure 7.1, is that duration measures the balance between reinvestment income and market gain or loss. The figure may be viewed first as illustrating an investment in a 10 percent zero-coupon bond with a maturity of 10 years, shown as the horizontal axis extending from the 10 percent mark to the 10-year maturity point. The zero-coupon bond has no coupon, and therefore there is no reinvestment income to affect the total return of this investment, which is 10 percent to the 10-year maturity. *Duration may be simply defined as a measure of the time to the receipt of a predetermined total-return objective.* In this case the total-return objective is to receive 10 percent in 10 years—hence the duration of a 10-year zero-coupon bond is 10 years.

Now consider investing in a 10 percent bond that pays a coupon every six months. The coupon will be reinvested at some rate, a rate that will be higher or lower than 10 percent depending on the level of market yields prevailing at the time of receipt of the coupon payment. (For a full discussion of the impact of reinvestment income on total return, see Chapter 6, particularly, "Reinvestment Impact on Value.")

FIGURE 7.1
Changes in Market Price versus Reinvestment Income

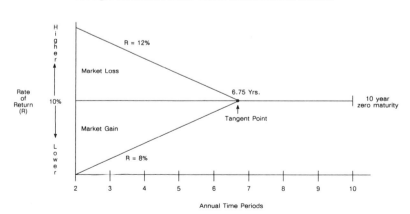

If market interest rates moved to 12 percent immediately following purchase of the 10 percent bond, there would be two impacts on our investment. First, we would incur a mark-to-market loss, obviously; but second, we would also be reinvesting at a higher reinvestment rate. In time, the ability to reinvest at 12 percent instead of 10 percent would eliminate the market loss. The point in time when that would mathematically occur is at 6.75 years, indicated on Figure 7.1 as the **tangent point**. If, on the other hand, interest rates immediately dropped to 8 percent, we would have a book market profit. But if we did not take the profit, reinvesting at the lower rate would in time erode our market profit—which would occur at the 6.75-year tangent point.

The tangent point, then, marks the time when we would realize our 10 percent total-return objective. This point in time is sooner than 10 years because with the addition of the combination of higher and lower reinvestment rates offset by market gains and losses the receipt of our target total return with a coupon bond is achieved in 6.75 years. This tangent point is therefore the derivative of the price/yield curve, as illustrated in Figure 7.2, which shows how price may be found from yield, and vice versa.

The mathematical definition of duration is given in equation (1).

FIGURE 7.2
Duration Tangent Line of 30-Year Bond at 10 Percent Yield

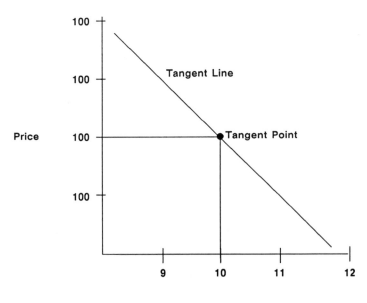

$$D = \frac{\sum\limits_{t=1}^{m} \dfrac{tC_t}{(1 + r)^t}}{\sum\limits_{t=1}^{m} \dfrac{C_t}{(1 + r)^t}} \qquad (1)$$

This formula is simply a calculation of the weighted average time to the receipt of each cash flow,

where
m = maturity,
t = number of periods,
r = periodic market discount rate,
C_t = cash flow to time t, and
$1 + r^t$ = present value to time t.

The time until the receipt (t) of cash flow is multiplied by the present value of the cash flow, expressed as $C_t /(1 + r)^t$. The sum of these components is divided by the sum of the weights, which is also the full price (including accrued interest) of the bond. The total is then multiplied by the frequency of the coupon payment (2 in the case of a semiannual coupon) to convert the periodic rate to years.

Duration Measures Time to Receipt of Value[1]

Duration may be understood initially as the weighted average time to the receipt of value, with value defined as the present value of the future cash flows discounted by a market discount rate; each series of cash flows is discounted by the weight of its sequential place in time. Figure 7.3 depicts the cash flows of an annual-pay 7-year bond. The shaded area of each box represents the present value of that cash flow. (These values are used in the calculation of duration.) The figure illustrates the cash flows as bond coupon payments balanced on a fulcrum with the fulcrum at the duration point.

Each box on the fulcrum represents the nominal amount of the coupon payment or cash flow to be received at that time. Each box also shows the discounted present value of each of the cash flows (shaded portion of box). Note that the present values of the cash flows are smaller for each subsequent box of cash flows. This is because the future value of a dollar (or dollars) is less as it is received farther into the future.

[1] This discussion is based on "The Analog Presentation of Duration," Salomon Brothers Inc., *Understanding Duration and Volatility*, September 1985, prepared by Robert W. Kopprasch.

FIGURE 7.3
Nominal and Present-Value Cash Flows
(weighted to duration point)

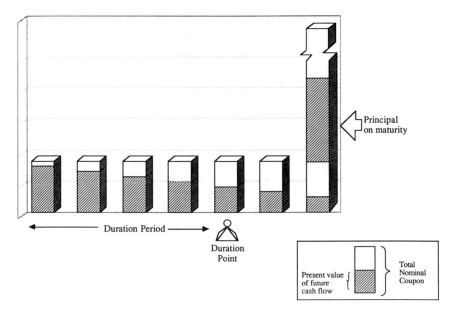

Source: This figure is based on a concept developed by Robert W. Kopprasch, Salomon Brothers, 1985.

The horizontal axis in the future is a measure of time. Each box represents a bond coupon payment for six periods, concluding with a seventh coupon payment that also includes the principal due on maturity of the bond. The duration is represented by the fulcrum, which shows the point where the present value "weights" of all the coupon payments, plus the final principal payment, are in balance. The fulcrum therefore represents the point in time where we receive our average time-weighted present value discounted by the market discount rate. The market discount rate is simply the IRR the market expects to receive for a given maturity bond—that is, 10 percent for a 10-year maturity Treasury. The duration of this 7-year 12 percent annual-pay bond is approximately 5.1 years.

Figure 7.3 can also demonstrate that the duration of a zero-coupon bond is equal to its maturity. For example, if there were only one cash flow, the principal on maturity—the fulcrum point—must lie at that cash flow. If Figure 7.3 were a zero coupon, only the last box to the right would remain, and the duration fulcrum would be beneath it.

Carrying this analogy to its logical conclusion, we see that if current market yields rise, the discount rate that will be applied to each of the future cash flows must be higher, and therefore the amounts in the shaded area in each container will be less. The more distant cash flows will be discounted the most, and therefore, the fulcrum would then have to be shifted farther to the left, indicating the duration of the bond is shortened. Note that the yield of the bond has now increased.

We may summarize some key concepts relating duration to the bond coupon and the market discount rate as follows:

1. The greater the bond coupon in relation to current market yields, the shorter the duration of the bond.
2. The lower the bond yield, the longer the duration.
3. The shorter the maturity of the bond, the shorter its duration.
4. The longer the maturity of the bond, the longer its duration.

The calculation of duration of a bond is illustrated by the simple example given in Table 7.1. The market value of this bond is par, or $1,000. Column (3) represents the weighted market value of the cash flows. The weights are derived by simply multiplying column (1) by column (2). In other words, the more distant the cash flow in terms of time, the heavier the period cash flow is weighted. Column (4) is the present value (PV) of the weighted values given in column (3) discounted back to a net present value (NPV) of 10 percent. The duration of this bond, then, is the sum of the time-weighted market values (4,790.79) divided by the market value of the bond, which is par, or $1,000. 4,790.79/1,000 = 4.79. The duration of this bond is therefore 4.79.

Using Duration to Measure Price

We can use this information to tell us how the price of the bond will change given a small change in yield. The duration number is the percentage by which

TABLE 7.1
Duration of $1,000 10 Percent Bond with Six Periods Priced at 100

(1) Years	(2) Cash Flow	(3) (1) × (2)	(4) Present Value Discounted at 10 Percent
1	100	100	90.91
2	100	200	165.29
3	100	300	225.39
4	100	400	273.21
5	100	500	310.46
6	1,100[a]	6,600	3,725.53
		Sum of PV of weighted cash flow =	4,790.79

[a] Principal of $1,000 paid on maturity at period six.

the price will change for a 100 basis-point change in yield. This bond has a duration of 4.79, meaning its price will change 4.79 points for a 100 basis-point change in yield. To illustrate, if market yields fall 100 basis points, theoretically the price will change from 100 to 104.79, and the market value increases from $1,000 to $1,047.90.[2]

Coupon Impact on Duration

If we have a higher coupon, for example, 11 percent, with market yields still at 10 percent, the duration of this bond will be shorter because we are receiving a higher coupon. The sum of the weighted market values of 11 percent at a 10 percent market rate bond is 4,931.18, and the bond will be priced at a premium of 104.4 to yield 10 percent. Its market value, therefore, is 1,044. The duration of this bond is 4,931.18/1,044 = 4.73 years. Finally, if we had a 9 percent coupon at a 10 percent market rate, it would be discounted at a price of 95.6 to yield 10 percent. Its weighted market value is 4,650.39. Dividing by the price of 956, we get a slightly longer duration of 4.86 because of the lower coupon.

Modified Duration

The **modified duration** of a bond is the percentage price change of the bond as the result of a small change in its yield.

$$D_{\text{mod}} = \frac{D}{1 + y/f} \tag{2}$$

where D = duration,

$\quad\quad y$ = yield to maturity (in decimal form),

$\quad\quad f$ = discounting frequency per year, and

$\quad y/f$ = periodic yield (in decimal form).

For semiannual-pay bonds, equation (2) becomes:

$$D_{\text{mod}} = \frac{D}{1 + y/2} \tag{3}$$

Modified duration can be used to estimate the percentage price volatility of a fixed-income security. The relationship follows.

$$\frac{\Delta P}{P} \times 100 = -D_{\text{mod}} \times \Delta y \tag{4}$$

---

[2]In fact, price increases and decreases are not symmetrical, as is demonstrated by the properties of convexity.

Percentage price change = − modified duration × yield change (in absolute percentage points). Δ = delta, which refers to "change in"—Δy means change in yield and ΔP means change in price.

Modified duration is a variation of the standard duration measure defined in equation (2). Once again, the higher the modified duration of a bond, the higher its risk. Modified duration gives the percentage change in price for a given change in yield.

Another concept used to measure the interest-rate sensitivity of a Treasury instrument is the **price value of basis point (PVBP)**. The PVBP is the change in the price of a bond for a basis-point change in its yield.

$$D_{mod} = \frac{\dfrac{-(P_2 - P_1)}{P_1}}{\dfrac{(P_2 - P_1)/100}{(1 + P_1/1200)}} \tag{5}$$

where P = price of the MBS, stated as a percentage, for a given
            yield and CPR speed,
        P_1 = current price of the MBS, and
        P_2 = current price after a change in yield.

Note that there is a minus sign preceding the numerator in equations (4) and (5). Recall that price is inverse to yield. Stated another way, the percentage change in price (the numerator) divided by the percentage change in the discount rate (the denominator) results in a negative number. It is therefore necessary to take the negative of the result to produce a positive duration number.

This may be expressed more simply as an absolute change in price and yield rather than as a percentage change, as in equation (6).

$$DA = \frac{-(P_2 - P_1)}{(r_2 - r_1)} \tag{6}$$

where r_1 = the discount rate at P_1 and
        r_2 = the discount rate at P_2.

DA is frequently referred to simply as

$$-dp/dy \tag{7}$$

with d representing delta, or "change in," P (price) and y (yield).

The duration measures described in equations (1) through (7) are the most commonly applied tools used to determine where on the price/yield curve a security should be priced. For example, if the duration of a security is five years, the security has the same relative risk and volatility of a 5-year maturity Treasury security which is at the 5-year point on the Treasury price/yield curve.

CONVEXITY

Convexity measures the *rate* at which duration changes with a change in interest rates.

We can define the price/yield curve by drawing a linear estimation of the tangent points derived from a series of duration calculations for small yield changes similar to the tangent point illustrated in Figure 7.2. Figure 7.4 gives the duration tangents and price/yield curve for a 10 percent 30-year bond. The duration of the bond is estimated by the straight line labeled "Duration at 10 percent yield." That is, the bond's duration, 9.46, has its tangent at the 10 percent yield point on the graph. The tangent point is used to derive a linear estimation of the change in price for a given change in yield.

FIGURE 7.4
The Price/Yield Curve of a Current 30-Year Bond at 10 Percent

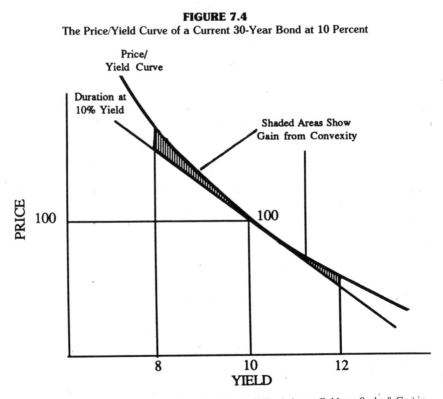

Source: Based on a concept developed by Stanley Diller (when at Goldman Sachs & Co.) in connection with his research on parametric analysis of MBS cash flows.

According to the duration line in Figure 7.4, a 200 basis-point change in yield (to 8 or 12 percent) indicates a price of 118.92 at 8 percent and of 81.08 at 12 percent. In fact, the actual price change is higher at both the 8 and 12 percent yield points than the duration line at these duration points has estimated.

Convexity explains the difference between the duration-estimated prices and the actual prices.

We may understand convexity quite readily if we observe how yield changes impact the duration fulcrum. To illustrate, we may use a bond with two coupon payments—like bond A—which was illustrated in Figure 6.2 (page 183). This bond is now shown as Figure 7.5 with its duration fulcrum.

When interest rates change, the bond starts to change in value. The change in yield causes a change in the present values of the coupon payments, but not equally—the coupon payment that is more distant changes by a greater amount.

When rates rise, the discounted cash flow of the more distant coupon payment declines more in value than that of the closer coupon. The present value weight of the near coupon therefore becomes greater, while that of the distant coupon becomes less. The duration fulcrum must therefore be shifted to the left to maintain the balance of our duration, as illustrated in Figure 7.6. This means the duration number of the bond becomes smaller, so when it is applied as a percentage to the base price to calculate the change in price, the price

FIGURE 7.5
Duration Fulcrum of Two-Coupon 3-Year Bond

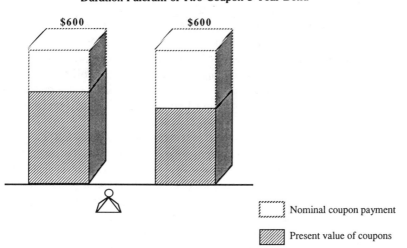

Nominal coupon payment

Present value of coupons

Note: The duration fulcrum is to the left of center, giving weight to the greater present value of the first coupon payment.

Source: This figure is based on a concept developed by Robert W. Kopprasch.

FIGURE 7.6
Duration as Rates Change

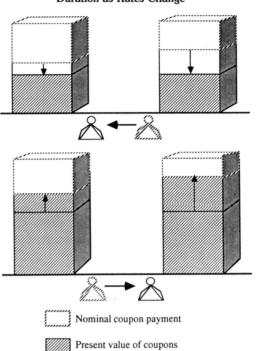

 Nominal coupon payment

Present value of coupons

Source: This figure is based on a concept developed by Robert W. Kopprasch.

change is somewhat smaller than before the rise in interest rates. In addition, since prices are falling, each calculation of the new price is off a smaller base.

Therefore, although the price is declining, it does so at a decelerating rate. This forces the duration tangent line to curl up as the bond falls to a discounted price.

When interest rates decline the reverse occurs. As rates fall, the present value weight of the more distant coupon increases faster than that of the nearby coupon, thereby causing the fulcrum to shift to the right, as also illustrated in Figure 7.6. As the duration number becomes greater it has a greater impact on the base price, which also becomes higher with each subsequent application. The price therefore increases at an accelerating rate in the declining interest-rate environment. Again, the duration tangent line is forced to curl up.

Note that the price/yield curve in Figure 7.4 is positively sloped and therefore is said to have **positive convexity**. Also note that with a *positively convex price/yield curve prices move inverse to the direction of interest rates*.

FIGURE 7.7
Mortgage-Backed and Treasury Price/Yield Curves

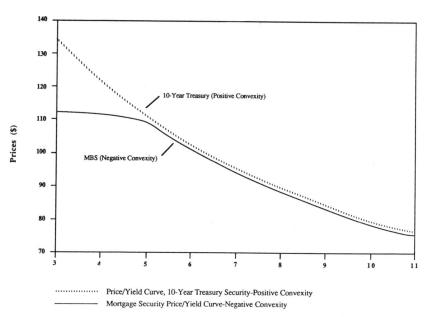

.... Price/Yield Curve, 10-Year Treasury Security-Positive Convexity
———————— Mortgage Security Price/Yield Curve-Negative Convexity

Figure 7.7 illustrates the price/yield curve of a MBS plotted against the Treasury. Note that unlike the Treasury price/yield curve, the MBS curve curls down at both extremes at price and yield. This curve is termed **negatively convex** because of its shape. Note another phenomenon associated with the MBS curve: *prices move in the same direction as interest rates*. Macaulay's duration cannot contemplate negative convexity, because in Macaulay's time there was no fixed-income security traded that had prepayments and an associated call option.

Negative Convexity of MBSs

The MBS has negative convexity because we always get—or do not get—the cash flows at the wrong time. See Figure 7.1, which illustrates how the duration concept is built on the trade-off between reinvestment income and market gains and losses. This relationship breaks down when the MBS trades up to a premium price. When rates are high we need the cash flows to reinvest at the higher yields, but when rates are high the prepayment speed slows down and so does the cash flow. Conversely, we get high cash flows when rates are low.

Because of this perversity in MBS cash-flow patterns, as well as the call option which gains value as rates fall, the premium-coupon MBS price becomes first compressed and then actually moves down—or moves in the same direction as interest rates—and therefore is said to be negatively convex.

The MBS investor's dilemma is best illustrated by the experience of **hedgers**, who for years wondered why they always lost money with MBSs hedges in a bull market. Hedging first came into its own with fixed-income portfolio managers with the routinely volatile markets introduced by the inflation of the late 1970s. Initially hedging was viewed as largely a matter of taking a short position in a security or commodity that looked and acted like what you owned and wished to hedge. During this time, Freddie Mac PCs and Fannie Mae MBSs were viewed as 10-year average-life securities and were therefore rather universally hedged against the 10-year Treasury bond traded on the Chicago Board of Trade (CBT). Although we now know that comparing a PC to the 10-year Treasury bond is only sometimes valid, in a bear market nobody really gets hurt because in bear markets the MBS performs reasonably well, except for deep discounts. Look again at the price/yield curves shown in Figure 7.7. Here, follow the price curves of a bull market by reading from right to left. The hedger who is short the Treasury against a long MBS position in a bull market has the worst of all worlds. The Treasury security (which he is short) is going up in price while the MBS, which is long, is going down in price as it becomes a premium. *The hedger is, in effect, losing the difference between the MBS and Treasury security price curves*, shown in Figure 7.7. Stated another way, if you are short both the standard-coupon bond and the call option in a bull market, you lose money on both.

ALTERNATIVE DURATION MEASURES

Clearly, we have to develop alternative ways to evaluate mortgage securities because Macaulay's duration will work only for current-coupon and moderate-discount MBSs,[3] and then only if prices do not change very much.

We shall examine four alternative evaluation techniques currently used by MBSs investors: (1) CPR-adjusted CFY; (2) volatility-implied duration; (3) prepayment-sensitive model; and (4) option-adjusted value theory.[4]

---

[3]Premiums and discounts are defined as moderate if the MBS coupon is within 300 basis points of the current coupon (the coupon of current new originations). Super-premiums and deep discounts are MBS coupons that are respectively higher or lower than the current coupon by 300 basis points.

[4]This discussion of alternative evaluation models is based in part on a special report by Morgan Stanley, *An Analysis of the New Valuation, Duration, and Convexity Models for Mortgage-Backed Securities*, January 1987.

CPR-Adjusted CFY

By the mid-1980s it was recognized that anticipated, or forecasted, prepayment rates were more genuine to the MBS investment consideration than the currently observed CPR. As previously stated, the observed current CPR in reality is more a reflection of the past than of the present. (See Chapter 5, "Lag Response of Prepayments.")

The CPR-adjusted CFY technique then applies a CPR forecast rate to a computerized cash-flow-yield model to adjust the period-by-period cash flows to the anticipated prepayment speed as measured by FHA, CPR, or PSA.

The duration value is determined by finding the yield that discounts the CPR-adjusted cash flows back to the current prevailing market price. Although a vast improvement over a long-standing practice of simply using the current observed CPR spread to generate the periodic cash flows, this technique is nevertheless a static model because it does not allow the cash flows to change or for price convexity to become negative. This approach is what some analysts refer to as the "Macaulay duration of the MBS." While it works well for current coupons and moderate discounts where the call option is latent, the approach does not serve well for premiums with an operative call option. Unfortunately, under no circumstances can a CPR-adjusted model produce a negative duration.

Volatility-Implied Duration

We have defined duration as a function of the sensitivity of price to value, measured in terms of changes in yield. Furthermore, by deriving a duration number defined in terms of years, we are really designating the point on the yield curve at which we are matched in terms of years. In other words, an MBS with a duration of seven years will have the *price risk and volatility characteristics of a 7-year Treasury*. If rates fall and prepayment speeds accelerate, the MBS will become a premium and will display the low-volatility characteristics of, for example, a 3-year Treasury; if rates rise, the MBS will take on the higher-volatility characteristics of a 10- or 12-year Treasury. *Duration, then, may be viewed as a measure of the relative price volatility of an MBS.*

Scott M. Pinkus, Vice President and Senior MBSs Analyst, Goldman Sachs, has extensively researched the price volatility of an MBS. One of his discoveries was that a single coupon—for example, a GNMA 10—displays dramatically different volatility characteristics as it passes through varying price cycles from current coupon to premium to discount. He found that the price relation between discounts and premiums through varying interest-rate paths is not linear but is better illustrated by a slightly curved line. Furthermore, he discovered that the curvature of the line representing the price relation between, for example, GNMA 8s and GNMA 13s increased significantly after the GNMA 13s passed through par and became a premium. He also discovered that the change in relative volatility between the two coupons changed more rapidly as the 13s became a premium. As the bull market continued, the GNMA 8 continued to rise in price (that is, displayed high price volatility), but as the GNMA 13 traded to higher levels it became *less volatile against the GNMA 8*; in other words, the GNMA 13 displayed what is defined as **price compression**.

Mr. Pinkus concluded that the relative price volatility of Ginnie Mae discounts versus premiums could be better measured by studying Ginnie Maes grouped within certain *price ranges* rather than by following Ginnie Mae coupon groups that would migrate over time from premium to discount and back. From this analysis, Mr. Pinkus derived the Ginnie Mae volatility curve presented in Figure 7.8.

Mr. Pinkus' findings are summarized as follows.[5]

- Discount Ginnie Maes are more volatile than current coupons and premiums. The faster prepayment rates associated with the higher-coupon securities (those priced at substantial premiums) shorten the average lives of these Ginnie Maes. Since shorter-term securities exhibit less price volatility than longer-term securities, we would expect Ginnie Maes priced at a substantial premium to be less volatile than lower-priced Ginnie Maes. In addition to the shorter average lives of higher-coupon securities, the severe prepayment risk associated with these securities also plays a major role in limiting their price volatility. While the prepayment risk with the current-coupon and slight-

FIGURE 7.8
GNMA Volatility-Implied Duration Curve

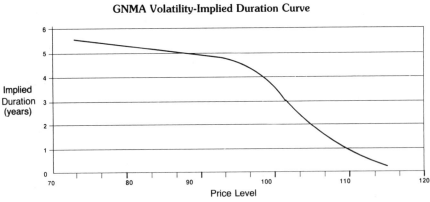

Source: From the *Journal of Portfolio Management,* Summer 1986. This concept was developed by Scott M. Pinkus, Vice President and Senior MBS Analyst, Goldman Sachs.

[5]From *The Journal of Portfolio Management*, Summer 1986.

premium Ginnie Maes is modest by comparison, it is sufficient to make these securities relatively less volatile than deep-discount Ginnie Maes.

• The price volatility curve is relatively flat in the discount area but falls sharply once it crosses par. While the price volatility of a discount Ginnie Mae declines slightly as its price increases, the price volatility of a current-coupon or premium Ginnie Mae declines rapidly as its price increases. As the price of a Ginnie Mae crosses above par, the prepayment risk associated with the security increases substantially as the implicit call option becomes in the money. The deeper in the money the call option becomes, the less volatile its price with respect to the current-coupon Ginnie Mae.

The Implied-Volatility Framework

Mr. Pinkus derived a volatility-implied duration model by comparing the price volatility of the current-coupon Ginnie Mae (defined as the coupon trading between 99.5 and 100) to a benchmark security the volatility characteristics of which could be defined in terms of classic Macaulay definitions. He selected the 10-year Treasury as his initial benchmark and defined the volatility relationships as follows.

$$\text{Relative price volatility of 10-year Treasury to Ginnie Mae current coupon} = \frac{\text{Duration of 10-year Treasury}}{\text{Implied duration of GNMA current coupon}}$$

Using the historical relative volatility analysis of MBSs coupon segments, Mr. Pinkus determined that the relative volatility ratio between the 10-year Treasury and the current-coupon Ginnie Mae is 1.45 percent. For example, if the duration of the 10-year Treasury is 5.93 years, the implied duration of the current-coupon Ginnie Mae is therefore 4.09 years (5.93/1.45). Once Mr. Pinkus found an estimate for the current-coupon Ginnie Mae, it in turn could become the benchmark security from which implied durations for other MBSs price-sector groups could be derived. Mr. Pinkus then compared his volatility-implied durations, as shown in Table 7.2.

TABLE 7.2
Macaulay versus Volatility-Implied Durations

	GNMA 8	GNMA 11	Implied Relative Volatility GNMA 8 vs. GNMA 11
Macaulay duration	5.4	5.8	0.93
Volatility-implied	5.2	4.2	1.24

Note that Macaulay's duration indicates that the GNMA 11 is more price volatile (longer duration) than the GNMA 8. Experience with actual price history of Ginnie Maes tells us this is emphatically not the case. The implied-duration calculation shows the discount 8 percent GNMA to be 24 percent more volatile than the higher-coupon 11. This implied-duration number is, in fact, representative of the duration relationship between 8 and 11 coupons as it has been derived by other techniques used to adjust Macaulay's duration for the impact of prepayments.

Prepayment-Sensitive Model

The prepayment-sensitive model utilizes a mathematical function that allows prepayment rates to change in response to interest-rate changes. An excellent example of this approach was developed by Steven Carlson, Vice President, Derivative Products Research Group, Shearson Lehman Hutton.

Mr. Carlson determined that if Macaulay's duration could be modified to be sensitive to changes in prepayment speed, we would have a valid valuation device for MBSs. He derived two components of a correction factor to be applied to the Macaulay calculation. The first part of the correction factor, which Mr. Carlson calls the E factor, captures the sensitivity of price to changes in prepayment speed.

The second part of the correction factor measures the sensitivity of CPR to changes in yield. This measure, which Mr. Carlson calls the S factor, needs to be estimated by the analyst. Together the terms E and S gauge the impact of a change in yield, which indirectly (yet instantaneously) affects price through changes in the market's perception of prepayment speed.

Mathematically, the correction factor may be expressed as

$$dP = \text{PVBP} + dY - (\text{PVCPR} \times S) + dY \qquad (8)$$

where dP = change in price,
     dY = change in yield in basis points,
     PVBP   = price value of a basis point,
     PVCPR = price value of a percentage of CPR, and
     S = absolute value of the change in the percentage of CPR per 100 basis-point increase or decrease in yield.

Corresponding to equation (8) is an alternative measure of duration [equation (9)], which Mr. Carlson calls *mortgage duration*:

$$\text{Mortgage duration} = D + (E \times S) \qquad (9)$$

where $D = \dfrac{-\text{PVBP}}{P} \times 100$, standard modified duration and

$E = \dfrac{\text{PVCPR}}{P} \times 100$, analogous to duration for CPR.

The following is quoted from a special report prepared by Mr. Carlson.[6]

Both equations can be derived formally using the equations for the price of a mortgage at a given yield and CPR.

Looking at the equation for mortgage duration provides the mathematical analogy to the basis introduced by prepayments. For discount mortgages, PVCPR is positive, since prepayments enhance value for that sector; the converse is true for premium mortgages—S is always positive. Therefore, the correction factor that adjusts standard duration for mortgage duration, $E \times S$, is negative for premiums and positive for discounts.

The mathematics allow us to be more specific about where mortgage duration makes a difference. For mortgages with prepayments that are insensitive to market moves, such as deep discounts, S will be small, and mortgage duration will be close to the standard calculation. For mortgages close to par, E is small because prepayments do not have a big impact on price. Mortgage duration for current coupons will also be close to the standard duration calculation. When applied to premium coupons, the mortgage duration calculation makes the most difference. The value of these mortgages is relatively more sensitive to the prepayment rate; the prepayment rate is also more sensitive to interest rates.

Option-Adjusted Spread[7]

The **option-adjusted spread (OAS)** method of MBS valuation separately values the call option and noncallable coupon bond components of the MBS. In Chapter 6 the composite market value of the MBS was defined as being equal to the value of the noncallable bond component of the MBS minus the value of the call option. Under the OAS methodology the value of the call is the option cost,

[6]Shearson Lehman Hutton, ''Assessing the Duration of Mortgage Securities,'' October 10, 1986.

[7]This discussion of the option-adjusted spread is based in large part on concepts developed in *An Analysis of the New Valuation, Duration, and Convexity Models for Mortgage-backed Securities* by David P. Jacob, Vice President, and Alden Toevs, Principal, Morgan Stanley, January 1987.

defined as additional basis yield spread. When the additional basis yield spread is added to the base yield spread of the MBS without an operative call (discount or current-coupon new production MBS) it defines the option-adjusted spread at which the MBS should trade against the Treasury price/yield curve. *The OAS then is the net spread that will on average be earned by the investor over time.*

Valuing the call option separately from the call-free MBS cash flows holds considerable appeal as a logical approach to the MBS pricing process. We know intuitively that if interest rates are rising, the call option has little value, and the sum of the callable and noncallable components (the option-adjusted price) will differ little from pricing the MBS to a cash-flow yield using a static speed assumption.

When interest rates are falling, however, the call option value becomes critical to the pricing process. The OAS pricing process becomes analogous to that of pricing a callable corporate bond. With a typical standard callable corporate bond, the value of the call option may be viewed as the sum of the discounted present values of all the cash flows that follow the exercise date of the call. Again, this confirms our intuitive approach to MBS pricing in that we know the present value of cash flows returned at par is very great if those cash flows were purchased at a discount. Conversely, if the cash flows were bought at a premium, the value becomes a negative—that is, a deduction from the price. In the case of a standard callable bond, cash flows that are received prior to the call are probably all that will be realized if rates decline precipitously.

The call option embedded in the MBS differs from that of a callable corporate bond in two major respects. First, the call attached to a corporate bond is a rational call. It will either be called or not depending primarily on an economic decision to replace the callable bond with cheaper money. As discussed in Chapters 5 and 6, the implied call of the MBS is irrational. The homeowner may exercise the call even when it is out of the money because the home is sold—the mortgage is prepaid for reasons unrelated to the presence or absence of an economic incentive to refinance. Conversely, the option may not be exercised when in the money either because the homeowner does not have the means to pay the transaction cost of refinancing or for other reasons unrelated to refinancing considerations.

Furthermore, underlying the MBS is a pool consisting of several individual mortgages, each containing a prepayment option. The MBS therefore consists of a multitude of options, each with a different propensity to be called depending on the human factors which influence the various homeowners holding a given option embedded within the pool.

The valuation of the call options bundled into an MBS pool is therefore a combination of an art and a science, requiring the investor to apply some intuition and interpretation to the valuation process. Principal among these is making a judgment call on the probable future course of interest rates and the impact that will have on prepayments.

Make no mistake about it, the empirical derivation of OAS contributes enormously to lending correct direction to the MBS valuation process. The factors that are critical to the derivation of OAS are a properly designed prepayment model and a correct assessment of price volatility ranges likely to be realized over the intended investment horizon. The options-based model incorporates all the critical variables applicable to the derivation of the price and basis-point yield spread to the Treasury curve at which the MBS should trade. These variables, as they were identified in the Jacob and Toevs study, include: (1) The relative level of current interest rates; (2) a process describing how current interest rates can change without creating artificial arbitrage opportunities; (3) a parameter of volatility to govern the size of period-by-period interest-rate changes; and (4) a functional prepayment model to translate the future interest rates into MBS cash flows.

In the Morgan Stanley report by Jacob and Toevs, the term "options-based" is construed as referring to the concept that an MBS pool is imbedded with a number of options associated with each of the mortgages that make up the pool. Each individual option may have slightly different characteristics, depending on how the homeowners react to the series of interest-rate paths through which an MBS pool will pass over time.

The report emphasizes that the level of prior interest rates has an important bearing on how homeowners will react to a change in interest rates today as well as on how many of the original mortgages are remaining in the pool today. As was pointed out in Chapter 5 in the section dealing with prepayments, an MBS pool will have its strongest reaction and highest measured prepayment rate the first time the WAC of the mortgages underlying the pool is thrust below the threshold for refinancing (overshooting) and will react with somewhat less vigor in subsequent interest-rate cycles (steady state). The collective options imbedded in the MBS pool may therefore be said to be *path-dependent.*

Finally, expectations of future volatility must be taken into account. The greater the analyst's expectations of relatively high volatility in interest rates, the more likely is the MBS pool to pass through a series of prepayment thresholds and accelerate the process of first overshooting and then pass through a series of interest-rate paths that may, with successive waves of bull and bear market volatility, achieve a steady state of prepayment speed within a short period of time. On the other hand, if the analyst anticipates a long period of relatively low volatility, the opportunity may exist for pent-up demand to refinance, thus magnifying the overshooting effect when a long-awaited opportunity to refinance finally presents itself.

The options-based price reflects the value of the options embedded in the

MBS. This price, however, may misstate the true value of the security because the cash flows have been discounted by a market discount rate based on the then-current Treasury yield curve. To bring the options-based price to a true market value, we must add a spread to the Treasury curve. As indicated earlier, we refer to the spread that equates these prices as the options-adjusted spread, or OAS.

Jacob and Toevs point out: "The OAS is not a spread off a specific Treasury issue, nor can it be added back to a specific Treasury to produce a yield for the MBS. Rather, it is a number that, when added across the Treasury yield curve, allows us to derive the market price of the MBS using the options-based methodology."[8]

OAS Analysis Applied to MBS Pricing

Figure 7.9 illustrates the total option cost and OAS basis-point yield spreads to the Treasury yield curve of GNMA 7 percent through 13.5 percent coupons.

FIGURE 7.9
Total Spread and OAS Components for GNMA MBSs 7% through 13.5%

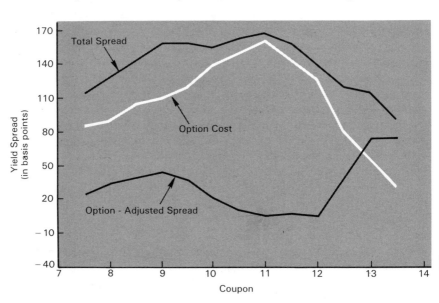

Source: Based on Drexel Burnham Lambert material distributed in connection with a presentation by Drexel at the MBS Conference, Institute for International Research, March 1988.

[8]Reprinted from *ibid*.

The total spread, shown in the curve at the top, is the yield spread derived using traditional duration measures. The option cost is the value of the call option derived by the options-based model. The curve at the bottom of the chart depicts the OAS.

Note that the total spread suggests the greatest yield spread value is in the 11 percent coupon, shown as trading at a yield spread in excess of 160 basis points over the Treasury curve. However, the 11 percent coupon, trading at a premium price, has its option very much in the money. As the option-cost curve illustrates, the option value (cost) of the GNMA 11 coupon is the highest of any of the coupons illustrated. The OAS of the GNMA 11 is less than 20 basis points, suggesting it is expensively mispriced. The investor is not getting a fair OAS here.

The GNMA 9 coupon, on the other hand, is showing an OAS of more than 40 basis points. Furthermore, it is trading at a discount, and its option is out of the money. This coupon therefore appears to be fairly priced.

Now note the 13 percent and 13.5 percent coupons. These coupons, also trading at premiums, show low option values and a relatively high OAS. They have been priced to premium prices for some time and are now experiencing prepayment burnout. Therefore, they are also mispriced, but this time the market is overestimating their prepayment speeds, meaning they are under-valued and represent an investment opportunity.

In summary, the prepayment model used in conjunction with the options-based model is saying the prepayment-speed assumption used to price GNMA 11s was too slow, for the GNMA 9s about right, and for the 13s and 13.5s too fast. So using a static, or the current observed, speed, the 11 and 13 and 13.5 coupons were mispriced; the options-based model, using a prepayment fore-cast, has identified the 11s as expensive and the 13s and 13.5s as undervalued when priced to an option value-adjusted price.

Conclusion

We may ask at this point, what does OAS mean? OAS is not a definitive answer to the selection of long-term values in portfolio restructuring. OAS gives us an estimate of the direction of value at one point in time; it is not something you can put in your pocket and earn forever—the relative option-adjusted values will change over the course of a year. But the OAS spread does trend to a mean of spread values that will be earned over time. Used consistently in a prudently managed portfolio, application of the OAS technique should lead to better than average portfolio performance measured in terms of total return.

8

Measuring Value without the Black Box

INTRODUCTION

A portfolio manager may participate in any market with one of two approaches, as either a trader or an investor, or both. Both approaches require, first, a careful assessment of risk; second, a definition of the time horizon, or holding period, of the trade or investment; and third, a decision to buy, sell, or remain neutral following a risk/reward analysis of the trading or investing opportunities available. Traders generally operate on a short-term horizon and seek profit opportunities in the market by identifying securities that on a relative value basis appear cheap (to buy) or expensive (to sell). Trading decisions are made primarily on the basis of price in the expectation the price will more likely than not increase or decrease within a relatively short time. Investors also consider price as a measure of relative value, but are more likely to seek securities that will provide a superior total return in yield over a longer time.

Trading and investing are a combination of art and science. Technology provides the information upon which good trading and investing decisions are made, but no technology can replace the risk/reward judgment call to make or not to make a trade or an investment based on the information provided. MBSs trading and investing require more technical information with far greater emphasis on the judgment call than with any other fixed-income security. It is for this reason, of course, that MBSs are priced to a considerable yield spread over Treasury and corporate bonds, with the opportunity for profit (and loss) also greater.

This chapter is in effect a wrap-up of Chapters 5, 6, and 7, with the objective to review some applications of the skills learned in those sections of the book. Chapter 5 reviewed the causes of prepayment speed and its impact on average life. Chapter 6 assessed the impact of changes in average life on price and how to calculate yield. Chapter 7 discussed several valuation techniques defined in terms of duration. This chapter presents the use of yield/duration curves to identify both value and risk/reward in MBSs trading and investing. The yield/duration curves provide a visual analysis of the impact of prepayments on yield and duration and, most important, illustrate how the MBS basis-point spread to the Treasury curve changes with varying prepayment patterns. These curves, then, provide in visual form the option-adjusted spread to the Treasury curve, which in the final analysis is what pricing is all about. Best of all, the curves enable portfolio managers who must make risk/reward investment decisions without access to a computer base to view a framework of relative values without the black box.

A RISK-VALUATION FRAMEWORK

Risk may be defined as the uncertainty and volatility of returns. The greater the uncertainty of realizing the return, the greater the risk of the investment. In a real sense, uncertainty may be measured in terms of the volatility of probable returns that may be realized on the investment. The more volatile the potential of realizing the expected return on the investment, the greater the risk of making the investment. This is not the same as defining risk in terms of price or yield volatility. The issue is more of defining risk relating the duration of the security to the time horizon of the investment. For example, an insurance company that purchased 10-year, zero-coupon Treasury bonds to match fund a predetermined time horizon such as a 10-year guaranteed insurance contract (GIC) might experience considerable price volatility during the holding period but would have a very low risk of total-return volatility—that is, in realizing the total return to the targeted holding period. On the other hand, if the time horizon were 10 years and it were funded with short-term Treasury securities such as the three-month bill, the return volatility would be very high because the investor would be faced with 39 reinvestment intervals over the holding period. There would therefore be great uncertainty of realizing a targeted return in this example—and therefore high risk—even though the price volatility of a three-month Treasury bill is very low. Thus one consideration is to predefine the holding period and seek the investment (or MBS) with the closest duration that will match it.

Investing with a Market View

The other consideration is sector selection based on a bullish or bearish scenario. Investing with an interest-rate outlook is particularly critical in MBSs investing because of the impact interest-rate changes have on prepayment speeds and how that factor will affect the return on the MBS. There is no faster way to ruin than to buy the wrong sector of the MBSs market for the interest-rate climate that ultimately prevails during its holding period—for example, buying premium-coupon MBSs at the start of a bull market.

RIDING THE MORTGAGE YIELD CURVE

The following discussion of relative value analysis is based on a series of figures that illustrate for various MBSs coupons how yield spreads to the Treasury curve and durations change as prepayment speeds change. The presumption is that in bull markets the speed of the MBS will increase, shortening its duration. In bear markets, prepayments slow down and the duration of the MBS is extended. As the duration of the MBS changes, the maturity of the Treasury to which the MBS is compared changes. For example, the base-case comparison for a Freddie Mac PC 10 percent coupon might be its yield spread to the 10-year Treasury, which has a duration comparable to the PC in the base-case pricing assumption. If rates fall and speeds accelerate, the duration of the PC shortens, making it more comparable to the 5-year Treasury. Or if rates rise, the PC duration may be extended to be comparable to the 10-year Treasury.

Typically, as speeds increase the yields of discounts increase, and the yields of premiums decrease in absolute terms. As speeds decrease the reverse is true. The essence of the valuation process is not only to predict whether the yield of the MBS will increase or decrease but also to accurately estimate whether the basis-point yield spread of the MBS to the comparable maturity Treasury narrows or widens. For performance-oriented portfolio managers the latter issue is regarded as the ultimate test of risk/reward. The yield/duration curves in the figures that follow clearly illustrate the risk/reward considerations that are key to maximizing portfolio performance. The figures all follow the same guidelines, and they are outlined in the explanation below.

Explanation

- The curves show relative economic value (as measured by yield to maturity) as a function of market risk (as measured by duration) for a wide range of possible future prepayment rates.
- Prepayments always increase from *right* to *left*.
- A ''central rate'' is chosen and is indicative of recent historical or near-term projected prepayment rates. This central rate is near the middle of each curve and is marked with a dot (•).

Unless otherwise indicated, the *left-hand* termination of each curve is at *twice* the central prepayment rate, and the *right-hand* termination is at *half* the central rate.

- Prepayment rates followed by a "P" are PSA rates; others are CPRs.
- "N" next to coupon denotes new productions; "S" denotes seasoned.

Purpose

- To compare alternative investments and identify swap opportunities.
- To construct "what if" scenarios for a wide range of future prepayment rates.
- To provide answers to a variety of questions concerning relative value and prepayment risk.

In general, the ideal is to find the MBS curve that remains the most in the northwest quadrant of the figure (highest yield, shortest duration). The poorest values typically lie in the southeast quadrant (lowest yield, longest duration). Risk is measured by lines that plunge the fastest to low yields; reward, by lines that rise to higher yields and shorter duration.

Discussion of Figure 8.1

Figure 8.1 illustrates the Treasury yield curve as it appeared on January 22, 1988. Superimposed over the Treasury curve are the yield curves of several Ginnie Mae coupons, including discounts and premiums and 15- and 30-year Ginnie Mae MBSs.

The curves clearly illustrate the impact of speed on both duration and yield at the same time. For example, the GNMA 15 loses yield dramatically with even a short change in duration as prepayments rise (implied bull market) and shows its bear market value as the yield increases with slowing speeds. It is particularly important to note that the yields of GNMA 12, 13, and 15 coupons all dive below the Treasury yield curve as their speeds accelerate, making these coupons high-risk substitutes for short-term investments. Sometimes investors purchase high-speed premium coupons as a proxy for short-term investments because of their short stated average lives. But if speed slows down, the investor will experience extension risk.

Note the GNMA 10 coupon, priced close to par, shows very little yield change as its duration shortens and lengthens, and it also holds a fairly even basis-point yield spread to the Treasury curve in a variety of interest-rate scenarios. The same is true of the GNMA 9 coupon, but note that its duration is longer and its yield lower than those of the 10 coupon. Holders of 9s would be wise to swap to 10s.

FIGURE 8.1

Ginnie Mae Yields to Maturity

(based on 1/88 3-month CPRs)

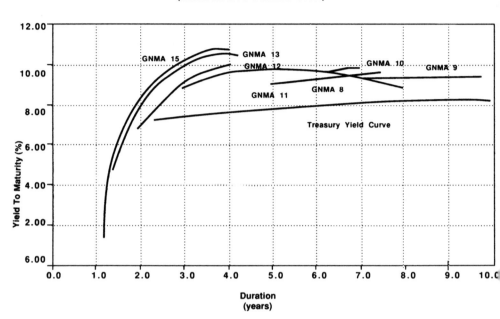

Source: Shearson Lehman Hutton Mortgage Securities.

Seeking and Holding Basis-Point Spread

Figure 8.2 illustrates an interesting pocket of yield spread against the 5- and 7-year points of the Treasury curve. Note that the GNMA 11 was trading at a wider spread than either the higher or lower coupons around it. The market may have been concerned that the relatively low speed of the 11s (11 CPR) offered undue risk in the event of a bull market, but the figure shows that the risk of rising speeds was not a poor risk/reward prospect. Compare the speed risk of the 11s with that of the 12.5s. This may have been an example of a mispricing opportunity with the 11s, which appear to have acceptable risk/reward at this level. Note that the 8s show good yield appreciation potential in the bull market, but the duration of the 8 is significantly longer than that of the 11, making it a poor risk/reward.

Figure 8.3 shows that by February 1988 the GNMA 11s had indeed both picked up yield and shortened duration. The GNMA 8s, meanwhile, remained at about the same yield but their duration extended a bit. At the same time, the GNMA 11s picked up some negative convexity and are showing a stronger risk

FIGURE 8.2
Ginnie Mae and Treasury Markets

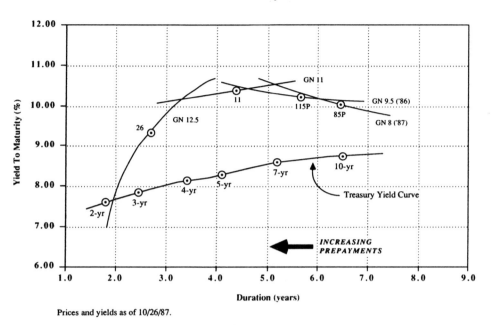

Prices and yields as of 10/26/87.

Source: Shearson Lehman Hutton Mortgage Securities.

(bull market)/reward (bear market) bias to a market call. A more conservative posture might be to swap to Freddie Mac PC 10s.

Figure 8.4 shows that in February 1988 the PC 10s had a duration about the same as the GNMA 10s and offered only a slightly lower yield but much less negative-convexity risk. A bear market-oriented investor would, however, have been better off staying with the GNMA 11s; or he could have swapped to the PC 11s, shortened duration by one full year point on the Treasury curve, and given up only a small amount of yield. But it is hard to win by staying neutral. In the MBSs market money is made by investing with a market view—and then being right.

Bull Market Investing

The principal investing considerations for bull market investors are as follows.

Coupon

• Low coupon to maximize return of discount.

FIGURE 8.3
GNMA New Production Yield/Duration Curve

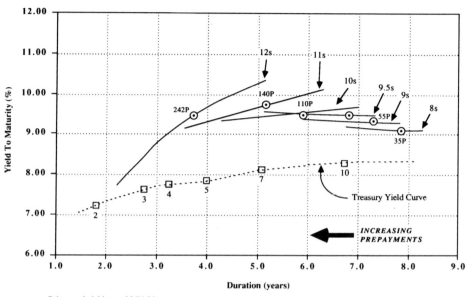

Prices and yields as of 2/22/88.

Source: Shearson Lehman Hutton Mortgage Securities.

- Low coupon to remain off the cusp; avoid or sell convexity (swap current or premium coupons for discounts).
- Moderate premiums are the most dangerous—call option is right at the money, on the fringe of the cusp.
- Tight WAC, especially for current or premium coupons.

Average Life/Duration

- Long average life/duration for call protection.

Type

- For current or premium coupons, Ginnie Mae over conventional; slower speed, better call protection. For discounts, conventional to maximize return of discount.
- Thirty-year over 15-year; longer average life.

Seasoned versus New

- New production offers call protection.

FIGURE 8.4
Freddie Mac PC New Production Yield/Duration Curve

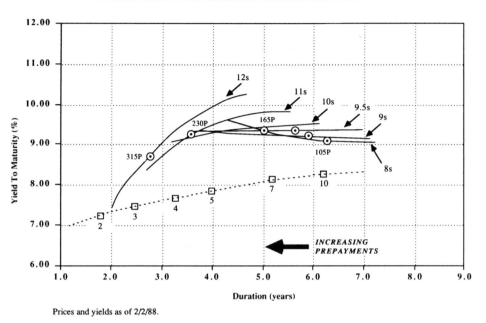

Prices and yields as of 2/2/88.

Source: Shearson Lehman Hutton Mortgage Securities.

Figure 8.5 illustrates a coupon swap for the bullish investor—selling FHLMC 10.5s to buy FHLMC 9.5s. This swap offers an 11 basis-point yield pick-up, reduces prepayment risk, and extends duration by one and a half years. Note the much greater negative convexity of the 10.5s versus the level yield maintained by the 9.5s. Note the swap also yields a dollar take-out of about 4¼ points. Also, the more bullish investor would prefer to swap down to a coupon selling below par, as are the 9.5s, priced at 99⁷⁄₃₂.

Figure 8.6 illustrates the use of a principal-only (PO) stripped MBS to create a range of synthetic coupons. The PO was stripped from GNMA 11.5 coupons, giving it strong speed characteristics in a bull market. By combining the PO with generic GNMA 11.5s, synthetic coupons may be created with no basis risk or prepayment risk because the collateral is identical for both parts of the synthetic combination.

Note the severe negative convexity of the generic GNMA 11.5 in the increasing prepayment (bull market) scenario. Bullish investors holding GNMA 11.5s could hedge the negative convexity by adding the PO in a 1 for 9 ratio (a $1 million position would be $100,000 PO and $900,000 GNMA 11.5s). If the investor is more bullish, the ratio of PO can be increased. For example, at a ratio of 3 for 7 (30 percent PO) the trade offers dramatic upside,

FIGURE 8.5
Freddie Mac PC Bull Market Trades

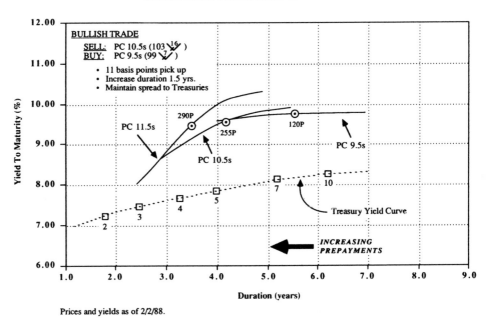

Prices and yields as of 2/2/88.

Source: Shearson Lehman Hutton Mortgage Securities.

potentially soaring to beyond 12 percent. With a downside risk of just below 9 percent, this trade has excellent risk/reward for the bullish investor.

Note also how well the synthetic 8.01 coupon performs against the seasoned GNMA 8 coupon. In a bear market the synthetic would yield only slightly less than the GNMA 8s at their minimum respective speed points (far right point on the curved lines) and would have a maximum bear market duration a full year shorter than that of the GNMA 8. In the bull market, the performance of the synthetic is far superior.

Bear Market Investing

The principal investing considerations for bear market investors are as follows.

Coupon

- High coupon to benefit from speed slowdown.
- Seek coupon on the cusp to gain benefit of cash-flow retention as it slides off the cusp.
- High WAC on discounts to maintain speed.

FIGURE 8.6
Synthetic Combinations: GNMA 11.5s and FNMA Trust 29 POs
(GNMA 11.5% collateral)

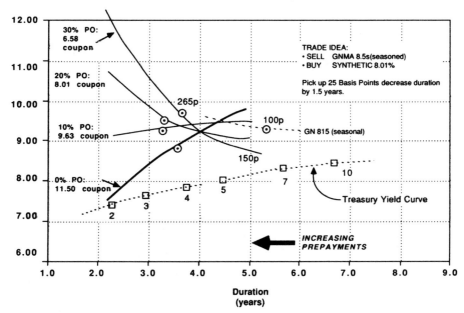

Prices and yields as of 1/26/88.

Source: Shearson Lehman Hutton Mortgage Securities.

Average Life/Duration

- Short average life/duration to minimize price volatility.

Type

- Ginnie Mae if premium coupon to extend cash flows for maximum recapture of premium points; conventional if current coupon to maintain shorter duration. Avoid discounts.
- Fifteen-year over 30-year to reduce duration extension.

Seasoned versus New

- Seasoned to maintain speed and shorter duration as coupons slide below the cusp.

Figure 8.7 shows the same coupons and curves as those in Figure 8.5 but illustrates a bear trade if the FHLMC 10.5s are sold to buy FHLMC 11.5s. The

FIGURE 8.7
Freddie Mac PC Bear Market Trades

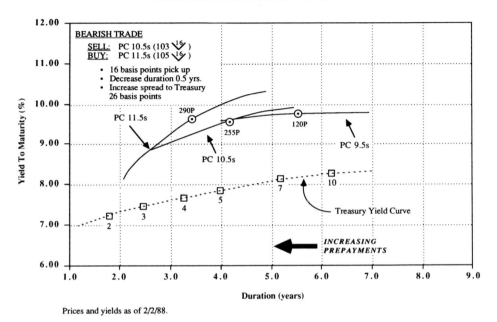

Prices and yields as of 2/2/88.

Source: Shearson Lehman Hutton Mortgage Securities.

investor picks up 16 basis points in yield and shortens duration by half a year. Significantly, there is a 26 basis pick-up in yield spread to the Treasury yield curve, which should hold well as speeds slow down and the high coupon remains on the books. Note how well the yield curve of the 11.5 performs, rising sufficiently to hopefully maintain yield spread to the Treasury as the duration of the PC 11.5 is extended along the Treasury curve, which will be moving to higher levels as rates increase in the bear market.

Sector Analysis

Figures 8.8 through 8.10 illustrate MBSs market sectors segregated by duration sectors as they appeared in January 1988. In Figure 8.8 the best relative value of all MBSs 11.5 coupons is in the FNMA 11.5. The durations of all three MBSs are about the same, but the Fannie Mae holds yield spread the best under bull and bear market conditions. Note in particular that even though the yield of the FNMA 11.5 declines in the bull market, it maintains a positive spread to the Treasury curve even at its high-speed point. Defensive investors then could

FIGURE 8.8
Under 4-Year Maturity Sector

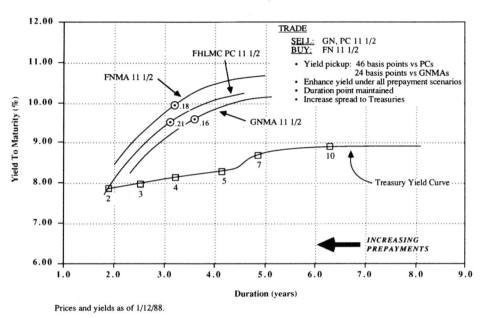

Prices and yields as of 1/12/88.

Source: Shearson Lehman Hutton Mortgage Securities.

endure a shortening of duration to two years and still own an MBS that offers a positive spread to the Treasury curve.

Figure 8.9 shows a more mixed performance, with a variety of coupons in the 4- to 6-year duration sector. The FNMA 9.5s and GNMA 10s, both new production pools, hold spread the best in bull and bear markets. Both FHLMC 8.5s and FNMA 11s have market bias, the former for a bull market and the latter for a bear market.

Figure 8.10 illustrates the 6-year and longer sector, with GNMA 9.5s showing the best relative value with the shortest duration and widest basis-point spread to the Treasury curve. Significantly, the GNMA 9.5s also hold yield spread the best in most prepayment scenarios.

The series of yield/duration curves points out that there are no fixed rules governing which MBSs will perform the best under certain circumstances. The ability to seek the best relative values through this approach will enhance portfolio performance over time. This technique makes it possible to identify relative values without relying on cut-and-dried rules of thumb that lead many market participants to miss opportunities to swap into cheap and out of rich

FIGURE 8.9
4- to 6-Year Maturity Sector

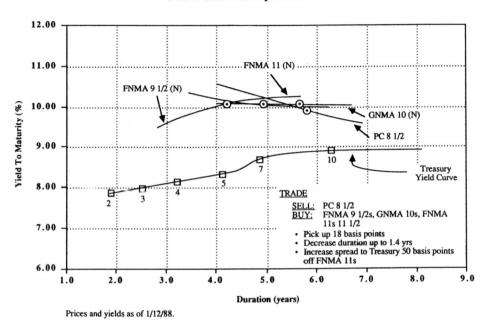

Prices and yields as of 1/12/88.

Source: Shearson Lehman Hutton Mortgage Securities.

securities as the securities may from time to time become under- or overpriced. The approach also allows the investor to apply some judgment through a visual analysis of market profiles. For the informed and alert investor this can be more rewarding than a table filled with option-adjusted spreads derived by a black box from assumptions that may not be fully revealed to the investor.

Some Guidelines for Swaps

When evaluating swaps look for more than high yield and short duration. Consider concerns such as whether you are buying or selling convexity. When examining prepayment projections, assess whether they appear conservative or somewhat aggressive—for example, a little high for the discounts and a little low for the premiums. Remember that much of the analysis you will see is prepared by somebody with something to sell, and it is human nature to err in favor of the story you want to tell. Understand how the durations of the MBSs have been calculated and what assumptions are behind them. If the presentation is based on option value-adjusted spreads be sure you are comfortable with all the assumptions (see Chapter 7 for a discussion of assumptions that lead to the derivation of option-adjusted spread).

FIGURE 8.10
Over 6-Year Maturity Sector

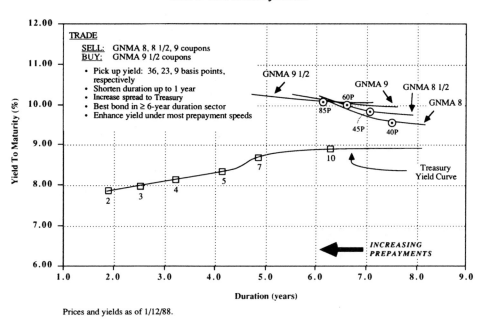

Prices and yields as of 1/12/88.

Source: Shearson Lehman Hutton Mortgage Securities.

In general, if MBS coupon spreads are narrower than usual, buy the high-priced item and sell the low-priced one. A narrow spread is usually the result of price compression where the high-priced item has taken on its maximum negative convexity. A market reversal will usually call for the lower-priced item to fall away, widening the spread and enabling you to buy it back cheaper.

If spreads are wider than usual, sell the high-priced coupon and buy the low-priced one. The lower-priced coupon will have the greater opportunity to trade up in price while the higher coupon becomes compressed. Upon reversal of the swap the profit comes from the price appreciation of the lower-priced coupon.

Concentrate swap activity in markets with volatility. Swaps should be done where the anticipated result can be realized fairly quickly. Without volatility there will be an extension in time to gratification, and time adds risk to the trade.

It often pays to be a contrarian. If high speed is going to favor your trade, avoid high-speed pools that may be approaching burnout, or slow-speed pools that can only speed up with market volatility.

When examining relative price spreads, determine whether superior price performance is from special demand (somebody is accumulating FNMA 10s for a $500 million arbitrage CMO). If you buy just as the demand has been filled, you will own expensive bonds, or perhaps a big seller of GNMA 12s has just completed a swap for lower coupons.

You May Be Able to Buy Cheap Bonds

Be aware of the availability of product. Avoid buying into a program swap that looks good on paper but after half the trade is executed you find you cannot fill the other side. You may get caught with one leg up and nowhere to put it down. In general, it is wise to stick with liquid items so that a swap trade can be reversed quickly. And avoid the fringes of the market, such as super-high premiums or seldom-traded coupons. Pricing of fringe items is usually sloppy at best, and they usually are bid low and offered high by the dealer market. Remember, in trading swaps you want to ride with the generic market so that anticipated price changes will more likely be realized. Exotic items representing unique value may be bought for portfolio holding to a predetermined holding period, but when trading remember that the larger the outstanding of the coupon group of your interest, the closer it will track the generic market.

III

SPECIAL MORTGAGE PROGRAMS

9
Fifteen-Year, Manufactured Housing, and Graduated-
Payment Mortgage Securities

10
Adjustable-Rate Mortgage Securities

11
Multifamily and Project Loan Securities

9

Fifteen-Year, Manufactured Housing, and Graduated-Payment Mortgage Securities

INTRODUCTION

Mortgage securities collateralized by mortgages with original maturities of 15 years have become increasingly popular with investors seeking shorter maturity. Investors looking for shorter maturity or duration may find it with mortgage securities backed by 30-year mortgages, which because of high prepayment rates have a short average life. Another alternative is seasoned loans, which have amortized down to short WAMs.

Some risks and limitations for investors are inherent in either premium or seasoned short WAM MBSs, however. Premium-coupon securities that are currently paying at a high prepayment speed have the potential for the prepayment rate to slow down significantly in a period of high interest rates. But the average life could be extended from a current one of 3 or 4 years to 7 or 10 years.

Short WAM, seasoned product has an advantage over the long WAM speed pool described above because a short WAM cannot be extended beyond its final maturity date. If, for example, the WAM is 200 months, the average life will tend to remain relatively short, even in periods of slow prepayment speeds. The limitation of short WAM, seasoned product is that it is seldom available in pieces of more than $5 million, which by their nature are usually discount-priced coupons, and so may not fit the buyer's investment objectives (for example, in a bear market).

The 15-year security has the advantage of a short final maturity at the time of its origination and will trade to an average life of 7 years even as slow-speed, new production loans. After two years of seasoning or more, the 15-year MBS is likely to trade to a 5-year average life. And even in times of high interest rates and slow speeds, the duration-extension risk is limited to a 7- or 8-year average-life range.

Mortgage securities collateralized by 15-year mortgages are issued under the Ginnie Mae guaranty as Midgets; and by Freddie Mac as Gnomes if issued out of Cash program pools, and as non-Gnomes if issued under the Guarantor swap program (see Chapter 3). Fannie Mae-guaranteed 15-year MBSs are called Dwarfs. Manufactured home (mobile home) securities are at present agency guaranteed only under the Ginnie Mae program, with original maturities of 15 years and 12 years.

CHARACTERISTICS OF 15-YEAR MORTGAGES[1]

Rising Popularity of 15-Year Mortgages

The 15-year mortgage gained popularity as lower mortgage rates made higher monthly payments more manageable and lower inflation rates reduced the advantage of borrowing long and paying down the principal in cheaper dollars. Borrowers quickly realized that 15-year mortgages offer lower mortgage rates, lower overall financing costs, and faster equity buildup than 30-year mortgages. As a result, originations of 15-year mortgages rose from $30 billion in 1985 to an estimated $80 billion in 1986.

Under a normal, upwardly sloping yield curve, the 15-year mortgage rate is generally 25–50 basis points lower than a 30-year rate because of its shorter maturity. More important, the faster principal paydown dramatically reduces total interest costs. As Figure 9.1 shows, the 15-year borrower pays down half of the principal during the tenth year, whereas the 30-year borrower does not reach the halfway point until the twenty-fourth year. Consequently, at the same mortgage rate, the 15-year borrower pays only 43 percent of the total interest cost paid by the 30-year borrower. In addition to reducing total finance costs, the faster principal paydown of the 15-year mortgage leads to faster equity buildup in the home. This provides 15-year borrowers with a ready source of funds for future needs through home equity loans or second mortgages. For example, as Table 9.1 shows, a 15-year borrower would accumulate $19,932 in paid-in equity on a 9 percent, $100,000 mortgage after five years, whereas a 30-year borrower would accumulate only $4,120.

To realize these benefits, however, the 15-year borrower must make substantially higher monthly payments. Consequently, the 15-year mortgage

---

[1]This discussion is from Shearson Lehman Hutton, *An Analysis of 15-Year Mortgage Securities*, April 1987.

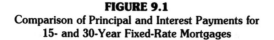

FIGURE 9.1
Comparison of Principal and Interest Payments for
15- and 30-Year Fixed-Rate Mortgages

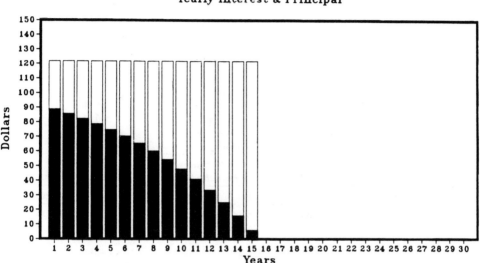

15–Year 9% Mortgage
Yearly Interest & Principal

Source: Shearson Lehman Hutton Mortgage Securities.

appeals to relatively affluent borrowers, such as dual-career families, who can manage the higher monthly payments. For example, at the same 9 percent mortgage rate, the 15-year borrower pays an additional $2.09 per month for each $1,000 of original principal. This imposes a substantial opportunity cost on the 15-year investor, since the additional principal payment could have been spent or invested elsewhere. As Table 9.1 shows, however, the interest savings on the 15-year mortgage more than offsets the foregone earnings because of the faster reduction of the original mortgage balance. Moreover, the net advantage of the 15-year relative to the 30-year mortgage increases over time and becomes much more significant after the fifth year. As a result, the 15-year mortgage appears particularly well suited for borrowers who expect to remain in their homes for several years.

In view of these advantages, 15-year, single-family mortgage origina-tions should increase in the years ahead. As of March 31, 1988, total outstand-ings of 15-year MBSs totaled about $67 billion, with $17,167,200 in Freddie Mac Cash Program PC Gnomes; $17,770,100 in the Freddie Mac Guarantor; $17,974,700 in Fannie Maes; and $14,015,100 in Ginnie Mae Midgets. The FHA/VA programs capture a slightly lower share because they are designed for

TABLE 9.1
Cumulative Net Advantage of a 15-Year Mortgage versus
a 30-Year Mortgage ($1,000 principal, 9% mortgage rate)

Year		*Cumulative. . .*	
	Net Advantage	*Foregone Interest Earnings on Principal*	*Interest Savings and Compound Interest*
1	.36	.72	1.08
2	1.59	3.17	4.76
3	3.81	7.62	11.43
4	7.18	14.35	21.53
5	11.85	23.71	35.56
10	62.12	124.26	186.38
15	183.62	367.24	550.86

Scheduled Principal and Interest Payments for 15- and 30-Year Mortgages

	15-Year Mortgage Monthly Payment: $10.15		*30-Year Mortgage Monthly Payment: $8.05*		*Difference 15-Year Minus 30-Year*	
Year	*Principal*	*Interest*	*Principal*	*Interest*	*Principal*	*Interest*
1	$ 33.05	$ 88.66	$ 6.83	$ 89.72	$ 26.22	$ −1.06
2	69.21	174.22	14.30	178.80	54.90	−4.59
3	108.75	256.38	22.48	267.19	86.27	−10.80
4	152.01	334.84	31.42	354.80	120.59	−19.96
5	199.32	409.24	41.20	441.57	158.12	−32.34
10	511.39	705.73	105.70	859.84	405.69	−154.12
15	1,000.00	825.68	206.70	1,241.63	793.30	−415.95
30	NA	NA	1,000.00	1,896.64	NA	NA

Source: Shearson Lehman Hutton.

lower-income households, which are less able to meet the higher monthly payments associated with the 15-year mortgage. Moreover, if FHA data are any indication, 15-year originations should increase along with refinancing activity. According to FHA data, borrowers are more likely to refinance into 15-year than 30-year mortgages. Refinancing accounts for approximately 30 percent of 15-year FHA-insured mortgage originations but only 11 percent of FHA-insured 30-year originations. This may reflect borrowers' ability to manage the higher monthly payments associated with 15-year mortgages after paying down a substantial portion of their original loan balances. The median loan amount of a 15-year mortgage is lower than that of a 30-year mortgage for both FHA-insured and privately insured conventional mortgages (see the nearby box, "A Profile of 15- and 30-Year Borrowers").

The share of 15-year mortgages in all conventional purchase-money mortgage originations has increased dramatically over the past few years. According to the Federal Home Loan Bank Board (FHLBB), which compiles

A Profile of 15- and 30-Year Borrowers
Part A: FHA Mortgages
1982—86

	15-Year	*30-Year*
Loan-to-Value Ratio (%)		
Less than 85	4.00%	6.18%
85–89	0.02	0.00
90–95	0.01	0.01
Greater than 95	95.96	93.80
Mortgage Amount ($000)		
Less than 25	9.74%	4.43%
25–35	16.96	12.52
35–45	19.54	19.80
45–55	19.60	21.21
55–65	14.73	18.06
65–75	11.55	13.37
Greater than 75	7.88	10.61
Median	$46,918	$51,245
Income ($000)		
Less than 25	16.71%	21.51%
25–34.9	28.54	34.38
35–44.9	26.27	24.36
Greater than 45	28.48	19.75
Median	$35,903	$29,143
Age (yrs.)		
Younger than 25	13.03%	20.18%
26–35	46.45	50.90
36–45	23.91	18.19
46–60	14.13	9.04
Older than 61	2.47	1.69
Median	32.7 yrs.	29.9 yrs.
Construction		
Proposed	5.95%	10.91%
Existing	94.05	89.09
Purpose of Mortgage		
Refinance	30.66%	11.10%
Purchase money	69.34	88.90
Total loan volume	16,691	247,291

Source: Department of Housing and Urban Development/FHA.

Part B: Privately Insured Conventional Mortgages
1983–86

15-Year						Age		
Loan-to-Value Ratio (%)	Loan Volume	Average Annual Income	Average Loan Amount	18–25	26–33	34–40	41–48	Older Than 49
80	8.89%	$71,523	$94,319	6.93%	27.18%	27.80%	19.76	18.19
90	65.25	48,039	60,393	12.81	42.52	23.17	11.87	9.63
95	25.85	42,717	53,607	19.42	41.01	19.44	11.43	8.67
	63,753[a]	48,751[b]	61,654[c]					
30-Year								
80	5.94%	$56,742	$81,389	7.42%	35.15%	23.96%	16.06%	16.33
90	46.85	46,398	69,990	13.68	44.94	21.91	10.47	8.51
95	47.21	39,618	61,687	21.97	45.57	18.34	8.10	5.78
	796,752[a]	43,811[b]	66,746[c]					

[a] Total loan volume.
[b] Weighted average income.
[c] Weighted average loan.
Source: Shearson Lehman Hutton.

data on all major lenders, the share of 15-year mortgages rose to 21 percent in 1986 from 17 percent the previous year. In contrast, this share stood at 9 percent in 1984 and at a mere 3 percent in 1980. In fact, the share rose as high as 28 percent in May 1986, despite the relatively narrow 30 basis-point differential between 15- and 30-year fixed rates at that time. However, it fell to 16 percent in December 1986, even though the 15- to 30-year rate differential widened slightly. This pattern suggests that 15-year borrowers value the rate differential less than the lower overall financing costs and faster equity buildup.

Significantly Lower Default Rates

Over their brief lifetime, 15-year mortgages have posted impressively lower default rates than their 30-year counterparts. As a result, many portfolio investors, including Fannie Mae, have aggressively purchased these mortgages in order to improve the quality of their portfolios. Although data on default rates for conventional mortgages are scarce, industry estimates place 15-year mortgage default rates at about half those of 30-year mortgages. In fact, significantly lower claim rates have already prompted one private mortgage insurance company to create a separate risk class for these mortgages to reflect their lower risk. Default rates for 15-year FHA-insured mortgages are even lower. As Table 9.2 shows, less than 1.2 percent of all 15-year FHA-insured mortgages resulted in claims during the 1982–86 period compared to 4.2 percent of all 30-year FHA-insured mortgages.

Several reasons explain the different default experiences. First, the average loan-to-value (LTV) ratio of a 15-year mortgage is significantly lower than that of a 30-year mortgage. Second, 15-year borrowers build up substantial equity in their homes faster than 30-year borrowers. Third, 15-year borrowers are generally more affluent than 30-year borrowers. Fourth, lenders may allow 15-year borrowers who face default to refinance into a 30-year mortgage.

To elaborate on these points: When Fannie Mae tightened its underwriting standards in August 1985, it estimated that 85 percent of all 15-year level-payment mortgages have down payments of 20 percent or more and that only 5 percent have down payments of less than 10 percent. Loans with LTV ratios greater than 90 percent are five times more likely to end up in foreclosure than those with LTV ratios between 80 and 90 percent. Moreover, 15-year borrowers pay down principal faster and, therefore, accumulate home equity faster than 30-year borrowers. As a result, they are less likely to walk away from their homes in the face of adversity. Furthermore, 15-year mortgages appeal to more affluent homeowners because they entail higher monthly payments. These borrowers often have recourse to other sources of funds and are less likely to default because of job loss. Finally, lenders may allow 15-year

TABLE 9.2
Claim Rates for 15- and 30-Year FHA-Insured Mortgages (1982–86)

	15-Year			30-Year		
	Insured	*Claims*	*Percent*[a]	*Insured*	*Claims*	*Percent*[a]
Loan-to-Value Ratio (%)						
Less than 85	668	16	2.40	15,284	733	4.80
85–89	4	0	0.00	10	0	0.00
90–95	2	0	0.00	27	1	3.70
Greater than 95	16,017	179	1.12	231,970	9,663	4.17
Total	16,691	195	1.17	247,291	10,397	4.20
Income ($000)						
Less than 25.0	2,789	59	2.12	53,192	3,530	6.64
25.0–34.9	4,764	65	1.36	85,020	3,348	3.94
35.0–44.9	4,385	33	0.75	60,234	1,950	3.24
Greater than 45.0	4,753	38	0.80	48,845	1,569	3.21
Total	16,691	195	1.17	247,291	10,397	4.20

[a] Claims as a percentage of loans insured for each category.

Source: Department of Housing and Urban Development.

borrowers to convert to 30-year mortgages, rather than default, if circumstances prevent them from meeting scheduled monthly payments. This drastic measure would lower the 15-year borrowers' scheduled monthly payments, thereby making debt service more manageable.

Issuance and Outstanding Volume

Issuance of 15-year pass-throughs increased dramatically during the past two years. Although Ginnie Mae 15-year mortgage pass-throughs (Midgets) were first issued in 1982, and both Fannie Mae and Freddie Mac began issuing 15-year pass-throughs in 1984, the total outstanding volume barely exceeded $5 billion by year-end 1984. In contrast, the outstanding volume of 30-year pass-throughs reached $285 billion by year-end 1984. Despite this slow start, 15-year pass-through issuance skyrocketed to almost $13 billion in 1985—more than doubling the size of the 15-year market. As Table 9.3 shows, this impressive performance continued. Issuance of 15-year pass-throughs climbed to $30 billion in 1986, expanding their outstanding volume to $49 billion. Nevertheless, the size of the 15-year market pales in comparison to the 30-year market. Issuance of 30-year pass-throughs topped $215 billion in 1986, bringing the total outstanding volume of these securities to more than $500 billion.

Agency Underwriting Standards for 15-Year Mortgages (Fixed-Rate Purchase Programs)

Commitment Guidelines	*Freddie Mac*	*Fannie Mae*
Minimum Commitment	None	$100,000 $250,000 for participations
Maximum Commitment	$25 million	None

Loan Eligibility		
Mortgage type	All mortgages to purchase owner-occupied, investor-owned, and second	Mortgages to purchase owner-occupied and second homes and to refi-

	homes; to refinance existing mortgages; and to finance energy and other improvements are eligible.	nance existing mortgages are eligible. These include fixed-rate, level-payment mortgages as well as GPMs, GEMs, and balloon mortgages. If the mortgage insurance premium is financed, then lenders may deliver only mortgages for owner-occupied, principle residences with no possibility of negative amortization.
Maturity	10- to 15-year	15-year original term
Loan-to-value (LTV) ratio	Maximum LTV ratio on original loans is based on lesser of purchase price or appraised value at time of loan closing. Maximum loan amount is the loan's balance at origination.	Maximum LTV ratio on original loans based on lesser of purchase price or appraised value at time of loan closing. Maximum loan amount is the loan's balance at origination.
Maximum LTV ratio	Ratio for owner-occupied refinanced mortgages is 90% of appraised value at the time of closing.	Generally 95%; however, if the mortgage insurance premium is financed, then the LTV ratio excluding premium cannot exceed 90%, but can be as high as 92% including financing.

Assumable	No	No
Private mortgage insurance (PMI)	Freddie Mac requires carrying mortgages seven years before removing PMI.	Fannie Mae requires removal of PMI when the LTV ratio reaches 80% as long as the borrower has an acceptable payment record, or if the borrower requests removal after a reappraisal indicates that the house has appreciated enough to lower the LTV ratio to 80%.

Source: Shearson Lehman Hutton.

Aggressive Agency Participation

The stunning increase in Fannie Mae and Freddie Mac purchases of 15-year mortgages during 1986 testifies to the rapid growth of the 15-year market. Fannie Mae purchased $20 billion of 15-year mortgages in 1986 versus $6.3 billion the previous year, while Freddie Mac purchased $22 billion and $6.1 billion of 15-year mortgages in 1986 and 1985, respectively. In both cases, purchases grew more than 200 percent. Although both agencies purchased approximately the same dollar volume of 15-year mortgages over the past two years, as shown in Table 9.3, Freddie Mac's 15-year issuance more than doubled Fannie Mae's. Fannie Mae capitalized on borrowers' growing preference for 15-year mortgages to increase the quality of its portfolio holdings and shorten its asset duration. Consequently, it retained the bulk of its 15-year mortgage purchases. Over the past few years, Fannie Mae has stressed the importance of portfolio investing, and the shorter-duration, higher-quality 15-year mortgage complements its strategy of risk reduction and duration matching.

In keeping with its mortgage banker-like role, however, Freddie Mac securitized most of its purchases. The agency emerged as the leading issuer of

TABLE 9.3
Issuance and Outstanding Volume of 15- and 30-Year
Mortgage Pass-Throughs as of December 1986 ($ billions)

| | | 15-Year Pass-Throughs | | | |
	15- & 30-Yr	Total	GNMA	FNMA	FHLMC
1972–81	$149.9	—	—	—	—
1982	54.2	*	*	—	—
1983	83.5	$2.6	$2.6	*	*
1984	60.1	2.6	1.2	$0.2	$1.2
1985	108.3	12.8	2.9	3.0	6.9
1986	254.0	38.3	7.6	8.8	21.9
Total Issuance	710.0	56.3	14.3	12.0	30.0
Outstanding at Year-end 1986	550.0	49.0	12.3	10.8	25.9

*Less than $100 million.

Sources: The Bond Buyer Government Securities Factor Service, FNMA, FHLMC, Ginnie Mae, and Shearson Lehman Hutton.

15-year pass-throughs in 1985 and now accounts for approximately half of the outstanding volume of these securities. Freddie Mac dramatically expanded its role in this market after inaugurating a daily 15-year auction in November 1985. Currently, Freddie Mac Gnomes—pass-throughs pooled by 15-year mortgages purchased through its Cash program—account for more than half its total issuance, which approached $22 billion in 1986. Non-Gnomes—15-year pass-throughs purchased through Freddie Mac's Guarantor program—account for the remainder. Furthermore, the agency issued the first CMO backed by 15-year mortgages in April 1986.

In view of the anticipated growth of the 15-year market, both agencies have enhanced their 15-year purchase programs. Fannie Mae began posting commitment rates for 15-year mortgages in December 1986, and both agencies now offer commitments on a 10-, 30-, 60-, and 90-day basis. Fannie Mae also allows lenders to specify a lower servicing fee—.25 percent rather than the standard .375 percent—for mandatory delivery of 15-year, conventional, fixed-rated mortgages. Moreover, Fannie Mae will purchase eligible fixed- and adjustable-rate 15-year mortgages that include a mortgage insurance premium as part of the mortgage loan balance.

Prepayment Rates

Prepayment rates for 15-year mortgage pass-throughs typically exceed those of comparable-coupon 30-year pass-throughs. More important, they generally rise faster in a falling-rate environment and are likely to fall faster in a rising-rate environment. In short, 15-year pass-throughs appear more negatively convex than comparable-coupon 30-year pass-throughs. Furthermore, 15-year pass-throughs season faster than their 30-year counterparts. In contrast to 30-year pass-throughs, which season after 30 months, 15-year pass-throughs season after 20 months. Consequently, they begin to prepay faster and much sooner than comparable-age 30-year mortgages.

There are several reasons for this difference. First, 15-year borrowers are more affluent than their 30-year counterparts (see box, "A Profile of 15- and 30-Year Borrowers," on p. 235). Therefore, they are more likely to have the financial wherewithal to meet the out-of-pocket expenses associated with refinancing. Second, they are older than 30-year borrowers and possibly more financially astute as a result. Although the median age of the 15-year borrower exceeds that of the 30-year borrower by only three years, 15-year borrowers are more likely to be 35 years old or older. In view of these characteristics, 15-year borrowers are likely to be more mobile as well.

Finally, 15-year borrowers accumulate home equity much faster than 30-year borrowers. As a result, they can refinance their mortgages to draw down paid-in equity much faster than 30-year borrowers. Although this does not explain the higher prepayment rates of last year for 1985 and 1986 originations, it should become a significant factor in the years ahead. The Tax Reform Act of 1986 gradually eliminates the deductibility of interest payments for consumer debt but leaves the mortgage interest deduction intact. As a result, the home will become a primary financing vehicle. Homeowners will draw down paid-in equity in their homes in order to obtain tax-deductible financing to purchase big-ticket items. Consequently, 15-year mortgages are likely to prepay faster than 30-year mortgages even in a flat-mortgage-rate environment.

Cash Flows

Despite faster prepayment rates, 15-year mortgage pass-throughs provide more stable cash flows than 30-year pass-throughs. As Table 9.4 shows, the average life of a 15-year pass-through falls much less than that of a 30-year pass-through in response to rising prepayment rates. In short, 15-year pass-throughs exhibit less duration drift than comparable-coupon 30-year pass-throughs. This predictability increases their value as collateral for both strips and CMOs. Moreover, it appeals to investors, such as insurance companies, that are extremely sensitive to early repayment of principal.

Duration drift occurs when the time-weighted return of principal changes substantially in response to changing mortgage rates. It affects 15-year pass-throughs less than 30-year pass-throughs because principal payments comprise a much larger portion of total monthly payments (see Figure 9.1). In contrast, scheduled principal payments comprise only a small portion of scheduled monthly payments for 30-year mortgages. Therefore, rising prepayment rates

TABLE 9.4
Average Life of Selected Mortgage Coupons under
Various Prepayment-Rate Scenarios (years)

12% Coupons

	Fannie Mae		Freddie Mac		Ginnie Mae	
PSA (%)	15-Year	30-Year	15-Year	30-Year	15-Year	30-Year
100	8.92	13.34	8.98	13.39	8.89	13.31
150	7.51	9.90	7.56	9.96	7.48	9.87
200	6.37	7.67	6.43	7.72	6.34	7.64
250	5.45	6.15	5.51	6.21	5.42	6.12
300	4.71	5.09	4.77	5.14	4.68	5.06
400	3.60	3.71	3.66	3.77	3.58	3.68
500	2.84	2.87	2.99	2.93	2.82	2.84
1000	1.17	1.17	1.23	1.23	1.14	1.14

9% Coupons

	Fannie Mae		Freddie Mac		Ginnie Mae	
PSA (%)	15-Year	30-Year	15-Year	30-Year	15-Year	30-Year
100	9.56	13.83	9.62	13.88	9.54	13.80
150	8.06	10.33	8.12	10.38	8.03	10.30
200	6.86	8.07	6.92	8.12	6.84	8.04
250	5.91	6.54	5.96	6.60	5.88	6.51
300	5.14	5.47	5.19	5.53	5.11	5.44
400	4.00	4.09	4.06	4.15	3.98	4.07
500	3.23	3.26	3.29	3.31	3.21	3.23
1000	1.57	1.57	1.62	1.62	1.54	1.54

Assumptions: WAMs = 336 months for 30-year and 156 months for 15-year FNMA, FHLMC, and GNMA 12s.

WAMs = 348 months for 30-year and 168 months for 15-year FNMA, FHLMC, and GNMA 9s.

WACs = 75 basis points above the coupon for FNMAs and FHLMCs, 50 basis points for GNMAs.

Delay: GNMA = 14 days.
FNMA = 24 days.
FHLMC = 44 days.

Source: Shearson Lehman Hutton Mortgage Securities.

dramatically accelerate principal return for 30-year pass-throughs, thereby substantially shortening their average lives.

Relative Value Analysis

Mortgage-to-Treasury yield spreads for 15-year pass-throughs behave in much the same manner as those of 30-year pass-throughs. For example, mortgage-to-Treasury spreads for current coupons in both sectors widened to approximately the same level—250 basis points—as mortgage funding pressure intensified in the summer of 1987 and gradually declined to the same level—100 basis points—as it eased. Figures 9.2–9.4 show mortgage-to-Treasury yield spreads for 15-year pass-throughs over selected intervals, based on data availability. (Because of their shorter maturity, 15-year pass-throughs are spread to the 7-year Treasury, whereas 30-year pass-throughs are spread to the 10-year Treasury.)

On the other hand, there are several important differences between 15- and 30-year pass-throughs. First, 15-year pass-throughs with coupons of 9.5 percent and below trade several points above comparable-coupon 30-year pass-throughs. Since the two securities offer equal coupon payments, the 15-year pass-through's higher dollar price lowers its yield to reflect its shorter maturity. This relationship reverses itself for coupons above 9.5 percent, since 15-year pass-throughs in this coupon range prepay substantially faster than their 30-year counterparts.

As a result, their prices compress well below those of comparable-coupon, 30-year pass-throughs. Second, holding all else constant, 30-year

FIGURE 9.2

Mortgage-to-Treasury Yield Spreads for 15-Year FNMA, FHLMC, and GNMA 8s*
(November 1986–March 1987)

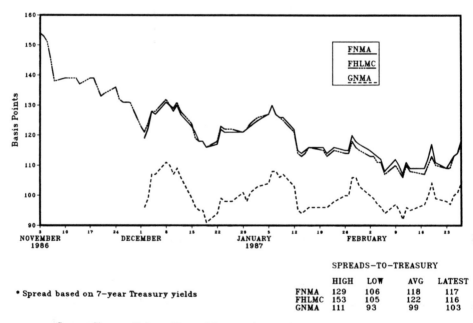

SPREADS-TO-TREASURY

	HIGH	LOW	AVG	LATEST
FNMA	129	106	118	117
FHLMC	153	105	122	116
GNMA	111	93	99	103

* Spread based on 7-year Treasury yields

Source: Shearson Lehman Hutton Mortgage Securities.

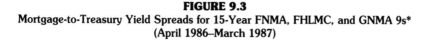

FIGURE 9.3
Mortgage-to-Treasury Yield Spreads for 15-Year FNMA, FHLMC, and GNMA 9s*
(April 1986–March 1987)

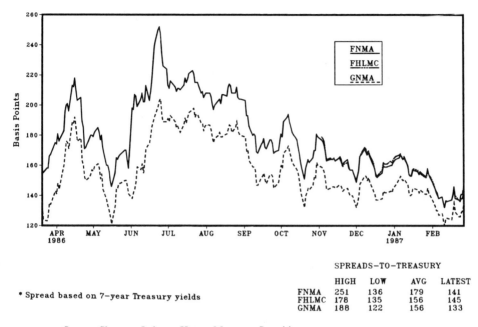

		SPREADS-TO-TREASURY		
	HIGH	LOW	AVG	LATEST
FNMA	251	136	179	141
FHLMC	178	135	156	145
GNMA	188	122	156	133

* Spread based on 7-year Treasury yields

Source: Shearson Lehman Hutton Mortgage Securities.

pass-throughs should command a wider spread to Treasuries than 15-year pass-throughs. Therefore, the yield spread between 30- and 15-year pass-throughs should exceed that between 10- and 7-year Treasuries. Investors demand the additional yield because of the longer duration and more volatile cash flows inherent in 30-year pass-throughs.

As market conditions change, however, the 30- to 15-year spread will widen or tighten to reflect investors' willingness to trade yield for potential price gains. For example, bullish mortgage investors prefer 30-year pass-throughs, relative to comparable-coupon 15-year pass-throughs, since their longer duration allows greater potential price appreciation during market rallies. (Bullish investors would, in general, prefer Treasuries, since they offer the greatest potential price appreciation in a market rally.) The 30- to 15-year yield spread would tighten under these conditions. In contrast, bearish mortgage investors prefer shorter-duration 15-year pass-throughs to minimize potential price losses in a market retreat. In this case, 15- to 30-year yield spreads would widen.

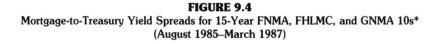

FIGURE 9.4
Mortgage-to-Treasury Yield Spreads for 15-Year FNMA, FHLMC, and GNMA 10s*
(August 1985–March 1987)

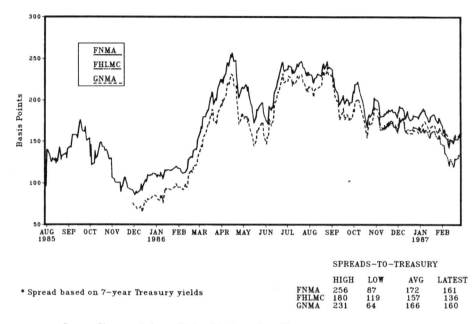

SPREADS–TO–TREASURY

	HIGH	LOW	AVG	LATEST
FNMA	256	87	172	161
FHLMC	180	119	157	136
GNMA	231	64	166	160

* Spread based on 7–year Treasury yields

Source: Shearson Lehman Hutton Mortgage Securities.

Liquidity

Because the 15-year market is relatively new, it is somewhat less liquid than the 30-year market. Nevertheless, it has become much more liquid over the past few years. In fact, the outstanding dollar volume of 15-year pass-throughs has grown tenfold since 1984 and now stands at almost $50 billion. Moreover, bid/ask spreads, a good indication of liquidity, have narrowed substantially since 1984. Bid/ask spreads for 15-year pass-throughs now compare quite favorably to those for 30-year pass-throughs, in view of the smaller 15-year market.

To some extent, these improvements reflect dealers' willingness to make a market in 15-year pass-throughs rather than fundamental changes in the market itself. The 15-year market still lacks some of the attributes that characterize a mature market such as the 30-year pass-through market. For example, investors do not understand 15-year pass-throughs as well as they understand 30-year pass-throughs.

Moreover, investors face liquidity problems among some of the higher-coupon issues. Since most 15-year mortgages were originated after 1984, the distribution of 15-year pass-throughs is skewed toward lower coupons. As Figure 9.5 shows, the bulk of outstanding 15-year pass-throughs—more than 70 percent—lies within the 8.5 to 9.5 percent coupon range. In fact, the generic (TBA) market for 15-year pass-throughs with coupons above 9.5 percent is virtually nonexistent. These coupons trade almost exclusively on a specified-pool basis.

Derivative Mortgage Securities

The various characteristics of 15-year pass-throughs just mentioned—in particular their greater sensitivity to changing mortgage rates and smaller duration drift relative to 30-year pass-throughs—should facilitate their use in constructing derivative mortgage securities. Nevertheless, illiquidity and higher dollar prices relative to 30-year pass-throughs have limited their use. For example, only a handful of CMOs have been collateralized by 15-year mortgage securities. Freddie Mac issued the first CMO backed by 15-year pass-throughs in

FIGURE 9.5
Outstanding Dollar Volume of 15-Year Pass-Throughs by Coupon
($ millions, March 1987)

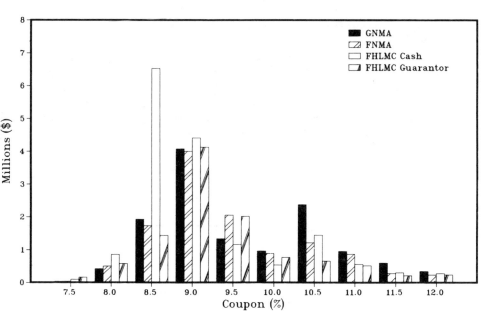

Source: Shearson Lehman Hutton Mortgage Securities.

April 1986. The total dollar volume of 15-year CMOs issued in the year since then, however, stands at only slightly more than $2 billion.

The 15-year mortgage appears to have a brighter future in the emerging market for stripped MBSs. Shearson Lehman Hutton issued the first stripped MBS using 15-year pass-throughs as the underlying collateral in February 1987. The $250 million offering was backed by FNMA 9s and was issued in the form of interest-only (IO) and principal-only (PO) securities. This innovative feature exploited both the relative cheapness of the collateral as well as its much more stable average life relative to 30-year pass-throughs.

In addition to CMOs and strips, 15-year pass-throughs could become the collateral of choice for REMICs issued with a senior/subordinated structure. Since the subordinated class services the senior class, the risk characteristics of the entire REMIC depend on the performance—particularly the default rates—of the mortgages used to collateralize the subordinated class. In view of lower default rates for 15-year mortgages, a REMIC with a subordinated class collateralized by these securities should receive a better rating than one collateralized by 30-year mortgages.

TYPICAL INVESTORS

Investors prefer 15-year pass-throughs to other comparable-quality intermediate-term securities because they offer higher yields. More important, 15-year pass-throughs have more stable average lives than comparable-coupon 30-year pass-throughs. Investors who shy away from 15-year pass-throughs typically do so because of their high dollar price relative to 30-year pass-throughs. Mutual funds and commercial banks, for example, are current yield buyers. Given the same coupon, they purchase the security with the lowest dollar price in order to maximize current yield. Therefore, these investors prefer 30-year over 15-year pass-throughs.

Insurance Companies

Insurance companies have always been and are likely to remain the largest buyers of 15-year pass-throughs. These securities offer high yields, good quality, and relatively stable average lives. Consequently, they satisfy several important portfolio needs. First, insurance companies are yield-oriented investors, and 15-year pass-throughs often offer much higher yields than comparable-quality securities in other sectors. Second, insurance companies are extremely sensitive to duration drift because they duration-match all liabilities. The majority of their liabilities are in the 7- to 10-year maturity range. Life and property/casualty portfolios have maximum maturities of 10–15 years, while most guaranteed income contracts (GICs) have slightly shorter durations, ranging from three to seven years. Therefore, 15-year pass-throughs are ideal investments: Their average lives correspond to the maturity of most insurance company liabilities, and they exhibit significantly less duration drift than comparable-coupon 30-year pass-throughs. Third, 15-year pass-throughs offer liquidity relative to other intermediate-term securities. In contrast to many high-quality corporates, 15-year pass-throughs are usually available in multiples of $1 million. Finally, 15-year pass-throughs offer insurance companies portfolio diversification. Most large companies have substantial holdings of corporate securities that meet their quality standards but cannot increase their holdings of these securities.

Savings Institutions

Savings institutions are already major investors in 15-year pass-throughs. Moreover, they are likely to expand their role in the 15-year mortgage market in 1989, both as originators and investors. The growing preference of borrowers for these shorter-duration mortgages offer savings institutions an opportunity to book high-quality assets while shortening duration. In addition, the 15-year pass-through market is more liquid than with other intermediate-term mortgage securities, such as CMOs.

GINNIE MAE MANUFACTURED HOUSING PASS-THROUGHS

Ginnie Mae is the only federal agency guarantor of securities issued against loans on manufactured homes. Ironically, Ginnie Mae **manufactured housing (MH) securities** are generally referred to as **"mobile home" securities** even though HUD specifically defines the difference between manufactured housing and mobile homes. In general, the term "manufactured housing" is used to describe living units produced off-site which have axles and wheels only for the purpose of transporting the unit to its designated site. The axles and wheels are then removed and the unit is affixed to the site, for all intents and purposes becoming immobile. Manufactured housing does not include modular housing or recreational vehicles, which are self-propelled or towed by passenger vehicles.

Ginnie Mae MH pools are designated by type with a letter suffix, as summarized in Table 9.5.

Each loan in the pool is to be secured by a MH unit or combination of a simultaneously acquired MH unit and developed manufactured home lot. For VA-guaranteed loans, the amount of the guarantee must be at least 50 percent of the loan balance at the time it is placed in the pool (35 percent for combination MH and property loans). There are two pool types: custom (minimum pool size $350,000) and multiple issuer ($250,000 minimum).

Mortgages of different maturities may be mixed in a pool provided that at least 50 percent of the component mortgages have an original term equal to the longest original term in the pool, and the shortest original term is within 60 months of the longest original term. Combination home unit and home lot loans are to have a minimum original term of 18 years. MH pass-throughs are classified into four types according to original term to maturity and type of underlying mortgage, as shown in Table 9.5.

Under the MH loan securities program, the issuer bears risks that exceed those on other Ginnie Mae pass-throughs. The additional risks involve contingencies associated with full collection in the event of default. The issuers–servicers are compensated for this additional risk with greater servicing fees, as follows.

Mortgages may carry mixed interest rates but must all produce the same pass-through rate when net of servicing fees. The servicing fee may run from 3 percent to 3½ percent on FHA loans and from 2¾ percent to 3¼ percent on VA loans (except for combination loans for which these ranges are 5 percent or lower).

CONVENTIONAL PASS-THROUGHS

Manufactured housing, or mobile homes, has been a source of low-income housing for many years. As an industry, the mobile home business has at times experienced severe losses as a result of widespread borrower defaults and losses on resale of the repossessed units. Despite these losses, MH has attracted lenders willing to accept credit risk in exchange for high yield and large servicing spreads.

The MH market, while relatively small compared to the residential

TABLE 9.5
Classification of MH Pass-Throughs

Type	Maturity (years)	Collateral
A	12	Single-wide homes
B	15	Double-wide homes
C	18	Combination single-wide homes and lots
D	20	Combination double-wide homes and lots

housing market, is significant in total dollar volume. Total outstanding MH debt is approximately $27.5 billion, with 10 percent securitized through Ginnie Mae guarantee programs. Residential mortgage debt outstanding is $1.5 trillion, with $500 billion or 33 percent in conforming securities (Ginnie Mae, Fannie Mae, and Freddie Mac).

Origination volume for MH declined recently in response to falling interest rates as potential buyers were able to qualify for site-built housing. However, as rates trend upward the universe of MH buyers will increase, and origination volume can be expected to rise again.

A recent development in the MH market is the securitization of nonconforming loans, which represent 90 percent of the total loans outstanding. This development mirrors the residential mortgage market where agency-backed securities gained investor acceptance before securities backed by nonconforming loans. In March 1987, Green Tree Acceptance, Inc., the largest single originator and servicer of MH loans, issued the first in a series of AA-rated pass-through securities backed by a geographically diversified pool of newly originated loans on manufactured homes. The securities were structured as monthly pass-throughs issued by a trust and supported by a limited guarantee of the servicer (Green Tree), in turn supported by letters of credit from two foreign banks, one with an AA debt rating. Although this transaction was privately placed, it is expected that the public market will ultimately be tapped.

Securities backed by MH receivables are recent additions to the cavalcade of securitized assets that can offer investors attractive and stable returns, short average lives, and acceptance credit protection.

Investment Characteristics of MH-Backed Pass-Throughs

Certificates for Manufactured Housing Contracts (MaHCS[sm], a service mark of Green Tree) are AA securities. They can be compared to similar MBSs in terms of yield, average life, and spread to comparable benchmark securities.

As with residential mortgages, nonconforming MH loans tend to prepay faster than conforming. However, in a comparison of residential mortgages to MH with the same underlying interest rate of approximately 13 percent, the MH loans were less likely to prepay. For example, the average CPRs in 1984, 1985, and 1986 for single-family GNMA 12.5s were 6.8, 9.6, and 36 percent, respectively, while the CPRs for GNMA MH 9.5s were 4, 6.6, and 8.9 percent. This apparent lack of response from MH owners to the dramatic drop in rates during this period could have been due to a variety of factors. Given the low average loan balance and shorter term of MH loans, even a large change in interest rates (200 basis points) would not lead to a significant change in monthly payments for the homeowner and therefore would create little incentive to refinance.

Loans on manufactured homes are often assumed to be identical to mortgage loans. The underlying collateral for each is a home, but the moveability of that home is misleading since about 95 percent of all manufactured homes do not move from their original sites. MH loans have the following characteristics:

- Fully amortizing loans, generally due-on-sale.
- Maturities ranging from 12 to 20 years.
- Current-coupon rates approximately 300 basis points higher than current-coupon mortgage rates.
- Average principal balances of approximately $18,000.

A technical distinction is often made that a loan on a manufactured home is "chattel" paper rather than an interest in real property like the mortgage on a site-built house. This difference leads to comparisons between MH loans and consumer receivables, which are also chattel. The distinction between chattel and mortgage paper affects the method of perfecting the lender's security in the collateral and the lender's remedy in default; in general, it is easier for a lender to foreclose on a chattel borrower than on a mortgagor. Both interests are secured by a promissory note backed by collateral, but chattel paper must be secured under the Uniform Commercial Code or state titling laws, whereas real property is subject to state estate laws.

The collateral securing the contracts is manufactured mobile homes rather than site-built residential homes. These assets depreciate rather than appreciate. Whereas a mortgage lender takes comfort in the fact that a borrower's home equity will generally grow over time due to loan amortization and property appreciation, the MH lender can anticipate a depreciated resale value of the unit in the event of a foreclosure. Equity buildup will not insulate the lender from losses in repossession. This effect is somewhat offset by the shorter-term loans and more rapid amortization of principal, yet the lender's best protection by far is quality underwriting and efficient servicing.

Credit Considerations

Securities backed by MH are rated by Standard & Poor's using the same kind of analysis employed for nonconforming mortgage loans. The two critical statistics for determining the level of credit enhancement required are loss severity and foreclosure frequency. Loss severity is the percentage of the outstanding balance recovered upon resale after repossession; foreclosure frequency is the percentage of a portfolio expected to go into foreclosure over its life. The product of these two numbers determines the level of loss coverage required to achieve an AA-rating level. For AA rating the agency assumes a lifetime foreclosure frequency and loss severity of 45 and 60 percent, respectively, yielding a loss-coverage level of 27 percent (.45 × 60). Thus, if one of every two loans defaults and there is a loss of $.60 on every $1 of defaulted principal, coverage will be provided for the investor. The comparable figures for AA-rated single-family residential securities are 10 percent foreclosure frequency and 40 percent loss severity, or a loss-coverage level of 4 percent. Clearly, the agency believes that the probable losses on MH loans will be greater than on mortgage loans, a supposition that is borne out by industry statistics (see Table 9.6).

The dramatically lower delinquency ratio for manufactured than for residential housing shows that servicers of MH loans are by necessity more active collectors of delinquent payments than residential servicers. A mobile home borrower, who is likely to have a low income, is less likely to regain current status than a delinquent residential borrower. This fact is reflected in higher foreclosure rates.

From a credit risk standpoint, the most important statistics are foreclosures and net losses, since the actual net losses on a foreclosure will determine the adequacy of the loss-coverage level established. Typical credit enhancement allows for advance of delinquent payments and defaulted principal up to an established level of disbursement net of any recoveries. Comprehensive data on net losses are difficult to locate. Using Fannie Mae as a proxy for residential housing, however, shows that losses on MH repossessions seem to be much higher than on residential housing.

The resale value of a mobile home, and hence the recovery rate on repossession, is estimated in a manner similar to that employed with used

TABLE 9.6
Comparison of Delinquencies, Foreclosures, and Net Losses for
Manufactured and Residential Housing
(percent of portfolio)

	Delinquencies		Foreclosures		Net Losses	
Year	MH (ABA)[a]	Residential (MBA)[b]	MH (GNT)	Residential (MBA)	MH (GNT)[c]	Residential (FNMA)
1982	2.82	5.52	1.09	0.57	—	0.01
1983	2.68	5.69	1.33	0.67	—	0.16
1984	2.44	5.65	1.27	0.68	1.24	0.32
1985	2.65	5.83	1.10	0.78	1.13	0.41
1986	2.97	5.56	1.10	0.90	1.64	0.38

[a]American Bankers Association.

[b]Mortgage Bankers Association.

[c]Green Tree statistics for nonconforming loans only.

Source: Shearson Lehman Hutton Mortgage Securities.

automobiles, for which the "blue book" value by model type is published by the National Automobile Dealers Association. This estimate of value can misstate the actual recovery because of temporal factors such as regional economic dislocation. An example would be the recent situation in oil-producing states such as Texas; repossession rates have been at a higher than normal level, and due to the glut of repossessed units the market for used units has been soft.

Credit-Rating Considerations

The available forms of credit enhancement for securitizing MH loans are comparable to those available for securitizing consumer and auto receivables transactions and include overcollateralization, limited guarantees by the issuer, and letters of credit. Unlike the residential mortgage market, MH has no insurers willing to provide pool insurance. This is primarily because of the drastic losses experienced by pool insurers during the early 1970s and early 1980s due to oversupply and concentrated losses in certain geographic areas. Also unlike the mortgage market, MH loans do not have primary mortgage insurance for homes with loan-to-value ratios in excess of 80 percent. The combination of usable credit enhancements mentioned above must provide all the required coverage for rating purposes.

The adequacy of this coverage can be assessed by comparing historical pool statistics to the proposed level of coverage and applying sensitivity analysis to varying levels of foreclosure frequency and loss severity. This sensitivity analysis could incorporate an investor's perception of such factors as geographic concentration and amount of used mobile homes in a particular pool. Furthermore, it is important for investors to assess not only industry statistics but also the record of the specific originator and servicers of the loans because there are quality differences.

The originator of the pool of loans backing the first AA-rated transaction, Green Tree Acceptance, currently has an annual foreclosure rate of approximately 1.6 percent and a loss severity of 30 percent. (An annual foreclosure rate of 1.6 percent would approximate a total foreclosure rate of 9.6 percent, assuming a six-year average life and cumulative net losses of approximately 5 percent.) A loss-coverage level of 24 percent was established for this program by the rating agency; this is adjusted downward over time to reflect paydowns and net losses.

A loss-coverage level and guarantee similar to that established for the MaHCS program would be sufficient to protect investors from principal losses under most scenarios (see Table 9.7). Up to the guarantee amount, these foreclosures would seem like prepayments to investors.

TABLE 9.7

Cumulative Net Losses (estimated) as a Percentage of Original Portfolio Balance
(assume 9% CPR, 12.74% WAC, 174-month WAM)

Loss Severity (%)	Years	30%	40%	50%	60%	70%
Annualized	3	5	7	9	11	12
foreclosure	5	8	10	13	16	19
frequency [a]	10	13	18	22	27	31
	20	19	26	32	39	45

[a] Percentage of portfolio outstanding.

Source: Shearson Lehman Hutton Mortgage Securities.

Comparison to Other Receivables-Backed Securities

MH-backed securities resemble receivables-backed securities in their required level of credit enhancements yet are closer to mortgage securities in average life and prepayment characteristics (see Table 9.8).

Future Developments

Multiclass securities backed by MH loans are now facilitated by a Treasury regulation enacted June 2, 1987, that qualifies them for election of REMIC status.

The securitization of MH loans can be expected to continue as portfolio holders seek to take advantage of securitization rather than sale in the less liquid whole-loan markets.

GRADUATED-PAYMENT MORTGAGES

Graduated-payment mortgages (GPMs) differ from standard, or level-pay, mortgages in that the monthly payments are not equal throughout the life of the loan. With the GPM, the payments are relatively low for the first few years and

TABLE 9.8

Comparison of MaHCS to Receivables-Backed Securities

	Approx. Term (mo.)	Approx. CPR (%)	Approx. Average Life (yr.)	Loss Coverage Required (AA)	Net Loss as % of Outstanding
MaHCS (Green Tree)	180	9–10	5–6	20–25	1–2
Auto receivables	36–60	12	2–4	5–10	.3–1
Credit-card receivables	18–24	NA	1–5	10–15	2–3
15-yr AA mortgage pass-throughs	180	6	7	4	.3–.4

Source: Shearson Lehman Hutton Mortgage Securities.

then increase in steps on specified anniversary dates. At the end of the graduation period the monthly payments level off at a significantly higher annual rate for the remaining life of the loan to its original maturity. The GPM was a creature of the high-interest-rate periods of the 1970s and 1980s and was created to provide affordable financing for homeowners who would have been unable to qualify for financing at the then high mortgage rates.

GPM Plans[2]

By changing the combination of graduation rate and graduation period, various types of GPMs with different levels of initial payments can be designed. For illustration, Figure 9.6 compares the payment stream and the unpaid principal balance of a fixed-rate level-payment mortgage and a Type III GPM loan per $1,000 of original principal amount. All mortgages have the same interest rate (13.5 percent) and amortization period (30 years). The five GPMs are as follows:

Type   I: a 5-year graduation period with a 2.5 percent graduation rate
Type II: a 5-year graduation period with a 5.0 percent graduation rate
Type III: a 5-year graduation period with a 7.5 percent graduation rate
Type IV: a 10-year graduation period with a 2.0 percent graduation rate
Type V: a 10-year graduation period with a 3.0 percent graduation rate

Two notable aspects of graduated-payment mortgages are shown in the upper panel of Figure 9.6. First, the initial payments of GPMs are lower than those of level-payment mortgages. After the graduation period, however, this relationship reverses. Second, the monthly payments of the GPM in the early years almost never cover the required interest payment on the loan. The difference between the monthly payment and the required interest is added, with interest, to the original principal balance—a process known as **negative amortization**. Consequently, the unpaid principal balance invariably rises during the graduation period rather than declining immediately, as in the case of a level-payment mortgage. It should be noted that GPMs do not necessarily involve negative amortization. At extremely low interest rates (4 percent or lower for the Type III GPM), the low initial payment *can* cover the required interest payment, and therefore no negative amortization is necessary. Moreover, when the graduation rate is rather small, negative amortization occurs only when interest rates are relatively high (at 8.5 percent or higher for the Type I GPM).

[2]This discussion of GPM plans is based on Joseph Hu, "Graduated-Payment Mortgage—An Alternative to Adjustable-Rate Mortgages," *Appraisal Review Journal*, Winter 1985.

FIGURE 9.6

Comparison of Payment Streams and Unpaid Principal Balances of a
Level-Payment Mortgage and Four GPMs* (first 10 years)

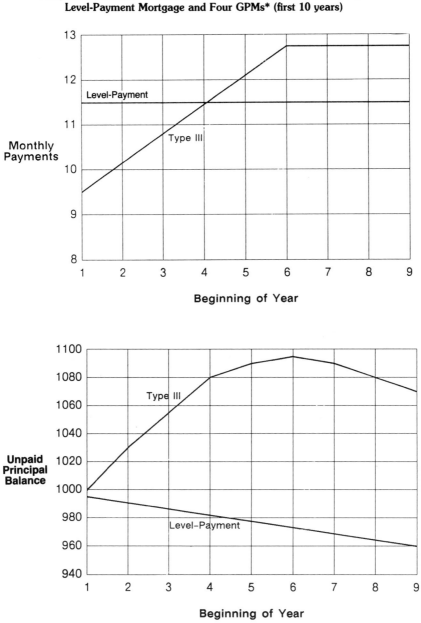

*Original mortgage loan amount: $1,000; interest rate: 13.5%.

The lower panel of Figure 9.6 compares the unpaid principal balance of a level-payment mortgage with those of the four GPM alternatives. For a GPM carrying a 13.5 percent interest rate, the unpaid principal balance peaks at the end of the graduation period—in other words, negative amortization lasts as long as the graduation period. In addition, the extent of the accumulation of the unpaid principal balance is inversely related to the level of the initial payment. At lower interest rates (below 10 percent for the Type III GPM), negative amortization *can* reach its maximum level before the graduation period is over.

The relationship between the initial payment and the unpaid balance provides a guideline to the design of a GPM. It is clear from Figure 9.6 that a GPM designed to help home buyers with a low initial payment carries the burden of a large unpaid principal balance after the graduation period. On the other hand, a conservatively designed GPM with a moderate accumulation of loan balance during the graduation period runs the risk of a cool reception by prospective borrowers because of its high initial payment. Currently, the most popular GPM is the Type III, which is a GPM with a 7.5 percent graduation rate and a five-year graduation period. Table 9.9 compares the monthly payment per $1,000 of principal for an 11.75 percent, five-year GPM to that of the level-payment mortgage with a payment that matches the initial payment of the specified GPM.

In view of the rising monthly payment and the growing unpaid principal balance of GPMs, two questions inevitably arise: (1) Can borrowers keep up with the scheduled increase in monthly payments? (2) Will house prices rise fast enough so that the loan-to-market-value ratio declines, or at least does not exceed the original ratio? Although there is no guarantee that the answers to

TABLE 9.9
Comparison of Monthly Payments and Unpaid Principal Balances
of a GPM versus a Level-Payment Mortgage

Year	*GNMA GPM 11.75%*		*GNMA 11.75%*	
	Beginning UPB	*Monthly Payment*	*Beginning UPB*	*Monthly Payment*
1	$1,000.00	$ 7.75	$1,000.00	$10.09
2	1,025.81	8.34	996.10	10.09
3	1,047.45	8.96	991.21	10.09
4	1,063.86	9.63	986.78	10.09
5	1,073.79	10.36	981.23	10.09
6	1,075.80	11.13	975.00	10.09
7	1,068.21	11.13	968.00	10.09

Initial LTV: 95%	Initial LTV: 95%
5 years later: 84%	5 years later: 76%
Refinancing at 9% mortgage rate	Refinancing at 9% mortgage rate
New monthly payment: $8.66	New monthly payment: $7.85
Savings: $2.47	Savings: $2.24

these questions will always be favorable, historical evidence instills optimism about the future patterns of income and housing prices.

The Ginnie Mae GPM Program

All GPM mortgages to be included in a Ginnie Mae pool must be insured by FHA (under Section 245 of the National Housing Act) and fall into one of two categories identified by the suffix GP or GT.

The GP suffix may apply to GNMA-I or -II programs and for mortgages on which monthly payments increase annually for no more than the first five years, which includes plans I through III.

The GT suffix applies only to GNMA-II and includes plans IV and V.

Minimum pool sizes are $500,000 for GNMA-I and -II custom pools and $250,000 for GNMA-II multiple-issuer loan packages.

The maximum servicing spread for GNMA-I GPMs is .5 percent and for GNMA-II, 1.5 percent.

10

Adjustable-Rate Mortgage Securities[1]

INTRODUCTION

Adjustable-rate mortgages (ARMs) are mortgage loans whose rates are reset periodically according an index linked to market interest rates. Although some adjustable mortgage loans were originated in the 1970s, ARMs first came into widespread use in the early 1980s. They were developed in response to the high and volatile interest-rate environment that followed the 1979 change in Federal Reserve operating policy. In addition, the 1982 deregulation of financial markets and the ensuing creation of money market mutual funds altered the liability structure of major mortgage lenders.

In particular, deregulation of the S&Ls and the introduction of federal agency-sponsored ARM purchase programs were the key to stimulating ARM loan production. The introduction of an ARM purchase program by Fannie Mae on June 25, 1981, followed by Freddie Mac's aggressive ARM purchase program beginning in 1982, gave impetus to the ARM origination market.

With deregulation of thrift deposits S&Ls were forced to compete with money market funds for deposits. The need to match volatile deposit-based liabilities with interest-rate–sensitive assets has been a priority for S&Ls since the FHLBB restructuring initiatives of 1981 and 1982 (see Chapter 1). At the same time, the federal agency ARM loan purchase programs provided a standardized program structure and a ready market for the ARM mortgage.

---

[1]This discussion of ARM securities is taken in large part from "A Guide to ARM Securities" by Wesley Edens and William Halapin, both Vice Presidents of Shearson Lehman Hutton.

Consumers overcame their reluctance to accept the interest-rate risk of an ARM with the early introduction of per-adjustment-internal and lifetime caps on the maximum interest rate or payment rate the borrower would have to pay. In addition, ARMs are characterized by relatively low initial, or "teaser," rates. Many ARM originators have a first-year rate 200–250 basis points below market yields for comparable fixed-rate loans. As a result, the home buyer is able to qualify for either a much bigger mortgage than would be possible with a standard fixed-rate loan or, in many instances, even to qualify for a mortgage. Since 1984, ARMs have represented between 40 and 60 percent of total residential loan originations (see Chapter 2, "The Whole-Loan Market").

For many lenders, floating-rate assets such as ARMs are attractive because their repricing frequencies can be designed to match the short maturities of their liabilities. Home borrowers are attracted to ARMs because the initial rate is often substantially below the interest rate on fixed-rate mortgages. Many lenders qualify borrowers on the low initial ARM rate, thereby greatly increasing the pool of potential home buyers (see Chapter 2).

Since 1983 over $500 billion in ARMs have been originated, compared with about $1 trillion for fixed-rate mortgage originations. Table 10.1 presents historical origination data comparing adjustable- and fixed-rate loan originations.

While about two-thirds of fixed-rate originations in the period 1983 through 1988 have been securitized, for two reasons only a small fraction of ARM originations have been used to collateralize securities. First, many ARM originators prefer to hold ARMs in their portfolios to match the duration of their short-term deposits and borrowings. For example, S&Ls hold about $250 billion of ARMs, more than 40 percent of their total residential mortgage holdings.

TABLE 10.1
Originations of One- to Four-Family Nonfarm Mortgage Loans
($ millions)

Year	Total Originations	FHA/VA	Total Conventional	Conventional ARMs	ARMs as a % of Total Conventional
1983	$ 201.9	$ 47.7	$ 154.2	$ 57.1	37%
1984	203.7	28.6	175.1	106.8	61
1985	243.1	44.0	199.1	99.6	50
1986	454.1	93.0	361.1	111.9	31
1987e	425.1	75.1	350.0	138.9	40
Total					
1983–87	$1,527.9	$288.4	$1,239.5	$514.3	41%
1988p	330	50	280	140	50

e = estimated; p = projected.
Source: HUD and Shearson Lehman Hutton.

Another reason for the lagging securitization of ARMs is the lack of standardization of the ARM loan structure. When ARMs were introduced there were dozens of types of loans with different adjustment periods, indexes, margins, and interest-rate caps. Such a variety made it difficult to aggregate a sizable amount of loans with identical characteristics for securitization purposes. More recently, there has been a movement toward a smaller number of more standard instruments, a direction encouraged by both Fannie Mae and Freddie Mac. In March 1986, Freddie Mac initiated a standardized ARM program by issuing PCs backed by constant maturity Treasury (CMT)-indexed ARMs. Freddie Mac continues to issue these securities, with $6 billion outstanding as of year-end 1987. In October 1987, Fannie Mae announced that it would begin a program to buy standardized ARMs based on a one-year constant maturity Treasury index and issue securities based on these ARMs. In mid-November, the agency said it would begin to buy ARMs based on the 11th District Cost of Funds Index. These developments should help to increase ARM issuance and provide greater liquidity in the securitized ARM market.

ARM STRUCTURAL CHARACTERISTICS

ARM loans and securities adjust to changing interest rates according to a formula tied to an index plus a margin—most ARMs have interest caps or payment caps, or both. A further common characteristic of newly issued ARM loans is an initial rate generally at or below the market yield value of the index plus margin.

Initial Rate

The **initial rate** is the mortgage interest rate that applies to the loan to its first adjustment interval. Most initial rates are now within 200 basis points of the index value in effect at the time of loan origination. This is particularly the case with ARM securities currently being issued under the federal agency guarantees and by the issuers of private pass-through ARM securities.

Indexes

Most ARMs are based on one of three types of indexes: yields on U.S. Treasury securities, cost of funds indexes (COFIs), and average mortgage rates. Treasury indexes include maturities of six months and one, three, and five years. COFIs include the FHLBB 11th District COFI and the National Median Cost of Funds at FSLIC-insured institutions. The most common average mortgage rate index is the average contract interest rate on conventional mortgage loans closed for purchasing previously occupied single-family homes from all major lenders. The coupon of an ARM is calculated by adding the margin to the index, subject to maximum and minimum coupon limits during the mortgage's life or in a defined period.

By far, the most common indexes for securities collateralized by ARMs are the one-year constant maturity Treasury and the 11th District COF.

The Constant Maturity Treasuries

The one-year **constant maturity Treasury (CMT)** index is based on the average yield of a range of Treasury securities adjusted to a constant maturity of one year. This yield is estimated from the Treasury's daily yield curve. The curve, which relates the yield on a security to its time to maturity, is based on the closing market bid yields on actively traded Treasury securities in the over-the-counter market. Five leading U.S. government securities dealers report these bond yields to the Federal Reserve Bank of New York. The index is computed on a weekly average, and the Federal Reserve Board calculates and publishes this yield in its weekly H-15 statistical release. The same process is employed for the three- and five-year CMT-based indexes.

11th District Cost of Funds Index

The **11th District Cost of Funds Index (COFI)** is based on the average cost of funds for member institutions of the 11th District of the FHLBB composed of California, Nevada, and Arizona. The index is computed by dividing monthly interest expense by average liabilities and multiplying by 12. It is released by the Federal Home Loan Bank of San Francisco at the close of business on the last business day of each month and refers to the preceding month. The interest rate on many ARMs indexed to the 11th District COF is adjusted monthly, with the rate at each reset based on the index three months prior to the reset date.

The 11th District COFI is calculated using liabilities of various maturities. Table 10.2 illustrates the composition of the 11th District COFI. Since the rates on long-term liabilities are locked in, the cost of these liabilities does not change as interest rates fluctuate. For this reason, index changes lag behind market rate changes. In periods of falling rates, the COFI tends to be above the one-year CMT, as was the case through most of the 1985–87 period. In technical terms, the flatter profile of the COFI means that it has less volatility than the Treasury index. Volatility, plotted in the lower panel of Figure 10.1, is a measure of how much an index fluctuated in a given period. The higher the number, the more the index fluctuated. (A volatility of 20 percent, for example, means that about two-thirds of the observations in the period lie within 20 percent of the average value for the period.) For the entire 1982–87 period, volatility for the COFI was below that of the one-year CMT. Volatility is an

TABLE 10.2
Components of 11th District Cost of Funds Index
(December 31, 1986)

Passbook accounts	5.4%
Transaction accounts	5.6
Money market deposit accounts	14.3
Fixed maturity, fixed rate	
Original maturity:	
6 months or less	23.7
6 months to 1 year	19.7
1 to 3 years	18.4
More than 3 years	10.3
Fixed maturity, variable rate	2.6
	100.0%

Source: Shearson Lehman Hutton and the Federal Home Loan Bank of San Francisco.

important determinant of the performance of ARM securities and is discussed in more detail in the section later in this chapter on ARM valuation and in mathematical terms in the appendix to this chapter (p. 283).

Margin

The **gross margin** is the yield spread, measured in basis or percentage points, by which the ARM loan rate is to exceed the index value. This is the rate paid by the homeowner. The **net margin** is the gross margin less the servicing spread. The cost of mortgage insurance and other securitization expenses is deducted to arrive at the net margin for securitized ARMs. The net margin plus the index rate is the rate passed through to the investor.

Reset Interval

The **reset interval** is the time period between adjustments in the ARM interest rate. The reset interval is generally the same for a given ARM. For example, the rate of a one-year ARM is reset annually and is adjusted up or down to the index value plus the margin. Because the ARM is reset at these predetermined intervals, the ARM market price is much less volatile than the price of a fixed-rate investment, although there is a risk that the ARM will become "capped out," as will be discussed below.

ARM Caps

ARM loans almost always carry a **cap** on the maximum percentage by which the interest rate and/or payment rate may change. Interest-rate–capped loans generally carry both a per-reset, or per-adjustment-interval, cap and a life-of-loan cap. Payment-capped loans generally do not have life-of-loan caps.

FIGURE 10.1
Constant Maturity 1-Year Treasury,
11th District Cost of Funds, Spread, and Volatility*
(monthly data from January 31, 1982 to December 31, 1987)

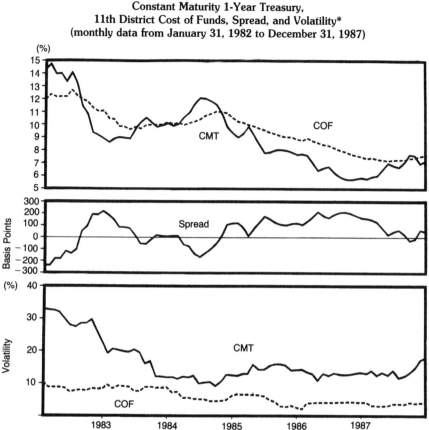

*Annualized standard deviation of monthly percent change in the rate of CMT and COF over a 12-month period, adjusted for serial correlation.

Source: Shearson Lehman Hutton Mortgage Securities.

Interest-Rate Caps

The most common **per-interval** interest-rate cap is 2 percent annually, which applies to both rate increases and decreases. For the mortgagor the ARM therefore has the same effect as if he had purchased an interest-rate cap. For example, consider a one-year ARM with an index value of 8 percent, a net margin of 175 basis points, and a 2 percent annual interest-rate cap. The index plus margin value is 9.75 percent. Assume that one year later the one-year Treasury yield has risen from 8 percent to 10.5 percent. The index plus margin value is now 12.25 percent. However, there is a 2 percent interest-rate cap—

therefore, the ARM interest rate may not increase higher than 11.75 percent (9.75 + 2 = 11.75). In this instance the effect is the same as if the investor had sold an interest-rate cap to the mortgagor, who holds the equivalent of an interest-rate cap to the investor at 11.75 percent. (Ginnie Mae ARM securities restrict the annual interest-rate cap to 1 percent.) The mortgagor thus saves the interest payments that would have been paid at any interest rate over 11.75 percent—and also deprives the investor of the same.

Life-of-Loan Caps

Most ARMs containing a per-interval interest-rate cap also have a **life-of-loan cap**—an absolute cap on the interest rate for the life of the loan. The life cap is sometimes stated as 5 percent, calculated from the initial rate as the base, but more often as a flat percentage, which is usually derived from the same calculation process. If the initial rate is set at a relatively low level, for example, below the index value, the life cap may impose a relatively low ultimate rate on the investor. To illustrate, suppose the index value at time of origination is 8 percent but the initial rate was set at 6 percent. A 5 percent life cap on a 6 percent initial rate would cap the loan out at 11 percent. Some ARMs provide for the life cap to be based on the index value, and a few base the life cap on the index plus margin.

Payment-Rate Caps and Negative Amortization

Many ARMs carry a payment cap instead of an interest-rate cap; a few have both types of caps. The **payment cap** restricts the maximum amount by which the monthly mortgage payment may increase at each adjustment interval. To understand the effect of the various caps, suppose interest rates rise 100 basis points. At the beginning of year 2, the index is 9.5 percent, and the index plus margin is 11.5 percent. Under the rate-cap structure, the mortgage rate would be limited to 10.5 percent because of the 2 percent rate cap. The monthly P&I payment necessary to amortize the loan at the 10.5 percent mortgage rate is $912.39. Under the payment-cap structure, the ARM rate is 11.5 percent, which would require a monthly payment of $986.80, but the increased monthly P&I payment is limited to $826.58. The interest component alone of an 11.5 percent coupon would be $951.09 on the $99,244 balance. With many, but not all, payment-capped loans, the difference is added back to the balance of the loan, resulting in negative amortization. If the payment-capped loan used for the example permits negative amortization, the unpaid interest is deferred and added to the outstanding balance. As a result of negative amortization, at the end of year 2 the outstanding balance would be $100,819.[2]

Interest-rate–capped loans never provide for negative amortization. Most

[2]Example provided by The First Boston Corporation, *The Valuation of Adjustable Rate Mortgages,* 1987.

payment-capped mortgages that take into account negative amortization stipulate that the negative amortization may not exceed some particular percentage of the original mortgage amount, for example, 125 percent. (Fannie Mae restricts negative amortization to 110 percent of the original loan.) There is also usually a requirement that the mortgage be recast every five years to adjust the monthly payment to fully amortize the unpaid principal balance (including any negative amortization) to the original maturity date of the loan (or in some cases to 40 years from the date of the loan). Recasting of the loan is sometimes called for earlier than the five-year period if negative amortization exceeds the allowable maximum (for example, 125 percent).

Negative amortization has been a cause of serious concern among ARM underwriters and investors because of the potential for the loan balance to increase to the point that the mortgage owed exceeds the market value of the house. Such an event could occur, for example, with a 95 percent original loan-to-value (LTV) loan on a house purchased for $100,000. The 95 percent LTV mortgage would be $95,000, but negative amortization could increase the mortgage balance up to 125 percent, or to $118,750. Thus, if for some reason home values did not increase, there could potentially be a credit problem.

Table 10.3 summarizes the characteristics of ARMs that are most commonly traded today.

FEDERAL AGENCY-BACKED ARM SECURITIES

All three federal agencies, Ginnie Mae, Fannie Mae, and Freddie Mac, offer ARM securities programs.

The Ginnie Mae ARM Security

What distinguishes the Ginnie Mae ARM from other ARMs is its form of guaranty, which is a U.S. government full faith and credit guaranty of the timely payment of P&I. Another distinction is that the Ginnie Mae eligible loan collateral is restricted to single-family residential home mortgages insured by FHA. The FHA mortgage collateral is significant because since FHA mortgages are fully assumable, the average life of a Ginnie Mae ARM might be longer than with ARMs collateralized by conventional loans.

In the reset percentage and frequency there are also differences between the Ginnie Mae ARM and other one-year ARMs. The Ginnie Mae reset is restricted by a 1 percent cap, whereas a 2 percent cap is typical of other ARMs. The reset frequency is annually, but Ginnie Mae has set only four yearly adjustment dates: the first day of January, April, July, and October. This schedule was set to allow originators time to accumulate large pools of loans with the same adjustment date. Ginnie Mae announces the allowable initial

TABLE 10.3
Characteristics of ARMs (percentage distribution)

	Fall 1986	Fall 1985	Fall 1984
Interest-Rate Index			
U.S. Treasury securities			
6-month bill	1	*	8
One-year CMT	45	64	49
Three-year CMT	11	7	9
Five-year CMT	*	2	2
FHLBB contract rate	11	15	12
Average cost of funds	28	11	18
Other	4	1	1
Payment-Adjustment Period			
6 months or less	8	3	5
One year	66	85	74
Three years	21	10	18
Five years	3	2	2
Other	2	*	*
Use of Borrower Protection Cap(s)			
Both adjustment-period and life-of-loan caps	97	90	88
No cap	1	4	4
Adjustment-period cap only	2	2	4
Life-of-loan cap only	*	4	4
Extent of Negative Amortization			
No scheduled negative amortization	97	96	91
Restricted negative amortization— 125% of loan amount	2	3	7
Unrestricted negative amortization	2	1	2

*Less than 1 percent.

Note: Components may not sum due to rounding.

Source: National Association of Realtors, Real Estate Finance Division, "Fall 1987 Residential Mortgage Finance Panel Survey."

rates that may be offered on the ARM, and the agency allows the margin over the index to be either 1 percent or 1.5 percent. Within these parameters Ginnie Mae ARM securities originators may offer various combinations of initial rate and index margin.

Fannie Mae

Fannie Mae was the first agency, in June 1982, to issue adjustable-rate pass-throughs, using California variable-rate mortgages (VRMs) as collateral.

In the summer of 1984, Fannie Mae began to issue securities backed by ARMs based on the more common indexes. Fannie Mae has been issuing ARM securities through its loan swap for MBSs program, permitting originators to exchange whole loans for securities guaranteed by Fannie Mae. In December 1987, Fannie Mae announced that certain ARMs could be included in specified Fannie Mae multiple-pool transactions (Fannie Mae Majors).

Through 1987, Fannie Mae had issued in excess of $14 billion in ARM securities based on a variety of indexes. The Fannie Mae securities with the highest issuance volume are based on the 11th District COFI ($10.6 billion issued), the one-year CMT index ($1.5 billion), and the National Median COFI ($1.1 billion).

Freddie Mac

Freddie Mac began issuing ARM PCs in March 1986. The agency accumulates the collateral for its Cash program ARM PCs by purchasing whole-loan ARMs from originators. It has been selling ARM PCs on an auction basis based on the one-year CMT through securities dealers. In the summer of 1987, Freddie Mac began issuing ARM PCs based on the one-year CMT through its Guarantor swap program.

The cycle of payments for MBSs is different for each security, depending upon the issuer of the ARM security. Table 10.4 illustrates the timing differences between the date the index is published and the date an investor receives the payment associated with the change for Fannie Mae and Freddie Mac securities. As the table indicates, an investor holding a Freddie Mac MBS receives the payment reflecting the latest adjustment 55 days after the interest rate has changed for the mortgagor. The holder of a Freddie Mac PC security receives the payment reflecting the latest adjustment 105 days after the interest

TABLE 10.4
Fannie Mae versus Freddie Mac Principal and Interest Payment Timeline

	August	September	October	November		December	
	1	1	1	1	25	1	15
Fannie Mae	Index published		Mortgage rates adjust	Borrower remits P&I[a]	MBS investor receives P&I		
Freddie Mac	Index published		Mortgage rates adjust	Borrower remits P&I[a]		PC investor receives P&I	

[a] November principal payment and October interest payment.
Source: Shearson Lehman Hutton.

TABLE 10.5
Ginnie Mae ARM
MBS Program Summary

Index	Weekly average yield on U.S. Treasury securities adjusted to a one-year CMT
Reset interval	Annual
Periodic caps[a]	Interest rate: 1.00%
	Payment: none
Lifetime cap[a]	5.00%
Pass-through margin	1.50%[b]
Index determination	Most recently published index 30 days prior to the interest-adjustment date for the pass-through
Collateral	Mortgages insured by the National Housing Act, Sections 203(b), 203(k), and 234(c)

[a]Interest-rate caps apply to both upward and downward movements in interest rates.
[b]A small number of Ginnie Mae ARM securities have margins of 1.00%.
Source: Shearson Lehman Hutton.

rate has changed for the mortgagor. Most pass-through securities payment cycles are structured like those of Freddie Mac.

Tables 10.5 through 10.8 summarize ARM securities associated with the federal agencies.

THE PRIVATE ARM MARKET

ARM loans may be purchased by investors in a variety of forms. From the investor's perspective, the transaction can be as simple as purchasing a Ginnie Mae ARM-backed security or as complicated as purchasing individual whole-loan ARMs.

TABLE 10.6
Freddie Mac CMT-Indexed ARM
PC Program Summary

Index	Weekly average yield on U.S. Treasury securities adjusted to a one-year CMT
Reset interval	Annual
Periodic caps[a]	Interest rate: 1.00% or 2.00%
	Payment: none
Lifetime cap[a]	6.00%
Pass-through margin	150–225 basis points
Index determination	Most recently published index 45 days prior to the interest-adjustment date for the pass-through
Collateral	One- to four-family, first lien ARMs meeting the requirements stated in the Freddie Mac Sellers' and Servicers' Guide

[a]Interest-rate caps apply to both upward and downward movements in interest rates.
Source: Shearson Lehman Hutton.

TABLE 10.7
Freddie Mac COF-Indexed ARM
PC Program Summary

Index	Monthly weighted average cost of savings, borrowings, and advances of the 11th District members of the Federal Home Loan Bank of San Francisco (11th District COF)
Reset interval	Monthly
Periodic caps[a]	Interest rate: set by Freddie Mac at origination Payment: changes annually with 7.5% limit
Lifetime cap[a]	125 basis points
Pass-through margin	Set by Freddie Mac at origination
Negative amortization	Limited to 125% of the original loan balance. If the limit is reached, the borrower's payment will be adjusted to fully amortize the loan within the remaining term.
Collateral	One- to four-family, first lien ARMs meeting requirements stated in the Freddie Mac Sellers' and Servicers' Guide

[a]Interest-rate caps apply to both upward and downward movements in interest rates. On each anniversary date divisible by 5, the payment is changed without regard to caps to fully amortize the loan within the remaining term.

Source: Shearson Lehman Hutton.

TABLE 10.8
Fannie Mae ARM
MBS Program Summary

Index	FHLB 11th District COF	One-year CMT	National Median COFI[a]
Reset interval	Monthly	Annual	Monthly
Periodic caps[b]			
Interest rate	None	2.00%	None
Payment cap	7.5%	None	7.5%
Lifetime cap[b]	5.00%[c]	Varies	Varies
Pass-through margin	1.25%[d]	1.50% to 2.25%	1.75%[d]
Negative amortization	Permitted[e]	None	Permitted[d]
Collateral	One- to four-family, first lien ARMs meeting requirements of Fannie Mae MBS Selling and Servicing Guide		

[a] The index is the National Median monthly COF ratio to institutions insured by the FSLIC, as computed from statistics tabulated and published by the FHLBB.

[b] Interest-rate caps apply to both upward and downward movements in interest rates.

[c] In a number of pools the maximum rate is established by the lender at origination.

[d] Indicated margins are for the majority of pools outstanding.

[e] Negative amortization is limited to 125% of the loan balance. If the limit is reached, the borrower's payment will be adjusted to fully amortize the loan within the remaining term. In a number of pools the amount of negative amortization is limited to 110% of the original loan balance.

Source: Shearson Lehman Hutton.

Whole Loans—100 Percent Participations

Until recently, originators sold most mortgages as whole loans. In a whole-loan transaction, the agreement between the buyer and seller normally includes only a limited number of representations and warranties. The recourse for the investor rests solely with the mortgage and with the real estate securing the mortgage. The investor takes physical possession of the legal documents and relies upon the seller to service the mortgage.

In an attempt to facilitate whole-loan sales, the mortgage industry developed a sales vehicle known as the **100 Percent Participation**. The concept evolved out of the thrift industry's practice of selling fixed-percentage interests in groups of mortgages. Purchasers of fixed-percentage interests received participation certificates representing their ownership of the mortgages. While 100 Percent Participation represents ownership of the whole loan rather than a fractional interest of it, the ease of execution of a participation sale still applies. Compared with a whole-loan transaction, the investor receives a participation certificate rather than legal documents for an individual loan. The legal documents, however, are held by an independent third-party custodian on behalf of the investor. Table 10.9 summarizes the typical terms of a whole-loan ARM.

Private Pass-Through ARM Securities

Private pass-through ARM securities are issued through more formal structures than either whole loans or participations. The usual issuance vehicle for MBSs is a grantor trust, defined by the organizing document under which the trust is formed. The trust indenture structures the trust composition, the duties of the parties involved in the trust, and the responsibilities of the trustee.

In a standard MBSs transaction, the trust consists of the mortgage loans, the pooling and servicing agreement, the custodial agreement, all pool and hazard-insurance policies, and a collection account. Investors in MBSs own a certificate that evidences pro-rata ownership of the mortgages in the trust.

A rated MBS includes cash flows from the mortgages in the trust, along with the insurance policies or other enhancements which provide sufficient assurance to the investor that payments of P&I will be made on the security. A MBS with a high rating provides greater assurance of payment than one with a low rating.

An increasingly popular form of mortgage pass-through security has a senior/subordinated structure as the form of credit enhancement. The level of subordination is directly linked to the quality of the underlying mortgage pool, which the rating agencies ultimately determine. This structure is used for the

TABLE 10.9
ARM Whole Loan
Summary of Terms

Pool balance	$25,000,000
Weighted average gross coupon	8.750%
Weighted average net coupon	8.125%
Current-coupon range	8.375% to 9.625%
Weighted average maturity	340 months (330–355 range)
Maximum original loan amount	$300,000
Minimum current loan amount	$125,000
Index	Weekly average yield on the one-year CMT
Weighted average time to next roll date	6 months
Net margin	200 basis points
Average loan amount	$175,000
Annual cap	2% per annum
Lifetime cap	Net ceiling rate of 14.00%
Property types	80% SFD, 20% Fannie Mae-approved condos
Property locations	25% CA, 20% WA, 10% VA, 10% MD, 5% PA, 2% or less in other states
Owner occupied	100%
LTV	Loans in excess of 80% are insured on amounts over 75% until balance is reduced below 80%; 95% LTVs have 25% coverage
Servicing	MBS: pass-through of P&I on 18th day of the month

Source: Shearson Lehman Hutton.

securitization and sale of conventional, nonconforming mortgage loans. The subordinated interests and other sources of cash flow ensure that the senior interests receive a complete share of mortgage pool cash flow. The ultimate exposure of the subordinated interest holder is limited to the initial principal balance of the subordinated interest.

The subordinated amount substitutes for the several tiers of credit enhancement typically provided by third parties in a standard, rated pass-through. The credit enhancements include pool insurance policy or a letter of credit, special-hazard insurance, bankruptcy insurance, and fraud coverage. The subordinated amount can be reduced over time based on the actual losses suffered by the pool through delinquency and foreclosure as well as on the decreasing credit risk associated with a seasoned pool of mortgages. Table 10.10 summarizes the terms of a typical AA-rated private ARM security.

TABLE 10.10
ARM AA Pass-Through
Summary of Terms

Pool balance	$100,000,000
Ratings	AA (S&P and/or Moody's)
Initial pass-through rate	7.5%
Net margin	175 basis points
Master servicer	Sample federal mortgage company
Originator	Sample federal S&L
Minimum original loan amount	$300,000
Minimum current loan amount	$125,000
Index	One-year CMT
Weighted average time to next roll date	7 months
Average loan amount	$160,000
Annual cap	2%
Lifetime cap	7.5%
Property types	Single-family
Property locations	25% CA, 25% DC, 25% MA, 10% NY, 15% NJ
Owner occupied	100%
LTV	80%
Credit enhancement	(1) Pool insurance policy provided by the sample federal mortgage company
	or
	(2) Subordination of 8.50% of the initial aggregate principal balance of the mortgage loans

Source: Shearson Lehman Hutton.

ARM VALUATION

Factors Affecting ARM Security Valuation

An ARM security coupon changes at each reset date to reflect market-rate changes. If the rate on the adjustable instrument were reset to reflect market rates each time rates changed, if there were no restrictions on rate changes, and if the instrument had no default risk, the price of the security would always be at par. In reality, ARM securities do not meet these idealized conditions. For example, most ARMs have interest reset dates at fixed intervals—every six months, one year, or three years. In addition, almost all ARMs have interest-rate ceilings and floors both at each reset date and over the life of the loan. Finally, ARM securities exhibit varying degrees of default risk. For these reasons, in order to be priced at par, the ARM security must yield more than a comparable-maturity Treasury security. Alternatively, an ARM security with a stated margin that is not enough to compensate for the differences from the expected Treasury yield will be priced at less than par.

The mortgage characteristics most important in determining the price of an ARM security are the interest margin over the index rate, caps, prepayment rates, the volatility of the interest-rate index, and the initial discount from the formula rate. Given these factors, the ARM security price is determined by the yield or net effective margin investors require to purchase the security.

Net Effective Margin

Returns on fixed-rate instruments are quoted as yields to maturity. For example, at the close on February 26, 1988, the 8⅝ coupon Treasury maturing in 1995 had a yield to maturity of 7.94 percent and a price of 103.50. The yield calculation takes into account the fact that the security was trading slightly above par, and this premium is amortized over the life of the instrument. If the security is held to 1995, the annualized yield is 7.94 percent. If the security is sold before maturity, the total yield is uncertain because the selling price may differ substantially from the initial price.

Performance of a non-Treasury security is often judged by the amount of basis-point yield spread over a Treasury security with a comparable average life. For instance, on February 26, the current-coupon Ginnie Mae was quoted as having a yield of 143 basis points above the 10-year Treasury. This means that if both the 10-year Treasury and the Ginnie Mae had an average life of 10 years, the Ginnie Mae would have an annualized yield of 143 basis points more than the Treasury security.

For an adjustable-rate security there is no equivalent for the yield to maturity of the fixed-rate security. Instead, since the coupon changes at each reset date, the annualized yield to maturity is a function of future market rates. An expected yield to maturity can be computed using implied forward rates from the yield curve.

Is there a standard of performance for an ARM security similar to the spread off the Treasury curve for fixed-rate securities? A yield to maturity cannot be calculated because the future path of short-term rates is not known. However, the relationship of the short-term yield of the ARM security to an index rate is known. For this reason, yields of ARM securities are discussed in terms of margins or spreads to a specified index rate. For example, one prevalent ARM security is backed by mortgages adjusted annually to 175 basis points over the one-year CMT. If the rate on the mortgages were, in fact, always 175 basis points above the Treasury and the security were priced at par, the investor would realize a margin or spread of 175 basis points.

The mortgages backing ARM securities often do not yield the stated margin over the index because of caps on interest adjustments and below-market initial rates. These factors were described in "ARM Valuation." In comparing relative values on ARM securities, a measure known as **net effective margin (NEM)** is used. NEM is the difference between the yield obtained by holding the adjustable instrument and that obtained from holding the security on which the index is based. The NEM over the life of the loan is the average of the NEMs for each period between rate resets.

For a freely floating security, with no restrictions on rate movements, the NEM is simply equal to the stated margin. ARM-backed securities with interest-rate caps, infrequent adjustment periods, below-market initial rates, and uncertain prepayments may have NEMs that differ significantly from the stated interest margin. These factors account for the fluctuating NEM on ARM securities as interest rates change.

If one of the ARM structural characteristics is varied while the others remain constant, we can predict the effect on either the price of the ARM or the NEM by evaluating the impact of this change on future cash flows of the underlying mortgages. Holding the NEM constant, we see that if the change reduces the expected cash flow, then the price of the security will fall; if it increases the expected cash flow, the price will rise. Holding all of the mortgage factors constant and changing the assumption about the NEM will also alter the price of the ARM security. The higher the NEM required by investors, the lower the price of the ARM security.

How will each of the factors just discussed affect the price of the security? This is a difficult question because the determination of price depends upon forecasting up to 30 years of cash flows, which in turn depends on the course of interest rates and prepayments. The following sections of this chapter focus on methods of ARM valuation.

Effects of Mortgage Characteristics on ARM Security Prices

Interest-Rate Caps and Volatility

The presence of interest-rate caps raises the possibility that, at some future reset date, the interest rate received by investors will be less than the expected return. In order to equate the actual return with the expected NEM, the price of the ARM security must fall. The greater the likelihood that the interest rate on the underlying mortgages will reach a cap rate, the higher the required NEM and, therefore, the lower the price of the security. Interest-rate caps could also have a favorable effect on cash flows if the caps prevent the mortgage rate from falling below a floor that is above the index rate plus margin rate on the ARM.

The probability that the mortgage rate will hit a ceiling or floor cap depends on the volatility of the interest rate used as the index and the range of rates allowed by the caps. Measurement of interest-rate volatility is discussed in detail in the appendix to this chapter. Very wide interest-rate–cap limitations coupled with a low-volatility index rate mean that the caps are less likely to affect the cash flows and the price of the ARM security. On the other hand, caps with low or tight margins and a highly volatile index suggest that caps are likely to be binding with greater frequency.

Figure 10.1 shows the historical volatility of two commonly used indexes for ARM rates, the one-year CMT and the 11th District COF. As the figure shows, the volatility of the one-year CMT has historically been much greater than that of the 11th District COF. Two percent annual and 5 percent lifetime caps are less likely to affect the future cash flow of ARMs linked to the COF than to the Treasury indexes. The importance of interest-rate caps is highly dependent on the index used to set the ARM rate.

Initial Discount

The amount by which the initial rate is discounted below the formula mortgage rate often has a significant impact on the initial price of the ARM security. Such a discount clearly reduces the cash flow in the first period to the reset. For this reason alone, the price of an ARM security collateralized by ARM mortgages with a discounted initial rate must be less than that of a security collateralized by fully indexed mortgages. In addition, the initial discount may affect cash flows in subsequent periods if the annual interest caps do not allow the mortgage rate to "catch up" to the rate on mortgages with no initial discount. Thus the interaction between the initial discount, rate caps, and index volatility is important in the determination of the ARM security price.

Impact of Prepayments

A shift in prepayment speeds on uncapped ARMs with no initial-rate discount and a required net margin equal to the index margin should not significantly affect the price of an ARM security. The security would be priced close to par, and prepayments can be invested at a market rate that is roughly equivalent to the mortgage rate. If the security is priced at a large discount, an increase in prepayments would have a favorable effect on the total return; a slowdown in prepayments would have an adverse effect.

Prepayment speeds are likely to reach extreme levels when interest-rate caps are effective. Prepayments would be expected to slow when the mortgage rate is capped out at a ceiling rate because the borrower is in effect borrowing below the market. When the mortgage rate is capped at a floor, prepayments would likely accelerate, since borrowers could refinance at lower market rates.

Sensitivity of Net Effective Margins and Prices to Changes in Interest Rates, Prepayments, and Index Volatility

Changes in three factors could affect the NEM and price of an ARM-backed security: (1) market interest rates, (2) prepayments, and (3) index volatility. These factors will be considered separately to measure the marginal effect of changing each of the key assumptions needed to compute prices and NEMs.

Interest Rates

Table 10.11 shows the effect of changing interest rates on the NEM of a Freddie Mac ARM security with an 8.50 percent coupon reset annually at a margin of 175 basis points above the one-year CMT. The top row of the table gives the projected interest-rate change in the one-year CMT (from an assumed current level of 6.63 percent); the figures in the left column are the months that encompass a 100 basis-point interest-rate change. Each entry in the table shows the NEM for a given interest-rate scenario. For example, a rise in the one-year CMT of 300 basis points over an 18-month period (100 basis points every 6 months) gives a NEM of 1.05.

In a scenario of constantly rising interest rates, the NEM will always fall because the adjustment of the ARM rate will lag behind market rates. Conversely, in an environment of falling rates, the NEM will be rising. The more rapid the increase in rates, the greater the negative impact on the NEM because a quick jump in the index rate increases the likelihood that the caps on the underlying mortgages will become effective.

Impact of Interest-Rate Change on Prepayments

Changing prepayment speeds affect NEMs under rising or falling interest-rate scenarios. The pattern of interest-rate changes with respect to changes in the pass-through rate determines the impact of prepayments on the NEM. When rates rise and then level off (as in the right half of the lower part of Table 10.11), faster prepayments are generally undesirable because more of the cash flow is at below-market rates. In the example in Table 10.11, if rates rise by 200 basis points in 2 months, the one-year CMT will be 8.63 percent and the fully indexed mortgage rate will be 10.50 percent. However, until the rate resets after 12 months, the pass-through rate continues to be 8.50 percent. After 12 months, the pass-through rate will be reset to the fully indexed level of 10.50 percent. With high prepayments in the first year, less of the collateral will earn a market rate of interest, hence the NEM will be lower. As shown in the table, a 6 percent CPR results in a NEM of 1.20; a 24 percent CPR NEM is .59.

In some extreme circumstances, higher prepayments will result in a higher NEM in a rising interest-rate environment. If the mortgage rate is continually being capped out and fails to reach the fully indexed rate, faster prepayments may raise the NEM. Also, if interest rates are flat and then rise, or rise at an accelerating rate, faster prepayments could increase the NEM.

All of these computations have so far assumed that the interest-rate scenario is given and will not deviate from the assumed path. In reality, interest rates may fluctuate widely around an expected path. Thus, even if the yield curve shows that interest rates are expected to rise by only 100 basis points in the next year, there is some probability that interest rates will rise or fall by much more than 100 basis points. This probability, known as interest-rate

TABLE 10.11

Static-Yield Scenario, ARM Net Effective Margin Analysis

Model Assumptions	
Price	101.00%
Initial index rate (CMT)	6.63%
Financing attributes:	
Finance reset interval	Monthly
Months in first reset	26
Security attributes	
Pass-through rate	8.50%
Adjustment margin	1.75%
Life cap	4.00%
Adjustment cap	2.00%
Reset period	Annual
Interest-free delay days	44
Months to first reset	12

Total Interest-Rate Change (CPR = 12%)[a]

Month	−300	−200	−100	0	+100	+200	+300	+400
1	2.04	1.75	1.57	1.38	1.19	1.01	0.70	0.39
3	1.90	1.69	1.55	1.38	1.21	1.08	0.86	0.66
6	1.71	1.59	1.53	1.38	1.23	1.18	1.05	1.01
12	1.62	1.56	1.48	1.38	1.28	1.20	1.13	1.08

Total Interest-Rate Change (CPR = 6%)[a]

Month	−300	−200	−100	0	+100	+200	+300	+400
1	1.98	1.76	1.62	1.49	1.34	1.20	0.96	0.71
3	1.87	1.71	1.61	1.49	1.35	1.26	1.08	0.92
6	1.73	1.64	1.59	1.49	1.37	1.33	1.23	1.19
12	1.68	1.62	1.56	1.49	1.41	1.34	1.28	1.23

Total Interest-Rate Change (CPR = 24%)[a]

Month	−300	−200	−100	0	+100	+200	+300	+400
1	2.14	1.72	1.43	1.15	0.86	0.59	0.18	(0.24)
3	1.91	1.61	1.41	1.15	0.89	0.70	0.41	0.16
6	1.62	1.47	1.37	1.15	0.93	0.85	0.69	0.64
12	1.48	1.40	1.30	1.15	1.00	0.89	0.82	0.77

[a] The horizontal axis indicates interest-rate changes (in basis points). The vertical axis indicates the number of months between each 100 basis points of interest-rate change; that is, for month 12, a 300 basis-point change in interest rates would occur over three years.

Source: Shearson Lehman Hutton.

volatility, is discussed further in the next section. However, volatility does have a bearing on the impact of prepayments on NEMs. Faster prepayments shorten the life of an ARM security and make it less likely that an interest-rate ceiling or floor will become relevant.

With an upward-sloping yield curve, interest rates are expected to rise, and a ceiling on the ARM collateral is more likely to be reached than a floor. In this context, faster prepayments are thus desirable because they reduce the amount of collateral that could be capped at a ceiling rate. A 6 percent CPR gives a weighted average life (WAL) of 5.5 years for the Freddie Mac security described in Table 10.12. Increasing the CPR to 12 percent, 18 percent, and 24 percent gives a WAL of 4.5 years, 3.7 years, and 3.0 years, respectively.

The interaction of prepayments, interest-rate volatility, annual and lifetime rate ceilings and floors, and interest-rate expectations is complex, and a more elaborate model incorporating prepayments is needed to accurately calculate NEMs.

Index Volatility

The spread-sheet approach to ARM evaluation discussed so far assumes the projected interest-rate path occurs with certainty. A more sophisticated model is needed to incorporate interest-rate volatility. Given an expected interest-rate path and an expected volatility around that path, an ARM pricing model can calculate the price of a one-year CMT ARM for a specific NEM or, alternatively, compute the NEM for a specified price. To illustrate the function of an ARM pricing model, the Shearson Lehman Hutton (SLH) ARM pricing model is described in the following paragraphs.

The SLH model works by simulating random interest-rate paths and computing a discounted stream of monthly mortgage payments based on the simulated rates. The price and NEM are based on the average of the discounted payment streams over several hundred simulations. In any month, the average interest rate over all of the simulations is equal to a projected interest rate, with a standard deviation equal to projected volatility. The projected interest rate could be based on forward rates, set equal to the current index rate, or set to a specific forecast.

The more volatile the index, the greater the probability that the mortgage rate will hit a ceiling or floor. With an upward-sloping yield curve, it is more likely that the interest rate will hit a ceiling than a floor. Even with a flat yield curve, there is an upward bias to rates in the SLH ARM pricing model. The reason is that simulated interest rates are constrained to be between 2.5 percent and 25 percent. As long as the initial index rate is below 13.75 percent [(2.5 + 250)/2], there will be an upward bias to rates and a greater likelihood that a ceiling rather than a floor will be reached in any given period. This means that rising volatility will result in a lower price given a fixed NEM.

Table 10.12 shows results of simulations for the FHLMC 7.25 percent coupon ARM security under two interest-rate assumptions. The table illustrates the effect of rising interest-rate volatility on price, holding all other factors constant.

In the first column, the one-year CMT rate was assumed to be 6.75

TABLE 10.12
Effect of Volatilty Changes on 7.25% FHLMC ARM Security

Volatility (%)	Price with Upward-Sloping Yield Curve[a]	Price with Flat Yield Curve[a]
0	98.78%	99.00
5	98.64	99.00
10	98.19	98.93
15	97.40	98.70
20	96.89	98.36
25	96.35	97.97
30	95.89	97.57
35	95.48	97.16
40	95.10	96.75
45	94.72	96.35
50	94.37	95.96

[a]Assumes 12% CPR, 2–6% interest-rate adjustment caps, and a NEM of 150 basis points.

Source: Shearson Lehman Hutton.

percent, projected to rise to 9 percent over a 36-month period. (This assumption was based on the shape of the Treasury yield curve in the first week of November 1987.) As expected, when volatility increases (holding the NEM constant), the price falls. An increase in volatility of 5 percent—from 15 percent to 20 percent—lowers the price by about one-half point. With a flat yield curve, volatility has a slightly less negative effect on price, as shown in column 2 of Table 10.12. An increase in volatility from 15 percent to 20 percent reduces the price about one-third of a point.

THE SLH ARM PRICING MODEL

Shearson Lehman has developed two computer models to describe the performance of an ARM. One uses a net effective margin for an adjustable-rate instrument given a specified degree of volatility. The other employs specific net effective margins under a discrete series of interest-rate movements.

The scenario analysis in Table 10.11 was developed from the static-yield scenario model. This model, with specific inputs including collateral and security characteristics and financing attributes, calculates a net effective margin for discrete changes in interest rates. The analysis in Table 10.12 was developed from a model that generates NEMs based on degrees of interest-rate volatility. Volatility is a measure of how much an index fluctuated in a given period. A higher volatility number means more index fluctuation. A volatility of 10 percent means that approximately two-thirds of the observations are within 10 percent of the average value for the period.

ACCOUNTING CONSIDERATIONS—FASB 91

Overview

The Financial Accounting Standards Board (FASB) Statement No. 91, "Accounting for Nonrefundable Fees and Costs Associated with Originating or Acquiring Loans and Initial Direct Costs of Leases" (FASB 91), established the accounting principles for nonrefundable fees and costs associated with lending, committing to lend, or purchasing a loan or group of loans. FASB 91 also addresses the accounting provisions for discounts and premiums associated with the purchase of debt securities. FASB's goal was to eliminate the different accounting treatments for similar lending transactions, particularly accounting for loan fees and costs, among finance companies, banks, and thrift institutions.

Accounting Provisions

Purchased Debt Securities

FASB 91 requires that premiums and discounts related to purchased debt instruments, such as ARMs, be amortized using the interest method. The amortization should be applied in the same manner as deferred fees and costs for loans originated by a financial institution.

Accounting for Purchases and Sales of Loans, Including Participations

An investor's initial investment in a purchased loan or group of loans is the amount paid to the seller plus any fees paid or less any fees received. Usually the initial investment differs from the related principal amount (par). This difference must be recognized as a yield adjustment over the life of the loan. All other costs, such as additional due diligence procedures performed by the purchaser, must be expensed as incurred.

Amortization of Deferred Fees and Costs

Net deferred fees and costs are to be recognized using the interest method. The objective is to arrive at a constant effective yield on the net investment in the loan over its term. The required amortization is the difference between the periodic contractual interest rate and the amount computed by applying the effective yield to the net investment on the loan. With respect to discounts related to purchased instruments, or, in the case of ARMs, loans purchased with "teaser" rates, discounts are amortized using the interest method.

Regulatory Accounting Considerations

Regulatory accounting procedures (RAP) include accounting regulations and practices that financial institutions must follow in filing periodic financial reports with their governing regulatory agencies. RAP requires commercial banks to account for loan fees and related costs for domestic lending activities in accordance with Generally Accepted Accounting Procedures (GAAP); therefore, FASB 91 does not present any conflicts.

FSLIC-insured institutions recognize loan fees for RAP purposes up to a certain amount at the time of origination, which is prohibited by FASB 91. Unfortunately, these differences are likely to continue.

Differences between RAP and GAAP reported numbers are increasingly important in the current environment as more thrifts seek public financing and accordingly must comply with GAAP for external financial reporting. The FHLBB is now more frequently conforming RAP with GAAP and is expected to adopt new measures to conform RAP with GAAP, including FASB 91.

APPENDIX

Volatility

While there are many ways to measure volatility, it is defined here as the annualized standard deviation of continuously compounded daily percentage changes in the one-year CMT over a 20-trading-day period, adjusted for autocorrelation.

The following example illustrates this point in mathematical terms. Given the interest-rate time series:

$$R_1, R_2, R_3, \ldots, R_{t-1}, R_t, R_{t+1}, \ldots \tag{1}$$

The continuously compounded daily change is written as:

$$ln(R_2/R_1), \ ln(R_3/R_2), \ \ldots, \ ln(R_{t-1}/R_{t-2}), \ ln(R_t/R_{t-1}),$$
$$ln(R_{t+1}/R_t), \ \ldots \tag{2}$$

There is generally a trend movement, or autocorrelation, associated with this series. This means that there is some degree of dependence from day to day in percentage changes. Equation (3) expresses this relationship mathematically:

$$\ln(R_t/R_{t-1}) = c\ln(R_{t-1}/R_{t-2}) + e_t, \quad -1 < c < 1 \qquad (3)$$

$$e_t = \ln(R_t/R_{t-1}) - c\ln(R_{t-1}/R_{t-2}) \qquad (4)$$

This equation is first-order autoregressive with c the coefficient of autocovariance and e_t the stochastic disturbance, or random shock.

In order to measure the volatility of the random-shock component of series (2), we need to remove the autocorrelated components from the original percentage-change series. We then can measure the annualized standard deviation of the random-shock series on a moving 20-business-day basis. Each point on Figure 10.2 corresponds to the volatility of the one-year CMT for the immediately preceding 20-day period.

FIGURE 10.2
Annualized 20-Day Volatility of 1-Year Treasury
(daily data from January 31, 1980 to February 5, 1988)

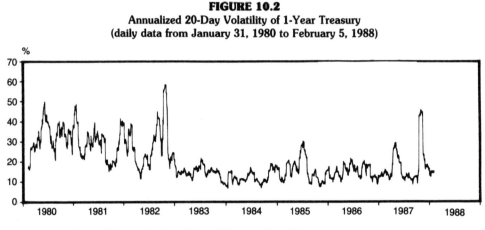

Source: Shearson Lehman Hutton Mortgage Securities.

11

Multifamily and Project Loan Securities[1]

INTRODUCTION

Multifamily loans are usually represented by conventional mortgages on multifamily rental apartments and may also be FHA-insured or HUD-guaranteed. The term **project loan** is used primarily to refer to FHA-insured and HUD-guaranteed mortgages on multifamily housing complexes, but includes as well nursing homes, hospitals, land development, retirement centers, and other types of development. Both federally insured and conventional multifamily and project loan securities are actively traded in the secondary market today. The predominant forms of conventional multifamily loan security traded in the MBSs market are those packaged under the Freddie Mac multifamily PC program. Many FHA-insured project loan securities are issued under the Ginnie Mae MBSs program, but some FHA-insured projects are also traded without the Ginnie Mae guaranty, particularly those sold by Ginnie Mae out of its Tandem plan portfolio.

High yields, call protection, and agency guarantees have contributed to growing investor interest in multifamily MBSs. These securities, traded in a large and active market encouraged by federal involvement in housing, provide an attractive alternative to other mortgage instruments and long-term corporate bonds. FHA insurance and co-insurance programs and Fannie Mae purchase programs have helped to standardize and increase the quality of multifamily

---

[1]This chapter is derived in large part from Shearson Lehman Hutton, *Multifamily Mortgage-Backed Securities: An Overview*, August 1987; prepared by Nicole A. Lowen.

loans. They now back Ginnie Mae, Freddie Mac, and Fannie Mae and privately issued MBSs with low and well-defined possibilities of prepayment. Like single-family pass-throughs, many multifamily securities are backed by agency guarantees, and the creditworthiness of privately issued deals is enhanced by the quality of the collateral. Multifamily securities can provide both traditional mortgage and corporate bond investors with an attractive combination of term, safety, and yield. This chapter introduces multifamily lending practices, loan types, and securitization programs and reviews the investment characteristics of multifamily MBSs.

MULTIFAMILY LENDING AND LOAN STRUCTURES

Multifamily lending differs from single-family underwriting in several ways. While the borrower's ability to meet payments is important for both types of loans, for multifamily loans the economic viability of the underlying collateral—the building—is critical. Revenues from the building determine its value and are generally used to repay the loan. Thus occupancy levels, the size of the rent rolls, and the building's expected remaining economic life are important underwriting criteria. Of course, in all cases the borrower's financial situation is also a consideration.

   The amortization schedule and term of multifamily loans are likely to differ from single-family residential mortgages. The typical single-family mortgage is level-pay and fully amortizing in 25 to 30 years. In comparison, most federally insured multifamily mortgages are fully amortizing in 35 to 40 years. Conventional multifamily mortgages often have original maturities of 10 to 15 years. Some of these mortgages do not fully amortize; instead, payments are calculated on an amortization schedule longer than the term of the loan, creating a final balloon payment.

   Unlike most single-family mortgages, many multifamily mortgages are structured with barriers to prepayment. The establishment of a **"lock-out"** period during which prepayment is prohibited is common with both federally insured and conventional multifamily mortgages. Additionally, multifamily mortgages often include prepayment penalties instead of, or following, a lock-out period. Prepayments may also be moderated because FHA-insured and co-insured mortgages are assumable, as are many conventional multifamily mortgages. In general, assumable multifamily loans are eligible for securitization by Ginnie Mae, Freddie Mac, and Fannie Mae. However, HUD, Freddie Mac, and Fannie Mae restrictions on secondary financing make assumption unlikely if the property has appreciated substantially since the loan was originated.

FEDERAL MORTGAGE PROGRAMS

Multifamily loan insurance and co-insurance programs were established under the National Housing Act of 1934 and its subsequent amendments. Through these programs HUD encourages private lending for multifamily housing by guaranteeing repayment of all (insurance) or part (co-insurance) of a loan's outstanding balance. The FHA is responsible for administering HUD's housing insurance, co-insurance, and rental assistance programs. Some programs originally offered enticements to issuers in the form of 20-year put options and to project owners through interest-rate subsidies. In addition, Section 8 Lower-Income Rental Assistance contracts, which enhance the economic viability of low-income projects, were available in conjunction with many programs. The National Housing Act contains separate provisions for insurance on purchase money and refinancing loans on completed multifamily structures, loans for rehabilitation of rental properties, loans for construction or rehabilitation of nonprofit and proprietary hospitals, and loans on nursing homes and intermediate-care facilities. The characteristics of the major insurance and co-insurance programs are summarized in Table 11.1. A more detailed profile of the FHA-insured project loan types is provided in the appendix to this chapter.

FHA Insurance and Co-Insurance Programs

FHA insurance and co-insurance minimize the cost of default to private multifamily issuers by reimbursing all or part of the outstanding principal balance of a defaulted loan. Under **co-insurance** the private lender and HUD share the risk on the loan. With FHA insurance programs, the issuer may declare the loan in default and assign it to HUD as early as 30 days after the first payment is missed. At that time the issuer begins receiving interest from HUD at a rate tied to the FHA debenture rates effective on the loan commitment and closing dates. When the claim is settled, HUD reimburses the issuer 100 percent of the loan's outstanding principal balance at default minus a 1 percent assignment fee. The claim proceeds are paid either in cash or in 20-year FHA debentures, according to the rules of the specific loan program. Loss to the issuer is limited to 30 days' interest plus or minus the difference between the FHA debenture and loan note rates.

While insurance programs attract issuers because of their high level of coverage, HUD administrative delays can make the programs unwieldy. To accommodate issuer demand, HUD has developed co-insurance options through which the issuer assumes a greater proportion of losses due to default in exchange for minimal FHA involvement in the origination, underwriting, and servicing of the multifamily loan. If a co-insured mortgage is declared in

TABLE 11.1
Major Federal Multifamily Insurance and Co-Insurance Programs

			Section of National Housing Act				
	223 (f)	207	220	221(d)(3) Below-Market Interest Rate (BMIR)	221(d) (3) and (4) Market Rate	232	242
Loan type	Purchase/ refinance	Construction/ substantial rehabilitation	Construction/ substantial rehabilitation	Construction/ substantial rehabilitation	Construction/ substantial rehabilitation	Construction/ substantial rehabilitation	Construction/ substantial rehabilitation
Structure type	Existing rental residences	Rental residences	Rental residences in urban renewal areas	Rental residences	Rental residences	Nursing homes, intermediate-care facilities	Nonprofit and proprietary hospitals
Program type	Insurance and co-insurance	Insurance	Insurance	Insurance	Insurance and co-insurance	Insurance currently, co-insurance proposed	Insurance
Original term (yrs.)	35	40 plus construction period	40 plus construction period	40 plus construction period	40 plus construction period	40 plus construction period	25 plus construction period
Length of lock-outs and prepayment penalties (yrs.)	Up to 10	Up to 10	Up to 10	Up to 10	Up to 10	Up to 10	Up to 10

Insurance claim payment type	Insurance: FHA debentures co-insurance: cash	Cash	Cash	Cash	Cash	FHA debentures	FHA debentures
Special features	Property must be at least 3 years old and not require substantial rehabilitation	Local or statutory limit by unit allows larger loan size	Section 8 rent subsidies allowed	Section 8 rent subsidies allowed, may have 20-year put, subsidized interest rate generally 3–5%	Section 8 rent subsidies allowed, may have 20-year put, regulations allow high LTV	Major moveable equipment may be included in balance	Major moveable equipment may be included in balance

Source: Shearson Lehman Hutton Mortgage Securities.

default, the issuer must foreclose or otherwise liquidate the mortgage before making a claim to FHA. The total losses to the issuer are 30 days' interest, 5 percent of the outstanding principal balance of the loan, and 15 percent of any additional losses related to the claim. If the issuer reinsures more than 50 percent of the risk, then FHA reimburses a lower proportion of losses. As in the insurance programs, the claim is paid in either cash or FHA debentures.

Put Option

To encourage lending institutions to supply long-term funds for multifamily projects, Section 221(d)(3) and (4) contracts originally offered a put option to the issuer. That is, the issuer can assign the loan to FHA 20 years after final endorsement in exchange for 10-year FHA debentures of equivalent face value. The rate on these debentures is approximately equivalent to the rate available on 8- to 12-year Treasuries at the put date. To value this put, most market participants price the debentures at 96. Many 221(d)(3) and (4) loans insured or co-insured before December 1, 1983 carry the put.

Section 8 Lower-Income Rental Assistance

Many of the buildings insured or co-insured by FHA also have Section 8 subsidies. Through this program HUD makes up the difference between fair market rent and the amount a low-income household can afford to pay. Funding for contracts covering new construction has not been available since 1983. The original Section 8 contracts were for five years, with an option to renew, in five-year increments, up to 20 years. Since 1979, however, HUD has structured all new Section 8 contracts as 20-year contracts. HUD approval of the sale or refinancing of a project with Section 8 assistance was also instituted in 1979, making prepayment unlikely for these projects. No authorization now exists for renewal of contracts beyond the original 20-year period. Some Section 8 contracts will expire within a few years, raising the possibility of large prepayments as project owners, free of HUD-imposed conditions, sell buildings or convert them to condominiums in newly gentrified areas.

Interest-Rate Subsidy Programs

During the 1960s and early 1970s, project owners were able to arrange both HUD insurance and a subsidized interest rate through Section 236 and Section 221(d)(3) below-market interest-rate (BMIR) loans. Both programs, now inactive, were designed to assist low-income housing and were often used in conjunction with Section 8 assistance. While loans insured under Section 236 generally carry a 7 percent mortgage rate, federal subsidies make the project owner's effective payment equal to a 1 percent coupon. Section 221(d)(3) BMIR loans generally carry coupons of 3–5 percent. While low-interest rates reduce the refinancing risk of these loans, expiration of Section 8 contracts may increase the level of terminations.

Conventional Loans

Freddie Mac and Fannie Mae have developed standard underwriting criteria for conventional multifamily loans. The two major types of mortgages are Plan A and Plan B. Plan A mortgages are fully amortizing in 10 to 30 years, are not assumable, and allow for full or partial prepayment with a penalty at any time. Plan B mortgages have original terms of from 10 to 15 years but are usually not fully amortizing. They are assumable and always have a lock-out period, after which prepayment is allowed with a penalty.

MULTIFAMILY MORTGAGE-BACKED SECURITIES

To foster a secondary market for multifamily mortgages, Ginnie Mae, Freddie Mac, and Fannie Mae have established purchase and securitization programs. Ginnie Mae multifamily pools are backed by the full faith and credit of the U.S. government. The Ginnie Mae **Construction Loan Certificate (CLC)** and **Project Loan Certificate (PLC)** programs are the primary means of securitizing FHA-insured and co-insured multifamily, hospital, and nursing home loans. Some $6.7 billion of these securities were outstanding as of mid-1987. The Freddie Mac and Fannie Mae programs, designed primarily for conventional multifamily mortgages, have also been popular with lenders and investors. As of June 1, 1987, the amount outstanding for securities backed by multifamily mortgages was over $5.9 billion for Freddie Mac and $1.7 billion for Fannie Mae. Additionally, in excess of $2 billion of securities backed by FHA-insured loans have been issued privately.

Ginnie Mae

The Ginnie Mae multifamily program allows lenders to securitize FHA-insured or co-insured loans that they have underwritten. CLCs are backed by a single, nonamortizing construction advance loan. They pay timely interest regardless of FHA insurance deductions or co-insurance losses and are either redeemed or exchanged for one PLC at or before their maturity date. In general, Ginnie Mae PLCs are backed by a single project mortgage. They are level-pay and fully amortizing with a coupon rate that is .25 percent or .45 percent below the mortgage rate, depending on how claims are repaid. Investors receive timely payment of principal and interest regardless of payments by the project owner; in case of default, investors receive 100 percent of the outstanding principal balance when the claim is paid, regardless of any deductions or losses the lender experiences. Ginnie Mae does not guarantee or require that prepayment penalties collected by issuers be passed through to investors, although they often are.

Freddie Mac and Fannie Mae Multifamily MBSs

Freddie Mac and Fannie Mae multifamily loan securitization programs are similar. Both require loans to be of general investment quality: rental income must be great enough to support the loan's debt service and other expenses, and the building collateralizing the loan must have sufficient value to return the lender's investment should a default occur. Since both Freddie Mac and Fannie Mae pools are backed by more than one mortgage, partial prepayments on the pools can occur once lock-outs expire. However, neither agency passes prepayment penalties through to investors.

Fannie Mae currently pools only conventional multifamily mortgages, although pools backed by FHA-insured project loans have been created in the past. Loans may be fully amortizing, balloon, or adjustable-rate with a term of from 7 to 15 years and an amortization schedule of up to 30 years. Fannie Mae requires a lock-out of five years from the mortgage origination date, with a prepayment penalty thereafter, and forbids partial prepayment.

THE FREDDIE MAC MULTIFAMILY PC PROGRAM[2]

Freddie Mac issued its first multifamily PC in September 1985, using as collateral for the PC multifamily conventional loans purchased under Freddie Mac's Plan B. Commencing in August 1986, Freddie Mac inaugurated a program of weekly auctions of its multifamily PCs, adding considerably to the trading activity of these PCs. The auctions were discontinued in 1987, however, because of a slowing of multifamily loan originations following disincentives to multifamily financing contained in the 1986 Tax Reform Act.

The Plan-B Mortgages

Most of the Freddie Mac multifamily PCs are backed by the Plan-B–type loans. All Plan-B mortgages purchased by Freddie Mac are first-lien, fixed-rate mortgages secured by rental apartment properties with five or more residential

---

[2]This description of the Freddie Mac multifamily PC program is based in part on information provided in Drexel Burnham Lambert Mortgage-Backed Securities Research, *MBSs with Call Protection*, September 8, 1986; prepared by David J. Askin, First Vice President, and Steven D. Meyer, Associate.

units. The properties are typically low-rise, or sometimes high-rise structures and townhouses, or co-op apartments.

The loans are not subsidized, insured, or guaranteed by the U.S. government or any federal agency, but they are underwritten to tight and standardized guidelines issued by Freddie Mac. Among other requirements, at least 80 percent of the property's units must be occupied, and the rental income of the property must cover operating expenses and the loan debt service before the loan may be considered for purchase by Freddie Mac.

The Plan-B Loan Terms

The maturity structure of the Plan-B loans is unique in that they are usually written with an amortization schedule of 30 years. However, the loans also generally carry a 10- or 15-year balloon maturity, and the multifamily PCs are sold with a stated maturity of 10 or 15 years with the balloon maturity guaranteed by Freddie Mac.

Call-Protection Feature

The multifamily PCs contain a call feature provided by a lock-out period contained in the underlying conventional mortgage, which is passed on directly to investors as a structural characteristic of the PC. The lock-out period is written in the loan as a specified length of time during which prepayment of the loan is prohibited. The lock-out period is usually from 54 to 66 months. After the lock-out period has expired prepayment is permitted, but the borrower must pay a prepayment penalty of 1 percent of the remaining unpaid principal balance of the loan. Because of processing lead time required to securitize the multifamily loans, the effective lock-out period of a newly issued multifamily PC is usually about four to five years.

The Multifamily PC

Multifamily PCs are issued as series 22 pools and are part of the Freddie Mac Cash program PC pools. (See Chapter 3 for a full discussion of the Freddie Mac PC Cash and Guarantor programs.) According to the Drexel Burnham report, the pools vary in size from $75 million to $80 million and contain from 62 to 742 loans. The average-size loan within the pools is about $1.2 million. WACs of the loans range from 10.23 to 12.89 percent, with a servicing spread range of from .96 percent to 3.13 percent. The WAM range is very tight, ranging from 355 to 360 months as of the issue date.

Multifamily PC Pricing Conventions

The multifamily PCs are generally traded to a 10-year prepaid-life assumption. The 10-year prepaid-life convention assumes no prepayments for the first 10 years, with the entire balance paid at the end of the tenth year. Unlike the 12-year prepaid assumption once applied to pools of single-family loans (see Chapter 5 for a discussion of the 12-year prepaid-life assumption), this convention provides a fair estimation of the cash-flow experience associated with multifamily pools. Unlike the single-family pools made up of single-family– home loans, multifamily pools contain a tighter window for the cash flows, with no prepayments permitted for the lock-out period followed by a 10- or 15-year maturity. Furthermore, the decision to prepay the loan offers a far more rational call option than that of single-family loans. The decision by the multifamily project owner to prepay or not will be based almost universally on purely economic considerations. This factor makes the WAC of the multifamily pool particularly significant when its associated PC is trading to a premium price.

PRIVATELY ISSUED POOLS

The Ginnie Mae Tandem program has enabled private issuers to create pools of multifamily loans without agency guarantees. Between 1975 and 1983, when the Tandem purchase program was discontinued, Ginnie Mae acquired over $35 billion in multifamily mortgages under its special-assistance mandate. The Tandem auction program was established to liquidate this portfolio. Most of the loans auctioned are older mortgages insured under Sections 221(d)(3) (both market rate and BMIR), 221(d)(4), 236, and 220. FHA project pools created from these loans do not carry a government guarantee, although the underlying loans retain their FHA insurance. Most of these pools are backed by 7.5 percent Section 221(d)(3) and (4) loans and carry a 7.43 percent coupon rate. Loans with Section 8 contracts are generally segregated into separate pools. By mid-1987, more than $2 billion of FHA project pools had been created. A liquid secondary market exists for these pools, although the supply is limited because Ginnie Mae has discontinued purchases of these loans.

INVESTMENT CONSIDERATIONS

Securities backed by multifamily mortgages provide a combination of term and stipulated call protection not found in single-family issues. Almost all multi-families are traded with a balloon prepayment assumption that is supported by the characteristics of the underlying loans. Ginnie Mae PLCs have 35- to 40-year original terms, and many are backed by loans with explicit call protection in the form of lock-outs during the first 5 to 10 years. If the project is also covered by a Section 8 contract, default or conversion to condominiums or cooperatives is unlikely because the properties are generally located in low-to-moderate-income areas, and the building's revenue depends, to a large extent, on the rental-assistance payments. Additionally, the decision to refinance or sell a multifamily property is complex, involving equity depreciation and tax considerations. Securities backed by Section 223(f) and market-rate Section 221(d)(4) loans and FHLMC 15-year multifamily securities trade to a 10-year balloon prepayment assumption. This takes into account lock-outs and the equity buildup necessary to make sale or refinancing attractive to a project owner. FHA project pools also trade with a zero prepayment assumption to maturity or to their put date. Multifamily securities are unlikely to experience partial prepayments, except Freddie Macs and Fannie Maes after the lock-out period expires.

In addition to call protection, multifamily MBSs also offer yield advantages over high-quality corporate bonds and alternative MBSs. For example, Ginnie Maes backed by Section 223(f) loans generally trade at a dollar spread to Ginnie Mae single-family pools. Current- and premium-coupon issues are priced 1 to 1½ points behind comparable-coupon single-family securities, while discounts are priced 1¾ to 2¼ points behind their single-family counterparts. This pricing gives true high current yield with both explicit and implicit call protection, a feature that single-family MBSs do not offer. FHA project pools have a low likelihood of repayment before maturity or their put date, if applicable, and provide attractive spreads to Treasury issues. Nonputable FHA project pools have recently traded between 100 and 150 basis points above the long Treasury. By comparison, AA utilities of the same maturity are currently trading at spreads near 110 basis points. Putable FHA project loans also offer advantageous spreads over the 10-year Treasury and corporate bonds with maturities near the projects' put dates.

THE PREPAYMENT HORIZON FOR MULTIFAMILY PROJECT LOANS[3]

Market-rate multifamily MPTs with amortization terms of 35 to 40 years are often priced with a 7- to 10-year prepayment assumption. This assumption has intuitive appeal: multifamily projects generally are sold or refinanced for purely economic reasons. For example, refinancing proceeds are often the least costly source of funds for necessary capital improvements. Prepayment is unlikely during the early years of the mortgage because of substantial tax and deprecia-

---

[3] This discussion of the prepayment horizon was written by Nicole A. Lowen and published in April 1988 in *Mortgage Finance Monthly*, a Shearson Lehman Hutton Mortgage Research publication.

tion advantages and, often, prepayment penalties. Partial prepayments are unlikely after these restrictions expire because second mortgages are prohibited for most types of multifamily projects.

Methods for Valuing Multifamily Projects

A multifamily project is primarily an income-generating investment for its owner. Rental income is used to repay the mortgage and cover operating expenses. Any remaining funds are the owner's return on investment. Multifamily mortgage underwriting standards determine a project's value and possible financing in two ways: debt-service coverage and loan-to-value (LTV) ratio. The first approach compares the after-cost income stream to the amount necessary to finance the property. Debt-service coverage is the ratio of net income to debt service. The LTV method compares the amount financed to the property's appraised value. The amount of financing that an owner can obtain will be limited by one or both of these methods.

Debt-Service Method

The cash flow from a multifamily structure available for debt service is its net operating income (NOI), which is the excess of net rental income after ordinary expenses. Ordinary expenses are administrative, operating, and maintenance costs (including taxes and hazard insurance), but not capital items such as roof and boiler replacement. Debt-service coverage (DSC) is the ratio of NOI to annual debt service, including any mortgage insurance premium (MIP). Because income and expense levels vary, and unexpected but necessary costs arise frequently in rental structures, the required level of debt-service coverage typically ranges from 1.1 to 1.2. Effective NOI (ENOI) is the portion of NOI dedicated to DSC. DSC of 1.1 means that the building owner must pledge approximately 91 percent of the building's NOI to repay the mortgage.

The debt-service percentage (DS%) is the sum of MIP and the mortgage constant (the annual debt-service payment due on each dollar of outstanding balance expressed as a percentage). Given the mortgage rate and term, this is easily calculated. The ENOI divided by the DS% determines the largest mortgage supportable by the project.

LTV Method

As in most mortgage agreements, borrowers are generally required to maintain equity in the multifamily project, resulting in a LTV ratio of less than 100 percent. The value of an income-producing property is determined by one of three methods: the income approach, which determines the present value of the projected NOI; the market-data approach, which employs recent sales of comparable properties as a benchmark; and the replacement-cost method, which equates value to the cost of constructing a comparable property, including the acquisition and financing of the land. The relationship between appraised value and NOI is called the capitalization ratio (cap rate). For example, if the NOI for a project is $800,000 per year and the value is $10 million, then the cap rate is 8 percent.

Determining the Likelihood of Prepayment

The prepayment horizon for a multifamily mortgage is more predictable than for a single-family loan because it does not depend on the demographic characteristics of the mortgagor. The decision to prepay a multifamily mortgage depends on the spread between the mortgage note rate and the current market rate and on tax and depreciation considerations. As soon as tax considerations warrant, or the owner has built up enough equity to increase the leverage of the investment profitably, a sale or refinancing will probably occur. The economic return to the owner is paramount: if the return of the structure is lower than alternative investments would provide, or if a different financing scheme offers higher returns, a prepayment will occur.

Even if an existing project is performing well, the owner may not hold the property indefinitely with the original financing. Since the property's value is likely to appreciate over time, the owner will desire to increase his leverage. Therefore, the owner has an incentive to extract equity from the property as soon as it is economically feasible. Also, because NOI is generally not large enough to cover capital repairs, owners may refinance to extract funds to maintain or improve the property.

Table 11.2 shows the likely prepayment horizon for a representative project loan. The horizon is determined by the number of years until NOI growth allows the owner to withdraw a substantial amount of equity from the project, given appreciation of the property at the same rate of growth as NOI and given current market rates. The analysis employs a simplified approach that ignores tax and depreciation considerations, focusing on the growth of cash flows and targeting maximum leverage for the owner.

Part A of Table 11.2 describes a hypothetical 11 percent GNMA project. The NOI and ENOI shown are the minimum necessary to support the $1 million mortgage using prudent underwriting standards. The capitalization rate, at a LTV of 85 percent, is 12.01. The excess of cash flow over debt service is 18 percent, or approximately $22,000 in the first year. Both NOI and the property value can be expected to grow, increasing excess cash flow and the owner's equity at the same time. Thus, it is likely that the property owner will refinance in several years, increasing leverage and extracting equity for other investments.

TABLE 11.2
Refinancing Horizon for a GNMA 11% Project Loan

A. Existing Financing (GNMA)

Balance	$1 million	LTV ratio	85%
Security rate	11%	Property value	$1.18 million
Term	420 months	Capitalization rate	12.01
Monthly payment	$9,565		
Mortgage constant	11.48%	NOI	$141,340
MIP	.50%	DSC	118%
Guarantor–servicer	.25%	ENOI	$119,779
Debt-service %	11.98%		

B. Refinancing Assumptions (GNMA)

Equity out	$200,000	Maximum mortgage balance	$1.24 million
LTV ratio	85%	Maximum property value	$1.46 million
DSC	118%	Term	420 months
MIP	.50%		
Guarantor–servicer	.25%		
Refinancing cost	2%		
Prepayment fee	2%		

C. Estimated Prepayment Horizon for Project Loans (years)

Annual Growth of NOI	Security Rate							
	16%	15%	14%	13%	12%	11%	10%	9%
1%	13	13	13	13	13	13	13	13
2%	13	13	13	13	11	11	11	11
3%	13	13	11	8	7	7	7	7
4%	11	10	8	6	5	5	5	5
5%	9	8	6	5	4	4	4	4
6%	7	6	5	4	4	4	4	4
7%	6	6	5	4	3	3	3	3

Source: Shearson Lehman Hutton, April 1988.

Part B of Table 11.2 shows the economics of refinancing the hypothetical project with a new Ginnie Mae project loan. In the early years, with little amortization of the existing mortgage, the new mortgage must be $1.2 million to extract at least $200,000. With refinancing costs and prepayment fees, the maximum mortgage amount grows to $1.24 million. Ginnie Mae financing allows a LTV ratio up to 85 percent; therefore, the maximum newly appraised property value under any scenario is approximately $1.46 million.

Part C of Table 11.2 shows a matrix of prepayment-horizon estimates for the original mortgage, given both the annual NOI growth rate and the horizon security rate. (The new mortgage rate is assumed to equal the security rate plus MIP and guarantee fees.) Besides finding the horizon where actual cash flows have grown enough to support the new mortgage, the analysis also considers two additional conditions. First, under high-NOI growth-rate scenarios, the time to prepayment is at least the number of years required for property value to grow to $1.46 million. This provides a floor for the estimate. The second condition sets a maximum value for the prepayment horizon. In low-growth-rate scenarios, NOI and the property value will not grow enough to support the maximum property value for many years. However, because the existing mortgage is amortizing, and assuming minimal property appreciation at 1 percent per year, equity will increase enough to allow for a $200,000 takeout after about 13 years. The analysis shows that a horizon of 7 to 10 years is possible under a wide range of refinancing rates if NOI grows in the 2–4 percent range. Under higher-growth scenarios, the horizon becomes shorter. These estimates are conservative because the analysis ignores substantial tax and depreciation advantages, which could cause the owner to hold the mortgage longer.

New Law Reduces Likelihood of Prepayments

On February 5, 1988, President Reagan signed into law the Housing and Community Development Act of 1987 (the Housing Act), which establishes a *de facto* two-year moratorium on prepayments for mortgages insured under the following sections of the National Housing Act (NHA): 236, 221(d)(3) BMIR, and 221(d)(3) with rent supplement or Section 8 subsidies. These programs required mortgagors to operate their properties as low-income housing for 20 years from final endorsement by HUD. After that time, owners were free to transfer the property to any use without HUD approval. In an effort to preserve the nation's low-income housing stock, however, Congress has imposed tight restrictions on prepayments for the two years following enactment of the Housing Act and intends to devise a permanent solution before the law expires.

HUD recently issued an interim rule, effective May 20, 1988, describing the procedures necessary to prepay project loans uninsured under the affected sections of the NHA. Prepayment is not specifically forbidden, but the owner must now obtain HUD approval for a plan of action relating to the low-income status of the property. HUD is instructed to approve a plan for prepayment only if it meets both of the following conditions: (1) prepayment will not materially increase economic hardship for current tenants or displace them unless comparable, affordable housing is available, and (2) sufficient alternative housing exists in the area that is decent, safe, and affordable. If a plan of action cannot be approved, the owner may request financial incentives from HUD, such as a rent increase to bolster the building's return. The restrictions are applicable to any mortgage that is or will within one year of the law's jurisdiction become eligible for prepayment.

The restrictions are tantamount to prohibiting prepayments because most owners applying for prepayment want to convert their buildings to market rent housing. Any such prepayment would naturally displace low-income tenants and at the same time shrink the local supply of low- and middle-income housing. Thus, any economically motivated prepayment is unlikely to be approved by HUD under the new restrictions. Congress clearly intends to enforce a moratorium: the law states that if the restrictions on prepayment are invalidated by any court, then no properties within the jurisdiction of that court may be prepaid for a two-year period.

A legal challenge to the restrictions is expected. Possible grounds for litigation include denial of due process and regulatory taking of property without just compensation. However, unless the matter is more clearly settled in the courts or by Congress, any project loans covered by the Housing Act are unlikely to prepay in the next two years.

APPENDIX[4]

Section 207: Multifamily Rental Housing

Section 207 represents the oldest of the HUD multifamily programs. Originated in 1934, this program represents one of the first in a long line of programs employed by HUD to encourage private investment in project housing. Although it is not considered a significant force in the market today, it continues to represent the foundation for many of the other HUD/FHA programs.

There are two major reasons for the less active status of the 207 program currently. First, the 207 program is a ''value-based'' rather than replacement-cost program. Therefore, the maximum mortgage amount of a Section 207 loan is determined by the HUD/FHA estimate of the project value. In most other programs, the maximum mortgage is based on estimated project replacement cost—a method that can provide greater flexibility in obtaining necessary financing. Another deterrent has been the inability to use a Builders' and Sponsors' Profit and Risk Allowance (BSPRA). The BSPRA allows the project's construction profit to be applied to the developer's mortgage equity requirement with little, if any, out-of-pocket expenditure. Instead, the project sponsor in the 207 program receives a lesser sum known as Builders' Profit, which does not offer the equity contribution or tax advantages of the BSPRA.

---

[4]Reprinted from Salomon Brothers, *An Anatomy of the FHA Project Market*, July 1987; prepared by Judy Hustick. Used with the permission of Salomon Brothers Inc.

Profile

Program inception	1934
Cumulative issuance[a]	$4,120 million (2,501 projects)
Insurance in force[a]	$1,240 million (579 projects)
Current status	Available, but rarely used
Maximum mortgage term	40 years
Types of mortgagors	Generally private, profit-motivated
Maximum mortgage amount[b]	90% of the estimated project value
Leverage	Builders' profit only
Form of FHA proceeds in event of default and assignment to HUD	Cash, debentures, or a combination of the two as determined by the HUD Commissioner at time of payment.
Prepayment	Full or partial prepayment is allowed without HUD consent, given 30-days written notice to the mortgagee.[c] There may be a prepayment charge if agreed upon between the mortgagor and mortgagee. This charge can be applied, however, only to prepayments in excess of 15% of the original face amount of the loan in any given year.

[a] Data through June 1987.

[b] Based on loan-to-value/cost ratio.

[c] In cases where the mortgage is originated to secure a loan made by a lender that has obtained funds for the loan through the issuance and sale of bonds and/or bond anticipation notes, the mortgage may contain prepayment restrictions agreed upon between the mortgagor and mortgagee and considered acceptable to the HUD Commissioner.

Section 213: Cooperative Housing

The Section 213 program, enacted in 1950, offers mortgage insurance on cooperative housing projects occupied or to be occupied by members of a nonprofit cooperative ownership housing corporation or trust. These loans may finance new construction, rehabilitation, acquisition, improvement, or repair of a project already owned; construction of projects composed of individual family dwellings to be bought by individual members with separately insured mortgages; and construction or rehabilitation of projects that the owners intend to sell to nonprofit cooperatives.

Profile

Program inception	1950
Cumulative issuance[a]	$1,606 million (2,022 projects)
Insurance in force[a]	$905 million (474 projects)
Current status	Active
Maximum mortgage term	40 years

Types of mortgagors	(1) A nonprofit housing corporation or trust that is formed either as a cooperative ownership or as an organization created to construct homes for members of the corporation or beneficiaries of the trust; or (2) a mortgagor who owns a project and intends to sell it to a nonprofit housing corporation or trust as described above.
Maximum mortgage amount[b]	98%[c] of the estimated project replacement cost
Leverage	Builders' profit
Form of FHA proceeds in event of default and assignment to HUD	Cash, debentures, or a combination of the two as determined by the HUD Commissioner at time of payment.
Prepayment	Full or partial prepayment is allowed without HUD consent, given 30-days written notice to the mortgagee.[d] There may be a prepayment charge if agreed upon between the mortgagor and mortgagee. This charge can be applied, however, only to prepayments in excess of 15% of the original face amount of the loan in any given year.

[a] Data through June 1987.

[b] Based on loan-to-value/cost ratio.

[c] 90% if the project is an "investor project," one which the mortgagor intends to sell to a housing corporation or trust.

[d] In cases where the mortgage is originated to secure a loan made by a lender that has obtained funds for the loan through the issuance and sale of bonds and/or bond anticipation notes, the mortgage may contain prepayment restrictions agreed upon between the mortgagor and mortgagee and considered acceptable to the HUD Commissioner.

Section 221(d)(3): Rental and Cooperative Housing for Low- to Moderate-Income Households

The 221(d)(3) program was initiated in 1954. It was intended to assist in the construction and substantial rehabilitation of rental and cooperative housing for low- to moderate-income households. There are two distinct groups of outstanding 221(d)(3) mortgages. The first are the below-market interest-rate (BMIR) loans. These were endorsed in 1961–72, most under limited dividend plans. HUD provided below-market-rate financing on these mortgages for sponsors of lower-income housing projects. Few had Section 8 subsidies. The claim rate on the BMIRs has been quite high. The BMIR program was subsequently replaced by the Section 236 mortgage interest-rate subsidy program under the HUD Act of 1968. Presently, no new mortgages are being insured under the BMIR program or under Section 236.

The second group of 221(d)(3) loans were endorsed under a market-rate plan. Most carry Section 8 subsidies. The claim rate on these has been significantly below the earlier BMIR loans.

Loans insured under the 221(d)(3) program and issued on or before November 30, 1983, may include a put or assignment option allowing the investor to exchange the loans, provided they are not in default, for 10-year FHA debentures. The option is exercisable during the one-year period following the twentieth anniversary of the mortgage. The face value of the FHA debentures will be set equal to the outstanding principal balance of the loan on the date of assignment plus accrued interest to such date. The coupon on the debentures will reflect the current "Federal rate." This rate is based on a six-month average of daily yields to maturity on outstanding U.S. obligations with 8 to 12 years remaining to maturity.

Profile	
Program inception	1954
Cumulative issuance[a]	$6,104 million (3,624 projects)
Insurance in force[a]	$4,392 million (2,547 projects)
Current status	BMIR program inactive, market-rate program active
Maximum mortgage term	40 years
Types of mortgagors	Private, nonprofit sponsors, public sponsors, limited dividend corporations, cooperatives, and investor-sponsored mortgagors; and general profit-motivated sponsors.
Maximum mortgage amount[b]	On limited dividend and profit-motivated project loans, 90% of estimated project replacement cost; 100% on nonprofit, cooperatives, and public sponsor projects.
Leverage	BSPRA allowed for limited dividend sponsors.
Form of FHA proceeds in event of default and assignment to HUD	Cash
Prepayment	Full and partial prepayment is allowed but only with HUD consent during the first 20 years of the mortgage term. Limited distribution mortgagors without rental supplement assistance may prepay without HUD consent thereafter. HUD consent, however, is still required for the remainder of the mortgage term on all other 221(d)(3) loans.[c] In cases of prepayment, there may be a prepayment charge if agreed upon between the mortgagor and mortgagee. This charge can be applied, however, only to prepayments in excess of 15% of the original face amount of the loan in any given year.

[a] Data through June 1987.

[b] Based on loan-to-value/cost ratio.

[c] In addition, in cases where the mortgage is originated to secure a loan made by a lender that has obtained funds for the loan through the issuance and sale of bonds and/or anticipation notes, the mortgage may contain prepayment restrictions agreed upon between the mortgagor and mortgagee and considered acceptable to the HUD Commissioner.

Section 221(d)(4): Rental Housing
for Low- to Moderate-Income Households

The Section 221(d)(4) program was initiated in 1959. It was created under a similar purpose as 221(d)(3) but with these minor differences: first, it was *only* a market-rate program (no BMIRs); second, it did not include cooperative housing; and third, the (d)(4)s insure only 90 percent of the replacement cost of the project in all cases, compared with (d)(3)s, which insure up to 100 percent of the project's replacement cost on nonprofit, public sponsor, and cooperative loans.

Loans insured under the 221(d)(4) program and issued on or before November 30, 1983, may include a put or assignment option allowing the investor to exchange the loans, provided they are not in default, for 10-year FHA debentures. The option is exercisable during the one-year period following the twentieth anniversary of the mortgage. The face value of the FHA debentures will be set equal to the outstanding principal balance of the loan on the date of assignment plus accrued interest to such date. The coupon on the debentures will reflect the current "Federal rate." This rate is based on a six-month average of daily yields to maturity on outstanding U.S. obligations with 8 to 12 years remaining to maturity.

Profile

Program inception	1959
Cumulative issuance[a]	$22,079 million (7,179 projects)
Insurance in force[a]	$19,721 million (6,188 projects)
Current status	Active
Maximum mortgage term	40 years
Types of mortgagors	Generally private, profit-motivated corporations, trusts, partnerships, or individuals. Nonprofit or public sponsors are eligible but are typically attracted to the 100% mortgage available under the 221(d)(3) program.
Maximum mortgage amount[b]	90% of the estimated project replacement cost
Leverage	BSPRA
Form of FHA proceeds in event of default and assignment to HUD	Cash
Prepayment	Full or partial prepayment is allowed without HUD consent, given 30-days written notice to the mortgagee.[c] There may be a prepayment charge, if agreed upon between the mortgagor and mortgagee, but the charge can only be applied to prepayments in excess of 15% of the original face amount of the loan in any given year.

It is important to note, that while HUD mandates no special prepayment incentives or restrictions under the 221(d)(4) program, many of the projects financed under this program receive subsidies that carry stringent restrictions greatly inhibiting the project owner's incentive to prepay the 221(d)(4) loan.

[a] Data through June 1987.

[b] Based on loan-to-value/cost ratio.

[c] In cases where the mortgage is originated to secure a loan made by a lender that has obtained funds for the loan through the issuance and sale of bonds and/or bond anticipation notes, the mortgage may contain prepayment restrictions agreed upon between the mortgagor and mortgagee and considered acceptable to the HUD Commissioner.

Section 223(f): Loans to Purchase or Refinance Existing Multifamily Projects

The Section 223(f) program, introduced under the Housing and Community Development Act of 1974, is a market-rate, unsubsidized mortgage insurance program that was created to facilitate the purchase and refinancing of existing multifamily projects. The 223(f) program was significant because it was the first HUD/FHA multifamily insurance program for existing projects that did not require a plan for substantial rehabilitation. To be eligible, projects must have been completed at least three years prior to filing. The vast majority of these projects serve middle- to upper-income tenants. Multifamily projects carrying a Section 8 contract are not eligible for 223(f) insurance. However, it is acceptable for individual tenants to be receiving assistance under Section 8. Initially, the 223(f) program was a full insurance program; HUD was responsible for all program administration and bore 100 percent of the risk in the event of delinquency or default. A co-insurance program was developed several years later under Section 244 of the National Housing Act under which the private lender and HUD share the risk on the loan and the lender takes over more of the underwriting and compliance responsibility.

Profile	
Program inception	1974
Cumulative issuance[a]	$5,672 million (1,157 projects)
Insurance in force[a]	$4,420 million (850 projects)
Current status	Active
Maximum mortgage term	35 years
Types of mortgagors	Generaly profit-motivated
Maximum mortgage amount[b]	85% of estimated project value. This amount can be raised to 90% if the project meets special eligibility requirements.

Leverage	None
Form of FHA proceeds in event of default and assignment to HUD	Debentures
Prepayment	Full or partial prepayment is allowed without HUD consent, given 30-days written notice to the mortgagor and mortgagee. There may be a prepayment charge if agreed upon between the mortgagor and mortgagee. This charge can be applied, however, only to prepayments in excess of 15% of the original face amount of the loan in any given year.
	It is important to note that while there are no HUD-mandated prepayment restrictions on the 223(f) loan, there may be other inhibiting factors to prepayment on such loans: (1) There are often high costs involved in prepaying a 223(f) loan. The refinancing fees involved in opting for another 223(f) loan are high and on many GNMA 223(f) loans, there are prepayment penalties.[c] Most common has been the "3-2-1" penalty; this involves a 3% penalty if prepayment occurs in the first year, 2% in the second year, and 1% in the third; such penalties are passed through to the investor; and (2) On some GNMA 223(f) loans, there are prepayment lock-outs for an initial number of years initially agreed upon by the mortgagor and mortgagee and written into the mortgage contract.

[a] Data through June 1987.

[b] Based on loan-to-value/cost ratio.

[c] Not imposed by HUD but by the GNMA issuer.

Section 231: Rental Housing for the Elderly or Handicapped

The Section 231 program was enacted in 1959 to provide insurance to finance the construction, purchase, and rehabilitation of rental housing specifically designed for the elderly. In 1964, the program was extended to include the handicapped. An elderly individual is defined as being 62 years or older, and a handicapped individual is considered to be any person with a long-term physical impairment that substantially impedes an independent living arrangement.

Profile	
Program inception	1959
Cumulative issuance[a]	$1,156 milion (499 projects)
Insurance in force[a]	$861 million (359 projects)
Current status	Active
Maximum mortgage term	40 years

Types of mortgagors	Public, private nonprofit, or private for-profit mortgagors
Maximum mortgage amount[b]	For new construction, 100% of estimated projected replacement cost if private, nonprofit, or public, and 90% if private, for-profit. For rehabilitation the same percentages apply but to estimated project value after completed rehabilitation rather than replacement cost.
Leverage	BSPRA on for-profit loans
Form of FHA proceeds in event of default and assignment to HUD	Cash, debentures, or a combination of the two as determined by the HUD Commissioner at time of payment.
Prepayment	Full or partial prepayment is allowed without prior HUD consent, given 30-days written notice to the mortgagee, on all public and on all private, profit-motivated 231 project loans. Prior consent from HUD is required on all private, nonprofit loans.[c] On all 231 loans, there may be a prepayment charge applied if agreed upon between the mortgagor and mortgagee. This charge can be applied, however, only to prepayments in excess of 15% of the original face amount in any given year.

[a] Data through June 1987.

[b] Based on loan-to-value/cost ratio.

[c] In addition, in cases where the mortgage is originated to secure a loan made by a lender that has obtained funds for the loan through the issuance and sale of bonds and/or bond anticipation notes, the mortgage may contain prepayment restrictions agreed upon between the mortgagor and mortgagee and considered acceptable to the HUD Commissioner.

Section 232: Nursing Home and Intermediate-Care Facilities

The Section 232 program, established under the Housing Act of 1959, was designed to help finance the construction and improvement of nursing homes and intermediate-care facilities. These are defined as units that can accommodate 20 or more persons that are unable to live independently but are not in need of acute care. The mortgage insurance may also cover the purchase of equipment necessary for the operation of the facility.

Profile	
Program inception	1959
Cumulative issuance[a]	$2,957 million (1,564 projects)
Insurance in force[a]	$2,165 million (800 projects)
Current status	Active
Maximum mortgage term	40 years
Types of mortgagors	Public, private nonprofit, or private for-profit mortgagors
Maximum mortgage amount[b]	90% of estimated project value

Leverage	Builders' profit
Form of FHA proceeds in event of default and assignment to HUD	Cash, debentures, or a combination of the two as determined by the HUD Commissioner at time of payment.
Prepayment	Full or partial prepayment is allowed without prior HUD consent, given 30-days written notice to the mortgagee on all profit-motivated 231 project loans.[c] Prior consent from HUD is required on all nonprofit projects. On both profit and nonprofit projects, there may be a prepayment charge applied if agreed upon between the mortgagor and mortgagee. This charge can be applied, however, only to prepayments in excess of 15% of the original face amount in any given year.

[a] Data through June 1987.

[b] Based on loan-to-value/cost ratio.

[c] In cases where the mortgage is originated to secure a loan made by a lender that has obtained funds for the loan through the issuance and sale of bonds and/or bond anticipation notes, the mortgage may contain prepayment restrictions agreed upon between the mortgagor and mortgagee and considered acceptable to the HUD Commissioner.

Section 236: Interest-Rate Subsidy Plan for Low- to Moderate-Income Households and Elderly Individuals

The Section 236 program, introduced in 1968, is a mortgage insurance program designed to enhance rental housing availability for low- to moderate-income families and elderly individuals through an interest-rate subsidy paid by HUD to lenders on behalf of project owners. Under the subsidy plan, the owner is responsible for a fixed debt-service cost of 1 percent while HUD is responsible for the difference between this and total debt-service costs on the loan plus the mortgage insurance premium. The owner of a project is expected to pass on the benefits of lowered debt-service costs to tenants in the form of lower rents.

Profile	
Program inception	1968
Cumulative issuance[a]	$8,045 million (4,240 projects)
Insurance in force[a]	$6,565 million (3,413 projects)
Current status	Inactive, suspended during the 1973 subsidized-housing moratorium
Maximum mortgage term	40 years
Types of mortgagors	Nonprofit organizations, limited distribution sponsors, builder-sellers organized to sell the project to a nonprofit organization after final endorsement, nonprofit cooperative housing corporations, or investor sponsors.

Maximum mortgage amount[b]	For nonprofit sponsors, builders, and cooperatives, 100% of estimated project replacement cost; 90% of replacement cost for limited distribution sponsors.
Leverage	BSPRA allowed for limited distribution sponsors.
Form of FHA proceeds in event of default and assignment to HUD	Cash, unless the mortgagee files a written request for payment in debentures.
Prepayment	There is a 40-year "lock-out"—a prohibition against prepayments without prior HUD consent—on nonprofit 236 loans and on limited dividend 236 loans which carry rental supplements. There is a 20-year lock-out on limited dividend loans without rental supplements.[c] HUD can override these lock-outs but only under specified circumstances.[d]

[a] Data through June 1987.

[b] Based on loan-to-value/cost ratio.

[c] In addition, where the mortgage is originated to secure a loan made by a lender that has obtained funds for the loan through the issuance and sale of bonds and/or anticipation notes, the mortgage may also contain a provision stating that prepayments are not to be made without the prior written consent of both the lender and the Commissioner for the full term of the mortgage.

[d] In no case will HUD allow prepayment during a lock-out if such action will result in the loss of a 236 project where such housing is still needed and not replaced with alternative housing and where tenants are not adequately provided with relocation assistance for comparable housing.

Section 242: Hospitals

The Section 242 program, enacted in 1968 and amended in 1970, provides insurance on mortgage loans to finance the construction and rehabilitation of for-profit and not-for-profit hospitals. The mortgage insurance may also cover the purchase of major moveable equipment.

Profile	
Program inception	1968
Cumulative issuance[a]	$5,981 million (244 projects)
Insurance in force[a]	$5,144 million (181 projects)
Current status	Active
Maximum mortgage term	25 years
Types of mortgagors	Private, nonprofit corporation or association, or a for-profit entity.
Maximum mortgage amount[b]	90% of estimated project replacement cost
Leverage	Builders' profit
Form of FHA proceeds in event of default and assignment to HUD	Cash, debentures, or a combination of the two as determined by the HUD Commissioner at time of payment.

Prepayment   For profit mortgagors, full or partial prepayment is
                                allowed without prior HUD consent, given 30-days
                                written notice to the mortgagee. For nonprofit
                                mortgagors, full or partial prepayment is allowed
                                only with HUD consent.[c] In either case, there may be
                                a prepayment charge if agreed upon between the
                                mortgagor and mortgagee. This charge can be applied,
                                however, only to prepayments in excess of 15% of the
                                original face amount in any given year.

[a] Data through June 1987.

[b] Based on loan-to-value/cost ratio.

[c] In addition, in cases where the mortgage is originated to secure a loan made by a lender that has obtained funds for the loan through the issuance and sale of bonds and/or bond anticipation notes, the mortgage may contain prepayment restrictions agreed upon between the mortgagor and mortgagee and considered acceptable to the HUD Commissioner.

IV

DERIVATIVE MORTGAGE-BACKED SECURITIES PRODUCTS: THEIR PROPERTIES AND USES

12
CMO Investing and Trading

13
IOs and POs: Stripped Mortgage-Backed Securities Cash Flows

14
Residuals: The Ultimate Derivative

15
Structured Arbitrage Strategies

12

CMO Investing and Trading

INTRODUCTION

The collateralized mortgage obligation (CMO) variation on MBS structure was formally introduced in June 1983 with issuance of the first Freddie Mac CMO. Since that historic event, more than $175 billion of all types of CMOs have been issued. In addition to Freddie Mac, CMOs have been issued by Wall Street securities firms, homebuilders, savings and loans, mortgage bankers, and life insurance companies.

Why have CMOs become so popular? The **CMO** reallocates mortgage pool cash flow in sequential order to a series of bonds (called tranches) with varying maturity characteristics which ride up the yield curve. The CMO therefore offers the mortgage originator, or in some cases a large portfolio seller, a highly efficient mechanism for the disposition of mortgages. For the same reason, CMOs offer the investor a wide variety of total-return and risk/reward opportunities over a broad spectrum of maturity and yield-curve point possibilities.

UNDERSTANDING THE CMO

To understand a CMO, the user must first have a clear understanding of the characteristics inherent in the underlying collateral. The characteristics of that collateral and the cash flows that are generated by it will determine the performance of the various CMO tranches.

As a first general point, the CMO, unlike other pass-through securities, brings the investor the benefits of a diversified mortgage securities portfolio. Theoretically, an investor seeking special collateral features such as predictable prepayment experience could do all the research and buy a $1 million pool of Ginnie Maes demonstrating the appropriate historical experience only to have that one pool be a statistical aberration. Now, with $1 million, an investor can buy CMO bonds in a specific tranche backed by a pool of $200 million or more and benefit from the statistical consistency of such a large pool. This diversity gives stability to the prepayment experience, which in turn provides cash-flow stability for the CMO.

Second, the investor must be attuned to economic and demographic factors that may alter the principal prepayment-speed profile of the CMO from its present state. The yield estimated for a CMO at time of purchase is a dynamic, not static, statement. The realized holding-period return of any mortgage-related investment, particularly of a CMO, will likely change—perhaps dramatically—over time as the underlying mortgage pool cash flow responds to factors that alter the principal prepayment speed. Those changes may or may not be in the investor's favor, but a significant part of the CMO investment decision must include an assumption of how future economic events are most likely to alter the yield and duration estimates of the investment made at the time of purchase.

A third key consideration is the coupon rate on the collateral: for example, whether the CMO is collateralized by MBSs or mortgages of a single coupon or whether it is collateralized by a range of coupons. The special-purpose or "arbitrage" CMOs formed by Wall Street dealers typically put securities of only one coupon rate in any single transaction—for example, all GNMA 12s or all GNMA 8s. This practice makes these CMOs easier to analyze, trade, and understand. When the CMO consists of a subset of GNMA 12s, for example, the prepayment experience of that subset will likely mirror that of all GNMA 12s. This single-coupon payment experience is referred to as the **generic paydown experience**. The broad public availability of this generic paydown experience allows the trading and investment community to make informed decisions about the value of the CMO bonds with information that is easily obtained from sources other than the dealer whose special-purpose corporation is issuing the CMO. The CMO may pay down slightly slower or faster than that of the generic experience. It is unlikely, however, that a variation from generic prepayment experience will continue for a prolonged period of time.

Collateral Considerations

A key consideration is whether the collateral type underlying the CMO tranche will tend to make the investment more conservative or more volatile with respect to prepayment-speed behavior. A CMO collateralized by Ginnie Maes, for example, will exhibit significantly different cash-flow variables than one collateralized by Freddie Mac PCs.

Investors should be wary of a CMO using a mixture of collateral types such as 25 percent Fannie Mae and 75 percent Freddie Mac; or 30 percent, 15-year–maturity MBSs and 70 percent, 30-year MBSs. The reason is simply that such a pool is almost impossible to track in terms of implied future speed performance. The investor who (wisely) endeavors to anticipate the probable future course of prepayment speed for the tranche representing the investment will find the task difficult when the collateral pool is a polyglot of different types of MBSs. For example, a CMO that was half GNMA 12s and half GNMA 11s would have an average coupon rate of 11½, but it would not likely display the cash-flow characteristics of an 11½ percent GNMA.

Number and Size of Tranches

The number of tranches that makes up the total CMO offering will have an impact on the length of the cash-flow window when principal payments are applied to the tranche. The most common form currently is the typical 4-tranche form of CMO structure, but there are several CMO issues with 6 to 10 tranches and one with 16. A CMO with a larger number of tranches will have very narrow cash-flow windows for each tranche—providing, in effect, "bullet maturities."

Tranche size is also a consideration. A CMO with a very large first tranche is not likely to achieve the short-maturity objective of the first tranche. With a large first tranche, there is a risk that during the life of the CMO speeds may slow to the point that the 3-year average life originally intended will become a 7-year average life. On the other hand, if the first tranche of a CMO issue is very small in dollar amount compared to the whole, very little in the way of prepayments is needed to retire the tranche. Therefore, a CMO issue with a few large tranches will tend to have less predictability with respect to the time required to generate sufficient cash flow to retire each tranche than one with many smaller tranches, which is more likely to produce smaller, bullet-maturity cash-flow windows.

CMO STRUCTURE

Table 12.1 illustrates the structure of a GNMA-collateralized CMO issued on August 11, 1986, by Ryland Acceptance Corporation.

The information in the top portion of Table 12.1 indicates that the issuer is Ryland Acceptance Corporation, the finance subsidiary of a major home-builder; that this is the 20th CMO for that issuer (showing the issuer comes to

TABLE 12.1
Ryland Acceptance Corporation

Series 20 $82,000,000 AAA
100% GNMA Collateralized

Settlement date	09/25/86	WAC	9.02%
First coupon	01/01/87	WAM	29.83
Distribution frequency	Quarterly pay (30-day delay)	PSA	100%

Class	Coupon	Amount	Stated Maturity	Average Life	Price	Yield	Spread to Treasury
20A	7.70	$17,775	10/1/96	2.3	99.30	7.49	2 yr. + 100
20B	8.50	17,660	7/1/01	5.5	99.31	8.43	5 yr. + 152
20C	9.00	38,600	1/1/08	10.9	97.30	9.30	10 yr. + 205
20D	9.00	7,965	10/1/16	21.6	82.16	10.00	20 yr. + 240

Source: Shearson Lehman Hutton Mortgage Securities.

market often and therefore is well known to the market); that the total size of the deal is $82 million; and that the security is rated AAA. Finally, we see that the CMO is 100 percent collateralized by GNMA MBSs.

More specific information given is that the settlement date is September 25 and that the first payment of P&I to the first tranche and of interest only to the following tranches will be January 1, 1987. The table also indicates that the frequency of P&I payments is quarterly with a 30-day delay. The delay is to give the trustee time to compile the information on all the payments made on the individual mortgages during the quarter and to prepare a collateral paydown status for distribution to the bondholders.

The WAC (weighted average coupon) is in fact the average note rate of the underlying mortgage collateral. The 9.02 percent WAC indicates that the mortgages are at rates below current market mortgage rates and are not now candidates for refinancing. The WAM (weighted average maturity) of 29.83 years confirms that the loans are new production loans, which will tend to pay at a slow rate for at least a year or more.

This offering appears to have some relative cash-flow stability. Note that the PSA assumption is 100 percent, which confirms a conservative estimate of the principal prepayment rate.

The structure of this typical CMO offers four classes of bonds, each with its own coupon and average-life assumption. The distribution of maturities walks up the yield curve with average lives corresponding to the 2-, 5-, 10-, and 20-year points on the curve.

The Pricing Process

The last column of Table 12.1 gives the basis-point spread to the Treasury curve point. The dealer's pricing determination was intended to target these levels of yield spread, and the dollar prices and coupons were derived to meet those yield-spread objectives—not the other way around. While the offering is held in syndicate the dollar prices given will hold. Once the offering is free to trade, it will trade to the stipulated basis-yield spreads to the comparable-maturity Treasury. This form of pricing enables the investor to invest at a known yield spread to the desired time sector of the yield curve (2 or 5 years, for example), rather than attempting to determine whether the dollar price is right.

CMO Cash-Flow Structure

Figure 12.1 illustrates the sequential pattern of cash flow through the four tranches of a typical CMO.

Note that the cash-flow window of each tranche starts when the last principal payment of the prior tranche has been made; peaks approximately midway through its cash-flow life; and then terminates, leading to the commencement of the cash-flow window for the succeeding tranche.

The start of the cash-flow cycle, or window, for a tranche is referred to as the **first call**. The time of the first call is the point at which, estimated by the speed model, the tranche will receive its first principal amount.

The mid-point of the cash-flow window is the estimated average life of the tranche. The average-life estimate is used to determine the time point on the Treasury yield curve that will be the reference point for calculating the cash-flow yield estimate used for pricing the tranche.

The end of the estimated cash-flow window is referred to as the **projected maturity** date. The investor may then use the estimated average life as a reference point for pricing purposes, with the projected first call and projected maturity date as estimates for the window during which cash flow will be received. As will be discussed further, these are only estimates and will change as economic and demographic factors cause the observed rate of principal payments, or cash flow, to accelerate or decline.

Z-Bond Class Structure

The fourth class of bonds, or tranche, is generally a **Z-bond**. The Z-bond receives no cash until all of the earlier tranches are paid in full. It does, however, accrete the coupon attributable to it during the period that other tranches are outstanding. The Z-bond's attributable coupon is accreted as an

FIGURE 12.1
How a CMO Is Structured

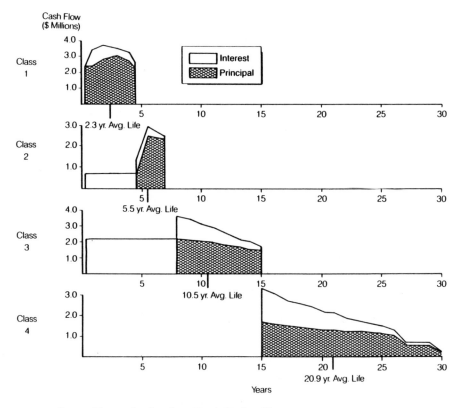

Source: Morgan Stanley; Janet Desel, Product Manager.

addition to its initial face amount. When all prior tranches have been retired, the Z-bond receives coupon payments on its then-larger principal balance, plus any principal prepayments made from the mortgage pool. Figure 12.2 illustrates the Z-bond cash flow.

The Z-bond tends to reduce some of the prepayment volatility of the cash flows on the earlier tranches. It differs from an ordinary bond in that it does not pay interest until all of the previous tranches have been completely paid off. The Z-bond accrues the interest as an addition to the unpaid principal due on the bond. Once all previous tranches have been retired, the accrual bond becomes a pass-through instrument. P&I, based on the accrued principal amount, is then paid to holders until the Z-bond is completely paid down, at which point the deal is closed. The interest on the Z-bond, received by the trust from the

FIGURE 12.2
Outstanding Balance of Z- or Accrual Class

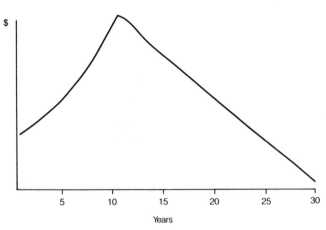

Source: Morgan Stanley.

underlying collateral, is used to pay down the earlier tranches, thus providing a dependable and thoroughly guaranteed cash flow to pay down the earlier tranches. Thus CMOs with a Z-bond tend to be more predictable than those without.

The amount of cash is considerable. Assume, for example, that $100 million of a 4-tranche $500 million deal is a Z-bond with a 10 percent coupon; the cash flow that would be applied to interest on that class, but used instead to pay down early tranches, is $10 million per year. Assume, further, that prepayments the first year would produce just under $6 million, the second year a little more than $18 million, and the third year slightly more than $27 million (100 percent of PSA experience). Scheduled amortization would provide additional cash flow to pay down the first tranche. The combined cash flow over three years would produce two-thirds of the amount required to pay off a $125 million first tranche, thus shortening the lives of the first three tranches.

At any point after issue and until they become the currently paying class, the principal balance of a Z-bond is the original balance plus accrued interest. When traded, the price applies to the then-current balance, not the original face amount; the balance is determined by multiplying the original face amount by the current factor. For legal purposes, the factor changes (accrued interest is added to principal) only on bond payment dates (for example, quarterly). For trade-settlement purposes, however, the factor increments daily. This procedure is necessary because the accrued interest is valued at the market price of the bond, not at par.

The Stated Maturity

Every CMO tranche has a stated maturity as well as the average life and projected maturity described above. The **stated maturity** is simply the date the last payment would occur at zero CPR—that is, if not a single mortgage prepaid. The CMO is what is referred to as a *pay-through* bond. That means the ability of the bond to be paid in full is dependent on the cash flow of P&I payments made by the underlying mortgages (which are guaranteed by either a federal agency or a combination of home equity, mortgage insurance, and the pool policy). To be absolutely conservative, the only safe assumption the trustee can make is to project the collateral cash flow on a zero prepay assumption. However, as past experience has demonstrated, there will always be some prepayments, so investors should not price a CMO to the stated maturity or zero CPR assumption.

The Reinvestment Assumption

The mortgages in the collateral pool pay monthly, of course. While some CMOs also pay monthly and others semiannually, most pay quarterly. The trustee is therefore able to reinvest the mortgage pool P&I between distribution dates. Again, to be conservative the rating agencies require the trustee to assume a relatively low reinvestment rate in the calculations to figure the funds that will be required to meet future bond payments. The reinvestment assumption most commonly used at present is 4½ percent the first year, 4 percent the second year, and 3 percent thereafter. Since CMO trustees have to date been able consistently to reinvest at rates higher than these assumptions, the excess is retained as a residual, which may ultimately be returned to the issuer or—as increasingly is the case—be sold by the issuer. (See Chapter 14 for a description of residuals.)

CMO PRICING AND INVESTMENT

Investors usually focus on the stated yield of a prospective investment and relate that to alternative fixed-income investments with comparable credit and maturity characteristics. Most fixed-income traders, including MBSs traders, think in terms of relative dollar price. They are not primarily concerned with the stated yield at a given moment; more typically, their focus is on determining the right dollar-price spread between a given Treasury issue and the 10-year or between GNMA 9s and GNMA 11s, for example.

Unlike fixed-income traders, CMO traders are concerned with determining the right basis-yield spread between the CMO and the comparable (duration-equivalent) Treasury, and which maturity Treasury is the right one. CMO investors should have the same focus. Table 12.2 shows approximate CMO-to-Treasury spreads for new-issue CMOs as they were priced in August 1988. The table shows the basis-point yield spread at which a particular CMO tranche would be priced to the Treasury security with a maturity closest to the average life of the CMO. Table 12.2 may be read as follows:

1. What is the price of a GNMA-collateralized CMO tranche with an average life of two years? See (1) in the table, which indicates the tranche should be priced to yield 85 basis points higher yield than the 2-year Treasury.
2. What is the price of the third tranche of a CMO collateralized by Freddie Mac PCs with a projected average life of 10.7 years based on the current observed prepayment speed of the underlying collateral? See (2) in the table, which indicates the tranche should be priced to yield 165 basis points higher yield than the 10-year Treasury.

Tracking Yield Spreads

The yield spread of a CMO to the Treasury will vary according to several factors: the nature of the underlying collateral; whether the price is at par, a discount, or a premium; and the implied outlook for speed.

Collateral Type

Ginnie Mae-backed securities enjoy the guaranty of timely payment of P&I by the full faith and credit of the U.S. Treasury. The Ginnie Mae guaranty is therefore the strongest.

TABLE 12.2
Indicative CMO New-Issue Levels
August 1988

Comparable Treasury	CMO Collateral Type		
	GNMA	FN/FH [a]	Whole-Loan AAA
1 yr.	70	85	125
2 yr.	85 (1)	95	135
3 yr.	95	110	145
4 yr.	120	140	175
5 yr.	125	145	180
7 yr.	135	150	200
10 yr.	155	165 (2)	220
20 yr.	145	160	195

[a]Designates FNMA or FHLMC collateral.

Source: Shearson Lehman Hutton Mortgage Securities.

Fannie Mae also guarantees timely payment of principal and interest, and although a strong agency, it is not full faith and credit. Freddie Mac guarantees the timely payment of interest and ultimate payment of principal with the exception of certain PCs issued under its Guarantor swap program designated for CMOs wherein timely payment of both P&I is guaranteed.

Conventional whole-loan–backed CMOs guarantee timely payment of P&I to the extent of home equity, private mortgage insurance, pool policy reserves, and other features of the trust indenture but are not agency-guaranteed. These CMOs are rated AAA by Standard & Poor's, however, and the strength of their credit should not be underestimated. Indeed, most sophisti-cated investors consider the AAA whole-loan CMOs as safe as the agency-guaranteed issues.

Because of these differences in collateral backing, GNMA-collateralized CMOs trade at the narrowest spreads; FNMA- and FHLMC-backed at some-what wider spreads; and whole-loan–backed at the widest spreads—given that maturity and speed considerations are equal.

Price Considerations

Par or discount-priced MBSs generally trade at a lower relative basis spread to the Treasury yield than do premium-priced MBSs. The same is true of CMOs. The wider yield spread commanded by premium-priced MBSs is, of course, related to the implied call option always present in a mortgage-related security.

The difficulty with the prepayment call option in the MBS is that it is *not predictable*. If an investor is short a call on a Treasury bond futures contract traded on an exchange and that option goes in the money, the investor knows the option will be called. Home mortgage borrowers do not always refinance, or repay, mortgages even when lower mortgage rates are available (mortgage prepayment options are in the money). And frequently they prepay mortgages when prepayment options are not in the money, but for other reasons—for example, the home is sold and the mortgage is not assumable. Thus the value of the option component in the MBS does not track a "rational" option-pricing model, but it is always there. For that reason, even an MBS coupon backed by mortgages that are not in the money with respect to current mortgage rates will, if the MBS coupon is trading at a premium price, trade at a wider spread to the Treasury than the par or discount security. (See Chapter 7 for more information on the value of the option in the MBS.)

Prepayment-Speed Considerations

Because of the inherent and uncertain risk associated with the mortgage prepayment option, CMOs that display observed relatively high speeds gener-ally trade at a relatively higher yield spread to the Treasury curve than CMOs with the same duration (same curve point) but with slower observed speeds. From that general observation everything becomes relative.

For example, increasing speed reduces the stated yield of premium-priced securities, but in time high speed will improve the stated yield of a discount. The reason is that increasing speed accelerates the pace at which mortgage pool cash flow is returned. If the investor pays a premium for an MBS or a CMO and the speed accelerates, cash flow purchased at a premium is returned faster than anticipated, resulting in the need to write off some premium that cannot be recaptured within the originally anticipated holding period. Also, since the duration is shorter than had been originally estimated, the investor has less time than was originally estimated to earn the higher coupon that now must be reinvested at a lower rate. The consequence is loss of yield.

On the other hand, if the MBS or CMO is bought at a discount and prepayments accelerate, cash flow purchased at a discount is returned at par sooner than anticipated, thus presenting the investor with a windfall gain. The returned principal will presumably also be reinvested at a lower yield than originally anticipated, but the rate is offset by a higher market price.

But everything is relative. If a premium coupon displays a slower observed speed than other premium coupons of similar duration, it may trade at a narrower yield spread than its peer group—and vice versa for the discount.

If the market perceives that future implied speeds are likely to slow down, the yield spread required of premium coupons will begin to shrink. There is, then, basis risk/reward in CMO investing. If the speed estimate is too low at the time of purchase, the required yield spread to the Treasury will widen as the market perceives that speeds are likely to accelerate. And if the CMO is purchased at a sectoral peak in speeds, the basis spread will shrink. If the investor buys a CMO at 200 basis points to the Treasury and that basis spread shrinks to 150 basis points, the price of the security will rise.

Summary of Key Points

Par price = new-issue yield to curve (see Table 12.2)

Discount-Priced Coupon
- Yield spreads generally lower than new issue
- Slower implied speeds = narrowing yield spreads
- Higher implied speeds = narrowing yield spreads

Premium-Priced Coupon
- Yield spreads generally higher than new issue
- Slower implied speeds = narrowing yield spreads
- Faster implied speeds = widening yield spreads

The key to CMO and all MBSs investing is that the yield, duration, and average-life assumptions given at the time of purchase are only ESTIMATES and are constantly subject to change as observed and even as implied speeds change.

CMO investing is a game of risk/reward. The successful player measures the probability of the risk—and whether it is a liveable one—before seeking the reward.

Measuring Risk/Reward in CMO Investing

The investor should compare the yield, average life, duration, and projected maturity at three speed assumptions for any CMO investment. The three speed assumptions should be the estimate at time of purchase, at a higher speed, and at a slower speed.

Table 12.3 illustrates a risk/reward sensitivity analysis for the second tranche of a GNMA-backed CMO priced at par.

The table presents a very conservative investment with little risk/reward to changing speed:

1. The CMO is priced at par, which means changes in speed have little impact on yield.
2. The CMO collateral is GNMA MBSs, which are backed by FHA/VA mortgages, typically the least sensitive to interest-rate and demographic changes.
3. The 9 percent pass-through rate on the MBSs means the mortgages are at 9½ percent, a rate too low to be subject to refinancing at rates that prevailed at the time the CMO was issued.
4. The basis spread to the Treasury increases when compared to the 4-year point on the curve only because the 4-year Treasury is at a lower yield than the 5-year Treasury.

TABLE 12.3
Shearson Lehman Hutton B-2 (second tranche)

Coupon	8.95%		
Stated Maturity	5/1/99		
Collateral	100% GNMA 9% MBS		
PSA assumption	75	100	125
Price	100	100	100
Average life (yrs.)	6.3	5.4	4.3
Duration (yrs.)	4.8	4.4	3.6
Yield (CBE)[a]	9.0	9.0	8.9
Spread to Treasury	5 yr. + 160	5 yr. + 160	4 yr. + 168

[a] CBE = corporate bond equivalent.

Source: Shearson Lehman Hutton Mortgage Securities.

Now consider a CMO with somewhat more volatile collateral—priced at a premium. Table 12.4 is a sensitivity analysis for a 12½ percent FHLMC-issued CMO third tranche priced at 109¼.

The assumed speed at the time of purchase is 550 PSA. The table shows that if the speed picks up to 600 PSA, the yield declines by about 20 basis points as the average life and duration shorten. This defines the risk. Is it acceptable? It might be. The important point is that even though the investor would give up yield with an acceleration in speed, the 9.24 yield may still be quite acceptable for a 3½-year average-life instrument. After all, if the prepayment speed picked up, it would probably be because market yields have fallen. Another consideration, however, is the basis risk. The computer shows the spread to the 4-year Treasury would be 154 basis points; but with an increase in speed it is likely the basis spread to the Treasury would widen, suggesting a drop in price.

In terms of reward, with slower speed the investor has a nice increase in realized yield to 9.84 percent. Again, the computer figures show a 200 basis-point spread to the 5-year Treasury. But with a drop in speed that yield spread should sink, leading to a price increase. This, then, would be a gratifying investment in a bear market.

Synthetic Discount CMOs

Finally, consider a CMO issued at a discount. This unique structure was introduced in 1987 as an outgrowth of the CMO floating tranche. Because of the need to overcollateralize the floater tranche to secure the cap, the fixed-rate tranches were structured with a discount coupon secured by high WAC collateral. Table 12.5 illustrates such a structure with the CMO Trust Series 16, class 4.

At the time these bonds were traded (summer 1987) the PC 9½s were actually paying down at a 3-month PSA of 552 percent. This speed was judged to be unsustainable, however, because the market had been in a bear mode for some time. The investor perceived that should the bear market persist, the

TABLE 12.4
FHLMC B-3 (third tranche)

Coupon	12½%		
Stated Maturity	9/30/13		
Collateral	12%–14%	conventional mortgages	
PSA assumption	450	550	600
Price	109¼	109¼	109¼
Average life (yrs.)	4.66	3.85	3.53
Duration (yrs.)	3.52	3.06	2.86
Yield (CBE)	9.84	9.45	9.24
Spread to Treasury	5 yr. + 200	4 yr. + 175	4 yr. + 154

Source: Shearson Lehman Hutton Mortgage Securities.

TABLE 12.5
CMO Trust 16-4 (fourth tranche)

Coupon	5.00%			
Stated Maturity	9/20/12			
Collateral	9% FHLMC PC			
PSA assumption	150	200	300	500
Price	81⅜	81⅜	81⅜	81⅜
Average life (yrs.)	5.65	4.35	2.97	1.83
Duration (yrs.)	4.80	3.83	2.72	1.73
Yield (CBE)	9.40	10.53	12.84	17.45
Spread to Treasury	5 yr. + 118	4 yr. + 245	3 yr. + 496	2 yr. + 987

speed on the underlying PCs might decline to 150 PSA at worst. The result would be a downside yield of 9.40 and a spread of 118 basis points to the 5-year Treasury, a yield and spread to the curve comparable to those available on seasoned short WAM PC 8s. At the time of purchase, based on the 3-month observed speed, the yield was 17.45 percent, or 987 basis points over the 2-year Treasury. Of course, the anticipation was that a high yield would not be realized for very long. The investor, however, could look forward to realizing a generous yield for however many months it might take for the PSA speed to slow to 150—if ever.

SELECTING THE CMO INVESTMENT

Once the investor has selected the type of CMO to buy (for example, FHLMC-collateralized or whole-loan–backed for highest yield); determined the desired maturity range on the yield curve (3 to 5 years, 7 to 10 years); and decided whether to make a discount, par, or premium-priced investment, the question is how to find the specific CMO that fits these needs.

Techniques of Investing

The investor will do best to define his objective by collateral and average-life sectors and to think in terms of GNMA versus Freddie Mac versus whole-loan collateral groups. The maturity bracket too should be defined by average-life sectors—3 to 5 years, 7 to 10 years, and so on. Investors are not well advised to try to find a specific tranche of a specific CMO issued some time ago. Accounts do not trade CMOs the way they trade generic MBSs coupons, so dealers are not likely to be able to find that particular tranche, and they will not short it. Major dealers, however, have several offerings that will fit a specific collateral type and average-life sector.

A next step is for the investor to define the yield spread to the target maturity sector of the Treasury curve that he believes is fair. A good way to do this is to make up a spread sheet that resembles Table 12.2. By tracking yield spreads of various CMO groups weekly one develops a good feel for what is available in the market.

Persons shopping for CMO investments should look for such criteria as agency-backed collateral with a 3- to 5-year average life at 110 to 150 to the curve or whole-loan collateral with a 7- to 10-year average life at 200 to 220.

Investors need to specify—usually with three or four major CMO dealers—whether they wish to see premiums (to take advantage of declining prepayment speeds) or discounts (to participate in a bull market). Several selections are likely to be offered that fit the investor's objectives.

FLOATING-RATE CMOs

In September 1986 Shearson Lehman Brothers introduced the concept of adding a floating-rate tranche to the CMO structure. In the summer of 1987 Congress amended the REMIC legislation, enabling the floater structure to be used in connection with multiclass REMIC issues.[1]

The floating-CMO class uses the **London Interbank Offered Rate (LIBOR)** as its index, usually the 3-month LIBOR rate. The interest rate on the floater is generally reset two business days prior to each CMO payment date. This rate is equal to LIBOR plus the spread, subject to an interest-rate cap. On each reset day, at 11 A.M. London time, the bond trustee determines the appropriate LIBOR rate by asking the London offices of four reference banks for their respective quotations. The four quotes are then averaged and rounded to the nearest 1/16th to arrive at the index rate. The interest calculations are then determined, assuming a 30/360 or actual/360 count basis.

The Variety of Floater Caps

A cap is the maximum interest rate allowable on a bond. Caps are not uncommon in the floating-rate debt markets. Adjustable-rate mortgage (ARM) pass-throughs have lifetime caps of 11–18 percent with maximum annual increases or decreases of 1–2 percent. Capped Euro and domestic floaters have lifetime caps of 12.5–13.75 percent on original-issue, 12-year securities. With floating-rate certificates of deposit lifetime caps are 7–13.25 percent on maturities ranging from 18 months to 7 years. CMO floater classes currently have the highest spreads of any capped LIBOR-based floaters at similar cap levels, regardless of rating.

[1]The discussion that follows is based largely on ''An Overview of Floating Rate CMOs,'' from Shearson Lehman Hutton, *Mortgage Finance Marketplace*, April 1987.

CMO floater classes have two possible cap structures:

1. *Step Caps:* Caps that are effective according to a calendar established at issue. The first floating-rate CMO was Shearson Lehman CMO Series D, which has step-up caps of 9 percent in year 1, 10 percent in year 2, 10.5 percent in year 3, 11.5 percent in year 4, and 12 percent in years 5 and beyond.

2. *Lifetime Caps:* Caps that are effective from issue through the life of the floating-rate class. These types of floaters make up the largest sector of the market, with caps ranging from 10.5 to 13 percent.

The coupon of a floating-rate class must be capped at some rate, because its only sources of payment are fixed-rate mortgages. Therefore, the existence of caps is not due to the discretion of the CMO issuer but rather is necessitated by the structures of a CMO.

Various techniques are available that allow floating-rate classes to be structured with higher caps. For example, if some of the fixed-coupon classes of a floating-rate CMO are issued with low coupons (relative to the collateral), more interest is made available for the floating-rate class. Consequently, the cap may be increased. Ryland Series 33, for example, has 9.5 percent Freddie Mac collateral. This simultaneous-pay floater class makes up half of the total issue and has a 13 percent cap. The other half of the issue consists of fixed-rate classes which all pay 6 percent. Note that half of 13 percent plus half of 6 percent equals 9.5 percent, which is the coupon on the collateral.

CMO Superfloaters: A New Hedging Vehicle[2]

Superfloater tranches of CMOs were introduced in late 1987 as a new alternative to interest-rate swaps or financial futures for hedging long-term assets that are funded with short-term liabilities. Superfloater tranches at issue yield less than LIBOR, but if LIBOR rises, the superfloater coupon adjusts upward by a multiple of the change in the LIBOR rate. Additionally, the principal prepayment changes in the underlying mortgage collateral change favorably for the investor in most interest-rate environments. Superfloater tranches are an excellent long-term portfolio hedge for the bearish investor: when combined with fixed-rate assets, superfloaters provide stability of returns over most interest-rate environments and, with rising interest rates, they add value to the portfolio.

---

[2]This discussion of superfloaters is taken from Shearson Lehman Hutton, "Mortgage Securities Market Update," June 1988. The article was written by Nicole Lowen.

Superfloaters differ from standard floating-rate CMO tranches in their rate-reset mechanism and in their investment applications. Floating-rate CMOs reset at a fixed spread over LIBOR on a periodic basis. For CMO superfloater tranches, however, the coupon rate is set through a formula that magnifies any change in the value of the LIBOR-based index. For example, the Ryland Acceptance Corporation Four Series 70-D superfloater class was issued with an initial coupon of 6.375 percent—75 basis points lower than LIBOR at the time of issue. After June 30, 1988, the coupon resets monthly at twice 1-month LIBOR less 7.875 percent, subject to a floor of 3.25 percent and a cap of 13.625 percent. If LIBOR increases (decreases) by 50 basis points, at the next reset date the coupon on the superfloater will rise (fall) by 100 basis points.

Like other floaters, floating-rate CMOs are an attractive alternative to short-term securities. Their frequent coupon resets provide market interest rates without the transaction costs incurred when reinvesting proceeds from maturing short-term assets. Superfloater CMO classes, however, should be purchased as an interest-rate hedge rather than as a stand-alone investment. The movement of the superfloater coupon works in tandem with the prepayment characteristics of the underlying mortgage collateral to the investor's advantage. As interest rates rise, the superfloater coupon adjusts upward faster than LIBOR. Since prepayments will slow in this case, the investor is doubly rewarded—the coupon resets at higher than market rates, and the weighted average life is extended, thereby maximizing the principal life when the yield return is at its highest. Conversely, in a falling interest-rate environment, the coupon on the superfloater declines faster than those of other floating-rate instruments, but the increasing prepayments passed through to the investor shorten the weighted average life and supply cash for alternative market-rate investments.

CMO superfloaters are an excellent hedge against rising interest rates when funding long-term assets with short-term liabilities. The stability of yield return that superfloaters can provide is illustrated by the return on assets (ROA), a measure of annual net income as a percentage of average book value (see Chapter 15). Table 12.6 compares ROAs for two hypothetical portfolios financed by one-month repurchase agreements. Portfolio 1 contains only GNMA 10s, while Portfolio 2 consists of GNMA 10s hedged with Ryland 70-D superfloaters. The hedged portfolio performs better when rates rise at least 200 basis points. Its ROA remains positive unless rates rise 400 basis points, at which point the superfloater coupon caps out.

In this example, an automatic dynamic hedge is created because the superfloater, which is collateralized by GNMA 10s, and the mortgage asset can be expected to pay down at similar rates. Thus the hedge ratio would require less frequent adjustment than a hedge using interest-rate swaps.

TABLE 12.6
Interest-Rate Return on Assets for Two Short-Funded Portfolios (in percents)

Interest-Rate Change (basis points)	Portfolio 1: GNMA 10s	Portfolio 2: GNMA 10s & Ryland 70-D Superfloaters
400	−2.14	− .20
300	− .62	1.03
200	.80	1.31
100	2.03	1.48
0	3.10	1.56
−100	4.01	1.63
−200	4.71	1.76
−300	5.12	2.50

Source: Shearson Lehman Hutton Mortgage Securities.

Inverse Floaters

Another variation on the floater-class structure is called an **inverse floater**. The interest rate of the inverse floater is reset (at the same time as the floater reset) to its own cap minus some multiple of LIBOR. As LIBOR rises, the interest rate of the inverse floater falls, allowing for a greater cap on the floater class. The inverse floating-rate classes and low-coupon classes appeal to investors seeking price appreciation. Table 12.7 compares changes in the effective rate of an inverse floater with those of a standard floater. Note that as the LIBOR rate increases from 0 to 15 percent, the effective rate on the inverse floater declines from 30 to 0 percent while that of the standard floater increases. In a period of declining LIBOR rates (bull market), of course, the realized yield of the inverse floater would increase.

TABLE 12.7
Possible Interest Rates on CMOs with a $20 Million Floating-Rate Class and a $10 Million Inverse Floating-Rate Class

LIBOR	0%	6%	15%
Inverse floater rate = 30% − (2 × LIBOR)	30%	18%	0%
Floater rate = LIBOR + 30 bp	.3%	6.3%	15.3%
Weighted average rate	10.2%	10.2%	10.2%

Source: Shearson Lehman Hutton Mortgage Securities.

Investment Strategies

CMO floating-rate class investors have a variety of structures from which to choose. The primary components to consider when investing in floater CMOs are cap, index, average life, and spread.

The spread over LIBOR for a floating-rate class should be higher in certain instances. Generally, floaters with longer average lives, more volatile average lives, or lower caps should have a higher spread. The underlying collateral will affect the volatility of the average life of the floating-rate class, thereby affecting its value.

Caps limit the interest payments on a floating-rate class and therefore must be compensated for by a higher spread over LIBOR than would otherwise be obtained. All else being equal, the lower the cap, the higher should be the spread to LIBOR. Also, the longer a floater remains outstanding, the greater its cap exposure, and the greater the potential for market spreads over LIBOR to change. Thus, again all else being equal, the longer the average life, the higher should be the spread.

Finally, for MBSs average lives can extend when interest rates rise. Thus the time of cap exposure may lengthen as interest rates approach the cap—an effect that is more pronounced for floating-rate classes with volatile average lives.

The prepayment speeds of premium-coupon mortgages are relatively high in a bull market environment, but may slow down considerably in a bear market. Discount-coupon mortgages exhibit relatively stable average lives over a wide range of interest-rate environments. Fifteen-year mortgages have less volatile average lives than similar 30-year mortgages. Thus, floating-rate classes with 15-year underlying collateral should trade richer (lower spread to LIBOR) than floating-rate classes with 30-year underlying collateral (assuming they have the same average lives and caps). Likewise, a floating-rate class backed by premium collateral should be compensated for its more volatile average life with a slightly higher spread than if it were backed by discount collateral, assuming other considerations remain constant.

Considerations by Investor Class

Thrift Institutions

Floating-rate classes provide risk-controlled arbitrage for thrift institutions. Many thrifts use MBSs as borrowing collateral under a repurchase agreement and with the proceeds purchase floating-rate classes. The thrift can then earn the spread represented by the difference between the repo rate and the floating-rate class coupon.

Life Insurance Companies

Life insurance companies are also looking to floating-rate classes. Many of these firms issue universal life policies, which like CMO floating-rate classes are typically interest-rate-responsive. Thus, floating-rate classes provide an attractive investment to back up universal life policy reserves.

European and Japanese Investors

These investors are familiar with the Euro-based floating-rate note market and capped floating-rate securities in general. CMO floating-rate classes provide higher spreads and better credit ratings at similar cap levels than their counterparts in the other floater markets. Consequently, European and Japanese investors have been significant participants in the floater CMO market.

Broad-based investor demand and explosive product origination have resulted in a widely traded CMO floater market. Generally, markets are quoted on a 1/8th spread in increments of $5 million and up. CMO floating-rate classes have become a significant part of both the CMO and floater markets. Floating-rate CMOs represent one of the most significant innovations since the development of the CMO itself.

PLANNED-AMORTIZATION CLASS (PAC) CMO TRANCHES[3]

The creation of **planned-amortization class (PAC)**[4] CMO bonds is another innovation in the CMO structure. A PAC can be viewed as a scheduled sinking fund mechanism. A PAC investor is virtually assured of receiving fixed payments over a predetermined time period under a wide range of prepayment scenarios. Typically, the PAC is the second tranche of a 4-tranche CMO.

While the PAC produces tremendous cash-flow certainty, it creates ambiguity for other maturity classes in a CMO.

[3]This section is based largely on a January 1987 Shearson Lehman Hutton research report, "Analysis of PAC CMOs," prepared by Kevin McDermott.

[4]This type of security has also been issued under the acronyms "PRO" (planned redemption obligation) and "SMRT" (stabilized mortgage reduction term). For simplicity, this discussion will use the initials PAC throughout.

Investor Considerations with PAC CMOs

1. The investor may view a PAC bond as similar to a callable sinking fund debenture. The average life and duration of a PAC vary little between prepayment rates of 12 and 419 percent PSA. The cash flow of a PAC bond is presented in Figure 12.3 under prepayment assumptions from 12 to 315 percent PSA.

2. Because of the principal-redemption schedule, however, the average life of a PAC bond lengthens slightly during prepayment speeds of 316 through 418 percent PSA. This extension occurs in the latter stages of the bond's life when the scheduled amortization of principal prepayments are not enough to meet the sinking fund schedule. The effect on the bond is generally positive

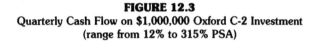

FIGURE 12.3
Quarterly Cash Flow on $1,000,000 Oxford C-2 Investment
(range from 12% to 315% PSA)

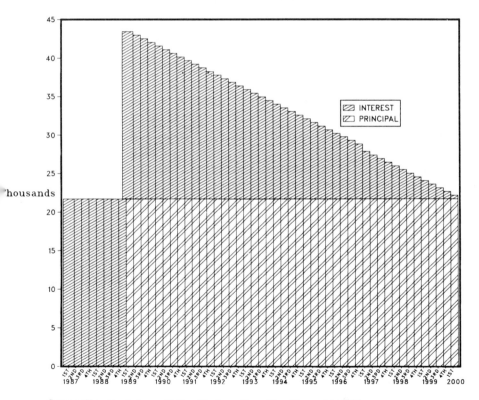

Source: Shearson Lehman Hutton Mortgage Securities, November 1987.

because the bond remains outstanding longer, when it is most beneficial for the bondholder. In other words, when rates drop significantly and prepayments rise to between 315 and 419 percent PSA, the bondholder retains the above-market coupon for an extended period of time.

3. If prepayments slow down, the average life (and duration) of the first maturity class in a PAC CMO lengthen considerably more than those of a standard CMO. Lengthening occurs because the sinking fund payment on the PAC must be met before any other maturity classes can receive principal payments. A further lengthening could occur if the PAC bond is entitled to a makeup for any shortfalls or deficits.

4. If prepayments accelerate, the average life (and duration) of an intermediate-maturity third class in a PAC CMO shortens more dramatically than those of a standard CMO. Within the structure of a PAC CMO, if the first class pays off as a result of rapid prepayments, the intermediate class then promptly begins to receive prepayments that are in excess of the scheduled sinking fund requirement of the PAC bond. In comparison, a standard intermediate class would receive principal payments only after all earlier classes have been retired.

5. The Z-class in a PAC CMO is also affected by an acceleration of prepayments. The average life (and duration) of the PAC Z-class is substantially shortened. In fact, at a prepayment rate of 320 percent PSA or faster, the Z-class is likely to be fully retired while the PAC remains outstanding.

6. Given the potential shortening of average life and duration, the later classes of a PAC CMO still have tremendous value if they are offered at a deep discount. In a declining interest-rate environment where prepayments accelerate, investors of these classes would most likely experience a substantial increase in cash-flow yields and market price.

The First Class of a PAC CMO

The first class of a PAC CMO has generally been an interest-bearing CMO with a 2- to 3-year average life. At first glance, the issue compares favorably with the first class of standard CMOs. Table 12.8 presents a detailed comparison of two similar deals brought to market in mid-September 1987.

Figure 12.4 illustrates the cash flows of the two CMOs in Table 12.8. It is evident from the figure that there is a significant difference between these two seemingly comparable CMOs: The Oxford C-1 becomes a much longer security as prepayments slow down. The lengthening will most likely occur when interest rates are rising—at a time when the investor least desires it. Therefore, the PAC CMO investor will be unable to reinvest as much principal at higher

TABLE 12.8
First-Class Standard CMO versus PAC Bond CMO

	Oxford Accept. Corp. Series III, C-1	Resident Mtg. Secur. Series II, 2-A
Coupon	7.93%	7.89%
Stated maturity	Nov. 20, 2010	Feb. 20, 2009
Collateral	FHLMC 9%	FHLMC 9%
WAM	28.50	28.50
Prepayment assumption	175% PSA	175% PSA
Average life	3.4 yrs.	3.4 yrs.
Duration	2.9 yrs.	2.9 yrs.
PAC bond in issue	Yes	No

Source: Shearson Lehman Hutton Mortgage Securities.

rates as is possible with the traditional CMO. If prepayment speeds were to fall to one-half of the pricing assumption (87.5 percent PSA), the average life on the Oxford C-1 would be 21 percent longer (6.74 years) than on that of the Residential 2-A class (5.57 years).

The priority of the sinking fund in a PAC bond causes classes like the Oxford C-1 to behave as shown in Figure 12.4. Because the sinking fund

FIGURE 12.4
Average Life of a Traditional CMO (Res MST II, 2A)
versus a PAC-Issue CMO (Oxford III, C-1)

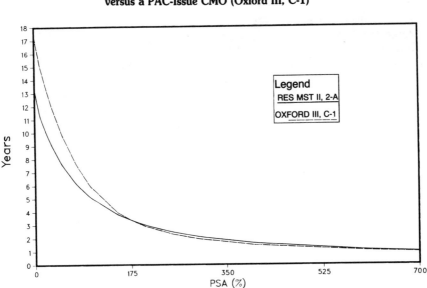

Source: Shearson Lehman Hutton Mortgage Research, November 1987.

schedule must be met before any other class can receive its principal payments, the C-1 is denied some or all principal payments under slow prepayment speeds. The traditional stability of the average life in a first-class CMO—scheduled amortization, Z-class contributions, and basic prepayments—is channeled to the PAC bond in times of need.

A further lengthening may occur if the PAC bond is entitled to make up shortfalls or deficits. In some issues, if a PAC bond's sinking fund payment is not met in one quarter, all subsequent principal cash flow is required to continue to go toward the PAC bond until both present and past sinking fund obligations are satisfied. This carryover effect will continue to deny the current-pay first-class CMO from receiving some or all of its principal distributions.

Third-Class CMOs (Intermediate-Term Average Lives)

Most PAC bonds are in the second class of an issue and are generally followed by a third class with an average life of approximately 10 years. A comparison of the third class in the Shearson Lehman C-3 with the third class of the now-familiar Oxford III-C deal is given in Table 12.9.

Figure 12.5 illustrates that as soon as one of these two bonds moves away from the pricing prepayment assumption, the result is a significant difference in average lives and durations. This is especially true when interest rates fall and prepayment speeds accelerate; the third class from the PAC CMO (Oxford III-C) then becomes a much shorter security, and its principal is paid off much earlier than is the case with the traditional CMO. This early payment is obviously to the disadvantage of the PAC CMO holder, because the above-market coupon is retired sooner than is usually expected. The holder will undoubtedly have to reinvest the funds at a much lower rate. At 500 percent PSA, for example, the third class of the PAC CMO has shortened from an average life of 10.8 years to 3.16 years, and its duration has decreased from 6.9 to 2.78 years. The traditional CMO, on the other hand, has only shortened from

TABLE 12.9
Comparison of Third-Class Standard versus CMO PAC Bond CMO

	Oxford Accept. Corp. Series III, C-3	Shearson Lehman CMO Series C-3
Coupon	8.95%	9.125%
Stated maturity	Aug. 20, 2012	Jan. 20, 2012
Collateral	FHLMC 9%	FHLMC 9.5%
WAM	28.50	29.1
Prepayment assumption	175% PSA	175% PSA
Average life	10.76 yrs.	10.93 yrs.
Duration	6.9 yrs.	6.95 yrs.
PAC bond in issue	Yes	No

Source: Shearson Lehman Hutton Mortgage Securities.

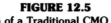

FIGURE 12.5
Duration of a Traditional CMO (SL C-3)
versus a PAC-Issue CMO (Oxford III-C)
(under varying prepayment assumptions)

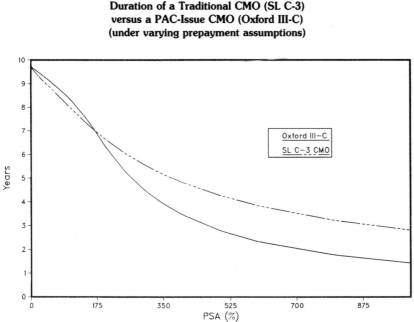

Source: Shearson Lehman Hutton Mortgage Research, November 1987.

an average life of 10.9 years to 5.34 years, and its duration has decreased from 6.95 to 4.26 years. The duration for a third class of the PAC CMO is cut in half at 400 percent PSA, while with a traditional CMO a speed of 700 percent PSA is needed to do the same thing.

To gain some insight into this behavior, we need to examine the mechanics of the principal distribution between the PAC bond and its accompanying third class. During each quarter, the PAC bond receives only the specified amount of principal described in the prospectus; any prepayments over that amount go to the current-pay CMO class. After the first class is completely paid off, the third class receives all prepayments in excess of the PAC bond's sinking fund requirement, thus causing a dramatic shortening of average life and duration. In direct contrast, the third tranche of the traditional CMO does not begin to receive principal distributions until the first and second tranches have been completely paid off.

Fourth-Class Z-Bonds

For comparison purposes, Table 12.10 is composed of two apparently similar Z- (deferred-interest) bonds.

TABLE 12.10
Comparison of Z-Bond Class Standard versus PAC Bond CMO

	Oxford Accept. Corp. Series III, C-4	Resident Mtg. Secur. Series II, 2-D
Coupon	8.95%	9%
Stated maturity	Nov. 25, 2017	Nov. 20, 2017
Collateral	FHLMC 9%	FHLMC 9%
WAM	28.50	28.08
Prepayment assumption	175% PSA	175% PSA
Average life	19.30 yrs.	19.15 yrs.
Duration	17.60 yrs.	17.50 yrs.
PAC bond in issue	Yes	No

Source: Shearson Lehman Hutton Mortgage Securities.

As Figure 12.6 depicts, when there is a significant drop in interest rates (accompanied by an increase in prepayments), the risk for a holder of Z-class bonds on a PAC CMO increases. The average life and duration shorten dramatically compared to the traditional CMO. There is an enormous decrease in both average life and duration between 250 and 400 percent PSA. Average life falls from 16.40 years to 6.28 years (-62 percent), and duration drops

FIGURE 12.6
Average Life of a Traditional Z-Bond (Res MST 2-D)
and a PAC-Issue Z-Bond (Oxford C-4)

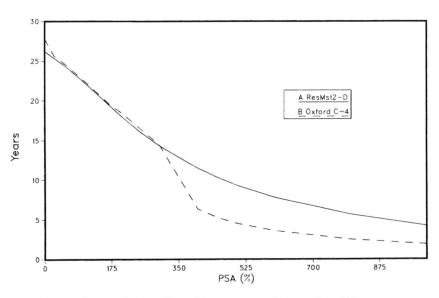

Source: Shearson Lehman Hutton Mortgage Research, November 1987.

from 13.85 years to 6.18 years (-56 percent). Meanwhile, the traditional Z-class CMO has had its average life shortened from 16.05 years to 11.47 years (-29 percent) and its duration decreased from 14.6 years to 10.53 years (-28 percent).

The duration of Z-class from the PAC CMO is halved at a prepayment speed of 340 percent PSA, while the traditional Z-tranche has its duration halved at 525 percent PSA. At 600 percent PSA the traditional Z-tranche is 2.31 times longer than the PAC CMO Z-tranche as expressed by their durations: 8.3 years versus 3.6 years.

Once again, this shortening can be better understood by observing the mechanics of the principal distribution system. Under a pricing speed of 175 percent PSA both the Oxford C-2s (the actual PAC bond) and C-3s will be fully retired in the year 2000. At that point, the C-4 class is the only remaining class and is entitled to all scheduled and prepayment principal until it too is completely paid off (as with a traditional CMO). As prepayments accelerate, the C-3s will be fully paid off well before the sinking fund schedule of the PAC bond has finished (May 20, 2000). Therefore any prepayments in excess of the sinking fund schedule will go directly to the Z-class. At speeds in excess of 320 percent PSA the Z-class will be fully retired by prepayments while the PAC bond is still outstanding. In effect, this fourth, and ostensibly last, class has become the third class. Although in theory the fourth class is the last to begin paying principal, it will be the next to last class to be fully retired. In a traditional CMO, this is not possible.

Pricing Considerations

Considering the severe negative convexity of the third and fourth classes of PAC CMOs, investors are likely to have serious reservations about such a security. Under one condition, however, the investor can utilize the PAC CMO's perverse behavior to his advantage—that is, to purchase these bonds well below par at a deep discount. Any investor who purchases a deep-discount security welcomes an earlier return of principal because he can realize a modest to major increase in the yield or rate of return. As prepayments increase, the discount accretes more quickly toward par, thereby increasing the yield or return on the investment. The return of principal on the third- and fourth-class PAC CMOs can be accelerated as much as three times faster than on traditional CMOs.

If an investor bought the Oxford C-3 at par for a quoted yield of 8.94 (using the 175 percent pricing speed) and subsequently rates fell sharply, so that prepayments rose to 600 percent PSA, the yield would actually have fallen to 8.77 percent, while the average life would have decreased from 10.8 to 2.28 years, thereby severely limiting any upward price appreciation. If the security was bought at a 10-point discount, the yield at 175 percent PSA would be 10.54 percent. A rally leading to a prepayment rate of 600 percent PSA brings about a yield of 13.47 percent. Furthermore, the security will most likely have experienced sharp upside price appreciation toward par. To take this hypothetical situation one step further, if the PAC issue was bought at a 20-point discount, the yield would jump from 12.41 to 19.22 percent!

Finally, if an investor bought Oxford C-4s at par with a pricing speed of 175 percent PSA, the yield would be 9.01 percent with an average life of 19.6 years. A major rally accompanied with prepayment speeds of 600 percent would bring the yield down to 8.84 percent and the average life down to 3.12 years. The same bond purchased at a price of 65.00 would yield 11.56 percent at 175 percent PSA and 21.77 percent at 600 percent PSA.

Targeted Amortization Class (TAC) Tranches

The TAC bond class is similar to the PAC except whereas the PAC structure provides call protection against increasing prepayment speeds, the TAC does not offer protection to extension risk from a reduction in prepayment speeds.

The TAC bond is designed to pay a specific or "target" amount of principal to the bond holder each month. If prepayments increase, the excess cash flows resulting from the higher rate of prepayments will be paid to the non-TAC class. If principal payments are reduced by a slowing of prepayment speeds, the TAC absorbs the available cash flows but goes in arrears for the amount by which it is short of the "target" amortization.

TAC bonds are particularly attractive to investors seeking high yield that could be at risk if prepayments accelerate, for example, with premium-priced collateral. Those who are concerned with extension risk can gain considerable protection by seeking TACs with new production or otherwise relatively slow-speed collateral where the risk of reduction in prepayment speeds is minimal. Table 12.11 illustrates comparative average lives for 10-year standard, PAC, and TAC classes.

Turbo POs: Derivative of Derivatives[5]

Turbo principal-only (TPO) bonds are zero-coupon tranches of REMIC CMO offerings that also contain PAC or TAC classes. TPOs display more leveraged prepayment sensitivity than regular POs because increases in prepayments on the pass-through collateral are directed disproportionately to holders of TPOs. TPOs are an excellent hedge for prepayment-sensitive mortgage securities such

---

[5]This discussion of Turbo POs is taken from Shearson Lehman Hutton, "Mortgage Securities Market Update," July 1988. The article was written by Steven J. Carlson.

TABLE 12.11
Average Lives of 10-Year Standard. PAC, and TAC Classes

Percent PSA	Standard	PAC	TAC
50	19.0	10.9	19.0
100	13.6	10.9	13.6
135	10.9	10.9	10.9
200	7.9	10.9	11.3
275	5.9	10.9	11.1
450	3.7	7.8	6.9

Source: Shearson Lehman Hutton Mortgage Securities.

as CMO residuals, interest-only bonds, and servicing portfolios. In addition, they offer payoff profiles that are similar to call options. This is particularly true for TPOs backed by current-coupon collateral that will experience significant increases in prepayments should interest rates fall.

The prepayment sensitivity of Turbo POs results from the structure of each CMO. The PAC or TAC bonds of a CMO have priority claim on return of principal and often provide the most stable cash flow and average life available in the market. PACs have first claim on principal payments from the CMO collateral, unless prepayments move beyond pre-established PSA limits. TAC bonds are repaid at the original-pricing prepayment rate. If prepayments increase, the payment schedule is maintained until all other bond classes have been retired. However, if prepayments are slower than the initial pricing speed, the average life of the TAC class is extended. As a result, TPOs from TAC offerings have greater protection from prepayment slowdown than those from PAC CMOs.

Because CMOs redistribute but do not reduce aggregate cash flow and average-life variability, the stability of the TAC or PAC class increases the average-life variability of non-TAC or PAC classes, such as TPOs. This greater variability of TPOs can work for investors, particularly in CMO offerings collateralized by current-coupon loans expected to prepay at relatively slow rates. Slow projected prepayments cause TPOs to have longer average lives and to be priced at greater discounts to par value than regular POs. If actual prepayments exceed the pricing speed, the prepayment sensitivity and deep price discounts of TPOs dramatically enhance returns. Therefore, derivative POs, particularly those backed by current-coupon collateral, provide performance profiles similar to a portfolio of serially maturing call options with varying strikes.

Table 12.12 illustrates the yield and average life of Ryland 76-C, a TPO from an offering with TACs compared to a hypothetical regular PO with the same underlying collateral (FNMA 9s) under various prepayment assumptions. The average life of the TPO varies from 21.45 years at the pricing speed of 135 percent PSA to 1.65 years at 300 percent PSA. The regular PO is much more

TABLE 12.12
Performance Profiles for Regular and Turbo POs

PSA	Ryland 76-C TPO		Regular 9% PO	
(%)	BEY (%)	WAL	BEY (%)	WAL
0	4.10	28.06	3.81	20.00
50	4.34	26.61	5.75	14.63
75	4.55	25.40	6.94	12.68
135	5.49	21.45	10.29	9.30
150	7.39	18.28	11.21	8.67
200	32.56	9.42	14.45	6.99
300	104.27	1.65	21.51	4.89
Dollar price: 30-00		48–24		

BEY = Bond equivalent yield.

WAL = Weighted average life in years.

Source: Shearson Lehman Hutton Mortgage Securities.

stable, varying from 9.30 years to 4.89 years. While TPO yield at 135 percent PSA is only 5.49 percent—480 basis points less than the regular PO—it increases dramatically as prepayments rise. If collateral prepayments reach 300 percent PSA, the regular PO yields 21.51 percent, but the Turbo PO jumps to 104.27 percent.

13

IOs and POs: Stripped Mortgage-Backed Securities Cash Flows

INTRODUCTION

Stripped mortgage-backed securities (SMBSs) are securities that redistribute the cash flows from the underlying generic MBS collateral into the principal and interest components of the MBS to enhance their use in meeting special needs of investors. Most SMBSs issued today are structured as principal only (PO) and interest only (IO), but the initial issues were designed as synthetic-discount and premium SMBSs. Synthetic-discount and premium MBSs were created by separating the P&I cash flows into a synthetic class. For example, the A class would consist of 99 percent of the principal and 45 percent of the interest cash flows (synthetic discount); the B class would consist of 50 percent principal and 33.33 percent interest (synthetic premium). (See Appendix C, which lists the 12 Fannie Mae synthetic-coupon issues as well as the fully stripped Fannie Mae SMBS Trusts 1 through 15.)[1]

The strip appears at first to be a complex deviation from the familiar generic MBS, but in reality it simply reaches to the fundamental components of the MBS collateral. In many ways the process of examining strip cash flows leads to a sound understanding of all MBSs cash-flow dynamics. Furthermore, a variety of investment strategies may be implemented with appropriate application of SMBSs. Among them are strategies that enable the investor to

[1]Regulated financial institutions for the most part must now restrict their involvement in SMBSs to hedging strategies and the use of SMBSs to enhance management-directed asset/liability restructuring programs—see "Regulatory Concerns with SMBSs," page 374.

profit from correctly anticipating the direction of interest rates, for hedging purposes, and to maximize portfolio yield.

POs have long, positive durations and respond well in bull markets. While the associated acceleration in prepayments leads to an increase in call-option value with resulting negative impact on the price and convexity of the generic MBS, the PO enjoys the benefit of acting like a high-speed, deep-discount MBS. IOs, on the other hand, with negative durations, perform best in bear markets, when virtually all other fixed-income securities are experiencing negative returns. Investors can also benefit from the unique convexity characteristics of strips. POs stripped from discount- or current-coupon MBSs and IOs stripped from high-coupon MBSs both have positive convexity, and as long as volatility remains high will outperform other MBS products whether interest rates are rising or falling. In a low-volatility market environment, negatively convex strips (POs stripped from premium collateral and IOs from current-coupon collateral) may be bought for high yield, but become risky investments if volatility increases.

This chapter examines SMBSs cash flows; the duration and convexity characteristics of strips; and the use of strips to hedge other assets—for example, by mixing POs with assets such as CMO residuals and mortgage-servicing income, which perform poorly in bull markets. Conversely, IOs may be matched against portfolio holdings of discount and current-coupon MBSs and mortgage loans to enhance their otherwise poor performance in bear markets. Maximizing risk/reward in strip investing and accounting and regulatory issues affecting SMBSs are also covered. (A full accounting for SMBSs is given in Chapter 17.)

RISK/REWARD IN STRIP INVESTING

This discussion underlines the price and yield benefits of increasing CPR speed to a PO and of slowing CPR speed to an IO. For reasons that will become clear, the strip investor may tend to seek for current investment IOs with collateral displaying a slow CPR and POs with high observed CPR.

Risk/reward analysis suggests the wisdom of a reverse posture. An IO displaying a slow CPR has little future reward—it is already at a slow CPR and has nothing but the potential to speed up in the next bull market. Perhaps a wiser course would be to seek an IO with collateral that has experienced a relatively high CPR for some months. High CPRs, as we know, cannot be sustained indefinitely, and in time the IO with high current speed is bound to pass through prolonged cycles of slower (and more normal) speeds.

With similar logic, a PO with collateral displaying current high CPR speed has maximum potential to slow down. The investor is likely to fare better with a PO displaying relatively slow speed—perhaps 8 to 10 percent CPR. Such a PO carries little risk of slowing down further. On the other hand, as the PO passes through bull market cycles, its CPR speed will likely break to higher levels, providing periods of high yield.

When trading strips it is important to remember that the greatest reward is realized when the underlying collateral is about to slide up on the cusp (for a PO) or to slide off the cusp (for an IO). The key is to weigh where the WAC of the underlying collateral is in relation to the threshold to induce refinancing—and what that means in terms of the investor's view on interest rates and the impact of the latter on the strip investment.

UNDERSTANDING STRIP CASH FLOWS

Stripped-coupon MBSs retain their discount (for POs) or premium (for IOs) propensities through all market cycles, with POs always displaying a bull market bias and IOs thriving in bear markets. To comprehend the nature of POs and IOs, the investor must divest himself of a coupon bond mentality and focus on the dynamics of the cash flows underlying the strip.

Principal-Only (PO) Cash Flow

Summary

Long (positive) duration.

Strong positive convexity.

All PO cash flow returned at par:

—Internal rate of return increases when PSA accelerates.

—Internal rate of return decreases when PSA slows.

Investor Uses

As a bull market play.

To maximize portfolio total return.

As a proxy for short WAM discounts.

To hedge PSA speed risk.

The PO consists of a stream of principal cash flows. These cash flows, which are purchased at a discount, are always returned at par—and the investor ultimately receives back all the cash flows. The value issue is one of timing: The sooner the cash flows are returned, the greater will be the present value of the future cash flows.

Assume the investor purchased a PO stripped from a GNMA 11 percent MBS at a price of $47. Figure 13.1 illustrates the principal cash flows of this PO strip at various CPR speeds based on $1 million notional[2] amount of GNMA-IIs.

Table 13.1 illustrates the annual cash flows of principal generated by $1 million notional amount of GNMA 11 percent MBSs. Note that no matter what the CPR speed, $1 million of principal is returned under all three CPR speed scenarios. The average life at 35 percent and 40 percent CPR is less than half that at 15 percent CPR, however, and note that the internal rate of return (IRR) at 40 percent CPR is almost three times that at 15 percent CPR. Also note that at 40 percent CPR almost 80 percent of the principal cash flows are returned in the first three years, while at 15 percent CPR about 40 percent are returned in the first three years.

The investor has paid $470,000 for $1 million notional amount of PO to

FIGURE 13.1
$1 Million Notional 11 Percent PO Strip, Principal Cash Flows

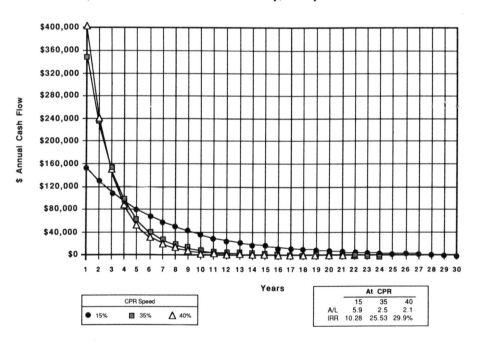

	At CPR		
	15	35	40
A/L	5.9	2.5	2.1
IRR	10.28	25.53	29.9%

CPR Speed: ● 15%   ▣ 35%   △ 40%

[2]The term "notional" refers to the PO or IO cash flow generated from $1 million "notional amount" of the underlying FNMA 9 percent MBS collateral. For example, with the IO there is no principal against which to discount the price, so the price is to the notional amount.

TABLE 13.1
GNMA 11 Percent PO Strip, Principal Cash Flows

Years	CPR		
	15%	*35%*	*40%*
1	$ 153,795	$ 352,900	$ 402,278
2	130,549	228,599	240,729
3	110,796	148,014	143,851
4	94,015	95,794	85,912
5	79,759	61,961	51,278
6	67,647	40,053	30,591
7	57,359	25,873	18,236
8	48,623	16,702	10,858
9	41,210	10,768	6,460
10	34,902	6,936	3,839
11	29,552	4,464	2,278
12	25,006	2,867	1,349
13	21,151	1,842	800
14	17,881	1,179	472
15	15,102	750	275
16	12,745	480	166
17	10,748	308	97
18	9,052	192	51
19	7,616	122	30
20	6,399	79	16
21	5,368	50	12
22	4,495	25	3
23	3,755	13	—
24	3,132	12	—
25	2,599	—	—
26	2,155	—	—
27	1,777	—	—
28	1,460	—	—
29	1,192	—	—
30	176	—	—
Total	$1,000,000	$1,000,000	$1,000,000
Average life	5.9 yrs.	2.5 yrs.	2.1 yrs.
IRR	10.28%	25.53%	29.9%

receive a stream of principal cash flows totaling $1 million to an estimated average life of 2.5 years for an IRR of 25.53 percent at 35 percent CPR. This cash-flow stream will be altered by interest-rate or demographic changes. For example, if interest rates fall (bull market scenario), the PSA speed will accelerate, returning the PO cash flows sooner. At 40 percent CPR the average life is shortened to 2.1 years, increasing the IRR to 29.9 percent. If interest rates rise (bear market), the return of cash flows will be deferred to an average life of 5.9 years if the CPR slows to 15 percent. Since cash flows received further in the future have a lower percentage value, the IRR is reduced to 10.28 percent.

PO as Bull Market Play

For investors who believe that prepayment speeds will increase—perhaps because of interest-rate expectations or seasonal factors in the housing market—high- or slight-premium POs offer a leveraged investment vehicle.

Example Purchase of POs backed by FNMA 9½s

WAC	10.20	
WAM	349	
Offered price	52.25	
Transaction ID	FNMA Trust 17	

	Speed	Average	BEY[a]
Pricing speed	165 PSA	8.6 years	9.54
Generic 6 month	255 PSA	6.1 years	13.79
Generic 3 month	268 PSA	5.9 years	14.41
Generic 1 month	318 PSA	5.1 years	16.81

[a] Bond equivalent yield.

The PO illustrated above is priced at 165 PSA. If the PSA speed rises to the higher generic speeds experienced over the past 1, 3, or 6 months by collateral underlying the PO, the bond equivalent yield (BEY) will be markedly enhanced.

PO Maximizes Portfolio Total Return

PO strips can offer attractive yields for investors who use total return (price performance plus cash-flow yield) to assess performance. Pension funds and insurance companies generally use a total-return approach. While POs have no interest income, prepayments returned at par can mean substantial incremental yield if they are paid faster than expected. As with any zero-coupon bond, the investor also gets the advantage of price accrual toward par.

Example Purchase of POs backed by GNMA 11½s

WAC	12.00
WAM	315
Offered price	70
Transaction ID	Shearson Lehman CMO TR 29

What are the total returns over a 12-month period if yields . . .
rise 100 basis points?   remain unchanged?   fall 100 basis points?

Speed Assumption 15 CPR	Speed Assumption 32 CPR	Speed Assumption 40 CPR
−2.8%	24.55%	31.16%

Compare this to a GNMA 11½ with the same speed assumptions at 105²⁴⁄₃₂:

9.73%	7.98%	7.65%

As illustrated above, the PO is strongly biased to return a very high yield in the bull market scenario (rates fall 100 basis points), but actually goes negative in the bear market. The generic GNMA 11½ performs just the opposite, yielding somewhat more in the bear market. The yield of the generic GNMA is lower in the bull market because it suffers negative convexity when rates are falling. The PO enjoys positive convexity, and therefore performs best when rates are falling.

PO as Proxy for Short WAM Discounts

Figure 13.2 (first seen as Figure 8.6) illustrates the yield/duration curves of seasoned GNMA 8½s and several synthetic coupons which may be created by

FIGURE 13.2
Synthetic Combinations:
GNMA 11.5s and Trust 29 POs (GN 11.5 coupon)

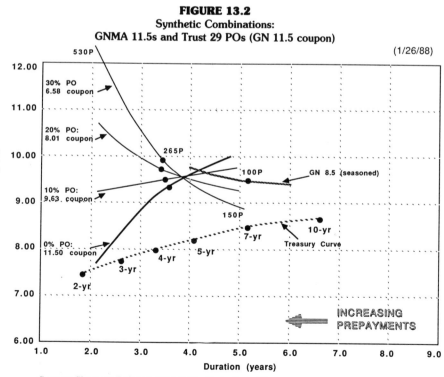

Source: Shearson Lehman Hutton Mortgage Securities.

FIGURE 13.3
Creating Synthetic Coupons Using
FHLMC PC 11.5 and FNMA Trust N-4 PO Strip

(12/7/87)

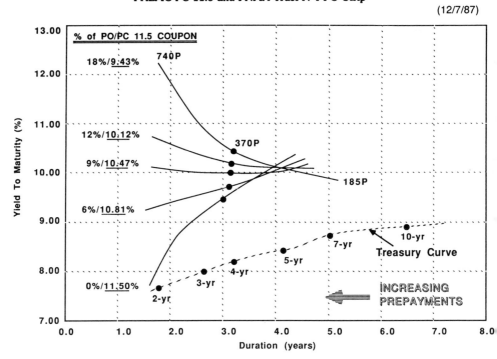

Source: Shearson Lehman Hutton Mortgage Securities.

mixing varying ratios of FNMA Trust 29 POs stripped from GNMA 11½s. Note the 8.01 percent synthetic coupon is close to that of the seasoned GNMA 8½s but has a shorter duration by more than a year and a half and offers far superior bull market performance.

POs may also be combined with premium collateral to create synthetic coupons that are comparable to current-coupon MBSs, but again with more favorable convexity characteristics. Figure 13.3 illustrates combining the SLCMO Trust N-4, a CMO issued privately by Shearson Lehman Hutton containing a PO stripped off FHLMC 11½ collateral. Note the 10.12 percent synthetic coupon performs extremely well in the bull market and performs better than a generic FHLMC 10 in a bull market environment—and markedly better than the FHLMC 11½ generic, which is shown as the bottom curve in Figure 13.3. The flat curve of the FHLMC 10 is illustrated in Figure 13.4, along with a range of Freddie Mac coupons.

FIGURE 13.4
Yield/Duration Curves, FHLMC PC 8 through 12.5 Coupons

(12/18/87)

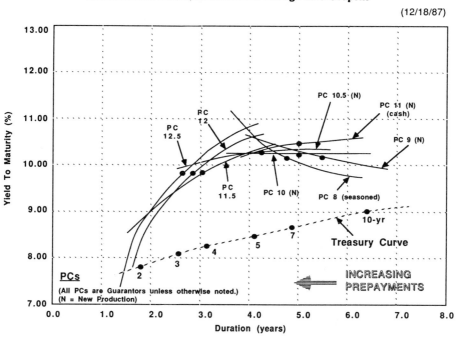

Source: Shearson Lehman Hutton Mortgage Securities.

Hedging Prepayment Risk with POs

Most fixed-income investors would not envision the need for a hedge in a bull market. When the MBS goes to a premium price, with a concomitant increase in prepayment speed, the MBS experiences negative convexity and a flattening or even decline in price. Since the PO thrives on an acceleration of prepayment speed, it serves as an excellent hedge for PSA (or CPR) prepayment-speed risk. Table 13.2 illustrates the respective gain and loss of a PO strip versus that of a generic MBS and indicates how the PO may be used as a hedge with various weightings.

Table 13.2 shows that the GNMA 11½ (Security 1) performs poorly in the bull market (− 100 basis points) because of its high CPR speed (30 percent) and enjoys a yield improvement to 10.4 percent in the bear market (+ 100 basis points) when the CPR slows to 7 percent. The PO (Security 2) performs in just the reverse, returning 20.3 percent in the bull market with a CPR of 25 percent.

TABLE 13.2
Bull Market CPR Hedge
Security 1: GNMA 11½ Percent MBS
Security 2: 11 Percent PO (hedge security)

Interest-Rate Scenario	HPR Security 1	CPR Scenario	HPR Security 2	CPR Scenario	100% Security 1 0% Security 2	90% Security 1 10% Security 2	80% Security 1 20% Security 2
− 100 BP	7.6%	30%	20.3%	25%	7.6%	8.9%	10.2%
Unchanged	8.7%	20%	6.4%	15%	8.7%	8.4%	8.2%
+ 100 BP	10.4%	7%	−22.5%	6%	10.4%	7.5%	4.6%

HPR refers to holding-period return. HPR calculates a one-year holding-period return including market profit and loss, a reinvestment assumption (6% for the above example), and the value of the principal and interest cash flows.

Interest-Rate Scenario   − 100 BP means Treasury yields decline 100 basis points.
                             + 100 BP means Treasury yields increase 100 basis points.

Source: Shearson Lehman Hutton Mortgage Securities.

The PO therefore demonstrates itself to be an excellent CPR speed hedge to protect the investor against dramatic increases in the CPR of generic MBSs portfolio holdings as they go to a premium price. Note alternative portfolios perform better in the bull market as the percentage of PO holdings is increased from 0 percent to 10 and 20 percent.

Protecting MBS Servicing with POs

Mortgage originators have long been familiar with the risk to servicing the value of a portfolio when prepayments accelerate as a result of refinancing when interest rates are falling. When mortgages under servicing by a mortgage banker are refinanced and paid off, there is, of course, a reduction in the number of loans held under servicing contracts. There is an obvious reduction in servicing income, with loss in value of the servicing portfolio which could be offset with the addition of POs. Bear in mind that the cash flows from servicing income are in reality a form of an IO.

Interest-Only (IO) Cash Flow

Summary

High current yield.

Negative mortgage duration.

Interest lives off principal:

—IRR increases when PSA slows.

—IRR decreases when PSA accelerates.

Investor Uses

As bear market-directed investment.

For high yield because of high volatility.

To hedge interest-rate–sensitive investments.

The IO consists of a cash-flow stream of interest. *The foremost consideration when investing or trading in IOs is that interest lives off principal: without principal no interest is generated.* Therefore, unlike with POs, no definitive amount of interest cash flow is returned with IOs. Simply stated, the longer the collateral life is extended, the greater will be the total of interest cash flows generated. Conversely, *if prepayment speeds accelerate dramatically, the interest cash flows returned could be less than the original dollars invested, resulting in a negative IRR.*

Assume the investor purchased an IO stripped off a FNMA 9 at a price of $47, to receive the interest cash flows back to an average life of 8.1 years at a

CPR of 10 percent. Table 13.3 illustrates the return of interest cash flows at CPRs of 8, 10, and 15 percent.

The table also displays the annual interest cash flows of the FNMA 9 IO at CPR speeds of 8, 10, and 15 percent. Note that the totals of interest cash flows are of dramatically differing amounts under the three CPR-speed scenarios.

At a purchase price of $47 and a CPR of 10 percent, the investor paid $470,000 to receive a cash-flow stream of interest totaling $706,626 to an average life of 8.1 years for an IRR of 7.42 percent.

As shown in Table 13.3, if the CPR speed slows to 8 percent, the total cash flows received increase to $823,597, improving the IRR to 9.65 percent.

TABLE 13.3
FNMA 9 Percent IO, Interest Cash Flows

		CPR	
Years	8%	10%	15%
1	$ 86,352	$ 85,502	$ 83,349
2	78,801	76,328	70,270
3	71,844	68,078	59,194
4	65,439	60,659	49,813
5	59,536	53,989	41,873
6	54,098	47,993	35,155
7	49,090	42,602	29,471
8	44,471	37,757	24,670
9	40,218	33,400	20,611
10	36,295	29,488	17,186
11	32,677	25,974	14,299
12	29,341	22,817	11,861
13	26,266	19,980	9,810
14	23,428	17,431	8,083
15	20,808	15,146	6,633
16	18,389	13,094	5,416
17	16,154	11,252	4,398
18	14,091	9,601	3,544
19	12,183	8,121	2,830
20	10,420	6,795	2,239
21	8,787	5,609	1,742
22	7,277	4,544	1,344
23	5,879	3,590	998
24	4,583	2,739	717
25	3,384	1,976	489
26	2,267	1,297	303
27	1,232	689	152
28	290	158	33
Total	$823,597	$706,626	$506,471
Average life	9.5 yrs.	8.1 yrs.	5.8 yrs.
IRR	9.65%	7.42%	1.75%

The interest cash flows are greater at the slower CPR speed because the average life is extended to 9.5 years. Conversely, if the CPR accelerates to 15 percent CPR, the average life is shortened to 5.8 years. With the shorter lifespan, the principal has less time to generate interest, which at the 15 percent CPR totals only $506,471, reducing the IRR to 1.75 percent.

Note from Table 13.3 that as the CPR increases, the total interest cash flow is not only less, it is less for each annual period. This is so because the principal is being paid down at an accelerating rate every year that the CPR speed is higher.

Table 13.4 and Figure 13.5 illustrate how dramatically the changes in prepayment speed affect the IO strip. In this case the collateral is of higher speed, and even a relatively small increase from 35 percent CPR to 40 percent CPR has a marked negative impact on the total interest cash flows. On the other hand, a slowdown from 35 percent CPR to 15 percent nearly triples the total sum of the cash flow. This latter speed slowdown illustrates the benefit the IO might be expected to enjoy in a rising interest-rate environment with its accompanying slowdown in prepayment speed.

FIGURE 13.5
$1 Million Notional 11 Percent IO, Interest Cash Flows

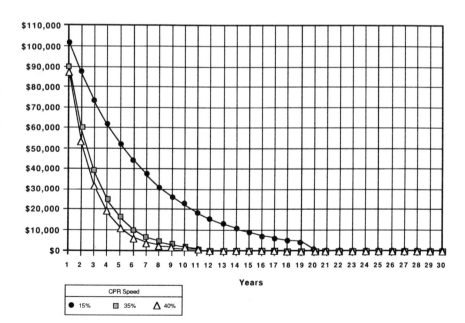

TABLE 13.4
GNMA 11 Percent IO Strip, Interest Cash Flows

Years	CPR					
	15%		35%		40%	
1	$102,016	16.0%	$ 90,818	35.4%	$ 87,823	40.3%
2	86,307	13.6	58,753	22.9	52,445	24.1
3	72,971	11.5	37,987	14.8	31,302	14.4
4	61,654	9.7	24,544	9.6	18,667	8.6
5	52,052	8.2	15,847	6.2	11,125	5.1
6	43,909	6.9	10,223	4.0	6,624	3.0
7	37,000	5.8	6,587	2.6	3,941	1.8
8	31,145	4.9	4,240	1.7	2,343	1.1
9	26,181	4.1	2,725	1.1	1,388	0.6
10	21,976	3.5	1,750	0.7	823	0.4
11	18,413	2.9	1,122	0.4	488	0.2
12	15,401	2.4	717	0.3	286	0.1
13	12,850	2.0	458	0.2	169	0.1
14	10,693	1.7	292	0.1	99	0.1
15	8,872	1.4	184	0.1	58	0.0
16	7,331	1.2	116	0.1	34	0.0
17	6,033	0.9	74	0.0	20	0.0
18	4,940	0.8	46	0.0	12	0.0
19	4,017	0.6	29	0.0	8	0.0
20	3,243	0.5	17	0.0	0	0.0
21	2,595	0.4	12	0.0	0	0.0
22	2,048	0.3	8	0.0	0	0.0
23	1,593	0.3	0	0.0	0	0.0
24	1,212	0.2	0	0.0	0	0.0
25	894	0.1	0	0.0	0	0.0
26	631	0.1	0	0.0	0	0.0
27	413	0.1	0	0.0	0	0.0
28	237	0.0	0	0.0	0	0.0
29	90	0.0	0	0.0	0	0.0
30	3	0.0	0	0.0	0	0.0
Total	$636,717		$256,560		$217,665	

IO as a Bear Market Investment

An investor with a strong rate or speed view can make a highly leveraged investment in IOs to exploit the opportunity.

For investors who believe that prepayment speeds will slow, based on the interest-rate environment or the housing market, the best purchase is either a premium-backed IO or an IO backed by collateral on the cusp of refinancability. (That is, where commonly held prepayment views are likely to alter substantially with small market moves.)

Example Purchase of IOs backed by FNMA 9½s

WAC   10.20
WAM   349
Offered price   47$^{16}/_{32}$
Transaction ID   FNMA TRUST #17
Prepayment speed at issue   165 PSA   9.47 BEY 8.6 average life
Expected speed in bear market   140 PSA   10.99 BEY 9.6 average life

IO as Portfolio-Yield Enhancer

Pension funds and insurance companies which have actuarially determined liabilities (and often guarantee yields) are good buyers of high-yield assets. In a neutral to bear market, IOs offer attractive yield opportunities as well as a bearish cushion.

Example Purchase of IOs backed by FNMA 9s

WAC   9.71
WAM   349
Offered price   47
Transaction ID   FNMA TRUST #17
Prepayment speed at issue   150 PSA   9.68 BEY   9.3 average life
Expected speed in bear market   125 PSA   11.14 BEY 10.4 average life

Illustrating Strip Cash Flows

Figure 13.6 illustrates the price curves of a generic MBS (top line) and the PO and IO. Note that the figure may be read as a bull market by scanning from right to left (from higher yields to lower) and as a bear market from left to right. The computer-generated PO and IO price curves confirm their respective bull and bear market bias. Note the generic MBS price curve rises until the price reaches over par, at which point it goes first flat and then slightly negative, a graphic illustration of negative convexity.

    Figure 13.7 illustrates in three-dimensional perspective the cash flows of POs stripped from 6 percent collateral to 12 percent in various interest-rate scenarios. The axis at the bottom left of the figure represents the coupons of the collateral underlying the PO strip. The left-to-right axis represents mortgage market yields, rising from 6 percent at the left to 16 percent at the right. The vertical axis represents projected prices for the PO. The highest PO value is found at the top left corner of the floating plane, which represents the PO strip cash-flow values. At the top left high point, the mortgage yield has reached its bull market low (6 percent); as we would expect, the PO stripped off the 12 percent coupon displays the highest performance. The 6 percent coupon,

FIGURE 13.6
Mortgage-Backed Security Price/Yield Curve

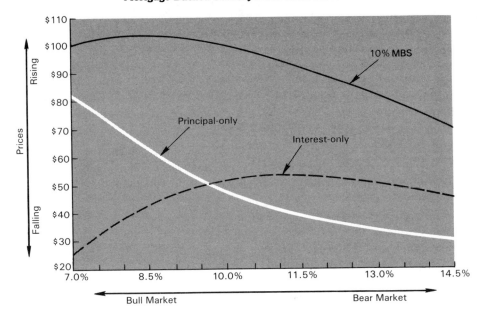

FIGURE 13.7
PO Sensitivity to Price and Yield
(coupons range from 6 to 12 percent)

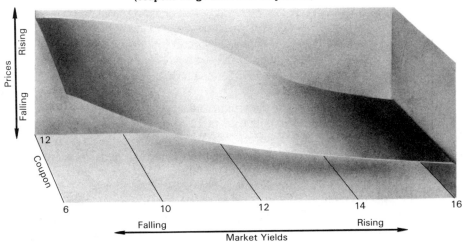

Source: Based on a model provided by Shearson Lehman Hutton Mortgage Research.

illustrated at the bottom left corner of the plane, also gains value in the bull market but sags below that of the 12 percent coupon. As mortgage yields rise, the PO cash-flow values decline, as illustrated by the plane that falls to the right (bear market) edge of the figure.

Figure 13.8 illustrates IOs stripped off MBS collateral with underlying coupons of from 6 percent to 12 percent. As would be expected, the IO performs the best in the bear market scenario, as depicted at the far right in the figure. The IO with the poorest performance is that stripped off the 12 percent MBS collateral, shown at the bottom left corner of the figure. The IO stripped from lower 6 percent collateral also loses value in the bull market, but as shown at the top left, holds up better than the higher-coupon strips.

The Refinancing Threshold

When interest rates decline significantly, the MBS trades to a premium, and prepayment speeds increase as homeowners refinance their mortgages. The threshold required to induce prepayments is first reached when the difference between the WAC of the mortgages underlying the security held is about 200 basis points higher than the current mortgage rate. As the spread between the WAC and current mortgage rate widens, the prepayments accelerate to a CPR of 50 or higher and then level off after six months or so. Most homeowners who can refinance will have done so within that time frame. In time, the CPR may be expected to fall back to a level of 30 or 40 or below as the pool ages, even if the MBS remains priced at a premium.

FIGURE 13.8
IO Sensitivity to Price and Yield
(coupons range from 6 to 12 percent)

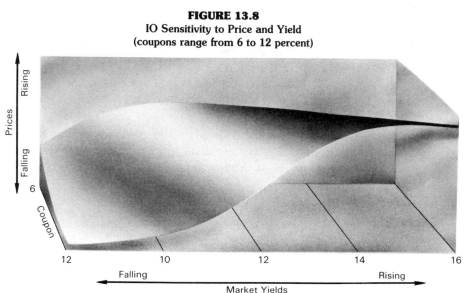

Source: Based on a model provided by Shearson Lehman Hutton Mortgage Research.

If shortly after the MBS has gone to a premium, interest rates increase to where the difference between the WAC and the current mortgage rate becomes 150 basis points or less, the CPR speed will fall dramatically, probably to 20 CPR or below.

Trading on the Cusp

When the CPR begins to accelerate because of refinancings (implied call in the money) it is said to be trading on the cusp. If interest rates rise again to the point where refinancings essentially cease (implied call goes out of the money), the MBS will be said to be off the cusp. It is when the MBS is perceived to be about to move on or off the cusp that market perceptions of speed changes have the most dramatic impact on any price.

For example, as the MBS is perceived to be approaching the threshold spread to induce refinancings, the market will anticipate higher prepayment speeds, and the price of the MBS will be significantly discounted in a short period of time to reflect the negative value of the faster return of cash flow. If the security held is a PO, the value response will be the reverse; the PO will rapidly increase in price as the market anticipates the benefit of receiving back the PO cash flows sooner. If the MBS is already on the cusp and experiencing high speed when interest rates increase, the market will tend to assign greater value to the MBS cash flows, anticipating a slowdown in speed with the MBS sliding off the cusp.

Strip Trading Axioms

- As the MBS is seen to be approaching the threshold for refinancing, the market anticipates higher prepayment speeds, and the price of the MBS will become negatively convexed.
- If the MBS is a PO, the market response will be the reverse; the PO will increase in price as the market anticipates receiving the PO cash flows sooner as the PO slides onto the cusp.
- If the security held is an IO and is already on the cusp (prepayment speed high), with rising interest rates the market will anticipate a slowdown in speed (IO slides off the cusp); price increases.

Summary

A trader anticipating rising interest rates will look for an IO that is trading on the cusp and will increase in price as speeds slow and the IO comes off the cusp. A trader anticipating falling interest rates will look for a PO that is off the cusp, anticipating that as speed accelerates the PO will go on the cusp and gain value as the cash flows accelerate.

IO Projected Price Performance

Figure 13.9 illustrates the projected price performance of an IO stripped off FNMA 9s. The figure is defined from the assumptions presented in Table 13.5.

The table illustrates the assumption that when interest rates are relatively low (10-year Treasury yield 7 percent), prepayment speeds will be high (PSA 195), and the price of the IO will be at its lowest (45⁸⁄₃₂). When prepayments are high, the IO offers a poor risk/reward profile and therefore trades at a wide yield spread (175 basis points) to the Treasury curve.

As interest rates rise, the market anticipates a slowdown in prepayment speed, and increases in price, as shown in Table 13.5. Concurrently, the risk/reward of the IO shifts to a favorable bias, leading to a narrowing in its yield spread to the Treasury curve to 125 basis points and ultimately to 100 basis points.

The IO reaches its high point in price (49⁸⁄₃₂) when the 10-year Treasury yield is 9½ percent. Beyond that point, the IO loses ability to increase in price even though the interest cash flows are growing larger (thus theoretically increasing in value) for two reasons: (1) even though the yield value of the IO is

FIGURE 13.9
FNMA 9 Percent IO, Projected Price Performance

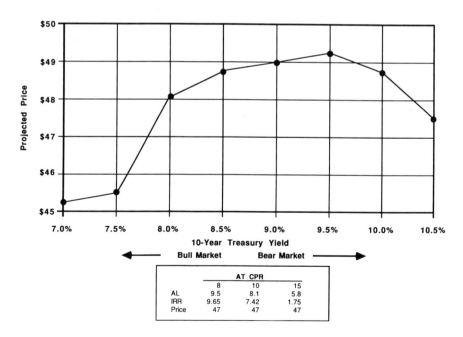

		AT CPR	
	8	10	15
AL	9.5	8.1	5.8
IRR	9.65	7.42	1.75
Price	47	47	47

TABLE 13.5
FNMA 9 Percent IO, Projected Price-Performance Assumptions

10-Yr. Tsy.	BP Spread to Tsy.	Projected PSA	Projected Price IO
7.00	+175	195	$45^{8}/_{32}$
7.50	+175	185	$48^{16}/_{32}$
8.00	+125	165	$48^{12}/_{32}$
8.50	+100	155	$48^{28}/_{32}$
9.00	+100	145	49
9.50	+100	135	$49^{8}/_{32}$
10.00	+100	130	$48^{28}/_{32}$
10.50	+100	130	$47^{20}/_{32}$

increasing, the IO trades at a price based on a yield spread to the Treasury curve, which is also increasing in required yield; and (2) once the prepayment speed has slowed significantly, the risk/reward bias again becomes adverse.

Once the bulk of potential slowing in prepayment speed has actually been realized, the investor is confronted with relatively little incremental value that can be gained with further extension of the cash-flow life. The IO therefore loses ability to maintain incremental yield value in excess of that demanded by the rising Treasury yield curve, and it falls somewhat in price.

The price curve illustrated in Figure 13.9, together with the assumptions provided in Table 13.5, suggest that the optimum time to purchase an IO is at the point when the underlying collateral is on the cusp, and therefore exhibiting a high CPR. When the investor can perceive that because of an anticipated slowdown in prepayment speed the collateral is about to slide off the cusp with a decline in CPR speed, the price of the IO will rapidly increase.

This projected price performance also suggests the IO may have limited value as an interest-rate hedge. The price-performance data given above show a price move of about 4 points from low to high in a market move where the underlying collateral might drop 10 points. The IO, however, offers strong positive value in the bear market, suggesting its greatest value may be as a strong enhancement to portfolio total return when rates are upwardly biased.

PO Projected Price Performance

The investor might be well advised to seek a PO with underlying collateral having a WAC below the threshold to induce prepayments. When the cycle of interest rates hits a bull market, the collateral will ride up onto the cusp, the CPR speed will accelerate, and the PO price is likely to rise quickly as investors anticipate the benefit of accelerating CPR speeds.

Figure 13.10 illustrates the hypothetical price performance of a FNMA 9 PO as yields range from 5.5 percent (peak of bull market) to 12.5 percent (bear market bottom). Table 13.6 displays the pricing assumptions used for Figure 13.10.

FIGURE 13.10
FNMA 9 Percent PO Strip, Price/Yield Curve

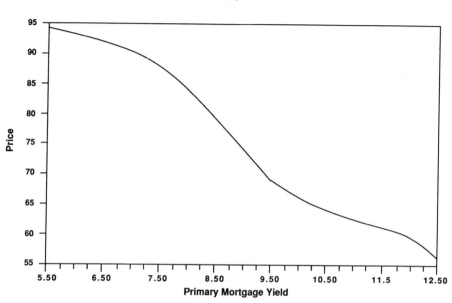

Table 13.6 indicates the PO will trade to a narrowing spread to the yield curve when rates are high. This is so because once interest rates have risen to a level to shut the refinancing window, the CPR speed drops dramatically. Once the window is shut, higher rates do not necessarily suggest that speeds will continue to slow at a decelerating rate. Once the PSA is below 150, there is little downside risk left in the PO.

The greater risk is when the PSA has achieved the high speed of 195 PSA. At that point there is little further upside, and the higher required yield spread to the Treasury curve (125 basis points) reflects the risk bias.

TOTAL RETURNS AND HOLDING-PERIOD RETURNS OF STRIPS[3]

Evaluating SMBSs requires a more prepayment-sensitive approach than the traditional determinations of cash-flow yield spread and total-return analysis. These familiar methods can fail to recognize the tremendous uncertainty of

---

[3]Reprinted from Shearson Lehman Hutton, "Dynamic Total Returns for Stripped Mortgage Securities," *Mortgage Finance Monthly*, September 1987. The article was written by Mohamad Sotoudeh, derivative mortgage products analyst.

TABLE 13.6
FNMA 9 Percent PO
Projected Price-Performance Assumptions

10-Yr. Tsy.	Projected Yield PO	Projected PSA	Projected Price PO
7.00	+ 125 to 7 yr.	195	$60^{14}/_{32}$
7.50	+ 125 to 7 yr.	185	$57^{27}/_{32}$
8.00	+ 125 to 10 yr.	165	$53^{20}/_{32}$
8.50	+ 125 to 10 yr.	165	$52^{6}/_{32}$
9.00	+ 115 to 10 yr.	155	$49^{25}/_{32}$
9.50	+ 100 to 10 yr.	145	$47^{16}/_{32}$
10.00	+ 80 to 10 yr.	135	$45^{10}/_{32}$
10.50	+ 80 to 10 yr.	130	$43^{12}/_{32}$

market liquidity and convexity attributes for stripped securities. SMBS evaluation needs a more dynamic total-return framework. This framework incorporates the impact of swings in yield-spread relationships to Treasuries as a result of changes in prepayment expectations and liquidity in various interest-rate environments. With this approach the investor can include his subjective view of liquidity and convexity in evaluating strips.

Traditional Holding-Period Returns for Strips

A traditional total-return analysis for a fixed-income security compares the original investment with the cash flow received over the investment horizon plus the sales proceeds at the end of the holding period. This technique examines the returns of the investment over a variety of interest-rate scenarios using three major assumptions:

- For a given level of interest rates, there is a corresponding prepayment rate.
- The yield spreads to comparable Treasuries remain largely constant over various interest-rate scenarios.
- Market liquidity at the end of the holding period is determined only by the assumed level of interest rates. That is, the security can be sold at the assumed yield level without any potential rise or fall in prices.

The total-return technique provides an understanding of the risk/reward profile of the security and therefore its appropriateness as a hedge or portfolio investment. This type of analysis for IO and PO securities of various coupons is shown in Table 13.7.

Some strips, such as premium-backed IOs, have performance profiles similar to those of debt options in that the returns vary asymmetrically with interest-rate movements. For example, the returns for GNMA 12.5 IOs change by as much as 45 percent when interest rates rise 100 basis points and by − 26

TABLE 13.7
One-Year Holding-Period Returns for IOs and POs under Three Interest-Rate Scenarios
(prices as of August 16, 1987)

	IOs					
Collateral	*Up 100 BP*		*Unchanged*		*Down 100 BP*	*Expected Return[a] (%)*
	Projected PSA (%)	*Return (%)*	*Projected PSA (%)*	*Return (%)*	*Projected PSA (%)*	*Return (%)*
FNMA 9	130	7.28	135	9.77	185	.01	5.69
FNMA 9.5	135	8.74	145	9.80	225	−6.51	4.01
GNMA 11	167	28.70	250	7.10	380	−17.68	6.04
GNMA 11.5	200	42.60	333	4.28	485	−21.49	8.46
GNMA 12.5	300	46.26	467	1.16	650	−25.30	7.37

	POs					
Collateral	*Up 100 BP*		*Unchanged*		*Down 100 BP*	*Expected Return[a] (%)*
	Projected PSA (%)	*Return (%)*	*Projected PSA (%)*	*Return (%)*	*Projected PSA (%)*	*Return (%)*
FNMA 9	130	2.55	135	8.91	185	27.91	13.12
FNMA 9.5	135	.29	145	9.65	225	33.78	14.57
GNMA 11	167	−7.39	250	10.60	380	28.18	10.46
GNMA 11.5	200	−8.09	333	11.72	485	25.66	9.76
GNMA 12.5	300	−3.47	467	10.96	650	20.46	9.32

[a]Expected return assumes equal probability for all scenarios.
Source: Shearson Lehman Hutton Mortgage Securities.

percent when rates fall 100 basis points, making them similar to puts on debt securities. This asymmetry of returns determines the relative value of the securities—the more asymmetrical, the greater the convexity. This concept can also be seen by comparing the security's expected returns (an average of the returns under rising, unchanged, and falling interest-rate scenarios) to the returns of the unchanged (flat) scenario. For example, Table 13.7 shows that the expected returns for GNMA 12.5 IOs at 7.37 percent exceed the flat rate of returns at 1.16 percent by as much as 6 percent. These IOs have positive convexity: the expected return is much greater than the flat rate of return.

It is important to note that spreads for strips are determined by the market's perception of their convexity and potential for price appreciation at currently projected prepayment rates. For example, the market is pricing GNMA 11½ IOs at a yield 406 basis points below the 4-year Treasury, and GNMA 12½ IOs at a yield 782 basis points below the same Treasury. The market pays a premium to own the higher premium-backed IOs because in a bearish market the decline in prepayment rate for GNMA 12½ IOs will be substantially greater than for GNMA 11½ IOs (see Table 13.8).

TABLE 13.8
IO and PO Spreads and Prepayment Rates
(prices as of August 16, 1987)

	Collateral Spread (bp)	IO Spread (bp)	PO Spread (bp)	WAL[a]	WAL[a] Equiv. Tsy. (yr.)	Prepay-ment (PSA%)
FNMA 9	120	215	125	10.2	10	135
FNMA 9.5	124	215	115	9.7	10	145
GNMA 11	112	−116	248	5.7	5	250
GNMA 11.5	90	−406	400	4.3	4	333
GNMA 12.5	52	−782	410	3.0	3	467

[a]WAL = weighted average life.
Source: Shearson Lehman Hutton Mortgage Securities.

From the relative spreads of the IOs for different underlying coupons it may be concluded that as interest rates rise, yield spreads will at some point become less negative for IOs. This point may be reached when the underlying coupon rate is 250 to 300 points above the current market coupon rate. This happens because the magnitude of further decreases in prepayment rates becomes smaller for any given rise in interest rates.

Consequently, IOs lose their potential for price appreciation. The yield spreads of the IOs, however, will also become less negative or even positive as the market rallies because the fall in prepayments slows for any further decline in interest rates.

The premium for convexity that the market commands on strips of different underlying coupons is also evident in the large spread variance of discount- and premium-backed POs. A comparison of the returns for FNMA 9.5 POs and GNMA 12.5 POs shows that for a drop of 100 basis points in interest rates, returns on FNMA 9.5 POs increase by over 24 percent, while returns on GNMA 12.5 POs increase by only 9.5 percent. Accordingly, the greater positive convexity of FNMA 9.5 POs allows them to be priced 295 basis points lower than GNMA 12.5 POs (shown in Table 13.8).

From the above observations, it is clear that at any given level, premium-backed IOs and discount-backed POs will trade at a premium and will therefore have more negative or tighter spreads to Treasuries. Conversely, premium-backed POs and discount-backed IOs will have wider or less negative spreads to Treasuries.

Dynamic Total-Return Analysis

Dynamic total-return analysis, like traditional total-return analysis, examines returns over different interest-rate scenarios using a prepayment model to determine appropriate prepayment rates. However, the dynamic-return model relaxes the constant-spread–relationship assumption and examines the effects of changes in the spread relationship on investment performance. Given current prices, a set of yield spreads is determined using projected prepayment rates for various stripped MBSs. A series of total returns for the investment horizon is calculated using the same formula as traditional total returns. The outcome is a matrix that reflects yield returns for a wide range of interest-rate and prepayment scenarios (see Figure 13.11).

To use the matrix, the point where the security is currently priced must be located. For the GNMA 11 IOs in Figure 13.11, the central point is at the current 10-year Treasury yield of 8.6 percent where the prepayment rate of the GNMA 11 collateral is projected at 15 percent CPR. The current yield spread of GNMA 11 IOs is −100 basis points to the 5-year Treasury. To determine the returns in a bearish market where the 10-year Treasury will yield 9.6 percent— a situation where GNMA 11s become less a premium and more a discount coupon—the spread to the 7-year Treasury will become more positive to make up for the lost convexity. Conversely, in a market rally where the 10-year Treasury yields 7.6 percent the spreads will likely become more negative to the

FIGURE 13.11
One-Year Total Returns (R) and Terminal Market Values* (A) for GNMA 11 IOs
(R in percent, A in 32nds; IO purchase price = 46.00;
prices as of August 16, 1987)

10-Year Treasury Yield (%)	10.60	9.60	8.60	7.60	6.60
Projected Prepayment (% PSA)	100	167	250	383	583
Weighted Average Life (yrs.)	10	7	5	3	3
Spread to Treasury					
−500	R = 92.25 A = 80 − 31	R = 60.43 A = 67 − 04	R = 30 A = 53 − 21	R = −27.95 A = 27 − 09	R = −50.02 A = 17 − 01
−300	R = 73.83 A = 72 − 01	R = 47.19 A = 60 − 18	R = 21.23 A = 42 − 07	R = −30.23 A = 26 − 00	R = −50.90 A = 16 − 16
−100	R = 58.91 A = 64 − 27	R = 36.3 A = 55 − 06	R = 7.21 A = 45 − 14	R = −32.33 A = 24 − 26	R = −51.6 A = 16 − 01
Unchanged	R = 52.51 A = 61 − 23	R = 31.48 A = 52 − 26	R = 6.32 A = 43 − 25	R = −33.21 A = 24 − 09	R = −52 A = 15 − 25
+100	R = 46.63 A = 58 − 28	R = 27.18 A = 50 − 21	R = 4.71 A = 42 − 08	R = −34.17 A = 23 − 25	R = −52.39 A = 15 − 21
+300	R = 36.37 A = 53 − 30	R = 19.47 A = 46 − 27	R = 2.90 A = 39 − 15	R = −35.84 A = 22 − 26	R = −53.35 A = 14 − 30

*Sales proceeds at the end of the holding period.

Shading indicates projected spread/market direction scenario.

Source: Shearson Lehman Hutton Mortgage Securities.

3-year Treasury to account for the convexity premium. The shaded diagonal band in Figure 13.11 shows the most likely direction of the returns, given yield-spread relationships for bullish and bearish environments. The dynamic total-return model provides additional insights because it allows the investor to examine the effects of convexity and potential liquidity conditions in different market scenarios.

MORTGAGE-DURATION CHARACTERISTICS OF STRIPS

Figure 13.12 illustrates the mortgage-duration[4] characteristics of strips. The baseline security is the current-coupon generic MBS, in this case a 10 percent GNMA. The duration of the GNMA 10 is depicted in the middle of the figure,

FIGURE 13.12
Mortgage Duration of IO and PO Strips
(IOs and POs stripped from 10 percent MBSs)

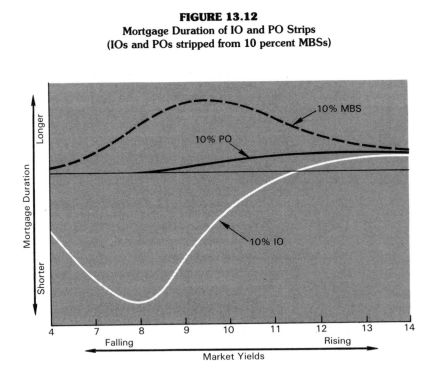

Source: Based on a model developed by Shearson Lehman Hutton Mortgage Research.

[4]For a description of mortgage duration, see Chapter 7, "Prepayment-Sensitive Model," and the discussion of the research study by Steven Carlson.

and since the 10 percent GNMA is the current coupon, the current market rate for mortgages is 10.5 percent. As we would expect, as mortgage rates increase, the duration of the security extends as the slowdown in prepayments extends its average life. The reader will recall from Chapter 7 that an increase in market yield tends to shorten the duration of noncallable fixed-income securities because of the improved reinvestment opportunity. This is not so with the MBS, because the extension of average life actually reduces the reinvestment opportunity for MBSs in the high-rate environments. Conversely, when interest rates drop, prepayments accelerate and the rapid return of principal shortens both the average life and the duration of the MBS. As was discussed in Chapter 7, the presence of the call option embedded in the MBS invalidates the application of standard duration; therefore, in Figure 13.12 mortgage duration has been used as a more accurate reflection of the relationship between price and yield.

Mortgage Duration of PO Strips

Figure 13.12 shows that the mortgage duration of the PO peaks at a market yield of about 9.5 percent, or when the PO has just slid into the cusp with the call option of the underlying generic 10 percent GNMA going into the money. It is at this point that market expectations of the benefit of the anticipated acceleration in prepayment speed is at its highest. At this point, the mortgage duration of the 10 percent PO is 25.7; that is, a 100 basis-point change in interest rates will result in a 25.7 percent change in price.

Since the PO is at the point of maximum option value, purchase at this level would offer poor risk/reward parameters because all the PO can do from this point is slow down; that is, with any market volatility it will lose value. Figure 13.12 therefore confirms the point made in the earlier discussion on trading off the cusp. The preferred time to buy the PO would be when the underlying generic is the current coupon and has not yet taken on option value. Similarly, reading the duration line farther to the left we see the impact of prepayment-speed burnout (see Chapter 5 for a discussion of prepayment cycles).

The Negative Duration of IOs

The duration line at the bottom of Figure 13.12 illustrates the **negative duration** of the IO. Note that as the underlying generic GNMA 10 approaches the cusp it takes on negative convexity. Recall the discussion of duration and convexity from Chapter 7. Positive convexity means the security changes price inversely to the direction of yield. Negative duration means the price moves in the same direction as interest rates. Thus when the IO has negative duration, its price increases as yields are increasing.

The IO reaches its maximum negative duration at the refinancing threshold (see Chapter 5) when the level of market interest rates is about 2 percent below the mortgage rate of the underlying MBS. When the mortgage duration has bottomed out, at about the 7 percent mortgage security yield point on the figure, any volatility will lead to a slowdown in prepayment speed and an improvement in price. This point therefore would represent the optimum risk/reward for purchase of the IO. As the duration line rises from this point to the right, the IO is gaining market value as the speed of the underlying generic MBS is slowing down. After the duration line crosses the zero line in the middle of the figure, the risk/reward of the PO becomes poor—it is now off the cusp and will be unable to slow down much more.

Because IOs have negative convexity they can be used in place of interest-rate swaps to hedge securities that display positive duration. Figure 13.13 illustrates the convexity characteristics of IO and PO strips from 10 percent MBS collateral.

FIGURE 13.13
Convexity of IO and PO Strips
(IOs and POs stripped from 10 percent MBSs)

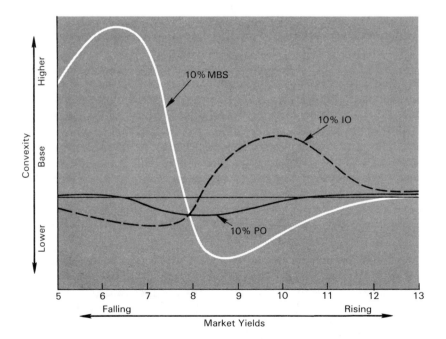

Source: Based on a model developed by Shearson Lehman Hutton Mortgage Research.

Hedging with Strips

SMBSs may be used to hedge interest-rate and prepayment-speed risks. Because IOs display negative duration, they may be used to hedge the interest-rate risk of fixed-income securities with positive duration. The durations of the respective securities must be carefully defined, however, because the durations of U.S. government and corporate bonds are measured by standard, or Macaulay's, duration, as may be discount-coupon MBSs, but SMBSs require a different duration model, as described in this chapter and more explicitly in Chapter 7. Furthermore, the hedging attributes of the strip are related to the response of prepayment speeds to interest-rate changes, which occurs over time with a response lag (see Chapter 5 for a discussion of the prepayment response lag associated with interest-rate changes). Since the price of straight fixed-income securities will respond instantaneously to a change in market yields, an interest-rate hedge utilizing strips will be effective only over a period of time—not for short-term trading positions.

Table 13.9 illustrates the use of an IO strip to hedge interest-rate risk. In Section A of the table, the security to be hedged is a 10-year Treasury bond, identified as Security 1. The hedging vehicle is an 11 percent IO strip, identified as Security 2.

The far left column of the table shows the current interest-rate environment as zero, with bull market scenarios identified as −100 basis points, and −50 basis points indicating the amount of decline in market yields in basis points. The bear market indicates rising yields as +100 and +50. Column 2 gives the holding-period return of Security 1, which includes a reinvestment assumption of 5.5 percent in the current market-rate scenario. The reinvestment rate increases or decreases by the same amount as the basis-point yield change for the respective interest-rate scenarios. The holding-period return also reflects market gains and losses (see Chapter 6 for a discussion of holding-period–return analysis).

The CPR scenario for the 10-year Treasury is not applicable because Treasury securities have no prepayments.

Note the HPR for the IO (column 4) is negative as its speed (column 5) increases. Columns 6 through 11 reflect varying ratios of the amount of IO to be included with the Treasury portfolio holding. Column 6 shows the HPR of the Treasury without any IO as a hedge.

The addition of the IO in increments of from 1 percent (column 7) to 20 percent (column 11) improves the portfolio HPR as interest rates rise, giving a portfolio HPR of 13.3 percent in the +100 basis-point-rate market, but as would be expected, the HPR does worse in the bull market when the IO is added. However, portfolio performance over a wide range of interest rates is enhanced with the addition of the IO, giving an HPR range of from 7.6 percent to 13.3 percent over a 4 percent swing in interest rates versus 1.0 percent to 13.6 percent for the Treasury security alone.

TABLE 13.9
Hedging Various Securities with IOs and POs: A One-Year Horizon Analysis

A Security 1: 10-Year Treasury Bond
Security 2: 11 Percent IO (hedging security)

Interest-Rate Scenario	Holding-Period Return Security 1	CPR Scenario	Holding-Period Return Security 2	CPR Scenario	100% Security 1 / 0% Security 2	99% Security 1 / 1% Security 2	95% Security 1 / 5% Security 2	90% Security 1 / 10% Security 2	85% Security 1 / 15% Security 2	80% Security 1 / 20% Security 2
					Holding-Period Returns of Alternative Portfolios					
−100 bp	13.6%		−18.6%	25.0%	13.6%	13.3%	12.1%	10.6%	9.1%	7.6%
−50	10.3		−5.1	20.0	10.3	10.2	9.6	8.9	8.2	7.4
0	7.1	(NA)	12.8	15.0	7.1	7.2	7.4	7.7	8.0	8.3
+50	4.0		30.7	10.5	4.0	4.3	5.5	7.0	8.5	9.9
+100	1.0		52.0	6.0	1.0	1.7	4.2	7.3	10.3	13.3

B Security 1: GNMA 8.5
Security 2: 11 Percent IO (hedging security)

Interest-Rate Scenario	Holding-Period Return Security 1	CPR Scenario	Holding-Period Return Security 2	CPR Scenario	100% Security 1 / 0% Security 2	99% Security 1 / 1% Security 2	95% Security 1 / 5% Security 2	90% Security 1 / 10% Security 2	85% Security 1 / 15% Security 2	80% Security 1 / 20% Security 2
−100 bp	13.0%	8.0%	−18.6%	25.0%	13.0%	12.7%	11.5%	10.1%	8.6%	7.1%
−50	10.8	7.5	4.2	20.0	10.8	10.7	10.1	9.4	8.7	8.0
0	8.6	7.0	12.8	13.5	8.6	8.6	8.8	9.0	9.2	9.4
+50	6.2	6.5	30.7	10.5	6.2	6.5	7.6	8.9	10.3	11.6
+100	3.9	6.0	52.0	6.0	3.9	4.5	6.8	9.7	12.6	15.3

C Security 1: GNMA 11.5
Security 2: 11 Percent PO (hedging security)

Interest-Rate Scenario	Holding-Period Return Security 1	CPR Scenario	Holding-Period Return Security 2	CPR Scenario	100% Security 1 / 0% Security 2	99% Security 1 / 1% Security 2	95% Security 1 / 5% Security 2	90% Security 1 / 10% Security 2	85% Security 1 / 15% Security 2	80% Security 1 / 20% Security 2
−100 bp	7.6%	30.0%	20.3%	25.0%	7.6%	7.7%	8.2%	8.9%	9.5%	10.2%
−50	8.2	22.5	14.6	20.0	8.2	8.2	8.5	8.8	9.2	9.5
0	8.7	20.0	6.4	15.0	8.7	8.6	8.6	8.4	8.3	8.2
+50	9.6	13.0	−4.9	10.5	9.6	9.4	8.9	8.2	7.5	6.8
+100	10.4	7.0	−22.5	6.0	10.4	10.1	9.0	7.5	6.1	4.6

Note: The reinvestment rate is assumed to be 5.5% in the flat-rate scenario and moves parallel to mortgage yields in alternative scenarios.

Source: Shearson Lehman Hutton Mortgage Securities.

Section B of Table 13.9 illustrates hedging a discount GNMA 8.5 percent coupon with the IO. In this case, the hedged HPR range is 7.1 percent to 15.3 percent over the 4 percent interest-rate swing, versus about 3.9 percent (bear market) to 13 percent (bull market) for the unhedged portfolio.

Hedging Prepayment-Speed Risk with POs

Section C of Table 13.9 illustrates hedging a GNMA 11½ with an 11 percent PO. Two key points should be noted: (1) this is a prepayment-speed hedge, so the prepayment lag response is about equal for securities 1 and 2. More important, (2) note the IO has been stripped off the same collateral as the security being hedged. *It is extremely important when structuring prepayment-speed hedges to use the same collateral base for both the hedging vehicle and the security being hedged.* If this is not done, the difference in prepayment response of a different collateral type could nullify the hedge benefit or even worse, exacerbate the prepayment risk. To illustrate, imagine trying to hedge the prepayment-speed risk of FHLMC 12s with a PO stripped off GNMA 8s.

The following discussion describes how an investor in MBSs, IOs, and POs can construct hedges to reduce prepayment risk.

Table 13.9 depicts the market value of a $100 investment in 11 percent IO, PO, and pass-through securities as a function of prepayment rate, assuming the securities' respective yields are kept constant. The analysis is based on 15 percent CPR as the pricing speed for all the securities. As shown, the pass-through and the IO decrease in value as the prepayment rate increases. Conversely, the PO security increases in value as the prepayment rate rises, making the PO security the one to buy when hedging the prepayment risk of a premium-coupon pass-through.

INVESTOR CONCERNS WITH SMBSs

SMBSs offer investors a wide array of investment, arbitrage, and hedging opportunities created by the unshackling of the effect of the mortgagor's prepayment option. Thus market participants can more efficiently exploit their assessments of interest-rate and prepayment expectations. Prudent investors in SMBSs, however, must appreciate that the inherent risks associated with IOs and POs are often greater than with generic MBSs. Failure to do so can lead to poor investment decisions and exposure to substantial loss—particularly with IOs. Principal among these concerns is the necessity of examining the strip within a sensitivity framework, subjecting the IO or PO to stress in a variety of prepayment probabilities. (For a discussion of sensitivity analysis testing MBSs to a range of interest-rate probabilities, see Chapter 6.)

SMBS PRICING METHODOLOGY

The SMBS is usually priced in terms of a basis-point yield spread to the comparable average-life Treasury at a projected prepayment-speed assumption. Because of the high degree of sensitivity of SMBSs to relatively small changes in prepayments, investors must carefully assess the risk/reward of mispricing that will result if the prepayment projection is incorrect. An error in the prepayment projection can lead to failure to realize the anticipated basis-point spread to Treasuries—either because the SMBS failed to achieve the targeted prepayment-speed requisite to generate the expected basis spread or the SMBS failed to realize the duration characteristics to place it on the anticipated maturity point on the yield curve (see Chapter 7 for a discussion of option-adjusted spread).

WAC and WAM considerations (see Chapter 5) are also more critical with SMBSs than with generic MBSs. The estimations of the impact of true WAM and WAC ranges on the prepayment projections all take on a more critical impact in IO and PO prepayment-sensitivity analysis.

REGULATORY CONCERNS WITH SMBSs

In April 1988, the Office of the Comptroller of the Currency (OCC) and some member banks of the Federal Home Loan Bank system issued guidelines to their respective regulated financial institutions. The guidelines warned of the inherent risks associated with trading in SMBSs and in residuals (see Chapter 14). In a memorandum to clients, Brown & Wood, Attorneys, summarized these guidelines as follows[5]:

> The Office of the Comptroller of the Currency has issued guidelines applicable to national banks regarding selection of securities dealers and unsuitable investment practices. [A copy of the guidelines is included in Appendix A.]
>
> Among other things, the guidelines warn that stripped mortgage backed securities (IO/PO securities) "cannot be considered as suitable investments for the vast majority of depository institutions." However, the guidelines conclude that stripped mortgage backed securities "may be appropriate holdings for depository institutions that have highly sophisticated and well managed securities portfolios, mortgage portfolios or mortgage banking functions." Such institutions are admonished, how-

---

[5]The following guidelines are reprinted from a memorandum issued by Brown & Wood, New York, N.Y., dated April 14, 1988, prepared by Daniel M. Rossner.

ever, to acquire stripped mortgage backed securities only in conformity with carefully developed and documented plans which have been approved by the institution's board of directors. Furthermore, the guidelines require that depository institutions that prepare their financial statements in accordance with GAAP report their holdings of such securities in accordance with FAS #91 which requires that the carrying amount of such securities on the institution's books be adjusted when actual prepayment experience differs from prepayment estimates. The guidelines contain similar warnings concerning asset backed residuals and long-term zero coupon and stripped products including STRIPS, TIGRs, CATS and Original Issue Discount Bonds.

In addition to discussing stripped mortgage backed securities, residuals and zero coupon bonds, the guidelines set forth steps to be taken by national banks in selecting securities dealers and criteria for distinguishing between investment activity and securities trading. The guidelines have been adopted by the Federal Financial Institutions Examination Council and by the Federal Deposit Insurance Corporation. It has been reported that the Federal Reserve Board and the Federal Home Loan Bank Board will adopt similar guidelines shortly.

Although the guidelines discuss the appropriateness for investment of various types of stripped mortgage backed securities, residuals and zero coupon bonds, they do not explicitly pass upon the legality of investment in any such securities. Accordingly, banks should continue to consult applicable law and regulations before investing in such securities. In addition, state-chartered banks should continue to consult with state regulatory authorities concerning any state guidelines regarding such securities.

APPENDIX A

Guidelines for Selection of Securities Dealers and Unsuitable Investment Practices[6]

Purpose

This issuance is to provide you with recommended procedures to be employed by all national banks when selecting securities dealers and to advise you of certain securities activities that the depository institution regulators view as unsuitable in an investment portfolio. The Federal Financial Institution Examination Council (FFIEC) recently endorsed the same policy statement. Adoption of the policy by FFIEC is intended to achieve uniform and effective supervision by institution investment portfolio managers. The following is the text of the FFIEC policy statement.

Background

The depository institution regulators have become aware of speculative activity which has taken place in a number of depository institutions' investment portfolios. Certain of these institutions have failed because of the speculative activities, and other institutions have been weakened significantly as their earnings and capital have been impaired and the liquidity of their securities has been eroded by the depreciation in their market value.

Speculative activity often occurs when a depository institution's investment portfolio manager follows the advice of securities dealers who, in order to generate commission income, encourage speculative practices that are unsuitable for the investment portfolio.

[6]Office of the Comptroller of the Currency, Administrator of National Banks.

Recommendations Concerning the Selection of a Securities Dealer

It is common for the investment portfolio managers of many depository institutions to rely on the expertise and advice of a securities sales representative for: recommendations of proposed investments; investment strategies; and the timing and pricing of securities transactions. Accordingly, it is important for the management of depository institutions to know the securities firms and the personnel with whom they deal. An investment portfolio manager should not engage in securities transactions with any securities dealer that is unwilling to provide complete and timely disclosure of its financial condition. Management must review the dealer's financial statements and make a judgment about the ability of the dealer to honor its commitments. An inquiry into the general reputation of the dealer also is necessary.

The board of directors and/or an appropriate board committee should review and approve a list of securities firms with whom the depository's management is authorized to do business. The following securities dealer selection standards are recommended, but are not all inclusive. The dealer selection process should include:

- A consideration of the ability of the securities dealer and its subsidiaries or affiliates to fulfill commitments as evidenced by capital strength and operating results disclosed in current financial data, annual reports, credit reports, etc.;
- an inquiry into the dealer's general reputation for financial stability and fair and honest dealings with customers, including an inquiry of past or current financial institution customers of the securities dealer;
- an inquiry of appropriate State or Federal securities regulators and securities industry self-regulatory organizations, such as the National Association of Securities Dealers, concerning any formal enforcement actions against the dealer or its affiliates or associated personnel;
- an inquiry, as appropriate, into the background of the sales representative to determine his or her experience and expertise;
- a determination whether the depository institution has appropriate procedures to establish possession or control of securities purchased. Purchased securities and repurchase agreement collateral should only be kept in safekeeping with selling dealers when (1) the board is completely satisfied as to the creditworthiness of the securities dealer and (2) the aggregate value of securities held in safekeeping in this manner is within credit limitations that have been approved by the board of directors, or a committee of the board, for unsecured transactions (see FFIEC Policy Statement adopted October 1985). Federal

credit unions, when entering into a repurchase agreement with a broker/dealer, are not permitted to maintain the collateral with the broker/dealer, reference part 703 of the National Credit Union Administration rules and regulations.

As part of the process of managing a depository institution's relationships with securities dealers the board of directors may wish to consider including in the financial institution's code of ethics or code of conduct a prohibition by those employees, who are directly involved in purchasing and selling securities for the depository institution, from engaging in personal securities transactions with the same securities firm that the depository institution uses for its transactions without specific board approval and periodic review. The board also may wish to adopt a policy applicable to directors, officers or employees concerning the receipt of gifts, gratuities or travel expenses from approved dealer firms and their personnel (also see in this connection the Bank Bribery Law, 18 USC 215 and interpretive releases).

Objectionable Investment Practices

Depository institution directors are responsible for prudent administration of investments in securities. An investment portfolio traditionally has been maintained by a depository institution to provide earnings, liquidity and a means of diversifying risks. When investment transactions are entered into in anticipation of taking gains on short-term price movements, the transactions are no longer characteristic of investment activities and should be conducted in a securities trading account. Securities trading of the types described in section I of the attached appendix will be viewed as unsuitable activities when they are conducted in a depository institution's investment account. Securities trading should take place only in a closely supervised trading account and be undertaken only by institutions that have strong capital and current earnings positions. Acquisitions of the various forms of zero coupon, stripped obligations and asset backed securities residuals discussed in section II of the attached appendix will receive increased regulatory attention and, depending upon the circumstances, may be considered unsuitable for a depository institution.

State chartered financial institutions are cautioned that certain of the investment practices listed in the appendix may violate state law. If any such practices are contemplated, the appropriate state supervisor should be consulted regarding permissibility under state law.

Appendix to FFIEC Supervisory Policy Statement on the Selection of Securities Dealers and Unsuitable Investment Practices

I. *Trading in the Investment Portfolio*

Trading in the investment portfolio is characterized by a high volume of purchase and sale activity, which when considered in light of a short holding period for securities, clearly demonstrates management's intent to profit from short-term price movements. In this situation, a failure to follow accounting and reporting standards applicable to trading accounts may result in a misstatement of the depository institution's income and a filing of false regulatory reports and other published financial data. It is an unsafe and unsound practice to record and report holdings of securities that result from trading transactions using accounting standards which are intended for investment portfolio transactions; therefore, the discipline associated with accounting standards applicable to trading accounts is necessary. Securities held in trading accounts should be marked to market, or the lower of cost or market, periodically with unrealized gains or losses recognized in current income. Prices used in periodic revaluations should be obtained from sources that are independent of the securities dealer doing business with the depository.

The following practices are considered to be unsuitable when they occur in a depository institution's investment portfolio.

A. "Gains Trading"

"Gains trading" is a securities trading activity conducted in an investment portfolio, often termed "active portfolio management." "Gains trading" is characterized by the purchase of a security as an investment and the subsequent sale of that same security at a profit within several days or weeks. Those securities initially purchased with the intent to resell are retained as investment portfolio assets if they cannot be sold at a profit. These "losers" are retained in the investment portfolio because investment portfolio holdings are accounted for at cost, and losses are not recognized unless the security is sold. "Gains trading" often results in a portfolio of securities with extended maturities, lower credit quality, high market depreciation and limited practical liquidity.

In many cases, "gains trading" has involved the trading of "when-issued" securities and "pair-offs" or "corporate settlements" because the extended settlement period associated with these practices allows speculators the opportunity for substantial price changes to occur before payment for the securities is due.

B. "When-Issued" Securities Trading

"When-issued" securities trading is the buying and selling of securities in the interim between the announcement of an offering and the issuance and payment date of these securities. A purchaser of a "when-issued" security acquires all the risks and rewards of owning a security and may sell the "when-issued" security at a profit before taking delivery and paying for it. Frequent purchases and sales of securities during the "when-issued" period generally are indications of trading activity and should not be conducted in a bank's investment portfolio.

C. "Pair-Offs"

A "pair-off" is a security purchase transaction which is closed out or sold at, or prior to, settlement date. As an example, an investment portfolio manager will commit to purchase a security; then, prior to the predetermined settlement date, the portfolio manager will "pair-off" the purchase with a sale of the same security prior to, or on, the original settlement date. Profits or losses on the transaction are settled by one party to the transaction remitting to the counter party the difference between the purchase and sale price. Like "when-issued" trading, "pair-offs" permit speculation on securities price movements without paying for the securities.

D. Corporate Settlement on U.S. Government and Federal Agency Securities Purchases

Regular-way settlement for transactions in U.S. Government and Federal agency securities is one business day after the trade date. Regular-way settlement for corporate securities is five business days after the trade date. The use of a corporate settlement method (5 business days) for U.S. Government securities purchases appears to be offered by dealers in order to facilitate speculation on the part of the purchaser.

E. Repositioning Repurchase Agreements

Dealers who encourage speculation through the use of "pair-off," "when-issued" and "corporate settlement" transactions often provide the financing at settlement of purchased securities which cannot be sold at a profit. The buyer purchasing the security pays the dealer a small "margin" that is equivalent roughly to the actual loss in the security. The dealer then agrees to fund the purchase by buying the security back from the purchaser under a resale agreement. Apart from imprudently funding a longer-term, fixed-rate asset with short-term, variable-rate source funds, the purchaser acquires all the risks of ownership of a large amount of depreciated securities for a very small margin payment. Purchasing securities in these circumstances is inherently speculative and is a wholly unsuitable investment practice for depository institutions.

F. Short Sales

A short sale is the sale of a security that is not owned. The purpose of a short sale generally is to speculate on the fall in the price of the security. Short sales are speculative transactions that should be conducted in a trading account, and when conducted in the investment portfolio, they are considered to be unsuitable.

Short sales are not permissible activities for Federal credit unions.

II. *Stripped Mortgage Backed Securities, Residuals and Zero Coupon Bonds*

There are advantages and disadvantages in owning these products. A depository institution must consider the liquidity, marketability, pledgeability, and price volatility of each of these products prior to investing in them. It may be unsuitable for a depository institution to commit significant amounts of funds to long-term stripped mortgage backed securities, residuals and zero coupon bonds which fluctuate greatly in price.

A. Stripped Mortgage Backed Securities (SMBS) consist of two classes of securities with each class receiving a different portion of the monthly interest and principal cash flows from the underlying mortgage backed securities. In its purest form, an SMBS is converted into an interest-only (IO) strip, where the investor receives 100% of the interest cash flows, and a principal-only (PO) strip, where the investor receives 100% of the principal cash flows. All IOs and POs have highly volatile price characteristics based, in part, on the prepayment of the underlying mortgages and consequently on the maturity of the stripped security. Generally, POs will increase in value when interest rates decline while IOs increase in value when interest rates rise. Accordingly, the purchase of an IO strip may serve, theoretically, to offset the interest rate risk associated with mortgages and similar instruments held by a depository institution. Similarly, a PO may be useful as an offset to the effect of interest rate movements on the value of mortgage servicing. However, when purchasing an IO or PO the investor is speculating on the movements of future interest rates and how these movements will affect the prepayment of the underlying collateral. Furthermore, those SMBS that do not have the guarantee of a government agency or a government-sponsored agency as to the payment of principal and interest have an added element of credit risk.

As a general rule, SMBS cannot be considered as suitable investments for the vast majority of depository institutions. SMBS, however, may be appropriate holdings for depository institutions that have highly sophisticated and well managed securities portfolios, mortgage portfolios or mortgage banking functions. In such depository institutions, however, the acquisition of SMBS should be undertaken only in conformance with carefully developed and documented plans prescribing specific positioning limits and control arrangements for enforcing these limits. These plans should be approved by the institution's board of directors and vigorously enforced.

In those depository institutions that prepare their published financial statements in accordance with Generally Accepted Accounting Principles, SMBS holdings must be accounted for in accordance with Financial Accounting Standards Board Statement #91 (FAS #91) which requires that the carrying amount be adjusted when actual prepayment experience differs from prepayment estimates. Other institutions may account for their SMBS holdings under FAS #91 or alternatively at market value or the lower of cost or market value.

Several states have adopted, or are considering, regulations that prohibit state chartered banks from purchasing IO strips. Accordingly, state chartered institutions should consult with their state regulator concerning the permissibility of purchasing SMBS.

B. Asset Backed Securities (ABS) Residuals

Residuals are the excess cash flows from an ABS transaction after the payments due to the bondholders and the trust administrative expenses have been satisfied. This cash flow is extremely sensitive to prepayments, and thus has a high degree of interest rate risk.

Generally, the value of residual interests in ABS rises when interest rates rise. Theoretically a residual can be used as a risk management tool to offset declines in the value of fixed rate mortgages or ABS portfolios. However, it should be understood by all residual interest purchasers that the "yield" on these instruments is inversely related to their effectiveness as a risk management vehicle. In other words, the highest yielding ABS residuals have limited risk management value usually due to a complicated ABS structure and/or unusual collateral characteristics that make modeling and understanding the economic cash flows very difficult.

Alternatively, those residuals priced for modest yields generally have positive risk management characteristics.

In conclusion, it is important to understand that a residual cash flow is highly dependent upon the prepayments received. Caution should be exercised when purchasing a residual interest, especially higher "yielding" interests, because the risk associated over the life of the ABS may warrant an even higher return in order to adequately compensate the investor for the interest rate risk assumed. Purchases of these equity interests should be supported by in-house evaluations of possible rate of return ranges in combination with varying prepayment assumptions.

Residual interests in ABS are not permissible acquisitions for Federal credit unions. Holdings of ABS residuals by other institutions should be accounted for in the manner discussed under stripped mortgage backed securities and should be reported as "Other Assets" on regulatory reports.

C. Other Zero Coupon or Stripped Products

The interest and/or principal portions of U.S. Government obligations are sometimes sold to depository institutions in the form of stripped coupons, stripped bonds (principal), STRIPS, or proprietary products, such as CATs or TIGRs. Also, Original Issue Discount (OIDs) Bonds have been issued by a number of municipal entities. Longer maturities of these instruments can exhibit extreme price volatility and, accordingly, disproportionately large long-maturity holdings (in relation to the total portfolio) of zero coupon securities appear to be unsuitable for investment holdings for depository institutions.

APPENDIX B

Federal Income Tax Considerations[7]

The following is a general discussion of certain of the anticipated federal income tax consequences of the purchase, ownership and disposition of Bonds. The discussion is based upon laws, regulations, rulings and decisions now in effect (or, in the case of regulations, proposed), all of which are subject to change or possibly different interpretations. The discussion below does not purport to deal with the federal tax consequences applicable to all categories of investors, some of which may be subject to special rules. Investors should consult their own tax advisors in determining the federal, state, local and any other tax consequences to them of the purchase, ownership and disposition of Bonds. For purposes of this tax discussion (other than the discussion of information reporting by the Issuer), references to a "Bondholder" or a "holder" mean the beneficial owner of a Bond.

REMIC Elections

Under the Internal Revenue Code of 1986 (the "Code"), an issuer of certain mortgage-backed bonds may elect to be treated as a "real estate mortgage investment conduit" ("REMIC"). The Prospectus Supplement for each Series of Bonds will indicate whether the Issuer intends to make such an election. The discussions below under the headings "REMIC Bonds" and "Non-REMIC Bonds" apply respectively to Bonds with respect to which a REMIC election will, or will not, be made.

---

[7]Information provided by Fannie Mae.

REMIC Bonds. Qualifications as a REMIC requires ongoing compliance with certain conditions. With respect to each Series of Bonds for which the Issuer intends to make a REMIC election, Cleary, Gottlieb, Steen & Hamilton, counsel to the Issuer, will deliver their opinion generally to the effect that, under then existing law and assuming compliance with the Indenture and the Trust Agreement, the Issuer will be a REMIC and the Bonds of such Series will be "regular interests" in the REMIC. Except as indicated in the next two paragraphs, the Bonds will be treated for federal income tax purposes as debt instruments that are issued by the REMIC on the date of issuance of the Bonds and not as ownership interests in the REMIC or the REMIC's assets.

In the case of each Series of Bonds with respect to which the issuer makes a REMIC election, in general, the Bonds will be "qualifying real property loans" within the meaning of section 593(d) of the Code, "real estate assets" within the meaning of section 856(c)(5)(A) of the Code and assets described in section 7701(a)(19)(C) of the Code, except that if, at any time during any calendar year, less than 95% of the assets of the REMIC consist of assets qualifying under these sections, then the portion of the Bonds that are qualifying assets under these sections during such calendar year may be limited to the portion of the assets of the REMIC that are such qualifying assets. The assets of the REMIC will include, in addition to the Certificates, money invested in reserve funds, if any, and payments on the Certificates held pending distribution of the Bonds. In general, the Certificates will be such qualifying assets. It is unclear whether payments on the Certificates held pending distribution or reserve fund assets would be considered to be part of the Certificates, or whether such payments or assets otherwise would receive the same treatment as the Certificates, for purposes of the foregoing sections. Interest on the Bonds will be interest described in section 856(c)(3)(B) of the Code to the extent that the Bonds are treated as real estate assets within the meaning of section 856(c)(5)(A) of the Code.

Furthermore, in the case of each Series of Bonds with respect to which the Issuer makes a REMIC election, Bondholders that would otherwise report income under a cash method of accounting will be required to report income on such Bonds under an accrual method, and gain from the sale of such Bonds that might otherwise be capital gain will be treated as ordinary income to the extent that such gain does not exceed the excess, if any, of (i) the amount that would have been includible in the seller's income with respect to the Bonds that are sold had income accrued thereon at a rate equal to 110% of the "applicable Federal rate" (generally, an average of current yields on Treasury securities), determined as of the date of purchase of such Bonds, over (ii) the amount actually includible in the seller's income.

Non-REMIC Bonds. In the case of each Series of Bonds with respect to which the Issuer does not make a REMIC election, although there are no regulations, published rulings or judicial decisions involving the characterization for federal income tax purposes of securities with terms substantially the same as the Bonds, Cleary, Gottlieb, Steen & Hamilton, counsel to the Issuer, will deliver their opinion to the effect that, assuming compliance with the Indenture and the Trust Agreement, the Bonds will be treated for federal income tax purposes as indebtedness of the Issuer, and not as ownership interests in the Collateral, or equity interests in the Issuer or in a separate association, taxable as a corporation.

In the case of each Series of Bonds with respect to which the Issuer does not make a REMIC election, Bondholders should be aware that the Bonds will be not "qualifying real property loans" within the meaning of section 593(d) of the Code, "Government securities" within the meaning of section 851(b)(4)(A)(i) of the Code, "real estate assets" or "Government securities" within the meaning of section 856(c)(5)(A) of the Code, or assets described in section 7701(a)(19)(C)(v) of the Code. Such a Bond will, however, constitute an "obligation . . . which is principally secured, directly or indirectly, by an interest in real property" within the meaning of section 860G(a)(3)(A) of the Code.

Original Issue Discount and Premium

General. All of the Compound Interest Bonds will, and certain of the other Bonds may, be issued with "original issue discount" within the meaning of section 1273(a) of the Code. Holders of Bonds issued with original issue discount should be aware that generally they must include original issue discount in gross income for federal income tax purposes as it accrues, in advance of receipt of the cash attributable to such income, under a method that takes account of the compounding of interest. The Code requires that information with respect to the original issue discount accruing on any Bond be reported periodically to the Internal Revenue Service (the "Service") and to certain categories of holders of such Bond.

Rules governing original issue discount are set forth in sections 1271–1273 and 1275 of the Code. The Tax Reform Act of 1986 amended these rules to provide that (i) the amount and rate of accrual of original issue discount on each Series of Bonds will be calculated based on a reasonable assumed prepayment rate (the "Prepayment Assumption") and (ii) adjustments will be made in the amount and rate of accrual of such discount to reflect differences between the actual prepayment rate and the Prepayment Assumption. The method for determining the appropriate assumed prepayment rate will eventually be set forth in Treasury regulations, but those regulations have not yet been issued. The legislative history of the Tax Reform Act of 1986 indicates, however, that the regulations will provide that the assumed prepayment rate for securities such as the Bonds will be the rate used in pricing the initial offering of those securities. The Prospectus Supplement for each Series of Bonds that includes Bonds issued with original issue discount will specify the Prepayment Assumption determined by the Issuer, but no representation is made that the Bonds will, in fact, prepay at a rate based on the Prepayment Assumption or at any other rate.

In general, a Bond will be considered to be issued with original issue discount equal to the excess, if any, of its stated redemption price at maturity over its issue price. The stated redemption price at maturity of a Bond other than a Compound Interest Bond is its principal amount (except as discussed below under ''Payment Lag Bonds'') and the stated redemption price at maturity of a Compound Interest Bond is the sum of all payments to be made on the Bond determined under the Prepayment Assumption. The issue price of a Bond is the initial offering price to the public (excluding bond houses and brokers) at which a substantial amount of the Bonds of that Class was sold. Notwithstanding the general definition of original issue discount, such discount will be considered to be zero in the case of any Bond if such discount is less than .25% of the stated redemption price at maturity of the Bond multiplied by its weighted average life. The weighted average life of a Bond would apparently be computed for this purpose as the sum, for all payments included in the stated redemption price at maturity of the Bond, of the amounts determined by multiplying (i) the number of complete years (rounding down for partial years) from the Closing Date until the date on which each such payment is expected to be made, determined under the Prepayment Assumption, by (ii) a fraction, the numerator of which is the amount of such payment and the denominator of which is the Bond's stated redemption price at maturity.

Rate of Accrual of Original Issue Discount. The holder of a Bond issued with original issue discount must include in gross income the sum of the ''daily portions'' of such original issue discount for each day during its taxable year on which it held such Bond. In the case of an original holder of a Bond, the daily portions of original issue discount will be determined as follows. A calculation will first be made of the portion of the original issue discount that accrues during each successive period (an ''accrual period'') that ends on a date corresponding to a Payment Date and begins on the day following the immediately preceding date corresponding to a Payment Date (or in the case of the first such period, begins on the Closing Date). The portion of the original issue discount accruing during any accrual period will then be allocated ratably to each day during the period to determine the daily portion of original issue discount for that day.

The portion of the original issue discount that accrues in any accrual period will equal the *excess,* if any, of (i) the sum of (A) the present value, as of the end of the accrual period, of all of the payments to be made on such Bond, if any, in future periods and (B) the payments made on such Bond during the accrual period that are included in such Bond's stated redemption price at maturity, *over* (ii) the adjusted issue price of such Bond at the beginning of the accrual period. The present value of the future payments referred to in the preceding sentence will be calculated (i) assuming that such Bond (and all other Bonds of the same Series) will be prepaid in future periods at a rate equal to the Prepayment Assumption and (ii) using a discount rate equal to the original yield to maturity of such Bond. For these purposes, the original yield to maturity of such Bond will be calculated based on the issue price of such Bond and assuming that such Bond (and all other Bonds of the same Series) will be prepaid in all periods at a rate equal to the Prepayment Assumption. For these purposes, the adjusted issue price of a Bond at the beginning of any accrual period will equal the issue price of such Bond, increased by the portion of the original issue discount that has accrued during prior accrual periods, and reduced by the amount of any payments made on such Bond in prior accrual periods that were included in such Bond's stated redemption price at maturity.

A subsequent holder of any Bond issued with original issue discount who purchases such Bond at a cost less than its remaining stated redemption price at maturity will also generally be required to include in gross income the daily portions of original issue discount, calculated as described above. However, if (i) the excess of the remaining stated redemption price at maturity over such cost is less than (ii) the aggregate amount of such daily portions for all days after the date of purchase until final retirement of such Bond, then such daily portions will be reduced proportionately in determining the income of such subsequent holder.

Premium. A purchaser of a Bond who purchases the Bond at a cost greater than its remaining stated redemption price at maturity will be considered to have purchased the Bond at a premium, and may, under section 171 of the Code, elect to amortize such premium under a constant yield method over the life of the Bonds (or if it results in a slower rate of amortization, over the period to an optional call date with reference to the call price for that date). It is not clear whether the Prepayment Assumption would be taken into account in determining the life of the Bonds for this purpose.

Payment Lag Bonds. Certain of the Bonds ("Payment Lag Bonds") may provide for payments of interest based on a period that corresponds to the interval between Payment Dates but ends one month prior to each Payment Date. Because of the lag between the end of the period during which interest accrues and the time such interest is required to be paid, the Service might take the position that (i) all or a portion of the accrued interest that is paid upon the purchase of a Bond should be treated as part of the overall cost of such Bond and not as a separate asset, the cost of which is recovered entirely out of interest received on the next Payment Date, or (ii) all or a portion of each interest payment must be included in the stated redemption price at maturity of the Bonds and accounted for as original issue discount. The principal consequence of analyzing a Payment Lag Bond in this manner would be to require a cash basis holder to report interest income from such Bond in whole or in part under an accrual method. Accordingly, applying this analysis would have little effect on holders of Compound Interest Bonds or Bonds with respect to which a REMIC election is made because interest on such Bonds must in any event be accounted for under an accrual method.

Variable Rate Bonds. Certain of the Bonds ("Floating Rate Bonds") may provide for interest that accrues (after the first Interest Accrual Period) at a rate that varies directly (though not necessarily proportionately) with an index of market interest rates (the "Index") such as LIBOR. Although not entirely certain, it is likely that the rules of the Code relating to original issue discount and bond premium would be applied to a Floating Rate Bond by assuming that such Bond will bear interest in all periods after the First Payment Date at a fixed rate equal to the interest that would be payable if the Index remained constant over the life of such Bond at its value as of the Closing Date (or possibly as of the date of pricing of the Bonds). Applying this assumption would effectively convert such Bond to a fixed rate bond to which the rules described above can be applied. If the rate of interest that is actually payable for an Interest Accrual Period differs from the assumed rate, then an adjustment would be made in the income of that period to reflect the actual rate.

Certain of the Bonds ("Inverse Floating Rate Bonds") may provide for interest that accrues (after the first Interest Accrual Period) at a rate that varies inversely with an Index. It is not clear how the original issue discount and premium rules of the Code will be applied to Inverse Floating Rate Bonds. One reasonable approach would be to apply to Inverse Floating Rate Bonds the method described in the preceding paragraph for taking account of the variable rate feature of Floating Rate Bonds.

One possible alternative would be to apply to Inverse Floating Rate Bonds rules for contingent payment obligations found in proposed regulations under the original issue discount sections of the Code. While those rules are complex, the principal consequences of applying them to

Inverse Floating Rate Bonds would appear to be that (i) the amount payable as interest on such Bonds on any Payment Date would be includible in income at the time when the amount of the interest payment becomes fixed, rather than over the period in which such interest accrues (in the case of accrual basis taxpayers) or at the time when the payment is made (in the case of cash basis taxpayers), (ii) the daily portions of any original issue discount represented by the excess of the principal amount of such Bonds over their issue price would be calculated as if the only payments to be made on such Bonds were the noncontingent payments thereon (including payments of principal) which would result in such original issue discount being accrued under a virtually straight-line method and (iii) any premium represented by the excess of the issue price of such Bonds over their initial principal amount would be required to be amortized without an election being made by holders at a rate that generally would not be slower than the rate of amortization of such premium under section 171 of the Code. If, for purposes of calculating the daily portions of original issue discount on such Bonds, the noncontingent payments on the Bond were considered to include the fixed interest payable on the first Payment Date in addition to the principal payments, then the daily portions would be increased but the holder would not be required to report such fixed interest as interest income in the first Interest Accrual Period. Application of the contingent payment rules to the Inverse Floating Rate Bonds would also make uncertain the character of gain or loss from sale of the Bonds (as ordinary or capital) and the method to be used by a subsequent purchaser of such Bonds to account for any difference between the cost of such Bonds to such purchaser and the basis that such Bonds would have at the time of the purchase in the hands of an original holder.

Market Discount

A holder who acquires a Bond at a market discount, that is, a discount that exceeds any unaccrued original issue discount, will recognize gain upon receipt of a principal payment, whether on the date on which such payment is scheduled to be made or as a prepayment. In particular, the holder will be required to allocate that principal payment first to the portion of the market discount on such Bond that has accrued but not previously been includible in income, and will recognize ordinary income to that extent. In general terms, market discount on a Bond may be treated, at the holder's election, as accruing either (i) under a constant yield method, taking into account the Prepayment Assumption, or (ii) in proportion to accruals of original issue discount (or, if there is no original issue discount, in proportion to accruals of interest at the stated interest rate). The Code requires that information necessary to compute accruals of market discount be reported periodically to the Service and to certain categories of Bondholders. In addition, deductions for a portion of the holder's interest expense on any debt incurred or continued to purchase or to carry a Bond purchased with market discount may be deferred. The deferred portion of any interest deduction would not exceed the portion of the market discount on such Bond that accrues during the taxable year in which such interest would otherwise be deductible and, in general, would be deductible when such market discount is included in income upon receipt of a principal payment on, or sale of, such Bond.

Notwithstanding the above rules, market discount on a Bond will be considered to be zero if such discount is less than .25% of the stated redemption price at maturity of such Bond multiplied by its weighted average remaining life. Weighted average remaining life presumably would be calculated in a manner similar to weighted average life (described above under "Original Issue Discount and Premium—General"), taking into account payments (including prepayments) prior to the date of acquisition of such Bond by the subsequent purchaser. If market discount on a Bond is treated as zero under this rule, the actual amount of such discount must be allocated to the remaining principal payments on such Bond and when each such payment is made, gain equal to the discount allocated to such distribution will be recognized.

Sales of Bonds

If a Bond is sold, the seller will recognize gain or loss equal to the difference between the amount realized in the sale and its adjusted basis in such Bond. Such adjusted basis generally will equal the cost of such Bond to the seller, increased by income reported by the seller with respect to such Bond and reduced by any amortized premium and the amount of distributions on such Bond received by the seller. Except as provided in the following paragraph and under "REMIC Elections—REMIC Bonds," any such gain or loss will be capital gain or loss provided such Bond is held as a capital asset.

Gain recognized on the sale of a Bond by a holder who purchased such Bond at a market discount would be taxable as ordinary income in an amount not exceeding the portion of such discount that accrued during the period such Bond was held by such holder, reduced by any market discount includible in income by such holder under the rules described above under "Market Discount."

For taxable years beginning after December 31, 1987, the preferential treatment currently afforded long-term capital gains will no longer be available.

APPENDIX C

FNMA Synthetic-Coupon SMBSs

Daily Strips Pricing Sheet

Issue	Class	P Pct.	I Pct.	Coupon	Price	Yield	Spread	Dur.	Mtg. Dur.	Speed
FNMA SMBS SERIES A	1	99.000%	45.000%	5.0%	79–29	9.66%	110/7 yr.	4.51	11.98	175.00
FNMAGL 11.00%	2	1.000%	55.000%	605.0%	26–22+	9.86%	130/7 yr.	4.08	−25.25	175.00
WAC 11.50% WAM 262										
PRICE: 105–26										
FNMA SMBS SERIES B	1	50.000%	33.333%	6.0%	80–29	9.81%	110/9 yr.	5.37	7.07	100.00
FNMAGL 9.00%	2	50.000%	66.667%	12.0%	108–07	10.53%	181/9 yr.	5.02	4.45	100.00
WAC 9.50% WAM 251										
PRICE: 94–18										
FNMA SMBS SERIES C	1	50.000%	33.333%	6.0%	80–29	9.81%	110/9 yr.	5.37	7.07	100.00
FNMAGL 9.00%	2	50.000%	66.667%	12.0%	108–07	10.53%	181/9 yr.	5.02	4.45	100.00
WAC 9.50% WAM 251										
PRICE: 94–18										
FNMA SMBS SERIES D	1	50.000%	35.294%	6.0%	81–05+	9.81%	110/9 yr.	5.30	7.10	100.00
FNMAGL 8.50%	2	50.000%	64.706%	11.0%	102–04+	10.73%	201/9 yr.	4.94	4.75	100.00
WAC 9.00% WAM 246										
PRICE: 91–21										

Security		(%)	(%)	(%)	Price	Yield	Term			
FNMA SMBS SERIES E FNMAGL 11.00% WAC 11.50% WAM 264 PRICE: 105–26	1	99.000%	54.000%	6.0%	85–27	9.49%	110/6 yr.	4.20	8.92	200.00
	2	1.000%	46.000%	506.0%	22–16	8.09%	–30/6 yr.	4.08	–25.83	200.00
FNMA SMBS SERIES F FNMAGL 9.00% WAC 9.50% WAM 238 PRICE: 94–18	1	50.000%	36.111%	6.5%	84–05 +	9.74%	110/8 yr.	5.25	6.56	100.00
	2	50.000%	63.889%	11.5%	104–30 +	10.65%	201/8 yr.	4.90	4.56	100.00
FNMA SMBS SERIES G FNMAGL 9.00% WAC 9.50% WAM 237 PRICE: 94–18	1	50.000%	36.111%	6.5%	84–06 +	9.74%	110/8 yr.	5.24	6.55	100.00
	2	50.000%	63.889%	11.5%	104–29 +	10.65%	201/8 yr.	4.90	4.55	100.00
FNMA SMBS SERIES H FNMAGL 9.00% WAC 9.50% WAM 238 PRICE: 94–18	1	50.000%	36.111%	6.5%	84–05 +	9.74%	110/8 yr.	5.25	6.56	100.00
	2	50.000%	63.889%	11.5%	104–30 +	10.65%	201/8 yr.	4.90	4.56	100.00
FNMA SMBS SERIES I FNMAGL 9.00% WAC 9.50% WAM 236 PRICE: 94–18	1	50.000%	36.111%	6.5%	84–07	9.74%	110/8 yr.	5.23	6.53	100.00
	2	50.000%	63.889%	11.5%	104–29	10.66%	202/8 yr.	4.89	4.54	100.00
FNMA SMBS SERIES J FNMAGL 11.00% WAC 11.50% WAM 257 PRICE: 105–26	1	99.000%	63.000%	7.0%	90–00	9.49%	110/6 yr.	4.16	7.25	200.00
	2	1.000%	37.000%	407.0%	16–23	10.17%	177/6 yr.	3.78	–23.54	200.00

(continued)

APPENDIX C

FNMA Synthetic-Coupon SMBSs (continued)

Daily Strips Pricing Sheet

Issue	Class	P Pct.	I Pct.	Coupon	Price	Yield	Spread	Dur.	Mtg. Dur.	Speed
FNMA SMBS SERIES K	1	99.000%	69.882%	6.0%	82–13	9.74%	110/8 yr.	4.99	6.50	100.00
FNMAGL 8.50%	2	1.000%	30.118%	256.0%	10–02	16.18%	754/8 yr.	3.52	−2.04	100.00
WAC 9.00% WAM 212										
PRICE: 91–21										
FNMA SMBS SERIES L	1	99.000%	61.875%	5.0%	78–17 +	9.66%	110/7 yr.	4.92	6.28	100.00
FNMAGL 8.00%	2	1.000%	38.125%	305.0%	8–19	27.06%	1850/7 yr.	2.66	− .38	100.00
WAC 8.50% WAM 202										
PRICE: 86–11										

Source: Shearson Lehman Hutton Mortgage Securities.

14

Residuals:
The Ultimate Derivative

INTRODUCTION

Residuals may be defined as remainder cash flows generated from the difference between the cash flows contributed by the pool collateral and those required to fund bonds supported by the collateral. They first came to the attention of secondary market investors as a by-product of the introduction of CMOs (see Chapter 12). The residual of a CMO may in a sense be viewed as the equivalent of the last tranche of the CMO—the residual is what is left over after the expenses of the bond issue and all its debt-service payments have been met. In practice, the residual holder is usually paid on each P&I distribution date because the CMO bond issue is structured throughout on a worst-case scenario. Whenever a distribution has been met in full, including payment to mandatory reserves and trustee expenses, the residual holder is entitled to any cash-flow remainder.

This chapter presents, first, a brief history of the secondary market for CMO residuals and then an analysis of the principal sources of residual cash flows and their sensitivity to changes in interest rates and prepayment speed. A review follows of the principal structural forms of CMO residuals, including CMOs with all-fixed, with fixed and floating, and with all-floating tranches. The chapter concludes with a discussion of hedging residuals with MBSs derivative products and with special-purpose liabilities such as interest-rate swaps and caps.

EVOLUTION OF THE RESIDUAL
SECONDARY MARKET

The developments that led to the creation of a secondary market for residuals stem from the requirements of the Grantor Trust mechanism for issuing MBSs. Virtually all pass-through MBSs are packaged with the mortgage collateral deposited in a **Grantor Trust**, which because of its totally passive nature, enables the MBS issuer to enjoy sale-of-asset treatment for tax and accounting purposes. Sale-of-asset accounting is particularly essential for mortgage bankers because with literally billions of dollars of loans under servicing, few such originators would be able to continue issuing MBS pools if the pools had to be carried on the books as debt issuance. One constraint of the Grantor Trust, however, is the IRS requirement that only a single-class Grantor Trust can be treated as a sale of assets.

Therefore, for the first years of their issuance, CMOs had to be structured as issuance of debt. To assure financing (debt issuance) status certain structural elements were introduced. Among these was to structure remittance of P&I payments to be distributed in some fashion other than monthly. Most issuers of the early CMOs elected quarterly distributions, but monthly distributions are quite common today. Another major structural element was retention of an equity interest in the collateral.

A party that retains an economic interest in the collateral remains "at risk," a key test in determining financing versus sale-of-asset treatment. This interest took the form of an equity, or ownership, position in the collateral, resulting in consolidation of the assets (the mortgage collateral) and the liabilities (the CMO bonds) on the issuer's balance sheet. This equity interest is what we now call a residual.

The requirement that CMOs be issued as debt restricted their use to the large, well-capitalized Wall Street firms which issued "arbitrage CMOs" under special-purpose corporations (see Chapter 12), builders who enjoyed other tax benefits (see Chapter 1), and some S&Ls which used the CMO as an economic means of liquifying below-market seasoned loans and preferred not to have sale-of-asset treatment (see Chapter 1).

The Owner-Trust Vehicle

Toward the end of 1985 the introduction of the owner trust as the CMO issuing entity made it possible to achieve off-balance sheet financing of mortgage collateral issued under a CMO. The owner-trust form of ownership may provide either owner-trust or partnership-style tax treatment. The owner-trust partnership allowed nonconsolidation of the CMO liabilities to the residual investor. Therefore, if the CMO issuer could sell 51 percent or more of the beneficial interest in the equity (or residual) of the CMO to a third party, the issuer could remove the collateral assets of the CMO from his balance sheet. With this development the secondary market for residuals was born.

In trust form, the CMO residual is an unregistered security that is placed privately by the issuer with investors. The form of the security is a certificate of beneficial ownership in the issuing trust. Many owner trusts that have been established to issue CMOs must be sold to qualified investors who will be able to meet ongoing net worth tests. These tests are different for each transaction, but all serve to effectively limit potential buyers to institutional investors who have adequate net worth. The fundamental reason for the requirement stems from the opinion of legal experts, who take the position that the CMO residual investors are the legal owners of the issuing entity. As such, they must be able to ensure that if the expenses of the trustee are not covered by residual cash flow, the residual owners will provide for those expenses. If the investors, as equity holders, did not have significant net worth, tax authorities might consider the CMO bond holders to be the real owners of the trust. In such a case both the collateral income and the bond interest might be taxable to the bond holders.

The TIMs Initiative

Determined to fulfill the dream of a multiclass pass-through, mortgage bankers and some friendly legislators undertook to amend housing legislation and the tax law to make it possible. In 1983 and 1984, the Mortgage Bankers Association and Fannie Mae spearheaded a lobbying effort leading to the TIMs (Trusts for Investment in Mortgages) initiative, but the effort folded under opposition by the investment bankers to the participation of Fannie Mae (see Chapter 1). Sears Mortgage Securities in 1983 structured a pass-through-type CMO, but the IRS issued a directive that such an issue would be taxed as a corporation (see Chapter 1).

The REMIC Impact

The pressure continued to build, however, and finally with the inclusion of the REMIC legislation in the 1986 Tax Reform Act a multiclass pass-through became permissible if the REMIC election was taken (for full discussion of the REMIC legislation, see Chapter 1). When first introduced, the REMIC election could be used only for the issuance of all-fixed-rate classes, but in 1987 legislative amendments permitted floating classes to be issued under the REMIC election as well.

Under the REMIC election, there are two classes of interests, the regular interests and the residual interest. The regular interests may look like the familiar tranches of a CMO or take other forms. The breakthrough for the residual secondary market was that under the REMIC structure the residual interest is a bond class in the multiclass REMIC offering and, therefore, may be freely traded, avoiding the awkwardness of the private placement process in the owner trust as described above. Furthermore, as part of the REMIC bond issue, the residual interest by definition is a qualifying real property loan investment.

SOURCES OF RESIDUAL CASH FLOWS

The residual interest (residual) represents the cash-flow remainder after all debt-service and administrative expenses of the bond issue have been met. Figure 14.1 illustrates the flow of funds for a generic CMO issue. The numbers 1, 2, and 3 on the figure specify the priority in the order of cash-flow distributions; note the residual holder receives distributions after priorities (1) and (2) have been met.

Fixed-Rate CMO Residuals—Bear Market Bias

The primary source of the residual interest derives from the coupon differential between the average weighted coupon of the MBS or mortgage collateral held in the trust and the weighted average of all the coupon payments due to be paid on the CMO bonds. In periods of a positively sloped yield curve the coupon differential could be considerable. Consider, for example, the coupon structure of the four-tranche CMO as illustrated in Table 14.1.

FIGURE 14.1
CMO Cash Flow

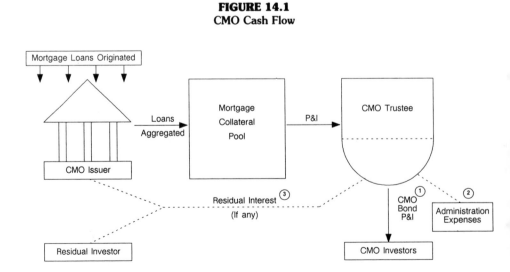

TABLE 14.1
Shearson Lehman CMO Series C
Pool Collateral: GNMA, FHLMC, and FNMA 9% and 9.5% Coupons

CMO Bond Class	Original Principal Balance	Bond Coupon Rate (%)	Stated Maturity Date[b]	Projected Maturity Rate[c]	Average Life (yrs.)	Bond Price
C-1	$ 51,883,386	7.45	7/20/99	7/20/90	2.11	99.95
C-2	68,000,000	8.25	4/20/06	1/20/95	5.62	99.99
C-3	67,500,000	9.13	4/20/10	4/20/01	10.95	99.58
C-4	11,259,875	9.45[a]	10/20/16	10/20/16	20.01	90.38
	$198,643,261	8.41			7.33	99.30
		(WAC)			(WAL)	(Aug. cost)

[a]Accrual bond class.

[b]Assuming reinvestment of cash flows at 4.5 percent year 1, 4 percent year 2, and 3 percent thereafter.

[c]Assuming reinvestment of cash flows at 6.5 percent for all years.

The WAC of the CMO tranches is 8.41 percent versus an average pass-through security rate of 9.17 percent on the MBS collateral. The weighted average life for the entire collateral pool is 7.33 years.

Of more specific interest, note that the coupon rate of the first tranche is only 7.45 percent, a spread of almost 1¾ percentage points below the 9.17 average net MBS rate received by the trust. This spread exists for a 2.11 average life *assuming the 165 percent PSA spread assumption is realized.* The next bond coupon is at 8.25 percent, about 92 basis points below the 9.17 percent MBS pass-through rate. The last two bond classes are above the average pass-through rate, but some pass-through coupons are as high as 9.5 percent. Clearly, most of the residual will be received while the first two bond classes are outstanding. The residual income is therefore front-end-loaded, which is typical of most fixed-rate CMO deals.

Residual Income Sensitivity to Prepayment Spread

It should now be obvious there are similarities between the residual in a CMO structured as above and on IO (see Chapter 13). In other words, if prepayments accelerate, the average lives of these first two bond classes will be shortened, thereby reducing the time for residual income to be generated, and vice versa if prepayments slow down. *Residuals of all-fixed–tranche CMOs therefore appreciate in value in periods of rising interest rates and rapidly decline in value when interest rates are falling.*

Table 14.2 displays a sensitivity analysis of the residual interest cash flows to varying prepayment-speed assumptions.

TABLE 14.2
Shearson Lehman CMO Series C
Residual Sensitivity Analysis

Residual Purchase Yield (%)	Residual Cost	Realized Residual Yield If PSA Speed Is:				
		100 PSA	*125 PSA*	*165 PSA*	*250 PSA*	*350 PSA*
11.00	$7,292,444	17.77	15.14	11.00	2.45	-0-
13.50	6,821,786	20.22	17.61	13.50	4.99	-0-
15.00	6,566,747	21.69	19.09	15.00	7.03	-0-
Total residual cash flow ($ millions)		14,107	21,410	10,417	7,811	6,100
Average cash-flow life (yrs.)		4.95	4.45	3.80	2.85	2.17

Source: Shearson Lehman Hutton Mortgage Securities.

The table shows that if the residual buyer purchased the residual at a price of $6,821,786[1] to yield 13.50 percent (see left columns at 13.50 purchase yield, cost = $6,821,786) *and if* the CMO collateral remains at 165 PSA for the term the residual is outstanding, the realized yield is 13.5 percent (see realized yields stated under 165 PSA column). The total cash flow received is $10,417,000 over an average life of 3.80 years. Now note that if the PSA speed accelerates to 250 PSA the realized yield is only 4.99 percent because the total residual cash flow is much less ($7,811,000) at the shorter average life (2.85 years). At 350 PSA, the residual purchaser does not even get back his original investment. If the PSA speed slows down, however, the total residual cash flow is greater (at 100 PSA, $14,107,000 to a 4.95-year average life). *The residual from a CMO of all-fixed–rate tranches is therefore clearly bear market-based*, similar to an IO except for the front-end-loading of the cash flows. The horizontal axes above and below the 13.5 percent base purchase-yield assumption illustrate the performance of the residual investment at lower and higher purchase yields. Figures 14.2 and 14.3 illustrate the residual cash flows at various PSA assumptions.

Other Sources of Residual Cash Flow

Other sources of residual income can arise from the requirements imposed on the Trust by the rating agencies. The agencies require that worst-case prepayment assumptions be applied to test the ability of the collateral cash flow to support the P&I requirements of the bonds under any economic scenario. Principal among these are:

[1]Since the residual has no principal component, the purchase price is stated first as a yield and then in dollars that represent the present value of the sum of the projected residual cash flows discounted at the purchase yield to the maturity projected by the PSA spread assumption.

FIGURE 14.2
CMO Residuals
Residual Cash Flow at Various PSA Assumptions

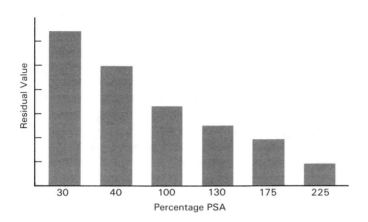

FIGURE 14.3
Residual Cash Flow at Various PSA Assumptions

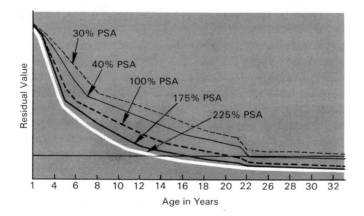

1. Discount-coupon collateral (coupon lower than CMO WAC) must be tested assuming no prepayments; therefore, any prepayments generate residual cash flows.

2. Premium collateral (coupon higher than CMO WAC) must be tested to a 100 percent prepayment assumption on the first CMO P&I distribution date; therefore, any extension of collateral life beyond the first distribution date generates residual cash flows.

3. Reserve funds and excess cash flow of the Trust are to be assumed reinvested at very low rates; such funds are generally reinvested at rates considerably higher than the rating agency's required assumption.

4. An assumption the coupon on a floating-rate CMO is at its cap rate immediately following issuance of the bonds. Since the cap is set well above interest rates prevailing at the time of issue, few CMO floaters have so far come close to hitting the cap rate.

Residual income is also generated from the time delay between receipt by the Trust of P&I payments made on the mortgages and when debt-service payments are remitted to the CMO bond holders. For a quarterly-pay CMO, for example, the excess could be considerable.

FIXED-FLOATER RESIDUALS— VOLATILITY ADVERSE

In September 1986, a floating-rate class was added to the CMO structure (see Chapter 12 for a description of floating-rate CMOs). The floater class introduced a fundamental change to residual cash-flow economics because now the coupon differential between collateral and bond coupon WAC became variable. From the viewpoint of the CMO issuer this was a dynamic innovation because the initial cost of the financing was reduced since the portion of the bonds issued as the floater class would be at an increment over LIBOR. Because LIBOR is a short-term money market index, its rate would be in close relation to short-term money market yields comparable to federal funds. The increment over LIBOR for the CMO floater bond varies from as little as 25 basis points to something less than 1 percentage point. From the bond investor's viewpoint the floater offers good protection against rising interest rates.

The considerations for the residual holder, however, now become mixed. In bear markets, the resulting slowdown in prepayment speed still provides the benefit of incremental residual income from that portion of the collateral allocated to the fixed-rate tranches. On the portion of the deal allocated to the floating class, however, a rising LIBOR rate reduces the spread between the CMO bond and collateral coupons.

Rating-Agency Considerations

As always, the rating agency requires that the collateral underlying the CMO bond issue be able to pay all investor obligations under a worst-case scenario. Therefore, for rating-agency purposes the floater class is assumed to be at the cap rate immediately upon its issuance. The combination of the bond coupons (including the floater at its cap rate) must not exceed the sum of the WACs of the underlying collateral. If the cap rate were 12 percent, for example, the WAC of the CMO bond coupons must average to something below 12 percent. If high-coupon collateral were available, the task might not be difficult, but such is generally not the case. Therefore, the fixed-floater is usually issued with discount-priced coupons in the fixed-rate tranches with the CMO sufficiently overcollateralized to support the total bond debt service, including the floater at its maximum rate-cap coupon.

Table 14.3 shows the structural details of the Shearson Lehman Series F CMO, in which the first class of the CMO is a floating rate which adjusts to 3-month LIBOR plus .625 percent.

TABLE 14.3
Shearson Lehman CMO Series F

COLLATERAL

Type	Pass-through Coupon	Mortgage Rate	Original Term to Maturity	Remaining Term to Maturity	Percent of Pool
FHLMC	9.50%	10.56%	360 mos.	339 mos.	100%

Projected PSA Speed		Prepayment History (PSA)				

1 Year	Long Term	1 Month	3 Months	6 Months	1 Year	Since Issue
120%	135%	211	258	275	280	202

BONDS

Bond	Original Principal Balance	Coupon	Stated Maturity	At 140% PSA Projected Maturity	Average Life	Yield Spread	Bond Yield	Bond Price
F-1(1)	$112,480,000	(2)	2/20/2018	2/20/2017	9.18	.625%	(1)	100.0
F-2	$27,460,000	5.00%	2/20/2009	8/20/1991	1.96	.950%	7.30%	94.6
F-3	$17,030,000	5.00%	11/20/2012	11/20/1994	5.46	1.250%	8.04%	86.1
F-4	$28,820,000	5.00%	11/20/2016	8/20/2004	11.34	1.400%	8.62%	74.9
F-5	$14,210,000	5.00%	2/20/2018	2/20/2017	21.72	1.500%	9.27%	61.1

(1) The sequence F-1 bonds pay down simultaneously with the sequence F-2 through F-5 bonds, which pay down in the order of their respective stated maturities.

(2) The F-1 coupon will be set on the second business day of the accrual rate and will be equal to 3-month LIBOR + .625 percent subject to a lifetime cap of 13 percent.

Source: Shearson Lehman Hutton Mortgage Securities.

Figure 14.4, which illustrates the CMO F bond structure, shows that the floating class pays parallel to all the sequential-pay fixed-rate classes.

Some structural characteristics of the Series F CMO that should be noted are that the fixed classes all have coupons of 5 percent; and the average life of the floater is the average life of the collateral, 9.5 years. The life cap is 13 percent.

RESIDUAL CASH-FLOW
SENSITIVITY ANALYSIS

Note that given a persistent rise in interest rates, the LIBOR-based coupon can, of course, rise higher than the highest mortgage coupon rate of the collateral—at least up to the cap rate assigned to the floater. Furthermore, if rates continue to rise over a prolonged period of time, there is a limit to how much the prepayment speed of the underlying collateral can slow down (see Chapter 5, "Overshooting to Steady State"). A further—and critical—consideration is that changes in the LIBOR rate occur instantaneously, but prepayment-speed changes take place over time. Therefore, a squeeze on the residual spread can occur very rapidly, but the benefit of slower prepayment speeds takes time to occur. Finally, there is yield-curve risk because the residual cash flows are impacted by events that take place at the short-maturity sector of the Treasury yield curve, whereas prepayment speeds are sensitive primarily to changes in the long-maturity section of the Treasury yield curve. For example, if short-term rates suddenly increase but long-term rates (mortgage rates) do not (flattening yield curve), the residual cash flows impacted by a rising LIBOR would be dissipated, but the residual tied to the fixed classes would enjoy no benefit from a slowdown in prepayment speeds. There are two consolations in

FIGURE 14.4
Shearson Lehman CMO Series F Bond Paydown Structure

Parallel Pay

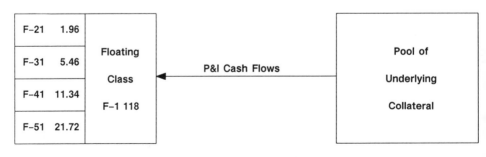

Source: Shearson Lehman Hutton Mortgage Securities.

the worst case: (1) the higher interest rates would generate substantial reinvestment income, and (2) the LIBOR rate is ultimately capped out. The ideal, of course, is a steep yield curve with LIBOR at a low rate with mortgage rates high (slow prepayment), giving maximum benefit to all residual cash flows.

Table 14.4 presents a sensitivity analysis for a similar fixed-floater CMO issue. The analysis shows in essence that with parallel yield-curve shifts (LIBOR and mortgage rates move together) the residual returns decline from the base-case (purchase) yield in both bull and bear markets. However, if LIBOR remains at 6.25 percent (base case) while mortgage rates rise, causing the prepayment speed to slow to 125 PSA or lower, the residual holder does very well. However, if the PSA remains at 165 while LIBOR increases to 8.25 percent, the residual performs poorly. The analysis clearly demonstrates that the cash-flow dynamics of this structure are LIBOR-driven.

Figure 14.5 dramatically puts into perspective the relation between residual value and mortgage and LIBOR rate changes. Mortgage rates are shown on the bottom left axis with rates increasing to the right; LIBOR rates are shown on the bottom right axis with rates rising to the left. Note that the highest residual value is at the top of the figure where LIBOR is low and mortgage rates are somewhat higher (positive yield curve), which are the results we would expect.

TABLE 14.4
Residual Sensitivity Matrix

CBE CASH FLOW YIELD AND
REALIZED NPV DISCOUNTED AT PURCHASED YIELD (IN THOUSANDS)
USING A PURCHASED YIELD OF 15.00%

LIBOR SCENARIOS

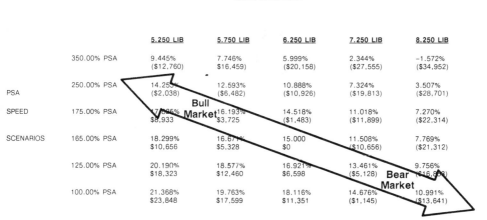

		5.250 LIB	5.750 LIB	6.250 LIB	7.250 LIB	8.250 LIB
	350.00% PSA	9.445% ($12,760)	7.746% $16,459)	5.999% ($20,158)	2.344% ($27,555)	−1.572% ($34,952)
PSA	250.00% PSA	14.25% ($2,038)	12.593% ($6,482)	10.888% ($10,926)	7.324% ($19,813)	3.507% ($28,701)
SPEED	175.00% PSA	17.095% $8,933	16.193% $3,725	14.518% ($1,483)	11.018% ($11,899)	7.270% ($22,314)
SCENARIOS	165.00% PSA	18.299% $10,656	16.671% $5,328	15.000 $0	11.508% ($10,656)	7.769% ($21,312)
	125.00% PSA	20.190% $18,323	18.577% $12,460	16.921% $6,598	13.461% ($5,128)	9.756% ($16,800)
	100.00% PSA	21.368% $23,848	19.763% $17,599	18.116% $11,351	14.676% ($1,145)	10.991% ($13,641)

Source: Shearson Lehman Hutton Mortgage Securities.

FIGURE 14.5
Residual Value Sensitivity to Market Yield and LIBOR Rates*

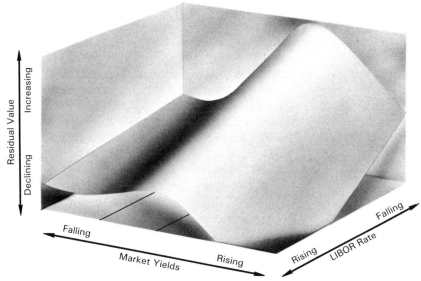

*The prepayment rate for the 9.5% CMO collateral priced near par is assumed to be 125% PSA. Prepayment rates are assumed to be a deterministic decreasing function of mortgage yield levels. If rates drop, prepayments increase rapidly, but cap out near 830% PSA. If rates increase, prepayments slow gradually to 75% PSA. Present value is obtained by discounting the projected cash flow at the mortgage interest rate. This simple prepayment relationship is not useful for forecasting exact price behavior. However, it provides a realistic model of residual value in varying market environments.

Source: Based on a model developed by Shearson Lehman Hutton Mortgage Research.

Residual Friendly-Floater Structures

If the floater is structured as parallel pay to only the first or second fixed classes (Figures 14.6 and 14.7), the risk to the residual holder is somewhat reduced because the average life of the floater class will, of course, be less (usually three to five years), thereby reducing the time of the residual investor's exposure to succeeding interest-rate cycles. The residual cash-flow income is still heavily LIBOR-driven, however. *The residual from a fixed-floater CMO is therefore stable market biased, generally performing poorly as interest-rate volatility increases.*

All-Floater Residuals—Bull Market Biased

In 1987 all-floater CMOs were created as an outgrowth of the stripping technology described in Chapter 13. The all-floater CMO produces a simplified although highly leveraged version of the fixed-floater CMO residual.

FIGURE 14.6
CMO Bond Structure

Parallel Pay

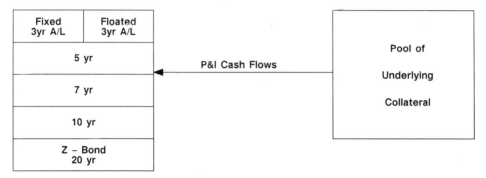

Source: Shearson Lehman Hutton Mortgage Securities.

The Shearson Lehman CMO Series M is a good example of the all-floater CMO. The Series M is a single-tranche, all-floater class with a residual. Its structure is as follows:

	Shearson Lehman CMO Series M
Pool Collateral:	FNMA 12.5% Coupons
Floater Coupon:	3-Month LIBOR plus 55 Basis Points
Cap Rate:	Life Cap: 12.25 Percent

The Series M sensitivity to LIBOR and PSA is illustrated in Figure 14.8. The base case for the sensitivity analysis is a 17 percent purchase yield,

FIGURE 14.7
CMO Bond Structure

Parallel Pay

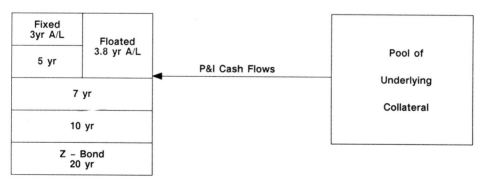

Source: Shearson Lehman Hutton Mortgage Securities.

FIGURE 14.8
Shearson Lehman CMO Series M
Residual Internal Rates of Return and Present Values
at a Purchased Yield of 17.00%
Speed on Vertical/LIBOR and Reinvestment on Horizontal Axis

	3.700% RNV 4.000% LIB	4.700% RNV 5.000% LIB	5.700% RNV 6.000% LIB	6.700% RNV 7.000% LIB	7.700% RNV 8.0005 LIB	8.700% RNV 9.000% LIB	9.700% RNV 10.000% LIB
850.00% PSA	10.968% $11,888	2.403% $10,556	−6.314% $9,224	−15.209% $7,893	−24.230% $6,585	−33.288% $5,349	−42.815% $4,126
650.00% PSA	31.082% $15,646	*Bull* 21.995% *Market* $13,826	12.756% $12,007	3.655% $10,260	−5.591% $8,540	−15.182% $6,828	−25.404% $5,118
550.00% PSA	40.324% $18,133	31.008% $15,994	21.896% $13,926	12.636% $11,882	3.127% $9,844	−6.744% $7,810	−17.255% $5,777
500.00% PSA	44.775% $19,594	35.582% $17,309	26.385% $15,069	17.000% $12,838	7.358% $10,612	−2.649% $8,388	−13.298% $6,165
340.00% PSA	59.234% $25,908	49.812% $22,885	40.217% $19,865	30.419% $16,846	20.367% $13,829	9.964% $10,811	−1.062% $7,795
240.00%	67.964% 31,667	58.287% $27,933	48.439% $24,200	38.392% $20,467	28.102% $16,735	17.479% *Bear* $13,003 *Market* 6.276% $9,271
140.00% PSA	76.369% $39,743	66.445% $35,010	56.352% $30,277	46.063% $25,544	35.539% $20,811	24.699% $16,079	13.550% $11,346

Source: Shearson Lehman Hutton Mortgage Securities.

500 PSA, and LIBOR at 7 percent. Note that LIBOR changes up or down have a much greater impact on the IRR than PSA speed changes. This is so with an all-floater because LIBOR changes are instantaneous and impact the entire bond issue, thereby overwhelming the effects of prepayment-speed changes.

Techniques for Hedging Residuals[2]

With the availability of stripped IO and PO SMBSs (see Chapter 13), a wide array of options is available as hedge vehicles for residual investors. This section briefly summarizes some applications of various hedging instruments which may be used as residual hedge vehicles, including SMBSs, as well as other hedging devices.

For simplicity in the analysis interest-rate changes will be considered the only variable. Also, interest-rate changes will be assumed as parallel shifts across the spectrum of the yield curve. Table 14.5 depicts a matrix of several possible hedge vehicles, rated by the effectiveness in hedging each of the four residual types discussed in this chapter.

Available Tools for Hedging Residuals

The performance characteristics of derivative mortgage securities can be utilized to hedge CMO residuals. Derivative MBSs have a variety of effects on return profiles, including:

[2]The discussion that follows, which includes available tools for hedging through special purpose liabilities, is reprinted from "Derivative Mortgage Securities: An Overview," Shearson Lehman Hutton, December 1987.

TABLE 14.5
Financial Instruments Suitable for Hedging CMO/REMIC Residuals

	Residual Structure Types			
	Fixed-Rate Current/ Discount Collateral	*Fixed-Rate Premium Collateral*	*Fixed-Floating*	*All-Floating*
Available Hedging Vehicles				
IO—current coupon	—	—	–	+ +
IO—premium coupon	–	—	+ +	+ +
IO—discount coupon	—	–	+	+
PO—current coupon	+ +	+ +	+ +	—
PO—premium coupon	–	+ +	–	—
PO—discount coupon	+	+	+	–
Reverse floaters	+	+ +	+ +	—
Buy interest-rate caps	+ +	—	+ +	+ +
Buy interest-rate floors	+ +	+ +	+ +	—
Sell interest-rate caps	–	+	–	—
Sell interest-rate floors	—	–	–	+ +
Interest-rate swap	–	—	+	+ +
Short swap	+	+ +	+	—
Callable swap	+	–	+ +	+ +
Swaption	+	–	+ +	+ +
Eurodollar futures	—	—	+	+ +
Options on Eurodollar futures	—	—	+	+ +
Yield-curve swap	+	+	+ +	+

+ = Usually complements the residual investment; + + is more useful than +.
— = Usually does not complement the residual; — is less useful than –.

- Modifying the price-yield sensitivity of the asset portfolio, thereby decreasing the need for more costly hedging techniques.
- Enhancing expected returns.
- Improving the stability of returns over different interest-rate environments and/or altering the performance profile to reflect the investor's needs.
- Altering the prepayment sensitivity of the asset mix.
- Modifying the convexity attributes of the portfolio.

Useful derivative securities for residual hedges include stripped securities of both IO and PO types, other CMO residuals, and inverse floating tranches from other CMOs.

Coupon-Only–Type Securities

IO stripped securities and servicing spread, both excess and normal, offer a negative interest-rate play depending on the collateral characteristics. Because their values increase as interest rates rise and fall as rates decline, these securities have a negative mortgage duration. Thus, their value often increases when more traditional fixed-income securities decrease in value. Furthermore, IO-type securities with sufficiently low projected prepayment rates also offer very high returns. Given these characteristics, coupon-only securities often provide an inexpensive alternative to using swaps to shorten the asset duration.

Principal-Only–Type Securities

PO stripped and deep-discount REMIC/CMO bonds offer a positive interest-rate play for hedging assets in structured arbitrage. As rates fall, PO strips increase in value. The performance of these derivative mortgage securities depends, like that of IOs, on the characteristics of the underlying collateral. The performance profile is not significantly influenced by the relationship between the mortgage coupon and current market interest rates—that is, whether the underlying pass-through collateral is priced at near-current (par value), discount, or premium coupon. Using principal-only strips protects a transaction as interest rates fall, in much the same way as using very short-term liabilities; in combination with other hedging vehicles principal-only strips can prove useful in stabilizing transactions.

CMO Reverse-Floater Bonds

Reverse floaters (see Chapter 12) offer an extremely bullish play and superior overall returns in falling interest-rate environments. Reverse-floater returns are inversely related to short-term interest rates. For example, for a given rise in the index, the coupon declines by some prearranged multiple. Reverse floaters offer a highly leveraged bullish play.

Superfloater Bonds

Superfloaters (see Chapter 12) offer good leverage in rising interest-rate environments. The floating rate increases according to a formula which is usually a multiple of the base LIBOR rate such as 2 times LIBOR minus 7.75.

Other Types of Assets

Interest-Rate Caps and Floors

Caps and floors provide a rich array of call- and put-option opportunities. Buying an interest-rate cap requires that a fee (premium) be paid initially in exchange for the right to receive payments if rates rise above a specified level (the strike). Payments received equal the difference between the prevailing rate level and the strike based upon the principal value. Cap value rises with interest rates. The risk in a falling-rate environment is limited to the up-front premium. Thus, caps can be useful in hedging against bearish interest-rate scenarios. Interest-rate floors, on the other hand, provide returns that rally as interest rates fall, with losses stopped out at the cost of premium in rising-rate environments. The premium is paid in exchange for the right to receive payments if rates fall below the specified strike. Floors have the same bullish impact on returns as some PO strips. Aside from their speculative potential, caps and floors are extremely useful in stabilizing transactions that might otherwise offer skewed returns.

Special-Purpose Liabilities

Short-term floating and fixed-rate financing provide varying degrees of protection against interest-rate fluctuations. Various forms of financing are available for integrated hedging. Long-term financing alternatives used to fix rates in structured arbitrage include swaps, swaptions, callable swaps, caps and floors, and longer maturities on some of these forms of financing.

- An **interest-rate swap** is an agreement to pay fixed rates in exchange for floating rates. Market quotations on the fixed side are expressed as spreads to Treasuries and on the floating side in relation to LIBOR. The net result of borrowing short and covering short financing with floating-rate interest swap receipts is to fix costs on liabilities over the maturity of the swap agreement.

- A **swaption** is a forward-swap agreement whereby the purchaser pays an initial fee for the option to enter into a swap at a later date at a specified rate. Investors who choose not to enter into a swap agreement at the outset of a transaction can hedge against rising interest rates for the cost of the swaption premium. A swaption requires a greater initial investment, but provides for the option of locking in favorable financing costs at a specific date.

- The **callable swap agreement** allows the fixed-rate borrower to terminate the swap at no penalty between the call date and maturity. The call premium as an up-front fee may be amortized over the life of the swap. The callable swap, like the standard swap, allows the purchaser to hedge against rising interest rates, yet it averts the high costs of an unexpected downward rate movement.

- Selling interest-rate caps and floors provides a financing vehicle that improves returns on relatively stable interest-rate scenarios. Selling a floor improves returns for flat- and rising-rate environments, but if rates fall the transaction returns suffer. Selling a cap enhances flat- and falling-rate scenarios, with declining returns if interest rates rise.

- Options on Eurodollar futures or the futures contract itself can be used to offset losses from LIBOR increases on floating-rate CMO residuals. Options

FIGURE 14.9

Profile Performance of Residual Types

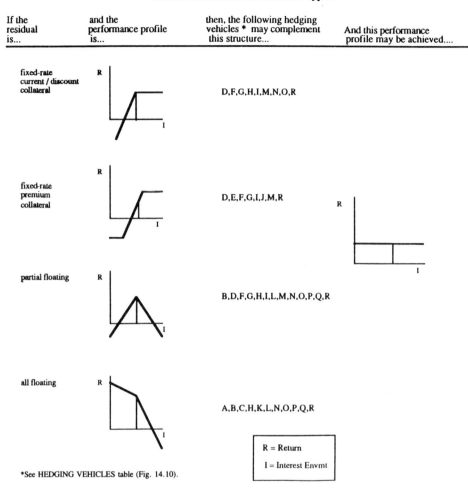

If the residual is...	and the performance profile is...	then, the following hedging vehicles * may complement this structure...	And this performance profile may be achieved....
fixed-rate current / discount collateral		D,F,G,H,I,M,N,O,R	
fixed-rate premium collateral		D,E,F,G,I,J,M,R	
partial floating		B,D,F,G,H,I,L,M,N,O,P,Q,R	
all floating		A,B,C,H,K,L,N,O,P,Q,R	

R = Return

I = Interest Envmt

*See HEDGING VEHICLES table (Fig. 14.10).

Source: Shearson Lehman Hutton Mortgage Securities.

versus the contract itself offer a lower boundary for losses (the option premium) with gains uncapped. However, futures contracts offer greater liquidity (lower bid/ask spread). These instruments can be useful for offsetting losses in floating-rate LIBOR-based residuals.

• Selling swaps short (reverse swap) provides an interesting twist on use of fixed-rate financing; that is, the investor pays floating rates and receives fixed-rate financing. These swaps dramatically boost stable interest-rate scenario performance and improve declining-rate returns. In rising-rate environments, however, they affect the transaction in much the same way as discount PO assets: as rates rise, returns are dramatically reduced.

- Yield-curve swap products can also assist in controlling exposure to yield-curve shape changes. The investor enters into a swap whereby the investor receives payments indexed to U.S. dollar 6-month LIBOR and makes payments based on the 10-year Treasury yield. The investor benefits from a flattening of the term structure, and vice versa.

Figure 14.9 depicts a performance profile of each of the four residual types, followed by a code that relates to specific hedging vehicles profiled in Figure 14.10. Rather than embark on a tedious discussion of each of the hedging possibilities, these profiles are presented to suggest the extent of hedging possibilities available in the market. More ambitious practitioners may wish to select a few possibilities to analyze on their own.

FIGURE 14.10
Hedging Vehicles

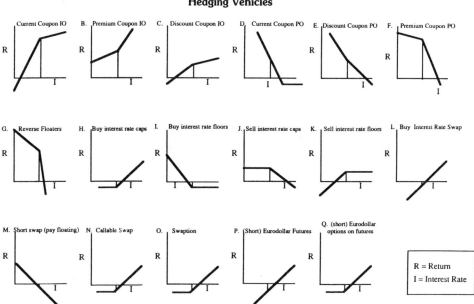

Source: Shearson Lehman Hutton Mortgage Securities.

15

Structured Arbitrage Strategies

INTRODUCTION

Thrifts, commercial banks, and other financial institutions are increasingly utilizing mortgage products in a series of transactions referred to as a structured, or risk-controlled, arbitrage. Structured arbitrage strategies have been utilized by S&Ls for many years, but recently other types of financial institutions have experimented with this form of transaction.

Structured arbitrage strategies appeal to S&Ls and banks because of three principal attributes:

- The ability to largely control the magnitude and direction of interest-rate risk.
- Effective generation of income through asset growth without large increases in general and administrative expenses.
- The capacity to add to earnings and realize significant returns on capital without adding credit risk to the institution's investment concerns.

OVERVIEW OF STRUCTURED ARBITRAGE STRATEGIES

A **structured arbitrage transaction (SAT)** or a **risk-controlled arbitrage (RCA)**, as it is referred to in the S&L trade, is a self-funding series of transactions that generally utilize mortgage securities as the primary assets. The assets acquired for the SAT are self-funded through a **reverse repurchase agreement (repo)** or other similar mechanism to finance the purchase of the assets. The reverse repo requires the institution executing the transaction to overcollateralize the SAT with an infusion of cash representing a "haircut." In effect the haircut is the equity investment contributed to the SAT by the executing institution. To complete the SAT, a series of interest-rate swaps or Home Loan Bank advances are generally utilized to extend the duration of the liabilities to match the duration of the assets purchased.

Figure 15.1 presents a view of the SAT cash flows as a whole. Note in the figure the respective patterns of fixed versus variable cash flows. The diagram

FIGURE 15.1
SAT Fixed and Variable Cash Flows

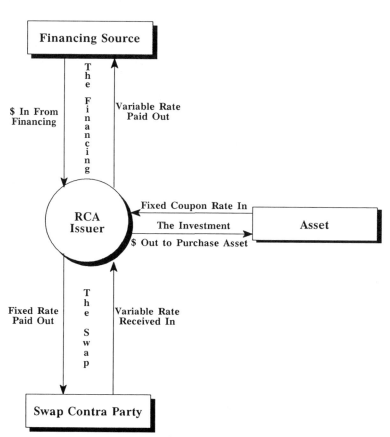

Source: Shearson Lehman Hutton Mortgage Securities.

shows that the fixed coupon rate received from the asset investment is offset with a fixed rate paid out on the liability—here an interest-rate swap; concurrently, the variable rate received from the swap offsets the variable rate paid out to finance the asset (the reverse repo).

The economics of the swap may be expressed as follows:

(Fixed Rate In) − (Fixed Rate Out) = The Gross Spread Fix-to-Fix

This relationship is referred to more generally as the mortgage asset spread.

The following discussion breaks the SAT down into its respective components in order to visualize more clearly the series of transactions that constitutes the SAT as a whole.

Step 1: Asset Selection. Purchase one or a series of high-yielding MBSs as the asset.

Step 2: Financing the Asset Purchase. A 90-day reverse repo may be utilized to finance the assets purchased to fund the SAT, using the MBSs as collateral for this short-term borrowing. The investor now receives cash back for the market value of the MBSs, *minus* a "haircut" created by the overcollateralization requirement. If, for example, the haircut requirement is 6.5 percent, $106,500,000 of MBSs will be delivered against $100 million of cash received back from the financing, leaving $6,500,000 cash invested in the transaction as the haircut, or equity, investment.

Step 3: Matching Assets to Liabilities. So far the transaction has created an attractive theoretical spread between the yield of the MBSs versus the cost of the repo, but it also represents a mismatch between assets and liabilities. For example, the MBSs might have an average life of 7 years versus 90 days for the reverse repo that is financing the purchase.

We will pause in the listing of overview steps to discuss various uses of the interest-rate swap in closing the asset/liability mismatch. The overview continues with Step 4 on page 420.

The duration of the liability can be extended by entering into an interest-rate swap using Treasury securities as the swap benchmark. In the swap the investor agrees to pay a fixed rate and receive in return a variable rate pegged to an index (usually LIBOR). The investor now has locked in longer-term fixed-rate financing and will receive back LIBOR as the variable-rate contra component in the swap.

In structuring the swap the SAT practitioner must use caution. The MBSs do not, of course, have a single maturity in seven years. In fact, because they are mortgage securities, they amortize principal monthly. We can, however, model the expected cash flows of the MBSs using the appropriate prepayment-speed assumption.

The interest-rate swap can be put on as a series, with the amount of swap declining somewhat each year to cash-flow match the amortization of the MBSs. Cash-flow matching is accomplished first by running out the monthly MBSs cash flows based on a speed projection. The annual changes in book value are then calculated (unamortized remaining unpaid principal balance × price). The weighted average annual change in book value dictates the amount of swap to be used as the hedge offset. A series of interest-rate swaps is then constructed to match the projected changes in book value to an assumed holding period. Table 15.1 illustrates cash-flow matching.

TABLE 15.1
Cash-Flow–Matched SAT

ASSETS

Type	Coupon	Yield[a]	Mortgage Duration (yrs.)	Price ($)	Face Amount ($ millions)	Market Value ($ millions)
GNMA	10.50	10.17	4.32	102.25	97,800	100,000
Avg./total		10.17	4.32	102.25	97,800	100,000

LIABILITIES

Type	Cost[b]	Maturity (mos.)	Modified Duration[c] (yrs.)	Swap Spread (bp)	Treasury Rate (%)	Notional Amount ($ millions)[d]
Repo	8.00	3	.25	0	0	29,132
Swap	8.12	12	.94	116	6.96	10,000
Swap	8.67	24	1.80	93	7.74	10,000
Swap	9.04	36	2.58	101	8.03	10,000
Swap	9.32	48	3.28	101	8.31	5,000
Swap	9.52	60	3.91	103	8.49	5,000
Swap	9.82	84	4.98	104	8.78	10,000
Swap	10.02	120	6.23	104	8.98	15,000
Avg./total	8.86		2.54			94,132
Initial investment (haircut)						5,868
Total liabilities						100,000

[a]Semiannually compounded yield under projected prepayment rates.

[b]The fixed cost on the interest-rate swaps excludes placement and credit intermediation fees that are typically paid by the fixed-rate payer.

[c]Swap-duration computation assumes a hypothetical bond with a face amount equal to the notional amount and a coupon rate equal to the all-in cost.

[d]All assets are reversed with the notional repo amount representing the net quantity of liabilities not swapped.

Source: Shearson Lehman Hutton Mortgage Securities.

In the example given in Table 15.1, a hypothetical structured arbitrage transaction begins with purchase of a portfolio consisting of GNMA 10.5 percent MBSs. To hedge the interest-rate risk in the mortgage portfolio, the investor matches the expected principal paydown of the GNMA 10.5 percent MBS with serially maturing interest-rate swaps. The top portion of the table shows the GNMA portfolio as the assets. The bottom portion describes the liability structure, including the notional amount that has been swapped for fixed rates via medium- and long-term interest-rate swap liabilities. Cash-flow maturity matching in this context is an attempt to immunize spread income over the life of the transaction. The amount assigned to each swap maturity approximates the expected paydown in the principal value of the GNMA due to prepayments and principal amortization for the time horizon of the SAT.

Cash-flow matching is generally regarded as the most conservative approach to the SAT structure, but it is not without risk. Should the prepayment speed of the MBS accelerate because of declining interest rates, the collateral cash flows will become greater for each year, and the average life shorter. The SAT will therefore be, in fact, overhedged with swaps that are likely to be at a high rate relative to prevailing interest rates. (An accelerating prepayment speed suggests interest rates have declined.) Conversely, if the prepayment speed slows, collateral life will be extended and the SAT will be underhedged.

Adjustments to the SAT can be made, of course, by buying or selling MBSs or swaps as needed to readjust the hedge, but this can be costly.

Duration matching will enhance the gross spread of the SAT because the swaps need not run so far out in maturity, as illustrated in Table 15.2.

When comparing the durations used for the assets and liabilities in Table 15.2, note that *mortgage duration* is used as the price volatility measure for the FNMA 9.5 because the impact of prepayment speed on price must be taken into

TABLE 15.2
Duration-Matched SAT with Swaps

ASSETS				
Type	*Yield*	*Mortgage Duration*	*Price*	*Haircut*
FNMA 9½	10.10	5.34	97.38	6.16%

LIABILITIES				
Type	*Cost*	*Repricing Maturity (mos.)*	*Modified Duration*	*Swap/Repo Amount ($mil.)*
Repo	6.95	3	.25	30,000
Swap	9.09	48	3.29	30,000
Swap	9.26	60	3.93	30,000
Swap	9.61	84	5.01	10,000

Source: Shearson Lehman Hutton Mortgage Securities.

account (see Chapter 7, "Prepayment-Sensitive Model," for a discussion of mortgage duration). Modified duration, however, is used for the repo and the swaps because government securities do not have speed (option component) considerations.

Figure 15.2 displays the asset/liability maturity structure of the sample transaction under alternative interest-rate scenarios. Maturity-matching techniques are widely used, but transactions can quickly become mismatched when SATs employ assets with embedded options, such as mortgage securities with valuable prepayment call options, especially current and premium mortgage pass-through securities. SATs with mortgage assets can become overhedged as rates fall and prepayments accelerate, decreasing the "duration" of the assets as the duration of the liabilities increases. Figure 15.2 shows this effect when interest rates drop 300 basis points. An asset with embedded options is often better hedged with purchase of financial instruments having option-like characteristics, such as stripped MBSs, or by duplicating the option characteristics through a dynamic hedging strategy. Such a strategy would require frequent adjustments to the SAT throughout the investment horizon.

Risk in duration matching also arises from a combination of basis risk and volatility risk. As market conditions change, the Treasury yield-curve relationship to the MBS may change such that the price volatility of the Treasury security relative to MBSs price volatility forms a different relationship.

FIGURE 15.2
Duration-Matched Swaps versus Interest Rates

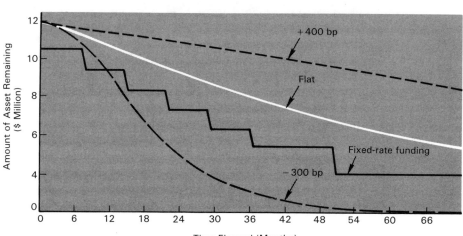

We have created a risk-controlled strategic arbitrage because the introduction of the interest-rate swap has matched the cash flows or durations of the
assets and liabilities, thereby dramatically reducing exposure to interest-rate
risk. Note that matching cash flows and matching durations are not necessarily
the same thing. We now return to the SAT overview with Step 4.

Step 4: Maximizing the Arbitrage Spread. A number of measures may be taken
to widen the arbitrage spread of an SAT while retaining the basic
structure just outlined.

a. Shorten the average life (duration) of the assets. For example, if
15-year–maturity MBSs are used instead of 30-year, the average life
can be shortened to a probable 5 years or less. By shortening the
average life of the asset, we reduce the amount of swap that will be
needed to lengthen the duration of the liabilities. This approach
helps in two ways: (1) reducing the total amount of the swap cost of
the transaction reduces expenses overall, and (2)—best of all—the
longer maturity swaps in the series are the most expensive, so that
here we can reduce the notional amount of swap for the last few
years of the swap series, thereby reducing the average cost of the
swap.

b. Hold the first year of the swap open-ended against the reverse repo.
Many institutions believe they can manage the first year of interest-
rate exposure reasonably well, and therefore the initiation of the
interest-rate swap series can be deferred a year.

c. Allow some asset/liability mismatch. For example, many institutions believe they can manage a mismatch of 70 to 80 percent, and
so further reduce the required amount of swap.

d. Add MBSs IO strips to shorten asset duration.

The IO strip has high negative duration because of its propensity to gain
value quickly in a bear market (prepayment speed slows, collateral life is
extended, and interest cash flows increase). Because of this characteristic,
being long on IO is the same as being short the market. The inclusion of the IO
in the SAT asset therefore shortens the duration of the asset (see Chapter 13 for
an analysis of IO strip cash flows).

CONSIDERATIONS IN USING IOs

The addition of the IO strip enhances the returns of the SAT—particularly in the
rising-rate scenario—making this arbitrage structure potentially suitable for
institutions that have portfolios with an asset/liability mismatch in the form of a

positive duration gap. A positive duration gap means that the longer-term assets decline in value at the same time that the costs of the shorter-term liabilities increase. This gap would be particularly vulnerable in a bear market, but with the addition of the IO the duration gap is shifted to the negative to produce more favorable results in the bear market. (Positive duration means price changes inversely to yield; negative duration means price changes in the same direction as yield; see Chapter 7.) IO strips, for example, exhibit negative duration because the value of the IO increases in a rising-yield environment (see Chapter 13). The IO does, however, provide poor protection in the declining interest-rate scenario because of the rapid increase in prepayments that adversely impacts the IO returns. A third type of structure might therefore be considered, one that would include a PO in addition to the IO to enhance the performance of the SAT in the declining-rate scenario.

Table 15.3 illustrates three SAT structures, one using FNMA 9½s alone and two IO combinations with ratios of 15 percent IO and 30 percent IO. The addition of the IO increases the initial yield on the SAT asset package by as much as 30 percent (from 9.83 percent to 10.12 percent) in the stable interest-rate environments.

In the table, as the percentage ratio of IO is increased, the notional amount of swap required is reduced from $95 million in the 100 percent pass-through SAT to only $55 million in the 30 percent IO SAT. Of greatest benefit, the amount of swap in the fifth and seventh years is greatly reduced as the ratio of IO is increased.

Interpreting the SAT Evaluation Model

Tables 15.4 and 15.5 illustrate a combination SAT using IOs and POs to achieve maximum performance in up and down markets. Table 15.4 describes the assets and liabilities of the SAT. The base asset is $61,188,000 face amount of FHLMC 10s with the addition of $44,753,000 face amount of IOs stripped from GNMA 11 percent and $42,247,000 face amount of POs stripped from FNMA 9 percent 15-year MBSs. The average mortgage duration of the asset package is .25 with an average modified duration on the liabilities of 1.11. Note the amount of interest-rate swap is greatly reduced because of the self-hedging attribute of this SAT contributed by the addition of the IO and PO strips. Note also that only two series of swaps are utilized, a two-year and a three-year.

Combination Analysis

The IO/PO combination SAT utilizes a relatively high-speed IO (245 PSA) and slow-speed PO (165 PSA). The purpose in doing so is to enhance the SAT transaction with derivatives that will be minimally affected by market scenarios

TABLE 15.3
Three Types of SAT Initial Structures
(balance sheets)

		ASSETS					LIABILITIES				
Type	Type	Yield (CBE %)	Mortgage Duration (yrs.)	Price (%)	Face Amount ($ millions)	Over-collatzn. (%)	Type	Cost (%)	Repricing Maturity (yrs.)	Modified Duration (yrs.)	Notional Amount ($ millions)
100% Pass-through	FNMA 9.5s	9.82	5.22	98-23	107.853	6.1	Repo	7.20	.25	.25	5
							Swap	8.29	2	1.81	5
							Swap	8.75	4	3.31	25
							Swap	8.97	5	3.96	30
							Swap	9.16	7	5.08	35
								8.89	5	3.90	100
85% Pass-through and 15% IO	FNMA 9.5s	9.82	5.22	98-23	107.853		Repo	7.24			
	FNMA 9.5 IOs	10.81	−3.69	46-00	34.938		Swap	8.29	2	1.81	5
	Total	9.97	3.88		127.191	6.7	Swap	8.75	4	3.31	20
							Swap	8.97	5	3.96	20
							Swap	9.16	7	5.08	25
								8.44	3.73	2.89	100
70% Pass-through and 30% IO	FNMA 9.5s	9.82	5.22	98-23	76.455		Repo	7.25			
	FNMA 9.5 IOs	10.81	−3.69	46-00	70.319		Swap	8.29	2	1.81	20
	Total	10.12	2.55		146.744	7.3	Swap	8.75	4	3.31	15
							Swap	8.97	5	3.96	10
							Swap	9.16	7	5.08	10
								8.04	2.32	1.87	100

TABLE 15.4
Combination SAT Using IOs and POs

									Repricing		
				ASSETS				LIABILITIES			
Type	CPN	Yield (CBE)	Mtg. Dur.	Price	Face Amnt.	Haircut	Type	Cost	Maturity (mos.)	Mod. Dur.	Notional Amount
FHLMC	10	9.81	4.67	100.75	61,188		Repo	7.02	3.0	.25	50,000
GNMA IO	11	9.22	−30.60	43.50	44,753		Swap	8.15	24.0	1.81	40,000
FNMA PO	9	8.95	12.37	64.00	42,247		Swap	8.60	36.0	2.60	10,000
Avg./total		9.48	.25	81.26	108,153	7.5%		7.63	14.7	1.11	100,000

which would be adverse to the IO or PO while exploiting maximum advantage of a beneficial scenario. Since the IO is already at a fairly high speed, it will not experience undue acceleration in prepayments until rates fall 200 basis points or more. On the other hand, in the rising-rate scenario, the IO has the potential to slow down significantly, thereby contributing substantial value to the SAT in a bear market. The PO is a relatively slow-speed current coupon and therefore will not give up much value in the rising-rate environment. The PO is, however, backed by 15-year collateral, which in the bull market will experience acceleration of prepayments faster than 30-year MBSs, and so contribute maximum value in the declining interest-rate scenario.

Interest-Rate Scenario Analysis

To evaluate its performance an SAT needs to be tested for different interest-rate scenarios and against a variety of cash-based as well as yield-spread measures.

Table 15.5 illustrates an interest-rate scenario analysis of the IO/PO combination SAT prepared by Shearson Lehman Hutton. The model tests the SAT for performance in the bull market assuming the Treasury yield curve falls 200 basis points (−200, left column) and also in a bear market, with the Treasury yield curve up 300 basis points (+300, right column). The model tests the SAT to a higher standard in the bear market because most investors are more concerned with the performance of the SAT in a rising-rate environment. The middle column, labeled "flat," reflects interest rates and spreads as they prevailed at the time the SAT was priced. Note the model also changes the PSA speed assumptions for the three interest-rate scenarios.

The return on equity is a high 22 percent going into the transaction and remains in double digits in both the rising and falling interest-rate scenarios. The IRR numbers are exceptional in all scenarios. The initial spread at 186 basis points is well above average, while both the mortgage asset and total asset spreads remain above 150 basis points in all cases. Particularly worth noting is the fact that the holding-period returns remain positive—even with rates up 300 basis points—a bear market that would cause very substantial market losses for

TABLE 15.5
Combination RCA Using IOs and POs

Rate scenario	−200	Flat	+300
Phase-in	12 mos.		10 mos.
Return on equity	11.74	22.07	12.58
IRR	14.49	35.98	17.41
Initial spread		1.86	
Mortgage asset spread	1.63	2.14	1.66
Total asset spread	1.50	1.91	1.53
Holding-period return	1.67	1.86	.11
Holding period		60 mos.	
Asset liquidation price	76.49	78.24	66.94
PSA speed assumptions			
PC 10	675	175	130
IO 11	610	245	85
PO 9	377	165	106

a portfolio with typical positive duration. Finally, the asset liquidation price remains reasonably close to the asset average combined purchase price of $81.26 in all three scenarios.

Figure 15.3 illustrates several possible scenarios for IRR that might be realized in the IO/PO combination SAT.

The IRR generated by the computer for up-down interest-rate scenarios assumes parallel yield-curve shifts—that is, the whole Treasury yield curve shifts up 300 basis points (bear market). In the real world, the yield curve is not likely to shift so evenly. Therefore, steepening and flattening yield curves are also illustrated. The Shearson Lehman analyst for comparative purposes also inserted a "likely scenario," representing a composite of probable interest-rate, yield-curve paths (dotted line).

Yield-Basis Risk[1]

Structured arbitrage transactions employ assets financed with liabilities that have various maturities and yield-spread relationships. For example, fixed-rate mortgage assets may be financed with reverse repos and interest-rate swaps to lengthen the duration of liabilities. As a result, SATs are exposed to many kinds of basis risk, perhaps the greatest of which is an overall steepening or flattening of the yield curve. The shape of the yield curve has a dramatic impact on performance because a sizable portion of SAT financing can be in short-term, floating-rate liabilities. In addition, for SATs that employ interest-rate swaps,

[1]The discussion of yield-basis risk and the SAT performance measures are taken from *Structured Arbitrage Transaction Analysis* by Steven Carlson, Vice President, Nirmal Singh, and Eric Fix, Shearson Lehman Hutton, January 1988.

FIGURE 15.3
Internal Rate of Return by Scenario Assumptions

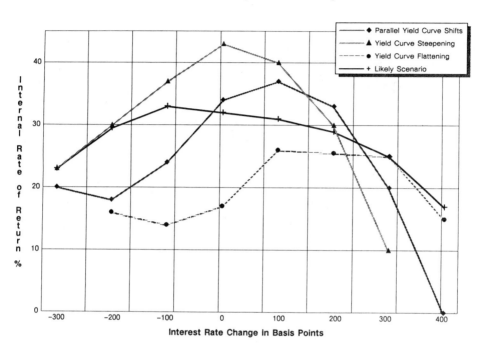

changes in the shape of the term structure influence performance. Changes in the basis between short- and long-term interest rates, therefore, strongly influence spread income.

For example, the short-term financing costs increase if the short end of the yield curve rises and decrease if it falls, all else equal. Figure 15.4 illustrates the impact of a 100 basis-point steepening or flattening over one year across all scenarios. This stress test indicates transaction sensitivity to yield-basis changes. If the yield curve flattens, returns are reduced in rising interest-rate scenarios. In the flat-rate scenario, return on investment (ROI) is reduced. Returns are enhanced as interest rates decline, primarily because higher short-term reinvestment opportunities become more important as a result of the rapid runoff of mortgage assets. If the yield curve steepens, returns are enhanced if rates remain stable or rise. This pattern is attributable to lower financing costs.

Other types of yield-basis risk can also influence the profitability of the transaction. For example, changes in the spread between the 3-month LIBOR payments received in the interest-rate swap agreements and the GNMA 30-

FIGURE 15.4
Sensitivity of SAT ROI to Yield-Curve Shape

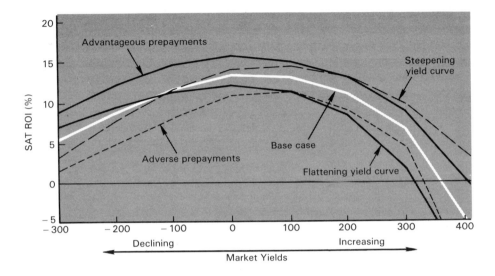

month repo rate paid add to the uncertainty of the transaction's performance (see Figure 15.5). The figure illustrates the impact of a 30 basis-point reversal in the LIBOR repo spread on the base-case ROI performance measure (the repo rate rises 30 basis points and LIBOR stays constant). A rise in the reverse rate systematically reduces returns. Another example of the effect of changes in yield-basis relationship on the transaction's profitability is the impact on the sale price of the securities remaining when the transaction is liquidated.

SAT PERFORMANCE MEASURES[1]

Two types of performance measures can be used to evaluate structured arbitrage transactions—book-based and cash-based. Book-based measures are used principally for accounting and regulatory purposes; cash-based measures are better for evaluating the financial performance of an SAT. The two cash-based measures—return on investment (ROI) and internal rate of return (IRR)—and the yield-spread measure of effective margin provide the best and most internally consistent indicators of investment performance.

FIGURE 15.5
Sensitivity of ROI to LIBOR/Repo Spread

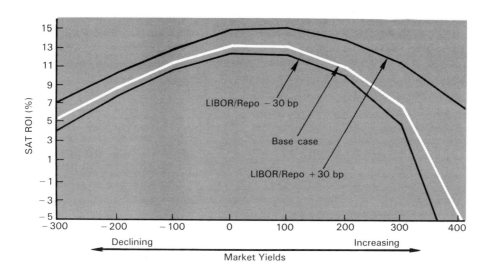

Book-Based Measures[1]

Book-based profitability measures—return on assets (ROA), cumulative book income, and book profit—do not provide SAT investors with sufficient information about the performance of the transaction. (ROA is the income booked each year divided by the average dollar-weighted annual book value of assets.) First, these measures do not recognize the time value of money; they ignore the fact that a dollar today is worth more than a dollar tomorrow. This defect can hamper comparisons of transactions, although time value is introduced to some degree in the reinvestment of cash proceeds over the horizon. Two transactions may be viewed as identical in absolute dollars earned, even though one has clearly superior cash-flow timing.

   A second difficulty is that the rigidity of accounting practices makes ROA, book profit, and some yield-based measures less valuable than their more comprehensive cash-based counterparts. For example, in cash-based analysis a premium paid for an option is recognized in the period it is purchased. Conversely, in book-based analysis, the premium cost is amortized over the life of the option.

   A third limitation of book-based measures, particularly for ROA, is the failure to offer insight on the total return of the transaction; that is, the liquidation value of the remaining SAT asset/liability position is ignored.

Cash-Based Measures[1]

The cash-based measures, particularly ROI and IRR, are concerned with the true financial characteristics of the transaction. The IRR measure assumes that net interest income generated by the SAT is reinvested at the same rate as the returns on the overall transaction, and that net cash flows are periodically doled out as dividends. A balloon payment is included at the end to value the assets and liabilities at current market prices. Dividends and the balloon payment are then discounted to equal the initial net SAT investment. The discount rate that equates the two is the IRR. Although conceptually they are kin, the ROI and IRR differ in their implicit reinvestment rates. Cash flows underlying the ROI are not paid out as dividends but accumulate at an explicit reinvestment rate. Theoretically, this rate should reflect the financial institution's investment opportunities in the given interest-rate environment.

The ROI is similar to the conventional holding-period return (HPR) measure. As applied to security analysis used in modern portfolio theory, HPR incorporates returns from cash flows generated by the security, reinvestment of these interim cash flows to the horizon, and liquidation value at the sale of the security. On the other hand, IRR is similar to yield to maturity (YTM). The YTM measure represents projections of total rate of return but under more restrictive assumptions. It assumes reinvestment at the rate produced by discounting cash flows on the transaction without regard to actual reinvestment opportunities.

The future-value orientation of the HPR/ROI measure, as opposed to the YTM/IRR's implied reinvestment, gives the ROI two positive features:

1. Reinvestments within an interest period occur at rates linked to the scenario, unlike IRR reinvestment. This feature is attractive for SAT strategies with a total-return orientation.
2. The future-value calculation implied by the ROI measure discounts cash flows as they are discounted in net present value (NPV) calculations. NPV allows for comparison of incremental opportunities by deriving a single number that can be ranked against all others. ROI inherits the robustness of this comparative approach.

The Initial Spread[1]

The initial spread is computed as the difference between the weighted average cash-flow yield (CFY) of the assets and the all-in costs of the liabilities, including fees and interest expense. The initial spread is a base-case assumption that does not take into account the impact of rising or falling interest rates.

Return on Assets

Return on assets (ROA) is computed as the cumulative annual book income of the SAT arbitrage as a percentage of the average balance of the SAT assets:

$$\text{ROA} = \frac{\text{Cumulative Book Income}}{\text{Average (Dollar-Weighted) Asset Balance}}$$

The cumulative book income is the coupon income and reinvestment income received from the assets of the SAT liabilities.

Effective Margin[1]

The **effective margin (EM)** equals the net earned spread, or margin, of income on the assets in excess of financing costs for a given interest-rate and prepayment-rate scenario. The effective margin is similar in concept to the asset yield less liability cost in a given interest-rate scenario, yet it goes beyond the simple yield spread and other spread measures commonly employed in asset/liability analysis. For a given interest-rate scenario, EM is the "add on" or "margin" that when added to cost of funds reduces the returns to zero. EM is the break-even financing spread under the particular interest-rate scenario.

The EM captures several yield-spread elements that give it a definitive edge over standard-yield and time and dollar-weighted spreads which are commonly used in asset/liability analysis. Specifically, EM captures:

- The impact of asset portfolio composition.
- The varying runoff rates on assets.
- The rolling nature of liabilities and changing cost structure as interest rates change.

Calculation of EM

EM is defined as the cost-of-funds "add-on" that satisfies the following identity:

$$\sum_{i=1}^{n} P_i \text{UPB}_i = \frac{\text{CF}_1}{(1 + \text{cof}_1 + \text{EM})} + \frac{\text{CF}_2}{(1 + \text{cof}_1 + \text{EM})(1 + \text{cof}_2 + \text{EM})}$$
$$+ \cdots + \frac{\text{CF}_T}{(1 + \text{cof}_1 + \text{EM}) \ldots (1 + \text{cof}_T + \text{EM})}$$

where n = number of securities in asset portfolio;
P_i = price of security i, for $i = 1, \ldots n$;
UPB_i = balance of security i, for $i = 1, \ldots n$;
CF_t = composite asset portfolio cash flow in period t, for $t = 1, \ldots T$;
cof_t = weighted average cost of funds/liabilities in period t; and
EM = effective interest margin on assets over liabilities.

Note: the tth period cash-flow receipt requires financing for t periods.

Example   A two-period asset priced at 100 yields 8 percent. It is funded with liability initially at 6 percent and rolled over at 10 percent.

$$100 = \frac{8}{(1.06 + EM)} + \frac{108}{(1.06 + EM)(1.10 + EM)}$$

$$Margin = .10\%$$

This example illustrates EM's recognition of the timing of raw interest margin. Had the 10 percent funding occurred initially and then been rolled over at 6 percent—the reverse of the above example—EM would be $-.06$ percent. A -2 percent margin in the second period is not as damaging as a -2 percent margin initially. This feature would be totally obscured in a dollar-weighted yield spread.

Book Profit

Book profit is cumulative book income plus any gain or loss on disposition of the assets (or mark-to-market) on termination of the SAT.

Return on Investment

Return on investment (ROI) is a measure relating future value of the SAT at the termination date to the actual initial cash investment. If the SAT is self-funded through financing of the assets via a reverse repo, for example, the ROI will be an attractive number. In the latter case the investment amounts to the haircut required under the repo. This may also be viewed as the equity in the SAT, in which case this return measure would logically be referred to as return on equity (ROE). In that sense, the equity is similar to a CMO residual (see Chapter 14).

Cash- versus Book-Based Measures[1]

Publicly held financial institutions—particularly thrifts—often concentrate on book-based ROA and certain spread-based measures.[2] This is motivated by the belief that stockholders focus on the difference between operating income and operating expenses, that is, the spread, without regard for nonrecurring gains and losses. As a result, some investors argue that ROA measures give them all the information necessary to make an investment decision. Nonetheless, there

---

[2]Accounting principles influence financial decisions and income recognition because they are concerned with tax issues and tax-related arbitrage. Although the accountant's definition of earnings provides a standardized means of relaying information about a firm's profitability, these earnings may not always conform to real financial earnings.

are often assets and liabilities remaining on the books beyond the intended life of the transaction which are essentially ignored by the ROA approach.

Whether the investor plans to liquidate a position or carry it on the books, any remaining assets/liabilities have earnings implications. A reasonable indicator of the ongoing performance of an asset/liability position is its liquidation value. Failure to incorporate the terminal asset/liability impact in the analysis provides an incomplete evaluation of the transaction. The ROI, the IRR, and the effective margin together provide rigorous and internally consistent means of addressing the terminal asset/liability problem by giving a more complete picture of the simulated performance. Because spread measures (ROA and other yield-spread measures) do not include the information, they leave out a critical component of thorough SAT analysis.

Rebalancing[1]

Rebalancing reflects the need to modify some of the components of the SAT position to adjust the hedge to changing market conditions. As such, rebalancing addresses three concerns: (1) Rebalancing may be an effort to counteract the development of duration mismatches in an originally well-hedged position. (A significant market move can lead to a divergence in asset and liability durations.) (2) Rebalancing may also redress errors in initial matching, or it may address the need for adjustment due to a change in management's perceptions about interest-rate direction and prepayments. (3) The SAT structure is positioned to benefit from the anticipated move rather than to immunize returns.

The ability of rebalancing to enhance returns depends upon whether management is proactive or reactive. If reactive—management examines the SAT position after the economic risk has become a reality—rebalancing is less driven by market opportunities than it is by the tax advantages of capital versus ordinary gains/losses because the damage has already been done. If the decision is proactive—management has successfully anticipated market moves—rebalancing is guided by the underlying economic value of the transaction. The realized gains/losses are then achieved through liquidations or greater net interest income. SAT investors must recognize that simulation is a static approach, necessarily requiring frequent re-examination as market conditions change.

Assets and/or liabilities can be liquidated or purchased to alter the performance of the SAT. Often analysis of total return starts with marking the SAT position to current market prices and examining the market net worth of the transaction (book performance is also analyzed). Such an approach typically evaluates net worth under the efficient market assumptions that assets can be traded freely and that the firm can purchase its debt in the open market at prevailing fair market value. While these assumptions may be unrealistic, they provide a starting point for analysis.

RISK CONSIDERATIONS[3]

Interest-rate risk for an SAT program is intended to be mitigated through the use of an appropriately designed hedging strategy that includes some combination of reverse repos, interest-rate swaps, and possibly IOs or POs (futures contracts, options, or caps might also be used). Even with appropriate hedging strategies, however, the following risks are present:

1. *Basis Risk.* Basis risk is the risk that the relationship between the assets and the hedge instrument (interest-rate swap, IO, PO, futures contract) will change. Because most hedges in SAT strategies are cross hedges, in which the instrument being hedged and the instrument underlying the hedging vehicle differ, there is a greater probability of basis risk being significant. If several different hedging instruments are used, or if the institution is using several different funding instruments, it can be argued that the basis risk can be adequately diversified.

2. *Yield-Curve Risk.* Nonparallel shifts in the yield curve can be hidden risks unless a thorough scenario analysis is undertaken. There is a risk that a change in the general level of interest rates will differ in magnitude for short-term versus long-term instruments; that is, that the yield curve will flatten or steepen. This risk can be hedged with more complex strategies that use a combination of long- and short-term interest-sensitive hedging vehicles. The idea behind this type of hedging strategy is to diversify the risk that long- and short-term interest rates may change by differing amounts.

3. *Prepayment Risk.* Prepayment risk is the risk that the MBS will prepay ahead of schedule as a result of a decrease in interest rates or for other reasons such as demographic changes or regional economic conditions. Sophisticated hedging techniques and pricing mechanisms can mitigate some of this risk. In periods of unusual economic circumstances, however, prepayment changes may not track historic patterns, thereby negating forecasted results.

   Prepayment risk is more of a problem if the liabilities are being hedged than if the assets are being hedged. The aim of liability hedging is to extend the duration of the liabilities by a swap or futures contract to a duration that is equivalent to the estimated duration of the assets. As interest rates vary the duration of the MBS will vary as a consequence of changes in the present value of the cash flows from the securities and because of changes in prepayment patterns. Therefore, the hedging instruments may have to be

---

[3]This discussion of risk is based in part on research working paper #128, "Risk-Controlled Arbitrage for Thrifts: Description and Associated Risks," by Edward A. Hjerpe, III, Office of Policy and Economic Research, Federal Home Loan Bank, May 11, 1987.

terminated, or hedge ratios may have to be adjusted to account for the change in the duration of the MBS.

On the other hand, if an institution is asset hedging, the change in the value of the hedging instruments is simply applied to the cost of the liability for the following period. As an example, the duration of a new current-coupon MBS could increase significantly with only a modest increase in mortgage rates because prepayments would quickly drop to a minimum level. Likewise, a decrease in interest rates may cause rapid prepayment of the MBS so that the durations would shorten significantly. This would leave the investor in an overhedged position. An overhedge is a more troublesome position to be in than an underhedge, especially if the investor is hedged with a swap. The swap duration would remain the same, but it would now be greater than the duration of the MBS. Terminating or buying out of a swap may impose large costs for an investor as the result of a decrease in the duration of an MBS. For this reason, swaps are the least flexible hedging instruments.

4. *Collateral Risk*. Collateral risk is the risk that more collateral or a principal payback will be required of the institution if the market value of the collateral decreases because of a change in prepayments and/or an increase in interest rates. This problem may not be significant since a decrease in the value of the securities should be offset by profits on a hedging position that could be used to cover the margin call. However, the cash flows from a hedging instrument and hedged asset or liability may differ in timing. This could lead to a temporary shortage of collateral and perhaps to a liquidity squeeze for the institution. In addition, the timing of receiving prepayments and interest payments for the MBS holder may lag behind the actual payment by the borrower. Again, this could lead to a collateral shortage.

For an investor with an unexpected collateral shortage an alternative is to unwind the leveraged position. For example, if a margin call must be met, the most recently purchased MBS could be sold in order to meet that call. If more margin were required later, another set of MBSs could be sold and more margin posted on each rollover of the collateralized borrowing. In theory, this unwinding should be able to be accomplished all the way down to the original investment.

5. *Refunding Risk*. Refunding risk is the chance that when a swap or a repurchase line of credit expires the spread between the cost of funds and the yield on the asset will have eroded. This risk is a problem only if the duration of the assets increases such that a higher cost of funds unexpectedly has to be locked in through additional hedging. This could lead to a smaller return on investments, but presumably never a negative return. If the hedged cost of funding becomes more than the yield on the asset, the strategy should be terminated.

Another form of refunding risk is the risk that an institution may be unable to borrow funds when its short-term liabilities have to be renewed. The problem may occur for even a very well-run program if a liquidity squeeze in the marketplace occurs as the result of some exogenous event. In this case, the institution may have to find an alternative source of funds, and that source may be more expensive.

6. *Implementation Risk.* The second major area of risk associated with an SAT program is implementation risk. Implementation risk is the risk that the program will be inappropriately managed. Potentially the riskiest aspect of an SAT strategy, the implementation risk, has several sources, including:

   a. *Incompetence.* The strategies involved require a great deal of technical expertise. Institutions that do not have this expertise should not participate in an SAT program. Rather, they should be willing to develop an expertise in this area and/or use someone with the capability to monitor the program before participating. It is not enough, however, to retain outside consultants for guidance in this type of strategy.

   Internal personnel must understand the mechanics and theory of the strategy. Additionally, a strong system of internal controls must be in place so management can monitor, evaluate, and supervise the investment program.

   b. *Fidelity Risk.* Most institutions employ an outside consultant to advise them of profitable opportunities and on appropriate hedges. The consultants can only advise, however. The institutions might choose to ignore the external advice. Further, if an investor wants to participate in some potential gains, he must leave his position open to some downside risk. Therefore, an investment manager may decide to hedge only 70 or 80 percent of the total portfolio, leaving the portfolio for upside gain on 20 to 30 percent but also the exposure to unlimited loss on the same percentage. Because of the high degree of leverage, the potential losses can be very large. Only competent and credible personnel should be allowed to manage this type of investment program. Again, a strong system of internal checks and balances must be maintained.

   c. *Churning Risk.* If an outside consultant is retained and the consulting fee is based on the trading activity of the institution, there is a greater incentive to advise the institution to make transactions that are not necessary or appropriate in order to generate commissions. A better arrangement is to compensate the consultants with an annual retainer fee that is independent of the trading activity of the institution. Consultants that are compensated based on the asset size of the institution may be inclined to lever the institution's initial investment to a greater extent, inflating the balance sheet, to generate larger consulting fees. An institution that retains an outside consultant should attempt to arrange a compensation that both parties are comfortable with and that does not create incentives for the consultants that might incline them to manage a riskier strategy than would otherwise be the case.

7. *Speculation versus Hedged Management.* Because the leverage potential is so great in an SAT strategy, some institutions may view it as a mechanism to outguess the market and make a large profit. For example, an institution could leverage an investment by several multiples and leave it unhedged. Thus, they stand to realize a large spread profit on the assets over the cost of short-term funding. However, they would be extremely susceptible to downside risk if interest rates increased or if large prepayments occurred on premium securities. A properly conceived SAT strategy is first and foremost a set of rules, guidelines, and parameters. Any implicit investment strategy based on outguessing the market is speculation, not SAT.

16

Using Mortgage Collateral as a Source for Earning Power

INTRODUCTION

Over the past several years, thrifts and commercial banks have acquired large amounts of MBSs either through outright purchase or by swapping their mortgages for Freddie Mac PCs (under the FHLMC Guarantor II program) or for Fannie Mae-guaranteed mortgage-backed pass-through. Apart from the benefit of having AAA-equivalent–rated securities guaranteed by a federal agency in their portfolios, there are other benefits which may not be generally known.

Principal among these is the ability to use MBSs as collateral for short-term financing through a reverse repurchase agreement or a dollar roll. Other short- and intermediate-term financing techniques may be beneficial as well.

An understanding of these benefits can be especially useful to an institution that has a large portfolio of below-market securities, a low level of net worth, or an adverse match of assets and liabilities in portfolio. When mortgage loans are swapped for securities, the securitization process makes the whole loans more marketable. Thus, in the event of a sudden shift in market conditions the securitized loans may be sold quickly. The sale of whole loans usually takes longer because of the lesser degree of standardization among mortgage loans, differences in underwriting standards, and the perception of greater risk associated with the lack of an agency guarantee. The securitization of the mortgages therefore reduces market risk, especially when timing is critical.

This chapter highlights ten methods of using MBSs as collateral for short- and intermediate-term financing and concludes with a detailed analysis of dollar rolls and the benefits and investor concerns related to the dollar roll method of financing.

USES OF MORTGAGE COLLATERAL[1]

MBSs are advantageous because they may be used as collateral for various types of borrowing. An institution may, with collateralized borrowing, obtain funds and relend them at rates higher than those currently being earned by loans in the portfolio. In many cases this can be done without selling the securities and booking an immediate accounting loss, which would impact net worth.

There are ten basic ways that a bank or S&L may raise funds by using MBSs as collateral. Which use is most advantageous is a function of the bank's particular charter, the size of the institution, the size of the block of MBSs available as collateral, the amount of money the bank wishes to borrow, the accounting system chosen by the borrower (RAP or GAAP), the degree of additional risk the borrower is willing to take, and whether there is taxable income.

These ten uses may be categorized into four subgroups: (1) a sale of assets defined as a deferred loss (under RAP accounting); (2) a financing transaction [reverse repurchase agreement, dollar roll, Federal Home Loan Bank (FHLB) advance, Federal Reserve discount window advance, commercial paper, and public tax and loan accounts]; (3) a bond and stock offering (mortgage-backed bond, pay-through bond, CMO and/or REMIC, and ARPS); and (4) interest-rate swaps (with Wall Street dealers or the Federal Home Loan Bank interest-rate swap desk).

Portfolio holders of MBSs may access these funds primarily through turning to several Wall Street dealers that specialize in this market or to the FHLB, the Federal Reserve Bank, Sallie Mae, or state and municipal public funds. A description of the ten uses follows.

Sale of Assets

1. Sale of Low-Coupon Securities under RAP and GAAP

Mutual thrifts regulated by the FHLBB may restructure their portfolios and regulatory net worth requirements by deferring gains and losses under regulatory accounting procedures (RAP). Under the FHLBB's RAP regulations, MBSs acquired before October 28, 1984, are eligible for loss deferral. Under certain

---

[1]This discussion is taken from David Olsen, *Uses of Freddie Mac Mortgage Participation Certificates* (Washington, D.C.: Federal Home Loan Mortgage Corporation, April 1985).

conditions, those acquired through a merger may be sold without recognizing a loss for financial statement purposes under the purchase method of accounting. In addition, under certain REMIC elections, fixed assets may be disposed of as a sale for tax purposes and at the same time be treated as a financing for GAAP income and balance sheet reporting purposes.

Financing Transactions

2. Reverse Repurchase Agreements

A reverse repurchase agreement is a simultaneous agreement by a portfolio holder to sell securities to a dealer and at the same time buy the securities back for settlement at a future date at an agreed-upon price. In effect, the portfolio holder is borrowing from the security dealer, and the borrowing is collateralized by the MBSs. The portfolio holder may then reinvest the funds for the term of the reverse repo. An arbitrage is often possible because the rates on Federal Funds and Eurodollar time deposits are generally higher than those on the MBS repo. It must be pointed out that the portfolio holder is not earning this arbitrage profit cost-free. Risk is increased because the amount of debt behind a given sum of money (the MBS) as well as the Federal Funds is increased, and the portfolio manager may not get the collateral back if the transaction dealer goes bankrupt. The repo-type transaction can most easily be done with broadly traded debt instruments such as Treasuries and federal agency-guaranteed MBSs.

3. Dollar Rolls[2]

An arrangement very similar to a reverse repurchase agreement is the fixed-coupon dollar roll. The **dollar roll** is a simultaneous agreement to sell a security held in portfolio with purchase of a similar but not identical security at a future date at an agreed-upon price. The securities sold and repurchased must have identical coupons and substantially similar maturities or WAMs.

The transaction is typically, but not always, rolled into a new transaction by a renewal of the dollar roll agreement. The seller receives cash at the time of the sale and then disburses cash at the time of repurchase. For thrifts regulated under FHLBB regulations, a fixed-coupon dollar roll may be treated as a financing only if the securities sold and repurchased have the same issuer, the same original stated maturity, approximately the same yield, and unpaid balances varying by no more than 2½ percent with backing by fixed-rate loans of the same type. The term of the agreement plus extension cannot exceed 12 months. Obviously, such tight restrictions can be met only with securities in a

---

[2]This description of dollar roll transactions is based on material distributed by Goldman Sachs & Company to its clients in 1985.

very liquid market, such as Treasuries and federal agency-guaranteed MBSs. As with reverse repos, the funds borrowed from the dealer may be reinvested to create an arbitrage. (Dollar rolls are discussed more extensively later in this chapter.)

4. Federal Home Loan Bank Advance

Thrifts regulated by the FHLBB may turn to their district bank for advances. Terms vary somewhat among the 12 district banks. Maturities of advances may be of almost any term up to 20 years, and collateral is generally required. For thrifts with net worth to liabilities (or assets) ratios in excess of 3 to 5 percent (the requirements vary among the 12 banks), it is not always necessary to identify specific collateral as long as the borrower certifies to the existence of collateral in the form of MBSs, mortgages, or other securities with a face value substantially in excess of all outstanding advances. When the ratio of net worth to liabilities (or assets) falls below the 3- to 5-percent level, borrowers are required to identify specific collateral and may even have to deliver the collateral to the FHLB. The collateral must have a market value of 110 to 125 percent of the outstanding advances. In these cases, MBSs are much more convenient as a source of collateral because of the reduced amount of paperwork and documentation required. Also, in some cases, mortgages converted into MBSs may have a greater computed market value than the mortgages as whole loans.

5. Federal Reserve Discount Window Advances

Commercial banks, of course, do not have access to FHLBB advances but may borrow from the Federal Reserve Bank. On the other hand, with the enactment of the Monetary Control Act of 1980, all thrifts now also have access to the Federal Reserve discount window because of the Fed's status as a lender of last resort. Loans are available for terms up to one year. Collateral is required in the form of MBSs, mortgages and other loans, and various other securities. Collateral for borrowings must be specifically identified. Therefore, paperwork and documentation may be greatly reduced by using MBSs instead of individual mortgages. This is especially true for borrowings with terms stretching to several months, because the collateral must in this case be delivered to the Fed. The interest rate at the discount window is typically much lower than that of other forms of borrowing, but the Fed is not obliged to lend and may turn the prospective borrower down.

6. Commercial Paper

A number of programs have been established to issue commercial paper collateralized by MBSs, with the first one having appeared in August 1984. The commercial paper is issued through a special-purpose corporation that is insulated from the thrift or bank. Commercial paper is a form of short-term borrowing for terms up to 270 days and is usually unsecured. Major buyers of promissory notes are insurance companies, bank departments, pension funds, and treasuries of public funds as well as corporations.

By collateralizing commercial paper with MBSs, the borrower is able to obtain a top rating on the commercial paper issue and thus borrow at a lower interest rate. Because the transaction appears to the thrift or bank as a repurchase agreement with the issuing corporation, it can be accounted for as a financing rather than as a sale of assets. This treatment avoids the necessity of booking a loss from a sale of mortgages at a discount. To obtain a top rating, the rating services usually require uncollateralized commercial paper to be backed 100 percent by bank lines of credit. However, when the borrowing is collateralized with MBSs, the rating services allow issuers to maintain lower standby lines of credit.

7. Federal Tax and Loan Accounts and Local Public Unit Deposits

S&Ls and banks may, in effect, borrow funds from federal, state, or local governments by bidding for their deposits at rates similar to commercial rates. Government treasurers require financial intermediaries to hold their tax and loan accounts. In accordance with federal and state laws, these deposits must be collateralized. Federally guaranteed MBSs are acceptable as collateral by the federal government and 19 state governments. The use of MBSs as collateral requires less time and paperwork than use of whole-loan mortgages. In most jurisdictions, the depository institution must establish a trust account to receive and hold the collateral. In some cases, collateral such as Freddie Mac PCs or Fannie Mae MBSs may be held in a single pooled trust account pledged to both the state and its subunits.

8. Mortgage-Backed Bonds, Pay-Through Bonds, and CMOs

These three types of bonds represent forms of longer-term borrowing. A mortgage-backed bond is a general debt obligation of the issuer payable from the issuer's general funds and secured by the market value of the collateral. The mortgages used as collateral provide protection to the bond holder. The collateral would be liquidated by the trustee in the event of default by the issuer, and therefore its market value must be maintained at a specific level.

A pay-through bond represents an obligation of the issuer to dedicate the cash flow generated by the collateral pool to repayment of the bond. The cash flow generated by the collateral, together with reinvestment income, must at all times be sufficient to provide for full repayment of the bond.

A CMO is a special type of pay-through bond that provides for cash flows generated by the collateral to be partitioned to create different maturity classes, called tranches. CMOs typically include four maturity classes (see Chapter 12). Payments of principal in each class do not begin until all previous classes have been retired. CMOs generally sell at spreads of from 110 to 250 basis points over the Treasury yield curve, the specific spread being a function of the maturity of the CMO defined in terms of its expected average life.

Since MBSs are more liquid than home mortgages, using them as collateral for bond issues may be an extremely efficient means by which to improve the rating of a bond issue. The major rating agencies typically require the market value of MBSs backing a mortgage-backed bond to be maintained at roughly 140 to 150 percent of the face value of the bond, whereas these agencies usually require MBSs serving as collateral for a pay-through bond to produce less than 105 percent of the cash flow of a pay-through bond. Thus, pay-through bonds can improve the efficiency of the PC collateral by obtaining a timely payment of principal guarantee on the bond from Freddie Mac.

With the introduction of the REMIC election in 1986, the senior/subordinated structure of credit enhancement for financing collateral has made these forms even more efficient (see Chapter 1 for a discussion of the REMIC election).

Bond and Stock Offerings

9. Controlled Adjustable-Rate Preferred Stock

The first **controlled adjustable-rate preferred stock (CARPS)** was issued in February 1984 for Coast Federal Savings and Loan of Los Angeles. The CARPS form of financing was designed by Mark Burton of Shearson Lehman Hutton. Over $1 billion have been issued, but CARPS has not been actively used in recent years because the S&Ls, the primary issuers of CARPS, have largely used up the eligible net operating losses (NOLs) that made the CARPS so attractive. Thrifts and banks could raise significant amounts of capital by establishing finance subsidiaries to issue CARPS. The stock may be effectively collateralized by MBSs. Capital can be raised at a relatively low cost if the institution is in a nontaxable position. Unlike interest payments on debt, the preferred dividend is not an allowable tax deduction for the issuing corporation. Adjustable-rate preferred stock is an equity security that offers a dividend with a periodically adjusting rate. In general, dividends are paid quarterly, and the dividend rate floats at a fixed margin below the highest of the 3-month Treasury bill rate, the 10-year constant maturity rate, and the 20-year constant maturity rate. Since it is anticipated that the dividends on CARPS will qualify for the 70 percent dividend exclusion[3] from the corporate income tax, taxable corporations will accept a lower yield on CARPS than they would on an otherwise comparable debt instrument. The FHLBB allows federally chartered thrifts to transfer up to 30 percent of the book value of assets to special-purpose finance subsidiaries.

10. Interest-Rate Swaps

Wall Street investment bankers and the FHLBs offer interest-rate swaps, of which a large proportion is secured by MBSs.

An interest-rate swap is a contractual agreement between two parties to exchange cash flows representing fixed and floating interest payments. Typically, the swap issuer agrees to exchange its variable-rate liability payments on some specified amount of principal for the fixed-rate liability payments of another party on the same amount of principal over a predetermined period.

There is no exchange of principal during the life of the transaction. As a result of the swap, the issuer now has fixed-rate liability payments to more closely match its fixed-rate assets, and the other party to the swap has variable-rate liability payments to more closely match the income on its variable-rate assets. Both parties may thereby protect the profitable spread between their interest income and their cost of funds.

Interest-rate swaps may be secured by Treasury securities, MBSs, or other securities. Interest-rate swaps for as little as $1 million and with maturities of up to 10 years may be made with an FHLB. Wall Street dealers generally require a minimum of $5 million to do a swap. Maturities range from 2 to 10 years.

Interest-rate swaps can create a closer maturity match between assets and liabilities by synthetically lengthening the maturities of existing liabilities without actually raising new funds. The FHLBs require collateral of 160 to 200 percent of the face value of the assets or—if net worth is low—100 to 125 percent of market value. In certain circumstances mortgages converted into Freddie Mac PCs or Fannie Mae MBSs have a greater computed market value than the mortgages as whole loans. The Wall Street dealers often require collateral for swaps, and MBSs are usually acceptable.

Reverse repos, dollar rolls, FHLBB advances, and public unit deposits have been the most commonly used of the ten collateralized borrowing methods described above. Thrifts and banks should consider their particular needs and seek that use which raises funds most cheaply, reduces interest-rate risk most efficiently, or produces the highest arbitrage income.

---

[3]The dividend exclusion is proposed to be reduced to 55 percent on January 1, 1989, to 52.5 percent on January 1, 1990, and to 50 percent on January 1, 1991, under legislation introduced by Dan Rostenkowski (D–IL), Chairman of the House Ways and Means Committee, as part of the technical corrections bill to the 1986 Tax Reform Act.

ARPS, MMPS, AND MMNs

Mortgages and MBSs may also be used to collateralize publicly traded issues such as **ARPS (adjustable-rate preferred stock), MMPS (money market preferred stock),** or **MMNs (money market notes)**. Although these forms of borrowing represent structured financings, as against the informal collateralized borrowing techniques outlined in "Uses of Mortgage Collateral," their structure is not complex and may be designed and prepared for marketing quite quickly.

ARPS

ARPS represents a recent financial innovation that offers unique advantages to both insurers and investors. This form was designed by the Chase Manhattan Bank in 1982 to provide an efficient source of financing to thrift institutions that would also appeal to investors seeking high-quality tax-advantaged securities. The result was a vehicle that makes ARPS attractive for corporate investors.

For the issuer, ARPS represents a means of raising funds at an overall cost as low as—or lower than—any of the more traditional sources. Moreover, the issuer has substantial flexibility in determining the amount to be raised and the eventual maturity of the stock. In addition, ARPS allows the thrift to employ lower-yielding assets without recording a sale and to realize net operating loss carryovers that might otherwise expire without benefit. Under certain circumstances, the structure of an ARPS issue may also add to the net worth of the issuing association.

For the investor, ARPS represents a floating-rate instrument with the highest-quality rating. ARPS is particularly attractive to corporations, in that 70 percent of the dividends may be excluded from taxable income. The issues are publicly traded and therefore provide liquidity as well.

ARPS Structure

A thrift intending to issue ARPS establishes a wholly owned or controlled subsidiary by contributing mortgage assets in exchange for the proceeds of the ARPS and all of the subsidiary's common stock. The subsidiary is usually incorporated, or at least conducts its business in a state that does not levy income taxes. In many states, a two-tier arrangement is necessary to comply with laws requiring all of the stock of first-tier subsidiaries to be owned by the parent thrift.

There are three principal reasons for issuing ARPS through a subsidiary rather than the parent. First, mutual institutions are precluded from issuing stock. Second, the highest investment rating can be obtained only if a new company is formed whose principal function is to service the preferred stock dividend. Third, the subsidiary structure contributes to the classification of ARPS as equity (not debt); the subsidiary has assets, few or no liabilities, and preferred and common stock, but the assets are not specifically pledged to support the ARPS.

The parent has substantial flexibility in choosing the assets it wishes to contribute to the subsidiary. A wide variety of mortgages, MBSs, and other instruments generating a predictable cash flow are permissible. One important requirement is that the overall composition of assets must be such that the subsidiary is not considered an investment company for purposes of current SEC registration regulations, thereby avoiding substantial operating limitations. To meet this criterion, the subsidiary must be deemed to be primarily engaged in real estate activities. Under recent SEC practice, this is achieved when 55 percent of its assets are composed of mortgage loans or whole pools of MBSs. Since much of a thrift's mortgage security portfolio represents its own originations, whole pools are often at hand. If they are not, the thrift can assemble whole pools from primary dealers engaged in the secondary market. The intercompany transfer of assets is not considered a sale, and thus low-coupon mortgages may be used without recognizing a loss.

The subsidiary then issues the ARPS, using the proceeds to pay the parent for the assets acquired. Earnings on the subsidiary's asset portfolio are reinvested as received in eligible assets, and the total earnings are used to service the quarterly ARPS dividend payment. The filing of consolidated returns by the parent uses the thrift's loss carryforwards to eliminate any tax exposure created by the subsidiary's earnings. When dividends are current and appropriate levels of assets are maintained, excess earnings can be distributed to the parent in the form of a common stock dividend.

Dividends on the ARPS are set according to a formula tied to Treasury indexes, subject to maximum and minimum rates. The ARPS generally carries a five-year no-call provision, callable thereafter at a premium that amortizes to par, usually in five years. This provision provides flexibility for the issuer should operating losses not provide sufficient tax-exposure coverage beyond some point in the future.

ARPS Tax and Accounting Concerns[4]

The thrift industry, in which many industries have large tax-loss carryforwards, is an ideal candidate for preferred-stock financing. With the availability of the 70 percent dividends-received deduction for corporate investors in preferred

[4]This discussion of tax and accounting concerns relating to ARPS is taken with permission from a presentation by A. J. Alexis Gelinas, Esq., of Brown & Wood. The material represents Section VI, "Adjustable-Rate Preferred Stock Payable from Mortgages (ARPS)," pages 31–34 of "Federal Income Tax Treatment of Mortgage-Backed Securities" by A. J. Gelinas, March 1985.

stock, the dividend that must be paid on the preferred is well below the rate at which the thrift can reinvest the proceeds. As long as tax-loss carryforwards are available to, in effect, shelter the reinvestment income from taxes, the nondeductibility of dividends paid on the preferred does not affect the economics of the transaction.

The Key Concept

Under the usual format, the parent transfers mortgages to a new subsidiary as a contribution to capital. Adjustable-rate preferred stock is sold to corporate investors who will be entitled to the 70 percent dividends-received deduction (thus reducing the tax rate on such dividends to 10.2 percent). The proceeds of the stock sale are used to purchase additional mortgages from the parent. The stock is perpetual preferred stock, but it may be redeemed at the option of the issuer after a specified period (for example, five years). The issuer must maintain an asset base equal to the original ratio of assets to stock outstanding. The stock will be subject to mandatory redemption if the value of the assets of the issuer falls below the required asset coverage.

The preferred stock has a liquidation preference but has no general voting rights during the period the required asset coverage is met. Consequently, the preferred stock should be considered nonvoting limited and preferred stock, and thus should not prevent the parent and the subsidiary from qualifying as an affiliated group eligible to file a consolidated federal income tax return [Code Section 1504(a)(4)]. Tax counsel have taken the position that the presence of contingent voting rights can be disregarded for this purpose. Thus, the income of the issuer can be sheltered by the net operating loss carryforwards of the parent.

1. A parent corporation's net operating loss carryforward will not be available to offset the earnings of its subsidiary if the carryforward losses are "separate limitation year" (SRLY) losses [Treasury Reg. B 1.1502-1(f)]. Generally, an SRLY loss is a loss incurred by an entity, such as a merger partner, that was not a member of the parent's consolidated group at the time the loss was realized or economically accrued.

2. Availability of the dividends-received deduction is conditioned upon the issuer having either current or accumulated earnings and profits equal to the amount of the distribution to shareholders. In certain transactions, the issuer has agreed to "gross-up" the dividends payment in the event the issuer has insufficient earnings and profits to ensure dividend treatment for distributions, or if (as discussed below) the preferred stock is reclassified as debt.

Major Tax Issues

In order for the tax benefits to be available, the issuer must be treated as a separate corporation for federal income tax purposes. Provided the requisite formalities are met and the assets of the issuer substantially exceed the value of the preferred stock, tax counsel have been satisfied that such would be the case.

It is also essential that the stock be treated as equity rather than debt for federal income tax purposes. Although there is some uncertainty, tax counsel have been able to render favorable opinions on this issue based upon the following factors:

  (i) Under its terms, the preferred stock is perpetual preferred, rather than a term instrument.
 (ii) Current dividends on the preferred stock are payable only if declared at the discretion of the board of directors of the issuer and, under local law, may only be paid out of legally available funds.
(iii) Holders of shares of preferred stock cannot compel redemption thereof at any time except in the event of certain contingencies which are not within their control (e.g., failure to meet the required asset coverage if distributions fail to qualify as dividends).

Care must be taken to ensure that the issuer will have sufficient current or accumulated earnings and profits (determined for tax purposes at the end of the tax year) to enable the distributions to the preferred stockholders to qualify as dividends. Distributions in excess of earnings and profits are treated as a tax-free return of capital, reducing the basis in the stock, but distributions in excess of basis are treated as capital gains (thus being taxed for corporations at a 34 percent rate rather than 10.2 percent for dividends). If issuers were no longer eligible to be included in the consolidated group (for example, if the voting rights of the preferred stockholders became exercisable), the issuer would incur federal income tax, which causes a reduction in earnings and profits.

MMPS

MMPS improves on the ARPS structure because MMPS adjusts periodically according to actual bids submitted by investors, while ARPS floats according to a preset formula. MMPS is therefore designed to always trade at par. A large part of the MMPS market is represented by issues of thrift-controlled subsidiaries.

Every 49 days the dividend rate on MMPS is adjusted in a "Dutch Auction" on the basis of bids submitted by present and prospective holders of the stock. (The 49-day rotation allows corporate investors—the prime market for MMPS—to claim the 70 percent exclusion on dividends under the longer holding period now required by the amended tax law.)

The Dutch Auction Procedure

The **Dutch Auction procedure** grew out of sixteenth-century tulip auctions in Holland. It works as follows: participants put in bids for a specified amount of the securities at whatever dividend rate they prefer. The lowest rate that would encompass enough of the bids to cover all of the securities offered then becomes the accepted rate. Bidders who submit a rate lower than the accepted rate receive the accepted rate. Those who propose higher rates lose out by not being able to purchase or hold the securities. In case there are not sufficient bids to clear the market, the rate is set according to a scale as follows:

Prevailing MMP Dividend Structure

Preferred Stock Rating	Maximum Dividend Rate
AAA/Aaa or AA/Aa	110 percent of the 60-day Federal Reserve "AA" composite commercial paper rate
A/A	125 percent
BBB/Baa	150 percent
Below investment grade	200 percent

Prevailing MMN Interest-Rate Structure

Debt Rating	Maximum Interest Rate
AAA/Aaa or AA/Aa	110 percent of 1-month LIBOR
A/A	125 percent
BBB/Baa	150 percent
Below investment grade	200 percent

If the winning bid rate from the auction is at or below the maximum rate, the winning bid rate will be the rate for that period. Any bid above the maximum rate will be treated as an order to sell. Conversely, if all existing holders submit hold orders, the rates are automatically set as follows:

- *100 percent MMP Hold Orders:* Rate is set at 59 percent of the 60-day Federal Reserve "AA" composite commercial paper rate.

- *100 percent MMN Hold Orders:* Rate is set at 100 percent of the 30-day Federal Reserve "AA" composite commercial paper rate.

The investor is required to sign a purchaser's letter agreeing that its MMPS will be transferred only through the Dutch Auction, to a broker–dealer or to another investor who has signed and delivered a similar letter. The letter stipulates that the MMPS certificates owned by the investor must be left at a clearing corporation, initially the Depository Trust Company.

As a result of the Dutch Auction innovation, the MMPS has become a lower-cost and more efficient means of collateralized borrowing for most institutions than the ARPS, therefore largely displacing the latter. In other fundamental respects the MMPS is similar to the ARPS, including the structural and tax accounting considerations.

MMNs

MMNs are intermediate-term securities with a floating-rate yield that is reset every 35 (or 91) days through the Dutch Auction in a manner similar to that used for MMPS, except for the basis of the rate scale, which is LIBOR for the MMNs in contrast to the MMPS, which uses commercial paper as the base.

MMNs, offered with an intermediate-term maturity, are redeemable by the issuer at par on each interest payment date (the day after each auction) on 30 days' notice. They are offered in denominations of $100,000 or $500,000 and in integral multiples thereof.

Through the Dutch Auction investors purchase and hold MMNs for 91 days with the option of selling the securities at par at the end of the period. Since the interest rate is the only variable bid in the process, investors are assured that they will receive par for any MMNs sold through the Dutch Auction. Investors who wish to hold MMNs for the next 91-day period must submit a hold order, indicating that they want to continue to hold the MMNs at whatever rate results from the Dutch Auction; or they submit no bid, in which case it is assumed that they have submitted a hold order.

The maximum interest rate a MMN auction can result in will be a percentage of the 3-month LIBOR rate, as announced on the auction date for the preceding business day, determined as set forth below based on the prevailing rating of such series of MMNs at the close of business on such business day:

Prevailing Rating	Percentage
Aa or Aa or below	110 percent
A/A	120 percent
BBB/Baa	130 percent
Below BBB/Baa	150 percent

If the winning bid rate from the Dutch Auction is at or below the maximum rate, the winning bid rate will be the MMNs' interest rate for that period. If there are insufficient bids to purchase all MMNs the interest rate for that period will be fixed at the maximum rate (any bid above the maximum rate will be treated as an order to sell MMNs). In this instance, any investors who wish to sell MMNs would sell only a pro-rata percentage of their holdings. Conversely, if all existing holders submit hold orders, the interest rate is automatically set at 100 percent of the interest equivalent of the 90-day Federal Reserve Aa composite commercial paper rate. Regardless of the winning bid rate, after the first auction MMNs may be called on any interest payment date with 30 days' notice.

Advantage to the Issuer

MMNs offer an attractive financing alternative for issuers of floating-rate debt. Specifically, MMNs provide the following advantages.

- MMNs are low-cost instruments. Because they afford investors liquidity at each Dutch Auction at par, investors should demand lower yields on MMNs than on standard fixed-rate notes.
- The Dutch Auction mechanism requires investors to compete in order to own the notes, thereby assuring that market forces work to achieve the lowest rate for the issuer.
- In the case of split ratings, the lower rating prevails.
- MMNs allow improved access to the floating-rate debt market.
- The flexible call features of MMNs allow an issuer to redeem the securities on any interest payment date.

Advantages to the Investor

MMNs are designed to attract traditional fixed-rate note investors as well as new investors for the following reasons:

- Through the Dutch Auction mechanism, MMNs minimize an investor's risk of principal in secondary market trading.
- Because of the Dutch Auction mechanism, MMNs afford an investor greater liquidity than is available with investments in most other floating-rate debt instruments.

DOLLAR ROLLS: TRANSACTION DESCRIPTION[5]

Dollar rolls offer MBSs investors an excellent opportunity to increase total return on a portfolio. A **dollar roll transaction** is one in which an institution sells a mortgage-backed pass-through security held in its investment portfolio to a dealer and agrees to repurchase a substantially identical security on a future

---

[5]This description of the dollar roll transaction is based on material distributed by Goldman Sachs & Company to its clients in 1985.

date at a specified price. At the time of the sale the institution receives cash, and when the security is purchased the cash is paid out. The difference between the sale and repurchase price represents the interest cost of the transaction and is referred to as **the drop**.

Dollar rolls may be used as a means of short-term financing or to generate income through arbitrage. The financing or arbitrage opportunity exists when an investor is able to borrow funds against pass-throughs held in portfolio at below-market rates; the proceeds raised by "rolling" the pass-throughs into a dealer are then invested at rates higher than the current reverse repo borrowing rate, with a maturity matching that of the dollar roll. The MBS holder thereby increases the total return on a rolled portfolio—either by making some otherwise dormant assets generate current income or by lowering his average cost of funds.

Although both regular reverse repos and dollar rolls involve the pledge of specific securities as collateral against cash borrowings, the similarities between the transactions do not extend much further. The term of a regular reverse repo may be as short as overnight or as lengthy as several months. During the transaction, the securities generally remain registered in the borrower's name. The borrower receives all income flows generated by the securities, which include prepayments as well as the contractual P&I. When the transaction matures, provided there was no preauthorized right of substitution, the dealer returns to the borrower the same collateral that was originally pledged. In contrast, most dollar reverse repurchase agreements are made for terms ranging between one and three months, although both shorter and longer transactions may be negotiated. During the term of the agreement the dealer is obligated to return to the borrower pass-throughs that are "substantially identical" to those pledged at the beginning of the transaction—but they need not be exactly the same. Substantially identical is considered to mean: (1) same type of security (GNMA for GNMA), (2) similar dollar value and principal amounts, (3) same coupon, and (4) maturity within two years of the original maturity. Dollar roll transactions presume on the part of both the institution and the dealer good delivery as defined by the Public Securities Association (see Chapter 4).

Economic Basis

It is precisely the flexibility of returning *substantially* identical rather than identical securities that creates the motivation for dealers to offer dollar roll financing, frequently at below-market levels. If a dealer needs a particular pass-through but either cannot or desires not to purchase the security outright, it can be borrowed through dollar roll. The dealer may be short a particular coupon needed to make a delivery, or a certain pool may have a characteristic for which a customer is willing to pay a premium price. The dealer expects to sell the pass-through rolled in at a slightly higher price than his cost of obtaining a similar pass-through to roll out; he creates incentive for security holders to roll their securities by sharing the expected profit in the form of lower financing rates.

Accounting Treatment

The FHLBB has ruled that conforming dollar rolls may be accounted for as financing transactions. The implication of this favorable accounting treatment is that no gain or loss needs to be recognized as a result of a dollar roll, provided the sale and subsequent repurchase involve substantially identical securities. The accounting for these transactions is described under GAAP in a statement of position by the Committee on Savings and Loan Associations of the American Institute of Certified Public Accountants (AICPA), dated 1982, and under RAP with Staff Memorandum R-48 of the FHLBB. The provisions of the FHLBB ruling and the position of the Committee on Savings and Loan Associations of the AICPA are essentially the same. (The FHLBB ruling is given on p. 456.)

Profit Evaluation

The profit potential of a proposed dollar roll may be analyzed as an arbitrage opportunity and is evaluated by comparing the revenue lost by not holding the pass-through with the reinvestment revenue earned on the cash borrowed. If looked upon as a means of financing, an implied repo rate is calculated for the transaction. In both instances, four revenue flows must be considered: (1) coupon payments; (2) prepayments; (3) reinvestment income; and (4) price spread, generally referred to as the drop. In a positive yield-curve environment, the drop is usually positive and is therefore revenue earned by the bond holder. The following formulas may be used to calculate the revenue flows.

1. Coupon Payments

Interest at the coupon rate of the pass-through is accrued during the life of the dollar roll and is payable to the dealer. From the bond holder's perspective, the coupon income is revenue lost.

$$\text{Foregone Coupon} = \text{Current Face Amount} \times \text{Coupon} \times (\text{Mortgage Days*}/360)$$

*Interest on MBSs is calculated on the basis of a 30-day month and a 360-day year.

2. Prepayment Value

Prepayments made during the term of a dollar roll transaction are collected by the dealer. Since all mortgages prepay at par, whether prepayments contribute or diminish the bond holder's net yield on the dollar roll depends on whether the pass-throughs are discount or premium bonds on the books of the entity doing the roll. In most cases, the bonds have been priced at a discount, and therefore prepayments represent an opportunity loss because the gain between the discount and par accrues to the dealer. If the bonds are valued at par, prepayments made during the term of the dollar roll have no cash-flow or current-yield effect. The loss due to prepayment on premium bonds is absorbed by the dealer and so represents an indirect gain to the party that initiated the roll. Premium bonds may be rolled in order to transfer the risk of prepayment to the dealer. All prepayments—whether on discount, par, or premium bonds—shorten the average life of the mortgage pool.

The value of the prepayments for mortgages priced at a discount or premium may be estimated by assuming that the current prepayment rate per month, quantified by CPR, will continue for the term of the dollar roll. Three-month average CPR is generally used, although market practice varies. This estimation may be worked out as follows.

$$\text{Amount of Prepayments} = \text{Current Face Amount} \times \text{CPR}$$

$$\text{Prepayment Value} = (\text{Par} - \text{Market Price}) \times \text{Amount of Prepayment}$$

3. Reinvestment Income

Unlike regular reverse repos and collateralized bank borrowings, dollar rolls assume the full market value of the underlying pass-through. There are no haircuts or excess margin requirements. A bond holder receives 100 percent of the current market price of the pass-through. These funds are generally invested and earn reinvestment income.

$$\text{Reinvestment Income} = \text{Cash Received} \times \text{Reinvestment Rate} \\ \times (\text{Number of Days}/360)$$

4. The Drop

The price spread may be either revenue earned or revenue lost to the bond holder, depending on whether the net of the sale and repurchase price is negative or positive. In either case, the value of the spread is simply the dollar value of the difference between the two prices.

The basic formulas are illustrated in the following example.

Assume Safe S&L enters into an agreement with Dealer to roll GNMA 10½s down $^{11}/_{32}$ from 10/19/88 to 11/16/88. On 10/19/88, the Ginnie Maes are selling at 94.00 and prepaying at 6 percent CPR, which is .2 percent a month. Safe can invest in Euro CDs for 30 days at 8.95 percent.

(1) Foregone Coupon $\quad = (.1050) (1,000,000) (^{27}/_{360}) = \$7,875.00$

(2) Prepayment Amount $= (\$1,000,000) (.002) = \$2,000$
    Prepayment Value $\quad = (1.00 - .94) (2,000) = \$120$

Total Revenue Lost $\quad\quad =$ Foregone Coupon ($\$7,875.00$)
                     $+$ Prepayments ($\$120$)
                  $= \$7,995.00$

(3) Cash Received $\quad\quad = (.94) (1,000,000) = \$940,000$
    Reinvestment Income $= (\$940,000)(.0895)(^{28}/_{360}) = \$6,545.44$

(4) Spread Profit $\quad\quad\quad = (^{11}/_{32})(1,000,000)/100 = \$3,437.50$

Total Revenue Earned $\quad =$ Reinvestment Income ($\$6,543.33$)
                     $+$ Spread Profit ($\$3,437.50$)
                  $= \$9,980.94$

Net Profit on Roll $= \$9,980.94 - \$7,995.00 = \$1,985.94$

An alternative way to evaluate a dollar roll is to calculate an implied repo rate. This calculation is a breakeven analysis that determines the rate of return that must be earned on the cash realized from the initial sale to recoup any cash-flow loss that may result from coupon, prepayments, or price spread. This rate can also be thought of as a cost of funds. In the example above, the implied repo rate would be calculated as follows:

Cash Received	$=$	$\$940,000.00$
Foregone Coupon	$=$	$\$\quad 7,875.00$
Prepayment Value	$=$	$\$\quad\quad 120.00$
Spread Profit	$=$	$\$\quad 3,437.50$
Required Investment Earnings $=$ Foregone Coupon $+$		
Prepayment Value $-$ Spread Profit	$=$	$\$\quad 4,557.50$

Let $R =$ the implied repo rate. Therefore,

Cash $(940,000) \times R \times$ Number of Days/360 $(^{28}/_{360}) = \$4,557.50$

$$R = 6.23 \text{ percent}$$

Dollar Roll Evaluation Worksheet

Let:

P	=	price of the pass-through, as a percentage of par,
C	=	coupon rate,
S	=	spread between purchase and sale price, in 32nds,
R	=	implied repo rate,
pr	=	assumed prepayment rate, or CPR, and
mmr	=	money market investment rate.

Implied Repo Rate

(1)   Foregone Coupon $= C \times 1,000,000 \times$ (Days*/360)

(2)   Spread Profit (Loss) $= S \times 1,000$

(3)   Value of Prepayment $= (100 - P) \times (1,000,000 \times \text{pr}/100)$

(4)   Required Investment Earnings $= (1) + (3) - (2)$

(5) $R = \dfrac{(4)}{P \times 1,000,000 \times \text{Days}**/360}$

Cash

(6)   Reinvestment Income $= P \times 1,000,000 \times \text{mmr} \times \text{Days}**/360$

(7)   Net Profit per Million $= (6) - (4)$

*30/360.
**Actual/360.

Prepayment Risk[6]

In the example on page 453 we assumed a 6 percent CPR. A faster prepayment rate increases the effective borrowing cost of rolling securities owned at a discount because Safe foregoes the opportunity of receiving the extra (prepayment) cash flows at par. On the other hand, if Safe were rolling MBSs purchased at a premium, such as GNMA 11s bought at $106^{14}/_{32}$, Safe wins because it avoids receiving the principal payments at par.

Table 16.1 extends the Safe S&L example in presenting a sensitivity analysis of the effective cost of borrowing under various prepayment-rate assumptions expressed as CPR. As is evident from the table, different prepayment rates can significantly change the effective cost of funds for GNMA 11s.

[6]This discussion is taken from Shearson Lehman Hutton, "Viewing Dollar Rolls as Collateralized Borrowing," May 1986, prepared by Steven Carlson, Vice President, Mortgage Research.

TABLE 16.1
Dollar Roll Cost of Funds at Various CPRs for Specified Drop Levels

CPR (percents)	$5/32$	$6/32$	$7/32$	$8/32$	$9/32$	$10/32$	$11/32$
0	7.92	7.53	7.14	6.75	6.36	5.97	5.58
5	7.57	7.18	6.79	6.41	6.02	5.63	5.24
10	7.21	6.83	6.44	6.05	5.66	5.27	4.88
15	6.84	6.45	6.06	5.67	5.28	4.89	4.50
20	6.44	6.05	5.66	5.27	4.88	4.49	4.10
25	6.02	5.63	5.24	4.85	4.46	4.07	3.68
30	5.57	5.18	4.79	4.40	4.01	3.62	3.23

Source: Shearson Lehman Hutton Mortgage Securities.

This fact makes the dollar roll a useful tool for institutions that anticipate prepayments will be greater over a given period. In addition to a prepayment-rate sensitivity, the table also shows the effective cost of borrowing at various dollar roll prices. As the drop increases the cost of funds decreases because the borrower repurchases the securities at a lower price.

The Delivery Put Option

The preceding analysis was based on the assumption that both parties to the dollar roll deliver exactly the notional amount of the transaction. In reality both parties have delivery tolerances because they can under- or overdeliver by 2.5 percent. The delivery tolerance effectively gives both parties put options: that is, the option—but not the obligation—to sell securities to each other. These two options influence the effective financing cost in opposite directions, but in unequal amounts. The value of Safe's option primarily depends on the time to the first settlement, in this case 7 days. A dollar roll executed closer to settlement will be a less valuable put option to the thrift. In contrast, the Dealer's option always has a longer maturity. The two put options also have different exercise prices. The difference is equal to the drop. In the example, Safe's option was "at the money" and the Dealer's option was slightly "out of the money."

Identifying the delivery features of the dollar roll agreement with options helps in determining the significance of their effect on the financing cost associated with a dollar roll. Put options on mortgages similar to the ones described above are traded over the counter, enabling a thrift institution explicitly to account for these elements in its financing decision if it so desires. The bid price of these two options as of May 15, 1988, was ¼ percent of face for Safe's implied put option (strike price of 106-14 within 7 days to expiration) and ½ percent of face value (strike price of 106-06 with 33 days to expiration) for the option written by Safe to the Dealer. The net value of the two options from Safe's perspective is the value of the option it owns less the value of the option the Dealer owns, or in this case, ($\frac{1}{4}$% $\times$ 100,000) − ($\frac{1}{2}$% $\times$ 100,000) = \$250. Treating this as an expected cost of borrowing raises the rate from 5.67 to 5.98 percent.

In practice, both parties cannot fine-tune their deliveries to fully exploit the ex-post value of their delivery options and as a result the ex-ante net cost of \$250 may not equal the expected net cost of the delivery options.

Another way to assess the impact of the options is to consider the ex-post effective borrowing cost under various combinations of price outcomes and delivery amounts.

Table 16.2 presents a matrix of cost of funds under alternative market price elections assumed as of May 21, 1988 and June 17, 1988. The matrix assumes that both parties to the dollar roll optimize their delivery election. That is, Safe overdelivers only if the market price is less than 106-14 on May 21 and underdelivers otherwise. The Dealer is assumed to behave similarly on June 17 except that its breakeven price is 106-08.

Federal Home Loan Bank Board R Memorandum: Opinion and Clarification

#R-48 SECURITIES TRANSACTIONS

A number of FSLIC insured associations are engaging in transactions involving the exchange of securities with different interest rates without properly accounting for such transactions. Previously, the Bank Board's Supervisory Agents have advised associations found engaging in these transactions as to the proper accounting. The purpose of this memorandum is to advise all FSLIC insured institutions on the proper accounting for such transactions.

The proper accounting treatment for these transactions depends on whether the transactions are to be treated as sales and purchases or as financing transactions. The issue turns on the application of existing accounting principles to the facts of the transaction. Where the risks of ownership are transferred to the buyer, or the security to be repurchased is not substantially identical to the security sold, the transaction involves a sale and purchase and is not a financing transaction. Thus, when transactions involve the exchange of securities with different coupon interest rates, the securities exchanged are not substantially identical and must be recorded as sales and purchases of security at market prices with profits and losses recorded in the period incurred.

TABLE 16.2

Effect of Optimal Delivery Price Election at Roll Out and Roll In Dates

Assumed Market Prices on May 21, 1988 (roll in)	Assumed Market Prices on June 17, 1988 (roll out)									
	105-14	105-22	105-30	106-06	106-14	106-22	106-30	107-06	107-14	
105-14	5.36%	5.05%	4.74%	4.42%	4.42%	4.42%	4.42%	4.42%	4.42%	Institution overdelivers $1,050,000 face
105-22	5.67%	5.36%	5.05%	4.74%	4.74%	4.74%	4.74%	4.74%	4.74%	
105-30	5.98%	5.67%	5.36%	5.05%	5.05%	5.05%	5.05%	5.05%	5.05%	
106-06	6.29%	5.98%	5.67%	5.36%	5.36%	5.36%	5.36%	5.36%	5.36%	
106-14	6.60%	6.29%	5.98%	5.67%	5.67%	5.67%	5.67%	5.67%	5.67%	
106-22	6.60%	6.29%	5.98%	5.67%	5.67%	5.67%	5.67%	5.67%	5.67%	Institution underdelivers $950,000 face
106-30	6.60%	6.29%	5.98%	5.67%	5.67%	5.67%	5.67%	5.67%	5.67%	
107-06	6.60%	6.29%	5.98%	5.67%	5.67%	5.67%	5.67%	5.67%	5.67%	
107-14	6.60%	6.29%	5.98%	5.67%	5.67%	5.67%	5.67%	5.67%	5.67%	
	Dealer overdelivers $1,050,000 face					Dealer underdelivers $950,000 face				

There are two types of transactions that have surfaced in the market-place recently: (1) dollar reverse repurchase agreements, and (2) loans of securities. In discussing these transactions, reference to Government National Mortgage Association (GNMA) securities is made only to serve as an example of the underlying security, and such reference should not be construed as delimiting this memorandum.

Dollar Reverse Repurchase Agreements

Dollar reverse repurchase agreements involving GNMA securities are generally written in the following two forms:

1. Fixed-coupon agreement. This agreement provides that the association is guaranteed delivery of GNMA securities having an identical certificate interest rate and a similar collateralizing pool of mortgages as the securities sold by the association.
2. Yield-maintenance agreement. This agreement provides that the association will receive GNMA securities that will provide the association a yield specified in the agreement. Consonant with the accounting principles expressed above, fixed-coupon agreements, where the transaction involves the exchange of GNMA securities which are from different GNMA pools, but the coupon interest rates are the same and the securities are substantially identical in other respects, may be accounted for as financing transactions. Yield-maintenance agreements, on the other hand, because they involve an exchange of securities with different coupon interest rates, must be accounted for as sales and purchases of securities at market prices, with profits and losses recorded in the period incurred. This conclusion is supported by observation of market practice which indicates that the several GNMA coupons are priced differently in the market.

Loans of Securities

Federal associations which engage in the practice of lending GNMA securities under the provisions of Federal Regulations 545.7-I, and state-chartered associations which do so under comparable state law, must account for such "loans" following the criteria set out above. For example, when the security delivered back to the association does not have the identical certificate interest rates as the securities loaned, the association must record this transaction as a sale and a purchase of securities at market prices (1/29/80).

17

Accounting Issues[1]

This chapter discusses two accounting issues:

- The accounting by investors for investments in IOs, POs, and residuals under generally accepted accounting principles (GAAP).
- A brief summary of the impact of a REMIC election on the accounting by the issuer of MBSs.

This chapter does not discuss:

- The federal income tax treatment of investments in IOs, POs, and residuals.
- The regulatory accounting practices of insurance companies, banks, savings and loan associations, or other regulated enterprises that invest in these securities.
- The accounting by the issuer for the issuance of IOs, POs, and residuals.

ACCOUNTING BY INVESTORS FOR INVESTMENTS IN IOs, POs, AND RESIDUALS

Background—Different Accounting Methods

Two accounting methods are used to account for investments in IOs, POs, and residuals depending on circumstances—the constant-yield method and the equity method. This section describes the methods and some of the implemen-

---

[1]This chapter was written by Benjamin S. Neuhausen, Partner, Arthur Andersen Company, Chicago, Illinois.

tation issues associated with them. Later sections of the chapter discuss accounting for each instrument and the circumstances under which each method is appropriate.

The Constant-Yield Method

The constant-yield method is described in FASB Statement No. 91, *Accounting for Nonrefundable Fees and Costs Associated with Originating or Acquiring Loans and Initial Direct Costs of Leases.* Under the constant-yield method, the investor records the investment at cost and, based on a projection of future cash distributions to be received from the investment, computes the estimated internal rate of return, or yield, over the life of the investment. During each period, the investor accrues investment income equal to the yield multiplied by the carrying amount of the investment. Distributions received are accounted for as reductions in the investment.

Statement 91 permits the yield computation to be made in either of two ways. One method is to compute the yield based on the contractual cash flows of the instrument, that is, assuming no prepayments of the underlying mortgages. The other method, which is permitted only when the investment represents an interest in a large number of similar loans for which the timing and amount of prepayments can be reasonably estimated, is to compute the yield based on estimated cash flows giving effect to estimated future principal prepayments.

If the first method (assuming no prepayments) is used, the investment balance should be adjusted each time a prepayment occurs so that the yield on the remaining contractual cash flows continues unchanged. The adjustment to the investment balance is recorded as a gain or loss in the period of the prepayment.

If the second method (reasonable estimates of prepayments) is used, estimates of prepayments, reinvestment income, and other factors will change over time. Periodically, the investor should revise the projections of future cash distributions and compute a new yield based on actual past distributions and the latest estimate of future cash distributions. The carrying amount of the investment should be adjusted to the amount that would have been recorded if the investor had recorded income using the latest estimate of yield. That adjustment of carrying amount is a gain or loss in the period the investor changes the estimated yield.

Example 1 (p. 466) illustrates the two methods for an IO in a pool of extremely simple loans. Both methods are shown to illustrate the differences. As noted below, with the facts in the example prepayments should be estimated.

For two reasons, accountants generally favor making reasonable estimates of prepayments whenever such estimates are feasible. First, the yield computed based on estimated prepayments reflects the economic assumptions used by the investor in making the investment decision and is, therefore, more relevant to readers of financial statements. The investor knows with certainty that some of the mortgages underlying the investment security will prepay. It does not make sense to account based on an assumption (no prepayments) that the investor knows to be false. Second, the method that assumes no prepayments overstates the yield in the early years for IOs and for most residuals, followed by losses when the inevitable prepayments occur. Accountants dislike accounting methods that inflate income in early years but result in losses or reduced income in later years.

The Equity Method

The equity method is described in APB Opinion No. 18, *The Equity Method of Accounting for Investments in Common Stock.* Under the equity method, an investor initially records an investment in another entity (investee) at cost. Each period, the investor records income and increases the carrying amount of the investment based on the investor's share of the earnings of the investee. Distributions received from the investee reduce the carrying amount of the investment.

The cost of the investment often differs from the investor's share of the reported book value of the investee. That difference should be amortized systematically over the life of the investment by a charge against income.

Market Value Entities

Some investors, because they operate in industries with special accounting principles, account for certain investments at market value. Examples include all investment of pension plans and mutual funds; broker–dealer investment positions; and insurance company, bank, and savings and loan association trading accounts. Theoretically, investors who use market value accounting could treat all distributions as reductions of the investment and then adjust the carrying amount of the investment to market value at each balance sheet date. In practice, however, these investors usually want to distinguish between investment income and unrealized gains and losses on investments. Accordingly, such investors should record investment income using either the constant-yield method or the equity method, as appropriate, treat distributions received as reductions of the investment, and then adjust the carrying amount of the investment to market value at each reporting date. Determinations of market value often will be difficult for IOs, POs, and residuals that do not trade frequently and are not similar to securities that do trade frequently. In these situations, market value may be estimated by projecting the remaining cash flows from the investment and discounting those cash flows at current market discount rates for similar securities.

Accounting for Investments in IOs

Investments in IOs should be accounted for by the constant-yield method. Statement 91 states that it applies to the accounting for discounts and premiums "associated with the purchase of loans and debt securities such as . . . loan-backed securities (such as pass-through certificates, collateralized mortgage obligations, and other so-called 'securitized' loans)." In addition, the accounting for investments in IOs was specifically addressed by the FASB Emerging Issues Task Force (EITF) in issue 86-38, *Implications of Mortgage Prepayments on Amortization of Servicing Rights,* subissue C, "Unanticipated Prepayments and Interest-Only Certificates." The EITF reached a consensus that Statement 91 applies to investments in IOs. Further, Task Force members indicated a preference for applying the constant-yield method assuming prepayments rather than applying the method allowed by Statement 91 that does not assume prepayments. The Task Force noted that under Statement 91, prepayments may be assumed only if certain criteria are met. Because IOs are strips of MBSs, the Task Force concluded that the underlying mortgages (rather than the IOs themselves) should be evaluated to determine whether the criteria in Statement 91 are satisfied.

The Chief Accountant of the SEC, who observes the EITF meetings, commented that the SEC staff expects public companies to assume prepayments in computing yield on IOs whenever the criteria in Statement 91 are satisfied.

Accounting for Investments in POs

Investments in POs also should be accounted for under the constant-yield method. The same sentence of Statement 91 quoted in the preceding section indicates that investments in POs are within the scope of Statement 91. As with IOs, it would be preferable to apply the constant-yield method assuming prepayments, looking to the underlying mortgages to determine whether the criteria in Statement 91 are satisfied.

If an investor were to follow the method allowed by Statement 91 that does not assume prepayments, the result would be a low computed yield with gains as prepayments occur.

Accounting for Investments in Residuals

The accounting for investments in residuals is more complicated than that for investments in IOs and POs, because residuals take different legal forms. Some residuals are in the form of specified interests in the cash flows from the underlying mortgages; others are in the form of ownership interests in the special-purpose trust or corporation that issued the MBSs.

If the residual is in the form of a contractual interest in the cash flows from the underlying mortgages, the investor should use the constant-yield method to account for the investment, based on the same sentence from the scope of Statement 91 quoted above. Neither the EITF nor the SEC staff has specifically addressed whether an investor should compute yield on residuals using an estimate of prepayments, but the analogies to IOs are strong. Most accountants would insist that an investor factor in estimated prepayments if the underlying mortgages satisfy the criteria in Statement 91.

If the residual is in the form of an ownership interest in the special-purpose trust or corporation that issued MBSs, the accounting depends on the level of ownership. If the investor holds more than a 50 percent interest in the issuer, the investor should consolidate the issuer in its financial statements. In this case, the investor steps into the shoes of the issuer and follows issuer accounting, which is outside the scope of this chapter.

If the investor holds an interest of 20 to 50 percent, the investor should use the equity method to account for the investment. The investor would need to obtain financial statements from the issuer to compute the investor's share of the issuer's net income and the investor's share of the issuer's book value. The difference between the investor's cost and the investor's share of the issuer's book value should be amortized by an accelerated method over the expected life of the mortgages in proportion to the expected pattern of earnings. If at any time the investor anticipates having to make contributions to the issuer to cover cash shortfalls of the issuer, the difference between cost and underlying book value should be amortized over the period of positive cash distributions, rather than over the life of the mortgages. The constant-yield method could be used as an alternative to the equity method if it could be demonstrated that the results of the two methods are substantially the same.

If the investor owns less than 20 percent of the issue, practice varies. The distributions received from the issuer need to be split in some systematic and rational way between income and return on investment. Either the equity method or the constant-yield method would be a systematic and rational way of computing how much of a distribution represents income and how much represents return on investment. Some accountants prefer the equity method because it follows the legal form of the investment (an ownership interest); others prefer the constant-yield method because they believe it more faithfully reflects the economics of the investment.

Other Issues

Impairment

Regardless of the method used to account for an investment in IOs, POs, or residuals, the asset should never be carried on the investor's balance sheet at an amount in excess of expected future cash flows. For purposes of this valuation ceiling, the future cash flows may be computed on either a discounted or undiscounted basis.

Income Tax Effects

The federal income tax treatment of investments in IOs, POs, and residuals is beyond the scope of this chapter. To the extent that the federal income tax treatment differs from the treatment under GAAP described in this chapter, deferred income taxes should be provided on the difference between the book and tax bases of the investments, in accordance with FASB Statement No. 96, *Accounting for Income Taxes*. In addition, if income for GAAP purposes exceeds taxable income for years through 1989, 50 percent of the difference is a preference item for alternative minimum tax (AMT) purposes.

THE EFFECTS OF A REMIC ELECTION ON THE ACCOUNTING BY THE ISSUER OF MBSs

This section summarizes briefly the accounting by issuers of MBSs and the effects of a REMIC election on the accounting.

The major accounting issue for an issuer of MBSs is whether the issuance should be accounted for as a sale of the underlying mortgages or as a borrowing collateralized by the mortgages. If the transaction is accounted for as a sale, the mortgages (or partial interests in the mortgages, if only partial interests are sold) are removed from the issuer's balance sheet and a gain or loss is recorded for the difference between the carrying amount of the mortgages and the proceeds received from investors. After the date of sale, the issuer's income statement does not reflect interest income with respect to the mortgages or interests in mortgages sold and does not reflect interest expense with respect to the MBSs. The issuer's income statement might reflect servicing-fee income and servicing costs, investment earnings on float, and losses under recourse provisions, if these features are present in the transaction. If the transaction is accounted for as a borrowing collateralized by the mortgages, the mortgages remain on the balance sheet as an asset and the proceeds received from investors are recorded as a liability. The issuer records interest income on the mortgages and interest expense on the MBSs over their lives. The issuer also will record servicing-fee income and servicing costs and investment earnings on float if these features exist in the transaction.

Which accounting method is followed depends in large part on the legal form of the transaction. If the MBSs are in legal form ownership interests in the mortgage collateral, for example, pass-through certificates or beneficial ownership of a trust that holds the mortgages, the transaction is accounted for in accordance with FASB Statement No. 77, *Reporting by Transferors for Transfers of Receivables with Recourse*. If certain criteria are satisfied, Statement 77 allows the transaction to be accounted for as a sale; if they are not satisfied, the transaction is accounted for as a borrowing. Generally, the criteria for sale accounting are easy to satisfy.

If the MBSs are in legal form debt instruments collateralized by the mortgages, for example, CMOs, the transaction is accounted for in accordance with FASB Technical Bulletin 85-2, *Accounting for Collateralized Mortgage Obligations (CMOs)*. If certain criteria are satisfied, Technical Bulletin 85-2 allows the transaction to be accounted for as a sale; if they are not satisfied, the transaction is accounted for as a borrowing. Generally, the criteria are difficult—though not impossible—to satisfy, and borrowing accounting is common.

An issuer can make a REMIC election with respect to either legal form of MBS. Statement 77 governs the accounting for issuances of pass-through certificates, with or without a REMIC election, and Technical Bulletin 85-2 governs the accounting for issuances of CMOs, with or without a REMIC election. The REMIC election makes it easier to structure transactions that qualify for sale accounting in at least two respects:

- Without a REMIC election, multiclass MBSs are feasible only for income tax purposes in the form of CMOs. Multiclass pass-through certificates, absent in a REMIC election, create adverse federal income tax consequences. Before the REMIC provisions became law, issuers who wanted the economic benefits of multiclass securities had to issue CMOs and deal with the more difficult sale accounting criteria of Technical Bulletin 85-2. With the REMIC election, it is feasible to issue multiclass pass-through certificates that can be accounted for under the easier criteria of Statement 77.

- Issuers often want to treat CMOs as borrowings for federal income tax purposes but as sales for GAAP purposes. Before the REMIC provisions became law, this was difficult to achieve because the attributes of the CMOs that caused them to be treated as borrowings for federal income tax purposes often violated the sale accounting criteria in Technical Bulletin 85-2. With a REMIC election, the issuer can structure a CMO transaction to meet the sale accounting criteria in Technical Bulletin 85-2 and elect to treat the CMO as a borrowing for federal income tax purposes.

AN EVOLVING AREA

The contents of this chapter are current as of early summer 1988. Both topics covered are part of an evolving area of accounting, and readers should be aware that the accounting rules may change. The FASB has on its agenda a project on accounting for financial instruments that includes one phase dealing with measurement of financial instruments and another phase dealing with when issuances of financial instruments linked to financial assets should be treated as sales of the assets and when they should be treated as borrowings collateralized by the assets.

Example 1: Applying the Constant-Yield Method with and without Assumed Prepayments

Assumptions

1. The pool of loans consists of 1,000 identical loans with the following terms:
   - All loans originated on January 2, 1989
   - $100,000 face amount per loan
   - 10 percent interest rate
   - Three annual payments in arrears of $40,211.48
   - No prepayment penalty
2. On January 2, 1989, the investor buys an IO backed by the entire pool for $13,014,866.77.
3. The investor expects ⅓ of the loans to be prepaid on the first annual payment date, ⅓ to be prepaid on the second annual payment date, and ⅓ to extend the full three-year contractual term.
4. At the first annual payment date, ½ of the loans prepay. Based on that experience and current interest rates, the investor now expects ½ of the remaining loans (¼ of the original loans) to prepay on the second annual payment date.

Amortization Table for One Loan

| | Beginning of Year | Annual Payment | |
Year	Principal	Interest	Principal
1	$100,000.00	$10,000.00	$ 30,211.48
2	69,788.52	6,978.85	33,232.63
3	36,555.89	3,655.59	36,555.89
		$20,634.44	$100,000.00

Investor's Economic Analysis

At inception, the investor expects to receive the following cash flows (in thousands):

Year		
1	$10,000.00	
2	4,652.57	(⅔ × $6,978.85)
3	1,218.53	(⅓ × $3,655.59)
	$15,871.10	
NPV @ 15%	$13,014.87	

Example 2: Investor's Accounting with Estimated Prepayments (in thousands of dollars)

1. Based on estimated prepayments, the investor expects a yield of 15 percent.
2. During the first year, therefore, the investor records interest income of $1,952.23 (15 percent × $13,014.87).
3. The $10,000.00 cash distribution reduces the asset to $4,967.10 at the end of the first year.
4. At the end of the first year, as noted previously, prepayments exceed expectations, and the investor revises his expected cash flows at the end of the second and third years to $3,489.42 and $913.90, respectively. This reduces the expected yield on the investment to 7.76 percent.
5. Under Statement 91, the investor adjusts the investment balance to what it would have been if he used a yield of 7.76 percent in the first year—$4,025.07—resulting in a loss of $942.03. (Stated differently, the first year interest income at 7.76 percent would have been $1,010.20 rather than the $1,952.23 that was recorded at 15 percent.)
6. During the second year the investor records interest income of $312.42 (7.76 percent × $4,025.07).
7. The $3,489.42 cash distribution reduces the asset to $848.07 at the end of the second year. Prepayments equal the estimate, so no adjustment is needed.
8. During the third year the investor records interest income of $65.83 (7.76 percent × $848.07).

Example 3: Investor's Accounting Based on Contractual Cash Flows (in thousands of dollars)

This example is presented to illustrate the constant-yield method applied based on contractual cash flows (no prepayments assumed). Based on the assumed facts, this approach should not be applied to this investment, because prepayments are estimable.

1. Based on contractual cash flows (no prepayments), the investor's yield on the $13,014.87 investment is 33.02 percent.
2. During the first year, therefore, the investor records interest income of $4,297.55 (33.02 percent × $13,014.87).
3. The $10,000.00 cash distribution reduces the asset to $7,312.42 at the end of the first year.
4. At the end of the first year, as noted previously, prepayments occur. The contractual cash flows for the remaining outstanding loans are $3,489.42 and $1,827.80 for the second and third years, respectively. The present value of the remaining contractual cash flows using the original 33.02 percent discount rate is $3,656.21.
5. Under Statement 91, the investor adjusts the investment balance to $3,656.21, resulting in a loss of $3,656.21. The asset is written down by 50 percent because 50 percent of the contractual cash flows is eliminated by the first year prepayment.
6. During the second year the investor records interest income of $1,207.29 (33.02 percent × $3,656.21).
7. The $3,489.42 cash distribution reduces the asset to $1,374.08 at the end of the second year.
8. At the end of the second year, more prepayments occur. The contractual cash flow for the remaining outstanding loans is $913.90, with a present value of $687.04 at 33.02 percent.
9. Under Statement 91, the investor adjusts the investment balance to $687.04, resulting in a loss of $687.04. The asset is written down by 50 percent because 50 percent of the contractual cash flows is eliminated by the second year prepayment.
10. During the third year the investor records interest income of $226.86 (33.02 percent × $687.04).

Comparative Summary of Income

Year	Estimating Prepayments	Not Estimating Prepayments
1	$1,010.20	$ 641.34
2	312.42	520.25
3	65.83	226.86
	$1,388.45	$1,388.45

GLOSSARY

ABS (asset-backed security): A security that is collateralized by loans, leases, receivables, or installment contracts on personal property (not including real estate).

Accrual bond: Also known as an accretion bond or a Z-bond in a CMO issue. A bond on which interest accrues, but is not paid to the investor during the time of accrual. Instead, the amount accrued is added to the amount of remaining principal of the bond and is paid at maturity.

Additional hedge: A protection against borrower fallout risk in the mortgage pipeline.

Adjustable-rate mortgages: See **ARMs**.

Adjustable-rate preferred stock (ARPS): Publicly traded issues that may be collateralized by mortgages and MBSs.

Alternative mortgage instruments: See **AMIs**.

AMIs (alternative mortgage instruments): Variations of mortgage instruments such as adjustable-rate and variable-rate mortgages (ARMs and VRMs), graduated-payment mortgages (GPMs), reverse-annuity mortgages (RAMs), and several seldom-used variations.

Amortization factor: The pool factor implied by the scheduled amortization assuming no prepayments.

ARMs (adjustable-rate mortgages): A mortgage that features predetermined adjustments of the loan interest rate at regular intervals based on an established index. The interest rate is adjusted at each interval to a rate equivalent to the index value plus a predetermined spread, or margin, over the index, usually subject to per-interval and to life-of-loan interest-rate and/or payment-rate caps.

ARPS: See **Adjustable-rate preferred stock.**

Average life: Also referred to as weighted average life (WAL). The average number of years that each dollar of unpaid principal due on the mortgage remains outstanding. Average life is computed as the weighted average time to the receipt of all future cash flows, using as the weights the dollar amounts of the principal paydowns.

Back fee: The fee paid on the extension date if the buyer wishes to continue the option.

Balloon loans: Mortgage loans that involve regular monthly payments for interest plus either no or partial amortization of the loan principal, so that at the end of the term of the mortgage there is a lump-sum payment of the remaining principal.

Basis risk: A risk that the price of a hedge tool does not move as expected relative to the increase or decrease in the market price of the hedged loan or security.

BEPR: See **Breakeven prepayment rate.**

BEY (bond equivalent yield): See ***Corporate bond equivalent (CBE).***

Book profit: The cumulative book income plus any gain or loss on disposition of the assets on termination of the SAT.

Borrower fallout: In the mortgage pipeline the risk that prospective borrowers of loans committed to be closed will elect to withdraw from the contract.

Breakeven prepayment rate (BEPR): The prepayment rate of a MBS coupon that will produce the same CFY as that of a predetermined benchmark MBS coupon. Used to identify for coupons higher than the benchmark coupon the prepayment rate that will produce the same CFY as that of the benchmark coupon; and for coupons lower than the benchmark coupon the lowest prepayment rate that will do so.

Builder buydown loan: A mortgage loan on newly developed property that the builder subsidizes during the early years of the development. The builder uses cash to buy down the mortgage rate to a lower level than the prevailing market loan rate for some period of time. The typical buydown is 3 percent of the interest-rate amount for the first year, 2 percent for the second year, and 1 percent for the third year (also referred to as a 3-2-1 buydown).

Buydowns: Mortgages in which monthly payments consist of principal and interest, with portions of these payments during the early period of the loan being provided by a third party to reduce the borrower's monthly payments.

Call option: The right to purchase a security at a predetermined price on or before a specified date.

Callable swap agreement: A provision allowing the fixed-rate borrower to terminate the swap at no penalty between the call date and maturity. Used in connection with residuals.

CARPS: See ***Controlled adjustable-rate preferred stock.***

Cash-flow yield (CFY): The monthly rate of return of the MBS derived by using the actual age, or WAM, of the mortgages underlying the pool, and projecting the monthly cash flows according to a prepayment assumption. The projected cash flows are then discounted to present value using a current market required rate of return.

CBE (Corporate bond equivalent yield): Also referred to as bond equivalent yield (BEY), CBE is an adjustment to the mortgage yield to reflect assumed semiannual payment of cash flows rather than monthly. Converting monthly MBS cash flows to semiannual equivalent allows a more meaningful comparison of MBSs values to corporate and government bonds. The conversion primarily reflects the benefit to the MBS holder of reinvesting MBS cash flows monthly rather than semiannually, as is usually the case with other fixed-income securities.

CFY: See ***Cash-flow yield.***

Claim letter: A request by the beneficial owner for payment of principal and interest paid to the currently registered owner.

CLC: See ***Construction loan certificate.***

CMOs (collateralized mortgage obligations): Debt issues with multiple classes of bonds. See ***tranches.***

Co-insurance: Under FHA a program in which the private lender and HUD share the risk on the loan.

Collateralized mortgage obligations: See ***CMOs.***

Conduit: An organization that buys mortgages from correspondents, packages the loans into collateral pools held by a trustee, and sells mortgage securities through the capital markets.

Conforming loans: Loans within the statutory size limit eligible for purchase or securitization by the federal agencies.

Constant prepayment rate (CPR): A measure of principal prepayments expressed as a ratio of prepayments to the prior month's outstanding principal balance.

Construction loan certificate (CLC): A primary program of Ginnie Mae for securitizing FHA-insured and co-insured multifamily, hospital, and nursing home construction advances.

Controlled adjustable-rate preferred stock (CARPS): An equity security that offers a dividend with a periodically adjusting rate. A prime way for banks and S&Ls to use mortgage collateral.

Convexity: A measure of the shape of the price/yield curve. Convexity explains the difference between the prices estimated by standard duration and the actual market prices of a security resulting from a change in market required yield.

Corporate bond equivalent: See *CBE*.

Current coupon: For Ginnie Mae securities, the pass-through rate applicable to the maximum allowable VA rate in effect at the time. The current-coupon Freddie Mac PC is that currently offered in the Freddie Mac Cash program PC dealer auctions.

Current loan balance: Also referred to as the current face, or the outstanding loan balance. The current monthly remaining principal of a certificate computed by multiplying the original face of the pool by the current principal balance (factor).

Cushion bond: With reference to MBSs, the tendency of premium-priced MBSs to hold price when market yields are rising because of the anticipated slowing of prepayment speed.

Cusp: The point where the price of the MBS reflects a current market interest rate where the mortgage loans underlying the MBS pool are presumed to have crossed the threshold for refinancing.

Custom pool: The single-issuer approach in which an individual issuer assembles a pool of mortgages against which he issues and markets securities, as in the GNMA-I program.

Delayed issuance pool: Refers to MBSs that at the time of issuance were collateralized by seasoned loans originated prior to the MBS pool issue date.

Delivery versus payment (DVP): A transaction in which the buyer's payment for securities is due at the time of delivery (usually to a bank acting as agent for the buyer) upon receipt of the securities. The payment may be made by bank wire, check, or direct credit to an account.

Depository Trust Company: See *DTC*.

Dollar roll: Similar to the reverse repurchase agreement—a simultaneous agreement to sell a security held in portfolio with purchase of a similar security at a future date at an agreed-upon price.

Drop (the): With the dollar roll transaction the difference between the sale price of a mortgage-backed pass-through and its repurchase price on a future date at a predetermined price.

DTC (Depository Trust Company): DTC is a user-owned securities depository which accepts deposits of eligible securities for custody, executes book-entry deliveries and records book-entry pledges of securities in its custody, and provides for withdrawals of securities from its custody.

Due bill: (1) A document delivered by the seller of a security to the buyer evidencing that any principal and interest received by the seller past the record date for that security will be paid to the buyer by the seller. (2) A document delivered by a seller to a buyer in lieu of securities, which evidences the seller's obligation to deliver securities to the buyer at a later date.

Duration: The weighted average time to the receipt of value of the future cash flows of a security weighted by the present value of each of the cash flows in the series. Duration is used to measure the relative sensitivity of the price of the security to a change in market required yield.

Effective margin (EM): Used with SAT performance measures, the amount equaling the net earned spread, or margin, of income on the assets in excess of financing costs for a given interest-rate and prepayment-rate scenario.

EM: See *Effective margin*.

Extension date: The day on which the first option either expires or is extended.

Factor: The proportion of the outstanding principal balance of a security to its original principal balance expressed as a decimal.

Fail: A trade is said to fail if on or after the settlement date the seller does not complete delivery of the securities to the buyer.

Fallout risk: A type of mortgage pipeline risk that is generally created when the terms of the loan to be originated are set at the same time as the sale terms are set. The risk is that either of the two parties (borrower or investor) fails to close and the loan "falls out" of the pipeline.

Federal Home Loan Mortgage Corporation: See *Freddie Mac.*

FHA prepayment experience: The percentage of loans in a pool of mortgages outstanding at the origination anniversary, based on annual statistical historic survival rates for FHA-insured mortgages.

First call: With CMOs, the start of the cash-flow cycle for the cash-flow window.

48-hour rule: The requirement that all pool information, as specified under the PSA Uniform Practices, in a TBA transaction be communicated by the seller to the buyer before 3 P.M. EST on the business day 48 hours prior to the agreed settlement date.

Forward delivery: A transaction in which the settlement will occur on a specified date in the future at a price agreed upon on the trade date.

Forward sale: A method for hedging price risk which involves an agreement between a lender and an investor to sell particular kinds of loans at a specified price and future time.

Forward trade: A transaction in which the settlement will occur on a specified date in the future at a price agreed upon on the trade date (see also *TBA*).

Freddie Mac (Federal Home Loan Mortgage Corporation): A Congressionally chartered corporation that purchases residential mortgages in the secondary market from S&Ls, banks, and mortgage bankers and securitizes these mortgages for sale into the capital markets.

Front fee: The fee initially paid by the buyer upon entering a split-fee option contract.

GEMs (growing-equity mortgages): Mortgages in which annual increases in monthly payments are used to reduce outstanding principal and shorten the term of the loan.

Generic: Refers to the characteristics and/or experience of the total universe of a coupon of MBS sector type; that is, in contrast to a specific pool or collateral group, as in a specific CMO issue.

Gestation repo: A type of reverse repurchase agreement between mortgage firms and securities dealers. Under the agreement the firm sells federal agency-guaranteed MBSs and simultaneously agrees to repurchase them at a future date at a fixed price.

Ginnie Mae: See *Government National Mortgage Association.*

GMCs (guaranteed mortgage certificates): First issued by Freddie Mac in 1975, GMCs (like PCs) represent undivided interest in specified conventional whole loans and participations previously purchased by Freddie Mac.

GNMA-I: MBSs on which registered holders receive separate principal and interest payments on each of their certificates, usually directly from the servicer of the MBS pool. GNMA-I MBSs are single-issuer pools.

GNMA-II: MBSs on which registered holders receive an aggregate principal and interest payment from a central paying agent on *all* their certificates. Principal and interest payments are disbursed on the 20th day of the month. GNMA-II MBSs are backed by multiple-issuer pools or custom pools (one issuer but different interest rates that may vary within one percentage point). Multiple-issuer pools are known as "Jumbos." Jumbo pools are generally larger and often contain mortgages that are more geographically diverse than single-issuer pools. Jumbo pool mortgage interest rates may vary within one percentage point.

GNMA Midget: A GNMA pass-through security backed by fixed-rate mortgages with a 15-year maturity. GNMA Midget is a dealer term and is not used by GNMA in the formal description of its programs.

"Gnomes": Freddie Mac's 15-year, fixed-rate pass-through securities issued under its Cash program.

Good delivery and settlement proce-dures: Refers to PSA Uniform Practices such as cutoff times for delivery of securities and notification, allocation, and proper endorsement.

Government National Mortgage Association (Ginnie Mae): A wholly owned U.S. government corporation within the Department of Housing and Urban Development. Ginnie Mae guarantees the timely payment of P&I on securities issued by approved servicers and that are collateralized by FHA-insured, VA-guaranteed, or Farmers Home Administration (FmHA)-guaranteed mortgages.

GPMs: See *Graduated-payment mortgages.*

Graduated-payment mortgages (GPMs): A type of stepped-payment loan in which the borrower's payments are initially lower than those on a comparable level-rate mortgage. The payments are gradually increased over a predetermined period (usually 3, 5, or 7 years) and then are fixed at a level-pay schedule, which will be higher than the level-pay amortization of a level-pay mortgage originated at the same time. The difference between what the borrower actually pays and the amount required to fully amortize the mortgage is added to the unpaid principal balance.

Grantor trust: A mechanism for issuing MBSs wherein the mortgage collateral is deposited with a trustee under a custodial or trust agreement.

Growing-equity mortgages: See *GEMs.*

Guaranteed mortgage certificates: See *GMCs.*

Guarantor program: Under the Freddie Mac program the aggregation by a single issuer (usually an S&L) for the purpose of forming a qualifying pool to be issued as PCs under the Freddie Mac guaranty.

Haircut: The margin or difference between the actual market value of a security and the value assessed by the lending side of a transaction—for example, a repo.

Hedgers: Those who engage in the use of a hedge; see *Hedging.*

Hedging: A technique employed by securities traders and investors to offset price risk by taking an opposite position from that of the position held; that is, to hedge a position in a security owned by selling short a like or substitute security such as a financial futures contract.

Immediate settlement: Delivery and settlement of securities within five business days.

Implied call: The right of the homeowner to prepay, or call, the mortgage at any time.

In the money: A call option that may be exercised to the economic advantage of the holder at the call option.

Interest-rate swap: An agreement whereby two parties agree to exchange payment terms, usually by exchanging fixed for floating, but may also be used to swap maturity terms, for example, 3-month LIBOR for 6-month LIBOR.

Internal rate of return (IRR): The value, measured in terms of yield, received on an investment to its maturity, including reinvestment income at the stated coupon rate of the security. The IRR takes into account the function of the coupon to price—i.e., discount or premium.

Inverse floater: A CMO tranche with a variable-rate coupon that is formulated to an index such that the coupon declines when the index value increases.

Investor fallout: In the mortgage pipeline, risk that occurs when the originator commits loan terms to the borrowers and gets commitments from investors at the time of application (or if both sets of terms are made at closing).

IO (interest only): The interest-only portion of a stripped MBS. With IO securities, all the interest distribution from the underlying pool collateral is paid to the registered holder of the IO based on the current face amount of the underlying collateral.

IRR: See *Internal rate of return.*

Irrational call option: The implied call imbedded in the MBS. Identified as irrational because the call is sometimes not exercised when it is "in the money" (interest rates at or below the threshold to refinance). Sometimes exercised when not in the money (home sold without regard to the relative level of interest rates).

Jumbo loans: Loans that exceed the statutory size limit eligible for purchase or securitization by the federal agencies.

Jumbo pools: Freddie Mac packages of pools in which the mortgage rates may be above or below the pass-through rate.

Lag response of prepayments: There is typically a lag of about three months between the time the WAC of an MBS pool has crossed the threshold for refinancing and an acceleration in prepayment speed is observed.

Level pay: The characteristic of the scheduled principal and interest payments due under a mortgage such that the *total monthly* payment of P&I is the same while characteristically the principal payment component of the monthly payment becomes gradually greater while the monthly interest payment becomes less.

"Lock-out": With PAC bond CMO classes, the period before the PAC sinking fund becomes effective. With multifamily loans, the period of time during which prepayment is prohibited.

Manufactured housing securities (MHSs): Loans on manufactured homes—that is, factory-built or prefabricated housing, including mobile homes.

Mark-to-market: The process whereby the book value or collateral value of a security is adjusted to reflect current market value.

MBSCC (Mortgage-Backed Securities Clearing Corporation): A wholly owned subsidiary of the Midwest stock exchange that operates a clearing service for the comparison, netting, and margining of agency-guaranteed MBSs transacted for forward delivery.

MBS Depository: A book-entry depository for GNMA securities. The depository was initially operated by MBSCC and is currently in the process of becoming a separately incorporated, participant-owned, limited-purpose trust company organized under the State of New York Banking Law.

MBS servicing: The requirement that the mortgage servicer maintain payment of the full amount of contractually due P&I payments whether or not actually collected.

MHSs: See *Manufactured housing securities.*

MMNs: See *Money market notes.*

MMPS: See *Money market preferred stock.*

Mobile home securities: See *Manufactured housing securities.*

Modified duration: The percentage change in price of a security that results from a small change in yield.

Money market notes (MMNs): Publicly traded issues that may be collateralized by mortgages and MBSs.

Money market preferred stock (MMPS): Publicly traded issues that may be collateralized by mortgages and MBSs.

Mortgage duration: A modification of standard duration to account for the impact on duration of MBSs of changes in prepayment speed resulting from changes in interest rates. Two factors are employed: one that reflects the impact of interest rates on prepayment speed and a second that reflects the impact of changes in prepayment speed on price.

Mortgage pipeline: The period from the taking of applications from prospective mortgage borrowers to the marketing of the loans.

MPTSs (mortgage pass-through securities): Securities representing an undivided ownership interest in an underlying pool of mortgages. The cash flow from the collateral pool is "passed through" to the security holder as monthly payments of principal, interest, and prepayments. The MPTS is the predominant form of mortgage-backed security traded in the secondary market.

Multifamily loans: Loans usually represented by conventional mortgages on multifamily rental apartments.

Multiple-issuer pools: Under the GNMA-II program, pools formed through the aggregation of individual issuers' loan packages.

Negative amortization: A loan repayment schedule in which the outstanding principal balance of the loan increases, rather than amortizing, because the scheduled monthly payments do not cover the full amount required to amortize the loan. The unpaid interest is added to the outstanding principal, to be repaid later.

Negative convexity: Describes securities that produce a negatively sloped price/yield curve. With negatively convex securities, price changes of the security are in the same direction as that of a change in yield.

Negative duration: A situation in which the price of the MBS moves in the same direction as interest rates.

Net present value (NPV): The current worth or value of a dollar amount to be received or paid over a period of time at a future date. The current worth is the price derived by discounting the future cash flows by a current market required yield.

Notification date: The day the option is either exercised or expires.

NPV: See *Net present value.*

OAS: See *Option-adjusted spread.*

Option-adjusted spread (OAS): The cost of the implied call embedded in the MBS, defined as additional basis-yield spread. When added to the base-yield spread of an MBS without an operative call produces the option-adjusted spread.

Option not to deliver: In the mortgage pipeline, an additional hedge placed in tandem with the forward or substitute sale.

Original face value: The principal amount of the mortgage as of its issue date.

Origination: The making of mortgage loans.

Out of the money: A call option that at the time offers no economic incentive to exercise the call.

Overshooting: The tendency of a pool of MBSs to reflect an especially high rate of prepayments the first time it crosses the threshold for refinancing, especially if two or more years have passed since the date of issue without the WAC of the pool having crossed the refinancing threshold.

PAC: See *Planned-amortization class.*

Pairoff: A buy-back to offset and effectively liquidate a prior sale of securities.

Pass-through rate: The net interest rate passed through to investors after deducting servicing, management, and guarantee fees from the gross mortgage coupon.

Permanent loan certificates (PLCs): Upon completion of construction projects, certificates that may be exchanged for CLCs. PLCs are issued with the suffix "PL" following the pool number.

P&I claim letter: See *Claim letter.*

Planned-amortization class (PAC): A CMO bond class that stipulates cash-flow contributions to a sinking fund. With the PAC, principal payments are directed to the sinking fund on a priority basis in accordance with a predetermined payment schedule, with prior claim to the cash flows before other CMO classes. Similarly, cash flows received by the trust in excess of the sinking fund requirement are also allocated to other bond classes. The prepayment experience of the PAC is therefore very stable over a wide range of prepayment experience.

PLCs: See *Permanent loan certificates.*

PO (principal only): The principal-only portion of a stripped MBS. For PO securities, all of the principal distribution due from the underlying collateral pool is paid to the registered holder of the stripped MBS based on the current face of the underlying collateral pool.

Pool factor: The outstanding principal balance divided by the original principal balance with the result expressed as a decimal. Pool factors are published monthly by the bond buyer for Ginnie Mae, Fannie Mae, and Freddie Mac MBSs.

Positive convexity: Describes securities that produce a positively sloped price/yield curve. With positively convex securities, price changes are inverse to the direction of changes in yield.

Price compression: The tendency of MBSs to lose ability to appreciate in price when the mortgage loans in the underlying pool have passed the threshold for refinancing.

Price risk: A type of mortgage pipeline risk created in the production segment when loan terms are set for the borrower in advance of terms being set for secondary market sale. If the general level of rates rises during the production cycle, the lender may have to sell his originated loans at a discount.

Price value of a basis point (PVBP): The change in the price of a security that results from a basis-point change in yield.

Principal-only security: See *PO*.

Product risk: A type of mortgage-pipeline risk that occurs when a lender has an unusual loan in production or in inventory but does not have a sale commitment at a prearranged price.

Production-flow commitment: An agreement by the loan purchaser to allow the monthly loan quota to be delivered in batches.

Project loan certificate (PLC): A primary program of Ginnie Mae for securitizing FHA-insured and co-insured multifamily, hospital, and nursing home loans.

Project loan securities: Securities backed by a variety of FHA-insured loan types—primarily multifamily apartment buildings, hospitals, and nursing homes.

Project loans: Usually FHA-insured and HUD-guaranteed mortgages on multiple-family housing complexes. Includes as well nursing homes, hospitals, and other development types.

Projected maturity date: With CMOs, final payment at the end of the estimated cash-flow window.

PSA: A prepayment model based on an assumed rate of prepayment each month of the then-unpaid principal balance of a pool of mortgages. Used primarily to derive an implied prepayment speed of new production loans, 100 percent PSA assumes a prepayment rate of 2 percent a month in the first month following the date of issue, increasing 2 percent per month thereafter until the 30th month. Thereafter, 100 percent PSA is the same as 6 percent CPR.

PSA: See *Public Securities Administration*.

Public Securities Administration (PSA): The trade association for primary dealers in U.S. government securities, including MBSs dealers.

Put option: An option giving the originator the right to deliver a loan or security at a prearranged price within an agreed-upon period.

PVBP: See *Price value of a basis point*.

RAMs (reverse-annuity mortgages): Mortgages in which the bank makes a loan for an amount equal to a percentage of the appraisal value of the home. The loan is then paid to the homeowner in the form of an annuity.

RAP: See *Regulatory accounting procedures*.

Rate lock: An agreement between the mortgage banker and the loan applicant guaranteeing a specified interest rate for a designated period, generally about 60 days.

RCA: See *risk-controlled arbitrage*.

Real estate mortgage investment conduit: See *REMIC*.

Rebalancing: A reflection of the need to modify some SAT components to adjust the hedge to changing market conditions.

Reclamation: A claim for the right to return or the right to demand the return of a security that has been previously accepted as a result of a bad delivery or other irregularity in the delivery and settlement process.

Record rate: The date that determines who is entitled to payment of principal and interest due to be paid on a security. The record date for most MBSs is the last calendar day of the month (however, the last day on which they may be presented for transfer is the last business day of the month). The record date for CMOs and ABSs varies with each issue.

Regulatory accounting procedures (RAP): Accounting principles required by the FHLBB that allow S&Ls to elect annually to defer gains or losses on the sale of assets and amortize these deferrals over the average life of the asset sold.

Remaining principal balance (RPB): The amount of principal dollars remaining to be paid under the mortgage as of a given point in time.

REMIC (real estate mortgage investment conduit): A pass-through tax entity that can hold mortgages secured by any type of real property and issue multiple classes of ownership interests to investors in the form of pass-through certificates, bonds, or other legal forms. A financing vehicle created under the Tax Reform Act of 1986.

Repo (repurchase agreement): An agreement of one party to purchase securities at a specified price from a second party and a simultaneous agreement by the first party to resell the securities at a specified price to the second party on demand or at a specified price.

Reported factor: The pool factor as reported by the bond buyer for a given amortization period.

Residuals: Remainder cash flows generated by pool collateral and those needed to fund bonds supported by the collateral.

Return on assets (ROA): A computation of the cumulative annual book income of the SAT arbitrage as a percentage of the average balance of the SAT assets.

Return on investment (ROI): In connection with SAT performance, a measure relating future value of the SAT at termination date to actual initial cash investment.

Reverse-annuity mortgages: See *RAMs.*

Reverse price risk: A type of mortgage-pipeline risk that occurs when a lender commits to sell loans to an investor at rates prevailing at application but sets the note rates when the borrowers close. The lender is thus exposed to the risk of falling rates.

Reverse repo (reverse repurchase agreement): An agreement of one party to purchase securities at a specified price from a second party and a simultaneous agreement by the first party to resell the securities at a specified price to the second party on demand or at a specified later date.

Risk-controlled arbitrage (RCA): A self-funding, self-hedged series of transactions that generally utilize mortgage securities as the primary assets.

ROA: See *Return on assets.*

ROI: See *Return on investment.*

RPB: See *Remaining principal balance.*

SAT: See *Structured arbitrage transaction.*

Scheduled cash flows: The mortgage principal and interest payments due to be paid under the terms of the mortgage *not* including possible prepayments.

Speed: A Wall Street dealer term that refers to the rate of principal prepayments of a pool of mortgages as calculated by the FHA, CPR, PSA, or other methods of measuring prepayments.

Split-fee option: An option on an option. The buyer generally executes the split fee with first an initial fee, with a window period at the end of which upon payment of a second fee the original terms of the option may be extended to a later predetermined final notification date.

Spot lending: The origination of mortgages by processing applications taken directly from prospective borrowers.

Stated maturity: For the CMO tranche, the date the last payment would occur at zero CPR.

Steady state: As the MBS pool ages, or four to six months after it was passed at least once through the threshold for refinancing, the prepayment speed tends to stabilize within a fairly steady range.

Strip mortgage participation certificate (strip PC): Ownership interests in specified mortgages purchased by Freddie Mac from a single seller in exchange for strip PCs representing interests in the same mortgages.

Strip PC: See *Strip mortgage participation certificate.*

Stripped mortgage-backed securities (SMBSs): Securities that redistribute the cash flows from the underlying generic MBS collateral into the P&I components of the MBS to enhance their use in meeting special needs of investors.

Structured arbitrage transaction (SAT): A self-funding, self-hedged series of transactions that usually utilize mortgage securities as the primary assets.

Substitute sale: A method for hedging price risk that utilizes debt-market instruments, such as futures, or that involves selling borrowed securities through dealers.

Swaption: In connection with residuals, a forward-swap agreement whereby the buyer pays an initial fee to enter a swap at a later date at a specified rate.

Tail: The odd amount in an MBSs pool.

Tandem programs: Under Ginnie Mae, mortgage funds provided at below-market rates to residential mortgage buyers with FHA Section 203 and 235 loans and to developers of multifamily projects with Section 236 loans initially and later with Section 221(d)(4) loans.

TBA: See *To be announced.*

Threshold for refinancing: The point when the WAC of an MBS is at a level to induce homeowners to prepay the mortgage in order to refinance to a lower-rate mortgage —generally reached when the WAC of the MBS is 2 percent or more above currently available mortgage rates.

To be announced (TBA): A contract for the purchase or sale of a MBS to be delivered at an agreed-upon future date but does not include a specified pool number and number of pools or precise amount to be delivered.

Tranche: Also known as class. CMOs generally have several tranches; each bond issued under the CMO is considered a separate tranche or class, each with different maturi-

ties and interest rates and/or accrual structures.

Variance rule: Specifies the permitted minimum or maximum quantity of securities that can be delivered to satisfy a TBA trade. For Ginnie Mae, Fannie Mae, and Freddie Mac pass-through securities, the accepted variance is plus or minus 2.499999 percent per million of the par value of TBA quantity.

WAC: See *Weighted average coupon.*

WAM: See *Weighted average maturity.*

Warehousing: The interim holding period from the time of the closing of a loan to its subsequent marketing to capital market investors.

WARM: See *Weighted average remaining maturity.*

Weighted average coupon (WAC): The weighted average of the gross interest rates of the mortgages underlying the pool as of the pool issue date, with the balance of each mortgage used as the weighting factor.

Weighted average life (WAL): See *Average life.*

Weighted average maturity (WAM): The WAM of an MBS is the weighted average of the remaining terms to maturity of the mortgages underlying the collateral pool at the date of issue, using as the weighting factor the balance of each of the mortgages as of the issue date.

Weighted average remaining maturity (WARM): The average remaining term of the mortgages underlying an MBS.

Wholesale mortgage banking: The purchasing of loans originated by others, with the servicing rights released to the buyer.

Z-bond: Also known as an accrual bond or accretion bond; a bond on which interest accretes interest but is not paid currently to the investor but rather is accrued, with the accrual added to the principal balance of the Z and becoming payable upon satisfaction of all prior bond classes.

Zero prepayment assumption: The assumption of payment of scheduled principal and interest with no prepayments.

Index

A

Accounting issues, 459-68
  impairment, 463-64
  income tax treatment, 464
  IOs, investments in, 462
  methods, 459-61
    constant-yield method, 460-61
    equity method, 461
    market value entities, 461
  POs, investments in, 462
  residuals, investments in, 462-63
Additional hedge, 87
Adjustable-rate mortgages (ARMs), 48-53, 54, 102-3, 260-84
  attractiveness of, 59
  convertible ARMS, 53
  FASB Statement No. 91, 282-83
    accounting provisions, 282-83
  fixed-rate pass-through issuance threatened by, 62-64
  Ginnie Mae, 122
  interest-rate adjustments, 59
  securitization of, 59
  security prices

    effects of mortgage characteristics on, 276-77
    factors affecting, 277
  SLH ARM pricing model, 281
  structural characteristics, 262-67
    caps, 264-67
    indexes, 262-64
    initial rate, 262
    margin, 264
  valuation, 274-81
    effective margin, 275-76
    factors affecting, 274-75
    index volatility, 280-81
    interest rates, 278-80
    prepayments, impact of, 277
Adjustable-rate preferred stock (ARPS), 443-46
  concept of, 445
  major tax issues, 446
  structure of, 443-44
  tax and accounting concerns, 444-45
    key concept, 445
    major tax issues, 446
Adjustments
  to pool cash flow, 148-51

for mortgage securities, 148-49
for prepayments, 150-51
for servicing spread, 150
Advertising, spot originations, 75
All-floater residuals, 406-8
Alternative mortgage instruments (AMIs),
71-72
American Southwest Financial Corporation,
15-16
Amortization, of deferred fees and costs,
FASB Statement No. 91, 282
Amortization factor, 167
APB Opinion No. 18, 461
Asset-backed securities (ABS), 44-45
residuals, as unsuitable investment practice,
382-83
Average life
bear market investing, 223
bull market investing, 220

B

Back fee, split-fee options, 84
Balloon loans, 71
Bank of America, 9
Banking Act, 27
Bartlett, William, 40
Basis-point spread, 218-19
Basis risk, 432
cash-to-futures basis, 84
hedging with OTC options, 84
substitute sales, 83
yield curve shape, 83
Bear markets
impact on holding-period return, 187-89
investing in, 221-24
Bear Stearns Mortgage Capital Corporation,
52
Below-market interest-rate (BMIR) loans,
290-91
Bid/ask spreads, 412
15-year pass-throughs, 246
Bi-weekly mortgages, 103
Bond equivalent yield (BEY), 149, 185
Book-based measures
limitations of, 427-28
versus cash-based measures, 430-31
Book profit, 430
structured arbitrage transactions (SATs),
430
Borrower fallout, 87
types of, 87
Breakeven prepayment rate (BEPR) analysis,
189-91
Builders' and Sponsors' Profit and Risk
Allowance (BSPRA), 300
Bull markets
impact on holding-period return, 187-89

investing in, 219-24
Buydowns, 71
definition of, 123

C

Callable swap agreement, 411
Call-protection feature, Freddie Mac
multifamily PC program, 293
Caps
adjustable-rate mortgages (ARMs), 264-67
interest-rate caps, 265-66
life-of-loan caps, 266
payment-rate caps, 266-67
Carlson, Steven, 208-9
Cash-based measures
internal rate of return (IRR), 426, 427, 431
structured arbitrage transactions (SATs)
book profit, 430
effective margin, 429-30
initial spread, 428-29
return on assets (ROA), 429
return on investment (ROI), 430
versus book-based measures, 430-31
Cash Flow Investment, REMIC collateral,
21-23
Cash flows
stripped mortgage-backed securities
(SMBSs)
illustration of, 357-60
refinancing threshold, 359-60
strip trading axioms, 360
Cash-flow yield, 177-79
Cash program participation certificates,
Freddie Mac, 124-25
Cash-to-futures basis, basis risk, 84
CATS, 375, 383
Centex Collateralized Mortgage Corporation,
52
Chicago Board of Trade (CBT), 13-14, 43,
47, 204
Churning risk, 434-35
Citicorp Homeowners Inc., 96, 98
Co-insurance programs, 287-90
Collateral
collateral risk, 433
REMICs, 21
Collateralized mortgage obligations (CMOs),
10-11, 313-41, 440-41
collateral considerations, 314-15
definition of, 313-14, 441
discount-priced coupon, 323
floating-rate CMOs, 327-32
floater caps, variety of, 327-28
inverse floaters, 320
investment strategies, 330-31
investor class considerations, 331-32
superfloater tranches, 328-29

investment selection, 326-27
  investment techniques, 326-27
planned-amortization class (PAC) CMO
    tranches, 332-42
  first class CMOs, 334-35
  fourth-class Z-bonds, 336-39
  investor considerations, 332-34
  pricing considerations, 339
  targeted amortization class (TAC)
      tranches, 339-40
  third-class CMOs, 335-36
  turbo principal only (TPO) bonds, 340-42
premium-priced coupon, 323
pricing and investment, 320-26
  collateral types, 321-22
  prepayment speed considerations, 322-23
  price considerations, 322
  tracking yield spreads, 321
reward of investing in, 324-25
risk of investing in, 324-25
structure of, 315-20
  cash-flow structure, 317
  pricing process, 317
  reinvestment assumption, 320
  stated maturity, 320
  Z-bond class structure, 317-19
synthetic discount CMOs, 325-26
tranches, number and size of, 315
Commercial paper, 439-40
Competitive Equality Banking Act (CEBA),
    36
Conduits
  definition of, 9
  evolution of, 9-11
    builder bonds, 10-11
    first modern conduits, 10
    pre-REMIC multiclass MBSs efforts, 10
    REMICs, 11
Conforming loans, 70
Consolidation trends, S&Ls, 98-99
Constant maturity Treasuries (CMTs), 263
Constant maturity Treasury (CMT) index, 59,
    122, 133
Constant prepayment rate (CPR), 43, 143,
    155, 167-72
  calculation of, 168
  converting between PSA and, 168-72
    seasoned loans, 169-72
  interest cash flow, 146
  mortgage cash flow, 144
  principal cash flow, 145
Constant-yield method, applied with and
    without assumed prepayments, 466-67
Construction loan certificates (CLCs), 122,
    291
Contingent cost nondelivery hedge, 88
Contractual cash flows, 143
  investor's accounting with, 467-68

Controlled adjustable-rate preferred stock
    (CARPS), 441-42
Conventional residential loan market, 72,
    77-78
Convexity, 192, 200-204
  definition of, 200
  negative convexity, 203-4
Cooperative housing, multifamily loans, 301-2
Corporate bond equivalent (CBE), 149
  conversion of mortgage yield to, 149
Corporate settlement transactions, as
    unsuitable investment practices, 380
Correspondent lending, spot originations, 75
Cost of funds index, FHLBB, 59
Coupon
  bear market investing, 222
  bull market investing, 219
Coupon-only-type securities, 409-10
Current-coupon security, 189
Cushion bond, 180
Custom pools, GNMA-II program, 120

D

Dall, Robert, 40
Dealer settlement procedures, 137
Debt-service coverage (DSC), multifamily
    projects, 296
Deficit Reduction Act (1984), 30, 51
Delayed issuance pools (DIPs), 173-74
Delivery, 136-41
  forward delivery, 136
Denominations, settlement, 138
Depository Institutions Deregulation
    Committee (DIDC), 24-25
Depository Institutions Deregulation and
    Monetary Control Act, 29
Depression era, mortgage banking during, 5-7
Derivative mortgage-backed securities
    products, 58, 311-435
  CMO investing and trading, 313-43
  residuals, 395-413
  stripped mortgage-backed securities cash
      flows, 343-94
  structured arbitrage strategies, 414-35
Discount-priced coupon, collateralized
    mortgage obligations (CMOs), 323
Dollar rolls, 438-39
Dollar roll transactions, 449-56
  accounting treatment, 451
  delivery put option, 455-56
  economic basis, 450-51
  evaluation worksheet, 454
  prepayment risk, 454-55
  profit evaluation, 451-54
    coupon payments, 451
    the drop, 452-53
    prepayment value, 452

reinvestment income, 452
The drop, 450, 452-53
Due bills, 141
Duration
  alternative duration measures, 204-13
  bear market investing, 223
  bull market investing, 220
  convexity, 200-204
  coupon impact on, 198
  CPR-adjusted CFY, 205
  definition of, 193
  measuring price by, 197-98
  measuring time to receipt of value by,
    195-97
  modified duration, 198-99
  option-adjusted spread (OAS), 209-12
    OAS analysis, 212
  prepayment-sensitive model, 208-9
  stripped mortgage-backed securities
    (SMBSs), 368-73
    IO strips, 369-70
    PO strips, 369
  volatility-implied duration, 205-7
    framework of, 207-8
Dutch Auction procedure, money market
  preferred stock (MMPS), 447-48
Dwarfs, 132

E

Economics of size, S&Ls, 99-100
Effective margin (EM), 429-30
  structured arbitrage transactions (SATs),
    429-30
    calculation of, 429-30
Elderly, rental housing for, 306
11th District Cost of Funds Index (COFI),
  133, 263
Emergency Home Finance Act, 28
Emergency Home Purchase Act, 47
Epic Mortgage Company, 23
Estimated prepayments, investor's accounting
  with, 467
Evaluation model interpretation
  structured arbitrage transactions (SATs),
    421-24
    combination analysis, 421-23
    interest-rate scenario analysis, 423-24
Extension date, split-fee options, 84

F

Fallout risk, 80-81
  hedging of, 87-88
Fannie Mae, 9, 45, 46-53
  adjustable-rate mortgage (ARM) purchase
    program, 14
  Fannie Mae Majors program, 132-33

federal agency-backed ARM securities,
  268-69
MBS development by, 12
MBSs product summary, 133-35
  guarantee, 134
  maturity, 135
  payments, 135
  pool composition, 134
  pool number, 134-35
megapools, 133
Reconstruction Finance Corporation, 45
synthetic-coupon SMBSs, 392-94
weighted average remaining maturity,
  129-30
Farm Mortgage Bankers Association
  (FMBA), 4
  creation of, 45
FASB Statement No. 77, 465
FASB Statement No. 91, 33-35, 282-83
  ARMS and, 282-83
    accounting provisions, 282-83
  commitment fees, 34
  impact on S&Ls, 35
  loan-origination fees, 33-34
  summary of, 33
  syndication fees, 34-35
FASB Statement No. 96, 464
Federal agency ARM securities, 267-70
  Fannie Mae, 268-69
  Freddie Mac, 269-70
  Ginnie Mae, 267-68
Federal agency MBSs programs, 107-35
  attack on, 17
  evolution of, 11-18
  Freddie Mac participation certificates
    (PCs), 13-14
  resurgence of, 17-18
  sponsorship, benefits of, 12-13
  and standardization of secondary market,
    15-17
Federal agency underwriting standards,
  15-year mortgages, 238-40
Federal Asset Disposition Association, 52
Federal Deposit Insurance Corporation
  (FDIC), creation of, 27
Federal Home Loan Bank Act, 27
Federal Home Loan Bank Board (FHLBB), 8,
  27, 45, 46
  adjustable-rate mortgages (ARMs) and, 14
  amendments to net worth regulation, 32
  R Memorandum, 456-58
    dollar reverse repurchase agreements, 458
    loans of securities, 458
Federal Home Loan Bank (FHLB), advances,
  439
Federal Home Loan Mortgage Corporation,
  See Freddie Mac
Federal Housing Administration (FHA), 3, 45

creation of, 6
function of, 6-7
insurance programs, 287-90
mortgage claim rates, 15- and 30-year
mortgages, 237
prepayment speed experience, 154
primary objectives of, 6
profile of 15- and 30-year borrowers, 235
Federal income tax, 384-94
adjustable-rate preferred stock (ARPS), 446
bond sales, 391
market discount, 390-91
original issue discount, 386-90
general rules, 386-87
payment lag bonds, 388-89
premium, 388
rate of accrual of, 387-88
variable rate bonds, 389-90
REMIC elections, 384-86
Federal Land Bank (FLB), creation of, 45
Federal National Mortgage Association
(FNMA), *See* Fannie Mae
Federal Reserve Bank
constant maturity Treasury (CMT) index, 59
discount window advances, 439
Federal Reserve Board, 36
Federal Savings and Loan Insurance
Corporation (FSLIC), 8
FHLMC, *See* Freddie Mac
Fidelity risk, 434
Fifteen-year mortgages, 103
agency participation, 240-41
cash flows, 242-43
default rates, 237-38
derivative mortgage securities, 247-48
future of, 248
issuance and outstanding volume, 238-39
liquidity, 246-47
prepayment rates, 241-42
relative value analysis, 243-45
rising popularity of, 232-36
typical investors in, 248-49
insurance companies, 248-49
savings institutions, 249
Financial Accounting Standards Board
(FASB)
FASB Statement No. 91, 32-35
commitment fees, 34
impact on S&Ls, 35
loan-origination fees, 33-34
summary of, 33
syndication fees, 34-35
Financial Institution Examination Council
(FIEC), 376
Financial Institutions Regulatory and Interest
Rate Control Act, 29
Financing transactions
mortgage collateral, 438-41

CMOs, 441
commercial paper, 439-40
dollar rolls, 438-39
Federal Home Loan Bank advance, 439
Federal Reserve discount window
advances, 439
federal tax and loan accounts, 440
local public unit deposits, 440
mortgage-backed bonds, 440
pay-through bonds, 440-41
reverse repurchase agreements, 438
First Boston, 39
First call, 314
First-class CMOs, 334-35
Fixed-floater residuals, 402-4
rating agency considerations, 403-4
Fixed-income securities, versus mortgage
securities, 61
Fixed mortgage rates, average spread between
adjustable and, 60
Fixed-rate pass-through securities, threat by
ARMs, 62-64
Fixed up-front fee (put) option, 88-89
Floating-rate CMOs, 327-32
cap structures, 328
floater caps, variety of, 327-28
inverse floaters, 320
investment strategies, 330-31
investor class considerations, 331-32
European investors, 331-32
Japanese investors, 331-32
life insurance companies, 331
thrift institutions, 331
superfloater tranches, 328-29
FNMA, *See* Fannie Mae
48-hour rule, 140-41
due bills, 141
reclamations, 141
Forward delivery, 136
Forward sales, 82-84
advantages/disadvantages of, 82
choosing between substitute sales and, 86
Fourth-class Z-bonds, 336-39
Freddie Mac, 8, 46-53, 107, 123-31
federal agency-backed ARM securities,
269-70
giant participation certificate exchange
program, 127-29
guaranteed mortgage certificates (GMCs),
131
MBS development by, 12
multifamily PC program, 292-94
call-protection feature, 293
Plan-B loan terms, 293
Plan-B mortgages, 292-93
pricing conventions, 293-94
participation certificates (PCs), 107, 124

cash program participation certificates,
124-25
guarantor program participation
certificates, 125-26
strip participation certificates, 127
PC product summary, 130-31
guarantee, 130
maturity, 131
payments, 131
pool composition, 130-31
product types, 126
program terms, 126-27
program to consolidate pools, 127-29
weighted average remaining maturity
(WARM), 129-30
Front fee, split-fee options, 84
F. S. Smithers, 39, 40

G

Gains trading, as unsuitable investment
practice, 379
Garn-St. Germain Depository Institutions
Act, 24, 30
Generally accepted accounting principles
(GAAP), 11
Generic pay-down experience, 314
Gestation repo, 77
Giant participation certificate exchange
program, Freddie Mac, 127-29
G.I. Bill of Rights, 28
Ginnie Mae, 8, 46-51, 115-23
adjustable rate mortgages (ARMs), 122
comparison of MBSs, 119
creation of, 8-9
dormant programs, 122-23
federal agency-backed ARM securities,
267-68
GNMA-I, 115-16
guarantee, 116
payments, 117
pool composition, 116
settlement and remittance, 117-18
Settlement Standard settlement, 118
GNMA-II, 15, 118-20
pool types, 118-20
programs, 120
graduated-payment mortgages (GPMs)
program, 121, 259
manufactured housing (MH) securities, 121,
249-55
MBS development by, 12
mortgage-purchase (Tandem) programs, 123
project loan securities, 121-22
SEC advertising rule, effect on funds, 38-39
serial note (SN) program, 122
Ginnie Mae Mortgage-Backed Securities
Trust, 15

GL pools, 132
GNMA, *See* Ginnie Mae
Gnomes, 126
Freddie Mac, 241
mortgage-related security, definition of,
16-17
See also Freddie Mac, participation
certificates (PCs)
Government National Mortgage Association
(GNMA), *See* Ginnie Mae
Graduated-payment mortgages (GPMs), 71,
255-59
Ginnie Mae GPM program, 259
GPM plans, 256-59
Grantor Trust, 396
Gross margin, 264
Growing-equity mortgages (GEMs), 71
Guarantee
Fannie Mae products, 134
Freddie Mac PC products, 130
GNMA-I, 116
Guaranteed insurance contract (GIC), 215
Guaranteed mortgage certificates (GMCs),
13, 131
Guarantor program participation certificates,
Freddie Mac, 125-26
*Guidelines for Selection of Securities Dealers
and Unsuitable Investment Practices*,
376-83

H

Handicapped, rental housing for, 306
Hedging
price risk, 82-84
forward sales, 82
substitute sales, 82-83
residuals, 408
available tools for, 408-10
CMO reverse-floater bonds, 410
coupon-only-type securities, 409-10
principal-only-type securities, 410
super-floater bonds, 410
stripped mortgage-backed securities
(SMBSs), 371-73
of prepayment-speed risk, 373
Hegemann, Steve, 40
Heritage Mortgage Corporation, 42
Hess, Edward, 40
Holding-period return analysis, 186-89
bull and bear markets, impact on HPR,
187-89
Holding-period returns, stripped
mortgage-backed securities (SMBSs),
364-66
Home Mortgage Access Corporation
(HOMAC), 9
Home Mortgage Disclosure Act, 29

Home Owners' Loan Act, 27
Home Owners' Loan Corporation (HOLC), 5-6, 45
Hospitals, multifamily loans, 309-10
Housing Act, 28
Housing Assistance Payments (HAP) contract, 123
Housing and Community Development Act (1987), 28, 29, 299
Housing-turnover rate, impact on prepayment speed, 165-67
Housing and Urban Development Act, 28
Howard Savings Bank (Livingston, N.J.), 15
Hu, Dr. Joseph, 96-97, 100, 165-66
HUD survivorship table, 172
Huntoon Paige and Company, 39

I

Immediate settlement, 136
Implementation risk, 434-35
   structured arbitrage transactions (SATs)
      fidelity risk, 434
      incompetence, 434
Implied call option of the MBS, 175
   valuing the call option, 181-82
Indexes
   adjustable-rate mortgages (ARMs)
      constant maturity Treasury (CMT), 263
      11th District Cost Funds Index (COFI), 263-64
Index volatility
   adjustable-rate mortgages (ARMs)
      valuation, 280-81
   effect on ARM security prices, 276-77
Initial discount, effect on ARM security prices, 277
Initial rate, adjustable-rate mortgages (ARMs), 262
Initial spread, structured arbitrage transactions (SATs), 428-29
In the money, 175
Institutional investors
   mutual funds, 37-39
   savings institutions, 23-36
Insurance companies, fifteen-year mortgages and, 248-49
Interest-only (IOs) cash flows, 353-57
   as bear market investment, 356-57
   investor uses, 353
   projected price performance, 361-62
   summary of, 353
Interest-only (IO) strips, 44
Interest-rate caps, 410-11
   adjustable-rate mortgages (ARMs), 265-66
   effect on ARM security prices, 276-77
   residuals, 410-11
Interest-rate floors, residuals, 410-11

Interest-rate risk, sources of, 79
Interest rates
   adjustable-rate mortgages (ARMs) valuation, 278-80
   prepayment speed, 156-57
Interest-rate subsidy plan, multifamily loans, 308
Interest-rate swaps, 411, 442-43
Intermediate care facilities, multifamily loans for, 307
Internal rate of return (IRR), 177, 426, 427, 431
   cash-based measures, compared to yield to maturity (YTM), 428
Internal Revenue Code, savings institutions and, 31
Inverse floaters, 320
Investor fallout, 87
Investors, new breed of, 100-101
Investors GNMA Trust, 15
Irrational call, 175

J

Jumbo loans, 70, 72, 74
Jumbo pools, 124

K

Kettenmann, Kurt, 40

L

Lag response of prepayments, 159
Leonard, Paul, 40
Level pay, 143
Life-of-loan caps, 266
   adjustable-rate mortgages (ARMs), 266
Lifetime caps, floating-rate CMOs, 328
Liquidity, fifteen-year mortgages, 246-47
Loan proceeds to appraised property value (LTV), 78
Lock-out period, multifamily mortgages, 286
London Interbank Offered Rate (LIBOR), 327
   LIBOR ARM, 102-3
Low- to moderate-income housing
   multifamily loans, 302-3
   rental housing, 304

M

Macaulay, Frederick, 192, 204
McGovern, Robert, 43
Manufactured home (MH) securities, 249-55
   conventional pass-throughs, 250-51
      credit considerations, 252-54
      credit rating considerations, 254-55
      future developments, 255

investment characteristics of, 251-52
Manufactured Housing Contracts (MaHCS)
  certificates, 251
Margin
  adjustable-rate mortgages (ARMs), 264
  reset interval, 264
Marine Midland Bank, 44
Marketing, mortgage loans, 88-78
Mark-to-market regulations, S&Ls, 94-95
Maturity
  Fannie Mae products, 135
  Freddie Mac PC products, 131
MBS servicing, 78
MDC Mortgage Funding Corporation, 52
Megapool program, Fannie Mae, 133
Midgets, Ginnie Mae, 233
Mobile home securities, *See* Manufactured
  home (MH) securities
Modified duration, 198-99
Monetary Control Act (1980), 439
Money market notes (MMNs), 443, 448-49
  advantages of, 449
    to investor, 449
    to issuer, 449
Money market preferred stock (MMPS), 443,
  446-48
  dividend structure, 447
  Dutch Auction procedure, 447-48
  hold orders, 447-48
  interest-rate structure, 447
Mortgage-backed bonds, 440-41
Mortgage-backed securities (MBSs)
  actual returns, 63, 64
  annualized returns, 60-61
  future trends, 91-104
  historical performance of, 59-66
  implicit call in, 43
  issuance levels, 63
  mortgage-to-Treasury yield spreads,
    stabilization of, 64-65
  pool characteristics, 108-12
    pass-through rate, 108
    payment delay, 110-12
    pool factor, 112
    pool issue date, 109
    pool maturity date, 109
    servicing speed, 108
    weighted average coupon (WAC), 108-9
    weighted average maturity (WAM), 110
  publicly offered privately issued MBSs, 67,
    68
  ranking of, 67
  sector analysis, 61, 62
  total returns versus Treasuries, 63
  versus corporates, 61-62
  versus Treasuries, 61-62
Mortgage Bankers Association, creation of, 45
Mortgage banking, 73-90

fallout risk, hedging of, 87-88
fixed up-front fee (put) option, 88-89
forward sales, 86
future of, 96-100
history of, 4-11
  conduits, evolution of, 9-11
  Depression era, 5-7
  post-World War II era, 7-8
  secondary market, birth of, 8-9
marketing, 77-78
mortgage pipelines, 79-84
  interest-rate risk, sources of, 79
  loan terms affecting price, 79-80
  pipeline risk, types of, 80-81
  price risk, hedging methods, 82-84
origination of loans, 74-76
servicing, 73-74, 78
  retention of, 78
split-fee options, 84-86
subpipelines, creation of, 89-90
warehousing, 77
Mortgage capital, future sources of, 101
Mortgage cash-flow calculations, pool cash
  flow, 146
Mortgage collateral, 436-58
  bond and stock offerings, 441-43
    adjustable-rate preferred stock (ARPS),
      443-46
    controlled adjustable-rate preferred stock
      (CARPS), 441-42
    interest-rate swaps, 442-43
    money market notes (MMNs), 448-49
    money market preferred stock (MMPS),
      446-48
  uses of, 437-49
    financing transactions, 438-41
    sale of assets, 437-38
Mortgage Guaranty Insurance Corporation
  (MGIC), 8, 9
Mortgage instruments
  future of, 102-3
    adjustable rate mortgages (ARMs), 102-3
    bi-weekly mortgages, 103
    fifteen-year mortgages, 103
    reverse annuity mortgages (RAMs), 103
Mortgage market, composition of, 55
Mortgage pass-through securities (MPTS), 12,
  107
  average life, 107
  first issue, 107
  principal and interest, 107
Mortgage pipelines, 73, 79-84
  interest-rate risk, sources of, 79
  loan terms affecting price, 79-80
  pipeline risk, types of, 80-81
  price risk, hedging methods, 82-84
Mortgage pool cash flows, 105-227

delivery and settlement, uniform practices
for, 136-41
federal agency MBSs programs, 107-35
measuring value, 214-27
price and yield, determinants of, 175-91
principal and interest, calculation of, 142-74
properties of mortgage securities, 192-213
Mortgages, history of, 3-4
Mortgage-to-Treasury yield spreads, 64-65
future of, 65-66
tightening of, 65
Mortgage yield curve, 216-27
availability of product, 228
basis-point spread, 218-19
bear market investing, 221-24
bull market investing, 219-21
sector analysis, 224-26
swaps, evaluation of, 226-28
Multifamily loans
cooperative housing, 301-2
federal mortgage programs, 287-91
co-insurance programs, 287-89
conventional loans, 291
FHA insurance programs, 287-89
interest-rate subsidy programs, 290-91
lower-income rental assistance, 290
put options, 290
Freddie Mac multifamily PC program,
292-94
call-protection feature, 293
multifamily PCs, 293-94
pricing conventions, 293-94
Plan-B loan terms, 293
Plan-B mortgages, 292-93
hospitals, 309-10
interest-rate subsidy plan, 308
investment considerations, 294-95
lending and loan structures, 286
low- to moderate-income housing, 302-3
rental housing, 304
mortgage-backed securities, 291-92
Fannie Mae, 292
Freddie Mac, 292
Ginnie Mae, 291-92
multifamily rental housing, 300
nursing home and intermediate care
facilities, 307
prepayments, 295-300
likelihood of, 297-300
privately issued pools, 294
purchase of existing multifamily projects,
305
refinancing of existing multifamily projects,
305
rental housing for elderly or handicapped,
306
valuing projects, 296-97
debt-service method, 296

LTV method, 296-97
Multifamily rental housing, 300
Multiple-issuer pools, GNMA-II program,
118-19
Mutual funds, 37-39

N

National Association of Realtors (NAR),
92-93
National Housing Act (1934), 287
National Median Cost of Funds, 262
Negative amortization, 256, 266-67
Negative convexity, 203-4
Negative effective margin (NEM), 275-76
sensitivity of, 277
Net margin, 264
Net mortgage finance demand, 92-93
Net present value (NPV), 177
New production
versus seasoned production, 158-59
bear market investing, 223
bull market investing, 220
1987 legislative and regulatory activity, 35-36
Non-Gnomes, Freddie Mac, 241
Notification date, split-fee options, 84
Nursing home facilities, multifamily loans
for, 307

O

Office of Management and Budget (OMB), 17
Olson, David, 97
100 Percent Participation, 272
Option-adjusted spread (OAS), 209-12
OAS analysis, 212
Optional hedge, subpipelines, 89-90
Option not to deliver, 87
Original issue discount
federal income tax, 386-90
general rules, 386-87
payment lag bonds, 388-89
premium, 388
rate of accrual of, 387-88
variable rate bonds, 389-90
Original issue discount bonds (OIDs), 375,
383
Origination of loans, 74-76
spot originations, 74-76
wholesale mortgage banking, 74, 76-77
Origination volume, S&Ls, 95-96
Out of the money, 175
Overshooting to steady state, 157
Over-the-counter (OTC) options market, 43

P

Pair-offs, 88

as unsuitable investment practice, 380
Parity, 112
Participation certificates (PCs), 107, 124
  cash program participation certificates,
    124-25
  guarantor program participation certificates,
    125-26
  strip participation certificates, 127
Pass-through rate, 108
Path dependent option, MBS pool, 21
Payment cap, 266
Payment lag bonds, federal income tax
  considerations, 388-89
Payment-rate caps, adjustable-rate mortgages
    (ARMs), 266-67
Payments
  Fannie Mae products, 135
  Freddie Mac PC products, 131
  GNMA-I, 117
Pay-through bonds, 320, 440-41
Pension funds, 37
  mortgage security investments, 36-37
Performance measures
  structured arbitrage transactions (SATs),
    426-31
    book-based measures, 427-28
    cash-based measures, 428-30
Per-interval interest-rate cap, 265-66
Permanent loan certificate (PLC), 122
Pieces, settlement, 138
Pinkus, Scott M., 205-8
Pipeline risk, 80-81
  fallout risk, 80-81
  price risk, 81
  product risk, 81
  reverse price risk, 81
Planned-amortization class (PAC) CMO
    tranches, 332-42
  first class CMOs, 334-35
  fourth-class Z-bonds, 336-39
  investor considerations, 332-34
  pricing considerations, 339
  targeted amortization class (TAC) tranches,
    339-40
  third-class CMOs, 335-36
  turbo principal only (TPO) bonds, 340-42
Planned amortization (PAC) bonds, 44
Pool cash flow
  average-life concept, 152
  fundamentals of, 143-52
    adjustments, 148-51
      for mortgage securities, 148-49
      for prepayments, 150-51
      for servicing spread, 150
    mortgage cash-flow calculations, 146
    principal and interest (P&I) payments,
      147-48
    remaining principal balance (RPB),

      146-47
Pool composition
  Fannie Mae products, 134
  Freddie Mac PC products, 130-31
  GNMA-I, 116
Pool day, 140
Pool number, Fannie Mae products, 134-35
Pool types, GNMA-II, 118-20
Premium-priced coupon, collateralized
  mortgage obligations (CMOs), 323
Prepayment rates, fifteen-year mortgages,
  241-42
Prepayment risk, 432-33
Prepayments
  adjustable-rate mortgages (ARMs), impact
    of interest-rate changes on, 278-80
  adjustments to pool cash flow, 150-51
  breakeven prepayment rate (BEPR)
    analysis, 189-91
  constant prepayment rate (CPR), 43, 143,
    155, 167-72
    calculation of, 168
    converting between PSA and, 168-72
    seasoned loans, 169-72
    interest cash flow, 146
    mortgage cash flow, 144
    principal cash flow, 145
  dollar roll transactions, 452
    risk, 454-55
  impact on valuation, 277
  multifamily loans, 295-300
    likelihood of, 297-300
Prepayment-sensitive model, 208-9
Prepayment speed
  age
    impact of, 157-59
      lag response of prepayments, 159
      new production versus seasoned pools,
        158-59
  calculation of, 167-74
    constant prepayment rates (CPR), 168
    converting between CPR and PSA, 168-72
    FHA experience, 172-73
    SMM, 167-68
  collateralized mortgage obligations
    (CMOs), 322-23
  constant prepayment rate (CPR), 155
  delayed issuance pools (DIPs), 173-74
  FHA experience, 154
  housing-turnover rate, impact of, 165-67
  interest rate changes' effect on, 156-57
    overshooting to steady state, 157
    threshold for refinancing, 157
    varying speed paths, 156
  measuring of, 153-67
  PSA standard, 155-56
  seasonal cycle, impact of, 159-62
  WAC, impact of, 164-65

WAM, impact of, 162-64
Price compression of premiums, 179-80
Price determinants, 176-80
  derivation of interest portion, 178-79
    pricing discount MBSs, 179
  derivation of principal amortization (AM),
    and prepayments, 178
  price to cash-flow yield, 176-78
  pricing par-priced MBSs, 179
  pricing patterns of premium-priced MBSs,
    179-80
Price risk, 81
  hedging methods, 82-84
    forward sales, 82
    substitute sales, 82-83
Price value of basis point (PVBP), 199
Pricing
  collateralized mortgage obligations
    (CMOs), 320-26
    collateral types, 321-22
    prepayment speed considerations, 322-33
  Freddie Mac multifamily PC program,
    293-94
  stripped mortgage-backed securities
    (SMBSs), 374
Primary dealer market, 39-53, 103-4
  asset-backed securities, 44-45
  derivative MBSs products, 44
  federal agencies and, 41
  Tandem plans, 41
  troubles faced by, 42-43
Principal and interest (P&I)
  calculation of, 142-74
  pool cash flow
    fundamentals of, 143-52
    payments, 147-48
  prepayment speed
    calculation of, 167-74
    measurement of, 153-67
Principal-only (PO) cash flow, 345-53
  as bull market investment, 348-49
  hedging prepayment risk with, 351-53
  investor uses, 345
  portfolio total return, 348-49
  projected price performance, 362-63
  protecting MBS servicing with, 353
  as proxy for short WAM discounts, 349-50
  summary of, 345
Principal-only (PO) strips, 44
Private ARM market, 270-74
  pass-through ARM securities, 272-74
    summary of terms, 274
  whole loans, 272
    summary of terms, 273
Privately issued conventional mortgages,
  profile of 15- and 30-year borrowers, 236
Privately issued pools, multifamily loans, 294
Private mortgage insurance (PMI) companies,
  47
Private pass-through market, 66-70
  by issuer, 69
  by structure, 69
  composition, 68-70
Proactive management, 431
Production-flow commitment, 76
Product risk, 81
Profit evaluation
  dollar transactions, 451-54
    coupon payments, 451
    the drop, 452-53
    prepayment value, 452
    reinvestment income, 452
Projected maturity date, 314
Project Loan Certificate (PLC), 291
Project loans, 72-73
Promotion, spot originations, 75
Public Securities Association (PSA), 118
Purchased debt securities, FASB Statement
  No. 91, 282
Put option, 88

Q

Qualified Mortgage, REMIC collateral, 21-23
Qualified Reserve Fund, REMIC collateral,
  21-23
Quartile distribution, of mortgage coupons,
  109

R

Rate lock, 74
Reactive management, 431
Real estate mortgage investment conduits
  (REMICs), 11, 53
  analysis of, 20-21
  appeal of, 20
  building blocks, 21
  collateral, 21
  compared to CMOs, 31-32
  interests, 22-23
    regular interests, 22
    residual interests, 22-23
  interests sold to investors, 21-22
    regular interests, 21
    residual interests, 21-22
  Tax Reform Act (1986), 18-19
Real Estate Settlement Procedures Act, 29
Realty ownership, S&Ls and, 100
Rebalancing, structured arbitrage transactions
  (SATs), 431
Receive and deliver (R&D), 139-40
Reclamations, 141
Reconstruction Finance Corporation, 45
Refinancing, multifamily loans, 305
Refunding risk, 433-34

Regular interests, REMICs, 21
Regulatory accounting considerations, FASB
    Statement No. 91, 282
Regulatory accounting procedure (RAP), 14,
    25-27, 48, 437
    impact on savings institutions, 25-27
    sale of low-coupon securities under, 437-38
Relative volume analysis, fifteen-year
    mortgages, 243-45
Remaining principal balance (RPB), pool
    cash flow, 146-47
REMICs, accounting by MBSs issuer, effect
    on, 464-65
Rental housing, multifamily loans, 306
Reported factor, 167
Repositioning repurchase agreements, as
    unsuitable investment practice, 380-81
Republic Bank of Delaware, 44
Reset interval, 264
Residential Funding Corporation (RFC), 10,
    49
Residential mortgage debt outstanding, 56
Residual cash flows
    sensitivity analysis, 404-13
        all-floater residuals, 406-8
        hedging residuals
            available tools for, 408-10
            techniques for, 408
        residual friendly-floater structures, 406
    sensitivity to prepayment spread, 399-400
    sources of, 398-402
        fixed-rate CMO residuals, 398-99
Residual interests, REMICs, 21-22
Residuals, 11, 58
    assets, 410-13
        interest-rate caps, 410-11
        interest-rate floors, 410-11
        special-purpose liabilities, 411-13
    definition of, 395
    fixed-floater residuals, 402-4
Residual secondary market
    cash flows, sources of, 398-402
    evolution of, 396-98
        owner-trust vehicle, 396-97
        REMIC impact, 397-98
        TIMs initiative, 397
Return on assets (ROA), 429
    structured arbitrage transactions (SATs),
        429
Return on investment (ROI), 430
    structured arbitrage transactions (SATs),
        430
Reverse-annuity mortgages (RAMs), 71, 103
Reverse price risk, 81
Reverse repurchase agreements (repos), 415,
    438
Reverse swaps, 412
Riley, William D., 40

Risk
    stripped mortgage-backed securities
        (SMBSs), 344-45
    structured arbitrage transactions (SATs),
        432-35
        basis risk, 432
        churning risk, 434-35
        collateral risk, 433
        implementation risk, 434
        prepayment risk, 432-33
        refunding risk, 433-34
        speculation versus hedged management,
            435
        yield curve risk, 432
Risk-controlled arbitrage (RCA), *See*
    Structured arbitrage transaction (SAT)
Risk-valuation framework, 215-16
    investing with market view, 215-16
Ryland Mortgage Securities Corporation, 11

S

S&Ls, 6, 8, 11
    future of, 93-96
        consolidation trends, 98-99
        economics of size, 99-100
        mark-to-market regulations, 94-95
        origination volume, 95-96
        realty ownership connection, 100
Salomon Brothers, 10, 14, 23, 39
Sandor, Dr. Richard, 43
Savings institutions, 23-36
    FASB Statement No. 91, impact on, 32-35
    fifteen-year mortgages and, 249
    Internal Revenue Code for, 31
    major legislative events affecting, 27-30
    net worth requirements of, 32
    RAP accounting, impact of, 25-27
    savings deregulation, 24-25
    secondary market activity, 26-27
    Tax Reform Act (1986), impact on, 31-32
Scheduled cash flows, 143
Sears Mortgage Securities Corporation, 50
Seasonal cycle, impact on prepayment speed,
    159-62
Seasoned loans, converting CPR and PSA of,
    169-72
Seasoned pools, versus new production loans,
    158-59
SEC advertising rule, effect on Ginnie Mae
    funds, 38-39
Secondary market
    birth of, 8-9
    historical highlights of, 3-53
    historical landmarks, 45-53
    residual secondary market
        cash flows, sources of, 398-402
        evolution of, 396-98

owner-trust vehicle, 396-97
REMIC impact, 397-98
TIMs initiative, 397
savings institutions, 26-27
standardization of, 15-17
wholesale-loan secondary market, 90-91
trading mechanism, 91
Secondary Market Enhancement Act
(SMEA), 16-17, 51
mortgage-related security, definition of,
16-17
Sector analysis, 224-26
Securities dealer, guidelines for selection of,
376-83
Securitization, ARMs, 59
Securitized mortgage market, profile of, 55
Sensitivity analysis
residual cash flows, 404-13
all-floater residuals, 406-8
hedging residuals
available tools for, 408-10
techniques for, 408
residual friendly-floater structures, 406
Servicemen's Readjustment Act, 28
Servicing of loans, 73-74
Settlement
dealer settlement procedures, 137
denominations, 138
immediate settlement, 136
investor considerations, 138-39
pieces, 138
variance rule, 137
Shared-appreciation mortgages (SAMs), 71
Shay, Rodger, 40
Shearson Lehman Mortgage-Backed
Securities Index (SL Index), 59-61
Sheppard, W. Stevens, 40
Short sales, as unsuitable investment
practices, 381
Single monthly mortality (SMM), 43, 155
Special mortgage programs, 228-310
adjustable rate mortgages (ARMs), 260-84
fifteen-year mortgages, 232-49
graduated payment mortgages (GPMs),
255-59
manufactured housing (MH) mortgages,
249-55
multifamily and project loans, 286-310
Special-purpose liabilities, 411-13
residuals, 411-13
Speed, *See* Prepayment speed
Split-fee options, 84-86
Spot lending, 74
Spot originations, 74-76
advertising and promotion, 75
correspondent lending, 75
types of loans, 75-76
Spreads

mortgage-to-Treasury yield spreads, 64-65
future of, 65-66
tightening of, 65
Standbys, definition of, 13
Stated maturity, 320
Step caps, floating-rate CMOs, 328
Strike price, split-fee options, 84
Strip participation certificates, Freddie Mac,
127
Stripped mortgage-backed securities (SMBS),
as unsuitable investment practice, 381-82
Stripped mortgage-backed securities
(SMBSs), 343-94
compared to MBSs, 343-44
definition of, 343
dynamic total-return analysis, 366-68
hedging, 371-73
of prepayment-speed risk, 373
holding-period returns for, 364-66
interest-only (IO) cash flows, 353-57
investor concerns with, 373
mortgage-duration characteristics, 368-73
IO strips, 369-70
PO strips, 369
pricing methodology, 374
principal-only (PO) cash flows, 345-53
regulatory concerns with, 374-75
reward in investing in, 344-45
risk, 344-45
strip cash flows
illustration of, 357-60
refinancing threshold, 359-60
strip trading axioms, 360
trading on the cusp, 360
Structural characteristics
adjustable-rate mortgages (ARMs), 262-67
adjustable-rate preferred stock (ARPS),
443-44
collateralized mortgage obligations
(CMOs), 315-20
cash-flow structure, 317
pricing process, 317
reinvestment assumption, 320
stated maturity, 320
Z-bond class structure, 317-19
Structured arbitrage transactions (SATs),
414-68
evaluation model interpretation, 421-24
combination analysis, 421-23
interest-rate scenario analysis, 423-24
IOs, use of, 420-26
overview of, 414-20
performance measures, 426-31
book-based measures, 427-28
cash-based measures, 428-30
rebalancing, 431
risk, 432-35
yield-basis risk, 424-26

Subpipelines
    creation of, 89-90
        hedging inventory risk, 89
        optional hedge, use of, 89-90
Substitute sales, 82-83
    advantages/disadvantages of, 82-83
    basis risk, 83
    choosing between forward sales and, 86
Superfloater tranches, 328-29
Swaps, evaluation of, 226-28
Swaption, 411
Synthetic-coupon SMBSs, Fannie Mae,
    392-94
Synthetic discount CMOs, 325-26

T

Tandem programs, 123, 294
Tandem project loans, 41
Tangent point, 194
Targeted amortization class (TAC) tranches,
    339-40
Tax Reform Act (1976), 29
Tax Reform Act (1986), 10-11, 18-23, 30-31,
    68-69
    private pass-through market and, 68-70
    savings institutions and, 31
Third-class CMOs, 335-36
Thompson, G. Adrian, 39
Threshold for refinancing, 157
TIGRs, 375, 383
TIMS (Trusts for Investment in Mortgages),
    10
To-be-announced (TBA), 136
    specified TBA, 139
    versus specified trades, 139
Total-return analysis, 182-86
    MBS versus Treasury cash flows, 185-86
    reinvestment, impact on value, 182-84
    volatility, 184
Tranches
    collateralized mortgage obligations
        (CMOs), number and size of, 315
    definition of, 126
Trusts for Investment in Mortgages (TIMs)
    initiative, 397
Turbo principal only (TPO) bonds, 340-42
12-year prepaid-life convention, FHA, 154

U

Unsuitable investment practices, 376-83
    asset-backed securities (ABS) residuals,
        382-83
    corporate settlement transactions, 380
    gains trading, 379
    pair-offs, 380
    repositioning repurchase agreements, 380-81

short sales, 381
stripped mortgage-backed securities
    (SMBS), 381-82
when-issued securities trading, 380
zero-coupon or stripped products, 383
U.S. League of Savings Institutions, 45

V

Valuation
    ARMS, 274-81
        effective margin, 275-76
        factors affecting, 274-75
        index volatility, 280-81
        interest rates, 278-80
        prepayments, impact of, 277
    multifamily loan projects, 296-97
        debt-service method, 296
        LTV method, 296-97
Variable rate bonds, federal income tax
    considerations, 389-90
Variable-rate mortgages (VRMs), 71
Variance rule, settlement, 137
Varying speed paths, 156
Veterans Administration (VA), 7-8, 28, 45
Volatility, adjustable-rate mortgages (ARMs),
    283-84
Volatility-implied duration, 205-7
    framework of, 207-8

W

WAC, impact on prepayment speed, 164-65
Wall, M. Danny, 93
Warehousing, 73
    mortgage loans, 77
Weighted average coupon (WAC), 17, 108-9
Weighted average life (WAL)
    duration and, 193
    mathematical expression of, 152
Weighted average maturity (WAM), 48, 110
    impact on prepayment speed, 162-64
    short versus long WAM, 231-32
Weighted average remaining maturity
    (WARM), 129
Westside Federal Savings & Loan, 42
When-issued securities trading, 380
    as unsuitable investment practices, 380
Whole loan market, 70-73
    alternative mortgage instruments (AMIs),
        71-72
    conventional residential loan market, 72
    project loans, 72-73
Wholesale-loan secondary market, 90-91
    trading mechanism, 91
Wholesale mortgage banking, 74, 76

Y

Yield-basis risk, structured arbitrage
    transactions (SATs), 424-26
Yield-curve risk, 432
Yield curve shape, basis risk, 83
Yield spreads
    between current-coupon Ginnie Maes and
        10-year Treasuries, 64-65
    collateralized mortgage obligations
        (CMOs), tracking of, 321

Yield to maturity, compared to internal rate of
    return (IRR), 428

Z

Zero-coupon bonds, 37, 317-19
    duration, 196
    as unsuitable investment practice, 383
Zero prepayment assumption, 111

Conversion of Monthly Mortgage Yield to CBE

If Mortgage Yield Is Between	Add for CBE	If Mortgage Yield Is Between	Add for CBE
7.72– 8.01	.13	11.42–11.62	.28
8.02– 8.30	.14	11.63–11.82	.29
8.31– 8.58	.15	11.83–12.01	.30
8.59– 8.85	.16	12.02–12.21	.31
8.86– 9.11	.17	12.22–12.40	.32
9.12– 9.37	.18	12.41–12.59	.33
9.38– 9.62	.19	12.60–12.77	.34
9.63– 9.86	.20	12.78–12.96	.35
9.87–10.10	.21	12.97–13.13	.36
10.11–10.33	.22	13.14–13.31	.37
10.34–10.55	.23	13.32–13.49	.38
10.56–10.77	.24	13.50–13.66	.39
10.78–10.99	.25	13.67–13.83	.40
11.00–11.20	.26	13.84–14.00	.41
11.21–11.41	.27	14.01–14.17	.42

Comparison of Primary GNMA, FNMA, and FHLMC Pass-Through Programs

Feature	GNMA-I	GNMA-II	FHLMC PC	FNMA MBS
Collateral	Primarily single-family residential mortgages. Mortgages have FHA, VA, or FmHA default guarantees. Newly issued mortgages (less than two years old)	Same as GNMA-I	Mostly conventional loans (single-family fixed-rate mortgages without government guarantees). New or seasoned mortgages. Some seasoned FHA/VA pools	Similar to FHLMC
Maximum mortgage amount	$153,200	$153,200	$168,700 (50% more for Alaska, Hawaii, and Guam)	$168,700 (50% more for Alaska, Hawaii, and Guam)
Original term	15–30 years	15–30 years	10–30 years (wide range of underlying maturities)	10–30 years (wide range of underlying maturities)
Guarantee	Full faith and credit of U.S. government for timely payment of P&I guaranteed by GNMA	Same as GNMA-I	Timely payment of interest and eventual repayment of principal guaranteed by FHLMC	Timely payment of interest and principal guaranteed by FNMA
Minimum pool size	$1 million ($500,000 for manufactured housing)	$250,000 multiple-issuer pools $1 million level custom pools $350,000 manufactured housing custom pools	$1 million for Guarantor $50 million for Cash, $500,000 for ARMs, $250,000 for Baby pools	$1 million ($250,000 for FNMA Majors)
Maximum servicing spread (basis points)	50 bp (except manufactured housing and project pools)	50–150 bp	Cash 200 bp Guarantor 250 bp	250 bp
Payment delay Actual Stated	14 days 45 days	19 days 50 days	44 days 75 days	24 days 55 days

With seasoned loans:

Pool age > 30 months

$$CPR = \frac{PSA}{100} \times 6$$

$$PSA = \frac{CPR}{6} \times 100$$

With new production loans:

Pool age < 30 months

$$CPR = (.2 \times m) \times \frac{PSA}{100}$$

$$PSA = \frac{CPR}{(.2\ m)} \times 100$$

where m = months the pool is outstanding.

The CPR/PSA conversion process is discussed on pages 169-171 of the text. The FHA, CPR, and PSA methods of measuring prepayment speed are defined on pages 153-156.

How Payment Delays Work
(primary market)

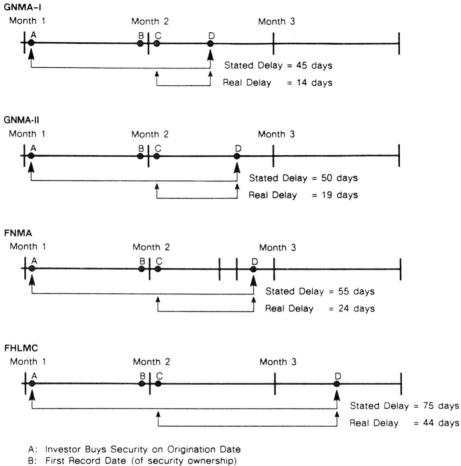

GNMA-I

Month 1 ... A

Month 2 ... B C

Month 3 ... D

Stated Delay = 45 days
Real Delay = 14 days

GNMA-II

Month 1 ... A

Month 2 ... B C

Month 3 ... D

Stated Delay = 50 days
Real Delay = 19 days

FNMA

Month 1 ... A

Month 2 ... B C

Month 3 ... D

Stated Delay = 55 days
Real Delay = 24 days

FHLMC

Month 1 ... A

Month 2 ... B C

Month 3 ... D

Stated Delay = 75 days
Real Delay = 44 days

A: Investor Buys Security on Origination Date
B: First Record Date (of security ownership)
C: First Payment Due From Homeowners
D: First Payment Actually Made to Pass-Through Investor

Source: First Boston Corporation Fixed Income Research.

Details of payment delays are found in the text on pages 110–112, and for GNMA (p. 116), FHLMC (p. 125), and FNMA (p. 132).

Most Commonly Traded Prefix and Suffix Designations

Ginnie Mae

Suffix	Program	Suffix	Program
SF	Single family	PL	Project loan
GP	Graduated payment	CL	Construction loan
MH	Manufactured housing (mobile home)	AR	Adjustable rate

Freddie Mac Single Family[1]

Prefix	Program
16, 17, 20, 22,	Cash
18, 25, 27, 29	Guarantor
21, 23, 26, 31	Guarantor

Fannie Mae Single Family[2]

Prefix	Program
AS	ARMs
CI	15-year
CL	30-year
GL	FHA/VA

[1]For other Freddie Mac prefix numbers see Table 3.4, page 128.

[2]For other Fannie Mae prefix numbers see the list on page 134.